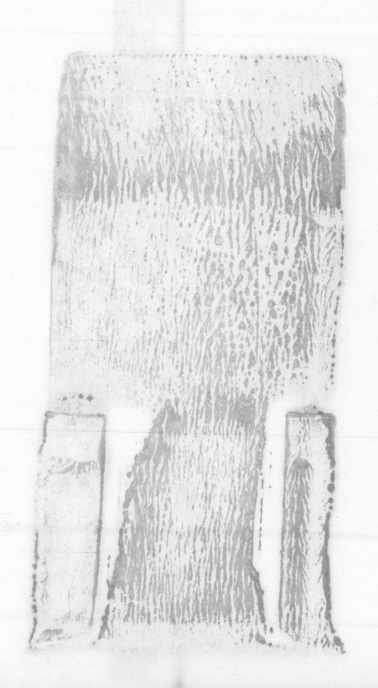

MALAYSIA · A SURVEY

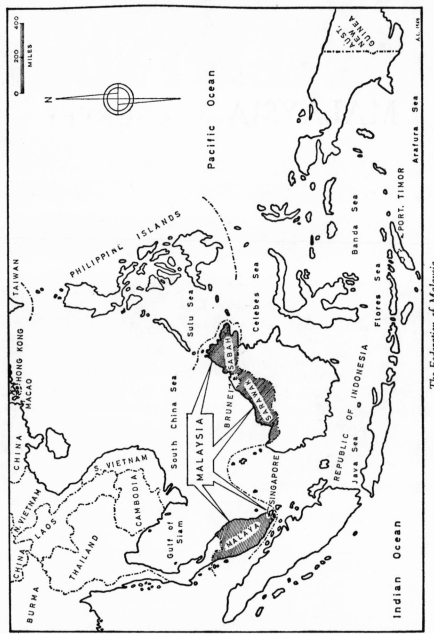

The Federation of Malaysia

MALAYSIA

A SURVEY

Edited by Wang Gungwu

FREDERICK A. PRAEGER, *Publishers*

New York · Washington · London

FREDERICK A. PRAEGER, Publishers
111 Fourth Avenue, New York, N.Y. 10003, U.S.A.
77-79 Charlotte Street, London W.1, England

Published in the United States of America in 1964
by Frederick A. Praeger, Inc., Publishers

Second printing, 1965

© Frederick A. Praeger, Inc.
Library of Congress Catalog Card Number: 64-24586

Printed in the United States of America

CONTENTS

CONTENTS

MAPS AND CHARTS

PREFACE

This volume was planned to appear soon after the formation of Malaysia and was the result of several discussions between me and several of my colleagues in the University of Malaya, notably Robin W. Winks and T. G. McGee. We agreed that we should not attempt to cover up-to-date events but to concentrate on the basic data for an understanding of the new country. Hence most of the papers have deliberately avoided the topical and immediate and I have kept the papers substantially as they were written, twelve months ago.

I now feel that, for the record, the most recent political position since the elections in Malaya in April 1964 should be briefly referred to; accordingly, the present position of parties in the Malaysian parliament and the composition of the cabinet are given overleaf. It is hoped that the reader can fit this material to the chapters of the book whenever and wherever relevant.

May 1964   WANG GUNGWU

THE MALAYSIAN PARLIAMENT, MAY 1964

Parties

Alliance (Malaya)	89	
Alliance (Sarawak)	20	125
Alliance (Sabah)	16	
People's Action Party (Singapore and Malaya)		13
Pan-Malayan Islamic Party (Malaya)		9
Sarawak United People's Party (Sarawak)		3
Barisan Socialis (Singapore)		3
Socialist Front (Malaya)		2
People's Progressive Party (Malaya)		2
United Democratic Party (Malaya)		1
Independent (Sarawak)		1
	Total	159

The Cabinet

Prime Minister, and External Affairs; Culture, Youth and Sports	Tengku Abdul Rahman
Deputy Prime Minister, and Defence; National and Rural Development; Lands and Mines	Tun Abdul Razak
Home Affairs; and Justice	Dato (Dr.) Ismail bin Dato Abdul Rahman
Finance	Tan Siew Sin
Works, Posts and Telecommunications	Dato V. T. Sambanthan
Transport	Dato Sardon b.Hj. Jubir
Agriculture and Cooperation	Mohamed Khir b. Johari
Health	Bahaman b. Samsuddin
Education	Abdul Rahman b.Hj. Talib
Commerce and Industry	Dr. Lim Swee Aun
Welfare Services	Haji Abdul Hamid Khan
Local Government and Housing	Khaw Kai Boh
Sarawak Affairs	Dato Temenggong Jugah anak Barieng
Labour	V. Manickavasagam
Information and Broadcasting	Senu b. Abdul Rahman
Minister without Portfolio	Dato Ong Yoke Lin

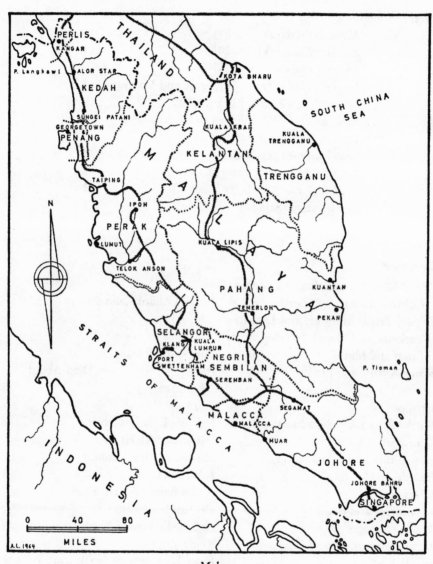

Malaya

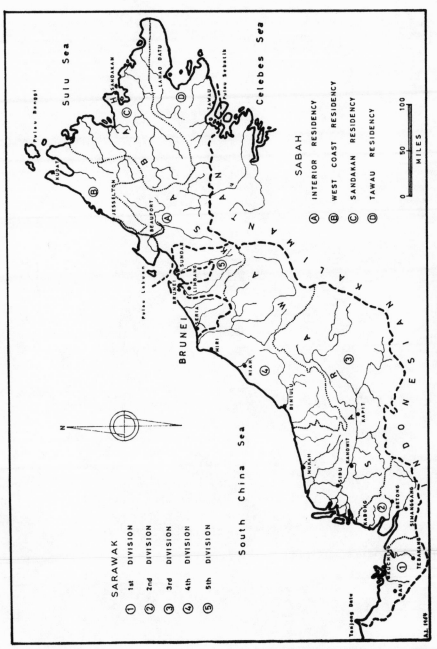

Sarawak and Sabah

Introduction

WANG GUNGWU

The word 'Malaysia' has been used since the nineteenth century as a synonym for the Malay archipelago. It was used to include all the islands of the southern half of South-east Asia, from the north-western tip of Sumatra across to the easternmost Spice Islands. The Philippines were usually not included, but the Malay peninsula was considered to be an integral part of it. This Malaysia had several things in common. The lingua franca of trade and communications was the Malay language and all the main languages indigenous to the area were related to Malay. Also, the majority of the people shared a similar way of life, a similar social and economic organisation and similar sets of customs and *adat* law. The people were physically homogeneous and most of them had for at least four hundred years shared a common religion, the faith of Islam.

The word 'Malaysia' was often used by European officials, and was particularly popular among natural scientists and globe-trotters of the second half of the nineteenth century and the early part of the twentieth. It is significant, however, that the word gradually fell out of use during this century. This was largely because Dutch and British administrative control had been extended to all the Malay areas which had remained independent and Malaysia was broken into parts of two European empires. In Malaya, for example, the name was retained only in a few government departments, notably the census compilers who continued to use it to describe immigrants into Malaya from the neighbouring islands of the Malay archipelago, and this somewhat technical usage has survived to the present day.

Since the Second World War, new names have come on to the map. Indonesia has replaced the Netherlands East Indies. Malaya has replaced the names of the several Malay states on the peninsula. For a number of years, there was talk of co-operation between Indonesian leaders and some of the Malay leaders in

15

Malaya. But the name 'Malaysia' was never used by them as a political concept. It was not until 1961 that the name was revived and almost instantaneously became the most potent subject of controversy in the region. This was when the Prime Minister of Malaya, Tengku Abdul Rahman, announced his intention to seek the political unification of Malaya and Singapore and the three territories of northern Borneo (Brunei, Sarawak and Sabah). This is very clearly a *new* Malaysia, for it consists of but a small corner of the Malaysia referred to in the past. And because there was a previous way of using the word, it has led to considerable difficulties and confusion among politicians in the territories concerned. This confusion has been increased by the use, in Malay, of a misleading translation, 'Melayu Raya' (Greater Malay Nation). It has led several political leaders to suggest that this Malaysia should embrace the whole of Indonesia and even possibly the Philippine Islands. It has also been argued that this extensive concept of Malaysia has historical foundations.

Indeed most of the islands, and parts of the mainland of South-east Asia as well, have shared a common history at some time or other during the past two thousand years. From the foundation in the second century AD of the Fu-nan Empire, which was based on the southern half of the Indochinese peninsula, close maritime relations have been maintained between mainland and island South-east Asia. These relations merely changed in emphasis during different periods. For example, after the fall of Fu-nan, the centre of that maritime world moved to Sumatra where the empire of Srivijaya dominated the region for probably over six hundred years. This in turn was succeeded by the Majapahit Empire with its centre on the island of Java. Then came the Malacca Empire which dominated the western half of the archipelago until the beginning of the sixteenth century. After this period three groups of Europeans imposed some kind of maritime trading organisation over parts of the archipelago successively: the Portuguese, followed by the Dutch, and then by the English. It is for this reason that Indonesia feels itself to be today the logical successor of the older empires.

There was in these maritime empires a continuity which is impressive, but at no time do we encounter the name of Malaysia as a political concept. Historically speaking, there has never been a state, kingdom or empire known as 'Malaysia' or 'Melayu Raya'. By this I mean that there has never been a political unit based on the idea of being Malay. The old empires have always been based on the range and efficiency of maritime power and the sovereignty of different ruling houses. The leaders today who argue for a political entity embracing Malaya, Indonesia and the Philippines are not thinking about maritime conquest or imperial power or even history, but really appealing to the modern concept of national destiny. In this idea of national destiny, there are of course both history and sentiment but even more important is the view that peoples of the same race and culture who use the same language or variants of the same language should be subjects of one single state.

All this, however, has nothing to do with the modest plan of the Prime Minister of Malaya to bring Malaya, Singapore and northern Borneo together. This smaller concept of Malaysia is strictly a political one. One can of course find common cultural features among all the peoples of the three areas and also argue easily for the economic and administrative advantages in having such a union. But the main object of the Tengku's plan is to achieve political stability in the heart of South-east Asia. Small countries are constantly in danger of being absorbed or over-run. Malaya has been troubled by the threat of communism for nearly twenty years and today, through Malaysia, it is hoped to find a more permanent solution to this threat. There is thus the question of the survival of a state, of a set of political values and of a political identity.

It cannot be denied that there are some fundamental difficulties about recognising the four territories of Malaysia as a new nation. Geographically and historically, northern Borneo has been quite separate from the Malayan peninsula and contacts in ancient times were probably few and far between. The main features the two regions share are similar flora and fauna, similar climate, similar culture and peoples; but these are also shared by the greater part of island South-east Asia. Since the fifteenth century, we can see two periods when the contacts between the peninsula and northern Borneo were increased and became also rather more special. The first period was when the Malacca Empire was instrumental in bringing Islam to Brunei. This was the result of trading relations and was to lead to further economic and cultural ties. But the bonds of religion and trade were not peculiar to the two regions. Again, they were features shared by most of the people of island South-east Asia. The second period, much more important and extending to our own time, was the period when both regions came under British rule in one form or another. The Malayan west coast was the first to be linked in this way through the Straits Settlements of Malacca, Penang and Singapore; not long afterwards, Sarawak came under the control of Raja Brooke. Then came the British move inland into the states of Perak, Selangor, Negri Sembilan and eventually Pahang, and about this time Sabah came to be dominated by the merchant adventurers of the North Borneo Company. Finally, to complete the work of colonial expansion, the British developed special relationships with Johore and the four northern states of Malaya at the beginning of this century. After the Second World War, both Sarawak and Sabah joined the other territories which were under the direct responsibility of the Colonial Office.

All this is well known and there is no need here to dwell on the various events and the complex motives of those responsible for them. The question most often asked by people in and outside of Malaysia is whether this common colonial experience is enough to bring the territories together and *keep* them together.

There is no simple answer to this. What the four territories have in common is extremely subtle. The peoples have each learnt many common lessons during the past century, about the importance of freedom and sovereignty, about the value of political and economic stability and about how to live peacefully in a plural society. The country has based its principles of government on the twin pillars of mutual tolerance among the various communities, and of respect for the law which protects the rights of all, whether they be the majority, the minority or mere individuals. The territories have come together mainly in order to protect these values in a region where there are many dictators and many types of tyranny; in other words, it may be said that they have come together not because of their common past but because they have become convinced that they have a common future.

Why then has Malaysia aroused so much controversy in South-east Asia, especially the bitter opposition of Indonesia? When the plan was first announced in May 1961, the Indonesian government made no protest. But when it was clear that Malaysia would definitely be formed, the situation changed rapidly. Soon after the abortive Brunei rebellion in December 1962, Indonesia announced its policy of confrontation. This is a policy which still continues today after the formation of Malaysia.

In order to understand the background of Indonesia's opposition, it is necessary to trace briefly the recent history of a new South-east Asian phenomenon: the rise of revolutionary nationalism. Twenty years ago, a handful of men saw themselves as the leaders of new nations in South-east Asia. Although the Japanese were then being defeated and the European victors about to return, these leaders saw that the region had left its colonial past behind and was about to enter the age of the nation-state. Three men were outstanding in creating the image of violence, bitterness and future glory for their countries: Aung San of Burma, Ho Chi Minh of Vietnam and Sukarno of Indonesia. Of the three men and the nations they created, Aung San is dead and his successors have led Burma into isolation; Ho Chi Minh won a terrible war and, rather than abandon communism, cut his country into half; Sukarno chose political unity at the cost of economic disruption and lives to enjoy his presidency for life. The three men set the pace of political revolution in South-east Asia and caught the imagination of a whole generation. Although today Aung San alone remains the youthful hero, and both Ho Chi Minh and Sukarno have grown old with the new orthodoxy, the momentum of their revolutionary politics is still with us and other nations have not been allowed to go their own ways. Of these nations who have grown at their own speed but cannot stay unaffected by their militant neighbours are the historic kingdom of Thailand, the republic of the Philippines, and the new monarchy of Malaysia. These three countries are all nonconformist and, in the eyes of the leaders of Burma, Vietnam and Indonesia, potentially subversive of the revolution they envisage for the region. Also, for reasons outlined earlier in terms of the historic empires of South-east Asia and the modern idea of national destiny, Indonesia has a special interest in the Malay peoples of Malaysia and the Philippines and is loath to see them uninspired by the same flaming ideals.

The core of the crisis, Indonesia's opposition to the creation of Malaysia, came into the open late in 1962. This opposition has been expressed in many forms. It was first put in terms of self-determination for the peoples of Sarawak, Brunei and Sabah. It then moved on to anti-colonial slogans and took the form of accusations of 'neocolonialism'. When this did not shake the Malayan government's determination to go ahead with the establishment of Malaysia, it appealed to sentiments of Malay brotherhood and brought the Philippines into opposition as well. By early August 1963, when President Sukarno met Tengku Abdul Rahman for the second time in Manila (the first time was in Tokyo in May and June), the opposition shifted its focus once again. Malaya was reminded of the principles of Maphilindo (the new partnership of Malaya-Philippines-Indonesia); there was a request for United Nations intervention in Sarawak and Sabah; and the long-term problem of military bases in South-east Asia was raised.

At this point, the Malayan government, still determined to establish the new federation, seized on the issue of the United Nations survey to bring Malaysia on to the world stage. On September 16, 1963, a few days after it was clear that the UN report on Sarawak and Sabah was favourable, Malaysia was inaugurated with a series of splendid ceremonies in the main cities of the new country.

For Indonesia, this was an affront to the ideals of revolutionary nationalism. Indonesian aims were being thwarted by the Malaysian leadership, a leadership that had emerged long after Indonesia had set the pattern for a revolutionary South-east Asia. Bitterly, and unperturbed by Malaysia's accepted position in the eyes of the non-communist world, the Indonesian government has ordered the continuation of the policy of confrontation. There is every reason to believe that this policy will be continued indefinitely as long as Indonesia remains committed to the final goal of destroying Malaysia. There are, on the other hand, a number of reasons why Indonesia expects Malaysia to fall apart. In addition to the threat of force, the support of armed rebels in Sarawak and 'piracy' in the Straits of Malacca and the economic 'strangulation' of Penang and Singapore, Indonesia places great hope on what it sees as the inherent weaknesses in Malaysia: its multistate system and its multiracial society.

The question of the inner political and economic structure of Malaysia is the subject of most of this volume. Let me first draw attention to the event which

19

shows up most clearly the problems of a multistate system. This is the decision made by the Sultan of Brunei not to sign the Malaysia Agreement in London on July 9, 1963. It was a decision which took everyone by surprise because in every way Brunei is part of, and even central to, the northern third of Borneo which now forms East Malaysia. It is both logical and necessary to consider Brunei when writing of Malaysia and it is with the greatest reluctance that references to Brunei in this volume have been kept to the minimum. Nevertheless, it has to be said that the Sultan's decision was not purely arbitrary but follows directly from the multistate nature of the new nation. This volume gives the historical background of this multistate system in the four chapters in Part Two and treats the subject more analytically in some of the chapters in Part Five. The implications of having such an exceptional framework in South-east Asia and the place of this multiple monarchy in the Commonwealth of Nations are examined in the last two chapters of Part Five.

As for the inner strains which derive from the multiracial society of Malaysia, this comes out clearly in most chapters of this volume. Particularly important are the two chapters in Part One on population and urbanisation and the two sets of studies in Part Three and Part Four. Part Three deals with the religion and culture of the various peoples and Part Four with the economic issues on which the future prosperity of Malaysia must hinge. It is hoped that, taken as a whole, the studies in this book will provide a sufficiently comprehensive picture of the new and hopeful nation in South-east Asia.

For this introduction, it is only necessary to touch on the most important problems which both friendly and hostile countries see as crucial for Malaysia during the next few years. Probably the most immediate and most important is nationalism, Malaysia's own nationalism. The drive towards independence during the years 1945–57 was led by Malay nationalist leaders who accepted the need to temper their nationalism with an appeal to the immigrant peoples to make their homes in Malaya. In their success in persuading the British to leave without a bitter and prolonged struggle, they have made it possible for the many races of the country to prosper without resort to violent nationalism. It is a measure of the success of this co-operation that the development of Malayan (as distinct from Malay) nationalism could have been as gradual as it has been. But this slow development left many issues unresolved. The most urgent of these has been brought to the surface by the crisis of Malaysia. This is the question of political loyalty. The assumption that proof of loyalty is needed only from the immigrant races has usually, and quite justly, referred to the Chinese and Indians. But Malaysia has now exposed the wider implications of this assumption, for Indonesians living in Malaysia are themselves immigrants and their loyalty, too, must be proved. The ramifications of this have yet to be fully grasped, but it is likely that *everyone* in Malaysia, whether indigenous or immigrant, will soon be tested and that the nation will emerge with a far more united people than was ever possible before. In this test, Malaysia will be greatly helped by a constitutional monarchy to which most Malays can be loyal and under which the immigrant subjects can hope for just protection.

In this growth of a multiracial nationalism, the new states in Malaysia have also important roles to play. Singapore has already shown itself sufficiently sophisticated to develop a multiracial loyalty in a predominantly Chinese city. It now has the task of demonstrating the significance of this loyalty elsewhere in the country. Sarawak and Sabah are yet to face their tests, but there are indications that they will both evolve their own versions of multiracial loyalty. Whether these versions will blend easily with the loyalty developed on the mainland must, in large measure, depend on the wisdom of the new national leadership.

To some observers, even more important than nationalism is the problem of economic development. The Malaysian government is committed to a policy of development which, if fully carried through, will have far-reaching social and political consequences. It aims at creating a rural landowning class and an urban capitalist class, which, together with the bureaucrats, lawyers, doctors, teachers and other professional men, will form the backbone of a loyal and conservative middle class. This is expected to be the answer to the revolutionary movements of Indonesia, whether nationalist or communist. If successful, it would appear to be the challenge to the Indonesian thesis of continuous revolution.

The Malaysian development policy, however, faces two immediate threats: the need to arm Malaysia and the need to divert funds from Malaya to areas of greater need in Sarawak, and to a lesser extent in Sabah. Both may have the effect of slowing down the projects already planned for Malaya and this may in turn have political repercussions on the mainland. But perhaps more fundamental to this policy is the question of the speed of development. In nineteenth-century capitalism in Europe and America, rapid growth was accompanied by ruthless exploitation of the industrial working class and the destruction of small-scale enterprise. No one would dare to advocate such a policy today when capitalism itself has been modified almost beyond recognition. But it is not yet certain how a new nation like Malaysia can reach a mature stage of welfare capitalism without undergoing the experience of an earlier stage. It does appear that the welfare state principle which governs Malaysian economic policy would be considerably strengthened if some of the basic forms of co-operative enterprise far better suited to the rural conditions of the country were systematically introduced.

Next to nationalism and economic development and related to both is the issue of education. The main problem here stems from the different standards achieved in different types of schools and in different parts of the nation. The contrast between some of the urban centres like Singapore, Penang, Kuala Lumpur and the majority of the rural areas in Malaya alone is sharp enough. But the contrast with the states in East Malaysia (northern Borneo) is even greater. In addition to this, there remains the question of national education and what this must eventually mean for all loyal nationals of Malaysia. The two features most relevant to the prospects of Malaysian nationhood are the national language and education for democracy. In both of these, the future must depend on the developments in Malaya where nearly three-quarters of the people of Malaysia live. And in Malaya, the leaders of the Alliance government are fully committed to the policy of establishing the national language as the sole official language by 1967. As for democratic institutions, the same leaders have pledged themselves to uphold the highest principles of parliamentary democracy. As if to emphasise their total commitment, they invited the Commonwealth Parliamentary Association to make its conference in Kuala Lumpur coincide with the opening of the new Malaysian Parliament buildings in November 1963.

This brings me back to the concept of Malaysia, not as 'Melayu Raya', but as a strictly political decision to find a more permanent place for democratic institutions in South-east Asia. This concept has been opposed, as one would expect, by international communism. It has also been opposed by Indonesia where parliamentary democracy has failed. Malaysia still has to solve the problems arising out of its multistate system and plural society and it cannot be denied that these problems are great indeed. But the democratic nations of the world wish Malaysia well and recognise that it has a historic role in South-east Asia. Malaysia is now expected to uphold some of the finest ideals of modern history: the ideals of freedom, of democratic representation and of equality before the law. These are values which deserve to survive.

PART ONE

Natural and Human Structure

1

The Environment

ROBERT HO

This chapter outlines environmental features of location, climate, evolution, topography and soils, indicating only in broad terms those physical aspects which seem most significant in the present context. The role of physical factors in human affairs has been overstressed in the past. Environmental determinism, even in a comparatively underdeveloped region such as that of South-east Asia, contributes very little at the moment to an appraisal of those human motives, actions and developments which are involved in the Malaysian Federation, and which form the major focus of attention in this book.

LOCATIONAL ASPECTS

All the countries examined here are small, even by regional and South-east Asian standards. Malaya and Sarawak, covering 51,000 and 48,000 square miles respectively, are the largest individual units of Malaysia, yet in aggregate are from one third to one fourth smaller than Burma. The Bornean territories of Sarawak and Sabah together make up only one sixth the area of Borneo. Altogether, Malaysia, with a total area of about 130,000 square miles, is just about equal in size to Thailand.

Broadly these lands occupy the concave and northern flank of a great arc formed by Sumatra, Java and the Lesser Sunda Islands. Being centrally located inside the Indonesian archipelagos, Malaysia has certain strategic advantages in internal lines of communication by sea. In peace, sea-borne traffic between Europe and Africa on the one hand, and China and Japan on the other, will prefer the transit of the Malacca Straits and South China Sea to the detour around the extensive Indonesian archipelagos, or to the traverse of narrower, more tortuous and coral-girt passages such as the Sunda and Sumba Straits. To some extent, also, the Malay peninsula may be considered as a link between the continental and insular parts of South-east Asia, which together provide short and sheltered coastal passages eastwards to Australia.

However, substantial distances separate Malaya and Singapore from the Bornean territories, indicating that difficulties of integration which confront divided nations such as Pakistan might also apply to Malaysia. Between Singapore and Tanjong Datu, the shortest distance between the Malaya-Borneo lands, lies four hundred miles of the South China Sea. Kota Bharu in north-east Malaya is almost a thousand miles in a direct line from Jesselton, and the whole territory of Sabah lies closer to Manila than to Kuala Lumpur.

In practice, communications between Malaysia are limited by more than sheer distances. Strong winds, of Beaufort Force 4 or more, and high seas, are regularly generated during the north-east monsoon season, preventing movement for periods of up to three weeks each year by small vessels. In the same season, shifting bars are built up at the mouths of all streams on the east coast of Malaya, thus limiting entry to ships of very shallow draughts. The opposing coast of Sarawak is, by contrast, such a gently shelving plain that ships of even moderate draughts have to lie well offshore, as at Miri. Apart from Singapore, the best natural havens serving the South China Sea are those in Brunei, Marudu and Darvel Bays, and these are furthest removed from major routes and centres of population.

In terms of inter-regional values, the Malaysian territories, especially those of Malaya and Singapore, are often cited as strategic lands, exercising some form of 'control' over seaways through the Malacca Straits and South China Sea. It has been suggested that Britain acquired them in the nineteenth century to safeguard, in the region, the shores of the route from India to China.[1] But command of these narrows by conventional forces might equally well be exercised from the adjoining territories of Sumatra and Kalimantan, while the strategic value of the Anambas and Natuna archipelagos, both Indonesian-controlled groups located almost equidistant between Malaya and Sarawak, hardly needs emphasis.

The special situation of Singapore calls for further comment. As the history of the Second World War and recent events in the state of Singapore indicate, its value as a military base is compromised by its overcrowded and Chinese-dominated population.[2] Locational values alone cannot explain the present economic status of Singapore, which could equally well originate from the deliberate maintenance of its well-known status as a free port. In the past, equally successful entrepôts at Djambi and Malacca served the South-east Asian region; and equally suitable strategic havens are immediately available nearby, at Rhio and Lingga. Equally satisfactory artificial ports, such as that built at Sihanoukville, could be rapidly erected by modern techniques. Singapore will continue to operate as a regional entrepôt only so long as other South-east Asian nations find it more convenient and cheaper than duplicating its facilities.

CLIMATIC ASPECTS

All the Malaysian territories lie between the 1°–7°N. parallels. The lengths of days at such latitudes vary little throughout the year; at Alor Star, which lies just north of 6°N. latitude, the difference between the longest and shortest days of the year amounts to 37 minutes, while at Singapore the difference is reduced to only nine minutes.[3] This may explain variations in rice yields, as varieties developed in more northerly latitudes often perform disappointingly when transferred to the near-uniform photo-periodic environment of Malaysia.[4]

Uniformly high temperatures also are typical of the region, as part of the equatorial belt. However, owing to the high incidence of cloud, which reduces the average number of sunshine hours received at, for example, Port Swettenham, to $6\frac{1}{2}$ per day, temperatures over 100°F. are rare. The high summer maxima characteristic of the subtropics are seldom experienced, and mean yearly temperatures range between 79° and 83°F. Diurnal ranges of temperature are characteristically much larger; while the annual range of temperature at Kuala Lumpur is only about 3°F., its mean daily range is 17·5°F. Departures from these means are mainly due to altitude, variations in ground cover, and aspect. More 'continental' regimes, with mean daily maxima and minima of 93°F. and 73°F. respectively, are recorded in western Malaya[5] in a belt of subdued relief and a leeward aspect in relation to the monsoons. Such anomalies are slight even by local standards, which differentiate the climatic year on the distribution of seasonal rainfall.

Like other equatorial countries, Malaysia 'is to be reckoned among regions with the highest and most regular rainfall in the world'.[6] As Chart 1 shows (page 28), only a few areas in south-central Pahang, Perlis and north Kedah,[7] and the Tawau plains at the head of Cowie Harbour, experience less than an average of 100 inches per year. The same areas also have one or at most two months each year when rainfall drops below 100 mm (3·94 inches), a monthly level that Mohr considers critical for soil-vegetation systems in the Tropics.[8] Nowhere else in Malaysia do rainfall regimes depart from the high and regular levels of the equatorial belt. Large areas have annual totals well in excess of 120 inches, rising to over 160 inches in the highlands of Sarawak and Sabah.[9]

Rainfall levels of this magnitude may be accompanied by what appear to be significant variations. On Malaya's east coast, rainfall variations of up to 40 per cent around an annual mean of 120 inches are recorded. All this means is that 96 inches may be recorded in a dry year, and 144 inches in a wet one; if distributed evenly, such rainfall would total 8 or 12 inches each month in a dry and a wet year

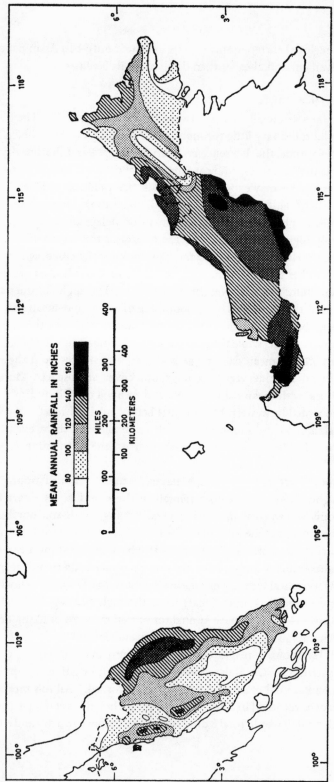

Figure 1: Total Annual Rainfall

respectively. However, occasional dry spells lasting for three to four weeks are common. Since the average rate of evaporation ranges from 40 to 60 inches per annum (3·33 to 5·0 inches per month), such spells can cause wintering in rubber trees and poor tillering in rice. Possibly the main effect of continual high temperatures and humidities is on human effort and energy and on the proliferation of fungal and bacterial diseases.

Except for a few stations, the distribution of rainfall in Malaysia seldom conforms to that experienced in typical equatorial regions, which have higher monthly averages at or just following the equinoxes. For many parts of Malaya and Borneo (Chart 2, page 30), the major peak of rainfall occurs during the north-east monsoon season, which is established in Malaya by late November, and in Sarawak by December. During this period, persistent north-easterly winds representing a zonal flow of subtropical easterlies, and reinforced by air from a high pressure system over Yunnan, may stretch all the way from Guam to Ceylon. These winds, often averaging 15 knots or more in brief surges, are separated from normal southern hemisphere westerlies by the Inter-Tropical Convergence Zone. Exceptionally heavy rains of six inches on each of two successive days appear to be associated with some form of eddy or wave-formation along this zone, affecting a belt 1° to 6°N., or 1° north and south of the ITCZ itself.[10] As this zone fluctuates considerably from the median position shown in Chart 2, the east coast of Malaya and the north-east coast of Borneo receive up to forty per cent of the whole year's rainfall in the period. Monthly falls then may rise to nearly twice those of the south-west monsoon season. However, the coast north of Brunei Bay as far as Kudat, being aligned parallel to prevailing surface winds, experiences its driest months at this season.[11] The persistent winds, working on the long stretch of unobstructed sea between the Malaysian territories, generate large swells. As indicated above, they build up sandbars at the mouths of rivers, and storm beaches on exposed coasts. They cause much turbulence and mixing of sea waters to all depths in the South China Sea, and a marked 'stacking' of water against the east coast of Malaya.[12] There is some evidence to suggest that catches of fish in this season are higher than at other times in the year.[13]

From May to September, south-westerly to southerly air streams are established over Malaysia. They originate as southern hemisphere subtropical or equatorial westerlies, pulled across the Equator to the intense low pressure cells developed over subtropical India and north Burma. As the season advances, the Inter-Tropical Convergence Zone moves north, ultimately beyond the Malaysian territories (Chart 3, page 31), which then lie completely under southern hemisphere air streams. However, these winds are feeble and less persistent than the north-east monsoon streams. The surface circulation often breaks down, allowing on occasion the penetration of tropical maritime (Pacific) air into the region

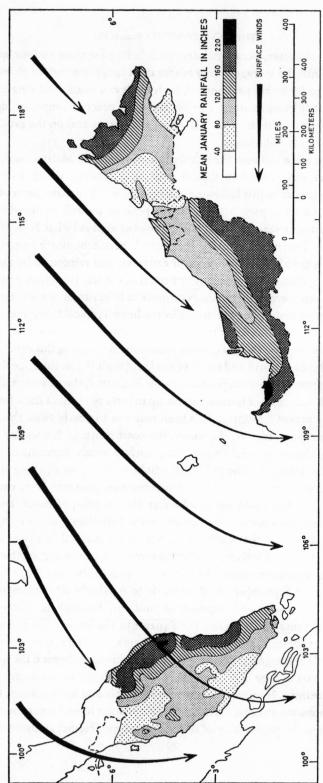

Figure 2: Rainfall and Surface Winds in January

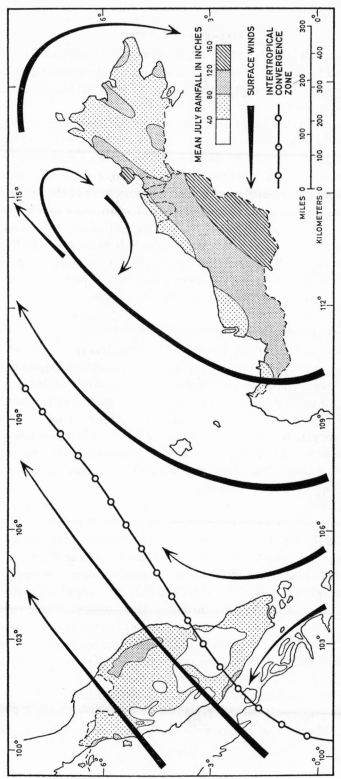

Figure 3: Rainfall and Surface Winds in July

as far west as north Borneo, and on others a resurgence of subtropical continental (subsident) air from the cell over south-east China.[14]   The season is generally dry for most areas in Malaya except for that part of the west coast around Malacca and Port Dickson.

Both monsoons may be thought of as abnormally strengthened modifications of zonal or planetary wind systems, which are fully re-established over Malaysia in April, and again in September.   In these periods, lasting for six to eight weeks each, indeterminate wind movements typical of the true doldrums predominate. Highly localised convectional rains are then common, bringing the largest proportion of annual rainfall to the north-west coast of Sabah.   Line squalls, known in Malaya as 'Sumatras', develop in these months, particularly at the end of the south-west monsoon period;[15] they bring high winds, heavy rains, and sharp falls in temperature.   Land and sea breezes are most in evidence during these inter-monsoon periods, and orographic control over rainfall patterns is then more clearly evident than at any other time in the climatic year.

GEOLOGICAL EVOLUTION

The Malaysian territories, together with Sumatra, Java and the rest of Borneo, form the largest exposed units of a partly drowned continent known as Sundaland.   The lower parts of this continent were submerged in comparatively recent (Pleistocene or post-Pleistocene) times, forming the shallow epicontinental seas around the higher islands and peninsulas of South-east Asia.   The edges of Sundaland are clearly defined at the Macassar Straits and on the Indian Ocean coasts of Sumatra and Java (Chart 4, page 33).   But connections with geological formations in Thailand, Burma and Vietnam are yet uncertain, and possible links with the Philippine arcs are still tentative.

In van Bemmelen's view,[16] Sundaland began with the formation of a geosyncline or marine trough which curved from the present Anambas islands into the headwaters of the Barito river (Chart 4, page 33).   The land mass bordering this trough to the west was Gondwanaland, and that to the east, Cathaysia.   Both continents have long since suffered complete erosion, drifting, or incorporation into the basic silicate melt of the world, but they contributed sediments to the geosyncline for most of the Palaeozoic era.   These sediments were then compressed and heavily intruded by igneous materials to form the initial land-core of Sundaland.   The subsequent growth of the continent has involved a repetition of geosynclincal formations evolving on the margins of the core, being filled in and compressed in turn.   To the south and south-west of the Anambas core, successively younger belts have been welded on to Sundaland, producing in turn the Malayan coulisses, then the Tigapuloh Mountains and Barisan Ranges of Sumatra, and finally, the yet incomplete orogenies represented by the Simaloe-

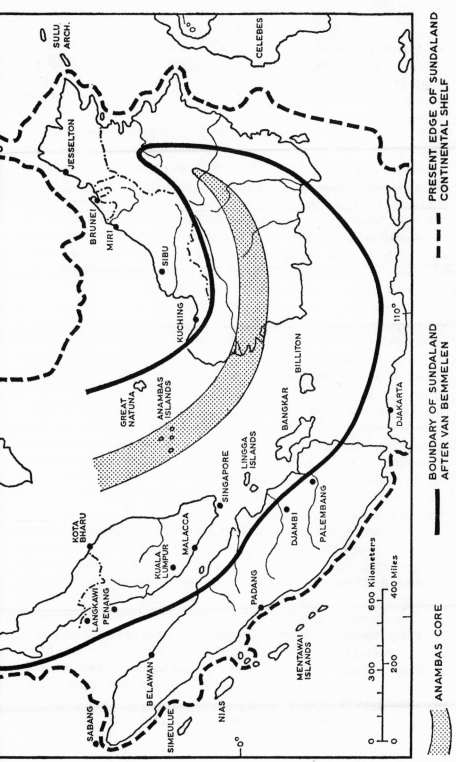

SULU
ARCH.

CELEBES

JESSELTON

BRUNEI
MIRI
SIBU

KUCHING

GREAT
NATUNA

ANAMBAS
ISLANDS

BILLITON

BANGKAR

110°

DJAKARTA

LINGGA
ISLANDS

SINGAPORE

DJAMBI

PALEMBANG

KOTA
BHARU

MALACCA

KUALA
LUMPUR

LANGKAWI
PENANG

PADANG

BELAWAN

MENTAWAI
ISLANDS

600 Kilometers

400 Miles

300   200

0°

SABANG

SIMEULUE

NIAS

0   0

PRESENT EDGE OF SUNDALAND
CONTINENTAL SHELF

BOUNDARY OF SUNDALAND
AFTER VAN BEMMELEN

ANAMBAS CORE

Figure 4: Core and Boundaries of Sundaland

Nias-Mentawei islands off western Sumatra.[17]   On the opposite flank of the core, a comparable sequence is known only from Sarawak and Brunei, where marginal geosynclines have been steadily displaced north and north-west, so that the axis of the present-day trough lies in the South China Sea, beyond the 2,000 metre bathymetric contour.

In what is now the Malay peninsula, land-building began in early Cambrian times with the southward extension of a geosyncline from Tenasserim into north-west Malaya.   By Silurian times, this trough had extended to at least the latitude of Kuala Lumpur, and in the early Carboniferous (Viseán) period, to the Kuantan area, where limestones were laid down in a shallow sea bordered by a volcanic coast.   Southwards, over Singapore and the Bangka-Billiton areas, the geosyncline appears to have shallowed, so that arenaceous and largely non-fossiliferous sediments become increasingly dominant.   In the vast period represented by the Palaeozoic, orogenic movements and partial infilling of the geosyncline must have produced a local geography of land and sea masses very different from that of today, but very little evidence of this has survived.   The present configuration of Malaya dates from major earth movements from mid-Mesozoic to late-Cretaceous times, when the geosynclinal sediments were folded along NNW–SSE lines. Massive granitic batholiths were emplaced in the anticlinal cores, and at their contacts with the sediments, lodes of tin were concentrated by hydrothermal processes.   Since the Mesozoic orogeny, Malaya has formed a stable and exposed part of Sundaland, and the axes of earth movements have shifted progressively further outwards to the south and south-west.   Apart from one basin deposit of Jurassic-Cretaceous age,[18] and equally restricted coal-bearing lacustrine formations of the Tertiary, no geologic deposits younger than the Triassic are known. But, as a result of eustatic fluctuations of sea level during the Pleistocene, Quaternary to Recent alluvials have been forming accretions marginal to the older, pre-Mesozoic formations.[19]

In the Bornean territories of Malaysia, the earliest deposits are of Devonian age, and are restricted to west Sarawak.   Here a complex history of sedimentation, folding and igneous activity occurred until the late-Cretaceous, when the major axis of activity migrated north and north-eastwards.[20]   An enormous trough, the North-west Borneo Geosyncline then came into existence, occupying an arc from the present Lupar Valley in Sarawak to the Trusmadi Mountains in Sabah.   In this trough, stages of sedimentation, basin-deposition, and uplift were each accompanied by folding and igneous intrusions of varying degrees of severity.   In such an unstable part of the earth's crust, with closely juxtaposed youthful mountains and deep marine troughs, relief energy was large, and thick deposits rapidly accumulated; 34,000 to 55,000 feet of shales and greywackes forming the Belaga Formation were accumulated between Upper-Cretaceous and Eocene times.

Deposition in central Sarawak ceased in the late Miocene, but continued until Oligocene times in north Sarawak and Sabah. Similarly, initial folding began in the late-Eocene in central and north Sarawak, moving to the Sabah area by Miocene times. In the Pliocene, extensive acid and intermediate pyroclastics were emplaced in the Hose and Nieuwenhuis Mountains and in the Linau Balui and Usun Apaul plateaux; they were followed by basaltic extrusions.

In general, the Bornean territories are geologically younger than the Malay peninsula.[21] Indeed, folding in central Sarawak and Sabah occurred as recently as the early-Pleistocene, following which the exposed landscape was bevelled in what is known as the Peneplanation Cycle. This in turn was followed by a general warping movement ranging from 2,500 to 300 feet, which initiated the Jerudong Cycle of erosion.[22] In Malaya a comparable sequence has not yet been identified, but marine benches and platforms at an altitude of about 70 metres point to an early-Pleistocene base level of this height. The submerged parts of Sundaland, particularly the apparently uniform depths of the bed of the South China Sea, and coastal alluvials of west Malaya that extend below present sea level, suggest, by contrast, a Pleistocene sea much lower than the present, which is the result of the final melting of ice sheets in post-Pleistocene or Flandrian times. This final eustatic episode has initiated the present cycle of erosion and deposition throughout the region.

TOPOGRAPHICAL ASPECTS

After the last episode in the geological history outlined above, streams everywhere in Sundaland began depositing alluvials far up-valley.[23] Gradually their drowned estuaries were filled in with broad floodplain deposits; then the surrounding shallow or epicontinental seas, formerly the lower, more base-levelled parts of Sundaland, began to be covered. In this way, the great coastal plains of western Malaya and of Sarawak and Brunei were formed, and in places are still extending seawards at a rate estimated at more than thirty feet per century. The high rate of deposition, normal in an equatorial region of heavy rainfall and intense erosion, has masked the effects of the Flandrian transgression. Indented coasts, usual in submerged lands, are rare in Malaysia, where smoothing of littorals by alluvials has so far advanced that all the territories together muster no more than about 3,000 miles of coastline. The deposits, which form about twenty per cent of Sarawak, and a slightly smaller proportion of Malaya, impinge directly against the older, highly eroded pre-Pleistocene landscape, which protrudes through its surrounding aprons of alluvials in the same way as islands stand above a shallow sea.

The older landscapes have suffered long continued weathering of equatorial intensity. In this environment, deep, kaolin-rich and clayey regoliths develop.

35

In addition, run-off is intense and stream densities high. Under these conditions, a fine pattern of drainage evolves, and streams quickly incise themselves through the weak regoliths to bedrock, producing steep-sided and youthful valleys which persist well into the mature stages of erosion. The sharp slopes normal to such regions are maintained, if not actually produced, by landslides which leave behind steep, curving tracks. Certain types of soil wastage may have similar effects on slopes.

The Malaysian landscapes are therefore dominated by steep and accidented topography, even though altitudes are subdued by comparison with those of other continents. Kinabalu, the highest point in the whole of the East Indies, rises to some 13,000 feet above sea level, while Murud in Sarawak and Tahan in Malaya are barely over 8,000 and 7,000 feet high respectively. But in Malaya, at least seventy per cent of the peninsula lies over 1,000 feet;[24] over forty per cent forms steep or actually mountainous land characterised by excessive soil drainage, lithosols, and severe erosion. Sabah is perhaps the most accidented of the Malaysian territories, reflecting its complex geological evolution and position at the unstable hinge-line between Bornean and Philippine structures. Collenette has shown that even the so-called Eastern and Western Lowlands of Sabah are really a series of isolated plains and terraces, interrupted by rugged extensions of the Western Cordillera and Central Uplands.[25] And while Sarawak has nearly three-quarters of its surface below the 300 metre contour, about sixty per cent of this apparent lowland consists of accidental scarps and hogsbacks.

The fundamental differences in environment presented by the youthful soils, sluggishly drained and flat plains on the one hand, and by the steep, incised uplands with mature soils on the other, are recognised in Chart 5 (page 37), which suggests, within the limitations of scale, the distribution of these two major relief types. An intermediate category of undulating relief is also differentiated but, in terms of area and cultural responses, is less significant. Major units within each of these relief types are described briefly below.

Malaya

1. *Plains.* The largest unit, and that most significant for human development, is the West Coast Plain, which extends nearly 600 miles from Perlis in the north to the Kukup peninsula in south-west Johore. The plain is interrupted by low hills only between Port Dickson and Malacca, and in places is more than 30 miles broad. Borings into the deposits at Parit Buntar in Perak did not penetrate beyond Recent alluvials at 200 feet, indicating the rapid build-up of this plain since the Pleistocene. It slopes very gently everywhere, gradients of one foot in 17 miles being typical. Its seaward and extending margins are bare mudflats, but inland, at heights determined by the depths and frequencies of tidal inundation, appear mangrove forests.

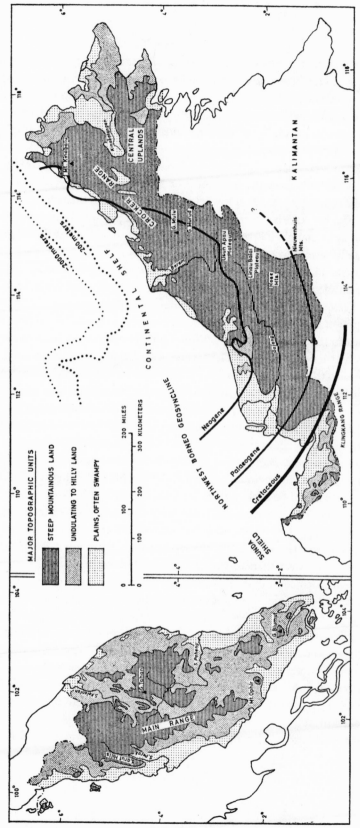

Figure 5: Major Relief Units

These give way in turn to fresh-water swamps such as those of the Trans-Perak and Krian regions, large areas of which have been cleared and settled by padi-growing farmers. Over the level plain, streams debouching from the hills meander broadly; complex patterns of levees, back swamps, abandoned channels and reworked deposits normal to all alluvial plains are found, and are topographically extremely slight.

Similar prograding coastal plains are found only between the Kuantan delta, southwards to Endau on the east coast of Malaya. Elsewhere, the east coast consists of a repeating pattern of low, curved sandy beaches thrown up by northeast monsoon breakers between low, but steep-sided promontories. Behind the beaches or 'permatang', drainage is ponded back into lagoons, but the whole belt is continually reworked by shifting streams attempting to maintain their outlets to the South China Sea. The belt is seldom more than five miles broad, but it forms a conspicuous region due to the open, savannah-type vegetation that colonises these near-sterile soils following deforestation.

Tongues of the plainland environment extend up the major streams, probably at least to the present 250 foot contour, which represents the head of deposition or actual level of an early-Pleistocene sea. Such inland extensions, most conspicuous in the Muar and lower Perak rivers among others, repeat on progressively smaller scales the patterns and landforms of the larger coastal plains. Yet they are not as extensive as might be thought, since Malayan rivers upstream of the coastal plain sectors occupy the youthful and pre-Pleistocene valleys. Alluvial formations in these valleys are further limited by colluvial deposits.

2. *Mountainous or accidented regions.* Scrivenor distinguished several coulisses, or ranges arranged on approximately parallel NNW–SSE strike lines.[26] This geological concept might be replaced for the present purposes by:

(a) The Main Range, a curved, high and complex feature running from the Thai frontier to about the latitude of Malacca. It is a conspicuous barrier, containing most of the 5,000 foot peaks of Malaya, and is asymmetrically disposed closer to the west than to the east coast. The highest parts of the Main Range are formed by granitic rocks exposed through aeons of erosion which have stripped off the overlying sediments now occupying flanking or synclinal positions in the range.

(b) Complex, generally lower, but highly accidented mountains forming most of upper Kelantan, inland Trengganu and Pahang. The highest peak in Malaya, Gunong Tahan, is found in this region, and is built of resistant quartzitic sediments. The regional NNW–SSE strike is present but difficult to recognise, and the heavily forested, landslide-scarred relief has so far repelled most forms of human occupancy.

(c) South of Malacca, the mountainous units lose topographic definition, appearing in isolated massifs such as that of Mount Ophir rather than in continuous ranges. Transverse movement along east–west lines is therefore easier in Johore and south Pahang than in north Malaya.

3. *Undulating regions.* In this category are the low uplands of south and central Johore and of south Pahang. These areas probably represent the marine platform cut by the early-Pleistocene sea which stood at or slightly above the 70 metre (240 foot) contour.[27] Continuing work in Malaya will probably reveal further extensions of this surface, which was first identified by its looser-structured, deficiency soils developed on what is now called the Older Alluvium. Topographically these areas offer special advantages to large-scale agricultural operations, and extensive oil palm and rubber plantations are located there.

Borneo[28]

In essentials, the Bornean territories consist of low coastal plains, backed by a foothill zone of varying width that rises to steep mountainous territory on the Kalimantan border. Large areas are still unknown, even reconnaissance by aerial survey being limited by the high incidence of cloud during the year.

1. *Plains.* An almost continuous fringe of coastal plain extends all the way from west Sarawak to Brunei Bay, being developed, as in the case of the west coast plain of Malaya, from alluvials laid down on the shallow, drowned Sundaland shelf. It occupies some twenty per cent of Sarawak and Brunei, and about 5,660 square miles of this, or twelve per cent of these territories, are peat swamps, as compared with three to six per cent for Malaya. The difference reflects the greater width and more difficult drainage of the Borneo plain, which has to transmit the waters of large rivers such as the Lupar, Rajang and Baram across, in some cases, fifty miles of subdued gradients.

From Brunei Bay around Sabah, only isolated coastal plains appear, such as those of the Klias-Crocker-Bandau areas at the head of Marudu Bay. The Eastern Lowlands include deltaic deposits of the Sugut, Labuk and Cowie streams, which have not yet coalesced into continuous coastal plains. In this relief category are also included the low, slightly dissected Pleistocene peneplanes of the Kinabatangan, Segama and Semporna lowlands.

2. *Mountainous or accidented regions.* In western Sarawak, steep but isolated ground is formed from resistant volcanic, igneous or limestone rocks. The Bau district, with its towering karst hills, and mineralised lodes (gold, silver, antimony and mercury), resembles the Kinta Valley of Malaya. South of west Sarawak, the Klingkang Range presents a bold, north-facing escarpment, being the northern limb of the Kotoengau syncline.

In the Second and Third Divisions of Sarawak, hogsbacks and conspicuous cuestas are developed on sandstones with a curved regional strike that was imposed by the North-west Borneo Geosyncline. At the point of maximum flexure, on the Kalimantan border, rise the 4,000 foot peaks and mesa-like surfaces of the Hose-Nieuwenhuis and Usun Apau-Linau Balui areas respectively.

In Sabah, the highest ground is formed by the Crocker, Witti and Trusmadi ranges, known collectively as the Western Cordillera. Eastwards is a triangular area of lower altitude but equally accidented relief formed on basalts of the Labuk and volcanics of the Tawau Highlands, among others. The Klias Hills and Sir James Brooke Range present steep, cliffed faces towards the coast. Trend-lines are complex, and whether they are linked to the Philippines via the Palawan or Sulu arcs remains to be investigated.

3. *Undulating regions.* In west Sarawak, land in this category is found on Tertiary sediments at an average height of 80 feet above sea level. Similar units can be recognised on the eastern side of Marudu Bay, and in the partly dissected basins of the Tenom, Sook, and Keningau in the Western Cordillera; the latter are probably graben or block-faulted basins, only slightly dissected by existing streams.

MAJOR SOILS[29]

It is generally recognised that soils of the Tropics are less fertile than those of arid or of temperate regions. Malaysian soils are no exception, since they have evolved in a continually hot and moist climate that has prevailed for at least the last million years. In most profiles, reserves of available nutrients are very small, and the organic matter that accumulates beneath a dense stand of lowland forest is usually no more than a few inches deep. When exposed, the whole accumulation, which may have taken years to develop, oxidises away in a few years. So rapid are pedogenic processes that mature characteristics such as deep, kaolin-rich residues and prominent sesquioxide horizons evolve quickly even in comparatively youthful parent materials. On long-exposed parts of the uplands, sedentary soils display more senile features such as gibbsitic horizons and desilicified residues rich in haematite. Finally, Malaysian soils have not, apart from limited areas in Sabah, had fresh accretions of volcanic material to counter the continual losses of nutrients in their equatorial environment.

More youthful soils are generally associated with alluvials where, in addition, freedom from erosion, location adjacent to water and a higher level of available nutrients result in a physical type that produces almost all the food of the region. Yet even soils in this environment pose serious problems of utilisation, since drainage is always difficult and soil acidity is often a limiting factor to cropping.

Within the two major physiographic-pedological groups mentioned above, further distinctions can be made on the basis of parent materials. In general, basic parent materials such as andesites and certain shales produce better soils, while acid rocks such as quartzites and granites weather down into pale, structure-

40

less residues of low base-exchange capacities. However, the soils described below are named in conformity with the pedological classification developed by the US Department of Agriculture for the world as a whole to permit comparisons with tropical regions outside Malaysia. No attempt is made to locate each group other than in broad terms, as there are no complete soil maps for the Bornean territories.

I. Major Soils of the Plains

1. *Organic Soils.*[30] These develop in low-lying parts of coastal and fluvial plains in Malaysia, wherever stagnant drainage and anaerobic conditions allow the accumulation of plant debris. In Sarawak, Anderson has shown how a prograding coastline may cause backing-up of streams inland; there the gradual rise of the water table initiates and maintains peats, which ultimately form bog plains estimated to occupy some twelve per cent of Sarawak and Brunei. In Malaya, peat formations or soils with more than sixty-five per cent of organic matter occupy three to six per cent of the whole peninsula. Tha largest Malayan formations are found in the west coast plains, accumulating in 'basins' between major rivers, in abandoned channels and in old lagoons. Depths of peat up to twenty feet are not uncommon, but average thicknesses range between four and eight feet.

All Malaysian peats (except for insignificant deposits at very high altitudes) are oligotrophic, that is, composed largely of partly decayed woody material which adds considerably to the difficulties of cultivation. The semi-liquid matrix shrinks rapidly on drying, ultimately collapsing irreversibly into a powdery mass. Even in their original state, therefore, peats possess low mechanical strength, forming poor bearing ground for tree crops. Many individual formations are also extremely acid owing to the presence of sulphur compounds. These obstacles to agriculture are incompletely resolved, even though pressure on available food-producing land in Malaya has extended padi-growing on to such soils.

2. *Low Humic Gleys.*[31] Most of the soils developed on alluvials of the coastal plains and floodplains of Malaysia fall into this group. Apart from having in common a high water table, soils of the group vary widely. Most commonly, they are grey to brownish clays, with strong gleyed horizons close to the surface. Mottling is common, even to the stage when ironstone concretions or 'batu kankar' are developed. With increasing organic matter, intergrades to ground-water gleys, semi-bog soils and mucks appear and, with increasingly coarser or sandier textures, humus podzols. These transitional soils occur on the margins of basins and of terraces respectively.

Some soils of the group are very fertile, such as the Selangor Series, with high levels of available nutrients for oil palms, and the prized rice-growing soils of north-west Malaya containing montmorillonitic clays. Others are almost sterile,

41

such as the deficiency soils of part of the Kelantan delta, and the extremely acid coastal soils of Tanjong Minyak in Malacca.

On very recent alluvials laid down at the littorals or on the banks of streams, immature phases of low humic gleys are found. Taxonomically these are azonal formations, showing very limited profile development: merely a fibrous black to dark grey topsoil overlying a light to dark grey clay subsoil, in which mottling and coarse soil structures gradually intensify with age. Many profiles are saline (halomorphic) and several contain crystalline gypsum at depth, indicating incomplete removal of alkaline, particularly sulphate, compounds. However, the rapid soil-forming processes normal to the Malaysian environment permit agriculture even on such immature soils, even though rice yields may drop below national averages.

3. *Podzols.*[32] Typical members of this group are found on sandy, excessively drained beaches and terraces on the coasts of east Malaya and lowland Sarawak. In a typical section, the ashy grey surface gives way at varying depths to an organic and iron-rich alluvial horizon. The clay content and nutrient status of the whole profile is very low, and the natural vegetation on such soil consists of heath forest, a climax lower and simpler than tropical rain forest. When cleared, it is replaced for long periods by open 'kerangas' and 'padang' vegetation of savannah type, indicating the poverty of the environment which offers little inducement for agricultural occupancy.

II. Major Soils of the Uplands

1. *Lithosols and Regosols* are developed on steep slopes everywhere in Malaysia where removal of weathered material downslope keeps pace with weathering, thus reducing the profile to a few inches of young, stony, and partly decayed material. Panton estimates that the group covers about 40 per cent of the total area of Malaya, and it probably occurs on a similar scale in the Bornean territories. Satisfactory use of these soils is confined to timber utilisation at intensities which do not initiate soil erosion.

2. *Red and Yellow Podzolic Soils* form the dominant group of upland and undulating regions in Malaysia, being evolved from a great variety of parent materials. The Rengam Series, formed from granite, is especially common throughout Malaya, and is probably closely related to the Jagoi Association of yellow to reddish-yellow, well to imperfectly drained, gritty loams and clays of Sarawak. Such soils, with moderate acidities, kaolinitic clays of low base-exchange capacity, and low reserves of plant nutrients, are surprisingly good agriculturally, possibly because their moderate structures and deep profiles allow plants access to the B_2 and Chorizons where further nutrients are continually being released by weathering.

Similar soils can be derived from shales, sandstones and greywackés. Subsoils with mottled zones, discrete ferruginous concretions, or iron pans may develop, depending on the composition of the parent material or on local ground-water drainage. On more acid parent materials, light-coloured and less fertile variants appear; such soils are usually coarser textured and more siliceous. In this category are some soils derived from the Older Alluvium, weathered material that has suffered two cycles of weathering on an early-Pleistocene marine plat-form; magnesium deficiencies develop in many rubber plantations located on these soils.[33]

3. *Latosols.* These are upland soils formed from basic igneous rocks and some sedimentary rocks rich in ferro-magnesian compounds.[34] As a rule, they are deep, uniform, red to dark reddish-brown loams or clay loams, with strong medium to crumb structures. They are excellent multipurpose soils, but unfor-tunately of limited extent only, occurring in central and east Malaya and in Sabah, where they are known as the Kuantan Series and Serian Association respectively.

4. *Limestone soils* include terra rossas or red earths, and rendzinas.[35] They are very limited in area and of moderate fertility, being more of academic than of practical significance, and their location on highly irregular karstic surfaces further restricts their use.

In many of the soils outlined above, lateritic horizons may evolve, since iron, and to a lesser extent aluminium, compounds, are easily mobilised in equatorial soils. These compounds are deposited in a zone within the profile over which the water table fluctuates.[36] The resulting formations rarely assume the vesicular morphology of Buchanan's classic laterite; pea-iron gravels, irregular concretions, or ferruginous coatings of soil aggregates are more common in Malaysia, some-times to the extent of forming continuous, indurated horizons. The density and thickness of the concretionary horizon or pan may restrict agriculture, parti-cularly if exposed through soil erosion, when it forms an impervious natural pavement at the surface.

This outline of the individual facets making up the physical environment of Malaysia might suggest a picture very different from the lush tropical world of the popular magazines. Certainly no attempt has been made to gloss over environ-mental problems of immediate significance such as are involved in increasing agricultural productivity from soils that are intrinsically poor, and in a climate that positively encourages fungal or bacterial attack. Less obvious, although just as germane, are the effects upon human effort of the equatorial climate, or the influence on future development of the low energy resources of Malaysia. Yet Malaya itself enjoys a degree of prosperity that is matched by few nations in Asia, showing how successfully environmental difficulties have so far been surmounted. It is worth remembering, with Toynbee, that human achievement probably needs some form of challenge or difficulty if it is to attain worthwhile levels.

43

2

Vegetation and Flora

M. E. D. POORE

The Malay peninsula and the islands of South-east Asia can boast the richest flora to be found on the surface of the globe, surpassing even the forests of the Amazon basin and the Congo. The variety of form in the Malayan forests is not immediately evident, however, as it is in the meadows of the European Alps or during spring in the Middle Eastern Steppes. For the outward aspect of the rain forest which covers most of the region is sombre and uniform; there is no seasonal flush of flowering and indeed many of the species flower rarely, while the scale of the trees is so vast that often the only indication to the wayfarer of a wealth of colour in the canopy are fallen petals on the forest floor.

Plant geographers, who study the distribution of plant species, find that each has its own geographical range which is determined in part by the climatic and soil conditions in which it can survive and partly by geological history. There is also a tendency for large numbers of species to be grouped in particular regions. One such is the area comprising the Malay peninsula, the Philippines, Indonesia and New Guinea. Rapid changes of flora occur at its limits.[1] There are, for example, 375 genera of flowering plants which reach their northern limit in the Kra Isthmus and 200 genera reach their southern limit in the same area; 664 occur in New Guinea and not in Australia, 340 in Australia and not in New Guinea. Similar discontinuities occur elsewhere round the margins of the region, but within it floristic boundaries are much less distinct. It is this region (the Malay peninsula, Borneo, Indonesia, New Guinea and the Philippines) which is known to plant geographers as Malaysia. The term was apparently first used by Zollinger in 1857, but he excluded east New Guinea.[2] Since then it has been applied to approximately the same area by a number of authors; but usage has now become stabilised by the setting up of the Flora Malesiana Foundation based in Leyden.

This organisation under the direction of Dr van Steenis has undertaken the colossal task of producing a definitive flora of the region. Three volumes have already appeared.[3] To the botanist, therefore, the term Malaysia means something different, and will always mean something different, from the political unit formed by the federation of Malaya and Singapore with the two territories in Borneo. This is no new problem. Political boundaries rarely coincide with those that are biologically natural.

There is no doubt, however, that there are close plant geographical links between the Malay peninsula and the western coastal strip of Borneo. In fact there are apparently greater floristic and vegetational similarities between west Borneo and the east coast of Malaya than there are between the two sides of the Main Range in Malaya itself. For example, there is a distinct Bornean element in the flora of South-east Johore; behind the sandbars on the east coast of Malaya there are swamps covered by the tree *Campnosperma coriacea*, a species which is very rare on the west coast of Malaya but is a feature of the developing stages of the Sarawak swamp forests; and the important kapur tree, *Dryobalanops aromatica*, which forms great forests on the east side of the Main Range in Malaya belongs to a genus which is better developed in Borneo. (There are two small pockets of this species west of the range in the passes near Kuala Lumpur, but it is thought that these may have been introduced from the east by aborigines engaged in the camphor trade.[4]) Corner gives many other fascinating examples of the similarities and differences between Borneo and Malaya, but all these are within the framework of the greater floristic unity which is the plant geographers' Malaysia.[5]

The reason for the local similarity between west Borneo and east Malaya probably lies in the geological history of the region. For in the Tertiary these lands were all part of the Sunda Shelf region and it is only comparatively recently that Borneo and Malaya have become separated by the submersion of the southern part of the China Sea. The sea here is shallow and there have been considerable fluctuations in the relative levels of land and sea during the Pleistocene.[6] Thus it is perhaps significant that many of the similarities between the two regions are of swamp and river plants.

THE LOWLAND RAIN FOREST

Before the advent of neolithic man the whole of this region was covered by evergreen tropical rain forest, a formation which depends for its existence on a climate which is essentially non-seasonal and in which the trees may grow continuously, interrupted by neither periodical drought nor cold. The lofty and luxuriant forest which grows under these conditions is hard to fell with primitive tools and does not burn readily; neither are the acid soils of Malaya very fertile even after forest clearance. Consequently settlement appears to have been sparse and, even in the last few centuries, has been mainly confined to the coast and navigable rivers. Even now official reports show that over 70 per cent of Malaya is forest covered, 73 per cent of Sarawak, 80 per cent of Sabah and 71 per cent of Brunei.[7] Such a proportion of forest is almost unique in the world today and carries with it some unique advantages.

If one flies over the lowland Malaysian forest, one sees a welling green surface like a choppy sea. The upper canopy is broken into crests and hollows. It is only in the mangrove, the swamps or the mountain forest that the canopy becomes nearly even. Bare rock or soil can rarely be seen except where precipices thrust their way through the forest cover, landslips leave their scars on steep slopes and banks of uncolonised mud or gravel appear along the rivers and the coast. The tree reigns supreme and the areas of scrub and grassland, bamboo thicket and ginger owe their existence to disturbance, usually by man. Consequently it is not surprising that many of the weeds of Malaysia are not native to the country; for example *Mimosa pudica, Eupatorium odoratum, Clidemia hirta* and the lawn grass *Axonopus compressus* all originate in South America.

Inside the forest the prevailing impression is of dim green light and innumerable smooth, straight trunks passing upward almost unbranched into the canopy. It is not particularly difficult to move except where a tree has fallen and let in the light, thus encouraging a vigorous young growth. Normally an occasional cut with a parang suffices to clear a way through the low shrubs and palms, and the light intensity on the ground is so low (often less than one per cent of that in the canopy) that nothing grows there but tree seedlings and the occasional shade-tolerant herb or fern.

The trees in the rain forest are not the largest in the world—*Eucalyptus regnans* of Australia reaches a greater height, and the Californian Redwood, *Sequoia sempervirens*, a greater girth—but the canopy is usually 140 to 160 feet or more high and many trees reach 12 to 15 feet in girth. Very many have an unbranched bole of 100 to 120 feet. If the structure of the forest is analysed, it is found that there are usually three layers of trees. The uppermost or emergents form the crests of the waves; the middle form the hollows of the waves; and the leaves of the lowermost are never fully exposed in the canopy.

Many of the forests in this region are very ancient. There is no evidence of catastrophic changes of climate in the Quaternary period, and much of the land surface has probably been covered continually with vegetation since it rose above the sea, some of it as long ago as the Jurassic. Certainly it appears that kinds of vegetation existed in the Tertiary which are comparable with those found today. But so far our knowledge of the history of the Malaysian flora is rudimentary; a great field of research is still open here.

Uninterrupted development and favourable environment have made the forest astonishingly rich in species. Counting only trees over three feet in girth I have recently found 381 species on 55 acres of forest in Pahang. Wyatt-Smith has listed 208 and 210 species respectively on two areas of four acres in Selangor and Malacca.[8] There are similar figures for Borneo. On 15 acres of the Semengoh Forest Reservation in Sarawak 250 species over two feet in girth have been found.[9] Consequently each species in these forests is represented by rather few individuals.

The most important family of trees in the Malaysian forests is the Dipterocarpaceae. Many of these are emergents and they provide the important timbers of chengal (*Balanocarpus heimii*), meranti (*Shorea* spp.), keruing (*Dipterocarpus* spp.), kapur (*Dryobalanops aromatica*), alan (*Shorea albida*) and others, as well as the illipe nuts of the Bornean species, *Shorea gysbertiana*. Many other families of tree contribute to the forest, some abundantly, some with one or two species only. Different families tend to be represented among the emergents and the lower storeys. In the former the most prominent are Burseraceae, Leguminosae, Anacardiaceae (which includes the poisonous rengas trees), Myristicaceae, Myrtaceae and Apocynaceae. Conifers are less common than broad-leaved trees and they are mainly confined to poorer habitats, mountain ridges and sandy soils. Genera represented are *Agathis, Dacrydium, Podocarpus* and *Phyllocladus*, the last confined to Borneo. Pine has been planted but does not occur naturally, although it is native in the Philippines, Thailand and Sumatra.

FORESTRY IN THE LOWLAND FOREST

Hitherto it has only proved economic to manage forest under (approximately) the 1,500 foot contour and large areas of the lowland Dipterocarp and mangrove forests are reserved for the growing of timber. Revenue from timber in all the territories is appreciable and much is exported over and above that used for internal consumption. For example nearly 99,500,000 cubic feet of timber were exported from the Federation of Malaya in 1960 and in the same year the value of forest products exported from Sabah was nearly $M 95 million. In Malaya it is estimated that the present yield from existing forest reserves will not meet the expected local demand in about forty years' time. Consequently silvicultural practices are being directed to producing an enriched forest in which the proportion of tree species which produce economic timber is higher than in the natural forest. This is brought about by weeding out the less valuable species. One phase of this forest rotation takes seventy years and so stability of policy is necessary if there is to be a return on the capital invested in the forest estate. It is probable, though, that competition for land with agriculture will make it necessary for the Forest Departments to attempt to manage economic forest in

47

the mountains, and research is starting on these lines. The productive mangrove forests are immune from this competition.

VARIETY OF PLANT FORM IN THE FOREST

The tropical forest is a treasure house of plant variation producing many plant forms which are not found in other less favoured habitats. Many of the trees have steep buttresses, huge flat flanges of wood which connect the upper surface of the lateral roots with the trunk and often spread yards from the base of the tree. Such occur in the kempas (*Koompassia malaccensis*), the keladan (*Dryobalanops oblongifolia*), many species of terap or breadfruit (*Artocarpus*) and others. Where buttresses are present the trunk itself narrows as it approaches the ground, so that the cross-section of the whole remains nearly constant. No one yet knows the purpose of buttresses. Another peculiarity is the possession of stilt roots as in *Xylopia ferruginea* and species of *Dillenia* and *Hopea*. Here the base of the trunk appears borne aloft on a number of separate woody roots. In the trees of mangrove and swamp in which this habit is most prevalent it may help to support the tree on shifting and unstable ground or to provide additional oxygen to the roots.

Many trees, too, bear flowers directly from burrs on the trunk, a habit known as cauliflory. On the trunks of *Dysoxylon* sp. in the family Meliaceae there are enormous clusters of flowers which develop into orange capsules with arillate black seeds. Big clusters of fruit in *Polyalthia* (Annonaceae) are produced from a single flower. *Saraca thaipingensis*, a tree in the pea family, so characteristic of streamsides in the Malayan foothills, bears tresses of orange flowers developing into sword-shaped purple pods two feet in length.

But perhaps the most remarkable diversity of all is shown by the figs,[10] where one genus produces small shrubs and trees, slender root climbers and vast banyans, where the fruits may be borne on the twigs, branches or even underground, and where pollination is carried out by minute wasps, each, perhaps, confined to one or two species of fig. Some of these remarkable plants begin as slender root climbers crawling up the trunks of forest trees with roots and leaves adpressed to the bark. Then they suddenly burgeon out, high above the ground, into woody branches with fruits and leaves of quite different form. A similar abrupt change of form is found in other climbers such as the climbing fern *Teratophyllum*. Some figs are among the giants of the forest. These are the strangling figs which start life in a small way as seedlings high in the branches of a forest tree. There they grow as epiphytes and soon send down long, slender, hanging roots which reach the ground. At this stage the direction of flow in the roots, which has hitherto been downwards, reverses, so flexible are plants in their functions. As soon as they reach the ground the roots thicken and multiply, eventually engulfing and

48

strangling the original host. Many stages of this predatory process can be seen in the Lake Gardens, Kuala Lumpur.

Because of the uniform climate few trees of the tropical forest are truly deciduous, though there is a tendency for more species to be so in areas with a seasonal drought such as Perlis and Langkawi. Leaf fall and flushes of new growth may be regular or erratic according to the species, and branches on the same tree often act independently of one another. The iron wood, *Mesua ferrea*, shows this well. Colour in the forest is more often that of young leaves than of flowers and the colours are often most vivid: red in *Elateriospermum tapos*, pale green to white in *Saraca* and blue in *Leptospermum*.

Although the trees are perhaps the most fascinating plants of the Malayan forests, interest is by no means confined to them. There are also many lianes and climbers whose long, knotted and coiled stems hang down among the trees and whose leaves and flowers are in the canopy. Especially conspicuous are the orange masses of the climbing species of *Bauhinia*. The stems have many peculiarities of growth which enable them, though thick and woody, to remain flexible and unbroken even though the trees on which they rely for support fall down. The vessels in the wood are wide and numerous, perhaps to allow the easy and swift transport of water to deal with rapid transpiration. A severed length of stem will readily yield pure water for drinking. The most obtrusive of the lianes are the rotans (palms of the genera *Calamus, Daemonorops, Korthalsia* and others) whose leaf tips are extended into long flagella armed with recurved thorns hanging down to scalp the unwary. Their leaf sheaths too are guarded with an armoury of spines. The rotans are among the most valuable of the minor products of the forests and are collected extensively by the local peoples for their own use and for sale.

An equal diversity is shown by other plants of the forest such as the herbs, epiphytes and parasites, but there is no space to deal with these here. Holttum in his *Plant Life in Malaya*[11] described many.

OTHER TYPES OF LOWLAND FOREST

The most luxuriant forests are typical of well-drained soils in the lowlands but other forest types occur on extreme soils such as marine clays, swampy peats, sands and limestone and quartzite outcrops. Only brief descriptions of the mangroves and peat swamps can be given here.

Mangrove forests occur mainly on the sheltered west coasts of Borneo and the Malay Peninsula. Here the land is extending seawards due to the offshore deposition of vast masses of alluvium. Rates of 10 to 12 metres per year have been measured in Indonesia[12] and it is likely that the rates in Malaya and Borneo are similar. The mangrove trees, many of which belong to the Rhizophoraceae, are remarkable, because they are capable of growing in heavy saline clays between the tide marks and they have many peculiar features associated with this environment. On the seaward side one frequently finds a fringe of api api (*Avicennia*) and *Sonneratia*, both characterised by the short, stout branch roots, aerophores, which grow in their thousands vertically upward from the mud—a habitat for mudskippers and countless crabs. These aerophores are full of spongy tissue and are thought to provide a reservoir of air for the roots growing in the intensely anaerobic clay. The species of *Rhizophora* are raised on stilt roots which make an all but impenetrable tangle in some parts of the mangrove forests. The fruits of *Rhizophora* and *Bruguiera* species are also unusual. They grow on the parent into cigar-shaped seedlings up to 15 inches long and fall in this state to the mud where they begin growth. This may assist them in starting growth in the high concentrations of salt which they find in the mud.

Behind the mangroves in Sarawak there are great peat forests. Peat does occur in Malaya also, but the forests are rather different. This peat is formed by the accumulation of the wood and leaves of trees under anaerobic conditions which prevent decay. As it forms the ground surface rises until the vegetation depends for its water entirely on rainfall and not on drainage from surrounding areas. Finally the peat assumes dome shaped contours. In the centre it may be as much as 30 to 40 feet deep representing a growth of some 40,000 years. Dr Anderson has established by boring in the peat that the swamp near Marudi, now 30 miles from the sea, has developed on mangrove clay.[13] These swamps are the locality of alan (*Shorea albida*), one of the most important economic timbers of Sarawak.

INFERTILITY OF FOREST SOILS

One would readily suppose that such a luxuriant forest must be growing on a soil of great fertility, but many projects for agricultural development have foundered on this assumption. In fact the majority of soils cleared from rain forest are acid, poor and require heavy fertilising to yield well. Why should this be? The clue is given by two features of the rain forest itself: most of the feeding roots of the trees are in the soil surface, and fallen leaves decay and disappear quickly so that there is rarely any accumulation of leaf litter and humus in the soil.[14] It seems that most of what one might call the 'fertility capital' of the site is in the living trees and not in the soil. The nutrients circulate rapidly; as soon as they are released from decaying fallen leaves and twigs, they go back into living roots and from there into the rest of the tree. No reserve remains in the soil as it does, for example, in temperate forest or grassland soils. This has an important bearing on the methods which should be used in clearing forest for agriculture. If the reckless cutting and burning of trees is followed by heavy rain, the accumu-

50

lated nutrients of the tree crop will wash away and only a small proportion will be left in the soil and tree roots. Nutrients can of course be replaced by fertilisers, but their loss is not a full measure of the extent of the damage. The forest top-soil has also developed over the course of centuries a structure and texture which contribute greatly to its fertility. This tilth is quickly lost when the soil is exposed to sun and beaten by rain, and it cannot be so readily restored. It is notable how slowly fresh vegetation reclothes eroded land in Malaya and Borneo. It should nevertheless be possible to develop methods of clearing which do the least un-necessary damage.

Shifting cultivation has been practised by aboriginal peoples over substantial areas in all parts of the region. It is estimated that 20 per cent of Sarawak, for example, is under shifting agriculture.[15] Areas of high forest are felled and burned, preferably on steep slopes to obtain a better burn, and the land is planted with hill rice, tapioca, vegetables and bananas. After harvest the land is aban-doned and allowed to recover fertility under forest regrowth. In Perak the people are being encouraged to plant forest trees before they leave a cultivated area. If the density of population is low and ample time is allowed for the land to recover before it is cleared again, there may be no erosion nor even loss of fertility; but the practice inevitably exterminates the majority of the slower-growing tree species from the site and reduces its potential as selection forest.[16] If the frequency of cultivation increases, the land deteriorates seriously, the risk of periodical fires increases and forest is replaced by unproductive lallang (*Imperata cylindrica*) or resam (*Gleichenia* spp.). Large areas in Sabah have been ruined in this way and parts of Malaya, round the Tasek Bera for example, are rapidly becoming degraded to this state. The same effect may be produced by any bad agriculture.

MOUNTAIN FORESTS

With increasing altitude the climate slowly changes. The mean temperature drops at the rate of approximately 1°C. for every 100 metres; the amount of cloud increases and the solar radiation consequently falls. The rainfall may also rise, although the highest precipitation is often to be found in the foothills and the mountains are drier. For instance the mean annual rainfall at Kampar (altitude 128 feet in the foothills) is 145 inches whereas that at the Cameron Highlands (4,750 feet) is only 104 inches. Associated with this change in climate the vegeta-tion of higher altitudes is lower in stature and less luxuriant; the wealth of tree species in the lowlands is replaced by a wealth of herbs and epiphytes in the mountains. The zonation has been described for the Malay peninsula by Wyatt-Smith.[17] At about 1,500 feet the lowland Dipterocarp forest is replaced by a hill Dipterocarp forest containing a rather different spectrum of species. *Shorea curtisii*, *Shorea platyclados* and *Dipterocarpus gracilis*, for example, become common and

51

many species of the lowland forest drop out, but the structure of the forest remains almost unchanged. At about 3,000 feet there is a striking change. The Dipterocarps become rarer, tree ferns more abundant and the forest is reduced to two storeys. This is the sub-montane forest. It still contains a large number of tree species, especially members of the Fagaceae (the oak family) and the Lauraceae (the cinnamon family). Indeed the area which includes Malaya, Borneo, Indochina and south China is richer in oaks than any other region in the world. It was in the sub-montane forest of Kinabalu that a remarkable new genus of the Fagaceae was found in 1961 by the Royal Society expedition under the leadership of Mr E. J. H. Corner. This has been named *Trigonobalanus* Forman[18] and is the first new genus of the family to be discovered for over a century. Two species are now known, *T. verticillata* from Kinabalu and Celebes and *T. doichangensis* from north Thailand (Forman: oral communication).* This new discovery is likely to add greatly to our knowledge of this important family and shows how much remains to be discovered about the Malaysian forests.

On high mountains montane rain forest begins at about 9,000 feet, but the boundary between this and sub-montane forest is lower on isolated mountain masses and exposed ridges. Here the sunshine is much reduced and the forest is often bathed in dripping cloud which deposits its water as it is blown through the branches of the ridgetop trees. Under these conditions the incessant drip of water within the forest makes it appear as though it were raining even though no rain is falling outside. The forest is low; the branches of the trees spreading and grotesque, matted thickly with liverworts, mosses, filmy ferns and epiphytic orchids. The ground is covered with thick peat formed by half-rotted wood and leaves. Often too there is another platform of peat in the crutch of the main branches. Characteristic of this forest is the family Ericaceae, a family more widespread in the Himalayas and the north temperate zone. Several species of *Rhododendron*, for example, occur as epiphytes or growing on the peat in the mountains of the Malay peninsula and there is a rich *Rhododendron* flora on Kinabalu. Mixed with these are conifers, especially *Dacrydium*, *Podocarpus* and *Phyllocladus* (the last only in Borneo). There is, too, a component of temperate species characteristic of the southern hemisphere: *Leptospermum* and *Baeckia* (Myrtaceae) and *Weinmannia* (Cunoniaceae). This whole flora, now isolated on high mountains in Malaysia, probably represents the remnants of a cool temperate flora which was more widespread and continuous during a cooler period in the past. This problem has been discussed by van Steenis[19] and further study will undoubtedly reveal more evidence about the geological, climatic and vegetational history of the region. In the mist forest there are many of the fascinating climb-

---

* *T. verticillata* has since been found by the author at Fraser's Hill in the Malay Peninsula and by P. S. Ashton in the Hose Mountains, Sarawak.

ing pitcher plants (*Nepenthes*). The tip of the leaves of these plants is modified into an upstanding pitcher which is often fantastically and beautifully ornamented round the rim. Insects enter the mouths of these pitchers and are trapped in the base. There their corpses are digested by enzymes secreted from the wall of the pitcher. In this way the plant obtains some of the nitrogen which is so deficient in the peat on which it grows.

Higher still the cloud cover often becomes less but the conditions are nevertheless very exacting for plant growth. The temperature falls nearly to the freezing point on practically every night in the year. Kinabalu is the only mountain which reaches this height in our region. This is a domain of shattered rock and sparse plant cover. Dwarf shrubs, sedges and grasses predominate and among them are found many which belong to circumboreal genera, *Potentilla*, *Carex*, *Agrostis*, *Gentiana* and *Euphrasia*, small but fascinating scraps of plant geographical evidence.

THE FUTURE

What does the future hold for this vegetation and flora? The population of the Malay peninsula is increasing at a rate that is, in the literal sense, terrific. This is due to the successes of modern medicine and the prevailing prosperity. Although the increase is not yet so rapid in the Borneo territories, it is only a matter of time before it becomes so. This multiplication is bringing in its train an increasing pressure on the forest. More space is required; more food must be grown; more productive uses must be found for the land. In recent years the pace of the forest clearance in Malaya has increased and many schemes of rural development for small-holders have been instituted.

In many parts of the world the potential of the land has been seriously impaired by centuries of misuse, and in the older civilised areas of the Middle East and China the rape of the earth has been continuing for millennia. Mistaken use of the land, poor cultivation, overgrazing and lack of appreciation of forest resources have all led to serious soil erosion, lack of water in the upper parts of river catchments, and flooding and drainage problems further down the river valleys. Only parts of the temperate regions have escaped relatively unscathed because there the climate is so kind that misuse does not bring severe retribution. In the devastated regions the effort to rebuild soil and restore fertility is both slow and expensive.

Malaya and the Borneo territories still have most of the cards in their hands and can profit by the great experience gained from the mistakes of others less fortunate—or less wise. A large proportion of the natural forest is still undisturbed and its soil capital is intact. A carefully planned policy of land use can retain the natural resources of the region. Agriculture and forestry, especially

53

the latter, require a period of stability if they are to develop. There is therefore urgent need for a national land use survey to decide what is the proper use for the various categories of land in the new Federation, in order that an overall land development plan may be prepared which will conserve soil and water resources. *Ad hoc* development can, and usually does, lead to patterns of land use which are harmful and later almost impossible to abandon.

The economic arguments for land use planning are obvious and compelling. It is not so obvious why areas of natural vegetation should be preserved undisturbed and unexploited. If representative areas of the various forest types of the Federation are to be preserved, it is urgent that they should be chosen as soon as possible. A good start has already been made with the Park Negara (the George V National Park) in Malaya and Bako National Park in Sarawak; and another has just been set up on Mount Kinabalu after the interest aroused by the Royal Society expedition to the mountain. Also many small but insufficiently protected areas have been demarcated in Malaya: the Virgin Jungle Reserves.

Many people are likely to ask why large areas should be, in the jargon of today, 'sterilised' and rendered 'unproductive' in perpetuity. The Malaysian forests are unbelievably rich and many species of potentially economic or decorative plants may remain to be discovered. The Chemistry Department of the University of Malaya is engaged in carrying out a survey of some of the chemical properties of Malayan plants and it is possible that chemicals of importance to medicine may be discovered as, for example, the alkaloid in *Rauwolfia*. Agriculturists and foresters constantly require a reserve of wild stock which may be crossed with cultivated varieties and so increase the genetic variability of the latter. An expedition has recently visited Malaya and Borneo collecting bananas for this very purpose. To destroy wantonly the source of so much potential would be criminal. During the next century the landscape of the Federation will be transformed beyond recognition. The natural forests of today will at best be rarities in a landscape of agricultural land, orchards and plantations. Even the managed forests will be transformed and will be quite unlike they are now. But a hundred years is too short a time to understand how the forests work and why certain kinds of tree grow where they do. Reserves will in the future serve as standards against which progress (or the lack of it) may be measured. We would dearly like to know today what the forests of the Middle East looked like 4,000 years ago. It should be remembered, too, that no efforts to conserve wild mammals, birds or insects can be successful unless large areas of the habitats in which they occur are also conserved. As the area of the forests decreases, so the popular demand for them as areas of recreation will increase. Now is the time to ensure that a representative sample of the best that Malaysia has to offer is available for posterity.

3

The Fauna

LORD MEDWAY

Physical relations between the Borneo territories and Malaya are closer than might at first sight be implied by their existing geographical separation. As explained in Chapter 1, geomorphically Borneo and the Malay peninsula, together with Java, Sumatra and the many smaller islands enclosed in this arc of land limited peripherally by deep sea channels, comprise the exposed parts of an extensive half-submerged south-eastern outgrowth of the Asian continent, known as the Sunda Shelf; the Philippine island of Palawan forms a northern promontory of this shelf. Recessions of the sea, associated with successive Ice Ages, periodically exposed much of what is now the South China Sea as dry land, affording close connections between the modern insular land masses.

Yet even at the periods of maximum lowering of sea level, the Sunda Shelf remained on the fringe of continental Asia, and apparently no eastward connection with the Australasian region was established. In modern times climatic factors reinforce the geographical isolation, for the narrow land connection of peninsular Thailand coincides with the transition from an equable, more or less perennially humid, equatorial climate prevailing in the land masses of the Sunda Shelf, to a monsoon climate marked by a distinct alternation of wet and dry seasons. The uniform climatic conditions of the Sunda Shelf account for close similarities in vegetation and in other ecologically important factors.

Due to these three influences—isolation from Asia, intermittent connection between the islands, and common climatic conditions—a characteristic fauna has evolved within the region, related to, but quite distinct from, the South-east Asian continental fauna. Despite local differences, the faunas of all existing land masses of the Sunda Shelf show closer affinities with each other than with the fauna of any other region. This faunistic coherence has led students of animal geography to recognise the area as a distinct subregion of the Oriental region, for which the name 'Malaysia' has become widely accepted.

This term was used loosely by a number of writers of the nineteenth century. It appears to have been defined in its existing zoological sense for the first time by C. Boden Kloss in 1918: 'Malaysian: pertaining to the Malay peninsula, Sumatra, Borneo and Java.'[1] In this sense the term has appeared in the titles of standard zoological works covering the region as a whole,[2] and has been employed widely in zoological literature.

Fortunately an alternative exists in the name 'Sundaland' (adjectivally 'Sundaic', or 'Sondaic'), which has also been used, less frequently, but with precisely the same connotation.[3] To prevent misunderstanding, it is proposed throughout this chapter to use the term 'Malaysia' only in its restricted sense, designating the new political federation, and to refer to the zoogeographical subregion consistently as 'Sundaland'.

ZOOGEOGRAPHICAL RELATIONS

The richness and complexity of animal life in Malaysia are unmatched in temperate regions. There are, for example, over 200 species of snakes recorded from Borneo and Malaya together,[4] over 550 birds (resident and migratory) from each territory,[5] and 192 mammals from the Bornean states alone.[6] This diversity is characteristic of most regions of tropical rain forest. For instance, Davis[7] has shown that the mammalian fauna of the lowland rain forest of the East Coast Residency of North Borneo (Sabah), comprising 135 species (including 58 bats), is almost three times as rich in species as the mammalian fauna of a temperate deciduous forest in the south-eastern United States (51 species, including 11 bats). But on the other hand (excluding bats, the distribution of which is poorly known), there is close similarity in the number of mammals in the lowland rain-forest fauna of north Borneo (77) and of a comparable region in the American tropics, as in Panama (71).

Invertebrate groups are still more richly represented. Although individually they may not be conspicuous, insects, spiders and other arthropods, molluscs and many soft-bodied invertebrates undoubtedly constitute the bulk of animal life in Malaysia. The study of most invertebrate groups has hardly progressed beyond the preliminary stages of collection and classification and, outside specialist literature, a general publication is available only on butterflies.[8] Vertebrates, being easier to collect and easier to determine, have attracted a greater share of attention, and the vertebrate faunas of Malaysia are adequately sampled, if not yet perfectly known.

Wholly terrestrial vertebrates—mammals, birds and reptiles—have relatively great freedom of movement over land, and during the Pleistocene were able to disperse widely in Sundaland. This is reflected in the high proportion of species still common to the two parts of Malaysia. Over half the lizards, snakes, resident birds and mammals of Borneo also occur in Malaya. This large group includes several animals widespread in South-east Asia such as the Two-horned or Sumatran Rhinoceros (now seriously threatened with extinction), Sambar and Barking Deer, the Brahminy Kite, the Cobra and Hamadryad. The majority however belong to the characteristic Sundaic fauna. These include the Flying Lemur, the Common and the Lesser Treeshrews, the Long-tailed or Crab-eating Macaque, the Banded Leaf-monkey, the Bearded Pig, many squirrels and rats, hornbills, the White-nest or Edible-nest Swiftlet, many barbets, bulbuls and babblers, and 34 species of snakes.

Of the animals not common to both Borneo and Malaya, some are species with Sundaic affinities, occurring elsewhere in the subregion (e.g. the Orangutan and the Sunda Islands Leaf-monkey in Borneo, the Siamang and the Common Bamboo Rat in Malaya). In addition a significant number of those occurring only in Malaya are continental Asian species whose range extends to the peninsula but not to the Sunda Islands. Familiar members of this group in Malaya are the Gaur or Seladang, the common grey-bellied squirrel (*Callosciurus caniceps*), and the White-breasted Kingfisher. Many of the smaller, less well-known mammals, birds and reptiles of this group are montane in distribution in Malaya (e.g. Bower's Rate Himalayan Striped Squirrel and the Red-cheeked Ground Squirrel).

There are very few endemic species of terrestrial vertebrate in Malaya, occurring there and nowhere else. There are no endemic mammals or birds, and only ten (out of a total of 127) species of snakes are listed as endemic by Tweedie.[9] The greater isolation of Borneo is reflected in the greater specialisation of its fauna, as evinced by the relatively high number of endemic species. Thirty-eight out of 192 species of mammals,[10] 28 out of 551 birds,[11] and about 33 out of 132 terrestrial snakes[12] are endemic to Borneo.

Certain endemic mammals of Borneo (the Proboscis Monkey, Mountain Ground Squirrel, and the Smooth-tailed Treeshrew) show affinities with forms from the Indochinese region. A discontinuous distribution of this sort may represent a limited invasion at some time in the past, perhaps directly overland along the north shore of the Sundaland peninsula at a period of its emergence. It may also arise by the localised extinction of intervening populations of an animal formerly much more widely distributed. Archaeological work has shown that the present distribution of at least two Malaysian mammals represents a relict pattern of this sort. One is the Orang-utan, which since historic times has been found only in Sumatra and Borneo, but which is known as a fossil in Pleistocene deposits in south China and Java.[13] The second is the Tapir, nowadays known only from Sumatra, Malaya and continental Asia to the north, but well represented among fossil animal remains excavated at Niah cave, Sarawak. The distribution of Tapir remains in this excavation indicates that it survived in Sarawak until at least 8,000 years ago.[14]

A single unerupted canine tooth of a juvenile Tiger has also been recovered at Niah cave from Neolithic levels.[15] In its present distribution, the Tiger does not reach Borneo. However, no other fossil remains of Tiger have been identified from deposits at Niah, or anywhere else in Borneo, and on the basis of this single specimen it is still an open question whether or not the Tiger too should rank among the extinct native fauna of Borneo.

LOCAL PATTERNS OF DISTRIBUTION

Within each of the two halves of Malaysia, the distribution of terrestrial animals is not even, and a number of localised patterns of distribution may be recognised. Characteristically, altitude is one important limiting factor. Throughout Malaysia, despite a small group of submontane forms which blur the boundary, specialised montane faunas occupy ground above 3,000 feet. In Malaya, several of the montane animals represent Asian species with Himalayan affinities. In Borneo, forms related to these also occur, but the majority of montane species are endemic. Many endemic Bornean species have been found so far only on the Kinabalu massif; others also occur on high ground elsewhere although they are absent from the intervening lowlands. The means by which these specialised forms have colonised groups of isolated mountain peaks across gaps of apparently unsuitable lowland terrain is not clear. The identification recently of a jaw of the normally montane Lesser Gymnure (*Hylomys suillus*) from Upper Pleistocene deposits now only a few feet above sea level at Niah Caves, Sarawak, indicates that ecological conditions at this period (perhaps generally depressed temperatures) permitted these now primarily montane mammals to colonise the lowlands as well.[16]

A second interesting feature of the montane fauna of Malaysia lies in the number of pairs of species with apparently similar ecology which are altitudinally exclusive in distribution. Many examples are found among mammals (especially rodents), birds, reptiles and amphibians, of pairs of species, morphologically quite alike, one of which inhabits the lowlands, the other the highlands. The factors controlling this pattern of distribution have not been studied.

As well as the altitudinal boundary at about 3,000 feet, other barriers to distribution may be recognised within the lowlands of Malaysia. In lowland Malaya, these are fundamentally according to latitude, despite the fact that the main physical feature of the country is the high central mountain chain running roughly north and south. A number of continental Asian species do not extend south of Perlis and northern Kedah (including Langkawi Island) where, unlike

58

most of Malaysia, there is a sharp distinction between wet and dry seasons; examples include the Stump-tailed Macaque, and a Kingfisher. This zone is particularly marked in the distribution of butterflies, and has been distinguished from Malaya proper under the name of 'Kedawi'.[17] Other strictly continental Asian animals, with Himalayan affinities, are found in the northern highlands of Malaya, but do not extend far south of Selangor.

In contrast to these patterns of rather abrupt limitation, the continental Asian grey-bellied squirrel, *Callosciurus caniceps,* is gradually replaced from north to south in Malaya by the Sundaic red-bellied Plantain Squirrel (*Callosciurus notatus*);[18] both are common pests of cultivated trees and plantations. A number of subspecies of both these squirrels are recognised in the Malay peninsula. The boundaries between these, and between the majority of subspecies of other mammals and birds occurring in lowland Malaya (excluding insular subspecies found on offshore islands), are also broadly latitudinal.

In Borneo, the boundaries are more closely related to topography. Among lowland birds and mammals, several have differentiated into local subspecies confined to Sarawak, apparently limited by the high ground of the central range. Another important faunal barrier is recognised in the region of the Baram river; and a number of subspecies have also been described from north-eastern Sabah. Certain very variable squirrels have differentiated into many locally distinct populations, which have been described as subspecies. The distribution of recognised subspecies of Prevost's Squirrel in Borneo indicates that the lower reaches of large rivers constitute total barriers to this squirrel, so that the population on one bank may be coloured quite differently to those on the opposite bank.[19]

The distribution of inland fishes of the primary fresh-water group, which cannot tolerate salt or even brackish water, is naturally still more strongly influenced by topography, particularly by the pattern of drainage during the Pleistocene.[20] As a result of the lowering of the sea during glaciation, the rivers of south-eastern Sumatra, southern Malaya and western Borneo from the Rejang southwards (possibly including also the Baram) were united at least once as tributaries of the great North Sunda river, the submerged channel of which can still be detected by soundings in the South China Sea.[21] At this time the fresh-water fish fauna of this group of rivers was essentially one, and this relationship is reflected in the present distribution of species. There are for instance many species of fish common to south Malaya and south-west Sarawak which are absent from north-west Malaya, where the fauna shows affinities with that of north-eastern Sumatra.

North of the Baram river, the fresh-water fish of the Bornean territories show an increasing endemicity, attributable to their greater isolation. The highest proportion of endemics is found in the Labuk-Segama catchment area, East Coast

Residency, with 58 species, of which 28 are endemic to Borneo, and **8** endemic within that one watershed. Three other fish from the Labuk-Segama catchment area have been found elsewhere only in Thailand, and a total of seven fish from Borneo (the other four being more widespread) exhibit this pattern of relict distribution, already noted among mammals.

ECOLOGICAL RELATIONS

In the evergreen tropical rain forest of the lowlands of Malaysia, the great majority of the native animals are specialised forest-dwelling forms. Comparatively few vertebrate species are able to exploit open country or cultivated land. For example, Harrison in Malaya, sampling mammal populations by ground-trapping techniques, obtained only three species from aborigines' rice-fields, as opposed to thirteen species from undisturbed forest, seven from secondary forest, and five from grass and bush land.[22] Many of those that do occur in open habitats are commensals or semi-commensals, closely associated with man (e.g. rats of the subgenus *Rattus*, the Tree Sparrow, the common estrildine finches that are pests of rice, and the frogs *Rana erythraea* and *Rhacophorus leucomystax*).

Stretches of mangrove forest also occur along sheltered coasts, associated with which is a specialised aquatic fauna. In both divisions of Malaysia a small group of birds, too, are more or less restricted to mangrove, and in Borneo the Proboscis Monkey is entirely dependent on coastal and fresh-water mangrove associations. Apart from the Proboscis Monkey, there are no other specialised mangrove forest mammals, and those found in this habitat in Malaya are the same versatile species that exploit open country and cultivated land.[23]

The structure of the lowland rain forest is such that there is a concentration of food supplies, in the form of growing shoots, leaves, flowers and fruit, in the upper storeys. In undisturbed forest there is only a very reduced carpet flora, and the ground level is largely devoid of living photosynthetic plant tissue. In relation to this, the fauna is rich in arboreal animals. For example, of 97 mammal species (excluding bats) from the forests of Malaya, Harrison recognised 48 per cent as arboreal, and 52 per cent as terrestrial.[24] A similar analysis has been given by Davis, who divided the 77 mammals of the lowland forest of North Borneo into 45 per cent arboreal, 52 per cent terrestrial, and 3 per cent aquatic.[25] Comparative figures from the characteristically more open temperate zone forest quoted by Davis are 15 per cent arboreal, 77 per cent terrestrial, and 8 per cent aquatic.[26]

Specialisation for flight may be regarded as an extreme adaptation for arboreal life, and flying or gliding forms are found among all vertebrate classes in Malaysia. Among mammals are the bats, which comprise 67 of the total number of 192 mammals of Borneo, flying squirrels and the Flying Lemur; among reptiles, the flying snakes (*Chrysopelea* spp.), the flying geckos (*Ptychozoon*) and flying lizards (*Draco*); among amphibians, several tree-frogs of the genus *Rhacophorus*. Such flying forms are generally more or less obligatorily arboreal, and may show associated adaptations of reproductive habit. The geckos affix their eggs in protected sites, well above ground, and the tree-frogs build aerial foam nests in which their larvae may undergo partial metamorphosis before hatching. The flying lizards, on the other hand, always descend to the ground to lay their eggs in the soil.

The scansorial and arboreal groups include a high proportion of animals dependent on vegetable matter for food. By contrast, strictly terrestrial vertebrates (excluding aquatic species) are either small animals of predatory habit (either carnivorous or, in the broad sense, insectivorous) or large animals prevented from climbing by their size, which have more varied feeding habits. Among mammals, the latter group includes browsers (elephant and deer), soil grubbers (pig), and carnivores (tiger). Cattle, which are grazers, find shelter in the forest, but feed largely in clearings and along the banks of rivers. Fossorial mammals are rare, being limited to bamboo rats and the mole which occur in Malaya only, but burrowing snakes are common, and cecaelians, legless burrowing amphibians, also occur.

It is naturally the ground fauna that is most effectively sampled by generalised trapping techniques. In Malaya, intensive trapping programs have been undertaken over a period of several years by the Institute of Medical Research, and the small mammals of the forest have been well sampled.[27] Results stress the fact, widely recognised as a characteristic of tropical rain-forest, that although the fauna is extremely diverse, in actual number of individuals the total population often does not exceed, and may even be smaller than, populations of similar animals in comparable habitats in the temperate zone. Figures derived from the small mammal trapping program of the Institute of Medical Research show a trapping success of 5 per cent (i.e. about five animals trapped per hundred trap-nights).[28] Comparable figures obtained from a briefer trapping program, undertaken in winter at the lowest point of the seasonal ebb in numbers, in deciduous woodland in Suffolk, England, where five mammal species were trapped (three rodents and two insectivores), give a much higher success rate of 19·5 per cent (229 trappings in 1,170 trap-nights).[29]

Under natural conditions a forest animal population in Malaysia characteristically remains stable at this fairly low density from year to year. On offshore islands with impoverished faunas, the resident populations (excluding breeding colonies of sea-birds) may be significantly more abundant. On the mainland, artificial conditions may periodically increase the populations of specialised animals to much higher densities. For instance, isolated trees may be completely

61

defoliated in a few days by phytophagous insect larvae, and ripening rice is often decimated by irruptions of rats or grain-eating birds. Also communally roosting or nesting animals such as bats or swifts are often found in great concentrations, both in natural sites and in buildings or tunnels. The populations of social animals of this sort may be limited in nature primarily by the availability of suitable roosting or breeding sites. Consequently human activity, in providing acceptable substitutes for natural roosting sites where these are in short supply, may be of direct benefit to them. For instance, the numbers of House Swifts (*Apus affinis*) must have increased enormously throughout Malaysia within the last few decades, solely due to the development of towns and the erection of large buildings, such as the station and offices of Malayan Railways at Kuala Lumpur, on which the birds nest in very large numbers.

DIURNAL AND SEASONAL PERIODICITY

About an equal proportion of animals in Malaysian forests are active by day as by night. Many matched ecological pairs can be recognised in the fauna, often from groups not closely related, which replace each other by day or night. The bats for example are highly diversified and include ecological counterparts to most diurnal birds. Among the bats there are many of fruit-eating forms, varying from very large flying-foxes down to small bats with a forearm length of under two inches, pollen- and nectar-eating forms, a great many insect-eating forms, varying from the large, high-flying Hairless Bat to the minute Flat-headed Bats which feed in the lower storeys of the forest, and (in Malaya only) the Indian False Vampire, which is a predator of non-flying vertebrates. Among terrestrial mammals, in the canopy the flying squirrels are the nocturnal counterparts of the diurnal typical squirrels and arboreal treeshrews (excepting the rare Pentail Treeshrew, which is nocturnal), and in the lower storeys and on the ground, rats are the counterparts of ground squirrels and other treeshrews. Among other vertebrates, the amphibians are characteristically nocturnal, skinks and arboreal lizards diurnal, the geckos chiefly nocturnal, and the snakes unspecialised.

Patterns of seasonal reproductive periodicity are equally varied. Although the Malaysian climate is very equable, there are in fact few localities (if any) in which it remains totally uniform without some degree of annually recurrent variation. Correspondingly many animals have restricted breeding seasons. In Sabah, data from a small collection of terrestrial mammals (excluding bats) suggested that breeding is seasonal, with a peak in pregnancy rate in July and August.[30] Throughout Malaysia, all colonies of microchiropteran bats inspected to date have proved to have restricted breeding seasons, closely synchronised both between members of one roost, and between different roosts of the same species in one district.[31]   Among birds, in Malaya, a limited number of investigations of single species have been undertaken.   Overall surveys indicate that most birds breed in the first part of the calendar year, commencing towards the end of the rains of the north-east monsoon.   From Borneo, less data are available, but the general pattern is similar.

The breeding of three species of swiftlet has been investigated at Niah Caves, Sarawak.   The two larger species (one of which builds the edible nests of commerce) both have long, annually recurrent breeding seasons, covering the months of September to April, during which eggs and young of all ages can be found on the same day in neighbouring nests.   The third species, the White-bellied Swiftlet, has three brief breeding seasons each year, during which reproductive activity is markedly synchronised both within and between different groups of nests.[32]   Further north, at Sandakan, the White-bellied Swiftlet has a rather different breeding season.[33]

On the other hand, Harrison has concluded that there is no breeding season among rodents and insectivores in central Malaya, but only irregular fluctuations in pregnancy rate which are broadly related to the amount of rainfall in any given month.[34]   Similarly, in a population of the frog *Rana erythraea*, at Kuching, Sarawak, adults were found in breeding condition at all months, the proportion varying from month to month over one calendar year without any obvious relation to climatic factors.[35]   No other accounts have been published of the breeding seasons of lower terrestrial vertebrates, but several workers are active in this field and have reports in preparation.[36]

The reproductive behaviour of the marine turtles that lay on the beaches of Malaysia, notably the Green Turtle and the Leathery Turtle, have been studied in some detail.[37]   The eggs of these turtles provide an important source of cheap protein, and there is a steady trade in them.   Partly due to this commercial interest, it has been possible to set up long-term conservation programs on the major turtle beaches.   Early results in Malaya have been rewarding.[38]

MEDICAL SIGNIFICANCE

Another major stimulus to research has stemmed from the growing realisation of the role of wild animal populations in relation to human disease.   Wild animals are significant in medicine from two aspects, firstly as vectors, and secondly as natural reservoirs, of disease-causing micro-organisms to which man is susceptible.   The principal vectors are blood-sucking flies and other arthropods. The classical example of these is the anopheline mosquito, vector of the protozoan parasite *Plasmodium*, which is the causative agent of human malaria.   Malaria is endemic in Malaya, and five species of *Anopheles* are known vectors.   Their habits and ecology vary, so that the significance of any one species in the transmission of malaria depends on local conditions of housing, vegetation, topography and other ecological factors. Some species are more susceptible to simple eradication techniques than others, and the danger exists that the elimination of a primary vector having close contact with man will leave unaffected a secondary vector which has only slight contact with man.[39]

Mosquitoes of *Anopheles* and other genera are also vectors of parasitic microfilaria, the causative agents of filariasis, another important disease endemic in Malaysia. Microfilaria can be transmitted by a very diverse group of mosquito vectors. For instance, microfilaria of *Wuchereria bancrofti* are known to be transmitted, over a wide area in Asia and the Pacific including Malaysia, by eleven mosquito species from four genera, including seven subgenera.[40] Control of both filariasis and malaria is being attempted by the elimination of mosquitoes. Problems in control are related to the ecology of mosquitoes, which has been studied intensively in Malaya,[41] and also to the appearance of resistance to insecticides which prevents the continuous use of any single preparation.[42]

Other parasitic arthropods are also significant as vectors of disease in Malaysia. The virus of scrub typhus, which is endemic, is carried by chiggers, larval trombiculid mites. These are parasitic only at the larval stage of their life, but are widespread and common in all types of habitat. In 1960 ten strains of virus, the pathogenic significance of some of which is uncertain, were also isolated from ticks in Malaya.[43]

It has long been recognised that these arthropod-borne viruses are endemic in wild mammals and other vertebrates, which thus form a natural reservoir for the maintenance of the diseases independent of the human population. It is a recent discovery that the rickettsia of leptospirosis is also endemic in forest animals in Malaya, and that this disease is a common infection of the human population in the country.[44]

It is now recognised, too, that the parasites causing filariasis, formerly thought to be specific to man, are also endemic in a number of wild mammals. During the period 1955 to 1960, in Malaya, infections of *Brugia malayi*, the principal pathogen of filariasis in the country, were recognised in the Long-tailed Macaque, all three native leaf-monkeys, the Leopard Cat, the Flat-headed Cat, the Common Palm Civet, the Small-toothed Palm Civet and the Pangolin, as well as domestic cats.[45] Equally disquieting was an outbreak of human malaria in a laboratory in the USA, which was ultimately traced to a *Plasmodium* of monkey malaria from Malaya. These and related parasites have been isolated from the blood of wild animals in Malaya, including monkeys. Investigations are continuing with the primary object of determining whether any other strains or species of monkey malaria are pathogenic to man, and whether human infections with monkey malaria occur naturally.[46]

HUMAN RELATIONS AND CONSERVATION

Direct predation of man by wild animals is of limited significance in Malaysia. Tigers still take a small but regular toll of the rural (chiefly aboriginal) population in Malaya, but are absent from the Borneo territories. Here, where rivers remain the principal means of communication, crocodiles are occasionally dangerous.

The same rural populations still obtain animal protein for food almost exclusively from hunting and fishing. Notwithstanding religious prohibitions, the flesh of wild pig, deer and cattle finds a ready market in urban areas, but there is little prospect that any of these could be 'farmed' economically in natural reserves in competition with domestic breeds in captivity. Game laws exist in all territories, but are difficult to enforce and rarely observed. Within human memory the populations of all bigger game mammals (pig, deer and wild ox) have been seriously depleted.

To a few communities, natural animal products are commercially important. In the earliest trade contacts these, in fact, were the major exports from all Malaysian territories. Early Chinese merchants took rhinoceros horn, hornbill ivory, kingfisher feathers, bezoar stones, coral and turtle shell,[47] many of which were also direct value objects to the native population. From perhaps the seventeenth century onwards, the edible nests of cave swiftlets were added to the list, and even in the nineteenth century revenue from the trade in birds' nests was a significant fraction of the budget of the Chartered Company of North Borneo.

Even today the prices of these exotica remain high, and continue to provide an incentive to the less advanced human communities of remoter areas. The perilous state of rhinoceroses, threatened with extinction the world over, is due entirely to the demand for their horns and other organs for quasi-medicinal purposes. In Malaya, the One-horned or Javan Rhinoceros is thought to be totally extinct (it never occurred in Borneo in historic times), and the Two-horned or Sumatran Rhinoceros is reduced to about fifty scattered individuals. In Borneo, the Sumatran Rhinoceros is now even scarcer, and it is very doubtful whether a viable population any longer survives. Men of the interior tribes in Borneo continue to hunt leaf-monkeys for their gall-stones, involving massive slaughter, and decorate themselves with ornaments of hornbill casques and feathers,[48] to the detriment of the species.

Edible birds' nests still command rewarding prices, and are regularly harvested, providing an important source of income in the districts where they occur in the Tioman archipelago, Sarawak and Sabah. A new trade has grown up in the capture and sale of wild animals for zoos and laboratories. It is this rather than any other factor that threatens the orang-utan.[49]

In a few cases exploitation has been controlled, and has been balanced with the natural productivity of the wild population. Harvesting of the marine turtle eggs on the beaches of Trengganu and the turtle islands of Sarawak is an example of successful control. Available evidence also suggests that birds' nest 'farming', which is still practised by traditional methods, does not dangerously deplete the swiftlet population, and in certain circumstances may even be beneficial.[50] Apart from these two exceptions, it is hard to believe that the existing fauna of Malaysia can survive unchanged over the years ahead in the face of the steady advance that it is hoped the human population will enjoy.

4

Population: A Preliminary Analysis

T. G. McGEE

The proposals for the creation of Malaysia have introduced several new considerations into the discussion of the population of the four territories.[1] Foremost amongst these considerations must be the question whether Malaysia can work out population policies which will benefit the people of the new nation to a greater extent than the present policies of the individual states. Unquestionably, the major problem which Malaysia faces is the formation of a policy which can weld the diverse ethnic groups into a loyal and united people. Malaysia is unique in the region because of the large size of its immigrant communities which form over fifty per cent of the total population (Table 1, page 68). Such a precarious balance greatly affects the policy-making of the indigenous elite who possess most of the political power. On the one hand, they must pursue policies aimed at satisfying the demands of the indigenous people for improved standards of living because their political power rests largely on the support of their own people. On the other, these policies must not so favour their people that the immigrant communities feel they must demand more political power.

The prime considerations affecting policy will be to prevent any great disturbance of the numerical balance between these two main groups and to ensure the indigenous peoples of their political power. Both these considerations were certainly of major significance in bringing about the formation of Malaysia. Internal political developments in Singapore led the Malay-dominated government of Malaya to fear that the state might be taken over by a strongly left-wing Chinese government. This prompted the Malayan government to propose what had formerly been unthinkable: a merger with Singapore. But this meant that the numerical dominance of the Malays would no longer exist, and this, in turn, led the government to press for a Malaysia incorporating the Borneo territories.

The addition of the indigenous peoples of the Borneo territories would produce 'a racial parity which Malaya stood to lose by merger with Singapore'.[2] This, together with the proposed distribution of seats in the federal parliament,[3] has meant that both the numerical balance between the indigenous and immigrant groups and the former's control of the political structure has been preserved.

TABLE 1. POPULATION GROWTH AND RACIAL COMPOSITION, 1921–60
(RACIAL COMPOSITION AS A PERCENTAGE OF POPULATION)

Year	Territory	Indigenous*	Chinese	Others**	Total Population (in thousands)
1921	Malaya	54·0	29·4	16·6	2,906
	Singapore	12·9	75·2	11·9	420
	Sabah	77·1	17·0	5·9	263
	Sarawak	No adequate information			
1931	Malaya	49·2	33·9	16·9	3,787
	Singapore	11·8	74·9	13·3	559
	Sabah	75·0	16·0	9·0	277
1939	Sarawak	73·7	25·2	1·1	491
	Malaysia	48·8	36·7	14·5	5,114
1947	Malaya	49·5	38·4	12·1	4,908
	Singapore	12·3	78·6	9·1	939
1951	Sabah	72·8	22·2	5·0	334
1947	Sarawak	72·4	26·6	1·0	546
	Malaysia	47·2	42·2	10·6	6,727
1957	Malaya	49·8	37·2	13·0	6,279
	Singapore	13·4	73·9	12·7	1,446
1960	Sabah	67·4	23·1	9·5	454
	Sarawak	68·8	30·7	0·5	744
	Malaysia	46·8	41·4	11·8	8,923

*Indigenous includes both Malays and those classified as Indigenous by the Borneo Territories Census.
** Other Races include all other races not classified as Indigenous or Chinese.

Whatever the arguments for or against this situation, the fact that it exists will have severe implications for federal population policy. The variations in size, density and ethnic concentration of the Malaysian population clearly point to the problems which may arise. For instance, the population of the over-crowded island port of Singapore is increasing at a rate which is faster than that of any of the other territories in the Federation. Despite ambitious schemes of housing and industrialisation[4] which are attempting to cope with this population increase, it seems likely that some kind of outlet will have to be found for this rapidly growing population. The Borneo territories which have low population densities and a shortage of labour would seem the logical place for this population to move. Yet the people there, afraid of being swamped by immigrants from Singapore, insist on keeping control of immigration into their territories. This then is one example of the conflict which may emerge between the political realities of Malaysia and the opportunity for a more logical population policy which it presents. However, it is possible that such problems will be merely part of the teething troubles of the new Federation, and with the success of a policy of integrating the major ethnic communities, a population policy which does not have to take accord of these problems of ethnic and political balance can be formulated. For the moment though these ethnic realities cannot be ignored, and the analysis of Malaysian population which follows takes full cognisance of them.

DEMOGRAPHIC HISTORY

The history of population growth in the Malaysian territories has been dealt with in a general fashion in several studies[5] and it is not proposed to treat the subject in any great detail here. Nevertheless, there are certain similarities in the demographic history of the area which must be emphasised if we are to understand the contemporary population problems.

The growth of population in the Malaysian region may be divided into five broad periods which reflect the relative importance of migration, fertility and mortality as growth factors.[6] The first important period of population growth occurred in the period several thousand years before Christ, when the Malay people came southwards from the mainland of Asia and pushed the nomadic aborigines away from the coastal areas into the mountainous interiors. This established the important division in the indigenous community of the area between the people of the mountainous interiors and those of the coast. Such a theory of the peopling of the Malaysian territories rests largely on the assumption that this immigration took the form of a large-scale filtering into South-east Asia which was wavelike in character. Recent work by Keesing[7] has thrown doubt on this wave theory and suggests that the original migration may have taken the form of one great movement of peoples, and that the broad differences which have come about have appeared because of genetic differences emphasised through interbreeding. Whichever of these two theories is correct, the importance is that this period gave rise to the fundamental difference between lowland and upland peoples which presents particular problems to population policy in the Malaysian territories today.

The second period saw the flourishing of Indianised Malay kingdoms, the introduction of Islam, and the early contacts of the Portuguese, Dutch and Chinese. Estimates of the early population of these Malay kingdoms are notably inaccurate. Tome Pires, a resident in Malacca between 1512 and 1515, estimated the population to be in the vicinity of 6,000 inhabitants of which the majority were Malays,[8] but it is unlikely that any of the other kingdoms in Borneo or the rest of Malaya approached this size at that time. The population increased during the following three centuries and this was largely due to the movements of people from Sumatra into the Malayan peninsula, particularly the Minangkabau groups who moved into the areas to the east and north of Malacca.[9] But in general, the demographic patterns of Malaysian society remained those of a traditional society during this period with high death and birth rates, and the population remained fairly stable.

The third phase is unquestionably of major significance for the present-day population patterns and problems of the Malaysian territories. This is the period which covers the extension of British power and control over Malaya and the Borneo territories from about 1786 to 1914. From the demographic point of view there are two main points to be made. The first is the importance of the large-scale Chinese, Indian and Indonesian migrations into Malaya during this period which created the plural society of today. These migrations reached a series of peaks of population influx. In the case of the Chinese the greatest migration was between 1880 and 1914. With the Indians the migration peak came somewhat later.[10] In part these migrations, particularly in the case of the Indians, were the result of demands for labour by the managers of European-owned tin mines and plantations, but large numbers of Chinese came under the impetus of their now countrymen recruiting labour to work in the tin mines of the west coast zone of Malaya. The migration of Chinese was also of considerable importance in the Borneo territories, but 'it should be noted that under the patriarchal rule of the Brookes, Sarawak was not opened either to capitalist development or large-scale immigration in the manner of Malaya or North Borneo' (Sabah).[11] The third important migration into the Malaysian territories was that of the Indonesians. This migration into Malaya and Singapore during the late nineteenth and early twentieth centuries concentrated primarily in the west coast states, forming an important proportion of the Malaysian population. They were particularly attracted to the new irrigation schemes for rice (such as Krian, which the British constructed in the 1890s), and formed most of the population. Thus by 1921 (Table 1, page 68), the immigrant groups made up substantial proportions of the total population of all the Malaysian territories.

The second major demographic characteristic of this period was that, while immigration led to a rapid growth in the total population, natural increase still remained low. Tropical disease had not yet been brought effectively under control and death rates in all groups remained high throughout the period. In addition, the migratory groups amongst the Chinese and Indians tended to be largely male and this contributed to low birth rates amongst the immigrant groups. This was not the case with much of the Indonesian migration (with the exception of Javanese labour) which tended to be characterised by family migrations; therefore birth rates were higher. This then was the most important period for the territories of Malaysia for it laid down the ethnic mixture which is the basis of the present-day plural society. Not only were the basic ethnic, economic and political cleavages built up in this period, but the basic patterns of distribution established then have persisted until today.

The fourth period of demographic growth from 1918 to 1947 saw some variations in the pattern of population growth between the Borneo territories and Malaya and Singapore. Although immigration did continue during this period, it was not so great as in the third phase and it tended to be much more female-dominated. This made the sex ratios amongst the immigrant groups more even, particularly those of the Chinese, and led to a rapid increase in the birth rate. In addition, the death rates of most of the groups in the Malayan peninsula, as well as the Chinese groups in the Borneo territories who were largely urban-based (and so more easily treated by western medicines), began to fall. Thus natural increase became a more significant part of the total population increase. But in the Borneo territories, the indigenous groups, who were largely located in isolated rural areas, did not experience the same drop in death rates. As they formed a substantial proportion of the population in the Borneo territories, this meant that these areas experienced a much slower rate of growth than Malaya and Singapore. For instance, in the period between 1921 and 1931, the populations of Malaya and Singapore increased by 32·5 per cent and 30·3 per cent respectively compared to a 5 per cent increase in Sabah for the same period. The Japanese invasion in the 1940s had a disastrous effect on population in the whole of the areas. Birth rates decreased and death rates increased with the decline of public hygiene in the big centres and the end of the war left a disastrous population situation in practically all territories.

The period since 1947 has seen the beginning of the latest phase of population growth. External immigration has ceased to be an important component in population growth of the territories although internal migration within the Malaysian territories has been of considerable importance, particularly in the case of Singapore. Practically all territories have experienced a rapid drop in mortality and patterns of constant high fertility, resulting in a rate of growth of over two per cent per annum throughout the area. But in terms of the population problems that may threaten Malaysia in the future, the most important rates of increase have been those of Singapore which average over four per cent in the period between 1947 and 1957. Saw Swee Hock points out the importance of internal migration from Malaya as an important component in this population increase.

71

'During the inter-census years 1947–1957, the actual population increase in Malaya was almost 1,373,000; but the natural increase was much larger, about 1,624,000 thus giving a migrational balance of 251,800. Of these it was noted that 141,700 went to Singapore and the remaining 110,000 migrated to outside countries.'[12] It is hardly surprising that Malaya experienced such a migrational deficit during these years because the unstable political situation brought about by the Emergency provided most unsettled conditions for the main immigrant group, the Chinese, many of whom were forced to leave the country. It is worth noting, however, that of the migrants who moved to Singapore since 1947, the majority group has been the Malays who formed forty-six per cent of the immigrant population.[13]

In view of their rather slow rate of growth in the period before the war, the most surprising increases in population have occurred in the Borneo territories. All the territories experienced a sharp rise in their rates of growth to over 3 per cent per annum. In part this was due to a remarkable fall in death rates, which accompanied the British colonial government's improved methods of health control. For instance, the crude death rates of Sabah fell from an average of 13·7 in the period between 1945 and 1949 to 8·3 in 1960. Sarawak recorded a death rate of 5·8 in 1960, but this figure is probably not a true indicator as it almost certainly indicates under-registration of deaths in the territory.[14] In Sabah, this natural population increase was swollen by the substantial immigration of Indonesians.

Thus throughout the whole of the Malaysian territory, as in many other South-east Asian countries, the population has reached a stage of high demographic potential in which large percentages of the population are in the youthful age groups and beginning to enter the reproductive age. This will bring the rate of population increase to an even higher figure unless social or economic developments bring a reduction in birth rates. It should be noted that this rapid increase is by no means equally shared by all the ethnic groups. The Murut community residing in Sarawak has one of the lowest rates of increase in the whole of the Malaysian area. On the other hand, the Chinese population of Singapore has one of the highest rates of increase in the world. Thus the problem of formulating a population policy for Malaysia is no simple one. Regional and ethnic differences in patterns of fertility, mortality and migration will mean that there must be close liaison between federal and state authorities and extremely careful planning.

THE PRESENT DEMOGRAPHIC POSITION

At present, then, Malaysia is a demographer's nightmare! Virtually every demographic process and structure occurs within this crescent of widely diversified territories. The population by 1960 had exceeded ten million and everywhere was increasing at a very fast rate of growth. As is obvious from Table 2 (below), the population is spread most unevenly between the main territories. The most striking contrast is between the heavily populated island port of Singapore with a population density of over 6,000 per square mile and the relatively sparsely settled territories of Borneo. To a large extent this can be explained by the degree of urbanisation of each of the territories.[15]

TABLE 2. THE MAIN DEMOGRAPHIC FEATURES OF THE POPULATION OF THE MALAYSIAN TERRITORIES

Territory	Population*	Density p.s.m.	Yearly Rate of Increase** 1953–60	Crude Birth Rate per 1,000 1960	Crude Death Rate per 1,000 1960	Natural Increase per 1,000 1960
Malaya	6,279,000	124	3·0%	40·9	9·7	31·2
Singapore	1,446,000	6,455	4·6%	38·7	6·3	32·4
Sabah	454,000	15	3·6%	32·9	8·3	24·6
Sarawak	744,000	13	3·3%	25·3	5·8	19·5

* Population at the last census date (see Table 1).
** All figures for rates of increase, crude birth rates, crude death rates and natural increase were taken from United Nations *Demographic Yearbook, 1961* New York, 1961.

The contrasts are even more striking when the general pattern of population distribution is investigated within the main territories. Over 83·5 per cent of the total population of Malaya is concentrated in the western states, and this trend towards concentration appears to be increasing. Kernial Singh comments that the western states registered an increase of thirty per cent during the period between the censuses of 1947 and 1957 compared with an increase of only twenty per cent in the eastern states. 'Furthermore, the government plans to open up new areas, in its effort to give land to the landless and diversify the agriculture, appear to be concerned chiefly with the more accessible western states.'[16] Singapore's internal population patterns require little comment, for much of the population is concentrated in the urban area of Singapore. Its importance in the Malaysian context rests on the fact that, though occupying less than one per cent of the land area of Malaysia, it has some sixteen per cent of the new Federation's total population. In the Borneo territories, however, these regional population contrasts are once again in evidence. The most important concentrations of population occur in the riverine valleys which run inland from the coast where the main towns are situated. Thus nearly a quarter of the people of Sarawak live in the Kuching-Serian area, and the density of people there is over 106 persons per square mile.[17] Similar patterns exist in Sabah where the population is concentrated around the main towns of Jesselton and Sandakan.

73

Almost as important as the features of total population distribution is the distribution of the main ethnic communities. The principal contrast is between the concentration of the Chinese in urban centres and the indigenous groups in the rural areas. The Chinese form over fifty per cent of the population in almost all the large urban centres in the Malaysian territories. The indigenous population, on the other hand, is located principally in the rural areas of Malaya, notably in the two rice bowl areas of Kedah and Kelantan and in other rice-growing areas in the west coast states such as Krian. In the Borneo territories where the indigenous communities are more ethnically divided, there is not such a clear-cut pattern, but the indigenous groups tend to be concentrated in the interior districts.

It is true that on a regional basis this generalisation does not always hold. The east coast towns of Kota Bharu and Kuala Trengganu in Malaya together with some of the smaller towns in the Borneo territories such as Bintulu in Sarawak have indigenous majorities. In addition, with independence, there has been an increasing movement of Malays to the urban areas and in particular to Singapore, but at present the broad pattern still holds and the Chinese dominate the urban centres. This pattern of population distribution has important political and economic implications. Politically, the most important result is the influence that this pattern of distribution has on the voting patterns of the main communities. For instance, in Malaya in 1959, almost one third of the Chinese voters were concentrated in eighteen urban parliamentary constituencies. By comparison only nine per cent of the Malay voters were located in the same urban constituencies.[18] Thus the immigrant groups have a most unequal pattern of representation in the electorate and if, as it appears, this pattern repeats itself in the Borneo territories, such inequality of representation will certainly continue. Thus, provided there are no wide splits amongst the indigenous groups, or substantial changes in the electoral boundaries which increase the number of urban constituencies, political control and power should remain with the indigenous groups.

This pattern of political control associated with the distribution of the two main communities also has implications for the economic policies which are followed. Because the indigenous groups draw their support primarily from the peasantry, they must follow economic policies which are directed to satisfy rural groups. Thus, for instance, the strongest and most publicised aspects of Malaya's program of economic development are the schemes of rural development. These are almost entirely schemes directed towards the Malay peasantry, and only recently have any suggestions for programs of aid for the Chinese rural dweller been put forward. It seems likely that such an emphasis will certainly be continued within the Borneo territories when the Malaysian state comes into being.

The inclusion of the urban, rapidly industrialising area of Singapore may mean that there will be some balancing of rural-directed federal policy. Nevertheless, the immediate problem of the Malaysian countries is to formulate policies which manage to satisfy the majority of the inhabitants while helping to build up a common sense of nationalism.

To understand these problems it is necessary to discuss the characteristics of the main ethnic communities of Malaysia. Although this chapter has chosen to divide the main ethnic groups of Malaysia into three broad groups—the indigenous communities, the Chinese community and the 'other races' groups—it must be emphasised that such divisions are largely arbitrary and mask considerable differences amongst these groups.

The Indigenous Community

In 1960, the largest of the three main ethnic communities in Malaysia was that comprising the indigenous groups[19] with 46·8 per cent of the population (Table 1, page 68). This represented, however, a declining proportion of the total Malaysian population, for in 1911 these groups had made up as much as sixty per cent of the population. Within this wider grouping of indigenous peoples, Malays formed by far the largest group, constituting over eighty per cent of the indigenous population, located principally in Malaya where ninety per cent of the Malays are found. In the post-war period the Malays have been increasing at a faster rate than any of the other indigenous groups, almost entirely from natural increase. Common ties of history, race and culture, the Malay language and the Islamic religion, a social structure in which the rigid division between the aristocratic elite and the great mass of the peasantry still persists—these factors unite to make the community one of the most unified in the Malaysian territories. It should not be imagined, however, that such ties enable the community to present a united front on all issues. Important regional factions exist which tend to break down this unified front. One example of this is in the east coast state of Kelantan, where the Pan-Malayan Islamic Party, a party advocating 'Malaya for the Malays', commands a large following. The revolt in 1963 of a large group of Brunei Malays against the proposed Federation of Malaysia indicates the regional tensions which exist in the Malay community.

The second largest group in the indigenous population are the Dayaks of Sarawak who form over seven per cent of the total indigenous population. These are commonly divided into two groups, the Sea Dayaks, or Ibans, who are by far the largest group, and the Land Dayaks. The Ibans are a predominantly rural people located in the Second and Third divisions of Sarawak. Their religion, language and culture are fundamentally different from that of the Malays, and they are extremely suspicious of the extension of Malay power,

75

particularly of the Brunei Malays. For instance, the Cobbold Commission reported that the Ibans reminded them 'that the record of Brunei rule in Borneo in the past centuries was far from encouraging and fears were expressed that the relative backwardness and inexperience of the Ibans might be used to their disadvantage by the more advanced and sophisticated Malays'.[20]

The remainder of the indigenous peoples is made up of a great diversity of linguistic, cultural and ethnic groups ranging from relatively large tribes, such as the Dusun of Sabah, to small groups of nomadic aborigines. In general, such groups are the least literate, the most economically backward, and the most politically unsophisticated of all the indigenous peoples. Their location is in the most isolated interior parts of the Malaysian territories, and the new federal state faces great problems in regard to improving their health, raising their standards of living and integrating them into the more advanced Malaysian society. Because of their relative isolation, they have not been affected by western medical measures as much as some of the other groups, and rates of population increase are very low. Perhaps the best example of such a group are the Muruts of Sabah who in the period before the war were fast declining[21] due to the introduction of malaria from Javanese labourers in the plantations. Recent statistics from the 1960 census indicate that this trend may have been halted by improved medical methods.[22] Extending medical care and welfare to all such groups throughout the Malaysian territories is a major task for the new Federation. The policies of the Aborigines Department of Malaya are proving particularly effective in this respect because not only are they directed towards improving the health of the aborigine groups, but also towards effectively integrating them, through schemes of education and training in agricultural techniques, into the wider structure of Malayan society.[23] In general, these comments point to an important division between the Malay-dominated territory of Malaya and the territories of Borneo with their large tribal majorities. The Federation of Malaysia is certainly being founded on the supposition that the indigenous groups will act as a unit to protect the political power which they are inheriting. The success of the Malaysian Federation will just as certainly rest on the ability of the indigenous groups to overcome regional tensions between the main groups and to formulate a policy which is acceptable to all groups.

The Chinese Community

Although the Chinese community is much more easy to define than the indigenous community, it is probably little more united. Of Malaysia's Chinese population, 60 per cent live in Malaya. Within this territory they are by no means extensively distributed, being concentrated in the two city ports of Penang and Malacca and the states of Perak, Selangor, Negri Sembilan and Johore. The largest concentration of Chinese is in Singapore. This group, which is unquestionably regarded with greatest suspicion by the other peoples of Malaysia, makes up 27 per cent of Malaysia's Chinese population. The remaining 13 per cent are in the Borneo territories. Regional tensions and structural divisions similar to those of the indigenous groups also characterise the Chinese community. Different waves of migration have led to regional and occupational concentrations of various dialect groups. Thus, for instance, the Teochew dialect group is heavily concentrated in the states of Kedah and Penang.[24] The Hokkiens have an 'urban habit and genius for trade and shopkeeping [and this with] their old association with the colony of the Straits Settlements accounts for their predominance in Singapore, Penang and Malacca . . .'[25] The main dialect community in the Borneo territories is the Hakka who, like their counterparts in Malaya, first moved into Borneo to take part in mining and farming.[26] Although these dialect groupings are no longer so important in terms of dividing the community they are important influences on the demographic and occupational patterns of the Chinese in various areas.[27] Patterns of historical growth have to some extent masked these dialect differences by new class differences. For instance, the longer-established, wealthy Straits Settlement Chinese have had a much longer association with the British and seem more willing to compromise with the aims of the new state to protect their economic interests than the proletarian Chinese migrants of later arrival. A second element in the Chinese community is a new and rapidly growing middle class who have frequently received an English education. The principal structural contrast in the Chinese community is almost certainly that between this group and the great mass of traditional Chinese dwellers who still persist in speaking Chinese, practising the various Chinese religions, and conforming to a traditional way of life. Regional differences among the Chinese are not so obvious as those between the various classes. Singapore with its strong left-wing parties, such as the 'Barisan Socialis' which draws much of its support from the Chinese proletariat, is obviously regarded as the main political problem area.

Because of its lower death rates and remarkably high birth rates, the Chinese community is generally regarded as having higher rates of natural increase within the Malaysian territories than the indigenous peoples. Certainly this is true of the Borneo territories where the death rates for the Chinese are often half those of the indigenous groups. This factor has contributed to rates of population increase which are almost twice those of the indigenous groups. For instance, the Chinese community in Sarawak increased by a total of 58 per cent in the period between 1947 and 1960, while the indigenous groups increased by only 28 per cent.[28] On the other hand, in the territories of Malaya and Singapore, the percentage of population increase was below that of the indigenous groups in the

77

period between 1947 and 1957. In Malaya this was due in part to substantial migration of Chinese both to Singapore and to outside countries. It may be partly attributed to a trend of fertility decline in urban centres which was already beginning to show in 1947[29] which appears to have continued, at least in Singapore, in the period between 1947 and 1957 (Table 3).

TABLE 3. SINGAPORE. PATTERNS OF FERTILITY, MORTALITY AND NATURAL INCREASE 1947-57[30]

	Crude Birth Rate per 1,000		Crude Death Rate per 1,000		Natural Increase per 1,000	
	1947	1957	1947	1957	1947	1957
Malays	48·1	47·3	17·8	10·0	30·3	37·3
Chinese	46·1	42·4	12·8	7·1	33·3	35·3

It is interesting to note the variation in patterns of fertility and mortality between the Chinese and the Malays in the urban centre of Singapore between 1947 and 1957. With the increasing urbanisation taking place in all territories amongst all groups, together with ambitious schemes for extending medical services, these statistics give some indication of the patterns which may emerge in the next few years in other Malaysian territories. In general, the birth rates of both groups tended to remain high throughout the period, although there was some tendency towards decline in the Chinese birth rate. The principal difference between the two communities was in the death rates. In 1947, the Chinese crude death rate was already quite low, and it has continued to drop. While a similar tendency is also apparent in the death rates of the Malays, these have not yet reached the Chinese level. The main reason for the higher death rate amongst the Malays is the high rate of infant mortality: almost three times that of the Chinese. It is notable, however, that, even allowing for their higher death rates, the Malays had a higher rate of natural increase than the Chinese in 1957. This may not necessarily be due to higher fecundity, but rather to the fact that the largely migrant character of the population tends to heavy concentration in the reproductive age group. Although Singapore is probably a rather atypical microcosm from which to draw population trends for the whole of the Malaysian region, it does indicate that the indigenous groups have a considerable potential for population increase which has not yet reached its peak.

The Other Race Groups

Foremost amongst these are the Indians. Limitations of space allow only brief mention of these groups which are located mainly in Malaya and Singapore. They still remain the most immigrant of all the communities with heavily masculine sex ratios and the closest links with their homeland. Although some middle-class Indians tend to be politically active in left-wing movements, the

78

Indian groups as a whole seem relatively willing to compromise and go along with the indigenous groups' ideal of the Malaysian nation state. Within the Borneo territories, the Indonesians form the largest community amongst the other race groups. Their migration, largely from the Indonesian territory of Banjarmasin into Sabah, has taken place only recently.

CONSIDERATIONS OF POPULATION POLICY

This brief treatment of the population of the Federation of Malaysia emphasises above all the bewildering diversity of its features. With the great variation in the prevailing levels of density, a tendency for the divergent patterns of fertility and mortality between the various groups to merge into a common pattern of high fertility and steeply falling mortality, Malaysia will almost certainly be faced not only with the problem of uniting these people, but also with the necessity of seeking measures to curb mounting population pressures in some parts of the state. While it is probable that some problems of agricultural over-population, in areas such as the Kelantan delta, may perhaps be dealt with by improvements in agricultural production, rural to urban migration, and new land development schemes, the main problem area will be Singapore. The unchecked control of population growth in Singapore could lead to a population of close to four million by AD 2000. Such a population projection assumes no immigration which, as it has already been pointed out, has shown a tendency to increase greatly throughout the period since the war.[31] Solutions to this problem are obviously related to wider questions of economic, political, and social policy throughout the region. In the strictly demographic sense, they most clearly hinge on the policies adopted towards the three components of population growth: fertility, mortality and migration. Mortality can be dismissed briefly. Almost all states today are dedicated to introducing health schemes and improvements in modern medicine which will lead to an increase in the life span of their citizens, greater health, and a lower rate of mortality. Any reduction in such policies would seem inconceivable.

The control of fertility is, however, a much more open question. The Malaysian territories are fortunate in that they have no large religious groups who are opposed to artificial methods of birth control, as exists in the Philippines, although early marriage and social traditions which encourage large families still largely persist amongst rural-based, peasant, indigenous groups. In the urban area of Singapore, where communication is not difficult, it should be possible to introduce measures of birth control and legalised abortion (so successful in Japan) which might lead to a substantial drop in the birth rate. It is possible also that increasing urbanisation and industrialisation, besides providing more employment opportunities, will also lead to a fall in birth rates, although much more research needs to be conducted in the Malaysian context before it can be definitely argued that such a fall will occur. Even if such measures were introduced, it is debatable if their effect would be felt soon enough to prevent the large increase in population which appears likely. The final alternative, then, is to attempt to alleviate some of this population pressure by allowing movement to other territories, particularly Borneo.

This will, of course, bring the Malaysian government face to face with the conflict between logical population policies and the present political realities which was mentioned in the introduction to this chapter. Neither Malaya nor the Borneo territories are willing to allow large scale movements of the predominantly Chinese population of Singapore into their territories. Malaya feels that movements of Singapore Chinese into their territory may upset the political and numerical balance between Malays and Chinese and has imposed restrictions on the voting rights of Singapore·citizens in Malaya.[32] The Borneo territories' fears are even greater, and they have demanded the right to control internal movement into their territories. It must be added that such demands are not presented by the indigenous groups purely for fear that their numerical dominance will be upset, but also by Borneo Chinese who are worried that their commercial hegemony may be disturbed by the wealthier and better organised Chinese interests of Singapore. These demands have been presented and accepted as one of the main features of the new Federation. For instance, the Cobbold Commission reported: 'It has been widely represented to the Commission by all races and communities in North Borneo [Sabah] and Sarawak that the small population of these two territories in relation to their size make it essential to provide them with protection against unrestricted movement of population from other parts of the Federation. We have no doubt that this is a legitimate and essential requirement.... In relation to the question of entry from any other Malaysian territory into Sarawak and North Borneo, we recommend that it should be subject to the control of the respective States.'[33] It is possible that such measures might prove little hindrance if they were not enforced rigorously, but few if any federations have persisted with measures to prevent freedom of population movement. One of the principal reasons for collapse of the short-lived West Indies Federation, which had grown out of a not too dissimilar situation, was the failure to reach agreement on the movement of population between the various territories.[34] It is to be hoped that such a similar problem will not obstruct the development of Malaysia.

In the ultimate reckoning, however, the future of the Malaysian Federation as an effective state or as a formulator of logical population policy will depend on its success in overcoming the diverse regional leanings and demands of its territories and the suspicious attitude of the various communities towards each other by wielding these diversities into a common Malaysian nationalism. At present it would appear that any program which attempts to bring about this national unity is going to be largely imitative of the present policy of Malaya; a program which includes such elements as the propagation of Malay as the national language, the formation of a national education system with Malay as the main medium of instruction, and the attempt to build up a culture which is largely based on elements of Malay culture. Such a policy, which can be labelled an assimilative or 'melting pot' policy, is ultimately aimed at destroying the distinct cultural elements of the immigrant communities and replacing it by something which is distinctively Malaysian.[35] In fact the cultural differences of the immigrant groups and their loyalty to Malaysia are two distinct attitudes, and it is possible for the two elements to exist. With the incorporation of Singapore with its large Chinese majority and the Borneo territories whose indigenous groups are by no means willing to accept a federal policy of assimilation such as that outlined above, the policy of creating a national unity will certainly have to become more flexible. Already, the demands of Chinese education in Singapore and the rights of other religions in the Borneo territories have received some recognition which indicates the beginnings of policy which might be labelled 'cultural pluralism'.[36]

The major point of this chapter has been to emphasise the cultural and ethnic diversity in Malaysia, which is characterised by severe economic and political inequalities between the various groups and the problems that this has created in forming a sensible and logical population policy for the new Federation. Population policy then is dominated by the aims and fears of the indigenous groups of the Federation. At the moment they are numerically dominant, but this may not always be the case. Population projections indicate that the immigrant communities will be in substantial dominance by the 1980s. For instance, United Nations estimates of the future population growth in the Malaysian region indicate that the Chinese population will be over nine million by the 1980s, whereas the indigenous groups will still not have reached nine million. It is true, of course, that by 1980 the immigrant groups may well be welded into a loyal Malayan citizenry, but their potential numerical dominance does mean that the ruling indigenous elite cannot afford to follow a policy which antagonises these groups so much that they cease to desire to belong to the Malaysian nation.

It is clear, then, that the success of Malaysia will rest to a large extent on its ability to put into practice a policy which can keep a satisfactory balance between the interests of the various groups while at the same time promoting the larger national aims. In the long run, it may well be that the greater ethnic diversity and regional variety of the Malaysian state may lead to an abandonment of the present 'melting pot' policy, and its replacement by a policy of 'cultural pluralism' which may prove to be the basis of a stronger and healthier state.

5

Urbanisation

HAMZAH-SENDUT

Early urbanisation in Malaysia is poorly documented. We know that about a thousand years ago, Indian cultural intrusions created important nucleated settlements which were capitals of miniature kingdoms and it is probable that these settlements were developed into commercial centres of vast hinterland areas and contained populations directly engaged in non-agricultural pursuits. But, beyond these broad generalisations, so little else is known that it is extremely difficult to say whether or not they marked the beginning of urbanisation in Malaysia. They existed as isolated 'cultural islands' while the other territories of the region were still the home of primitive cultivators, employing stone tools and pointed 'dibble' sticks for agriculture.

Available literature, however, suggests that the development of towns in Malaysia gained a new impetus during the early fifteenth century when Malacca rose from an insignificant, typical fishing village to become a centre of international interest, trade and intercourse. At about the same time, the town of Brunei grew in importance and was at the peak of its fortunes in 1521 when it became the political and commercial centre of northern Borneo. Malaysia was then a region of twin capitals but with the intensification of trade during the following period other towns grew to change the pattern. A number of capitals of Malay tribal states in Malaya became functionally important and could merit the term 'town' or 'urban centre', and, while the Dutch established trade centres in Borneo, British trading stations also appeared in Brunei and at Balambangan, an island north of Marudu Bay. Other population agglomerations were created so that by the early nineteenth century many coastal settlements had developed into fully fledged towns. Present-day towns have grown in number and size as a result of the rapid development that took place during the latter part of the nineteenth and in the early twentieth centuries, the impetus for growth being the exploitation of tin and cultivation of pepper and rubber in Malaya, and the exploitation of petroleum and cultivation of tobacco and other cash crops in the Borneo territories. The consolidation of British interests in Malaya and Singapore, in Sarawak in the shape of the 'White Rajah', and in Sabah by the North Borneo Chartered Company, was followed by stable government, minimal internal bickering among petty Malay chieftains, expanding commercial trade and an enormous immigration. These were important factors fostering the growth and development of towns. But as new towns were developed, some older towns declined in importance; Malacca town was replaced by George Town, Penang, as a trading centre, and later by Singapore; as the town of Brunei declined, the ports of Jesselton and Labuan assumed a new significance.

DEFINITION OF URBAN CENTRES

Definitions used in distinguishing urban centres from rural areas usually differ from country to country, but from the United Nations Yearbooks it may be noted that, for several South-east Asian countries, population size is a widely accepted criterion for demarcation of urbanisation. A certain designated size is set as being more significant than other arbitrary levels and the minimum population requirement appears to vary from 1,000 persons in Malaya to 2,500 persons in Thailand and 3,000 persons in Sabah. In general, however, it may be said that the demarcation criteria were relics of the past and the choice was established by previous colonial governments. Burma, Malaya and Sarawak adopted almost identical statistical criteria because at one time or other they were all three under the suzerainty of the United Kingdom. The statistical criterion of 3,000 people employed in Sabah does not differ appreciably from the figure of 3,500 persons for the United Kingdom; while the figure of 2,500 persons which the Philippines is known to have used is about the size for demarcation of urbanisation in the United States.

Besides size, legal and administrative criteria are also being used to identify South-east Asian urban centres. In the Philippines, for instance, only chartered cities and administrative centres of municipalities are recognised. In Singapore, Sabah and Burma, urban areas are those populated settlements which are designated as such either by state laws or by executive decree. In this sense, urban status is bestowed from above in the same fashion that towns acquire city-rank. For example, the British Crown conferred the title of 'city' on Singapore in 1951 and on George Town, Penang, in 1957.

There is, however, no satisfactory definition of the term 'urban' and 'rural' which could be uniformly applied to all the territories of Malaysia. While urbanisation is generally accepted as a demographic process, the statistical criterion of

83

size of population agglomeration employed by governmental authorities varies with each state. Censuses in Malaya since 1931, for instance, have adopted the arbitrary figure of 1,000 persons so that the urban population constitutes people living in settlements with 1,000 or more inhabitants. The urban population of Singapore comprises those people residing within the administrative boundary of Singapore City, which contained a little over 900,000 persons in 1957. For the territory of Sarawak, only the residents of Kuching, Sibu and Miri, the three largest towns, are taken into account, while the urban population of Sabah is taken to include only those towns with more than 3,000 inhabitants. Based on these varying statistical criteria, therefore, the degree of urbanisation is observed to differ from 12·5 per cent (1960) in Sarawak to 63·1 per cent (1957) in Singapore; it was 14·9 per cent (1960) in Sabah, and 42·5 per cent (1957) in Malaya (Table 4 below). The urban population of these territories added together accounted for 3·8 million people or approximately 42 per cent of the total population of Malaysia in 1957–60.[1] The percentage of population living in places of 20,000 and 100,000 inhabitants during the same period, was about 34 per cent and 18 per cent respectively. The disadvantage of using the last two criteria is that they tend to conceal the actual rate of urbanisation in the region and underestimate the importance of comparatively small towns as centres which are functionally dependent upon the rural hinterlands. They are, nevertheless, useful for international comparison of absolute levels of urbanisation.

TABLE 4. TOTAL URBAN POPULATIONS

Territory	Year	Total	Urban	
			Number	Percentage
Malaya	1947	4,908,086	1,301,376	26·5
	1957	6,278,758	2,679,673	42·5
Singapore	1947	938,079	679,953	72·5
	1957	1,445,929	912,343	63·1
Sabah	1951	334,141	44,833	13·4
	1960	454,421	67,674	14·9
Sarawak	1947	546,385	58,880	10·8
	1960	744,529	93,559	12·5
MALAYSIA	1947	6,726,691	2,085,042	31·0
	1957–60	8,923,627	3,753,249	42·1

Definitions of 'urban' for the purposes of this table:
    Malaya: Towns with over 1,000 inhabitants.
    Singapore: Singapore City population.
    North Borneo: Towns with over 3,000 inhabitants.
    Sarawak: Kuching, Sibu and Miri.

URBANISATION: Hamzah-Sendut

CHARACTERISTICS OF URBAN POPULATION

Malaysia may be said to be urbanised to a high degree although it is primarily engaged in agricultural production. From the standpoint of Asia in general, the percentage of people living in towns of more than 20,000 inhabitants is above the average; even as early as 1950 Malaysia contained about 24 per cent of its population in towns of more than 20,000 people compared with the continent of Asia's average of 13·1 per cent. This figure also made it a highly urbanised region in South-east Asia where the Philippines was 12·7 per cent urbanised in 1950, Burma 10 per cent, Indonesia 9·1 per cent, Cambodia, Laos and Vietnam together 8·0 per cent, and Thailand 7·6 per cent.[2]

The degree of urbanisation, however, varies considerably with the component states of the region. It is low in Sarawak and Sabah but comparatively high in the other two territories. The highest concentration of town-dwellers was recorded in Singapore in 1957 with Malaya a good second. This situation remains unchanged even when towns of over 20,000 inhabitants are taken into account (Table 5). Data also reveal the extent of concentration of the urban population in the capital cities, especially that of Singapore. The importance of Kuala Lumpur, Kuching and Jesselton in accounting for the high rate of urbanisation in their respective areas is also not to be underestimated. These capital cities together contain a high proportion of the urban people of Malaysia, and Singapore City alone accounts for nearly 40 per cent of the entire urban population. From another standpoint, about 55 per cent of the urban residents are found in Malaya, with about 6 per cent in Sarawak and Sabah together. In fact, the city of George Town, Penang, has a population greater than the total urban population of the two territories in Borneo. This imbalance reflects variations in the distribution of the total population within the region. Another reason is that both Malaya and Singapore have had the advantage of an early start, many areas having been the focus of earlier immigration and centres of settlement ever since they became accessible to economic development. On the other hand, the growth of urbanisation in Borneo has been impeded by the mountainous terrain, the undeveloped interior and general isolation from the world trade routes. The lack of efficient communications is specially conspicuous as a retarding factor.

There are no railways in Sarawak and remarkably few roads, because of the shortage of good roadstone and poor nature of the terrain. Traditionally, transportation is by river. Sabah, on the other hand, is better off because it not only has railways and 250 miles of metalled roads but also an air service linking isolated inland areas. The growth of towns, however, has been fostered mainly by coastal sea-traffic. In contrast, Malaya and Singapore have a network of over 6,000 miles of hard surfaced roads linking all the towns in the area; forty-one shipping lines

85

TABLE 5. URBAN AREAS WITH 100,000 AND MORE, AND 20,000 AND MORE INHABITANTS

Territory	Date of Census	Total Population (in thousands)	Towns of 100,000 + Inhabitants			Towns of 20,000 + Inhabitants		
			No.	Population Aggregate (in thousands)	% of Total	No.	Population Aggregate (in thousands)	% of Total
Malaya	1947	4,908	2	365	7·4	15	837	17·1
	1957	6,279	3	677	10·8	21	1,307	20·8
Singapore	1947	938	1	680	72·4	1	680	72·4
	1957	1,446	1	912	63·1	1	912	63·1
Sabah	1951	334	0	0	0	0	0	0
	1960	454	0	0	0	2	51	11·2
Sarawak	1947	546	0	0	0	1	38	6·9
	1960	745	0	0	0	2	80	10·7
Total Malaysia	1947	6,726	3	1,045	15·5	17	1,555	23·1
	1957–60	8,924	4	1,589	17·8	26	2,350	26·3

and seventeen miles of dock railways assist the growth and development of several coastal towns and the general spread of urban development.

Demographic statistics indicate that as the total population of the region rises, the number of people living in towns also increases. Over a period of ten to thirteen years, between 1947 to 1957–60, the total population of Malaysia showed an increase of 32·8 per cent from 6·7 million to 8·9 million people, while the urban population rose by 76·2 per cent from 2·1 to 3·7 million people. A similar pattern of population growth is also evident in three of the territories (Table 6, below), the exception being Singapore where the city showed an increase of population of 34·1 per cent compared to the total population rise in Singapore Island of 53·1 per cent. The proportion of the island's population within the city fell from 72·4 per cent in 1947 to 63·1 per cent in 1957, which reflects the Singapore government's attempts to develop the rural countryside as well as to relieve congestion within the city.

TABLE 6. COMPARATIVE GROWTH OF TOTAL AND URBAN POPULATION OF MALAYSIA

Territory	Period	Total Population Increase in %	Urban Population Increase in %
Malaya	1947–57	27·9	105·9
Singapore	1947–57	53·7	34·1
Sabah	1951–60	35·9	51·1
Sarawak	1947–60	36·4	61·0
Malaysia	1947/57/60	32·6	80·0

Among the territories of Malaysia, Malaya shows the greatest difference between total population and urban population increases. While the former rose by 27·9 per cent between 1947 and 1957 the latter increased by 105·9 per cent. Apart from natural increase of population in towns, this phenomenal growth may be explained by the artificial acceleration of urbanisation following the Emergency[3] which began in 1948. About half a million scattered rural dwellers were resettled into 440 compact villages of which 70 had a population of more than 2,000 people each.[4] Many of these settlements have thrived as semi-urban nuclei, so that in effect a small 'urban revolution' was initiated to force the pace of urbanisation in the country.

Another important aspect of the urban population of the Malaysian region lies in its distribution by sex. This is distinguished by the presence of a greater number of males than females in urban areas, the ratio being 1,103 males per 1,000 females in 1957–60. It is also observed that there is a tendency for the population to become less masculine especially since the Second World War; the proportion of males in 1957 has shown a decrease since 1947 (Table 7, page 88) and the

87

difference in the sex ratio is no longer considerable. Whereas the urban male population increased by 73·7 per cent, the urban female population has risen by 87·4 per cent and the trend towards parity may, in fact, reflect the sex composition of the migrant population from the rural areas and villages to the towns.

TABLE 7. SEX COMPOSITION OF THE URBAN POPULATION

Territory	Date of Census	Total Population		Urban Population	
		Females per 1,000 males	Males per 1,000 females	Females per 1,000 males	Males per 1,000 females
Malaya	1947	891	1,122	849	1,188
	1957	939	1,065	912	1,096
Singapore	1947	821	1,206	827	1,209
	1957	895	1,117	884	1,131
Sabah	1951	938	1,065	781	1,280
	1960	920	1,196	882	1,131
Sarawak	1957	943	1,167	860	1,163
	1960	981	1,019	964	1,038
Malaysia	1947	859	1,162	838	1,193
	1957–60	934	1,071	906	1,103

Rural-urban migration may have included a high proportion of females, from which it could further be inferred that there are at present fewer restrictions against women seeking employment in the towns than there were before the Second World War.[5] It should be noted, however, that these observations are tentative, and if more data were readily available it would be interesting to find out whether the population of Malaysia tends to become less masculine and more feminine as the size of towns increases. Urban sex ratios among the major communities in the region also require further study. With regard to age distribution, the findings for Malaya and Singapore for which data are available seem to indicate that urban areas carry a disproportionately big share of youthful population. For instance, about 40 per cent of Kuala Lumpur's population is below the age of fifteen and this would indicate the prevailing pattern in the whole of Malaysia. In addition to having a high proportion of persons between six and fifteen years of age, all towns also show a small percentage of people above sixty years of age.

An analysis of the racial composition of the urban population shows clearly the preponderance of Chinese over the indigenous population, there being 2·5 million Chinese compared to 0·9 million indigenous people. The other communities constitute less than 0.5 million people (Table 8). Whereas 66.9 per cent of the Chinese community lived in urban areas only 22·8 per cent of the indigenous people did so in 1957 and the disparity is more obvious in Singapore than in any other territory, where the Chinese outnumber the indigenous population by seven to one. They appear to be more urbanised in Malaya and Singapore combined than their counterparts in Sarawak and Sabah (Table 9, page 90).

TABLE 8. RACIAL COMPOSITION OF THE URBAN POPULATION (IN THOUSANDS)

Territory		Indigenous	Chinese	Others	Total
Malaya	1947	275	812	215	1,301
	1957	604	1,704	360	2,680
	% increase	119·6	109·8	67·4	104·3
Singapore (City only)	1947	73	537	70	680
	1957	101	710	102	912
	% increase	38·3	32·2	45·7	34·1
Sabah (Sandakan	1951	4·4	18·8	3·0	26·2
and Jesselton only)	1960	9·1	35·8	5·6	50·5
	% increase	106·9	90·4	86·6	92·8
Sarawak	1947	21·9	34·8	2·2	58·9
	1957	23·5	67·4	2·7	93·6
	% increase	7·3	93·6	22·7	61·0
MALAYSIA	1947	374	1,403	290	2,066
	1957	946	2,517	471	3,737
	% increase	152·9	79·4	62·4	80·8

While it is true that the Chinese have always shown a preference to living in urban localities they have, however, increased at a slower rate than the indigenous people. For Malaysia as a whole, the rates of increase were 79·4 per cent and 152·9 per cent for the two communities respectively; data in Table 9 also indicate great increases of the indigenous urban population in Malaya and Sabah. In actual numbers for all territories, however, the urban Chinese rose by 1·1 million compared with a rise in the number of the indigenous people of 572,000.

Although numerically the increase of the non-immigrant people is less significant than that of the Chinese, it suggests nevertheless a new trend in urbanisation in Malaysia. Townward movement of the indigenous people could perhaps be an important determinant of the growth rate of towns in the future because the proportion of foreign-born persons in each of these territories under consideration is becoming smaller and immigration has been of minor importance. It is almost superfluous to repeat that data adequate for the study of rural migration are not available but observations confirm what is already known.

TABLE 9. INDICES OF URBAN CONCENTRATION FOR THE INDIGENOUS AND CHINESE COMMUNITIES
OF MALAYSIA

Territory	Year	Indigenous			Chinese		
		Urban	Total	Index	Urban	Total	Index
		in thousands		%	in thousands		%
Malaya	1947	275	2,428	11·3	812	1,885	43·1
	1957	812	3,125	19·3	1,704	2,334	73·0
Singapore	1947	73	116	62·9	537	730	73·5
	1957	101	197	51·2	710	1,091	65·1
Sabah	1951	4·4	243	1·8	18·8	74	25·4
	1957	9·1	306	2·9	35·8	105	34·0
Sarawak	1947	21·9	396	5·5	34·8	145	24·0
	1957	23·5	507	17·0	67·4	229	29·2
MALAYSIA	1947	374	3,183	11·7	1,403	2,834	49·5
	1957	946	4,133	22·8	2,517	3,759	66·9

Note: Index of urban concentration in percentage equals

$$\frac{\text{urban population of a particular community of the country} \times 100}{\text{total population of that community in the country}}$$

The causes of these movements into the towns appear to be both social and economic. On the one hand, the rural areas lack adequate lighting, provide sparse health facilities, poor sewage systems and inefficient methods of water supply. Rural education is generally considered inferior, and where schools exist they are often ill-equipped. On the other hand, the towns generally have available such facilities as adequate shopping areas, entertainment, piped water supply, electricity, proper sanitation, good schools and roads.

ECONOMIC IMPLICATIONS OF URBANISATION

Of the territories of Malaysia, Singapore Island is the only state that exhibits a high level of urbanisation as well as industrialisation. With urban population increases, the labour force engaged in industries and non-agricultural activities has shown a rapid rise since 1947. Nevertheless, it should be noted that Singapore City has not been able to absorb all the population within its boundary, with the result that the government has had to create a new industrial estate at Jurong, a few miles outside the city. Plans are also in hand to develop similar estates at Sembawang and Woodlands and possibly in two other areas.

Malaya also shows a comparatively high rate of urbanisation but, unlike Singapore in many respects, its industrial occupations are essentially primary. In 1947, primary industry (agriculture, forestry and fishing) accounted for more than

50 per cent of the economically active population and the proportion showed no major change ten years later. Manufacturing still remained limited by 1957,[6] so that with the Emergency and other forces accelerating the push of the rural people into towns, the problem of unemployment and underemployment is sufficiently serious to merit continuous government attention.

In contrast to these two states, Sabah and Sarawak are less urbanised, and also their level of urbanisation is closely associated with the tertiary pattern of occupation structure. It can be observed that a great many people in Kuching, Jesselton and Sandakan are engaged in the retail trade, supplying Asian foods, hotel and restaurant service, domestic employment and 'fringe' services.

Thus, it appears that in Malaysia as a whole, like many other developing countries, there does not exist any close correlation between urbanisation and industrialisation. While it is true that the rate of urbanisation is comparatively high, there is only a small movement of people away from agricultural activities into industrial employment. Nowhere in this region does the high proportion of population living in towns reflect levels of industrial development. In this respect, the growth pattern of urbanisation in Malaysia as a whole differs from that of the United Kingdom, France or the United States, where growth tendencies indicate a close interaction of industrial development and urbanisation. Instead, in all the territories there appears to be a general lack of industries and there is considerable underemployment, at least in the major towns. Economically speaking, the rapid rise of urbanisation in Malaysia merely reflects a shift of people from low-income work in agriculture into another sector of employment, namely urban employment such as petty trading, taxi-driving, trishaw-peddling, hawking of foodstuffs and domestic service etc, which are also of low productivity. The question may then be posed as to whether the region as a whole is already at a critical stage of urban development before being overurbanised through further rural-urban migration.[7]

Another important economic aspect of urbanisation in Malaysia relates to the concentration of urban populations in the capital city of each of the constituent territories (Table 10). Jesselton and Kuala Lumpur showed population increases of more than 50 per cent each during the inter-census decade. The economic reasons for the rapid growth of the capitals seem obvious, but what is seldom recognised is that these increases strain not only the existing social overheads but also the economic infrastructure of these towns. In Malaya, on the other hand, a new pattern of development is apparent, for, in addition to the rapid growth of population in Kuala Lumpur, the small towns between 5,000 and 10,000 population show a greater concentration of people;[8] they grow faster than the medium size towns while still lacking the suitable technical, social and economic environment for the location of both small scale and large scale industrial enterprises.

91

TABLE 10. RATE OF GROWTH OF THE FOUR CAPITAL CITIES OF THE CONSTITUENT TERRITORIES

Territory and Capital		Population (in thousands)		Increase %	Urban % of Population of Malaysia 1957	% of Urban Population of Country 1957
Malaya	Kuala Lumpur	1947	176·0			
		1957	316·2	79·5	8·3	11·8
Singapore	Singapore City	1947	680·0			
		1957	912·3	34·1	24·3	63·1
Sabah	Jesselton	1951	11·7			
		1960	21·7	85·5	0·6	32
Sarawak	Kuching	1947	38·0			
		1957	56·0	47·3	1·5	59·8
Total for four capitals		1947	905·7			
		1957	1,306·2	44·2	14·8	

The impact of urbanisation on labour mobility, income, levels of living, saving and capital formation in Malaysia is difficult to assess because of the lack of data, but certain generalisations which apply to South-east Asia as a whole may also hold for much of the region although actual situations may vary with different racial groups. First, the movements of people from the countryside—rural Malays in Malaya and the indigenous tribes in Sarawak—clearly indicate some kind of labour mobility; the greater proportion of people at present working in the police force, government administration, public transport, and to a certain extent in manufacturing and processing industries, was recruited from agriculture. Secondly, while it is generally true that the urban working force receives a relatively higher level of income than the rural people, it must be noted that the same working force has a large number of dependants to support. In other words, the 'dependency burden' of townward migrants who leave their dependants in the rural areas is high, for not only have they to support themselves in a new environment but also their wives and children who are not with them. Finally, urbanisation in Malaysia is a process of modernisation, not only of the way of living of the people but also of their consumption habits. For instance, it has been observed that the urban migrants of Kampong Bahru, an exclusive Malay settlement area in Kuala Lumpur, take to eating breakfast before going to work, whereas they were used to going without it in the rural areas. It should be noted also that urbanisation in general has created new wants in many other directions.

SOCIAL IMPLICATIONS

The social implications of urbanisation in Malaysia have multifarious aspects[9] which comprise changes in family size, structure and stability, religious practices and beliefs, social stratification, social controls and the role of women in a changing society. Much more pertinent to the Malaysian political context is the question of integrating, in the urban setting, the immigrant with the indigenous communities. Information on these and other social phenomena is sadly lacking and it is not possible to establish broad generalisations on the subject. Besides, much depends on the particular situation and the educational and cultural level of the various ethnic groups under study. Certain brief comments, however, appear relevant.

First, there is as yet no conclusive evidence to show that family size declines with urbanisation although the author's preliminary investigations of some towns in Malaya indicate a lowering of fertility amongst both the Chinese and Indian urban dwellers. Birth rates are high in all towns, and the low income groups in particular have larger families than those in the high income brackets. Among the Malays of Malaya, this may be due to the presence in the towns of families born in the rural areas. If only town-born parents are considered, the differential between the two social groups may not be apparent. Among the more stabilised urban communities such as the immigrant groups, the number of housewives working outside the home is increasing and this may be a factor, among other factors, leading to a limitation on family size. As regards family structure there is no observable change and there is as much visiting of relatives and helping of relatives as before; kinship ties between urban dwellers and their relatives in the rural areas have not been dissolved because of the ease of movement and communication which motorcars, public transportation and, to a certain extent, telephones provide. Besides, the rural families that migrate to the towns are not necessarily the poorest of the countryside; rather, they comprise the intelligent and more progressive of the rural people.

The problems associated with personal disorganisation resulting from urbanisation could also be enumerated but of greater importance, both socially and economically, is the preponderance of children below the age of fifteen. It means that not only have schools and social amenities to be found for them, but also sources of future employment to meet their needs when they come into the working age group. The mobility of low income families to secure decent housing and the development of slum and squatter areas are twin problems attendant upon rapid urbanisation in Malaysia; the difficulties come not only from their economic situation but also from many of the social repercussions. Furthermore, state governments and local authorities have insufficient resources to solve these problems and the purchasing power of the squatter is too low to afford any alternative accommodation. Finally, there is the lack of adequate community facilities, including physical facilities (such as water supply, sewage systems and transportation) and public and social services. Although deficiencies in the distribution and quality of public services may be more acute on the periphery of such big towns as Singapore City and Kuala Lumpur than in other sectors where the population is concentrating, the deterioration of community facilities as a consequence of rapid urban growth may altogether affect the balanced development of many towns in the new Federation.

URBANISATION AND TOWN PLANNING

Brief remarks on the recent development of main towns in each of the territories may be instructive. Jesselton is the capital of Sabah, though its population is less than that of Sandakan, the largest town in the state. Founded in 1896, it grew up slowly from the swampy forests. In 1931, it had a population of only 4,745 people. With the increased use of the railways, the development of roads to Kota Belud, the extension of settlement by Chinese immigrants and the growing importance of rubber, Jesselton grew in significance. In 1961, its population was about four and a half times that in 1931. It assumed the status of capital in 1946.

The most striking development in post-war Jesselton is the increase in size of both the number of inhabitants and buildings. These include three banks, two cinemas built on land reclaimed from the sea, extensive office buildings erected by business houses, godowns, markets, a large community centre with a stage and bar, and two hotels. Four-storey blocks taking shape along the waterfront at the beginning of 1962 included new hotels, shops and offices. In the port area, a new 650 ft. wharf can accommodate one ocean vessel, one vessel of 3,000 tons, and two coastal vessels. At its entrance is a modern Customs House. A considerable expanse of newly reclaimed land nearby provides space for large warehouses and bulk oil-storage depots, and further expansion is proceeding in this direction.

Sandakan, the former capital and centre of the flourishing timber industry on the east coast of Sabah, has a population of 28,000 people. It is the state's biggest port, with a beautiful, naturally protected harbour. In 1960, its 740 ft. wharf handled 2·7 million gross tons of shipping: an increase of 0·5 million gross tons over the previous year. Here the timber, rubber, cutch and copra of the Labuk and the Sandakan peninsula are exported to all parts of the world. As in Jesselton, the town has been rebuilt in multi-storey reinforced concrete after the destruction caused by the Second World War, and land is being reclaimed to provide for the town's growth.

Kuching, the capital of Sarawak, is situated on the Sarawak River, about eighteen miles from the sea, in flat country with ranges of hills to the south and east. The main part of the town with its wharves and warehouses, commercial and government buildings, shops and churches, lies on the south bank of the river. An increasing number of new residential areas have developed and these projects have helped to ease overcrowding in the commercial-residential area of the town. An important port, Kuching can be reached by vessels of up to 2,500 tons and is a regular point of call for ships from Singapore, Hong Kong and other ports in South-east Asia. A new port area has just been constructed at Tanah Puteh, two miles downriver, to ease much of the congestion at the waterfront in the town centre.

Singapore City is South-east Asia's main commercial market, an international clearing-house and an entrepôt for Malaya and for other parts of South-east Asia. To meet the needs of its expanding population, many housing estates have been established either by public or private finance outside the city limits and there has also been the erection of a number of factories, producing or assembling commodity items ranging from biscuits to motorcars and tractors. The establishment of British military cantonments at Jurong, Sembawang and Changi attracted a proportion of workers from the city, and with the full implementation of the Singapore City Master Plan, decentralisation of population and industries will receive additional stimulus. With the already heavy concentration of population in the rural areas, the whole of the island will be urbanised and eventually transformed into one great conurbation of Singapore.

Kuala Lumpur, the capital of Malaya, is a busy commercial and administrative centre. Its population of 176,000 in 1947 rose to 316,000 in 1957, an increase of 80 per cent. This high rate of increase in the population can be attributed to the growth of secondary industries. Excluding palm oil and rubber estate factories, almost 85 per cent of the total number of factories in the state of Selangor are in Kuala Lumpur itself or within a very short distance of it. Kuala Lumpur, and the nearby 'new town' of Petaling Jaya, have many advantages and attractions for industrial development over other areas since Kuala Lumpur is not only centrally situated and the federal capital, but also contains many facilities for industrial development.

These brief descriptions admittedly do not do justice to the important roles that these towns play in their respective areas, especially Singapore City and Kuala Lumpur, but they give a satisfactory picture of recent developments.[10] It is clear that in spite of the smallness of their size compared with European and American cities, these towns are also facing problems of physical planning. The consequences of the rapid rate of urbanisation are becoming more visible in the second half than in the first half of the twentieth century. In Singapore and the big towns of Malaya, slums and squatter areas, excessive urban densities, uncontrolled

95

land use and speculation, inadequate urban services, deficient educational facilities and the lack of employment services, are evident in varying degrees of intensity. Obviously these problems are also beginning to affect some towns in Sarawak and Sabah; in fact, they affect not only dwellers in the individual towns but also those in the entire region. It is clear that the planner alone cannot make any effective contribution to the problem, much less attain the desirable goals of town development, unless the new federal government, the state governments and the local authorities in each of the constituent territories co-ordinate their economic, social, administrative and physical planning program. In a developing country such as Malaysia, the improvement of the urban environment entails a corresponding development of the rural areas.

PART TWO

The Historical Background

6

Early History

ALASTAIR LAMB

Malaysia today links mainland South-east Asia and island South-east Asia. It also forms a single political entity astride the main sea route between China and the West. It is thus in a very real sense the cross-roads of South-east Asia. Its strategic geographical position was apparent to European powers ever since the Portuguese first ventured into eastern waters. From 1511, the European nation which held Malacca enjoyed a real measure of control over the commerce of the Malacca Straits which join the China Seas to the Indian Ocean. The British in the eighteenth century came into contact with Malaysia in their search for ports outside China whither could come Chinese merchants to sell their wares free from the obstructions of the Manchu bureaucracy. In this quest the British straddled the entire extent of modern Malaysia, with settlements at Penang and at Balambangan on the Sulu Sea.

The economic importance of Malaysia, so apparent to the Portuguese, Dutch and English, was also clear in earlier times; and we can today reconstruct in significant detail the economic history of this region over at least a thousand years before the coming of the European. We cannot, however, say a great deal about the political history of Malaysia except in the last two centuries or so of this period. Political history can only be written on the basis of documentary evidence. We need to know something about the names and chronologies of dynasties, the policies and ambitions of kings and ministers, the conflicts between states. We need, in fact, a corpus of indigenous historical texts which is almost completely lacking in Malaysia. Neither Malaya nor that part of Borneo which came under British rule has so far produced a dated inscription earlier than the fourteenth century AD.[1] Malay histories do exist, but they throw little light on events before the beginning of the fifteenth century AD. Javanese sources extend our knowledge back for a further century, but, as far as the Malaysian region is concerned, in no great detail.

The historian of pre-European Malaysia, in fact, cannot rely on local texts and chronicles in the way that the historian of, say, medieval England can. He is obliged to supplement his indigenous sources with information gleaned from sources of non-Malaysian (and generally non-South-east Asian) origin. There are many of these. The Chinese have been in contact with South-east Asia since early in the christian era; and there is no shortage of references to South-east Asian place names in Chinese historical literature. The muslim world of the Middle East came into trading contact with the further shores of the Indian Ocean and beyond; and by the late eighth century AD Arab and Persian literature was becoming aware of the existence of South-east Asia. Indians, perhaps from some period before the opening of the christian era, traded across the Bay of Bengal; the information so derived has found its way into several texts and inscriptions. Finally, while Malaysia itself lacks documents and inscriptions, some of Malaysia's neighbours are rather more fortunate. In Cambodia, Vietnam, peninsular Siam, Java, Sumatra and Indonesian Borneo, for instance, there have been discovered during more than a century of research a fairly impressive epigraphical corpus which, after careful examination by modern scholars, has been made to throw some light on the evolution of the territories which now make up Malaysia.[2]

To this literary and epigraphical evidence we must add the information derived from archaeological research. Malaysia is far less fortunate than some of its neighbours in its heritage of ancient monuments. It possesses no great Hindu or Buddhist structures to compare with Angkor in Cambodia or Borobodur and Prambanan in Java. This lack has meant that during the period of colonial rule the incentive for the establishment of an ambitious archaeological and museum service was weak. Malaya and British Borneo, it is true, produced their museums. The work carried out by the staff of the Raffles Museum, Singapore, the Perak Museum, Taiping, and the Sarawak Museum, Kuching, has over the last half century been remarkable both for its quality and its quantity. However, Malaysia has not been able in the past to compete with the archaeological and cognate work which was sponsored by the French in Indochina and the Dutch in Indonesia. A great deal more needs to be done both in Malaya and in Borneo before a satisfactory archaeological basis for historical interpretation is established. Yet enough is known both to suggest the fundamental shape of Malaysian pre-European history and to indicate that some of the prevailing interpretations of the literary and epigraphical sources can only be accepted with caution.

The final elucidation of the pre-European history of Malaysia will involve a careful synthesis of, on the one hand, archaeological, anthropological and linguistic evidence, and on the other of the results of research into the inscriptions and the non-Malaysian texts. To date, a distinct gulf exists between these two categories of source material. The texts are full of references to place names which it has been deduced must be located in South-east Asia. They give quite a lot of historical information about some of these places, but they rarely tell us quite enough to locate the place names with certainty. The history derived from the texts is to a considerable extent a history in search of a country. The scholarly literature on the location of place names from Chinese, Arabic and Indian sources in South-east Asia is very extensive, the product of many able minds. It is, however, still surprisingly inconclusive and speculative. The history derived from archaeological investigation in Malaysia is quite precise, as far as it goes, but it does not give us anything very substantial in the way of names and dates. From archaeology we get a good picture of the sort of sites where settlement took place in pre-European Malaysia, and of the kind of trade which brought wealth to the region. We can trace the rise and fall of settlements. We can see the measure of influence from China and India. We cannot, however, find out with certainty what the settlements were called.

Archaeology and the texts, while they may not as yet have been reconciled in detail, are in general agreement as to the role which Malaysia played in the commerce and civilisation of pre-European South-east Asia. They leave us in no doubt that, from at least the opening of the christian era, the region was in some form of contact with both the Chinese coast and the major trading ports of the Indian Ocean. They show clearly that out of the interaction of these eastern and western contacts emerged a cultural and political evolution culminating in the Malaysian states which were found by the Europeans in the early sixteenth century.

In the centuries immediately before the opening of the christian era, Chinese influence, both political and cultural, began to penetrate into what is now Vietnam. In Tongking and along the Annamese coast, Chinese colonies emerged and Chinese culture blended with that of the indigenous peoples in regions beyond the direct political control of the Chinese dynasties. One consequence of this process would seem to have been the development of the Dongson culture, named after its type-site in Tongking. The culture is known chiefly for its bronze drums, bells and other artifacts which show in their decoration a blend of Chinese and indigenous Vietnamese motifs. The Dongson bronzes relate in many ways to the pottery of the late neolithic period in sites scattered widely over South-east Asia—in Thailand, Malaya, the Philippines, Sarawak, the Celebes and elsewhere. Dongson-type motifs still survive in the traditional arts and crafts of the aboriginal peoples of South-east Asia. The Dayak peoples of Malaysia have produced many examples of what has been described in the literature as Dongsonian influence.

101

The problems of the implications of the Dongson culture are far from solved at present; but it would seem that we have here two elements at least. On the one hand, throughout much of South-east Asia from late neolithic and early metal age times there existed a basic culture with Dongsonian affinities, having many local variations, of which traces can still be detected among many of the aboriginal peoples (that is to say the peoples who have resisted to some extent the influences of Hinduism, Buddhism and Islam). On the other hand, from the centres of Dongsonian culture in Indochina were traded bronze objects, drums, bells and the like, over a wide area. Dongson-type bronzes are known from Malaya, for example, with the drums and bells from near Klang in Selangor and the drum from the Tembeling river in Pahang. Such bronzes have been excavated from sites in many parts of Indonesia. In Laos and Burma Dongson bronze drums were imitated locally, and their manufacture has continued up to modern times.[3]

The distribution of Dongson bronzes is as yet not fully understood. There are still arguments as to whether these objects were exported from the Tongking region or were made locally by craftsmen who emigrated from Indochina and established foundries far from their homeland. What is certain, however, is that the spread of Dongson artifacts over such a wide area indicates that before the opening of the christian era much of South-east Asia was in some form of commercial contact with the southern fringes of the Chinese world. To what extent the Chinese themselves participated in these relationships is not known. Many parts of South-east Asia, including Java, southern Sumatra and the extreme southern tip of the Malay peninsula, have yielded earthenwares which have been identified as Chinese of the Han Dynasty. Some of these wares certainly are this; others, as for example the sherds found at sites along the Johore river in Malaya, are probably of much later date and reflect no more perhaps than the survival of an old tradition.

At about the same time as the Dongson culture was reaching its apogee, South-east Asia was coming into contact with regions to its west across the Indian Ocean. The process whereby this came about is no better understood than are many other aspects of the early history of this part of the world; but it is now widely accepted that the rise of empires in the Middle East and the Mediterranean was involved. By the sixth century BC the Achaemenian Empire in Iran had extended its boundaries to the Indus valley, thus linking the Indian subcontinent to the Mediterranean. In the fourth century BC the Achaemenians fell beneath the onslaught of Alexander the Great, whose Indian conquests were by the very end of the century snatched from Greek hands by the Maurya dynasty, the founders of India's first great empire.

In Maurya times overland contacts between Iran and India continued, and to these trade routes were added, with the expansion of the Han dynasty of China into Central Asia, overland links with the Far East. By the beginning of the christian era, with the Mediterranean united under Roman rule, it is certain that trade on a significant scale was being carried on between the remote corners of the Eurasian continent.

It was inevitable that this land commerce should be supplemented by the exploitation of the sea routes of the Indian Ocean and China Seas, where the operation of the monsoons facilitated regular navigation. By the first century BC, and probably much earlier, the Mediterranean was in contact with India by sea. Ports engaged in this trade were emerging on the shores of the Red Sea and, it seems very likely, on the Persian Gulf as well. Early in the christian era, Mediterranean merchants were well aware of ports on the eastern shores of peninsular India. It is possible, even, that Roman or Alexandrian merchants had already established agencies here—or so the evidence of excavations at Arikamedu (on the east coast of India south of Madras) would suggest. By the third century AD Mediterranean trade had been extended even further afield into mainland South-east Asia, as attested by the presence of Graeco-Roman objects in surprisingly large numbers in Siam and Indochina, and particularly in the neighbourhood of the delta of the Mekong. Here, at the site of Oc-eo, the French since 1940 have excavated an astonishing quantity of small objects clearly of Middle Eastern or Mediterranean origin of this period, including a number of engraved seals.

By the second century AD, South-east Asia was sufficiently well known to the Mediterranean world as to have earned a place in geographical treatises. The writings of Claudius Ptolemy contain a detailed, though by no means clear, treatment of the lands to the east of India. His Golden Khersonese is so similar to the Malay peninsula in shape that most modern scholars have not hesitated to make this particular identification. Recently, however, the French archaeologist Malleret, on the basis of his work at Oc-eo and other Indochinese sites, has come to believe that Ptolemy, when he described the Golden Khersonese, actually had in mind the region of the Mekong delta.[4] He argues that the most impressive evidence of contact here with the Mediterranean is not matched by archaeological evidence from the Malay peninsula. Indeed, as he points out, the entire archaeological basis for 'Roman' (i.e. Mediterranean) contact with the Malay peninsula in early christian, or pre-christian, times is to be found in some vitreous beads from Johore and some sherds from a cave site in the extreme north-west of Malaya which have been described as 'Attic'. He observes, as have also other scholars, that the 'Attic' sherds may well be Indian, and that the 'Roman' beads, even if of genuine Roman manufacture, need not have come to South-east Asia in Roman times. There is good evidence that South-east Asia remains even now a potential market for beads of ancient pattern, as witness the taste in these objects of some of the peoples of northern Borneo. Since the history of Malaysia as found in most

of the existing school texts begins with an account of the 'Malayan' Golden Khersonese, Malleret's conclusions may not readily be accepted. They cannot, however, be ignored.

The archaeological evidence is very strong that the first great western trade
contact with South-east Asia was with the Mekong delta region, which the
Chinese were soon to refer to as the kingdom of Fu-nan. Moreover, archaeology
suggests that with this commercial activity came the importation into South-east
Asia of Indian cultural and religious forms, giving birth to Indianised South-east
Asia, what has often been described as 'Greater India'. The problems of how and
why these Indian influences found their way across the Bay of Bengal have attracted the attention of many scholars, and the subject is still one fraught with
controversy.

We will now have to consider briefly two questions. Firstly, how and why
did Indian culture take root among the peoples of South-east Asia? Secondly, by
what routes did that culture travel across the Bay of Bengal? The answers to
these questions will affect profoundly our picture of the nature of the early
history of Malaysia.

Many explanations have been offered for the creation of 'Greater India'.
Some scholars have seen as its basis the physical migration of Indian populations
and the extension of Indian political power, resulting in the creation of Indian
colonies in the same sense that the Americas were the site of colonies of Europe.[5]
Other scholars have turned to a more subtle interpretation of the scanty evidence.
They see Indian (and Ceylonese) ports as essential elements in the gradual expansion eastwards of maritime trade in the Indian Ocean, and postulate that, in the
first stages of this economic process, Indian traders played a dominant role.
Indian traders, and Indian adventurers (who, by virtue of their superior skill in
war and administration, were able, like James Brooke in Borneo many centuries
later, to carve out for themselves South-east Asian kingdoms), gradually planted
across the Bay of Bengal many of the aspects of their own culture. They intermarried with South-east Asian ruling families. They brought their scribes and
priests into a non-literate society. They demonstrated that their abilities in the
fields of government and commerce were the product of their religious systems,
thus identifying the Indian religions with political success. Their influence was
profound and durable, but it did not result in the obliteration of the indigenous
cultural life. Rather, it created amalgams of Indian and South-east Asian cultures
which, by a process of evolution, became virtually new cultures, superficially
Indian but in reality something rather different from anything to be found in
India proper.

This particular theory of Indianisation in South-east Asia is now favoured,
though with many variations in detail, by the majority of scholars outside India.

104

No scholar to date, however, has managed to disentangle entirely the Indian and non-Indian elements in any one of the major South-east Asian culture groups, and it may well be that this is a task beyond human capabilities.

From the point of view of the early history of Malaysia, the routes whereby Indian influences migrated to South-east Asia are of great importance. If these influences followed the shipping lanes through the Malacca Straits, then they may well have resulted in the creation in the Malay peninsula and in northern Borneo of Indianised states which antedate the emergence of Fu-nan in the region of the Mekong delta. If, as Dr Quaritch Wales has argued, the early Indian traders and adventurers made their way eastwards across the Isthmus of Kra, thus avoiding the navigation of the Malacca Straits, then one might well expect to find the presence of extremely early Indianised states along the Isthmus and on the coast of the extreme north-west of what is now Malaya. The history texts now used in many Malaysian schools, using a priori arguments of this kind, have postulated the existence of such states, and have interpreted the rather confused archaeological evidence in this light.

Unfortunately, the weight of archaeological evidence is opposed to any such hypotheses. There is nothing in Malaya or Borneo to compare with the great mass of Middle Eastern and Mediterranean objects of early christian date from Oc-eo; and we must at present, failing fresh discoveries, assume that Indochina saw the flourishing of political organisations of an Indian type before such bodies politic had taken root elsewhere in South-east Asia. If it is necessary to postulate a chain of Indianised states linking Fu-nan to India, then these most probably lie across Burma, Thailand and Cambodia.

Once established in Indochina, of course, the Indianised form of political organisation spread rapidly throughout South-east Asia. Early inscriptions from Java and Indonesian Borneo suggest that by the fifth century AD, perhaps, Indianisation was making itself felt widely in island South-east Asia. It may be that at about this period—the fifth or sixth century AD—the first of a long history of settlements was founded in the Malayan state of Kedah on the mainland opposite Penang.[6]

We have noted the probability that in the process of cultural diffusion throughout South-east Asia, trade played a vital part. We must now consider that trade in some detail. J. C. van Leur, one of the most brilliant of all the Dutch historians of Indonesia, once observed that South-east Asia in pre-European times could be divided into two categories of regions; on the one hand, those with large populations supported by rice cultivation, as in Java, central Thailand, Cambodia and the Mekong delta; on the other hand, those with small populations, mainly confined to coastal settlements based on fishing and on trade between the outside world and the aboriginal peoples of the interior jungles.[7] In the first category, the regions of elaborate agriculture, there emerged quite early in the christian era forms of political organisation which were sophisticated and capable of giving rise to ambitious projects of public works of both practical and religious utility. The proliferation of Khmer temples, some of which date from the seventh century AD, and the staggering extent of the Khmer irrigation system with its great artificial lakes and canals, are examples of the type of physical remains which van Leur's first category left behind. In this kind of region there would from quite early times have been a demand for imported luxury goods (like the carnelian seals found at Oc-eo), for imported food in certain circumstances; and here there would be local manufacturing industries, ceramics, textiles and the like, giving rise to an export trade.

Van Leur's second category of region, into which Malaysia falls, presents a very different economic picture. Here we can expect to find no large populations, and hence, no great markets for manufactures. The urban communities are small and few and far between, and they are trading centres, not centres of extensive territorial government; they have no need for the pompous architectural magnificence of Angkor. Outside the coastal towns we need not expect to find large populations living under the sway of a heavily Indianised culture. Such populations as there are still live very much as they have done since neolithic times, though doubtless trading with the outside world for worked metal objects and for a few luxury items such as glass beads and ceramic vessels of ritual (usually funerary) import. Naturally, these interior peoples not being entirely isolated from the coastal towns, we can expect to find among them some traces of Indianised influence in their language and in, perhaps, the manner of their expression of religious concepts: but they will not really be Indianised in the sense that the inhabitants of the coastal centres will almost certainly be. The contrast between coast town and interior village, indeed, would have been in van Leur's second category almost as is now the contrast between Kuching town and an upriver Dayak village in Sarawak.

Why, in early times, did traders bother with the 'aboriginal' peoples of van Leur's second category when they had at hand the great populations of Java and the Khmer empire? The answer to this question is simple: the regions of van Leur's second category, though generally unsuitable for rice cultivation, were often rich in natural resources, minerals like gold and tin, jungle products like resins, gums and saps, not to mention the wide variety of spices and aromatic substances which have their origin in the tropics. These substances, particularly the resins and spices (some of which had medicinal uses), were much sought after not only in the regions of van Leur's first category but also in the great centres of civilisation of the known world, in China, India, the Middle East and the Mediterranean. It is not surprising, therefore, that the countries of van Leur's second category were visited by traders from distant lands in pre-European times for almost those very reasons which later brought here the Portuguese, Dutch and English.[8]

The countries adjacent to the Malacca Straits had a second economic importance arising from their geographical position rather than their natural resources. The Malacca Straits are a bottleneck in the sea route between the Far East and the Middle East. The long tongue of the Malay peninsula divides the monsoon system of the China Sea from that of the Indian Ocean. Once traffic started going through the Malacca Straits rather than bypassing it on the overland crossing of the Kra Isthmus and regions to the north, it was inevitable that, in the general neighbourhood of the Straits, settlements should arise to serve as entrepôts.

The commerce passing through the Straits, as indeed that on the overland bypasses, clearly was made up of two distinct elements. On the one hand, there was the long distance through-traffic: the carrying, for example, of Chinese manufactured goods, silks and, by the seventh or eighth centuries AD, ceramics for the great markets of the Middle East. On the other hand there was a trade with the interior peoples, in which eastern and western manufactures were exchanged for local produce. We can see these two components quite clearly in the more recent economic history of South-east Asia. The British East India Company, for example, regarded its settlement at Penang both as a means of trade with Malaya and the surrounding areas and as a place where British merchants could meet the Chinese junks and buy the Chinese tea, silk and porcelain without having to face the obstructive tactics of Chinese port authorities. In this trade with China, the non-Chinese local component was of great importance. Since China in the eighteenth century, as indeed at almost every period in her previous history, sold more than she bought, foreign merchants in the China trade constantly faced balance of payments crises. The local South-east Asian trade was, therefore, as a possible source of specie or of goods which could be exchanged for Chinese wares, regarded as a means for financing the China trade without exhausting the bullion reserves of the home country. There can be no doubt that this argument, which lay behind some of the proposals for British settlements in South-east Asia in the eighteenth century, at Balambangan in Sulu, for example, or at Penang, had considerable force in a much earlier period.

By the end of the T'ang dynasty in China the mechanism of South-east Asian trade along these lines was fully functioning. Traders from the Middle East, from ports on the Red Sea and the Persian Gulf, were trading with China; and, it seems, Chinese traders were visiting eastern South-east Asia in considerable numbers, though it does not seem likely that in T'ang times many Chinese actually passed west of the Malay peninsula and the Malacca Straits. By the end of the T'ang period the flow of traffic along this great maritime route between China and the western shores of the Indian Ocean had reached considerable proportions. The prosperity of many Middle Eastern ports depended very largely on the China trade. The port of Siraf in the Persian Gulf, for example, had by the tenth century grown so rich in this commerce that its taxes provided one sixth of the total revenues of the province of Fars, then the centre of Iranian civilisation. At the site of Siraf today traces of this prosperity can still be seen in the sherds of T'ang dynasty porcelains which litter the old waterfront. Chinese sherds here are almost as common as sherds of Islamic wares. Siraf in this respect is by no means unique. Chinese wares of this period have been found in the ruins of Fostat (Old Cairo) in Egypt and of Samarra, north of Basra in Iraq. They occur in a number of sites—Brahminabad for example—by the mouths of the Indus, and have been reported from Quilon (Kullamalai) in south-west India and from sites in Ceylon. By Sung times Chinese wares became even more widely distributed. Sherds of Sung ceramics abound at a large number of port sites in the Persian Gulf on both shores. On Bahrein Island excavators of prehistoric settlements have had to dig through many feet of the debris of this article of Chinese trade. At this period moreover, Chinese wares had already established themselves along the coast of East Africa, where in the region of Zanzibar and Mombasa, for instance, they were widely traded.

In Malaysia the development of the east-west maritime trade resulted in the creation of three main types of settlement. First, we have the true entrepôt, the meeting point for ships from either side of the Straits and the peninsula, where eastern and western goods were exchanged. Some of these entrepôts may well originally have been confined solely to the long distance trade, though, inevitably, they soon became points of collection for local products. Second, we have what might be termed subsidiary entrepôts, places where local produce was collected and imported manufactures, like beads, metals and ceramics, distributed. Such entrepôts would act as satellites to the main trade centres. Finally, we have ports involved in specialised trading systems separate from the main east-west routes. For example, there is evidence that from Sung times, and perhaps earlier, the Chinese were trading with Sarawak, exchanging ceramics and beads for local products including, it is possible, the substance which forms the basis for bird's nest soup. Some of these Sarawak ports, the evidence suggests, were not directly, or even very closely, related to the main east-west traffic. They involve a specialised Borneo-China relationship which may well be considered as a coherent trading system in its own right.[9]

In recent years a number of the major entrepôts in the Malay peninsula have been explored archaeologically. At Takuapa, on the western side of the Kra Isthmus, just north of the present Malayan border, there has been revealed the site of a trading port where merchants from India, the Middle East and China met to exchange goods during the period of the T'ang dynasty. The Indian aspect is indicated by a Tamil inscription which describes the founding here of an establishment by some south Indian merchant guild. Middle Eastern participation is shown clearly enough by the discovery of large quantities of glass and glazed ceramic fragments which most probably originated from the Persian Gulf, perhaps from the great Persian trading port of Siraf. Chinese trade is represented by quantities of stoneware and porcelain sherds of characteristic T'ang dynasty types. A similar assemblage of objects, but of somewhat later date, Sung or Yuan dynasty, has been excavated in Kedah in Malaya, especially at the port site of Pengkalan Bujang on the estuary of the Merbok river.[10]

These major entrepôts appear to have been Indianised. In the neighbourhood of both Takuapa and Pengkalan Bujang are the remains of temple structures of hindu or buddhist type, along with pieces of sculpture and other objects which the student of Indian culture would have no difficulty in recognising. In the Malaysian regions, however, it is unlikely that developed Indianised culture extended far beyond the limits of the actual entrepôt towns, which may perhaps be compared to the Greek city states of antiquity in remote places like Spain and the Black Sea, which were islands of Greek civilisation in a barbarian ocean. It seems certain that the degree of Indianisation in places like Kedah in Malaya, even as late as Yuan times, had penetrated far less into the rural areas than was the case in Cambodia or Thailand.

In many cases the satellite entrepôts may have also been influenced to some extent by Indian cultural forms, but clearly to a lesser degree than the main entrepôts. Archaeological sites like Kuala Selinsing in Perak, Malaya, and Santubong, Sarawak, have produced both evidence of an active commerce with non-Indianised peoples as well as a few Indianised objects such as an engraved carnelian seal from Kuala Selinsing and a small stone Buddha from Santubong. Finds such as these, however, probably indicate more the presence of traders from Indianised regions than the actual establishment of Indianised culture. In the centres of direct trade between China and South-east Asia, like some of the Santubong sites and the Niah caves in Sarawak, evidence of Indianised influence may be totally lacking.

The archaeological evidence for this threefold classification of trading sites in Malaysia is by now surprisingly abundant; and it is of the greatest importance for our interpretation of the history of the region over the seventh to thirteenth centuries. During this period the non-Malaysian sources suggest the presence of a political entity generally referred to as the kingdom of Srivijaya. This embraced much of Sumatra and Malaya, and may well have included parts of Borneo and other regions of island South-east Asia. A group of inscriptions from the

Palembang region in Sumatra, which are dated to the end of the seventh century AD, suggest that at this time Srivijaya was already an expanding state in Sumatra. These inscriptions are, incidentally, in the Malay language though with much Sanskrit enrichment. In the late eighth century an inscription in Sanskrit from the Isthmus of Kra region, generally described as the Ligor stele, refers to the union of Srivijaya with the Sailendra dynasty then ruling in Java. Thereafter, until the thirteenth century, Chinese sources refer to Srivijaya as a region in political and commercial contact with the Chinese coast. In the tenth and eleventh centuries, from Indian sources, we learn of close relations between Srivijaya and India, both at the centres of buddhist learning in the Pala country of the north-east, and along the Coramandel coast. In the eleventh century, so Tamil inscriptions indicate, the rulers of the Chola dynasty of South India undertook naval operations against Srivijaya and reduced it to a dependent status.[11]

The precise significance of these references to Srivijaya is still the subject of considerable argument amongst scholars. It seems fairly certain, however, that Srivijaya was a term implying an assemblage of mainly entrepôt-type Indianised centres in the region of the Malacca Straits and the islands to the east which at various times came under the influence of, or was subjected to attack by, neigh- bouring states. The subject is extremely complex, and the sources are often obscure, but one fact seems clear: the life of Srivijaya was based on trade. When the Tamils say that they conquered the states of Srivijaya, they probably mean no more than that they had established, or attempted to establish, a commercial monopoly much as the Portuguese and the Dutch were later to attempt to do.

Because in the Srivijayan area we do not find many large centres of population and elaborate systems of irrigated cultivation, conquest here meant something very different from conquest in Cambodia or Thailand. Sea power and the pos- session of one or two bases would suffice to establish control in military terms. Political influence would tend to be exercised rather through systems of alliances than through actual physical occupation. The prize was not land but trade, and the object of policy was the control of routes not areas. We see many examples of just this kind of political structure in the parts of island South-east Asia which came under European control, and to find the same phenomenon extending back in time to before the coming of the Europeans should cause no surprise. As in European times, so earlier we may suppose that the establishment of a satisfactory commercial monopoly was no easy task. It is likely that an entrepôt too heavily taxed or too rigidly controlled soon ceased to be an entrepôt, and that the trade migrated elsewhere. Archaeology certainly indicates that many of the sites of such trade were in fact occupied for a relatively short period. Takuapa, so its ceramics would indicate, lasted from the eighth to tenth centuries, Pengkalan Bujang from the eleventh to thirteenth centuries. The same phenomenon of mobility of centres of trade can be observed in the case of entrepôts in the Persian Gulf, for example, where between AD 1000 and AD 1600 we see Siraf giving way to Qais, Qais to Old Hormuz, Old Hormuz to New Hormuz, and New Hormuz to Bandar Abbas.[12]

With the coming of the Yuan dynasty to China in the latter part of the thirteenth century the political organisation of South-east Asia underwent a number of significant changes. Mongol attacks disrupted the old established powers of the mainland and gave opportunities for new states to emerge. The great Khmer and Cham kingdoms, for example, declined rapidly after this period in the face of attack from the Thais and Viets. Island South-east Asia was likewise affected. The Yuan period seems to have seen a great increase in the tempo of Chinese trade; and there is hardly an island in the whole archipelago which has not produced abundant evidence of extensive Chinese contact from the thirteenth century onwards. The Mongol Yuan dynasty even attempted a direct intervention into the islands. Its efforts to occupy Java failed, but the political consequences of this campaign were none the less profound. In the fourteenth century we see a Javanese state, Majapahit, attempting what might almost be described as a counter-attack, and in the process endeavouring to secure a commercial monopoly over the Srivijayan entrepôts. Majapahit dominance was short-lived, and by the fifteenth century it had been replaced on the trade routes of the Malacca Straits by the Malacca sultanate, and along the Borneo coasts by such states as Brunei.

In Yuan times a new influence, apparently from the west, made itself felt in island South-east Asia. Islam, which through Persian and Arab merchants (and perhaps Chinese muslim traders as well) had been in contact with this region since the late seventh century, finally, in the late thirteenth century, began to take root. No doubt an important factor was the Islamic conquest of India which progressed rapidly throughout the thirteenth century; and it seems that in one sense the coming of Islam was really a continuation of the process of Indianisation. Islam spread rapidly in the regions of the entrepôts and trading centres of the Srivijayan type, following the trade routes, spreading through dynastic marriages between local ruling families, encouraged by commercial advantage. The expansion of Islam in South-east Asia little resembled the rapid advance of the religion, along with the Arab armies, in the Middle East in the seventh century AD. Its impact on the centres of population on the mainland of South-east Asia was slight, and in the Malay peninsula and the islands its spread inland from the coasts amongst the non-Indianised peoples was slow. In some regions of island South-east Asia the process still goes on. It is probable that the basic stimulus for the coming of Islam to South-east Asia is related to the great expansion in world trade which was under way by the end of the thirteenth century, encouraged

111

by the formation of the Mongol empire and by the increasing prosperity of Europe.

Shortly after the Malacca sultanate, the Islamic successor to Srivijaya and Majapahit in the control of the entrepôts of the Straits of Malacca, had established itself, the Portuguese began to seek ways to participate directly in the maritime trade of the Indian Ocean. In 1511 the Portuguese captured Malacca and opened the modern age of European influence in South-east Asia. The Portuguese, however, were following well established paths; and it is really the increase in documentation which makes post-Portuguese South-east Asian history seem so different from what went on before 1511. The Europeans, of course, added new political elements, and they brought with them their technology; but they did not create a fundamental change in the basic factors of trade, population and products.

7

The Historical Background, 1500-1815

D. K. BASSETT

The basic problem of the present chapter is that of giving a historical unity to a region which derives its significance from a contemporary political creation. During the period covered, Malaya and Singapore were parts of the Malacca and Johore empires, or were known by the names of a number of Malay sultanates, while Sarawak and Sabah were parts of the Brunei empire. Lacking the unity later superimposed by a common British administration, the indigenous sultanates of Malaysia were inspired by varying ambitions and subjected to distinctive pressures. The Johore sultanate, as the obvious successor of the Malaccan empire, bore the brunt of the Portuguese invasion of South-east Asia. Brunei, by way of contrast, enjoyed peaceful relations with the Portuguese, who had dispersed their strength and lost much of their crusading ardour by the time they reached the north-west coast of Borneo. The uneasy balance of power, punctuated by Malay and Achinese sieges of Malacca and Portuguese punitive expeditions to Bintang and the Johore river, which characterised the Malacca Straits in the sixteenth century, had no parallel in Brunei. Indeed, local Portuguese officials regarded Brunei as a friendly provisioning port for royal ships bound from Malacca to the Moluccan garrisons. After the Spaniards settled on Luzon in 1570 the Manila government made a few abortive attempts to assert Spanish suzerainty over Brunei, but ultimately the depredations of the Moros of Sulu and Mindanao on the Visayan Catholic missions proved a more engrossing problem.

The Protestant nations in their turn esteemed Malaya more highly than north-western Borneo. The Dutch East India Company received Malay help in attacking Portuguese Malacca in 1606 and 1641, but Dutch anxiety to encourage Brunei in its hostility to Spain was never sufficiently acute to justify the expense of an official Dutch embassy to Brunei.[1] Nor did the Batavia government send its own ships to Brunei; it preferred to rely upon the visits of Bornean vessels to Batavia and the occasional voyage of a Dutch burgher to Brunei. Finally, the English East India Company, which maintained an extensive trade in Indonesia for eighty years in the seventeenth century, showed no interest whatever in Brunei. The British 'country' traders[2] who edged their way into the peripheral areas of Indonesia in violation of Dutch claims of monopoly in the early eighteenth century were scarcely less curt in their references to Brunei. It was only after the expansion of British trade with Canton in the second half of the eighteenth century that the need for an intermediate station in the China Sea focused British attention on northern Borneo.

The absence of any marked European interest in north-western Borneo *per se* provides an obvious contrast with the importance attached to the Malacca Straits region by the Portuguese, Dutch and English in turn. The strategic value of the Malacca Straits to the Portuguese as the customary route between Goa and Macao, and to the Dutch as a narrow sea lane in which inter-Asian trade could be controlled and taxed, is sufficient explanation of their determination to maintain naval supremacy there. Brunei could not command European interest on locational grounds, because even in the eighteenth century East Indiamen preferred to hug the Indochina coast on their voyages to Canton. But European indifference to the *commercial* potentialities of Brunei would suggest that the trade there was regarded as trivial compared to other Malay-Indonesian ports. This is not an unreasonable conclusion in view of the remarkable speed and often misplaced enthusiasm with which the Dutch and English sought out markets in comparative backwaters of the archipelago. Both companies opened factories in large trade centres such as Bantam, Djakarta, Macassar, Jambi and Palembang, but they also ventured their capital in lesser places such as Indragiri, Sambas, Sukadana, Landak, Banjarmasin, Japara, Johore and Kedah. Brunei, apparently, did not merit even the initial capital outlay. The port might serve as a classic example of a limited entrepôt unaffected either by the monopolistic designs or the commercial stimulus of extensive European contact. In this respect Brunei is similar to the river ports of Pahang, Trengganu and Kelantan, in which official European organisations, royal or commercial, took almost no interest. By way of contrast, the Malay states bordering on the Straits of Malacca and Singapore were deeply involved in the perennial disputes for the control of the sea route and in the resistance to Portuguese and Dutch monopolisation of local tin and pepper exports.

The political and commercial importance of the Malacca sultanate at the beginning of the sixteenth century was incomparably greater than that of Brunei. After a century of existence, Malacca was the greatest entrepôt of South-east Asia by virtue of its position on the straits and at the meeting place of the monsoons.

The most important aspect of trading activity at Malacca was the exchange of Indian piece-goods for the spices, aromatics and dyewoods of the Indonesian islands. Although Malacca acknowledged the suzerainty of Peking as a safeguard against Thai aggression, its trade connection with China was less extensive than that with India. A maximum of ten Chinese junks visited Malacca annually, bringing silk, musks, camphor, copper and ironware to exchange for pepper and other local commodities. The Malacca sultanate had adopted Islam as the official religion early in the fifteenth century and had given an impetus to the propagation of the new faith in the coastal regions of the Malay peninsula, eastern Sumatra, northern Borneo and Java. By 1511 Malacca claimed suzerainty over the Malay archipelago from Kedah and Trengganu to Lingga and over the Sumatran gold-exporting kingdoms of Rakkan, Siak, Indragiri and Kampar.

The contemporary limits of Brunei's political influence in Borneo are less well-defined. The two other great kingdoms of the island were Laue on the south-west coast near Sukadana, and Tanjongpura, which Cortesao places at Tanjong Puting on the south coast.[3] Both these kingdoms were Javanese-dominated in the early sixteenth century, although they exported diamonds, gold and rice to Malacca.[4] Brunei, which had recently accepted Islam, also contributed to the trade of Malacca by exporting camphor, wax, foodstuffs and gold in return for Bengal and Coromandel piece-goods and beads. It seems unlikely that Brunei possessed as extensive an administrative structure as Malacca, which had to handle a much larger cosmopolitan population. There seems to have been only one *shahbandar** at Brunei as compared to four at Malacca, but their duties were the same, as were those of the respective *bendaharas*, *temenggongs* and *laksamanas.*** Certainly, Pigafetta's description of Brunei in 1521 suggests the existence of a competent secretariat and an impressive ritual of government. The opulence of the ruling class was also reflected in the furnishings of the royal palace and the dress and weapons of the courtiers.[5] While Pigafetta's estimate of Brunei town as containing 25,000 households is probably exaggerated, his description of the city's wooden, easily movable houses mounted on piles in the river is echoed by Pedro Teixeira and van Noort's Dutchmen in 1600 and by Thomas Forrest in 1776.[6] Pigafetta and Forrest also commented upon the itinerant, water-borne, female food-vendors of Brunei, sheltering beneath their broad hats.[7] Indeed, there seems to have been no drastic change in the external appearance of the town over three centuries.

---

* *Shahbandar*: The port officer responsible for the reception and treatment of foreign merchants.
** *Bendahara*: the chief minister of state who controlled the treasury and was also chief justice; *temenggong*: the city magistrate and head of the police; *laksamana*: the admiral of the fleet.

The Portuguese capture of Malacca in August 1511 did not have the far-reaching results anticipated by the conquerors. Sultan Mahmud lost his capital and a great deal of his confidence, but not the loyalty of his vassals.[8] After several years as a fugitive, he settled at Bintang,[9] from whence his *laksamana* organised highly successful raids on the exhausted Malacca garrison and on the Portuguese rice ships which put into Pahang *en route* from Siam. It was only by a chance combination of forces and dogged siege work that the fourth Portuguese attack on Bintang was successful in 1526. By that time a Portuguese attack on the rising sultanate of Acheh had been heavily repulsed, the Portuguese garrison in the north Sumatran kingdom of Pasai had been expelled by the Achinese, and the projected Portuguese fortress at Sunda Kalapa (Djakarta) had been foiled by the Javanese sultanate of Demak. In the Moluccas, the Spanish successors of Magellan and Pigafetta made their appearance in 1527, and occasional Spanish trans-Pacific expeditions remained a source of irritation to the Portuguese commandant of Ternate until the implementation of the Treaty of Saragossa in 1533.[10]

In these circumstances the Portuguese government at Malacca was disinclined to add Brunei to its list of enemies, particularly when the north Borneo route to the Moluccas was the one most favoured by the Portuguese.[11] Dom Jorge de Menezes seems to have inaugurated the use of the Brunei route to Ternate in 1526, after which it became customary for the prospective Portuguese captain of the Moluccas to pay a short courtesy call on the sultan of Brunei during the outward voyage.[12] As early as 1523 Dom Jorge d'Albuquerque assured the king of Portugal that Brunei 'is not a country about which we should bother ourselves, except if travelling from Malacca to the Moluccas',[13] but Portuguese relations with the sultan remained sufficiently close for the Spaniards to fear a combined attack by them on Luzon in 1573.[14] When Francisco de Sande's Spanish armada captured Brunei in 1578, the Spaniards found not only cannon bearing the Portuguese royal arms in the town, but a letter from Dom Sebastian to the sultan encouraging him to write to Malacca for his needs. Four months after de Sande withdrew from Brunei, the usual Portuguese squadron called there and its commander was invited to join the war against Spain. As a Catholic he declined, but he purchased slaves and provisions amicably and left a Malabari factor to despatch wax, camphor and tortoise-shells on local vessels to Malacca.[15] Portuguese ships rarely returned from Ternate to Malacca via north Borneo because cargoes awaited them in the Bandas and the friendly east Javanese port of Panarukan.

Brunei was probably visited also by the ships of Portuguese private traders, although Pedro Teixeira's claim that the limited export trade of Brunei was entirely in Portuguese hands in 1600 is certainly exaggerated.[16] When Portuguese missionary activity developed in the Moluccas after 1546, Jesuit fathers used the

Brunei route safely, but a Spanish Franciscan from Manila was murdered in Brunei in 1587.[17]

The commerce of Brunei with Malacca was inherited by the Portuguese after 1511,[18] although that between Malacca and Laue seems to have lapsed until 1527. Malacca lost much of its trade prior to the fall of Bintang in 1526 and there was an exodus of Malays, Gujeratis, Javanese and Chinese to other ports. But the relative tranquillity of the second quarter of the century and the reform of tariff policy brought a revival of prosperity. Urdaneta wrote of Malacca's trade in glowing terms after his visit in 1535,[19] and the energy with which the Portuguese traded or fought in Siam, Pegu, Patani, China, Japan and the Moluccas during this period suggests that they did not regard the occasional Achinese, Javanese and Malay attacks on Malacca with the alarm which the dramatic sense of Portuguese chroniclers might represent. The Achinese 'sieges' of Malacca in 1537 and 1547 were little more than night raids and, with the exception of an unnecessary war in 1535–6 and a siege in 1551, the Malays maintained peaceful relations with the Portuguese from 1526 to 1586. Offensive measures invariably originated with the Asian states, because the Malaccan Portuguese, despite their verbal braggadocio, preferred to reap the profits of East Asian trade than fight Islam in the Albuquerque tradition. The admission of the Portuguese to Japan (1543) and the legalisation of the Portuguese trade with China (1554) must have strengthened this attitude of mind by conferring upon them the lucrative role of indispensable middlemen between these kingdoms.[20]

The grudging tolerance which usually prevailed between Portuguese Malacca and Johore was not shared by the north Sumatran sultanate of Acheh. The Achinese devastation of Johore Lama in 1564 inaugurated a period of Achinese ascendancy in the Straits which lasted until 1641. The temporary elimination of the Malays as a political force in 1564 and the unusual circumstance of a Malay-Achinese *entente* in 1571–9 exposed Malacca to unprecedented danger. Malacca survived the Achinese sieges of 1573, 1575, 1627 and 1629 because the threat to the vital sea route to Macao and Nagasaki stirred Lisbon and Goa into despatching naval reinforcements to the Strait. The Malays sought a Portuguese alliance against Achinese attacks in 1570 and 1582–3, and the Portuguese devastation of Johore Lama in 1587 was in some respects an anomaly caused by Lisbon's determination to eliminate Johore Lama as a rival entrepôt to Malacca. The policy had little support in Malacca, where the predominant fear was that of a Malay-Javanese rapprochement comparable to that of 1571–9. Fortunately for the Portuguese, Acheh relapsed into one of its periodic dynastic disputes and they were able to harry the Malays to their new capital of Batu Sawar.

Acheh re-emerged under Iskander Muda (1607–36) as the effective suzerain of Perak, Kedah and Pahang, all of which were conquered in 1617–20, with dama-

117

ging effects on the overland pepper trade to Patani. Batu Sawar was devastated by the Achinese in 1613 and the sultan of Johore died a fugitive in 1623. It was only after the reversion of the Achinese throne to the female line in 1641 that Johore dared to assert its traditional hegemony over the east coast of Sumatra. Pahang resumed its connection with Johore, but Kedah gravitated towards Siam, and Perak remained an Achinese dependency until the 1660s.

One consequence of the political turmoil in the Straits of Malacca and Singapore may have been a strengthening of Brunei's connections with the more peaceful ports of the South China Sea. The only reference to Bornean intervention in Malay affairs in this period is an unsubstantiated rumour that Brunei planned to support Pahang against Johore in 1613.[21] Chinese imports to Brunei were extensive by 1521[22] and the exodus of Chinese traders from Malacca to Patani may have encouraged this connection. The opportunity to purchase Chinese *cash* in Brunei for investment in the Moluccas was one reason for Portuguese visits by 1530.[23] When de Sande captured Brunei in 1578 he noticed the large number of merchants there from the ports on the opposite side of the China Sea, and his subordinate de Arce encountered two Chinese junks off Labuan in March 1579.[24]

The strongest evidence of Chinese commercial pre-eminence in Brunei is provided by van Noort's Dutchmen at the turn of 1600. The Chinese pilots from Changchou and Canton who brought van Noort's ships south from Manila knew Brunei well and conversed fluently with the local 'wachtmeester' (*shahbandar?*). It was a Patani Chinese, in great favour with the sultan, who welcomed the Dutchmen to the port. It is significant, too, that the local demand was for Chinese silks and that the Dutch cloth was regarded with indifference.[25] There is ample evidence, both in the van Noort accounts and in other contemporary Dutch sources, of the strong trade connections between Brunei and Patani. The Patani Chinese imported pepper to Brunei and exported camphor, slaves, sago, wax and bezoar stones. By the early seventeenth century Patani was the leading entrepôt for the purchase of Chinese commodities outside Canton.[26] The Dutch were quick to settle there and it was through ambassadors to Patani that the sultan of Brunei extended his invitations to trade to the Dutch Company in 1604 and 1614. As an incentive he proposed to treat them on the same basis 'als de Pataniers'.[27]

The Dutch Company never responded to this appeal. Its coolness is in marked contrast to its alliance with the Moros of Sulu and Mindanao against the Spanish government in the Philippines prior to the Hispano-Dutch peace of 1648. The only known proposal for co-operation between Brunei and the Dutch against the Spaniards occurred during Maerten Gerritsz. Vries's campaign in the Philippines in 1646–7. It seems to have been abortive.[28] The authorities at Batavia evinced some concern whenever it was rumoured that Brunei's hostility to Spain was waning, but Brunei's contribution to the harassment of the Philippines remained essentially an unrelated, spontaneous affair.

There is no concrete evidence that the Dutch Company sent a ship or a Dutch embassy to Brunei after van Noort's visit in 1600–1. Van Dijk's assumption that the Company must have traded in Brunei in 1604–8 rests on a contemporary knowledge of local products available to any reader of Linschoten.[29] Far more significant is the continuing Dutch ignorance of the navigation of north Borneo and the advice of Hendrik Janssen, the Dutch agent at Patani in 1614, that the trade of Brunei would not cover the expense of a factory.[30] In 1634 Harman Gerritsz. apparently explored the north Borneo route in order to permit the despatch of reinforcements from Batavia to the Moluccas outside the usual monsoon, but his discoveries do not seem to have been utilised.[31] On the contrary, Governor-General Hendrik Brouwer confessed to a rudimentary knowledge of Borneo in January 1636, and although van Diemen promised to explore its riches two years later, his attention was focused on the pepper kingdom of Banjarmasin rather than Brunei.[32] Embassies from Brunei were welcomed at Batavia and Dutch Malacca between 1650 and 1721, and probably later, but in 1718 the Batavia government held a poor opinion of the products of Brunei.[33]

The Spanish attitude to Brunei was less passive than that of the Dutch because of the raids on the Visayas by the Camucones or 'Orang Tedongers', who were nominally subjects of Brunei living on the islands off north Borneo. These attacks were particularly severe in the first seventy years of the seventeenth century, but seem to have eased after Brunei made friendly overtures to Manila in 1679, 1684 and 1705.[34] The degree of the sultan of Brunei's complicity in these raids is difficult to assess and the relaxation of Camucon pressure may reflect the interposition of Suluk and Ilanun power rather than a positive act of restraint by Brunei. Certainly Sultan Alimuddin of Sulu collaborated with the Spaniards to inflict a crushing defeat on the Camucones *outside* Brunei in 1746, and the 'Orang Tedongers' were as feared in Brunei in 1776 as elsewhere.[35] In any case, the depredations of the Camucones in the Visayas were overshadowed in the seventeenth century and first half of the eighteenth century by those of the Moros of Sulu and Mindanao. It was in the latter islands that the Spaniards strove, with some success, to assert their religion and government. Only two important punitive expeditions were sent against Brunei. That of de Sande in 1578 was inspired by a simple zeal to extend the Spanish empire and did little more than provide future historians with interesting details of Brunei's town and navy.[36] De Monforte's expedition of 1649 ravaged Banggi and initiated Jesuit missionary activity in Borneo, which soon lapsed in the absence of military support.[37]

During the peaceful interludes, vessels from Brunei maintained their traditional trade with Luzon by importing palm-mats, slaves, sago, glazed jars and camphor to Manila in exchange for wine, rice and cotton cloth.[38] In Spanish eyes, however, the Brunei commerce was trivial compared to the famous Canton-Manila-Acapulco silk trade, the Portuguese and Armenian trade from India, and later a considerable trade with Java. 'There is nothing special to be said of them,' wrote Antonio de Morga of the Brunei merchants and others in 1609, 'except that care is exercised in receiving and despatching them well, and seeing that they return quickly to their own countries.'[39]

The Dutch government at Malacca, faced with the task of restoring the prosperity of the battered town it had wrested from the Portuguese in 1641, and lacking the easy profits of a Pacific galleon trade, could not adopt the nonchalant *laissez faire* attitude of the Manileños. Dutch efforts to compel passing Asian and Portuguese ships to pay duties at Malacca, and to monopolise for the Company the local trade in piece-goods, tin and pepper cannot be elaborated here. Suffice it to say that even when Dutch naval coercion in the Strait was at its height in the seventeenth century, Malacca showed an annual deficit of fl. 50–80,000, which rose to fl. 100,000 in the decade before the British capture of Malacca in 1795. In order to make Malacca pay, the Dutch government had to obtain about 700,000 lbs of tin per annum and a steady turnover of gold and pepper from east Sumatra. This target was achieved in 1649 by a blockade of Acheh, Kedah and Perak, but never again. Kedah, Junk Ceylon* and Banggeri, where the Dutch claimed the right to half or all the tin production by virtue of treaties signed in the 1640s, were too far north for effective supervision by Dutch sloops. The trade there remained predominantly in Indian hands. Later Dutch attempts to extend the monopoly to Johore and Selangor were foiled by the fighting spirit and commercial acumen of the Bugis. In practice, the Dutch confined themselves to a more limited sphere of control in the centre of the Strait, based on the tin of Perak, the pepper of Indragiri and Bengkalis, and the gold of Siak.

Official British interest in the Malay peninsula prior to 1770 was checked by the severity of Asian competition and the rudimentary nature of the economy. Most states had sizeable stocks of rice, pepper, gold and tin for export, but the process of exchange was piecemeal and cumbersome. The market for Indian cloth was small, as Davies and Portman reported from the English Company's unsuccessful factory in Kedah in 1670, and as Thomas Bowrey complained of Junk Ceylon in 1675.[40] 'A Ship's Cargo is a long Time in selling, and the product of the Country is as long in purchasing', confirmed Alexander Hamilton of Junk Ceylon in 1727.[41] Acheh was regarded by most Englishmen as a much superior entrepôt to the Malay peninsular ports, but it was precisely to avoid the delay of piecemeal trading that the Madras Association commenced handling imports of Indian and British merchants to Acheh in bulk in 1770.[42]

---

* An island off the Indian Ocean seaboard of Siam, now known as Phuket.

The maintenance of the British connection with the Malay states was delegated to the British 'country' traders between 1675 and 1770. They specialised in the export of elephants from Kedah and Junk Ceylon to India, but also shipped pepper, tin and rattans from those ports and Acheh. Occasional British visits were made to Johore, Pahang and Trengganu, but these were incidental to voyages to Siam and China, and were not intended to develop permanent trade relationships. The British country trader avoided Perak because of the effectiveness of the Dutch guardships and the murderous reputation of the inhabitants. The tendency of contemporary British writers to characterise the Malay as treacherous, cruel and lazy[43] probably reflects the turbulent ill-disciplined society of the Malay states at that time, but it may also spring from a division of economic function which brought the Malays to European attention only in the most unfavourable form.

The proto-Malay sea folk or 'Salettes' were certainly pirates and slave raiders. Bowrey mentioned their depredations near Junk Ceylon and Pulo Sembilan and Hamilton commented upon their base in the Redang Islands between Trengganu and Patani.[44] They were the Malayan equivalent of Brunei's Camucones. But there must have been another or overlapping group of seafaring Malays who distributed household necessities to the local river kampongs and islands. A Flemish supercargo whose ship touched at Johore in July 1723 described the inhabitants as possessing 'une extrême passion pour le Commerce' and an activity which rendered the neighbouring islands virtual colonies of Johore.[45] It was on Malay and Javanese perahus (small sailing boats) that rice, salt, Javanese cloth, sugar and tobacco, iron pans, gold thread, arrack and sail cloth reached Batu Bara, Bengkalis, Rakkan, Muar, Batu Pahat, Siantan and elsewhere. Contemporary Europeans did not participate in this trade and would not describe it, but the records of the Dutch government at Malacca indicate its existence. Similarly, the bulk of the Malay peasantry must have followed a legitimate occupation. Their bullocks, ducks, chickens, rice, coconuts, plantains, fish and fruit supplied not only passing ships, but a sizeable transient and resident population of merchants and seamen. In this respect the Malay agricultural economy was rather more than a subsistence one, although few European sea captains speculated much about the cultivators of the provisions they bought. Pahang, Kedah and Trengganu were noted for their abundance,[46] and by the middle of the eighteenth century the last two states were recognised provisioning ports for East Indiamen bound to China.

The Indians and Chinese attracted European attention because the export side of the economy was in their hands. Over seventy Chulias were killed in the Malay-Siamese riot in Junk Ceylon in 1677, and it was against Chulia competition in Acheh, Kedah and Johore that Bowrey uttered his diatribe.[47] The chief *shahbandar* of Kedah at that time was a Chulia. When Monckton visited Kedah in 1772 four Chulias attended his audience with the sultan. The Chulias were the best customers for the sultan's elephants and they sold their piece-goods twenty per cent cheaper than those offered by the Madras Association which Francis Light represented. Despite the bogy of Dutch or Danish intervention raised by Light, the real opposition to British settlement in Kedah came from the Chulias.[48] The Indians also formed the nucleus of the export trade of Acheh in the seventeenth and eighteenth centuries. In Johore in 1718 it was the Malabar merchants who were 'of greatest use and profit' to the kingdom. They sometimes came there on their own ships, but usually freighted their goods on Danish or British country vessels as a protection against Dutch guardships.[49]

Johore apparently marked the eastern limit of Indian navigation in the eighteenth century, and the settlers in Johore were Chinese, not Indian. The distinction between Chinese trade in the seventeenth century and Chinese settlement in the eighteenth century is an important one. Hamilton, who visited Johore on numerous occasions between 1695 and 1719, found a thousand Chinese families settled there, besides a much greater number who traded to Johore from other parts. Half the population of Kuala Trengganu in 1720 was Chinese. The Chinese were the pepper cultivators in both states and also managed the gold mines of Trengganu. The Trengganu Chinese owned several junks and traded with Siam, Cambodia, Tongking and Sambas in Borneo.[50] Sambas was itself an area of growing Chinese activity in Hamilton's time, depending upon Chinese imports of Surat piece-goods from Johore and Malacca.[51] Chinese miners moved into the Sambas and Mampawa districts from Brunei about 1740–5 and had formed autonomous *kongsis** by 1760.[52] There are two final pieces of evidence of marked Chinese infiltration into Borneo and Malaya. After Monckton visited Riau in 1772 he described the Chinese as swarming in the Strait like bees and constituting the life of the trade there.[53] Thomas Forrest gave equal praise to the Chinese in Brunei in 1776. The pepper gardens at Brunei and on the Putatan river were entirely in their hands. Between four and seven Chinese junks of 500–600 tons came to Brunei every year from Amoy to collect ebony-wood, camphor, rattans, seaslugs, tortoise-shells and birds' nests. The Chinese held market either on their junks or at shops in the town, and even maintained a local dockyard at which they built junks of 500 tons.[54]

The Bugis were another vigorous addition to Malaysian society in the eighteenth century. Finding few commercial outlets in Celebes after the Dutch conquered Macassar in 1667–9, they became mercenaries and traders in Palembang, Borneo and the Malay peninsula. In 1681 Bugis help was sought by a

---

* A *kongsi* is an association of Chinese based on regional, occupational or dialect ties.

claimant to the Kedah throne and by 1700 a Bugis yamtuan* ruled on the Selangor river. Hamilton foiled a Bugis attack on Trengganu in 1719, but the town was overrun and the rajah killed in 1720.[55] The main centres of Bugis power were Selangor, where Rajah Luma became the first Bugis sultan in 1745, and Riau, the capital of the Johore empire, into which the Bugis infiltrated in 1717 as the supporters of Rajah Kechil against Sultan Abdul Jalil. By a shift of allegiance to Abdul Jalil's son Sulaiman, they secured the important administrative posts of the state and a Dutch war in 1756-8 failed to shake their domination. The Bugis leaders Daing Camboja (1761–77) and Rajah Haji (1777–84) were successively the vice-kings of Riau. In 1770 Rajah Haji negotiated a marriage between the sultan of Selangor and the daughter of the sultan of Perak, despite the Dutch garrison at Tanjong Putus on the Perak river; and in 1771 he attacked Kedah and drove the sultan into Perlis. Siantan in the South China Sea was also a resort of the Bugis leaders,[56] and Rajah Haji was assisting in a local war in Pontianak when he was called to Riau to succeed Daing Camboja in 1777.[57] Forrest employed three Bugis to caulk his famous *Tartar Galley* at Brunei in 1776 and the Bugis also controlled the east Borneo opium entrepôt of Passir at that time.[58]

The period of Bugis political supremacy in the Johore empire and western Malaya coincided with a marked increase in British country trade to those areas. After the Seven Years War (1756–63), British country sea captains, mainly from Madras and Calcutta, expanded their trade with Junk Ceylon, Kedah and Kuala Selangor and began new operations in Acheh and Riau. By the 1770s, and particularly during the government of Rajah Haji, Riau became an important entrepôt, where British, French and Portuguese ships could sell opium and piece-goods, and purchase Bangka tin and Sumatran and Borneo pepper for shipment to Canton. The tin and pepper that reached Riau after August were picked up by the European ships on their return voyage from China to India. The Dutch governors of Malacca, who were unable to conquer Riau until October 1784, admitted openly the commercial stagnation of Malacca in consequence.[59] Two years after Riau fell, they were confronted with the British free port of Penang, which they were unable to obliterate by violent means. The pleas of Malaccan officials for the adoption of a competitive policy to ruin Penang made no impression at Batavia before the British captured Malacca in 1795.[60]

A common feature of the histories of Malaya and north-east Borneo after 1760 was the development of *official* British interest in those regions. Put simply, the East India Company sought to establish a British settlement either near Malacca Strait or in the lands bordering on the South China Sea. The settlement was to be an entrepôt where South-east Asian produce could be collected for shipment

---

* Yamtuan = ruler (Malay)

to Canton to help finance the Company's growing investment in tea. It was also hoped to attract to the British factory Chinese merchants not represented in the Co-hong at Canton and persuade them to introduce British cloth into the colder parts of China. Thirdly, the settlement was designed as a centre for the peaceful expansion of British trade and influence in the Dutch Indonesian empire.[61] An additional factor in British policy was the strategic necessity for a naval base on the eastern side of the Bay of Bengal, from which to protect the Coromandel Coast against French ships based on Mauritius and Acheh. The strategic element in British policy was stimulated only in times of crisis, and from 1760 to about 1780 the solution of the Canton deficit was the predominant consideration.[62]

The suggestion that the Sulu archipelago was a suitable locality for the proposed British entrepôt originated with Alexander Dalrymple, a former deputy-secretary of the Madras government. In January 1761, with the approval of Governor Pigot of Madras, Dalrymple signed a preliminary treaty with the sultan of Sulu giving the Company the choice of a site for a factory and local freedom of trade exclusive of other Europeans. On a second visit in January 1763 he took possession of Balambangan.[63] There followed a period of disappointing trade and waning enthusiasm on the part of the Madras government and the directors. Official attention was diverted to the Cornish-Draper expedition which captured Manila in October 1762 and to a scheme to seize Mindanao after Manila had fallen into British hands. In the event, Manila was restored to Spain by the peace treaty and the Mindanao venture never materialised. But the temporary occupation of Manila also brought into British hands the dispossessed and rightful sultan of Sulu, who was a Spanish prisoner. In return for his reinstatement by Dalrymple in June 1764, he ceded to the East India Company all northern Borneo from Kimanis to Terusan Abai, together with Labuan, Palawan and Banggi.[64]

Dalrymple then used his position as deputy governor in charge of the British evacuation of Manila to ship a number of Chinese families and Indian Army sepoys to Balambangan. The directors deplored his precipitancy because of possible diplomatic repercussions with Spain, and after an attempt to justify his action Dalrymple left their service. Finally, after a preliminary survey, John Herbert opened a proper settlement at Balambangan in December 1773, with subsidiary factories at Palawan, Sulu and Labuan. The rudimentary nature of local trade and the peculation of Herbert ruined the enterprise. Before the directors could dismiss him, Balambangan was devastated by a Suluk raid in February 1775. The temporary headquarters at Labuan was closed in 1776.[65] The official British connection with Borneo then lapsed until Farquhar's brief occupation of Balambangan in 1803–5 to offset the return of the Moluccas to the Dutch. British military commitments elsewhere were too pressing to maintain the post.[66]

While the British directors were still nerving themselves to send Herbert to

Balambangan, their interest was drawn to Acheh by the current activities of the Madras Association of Merchants, and to Kedah by the exaggerated eulogies of Francis Light. In the hope of getting commodities for China, the Madras government sent Desvoeux to Acheh and Monckton to Kedah in February 1772. Monckton also went down to Riau and Trengganu in August–September 1772. Both missions failed, not because of the incompetence of Monckton and Desvoeux, but because the Company and the sultans expected conflicting benefits from the projected treaties. The Company desired a defensive alliance only, to be paid for from the sultan's revenues, but the sultan of Kedah demanded British help to attack the Bugis of Selangor and the sultan of Acheh had mortgaged his revenues five years ahead. Again, the Company was interested only in bulk purchases of pepper and tin from the sultans, but Monckton and Desvoeux made it clear that the sultans of Kedah and Acheh lacked the acumen, inclination and organisation for such an arrangement. The British envoys concluded quite correctly that the commercial potentialities of Kedah and Acheh had been grossly misrepresented. The Bugis of Riau did not need British protection and the rajah of Trengganu balked at the prospect of paying for it from his revenues. The negotiations failed in every case.[67]

During the next few years Francis Light championed his new home of Junk Ceylon as the potential British entrepôt in the eastern seas. Warren Hastings filed his recommendations in his private papers,[68] but did nothing because the renewal of the war with France engaged his attention. The naval battles of Suffren and Hughes for the mastery of the Indian Ocean revived the strategic element in British policy. Thomas Forrest, the commander of the Bengal Marine, set out to survey the Andamans in June 1783, but missing them, returned from his exploration of the Mergui archipelago with recommendations for British naval bases at Cheduba off Arakan, at St Matthew off the Pakchan estuary, and at Penang. In April 1784 he conveyed to Hastings Rajah Haji's offer of a site for a British commercial agency at Riau, but before Forrest reached Riau with the British acceptance, Rajah Haji was killed besieging Malacca by the men of van Braam's relief fleet. The Dutch warships moved on to capture Kuala Selangor and Riau in August and October 1784. The Dutch successes were temporary, but British official and private circles were gripped by a fear of Dutch domination of the Malay states and the best sea route to China.[69] This phantom prompted Macpherson, the acting governor-general, who personally favoured Junk Ceylon, to accept the offer of Penang conveyed from the sultan of Kedah by Francis Light. Light took possession of the island as the superintendent in August 1786.

Penang never became a naval base because the British Admiralty lost interest in the scheme by 1807, but as a port Penang flourished at the expense of Dutch Malacca. This was particularly the case after British troops occupied Malacca in

August 1795 to prevent the town from falling into the hands of revolutionary France.[70] The British occupation of Java in 1810 affected Penang's prosperity by making Batavia an attractive market for British shipping from India and lessening the incentive to smuggle Indonesian produce to Penang. A definite conflict of interests developed between Raffles, the British lieutenant-governor of Java, and the Penang government. Raffles was particularly anxious to impress upon the directors the commercial value of the island under his charge so that they might be more inclined to retain it at the end of the war. For this reason he deplored the smuggling of Bangka tin to Lingga and Penang rather than its legal delivery to Batavia, and on one occasion provoked protests from the Penang government by his expedition against the Lingga seafarers.[71] It is noteworthy, too, that the Penang government minimised the damage to British commerce from piracy in Malaysian waters, and that British country traders preferred to risk their ships in the turbulent ports of Borneo and the Riau archipelago than support Raffles' project for an orderly, but government-controlled trade in Borneo.[72] The latter arrangement would presumably curb the interloper and strengthen the commercial bargaining position of the Java government.

If Java had to be restored to the Dutch, Raffles planned to nullify this setback by creating in advance areas of British influence and protection in the outlying Indonesian islands. He made a careful distinction between Java, which the Dutch had held in full sovereignty in 1811, and those lands in which their legal pretensions had lapsed or never existed. Borneo, from which the last Dutch garrison had been withdrawn by Daendals in 1809, was an example of lapsed rights.[73] In addition to sending Alexander Hare as his commissioner to Banjarmasin in 1812, Raffles launched two naval expeditions against Sambas to suppress piracy in 1812–13. He then began his plan to restrict British commerce in Borneo to Banjermasin, Brunei and Pontianak, to the last of which he had sent John Hunt as his commercial agent in March 1813. Captain R. C. Garnham, who visited Borneo as Raffles' special commissioner in September 1813, declared Sambas a British protectorate and induced the sultan of Brunei to accept Raffles' restriction of trade.[74]

Irwin suggests that the collapse of Raffles' proposed Borneo protectorate was caused by the hostility of the new governor-general, Lord Moira, but even his predecessor, the amenable Lord Minto, referred the restriction scheme to London in July 1813.[75] Moira, who was certainly no friend of Raffles, condemned the extension of British influence in Borneo as likely to cause tension later with the Dutch, and gave only grudging approval to Hare's settlement at Banjarmasin. The Secret Committee in London described Raffles' whole proceeding as 'impolitic, and injudicious', and disavowed even Hare's treaty with Banjarmasin.[76] In any case, British foreign policy under Castlereagh favoured the creation of a strong Netherlands, and to promote this end the Dutch Indonesian possessions and Malacca were restored to the Dutch by the Convention of August 1814. Raffles was relegated to the lieutenant-governorship of decrepit Bencoolen, from whence he tried with considerable ineptitude to challenge the restoration of Dutch authority in Padang, Palembang and Semangka Bay.[77] Hare's lands in Banjarmasin were declared forfeit and Dutch sovereignty was proclaimed there in January 1817. Similar proclamations were made at Pontianak and Sambas in August and September 1818.[78] These events, and comparable Dutch moves in the Malay archipelago, were the saving of Raffles, because they convinced Lord Hastings, the governor-general, that Dutch pretensions were as excessive as Raffles suggested. Raffles was given his head after his visit to Calcutta in the autumn of 1818 and he founded Singapore three months later.

8

The Nineteenth Century

MARY TURNBULL

In the course of the nineteenth century all the present Malaysian territories, with the exception of the unfederated Malay states, were brought under some form of official British recognition. In the year when Singapore was founded prospects of British expansion in South-east Asia were far from promising. Raffles' plans for retaining Java as a British colony had failed, and his subsidiary scheme for establishing British influence in Borneo lay in ruins. In the peninsula, Malacca had been returned to the Dutch. The East India Company still owned Penang, but all hopes of establishing a naval base there had vanished, and there were constant attempts at retrenchment and rumours that the station was to be abandoned altogether. The infant settlement of Singapore appeared to have no brighter future than any of Raffles' other brain-children. The Dutch authorities in Batavia were irritated, but confident that once again the Company would repudiate this embarrassing venture. It would have been foolhardy to predict at that time that by the end of the century British authority would be so extensive in South-east Asia. The dogged efforts of individuals like Raffles and Brooke, and the gradual accumulation of unofficial economic interests in the Malay hinterland that cried out for protection, created a situation in which the British government was dragged at first reluctantly to intervene, and from which it could rapidly extend its power in the Malay world later in the century.

At the end of the Napoleonic Wars, the British government was prepared to sacrifice its interests in the East in order to build up the Netherlands in Europe. Had the Dutch pressed home their objections to Singapore immediately, it is more than likely that the settlement would have been abandoned, but by the time negotiations came to fruition, the port was a proven economic success, and the British were anxious to retain it to protect the China route.[1] Under the

128

terms of the Anglo-Dutch treaty of 1824, Singapore remained a British possession. In an attempt to settle territorial and commercial differences, the treaty arranged for Britain to cede Bencoolen to the Dutch in exchange for Malacca, thus cutting the British off from future political interference in Sumatra, and putting an end to Dutch political connections with the Malay peninsula. The status of the rest of the archipelago remained ambiguous. One clause which prohibited the British from interfering in the islands south of Singapore, undoubtedly referred at the time to the islands of the Riau-Lingga archipelago, but in later years the Dutch tried to extend the term to embrace every island in the Malay archipelago which extended southwards beyond the latitude of Singapore, and this included Borneo. By the middle of the century even the British Foreign Office was confused over the interpretation of this provision of the treaty.[2]

It was a long time before the issue became important, for the East India Company was not interested in the treaty as a means for extending its own power in the peninsula or the archipelago.[3] It had no intention of treating Sultan Hussein of Johore as its vassal. Hussein was recognised by Raffles for the sole purpose of establishing some form of legal claim to Singapore, and once this was secured, the Company would willingly have washed their hands of him. Each governor in turn whittled down the claims of Hussein and his successors until the title became extinct.

The Company was equally anxious to come to some arrangement which would keep it out of trouble in the northern Malay states, but at the same time check Siamese aggression. In the second decade of the nineteenth century, the Siamese revived former ambitions with intrigue in Perak, followed in 1821 by the overrunning of Kedah. The merchants of Penang feared for the safety of the settlement and wanted more favourable trading conditions with neighbouring states, an ambition which was shared by the energetic Robert Fullerton, who was appointed governor in 1824. Fullerton bluffed the Siamese into withdrawing an attack on Selangor and Perak, and tried to use the mission of Henry Burney, whom the East India Company despatched to Bangkok in 1825 to negotiate a treaty, to extend British influence in the northern Malay states. Burney had to leave Kedah in the hands of the Siamese, but he gained Siamese recognition of the independence of Perak and Selangor. Fullerton thwarted attempts made by the Siamese in 1826 to get round the terms of the treaty, and his agent made agreements with Perak and Selangor guaranteeing British support for their independence. This was contrary to the non-intervention policy of the East India Company, which angrily repudiated the treaties in private, but did not do so publicly. Although never ratified, the treaties of 1826 remained the basis of the Company's relations with Perak and Selangor and the guarantee of their independence. The position of Kelantan and Trengganu was left vague by the Burney treaty and throughout the nineteenth century the Siamese exerted a strong influence in those states, but they were in any event of minor importance to the trade of the Straits Settlements.

The East India Company was interested in the Straits Settlements solely as a protection to its valuable China trade and as collecting centres for Straits produce to help pay for that trade. In 1826, the three stations of Penang, Malacca and Singapore were grouped together to form the Straits Settlements Presidency, in the vain hope that their administration would be more economical, but the Presidency fell victim to the sweeping retrenchment by which the governor-general succeeded in restoring the Company's solvency after the financial blow suffered through the Anglo-Burmese War. In 1830 the Presidency was abolished and the Settlements reduced to a Residency subsidiary to the Presidency of Bengal. Three years later the Company lost its monopoly of the China trade and with it all interest in the Settlements. For the next three decades they were administered with the minimum of effort and cost. The Company grudged the funds needed for military defence, for naval protection, for the suppression of piracy, and for the provision of a strong police force to control the cosmopolitan and unruly immigrant population. The Company's only use for the Settlements in fact was as a convict station, and Calcutta was rigid in its determination not to be drawn into time- and money-consuming adventures in the Malay hinterland.

Certainly Calcutta had no intention of becoming involved further afield in the archipelago, and the foundation of British influence in Borneo was the work of private individuals, notably of Sir James Brooke.[4] It was quest for adventure that brought Brooke, a former military officer of the East India Company, to the East. In the prospectus of his intentions that he published shortly before his departure from England, he praised Raffles' policy, which had since been abandoned in the archipelago. Originally Brooke hoped to found a colony in northeast Borneo to promote trade and missionary work. When he reached Singapore, he decided to divert his attentions to Sarawak. This province was part of the sultanate of Brunei, then ruled by Omar Ali Saifuddin, a weak, middle-aged man, very much the puppet of other royal intriguers. More forceful was his uncle, Hashim, rajah muda* and regent, who had been trying since 1837 to suppress a revolt in Sarawak which had broken out among the Dayaks as a result of oppression by the Brunei nobles. Finding it impossible to quell the rebels, Hashim appealed to the British for help, and a group of Singapore merchants, who were tempted to take advantage of this situation, persuaded Brooke to visit the country. After some hesitation, Brooke agreed to help suppress the revolt in return for the right of trade and government in Sarawak and the title of rajah. Despite the reluctance on the part of the Brunei officials to carry out their part of the bargain,

---

* Crown Prince.

Brooke obtained his document and became ruler of Sarawak in 1841. The Dutch authorities at Batavia were angry, but no official complaint was made by The Hague to London, and the British government paid no attention to Brooke's venture.

It was to be the major weakness of Brooke's position that he had no official recognition or backing from Britain or any other European power. His relationship with the sultan of Brunei was uncertain, and in his early years he was at the mercy of Brunei politics. In 1846 the massacre of Hashim and all his party in Brunei was followed by an attempt on Brooke's life. He was saved by the Royal Navy, which blockaded Brunei, put down the new ruling clique and forced the sultan to confirm Brooke's title to Sarawak and to cede Labuan to Britain. But the support was on an *ad hoc* basis. When Brooke visited London in 1847, he was lionised as a national hero and appointed governor of Labuan, but he failed to obtain any concrete advantage for Sarawak. The British government would not recognise him as an independent rajah nor take Sarawak over as a protectorate, and Brooke was left in the same precarious position.

His administration was marked by sound common sense. He fixed taxes, laid down freedom of trade, abolished river dues and did away with forced labour. He administered justice personally and informally, using a set of simple legal rules. But simplicity of administration does not always lead to efficiency, nor conscientious humanitarianism to economic prosperity. Brooke was no financier, and throughout his rule he was dogged by heavy debt. While he had extravagant hopes of developing Sarawak's supposed rich resources, Brooke was unwilling to allow the existing way of life to be disrupted by the introduction of foreign capital. Consequently the Eastern Archipelago Company, which was designed to attract commercial support in Britain, was doomed from the start, even had Brooke not chosen an agent as malicious as Henry Wise. The attack upon the rajah which Wise fostered revealed the weakness of Brooke's position, unprotected by the British government and yet open to attack in Parliament. At first Rajah James encouraged Chinese immigration, but in 1857 the Chinese rose, destroyed much of Kuching and murdered several of Brooke's officials. With the help of the Dayaks, the rising was quickly suppressed. It was a local affair, sparked off by interference with Chinese interests in Sarawak. But Brooke regarded it as part of a general rising among the Chinese in British territories in South-east Asia, and afterwards the Chinese were never encouraged to settle in Sarawak again.

Late in 1857 Brooke went to England. With intrigues among the Malays and a commercial slump following the withdrawal of the Chinese, the plight of the Sarawak government seemed desperate. Brooke toured the country, appealing for protection for Sarawak and urging its union with the Straits Settlements to form one Crown colony. A petition in support of Brooke's plan was drawn up and signed by the mayor of Manchester and many leading merchants and industrialists, but found no hearing with the British government.[5] Failing in his bid for British protection, Brooke approached the Netherlands and France with no greater success, and he toyed with the idea of appealing to Belgium. In 1863 Britain acknowledged Sarawak as a state independent of Brunei, but would not accept it as a British protectorate. James Brooke continued to try to induce Britain to take over Sarawak and in 1868 in the last months of his life was also negotiating with Italy for protection.

Meanwhile the neglect by Calcutta in many ways favoured the development of the Straits Settlements, and particularly Singapore, which soon came to justify Raffles' dream as being the hub of trade in the Far East, a free port without duties or even port charges.[6] The revenue of Singapore, which had only amounted to $M 620 a month in 1820, increased by 1843 to over $M 15,000 a month, and the population, which in 1823 totalled less than 11,000, rose in twenty years to 57,000. Thousands of Chinese migrated to the Settlements each year, and gradually trade was built up with the interior. As early as the mid-1830s Chinese pepper and gambier planters began to move to the river valleys of Johore, and Chinese miners were already leading a precarious existence in the tin mines of Sungei Ujong in Negri Sembilan. From the middle of the century, with the opening of the tin fields of Larut and Selangor, Chinese miners flocked in thousands to the interior. More than half of them died of disease within a year, and the others were at the mercy of Malay chieftains and of their own rival clans, but the rewards for the fortunate few were substantial. The trade was dominated from the Straits Settlements by rich Chinese traders, often backed by capital from the European merchants,[7] and by 1863 the Singapore government estimated the trade between the Straits Settlements and the Malay states to be worth nearly one million pounds sterling a year.[8] This highly profitable but risky private trade sometimes involved the authorities in trouble. On occasion disputes between rival Chinese factions in the tin mines spread to the Straits ports and threatened the peace, particularly in Penang, where the secret society leaders could muster forces hundreds strong. Sometimes the miners clashed with Malay chiefs.

The settlements which had been made with the Dutch and the Siamese in the 1820s were intended as final arrangements to keep the Company out of trouble in the Malay peninsula. In fact they created a situation which was bound eventually to lead to intervention. The northern states, where Siamese influence was strong, remained fairly peaceful. For many years the ex-sultan of Kedah was a worry to the authorities in Penang, where he hatched several plots to regain his throne, some of them involving merchants in the settlement. The failure of armed insurrection induced the ex-sultan to change his tactics. In 1841 he sued for pardon, and in the following year Bangkok reinstated him as sultan of Kedah, but under strict control from Siam. The rulers of Kedah made no further attempts to throw off Siamese tutelage, and throughout the rest of the nineteenth century the country enjoyed peace and growing prosperity. The north-east states of Kelantan and Trengganu took many years to recover from the exactions made by the Siamese early in the nineteenth century. Their relationship with Siam continued to be ambiguous. In 1862, the suspicion that Bangkok intended to dethrone the sultan of Trengganu and substitute its own nominee led the Straits government to bombard Trengganu, in order to force the withdrawal of this Siamese puppet. If the Siamese had indeed any intentions of reviving their ambitions in the Malay states, this action discouraged their schemes. There was no further interference in the internal affairs of the states either by the Siamese or the British until the last years of the century. But peace did not bring good government nor justice of administration. Trengganu remained a poor, backward state, and trade between Kelantan and Singapore continued to be subject to hazards.

By the 1850s the political situation in those states which were not left under Siamese influence had produced a problem which the British authorities in Singapore could not continue to ignore. In the south, Sultan Hussein of Johore had no authority among the other Malay rulers, although one section of the European merchants of Singapore saw in him a useful tool for intrigue. The sultan in Rhio was forbidden by the Dutch to interfere in the peninsula, and this political vacuum encouraged the bid for independence by the subordinate chiefs, the temenggong of Johore and the bendahara of Pahang.

The temenggong by the middle of the century was a wealthy and powerful figure. The holders of the office were all men of ability and they gained the confidence of most of the British governors and of an influential section of the European mercantile community. The governors in turn built them up as rulers of Johore, since they saw in them the most effective means of developing a Malay state without the need for British political intervention. Eventually in 1885 the temenggong was recognised as sultan of Johore, and it was only the expansion of British influence in the Malay hinterland in the last quarter of the century which thwarted his schemes for bringing more of the peninsula under the control of Johore.

In Pahang, Bendahara Ali, who ruled for more than fifty years, brought peace to the country, and under his rule the state developed a profitable trade with Singapore. Civil war broke out after Ali's death in 1857, when one of his younger sons, Wan Ahmed, revolted against the new bendahara.[9] Singapore merchants became involved, and one European firm lent large sums to the bendahara, in return for valuable concessions in the Kuantan tin mines. By that time the bendahara had alienated all his powerful chiefs, and in 1863 Wan Ahmed gained

133

control of Pahang, became the new bendahara, was eventually recognised by the Singapore government and adopted the title of sultan. He repudiated the arrangement made by his predecessor over the tin mines, and the episode led to unrest and a renewed pressure in Singapore to establish some control over the chiefs of the hinterland.

In the independent states of western Malaya, the situation was even more tense, for the states were left in anarchy, while the rich tin deposits in Perak, Selangor and Sungei Ujong encouraged the influx of Chinese miners. Chinese immigration and the development of tin mining, in which subordinate chiefs often proved more competent than the sultans, finally undermined the tottering administration of the states. In all three states by the 1860s there was civil strife, in the midst of which the Chinese miners risked dispossession and slaughter, and their backers in the Straits Settlements faced financial ruin.

For many years the trade of the Straits Settlements flourished, but owing to the closely guarded policy of free trade, the government gained almost no share in this rising prosperity. In an attempt to prune expenses, administration was lax and inefficient. This was a positive advantage to the progress of the Settlements in the early decades, but by the middle of the century sections of the European mercantile community were growing restive under Indian rule. While fears of international war grew, the Company's parsimony had left the Settlements defenceless. There were fears of internal unrest, for the immigrant Chinese were organised by their secret societies, and the police force and judicial system were inadequate to control them. There were growing fear of convicts and resentment at being used as a penal settlement. Above all there was concern that the policy of uniformity which the government of India favoured from 1854 onwards would force the use of the rupee currency and introduce trade dues. The outcry among the European merchants in Calcutta following the Indian Mutiny for abolition of the Company was echoed in the Straits, and in 1858 a petition for transfer to the direct rule of the Crown was presented in the British Parliament.[10]

This apparently simple request was to lead to years of debate. The British government was not keen to take over a settlement that could not pay its own way, particularly at that time when the policy was to cut down commitments for military defence in overseas colonies. The issue was kept alive by an enthusiastic minority of the merchants, who thought that a colonial governor with a local legislative council would encourage and protect the expansion of trade in the neighbouring territories. Eventually the British government agreed grudgingly to the transfer, provided the Settlements paid their own expenses, but there was no intention of reversing official policy. The change did not bring immediately the advantages which the agitators for transfer had wanted. The Legislative Council was a disappointment because it was dominated by the official majority.

The governor was rigidly controlled from the Colonial Office, which at first was as adamant as the Indian government in steering clear of commitments in the Malay peninsula.[11] By that time, however, the policy of non-intervention was dangerously out of date. Selangor was plunged into civil war in the 1860s, when the influx of Chinese tin miners added to the chaos which had already been caused by the breakdown of the sultan's authority and wars between rival chiefs over tin and trade dues. Merchants from the Straits Settlements took advantage of the strife to supply and arm the contestants, and the collapse of government and consequent increase of piracy threatened the trade of the Straits Settlements. In 1861 the yamtuan besar* of Negri Sembilan died, and the local federation disintegrated when no unanimity could be obtained on appointing a successor. In Perak the authority of the sultan had broken down completely by the 1860s, and various petty chiefs who had risen to power and wealth through the tin trade had virtually established their independence. In 1871, when the sultan died, the normal heir was passed over, and civil turmoil was intensified.

By 1873 the Chinese merchants in the Straits Settlements were petitioning the British government for protection for their interests in the interior. Fearing intervention by Germany if the peninsula were left a political vacuum, the Colonial Office took advantage of the appointment of a new and well-trusted governor, Sir Andrew Clarke, to modify its policy. Clarke was authorised to investigate and report on the advisability of appointing British residents in some of the Malay states. Finding the situation on the spot serious, and under pressure from the Singapore merchants, the new governor exceeded his instructions. At a meeting which he called of the conflicting Malay chieftains and the secret society leaders at Pangkor early in 1874, an agreement was signed, whereby they agreed to keep the peace in Perak. The British nominee was confirmed as sultan and agreed to accept a British resident at his court. The next month a particularly daring case of piracy led Clarke to insist on the sultan of Selangor's taking a British resident, and later that same year the dato klana of Sungei Ujong asked for one to be appointed in his state.

These moves were designed in theory to end trouble without committing the British to any expensive intervention. In practice they meant that in future the British had the alternative of advancing to establish control over the whole country or of withdrawing altogether. Further intervention came more quickly than was anticipated, for the first British resident of Perak, J. W. W. Birch, aggravated the anti-British resentment, which was already strong among the Perak leaders as a result of the treaty that had been thrust upon them. Birch launched a full-scale attack upon the financial privileges of the chiefs and on the practice of

---

* Paramount ruler: Negri Sembilan was a federation of nine small states, of which Sungei Ujong was the largest.

slavery, and in 1875 he was murdered as a result of an intrigue against him in which all the major chiefs of Perak, including the sultan, were involved. In the retribution that followed nearly all the Perak leaders were removed, and the opportunity was created for a clean sweep to be made in administration. The new resident, Hugh Low, had spent nearly thirty years in Sarawak and Labuan, when he was appointed to Perak in 1877.[12] He brought with him the integrity, the concern for the welfare of the local population and reliance on simplicity of administration, which were the stamp of the Brooke regime in Borneo. Sir James's attempt to unite Sarawak with the British settlements in Malaya twenty years before had failed, but indirectly he left his imprint on the British administration of Malaya, for Low's work was to set the pattern for development in Selangor, in Sungei Ujong and in the other states of Negri Sembilan which gradually came under British protection. In Pahang an attempt to put down lawlessness and cruelty by establishing a British agent to draw up more humane law codes broke down, and in 1888 the sultan reluctantly agreed under great pressure to accept a British resident.[13]

On the whole, the early residents worked with enthusiasm, integrity and energy in introducing a rudimentary administration, reforming revenue collection, providing judicial tribunals and abolishing slavery. They were supposed to submit a diary of their activities each month to Singapore, and to send annual reports. But it was impossible to secure uniformity, and in 1895 the British government agreed to a federation of the four states of Perak, Selangor, Negri Sembilan and Pahang. They were to have a common civil service, an advisory council of sultans, and a resident-general to supervise the residents. In effect the rulers kept merely the trappings of authority, the residents lost their powers of initiative to the resident-general, and although the federation remained on paper a government by advice and agreement, in practice the foundations were laid for uniform government on the usual colonial lines.[14]

Meanwhile the expansion of British influence in Borneo followed an independent course. When the first white rajah died, he left Sarawak in a weak position, independent but unprotected, and with a substantial financial deficit. But the country was at peace, and the oppression and cruelty which Brooke found there a quarter of a century before had vanished. It was during the long rule of his successor that administration in Sarawak was organised on an orderly basis. The country was divided into three divisions, each under a European resident, with his own divisional council attended by the local chiefs, while a Council Negri, consisting of the chiefs and the leading European and local officials, met regularly in Kuching.

The Brooke family aspired to take over the whole of Brunei, which covered the coastal areas of much of modern north-eastern Borneo, but the British government opposed this encroachment.   Since many of the tribes were in open revolt against the sultan of Brunei, Charles Brooke suggested that Britain might take over Brunei as a protectorate if she would not allow Sarawak to absorb her territory.   But the British government's hostility to Sarawak's ambitions intensified from the 1870s, with the appointment of Treacher as governor of Labuan and the growth of rival interests in Sabah.[15]

An American company had made the first unsuccessful attempt to develop Sabah in the 1860s.   Its leases were bought up by the Austrian consul in Hong Kong, who proposed, with the help of two London merchants, to develop the territory and then to sell it to any interested European power.   Treacher insisted that they should not dispose of the territory without British approval, and it was with this proviso that he negotiated a new agreement for them with the sultan of Brunei.

The United States, Spain and Holland objected to this venture as infringing their prior rights, while Charles Brooke travelled along the coast with a warship, advising the inhabitants to resist.   He was reproved by Treacher and by the British Foreign Office.   Meanwhile the sponsors of the scheme for 'North Borneo' (Sabah), deciding it would be impossible to sell their rights to a foreign power, applied for a royal charter.   This was granted in 1881, on the understanding that the British government would not be involved in any expense.   The British North Borneo Chartered Company was to remain British, it could not transfer its rights and territory without permission from London, it was to suppress slavery but otherwise was not to interfere with the religion or customs of the local population, and it was to accept the decision of the British government in the event of any disagreement with the people of Borneo or with powers outside the country.   The chief representative of the Company in Borneo was to be appointed subject to approval of the British government, and Treacher became the first governor.

Both the rajah of Sarawak and the North Borneo Company in Sabah looked longingly at the territory remaining to the sultan of Brunei, and eventually in 1888 Sarawak, Brunei and Sabah all became British protectorates.   The governor of Singapore was made high commissioner for the Borneo Protectorate, and soon the relationship between Sarawak and the British North Borneo Company changed to one of friendly rivalry.   Labuan, a decaying Crown colony, was handed over to the Company in 1890 and continued to be an expensive liability.

The relationship of Britain with its various dependencies in the Malay peninsula and Borneo was in different forms and the paths by which the connection was established lay in different grooves.   There was at the close of the century no common purpose and no definite end in view, but a link had been established between the disparate territories that were to form the future Malaysia.

9

Political History 1896–1946

DAVID McINTYRE

The dominant theme in the political development of the Malaysian territories in the half-century from 1896 to 1946 was the attempt, and the failure, of British officials to unify the administration of the various states. The attempt failed chiefly because in these years two major movements of world history affected the region simultaneously: the final phases of European imperialism and the upsurge of Asian nationalism. While the expansion of British control in Malaysia continued up until the 1914–18 war, in other parts of Asia the pattern of British power was already changing. Consequently a curious uncertainty of aim can be discerned in Malaysia during the years leading up to the 1939–45 war.

At the close of the Victorian era, Britain stood firmly astride the trade route to China. Although politicians in London keenly felt the vulnerability of their world-wide interests and sought the friendship of the United States and of France, and gained the alliance of Japan in 1902, British representatives in South-east Asia confidently pushed ahead with British expansion. Indeed, Sir Frank Swettenham's accession to Government House in Singapore in 1901 seemed to symbolise a new mood of optimism. Since coming to Malaya in 1871 Swettenham had played a large part in the growth of the 'resident system' and had been one of the chief architects of the Federated Malay States. Now he crowned his career by presiding over all Britain's interests in the region.

As governor of the colony of the Straits Settlements he also became high commissioner for the Federated Malay States, thus supervising an administrative system which defied exact constitutional definition. The rulers of Perak, Selangor, Negri Sembilan and Pahang had accepted British residents, whose advice was to be taken on all matters except Malay custom and religion. But 'advice' had merely become a word for effective British control. Moreover, when the need

138

for highly trained specialist officers and the creation of a centralised administration were thought necessary, the so-called 'Federal Agreement' of 1895 was accepted by the rulers of the four states. Here again, Federated Malay States became the name for what was really an administrative *union* controlled by a resident-general and secretariat in Kuala Lumpur.

As high commissioner for the Borneo Protectorates, the governor watched over Britain's growing influence in the remnants of the Brunei sultanate, which had once ruled the northern part of the island. The sultan's territory had, by the close of the nineteenth century, already been reduced to a few thousand square miles close to the town of Brunei. The territory to the west was ceded gradually to the rajahs of Sarawak; that to the east given up to the British North Borneo Chartered Company. Since 1888 the now tiny sultanate and the two large 'private-enterprise states' were formally under British protection.[1] Indeed if it had not been for the Foreign Office, Brunei would probably have disappeared. But after the Lawas valley was detached from the sultan (first on lease to the chartered company in 1902, then transferred to Sarawak in 1905) further territorial adjustments were prevented. The sultan of Brunei, however, was forced to accept a resident in 1906 and to take his advice in all matters apart from religion.

In the Malay peninsula the expansion of British control was allowed to proceed. For a number of years Straits Settlements officials had wanted to bring the northern states of Kedah, Kelantan and Trengganu under British control. But as these states were recognised as 'tributaries' of Thailand, and as Britain wished to maintain Thai integrity, the Foreign Office vetoed the move. The possibility of intervention by other western nations, however, caused a rapid reversal of policy in 1901. Swettenham was empowered to exert pressure on Bangkok, and although an agreement of 1902 recognised Thai rights, it provided that the Thai advisers in the four northern states of Trengganu, Kelantan, Kedah and Perlis could be British officers. Kelantan accepted such a British adviser in 1903; Kedah and Perlis received financial advisers. In 1909 even the fiction of Thai sovereignty was ended. The four states were 'transferred' to British Malaya, and their rulers eventually accepted British advisers. Kelantan formally accepted protection in 1910. In the same year the sultan of Trengganu agreed to receive an agent, similar in function to a consular officer. In Kedah, officers from the Federated Malay States took over as the financial advisers, although a treaty formally providing for an adviser was not signed until 1923. The Perlis treaty followed seven years later. In the southern part of the peninsula, the last state to come formally under British control was Johore, which in some ways had always had the closest relations with the Straits Settlements. An agent with consular powers, provided for under the 1885 treaty, had not been appointed, but in 1914 Sultan Ibrahim agreed to accept an adviser-general, whose advice would

139

be followed as in the Federated Malay States. Gradually Johore and the four northern states came to be referred to as the 'Unfederated States'.

Thus the limits of British expansion in Malaysia were reached in the decade before the 1914–18 war. Yet the legal basis for British rule was most diverse; administrative methods also varied, and they were not always accepted without protest. British sovereignty was confined to the small settlements of Singapore, Malacca, Penang (with Province Wellesley) and Labuan,[2] which constituted a single Crown colony, where the governor ruled autocratically advised by an executive council of nine (whose advice he could reject provided he consulted the Secretary of State for the Colonies). Laws were approved by a legislative council of thirteen officials and thirteen nominees of the governor, who, in case of need, possessed the right to the casting vote. In the Federated Malay States the rulers remained sovereign, but in practice government was largely controlled by the residents. Although state councils, where the proceedings were in Malay, had provided a link between the aristocracy and the administration, the system changed after the creation of the 'federation'. By the early years of the twentieth century it appeared that instead of the rulers' governing with the advice of the residents, the residents carried on the government under the supervision of the resident-general, with reference to the rulers only when it was thought necessary. Yet when British control spread in the unfederated states the rights of the sultans were not encroached upon to the same degree as in the federated states; the forms of 'advice' appeared to be better respected. The advisers, in fact, acquired much the same position as the residents, but for various reasons these states retained their Malay character.

In Borneo the constitutional position was equally diverse. The protected state of Brunei was in a similar position to the Unfederated Malay States. The governor of British North Borneo (Sabah) ruled as a benevolent autocrat. He was served by a small advisory council of five officials, plus one planter and one Chinese; a legislative council was created in 1912. Rajah Charles Brooke of Sarawak has been called a 'model enlightened despot'. An austere, eccentric man, who prohibited his district officers from possessing armchairs, he was, in his way, devoted to the peoples of Sarawak. Leading Malays and officials were consulted regularly in the Supreme Council, and a wider group of chiefs, officials and settlers sat on the Council Negri, but the government always centred on the rajah or his deputy. At the same time Charles Brooke deprecated the mood of racial arrogance which infected many colonial administrators in the late Victorian era: 'Before we reach the middle of the century', he predicted in 1907, 'all nations now holding large Colonial possessions will have met with severe reverses. . . . India to a certainty will be lost. . . .'[3]

Brooke was not alone in forecasting the end of European hegemony. As the nationalists of China prepared to overthrow the Manchus and restore the integrity and dignity of China, the Chinese in Malaya were exhorted to support the revolutionary movement. Dr Sun Yat Sen first visited Malaya in 1900 to rouse the patriotism of the immigrant communities, and after the formation of the Kuomintang in 1912, thirty branches were registered in Malaya. This political awakening of the Chinese in Malaya was naturally focused on China, and was not directed against the state governments. Dissatisfaction among Malays, however, arose because of the growth of British control. As government in the Federated Malay States was increasingly controlled by the residents and resident-general, the rulers found their only real powers confined to muslim affairs. This tended to strengthen the institutions of orthodox Islam, which led, in turn, to attempts at religious reform among Malays, led by students who came under the influence of Egyptian muslim reformers while attending the Al-Ahzar University, Cairo. In 1906 the Malay newspaper *Al-Imam* (The Leader) was founded in Singapore by returning students, to attack the backwardness of Malays, and to promote interest in modern science and in world events among muslims.

In Borneo, several leaders arose to resist the encroachments of the new governments. Mat Salleh, of mixed Sulu and Bajau origin, led a considerable revolt against the British North Borneo Company from 1895 to 1900; in Sarawak the Dayak, Banting, resisted the rajah for fourteen years before submitting in 1907. Outbreaks of various kinds continued from time to time, such as the Murut rising of 1915.

Of more immediate practical significance for the development of policy was the growing dissatisfaction among Malay aristocrats, who felt that British civil servants were overcentralising the Federated Malay States. At the conference of rulers in 1903, Sultan Idris of Perak suggested that the 'federation' should be loosened and the growing power of the resident-general checked. An attempt was therefore made to restore, in some way, the rulers' powers, while preserving the advantages of central government services. In 1909 Sir John Anderson, the high commissioner, reminded officials that they were 'here in a Malay country as the advisers and counsellors of its Malay sovereigns'.[4] In an attempt to enhance the latters' position he negotiated the Federal Council agreement, providing for a federal council consisting of the high commissioner, the four rulers and residents, four nominated 'unofficials' and the resident-general (now renamed 'chief secretary'). But this change only served to further depress the powers of the rulers. Legislative power now tended to be taken out of the hands of the state councils by the Federal Council, which the sultans were not able to dominate. A genuine attempt at 'decentralisation' was delayed because of the 1914–18 war.

141

Malaysia was not directly endangered by the war, although there was some momentary excitement. The German cruiser *Emden* dislocated shipping in the Bay of Bengal and even raided the port of Penang, and in 1915 Indian troops of the 5th Light Infantry mutinied in Singapore. The interruption of trade through shipping shortages, and the need to liquidate German economic assets, caused administrative problems. In some cases, particularly in Sabah, the civil service suffered when its officers left to fight in Europe.

Yet in the long run the 1914-18 war marked a significant divide. Although, with the mandates of the former German colonies and the partition of the Middle East, the British empire reached its greatest physical extent, British economic and military power had declined markedly in relation to the United States. In 1917 the Bolshevik revolution and President Wilson's Fourteen Points presaged, in their different ways, the end of European supremacy. While Britain tried to maintain its power in the 1920s, its allies forced it to give up its Japanese alliance, and already in India and parts of Africa the goal of eventual self-government for its colonies was accepted.

The Malaysian territories, however, were chiefly protected states. Britain's policy here was less clear. On the one hand it was decided in 1921 to create a first class naval base in Singapore to strengthen British power in the region; on the other hand the policy of decentralising the Federated Malay States was resumed. Sir Lawrence Guillemard, high commissioner from 1920 to 1927, mooted the idea of a Malayan union, which would yet preserve the individuality of the states. It was found that the central bureaucracy had been overdeveloped in the prosperous pre-war years. Guillemard announced to the Federal Council in 1925 that the rulers, councils and residents of the federated states should have powers more akin to their unfederated neighbours. In a sense these proposals first awakened the spirit of political controversy in Malaya, although at this stage it was largely confined to the ruling elite. Decentralisation was opposed by Chinese and European unofficials in the Federal Council, and by the planters, who all cherished the efficiency of the central secretariat. Thus, although in 1927 the sultans left the Council, to meet occasionally in a ceremonial 'Durbar', and the form of the annual estimates was altered to show certain reserved state services separately, Guillemard's reforms had little practical effect.

Nevertheless, the decentralisation debates of 1925-7 posed a fundamental dilemma in Malaya both for the civil servants and the local communities as to their ultimate goals: should they build a unified modern state or preserve the existing small Malay states? On the one hand a proposal was made by Tan Cheng Lock, the wealthy Chinese leader, who suggested in the Straits Settlements Legislative Council in 1926 that the goal should be a unified, self-governing British Malaya. On the other hand, the clearest statement of official policy was made by Sir Hugh

142

Clifford, high commissioner 1927-30, who said the position of the Malay sultans was sacrosanct, that a democratic regime comprehending the immigrant peoples was out of the question and would represent a 'betrayal' of the Malays.[5] This view largely dominated British policy until the 1939-45 war.

In this atmosphere the unfederated states were regarded as the desirable model. Kedah, which had a British adviser, but a largely Malay civil service, was looked upon as an ideal Malay state. In fact, in 1931 the high commissioner, Sir Cecil Clementi, announced that the federated states had departed from the intentions of their founders and should be restored to the status of their neighbours as the first move in the creation of a Malayan union in which the territories in North Borneo might also be included. The next step then should be a customs union in which the Straits Settlements could join, thus creating a unified British Malaysia. But Clementi's proposals provoked bitter opposition on all sides. The Straits Settlements clung to the doctrine of free trade; the rulers of the unfederated states feared they might be pushed into a union without consent; the planters and businessmen were anxious lest the efficient services at Kuala Lumpur might disintegrate. Although a start was made by renaming the chief secretary, 'federal secretary', and lowering his status, and by giving the states more powers in such matters as health and public works, very little real decentralisation took place and union made little progress.

The civil servants, planters and businessmen who debated the future of Malaya did so with little reference to the wishes of the inhabitants. Nevertheless the various communities became more and more politically sensitive in the 1930s. Malay activity moved into two main channels. After the first Malay was nominated to the Straits Settlements Legislative Council in 1924, the Singapore Malay Union had been formed to back up his representation of Malay views. Similarly, in the Federated Malay States Council, a group of English-educated Malays were active, particularly in urging the promotion of their compatriots in the civil service. After 1937 Malay politico-cultural associations sprang up in all the states and a Pan-Malayan conference was held in 1939. At the second conference in 1940 the Malay Associations of Sarawak and Brunei were also represented.

These associations emphasised cultural unity and co-operated with the regime. Students who went to Egypt in the 1920s were influenced by Pan-Islamic nationalism in the Middle East and took a more radical stance in Malaya. One group of reformers looked to Sukarno's Indonesian National Party and envisaged unity and freedom for the entire Malay archipelago. The radical Union of Malay Youths (Kesatuan Malayu Muda), founded in 1937, attracted a growing Malay-educated intelligentsia from the technical colleges and teachers' training college. In 1941 one hundred and fifty of its leaders were arrested under defence regulations.

Among the Chinese the Kuomintang remained active. In the period when Chiang Kai Shek accepted communist co-operation, a growth of anti-British propaganda led to the banning of the Kuomintang in Malaya. But with the purging of the communists in China in 1927, the Malayan Chinese also divided. The left wing joined the existing nucleus of the Malayan Communist Party, dedicated to erecting a Malayan people's republic. The party was active in trade unions, and responsible for unrest and sabotage, in the mid-1930s. Middle class Chinese became (legally again) members of the Kuomintang of China. Their interest was still centred on China, and after the Japanese invasion large sums of money were sent ostensibly for relief work in China.

The Indian communities in Malaya formed associations which were largely non-political. Working conditions of Indians were watched over by an agent from the government of India appointed in 1923; there were also some Indian newspapers published in Malaya. Nehru caused a slight stir when he referred to Malaya, on a visit in 1937, as a 'political backwater'. Soon after his visit a Central Indian Association was formed in Kuala Lumpur, but it indulged in little real political activity.

Thus when the 1939–45 war shattered the relative calm of South-east Asia, there was no 'Malayan nation' to resist the Japanese. The British-controlled governments had presented an effective façade to the world; law and order had been maintained, economic growth encouraged, and many of the services of a modern state erected. Old Malayan hands might perhaps regard the inter-war years as a 'golden age' of mild, beneficent rule. Yet much was obviously lacking. Chinese, Indian and European communities had, with few exceptions, no loyalty to Malaya as such. Above all there had been no genuine political advance, no preparation for the franchise—largely because of the complex communal situation. No clear political goal had been set forth for Malaya, in contrast to other parts of the British empire. Thus, one former civil servant has described Malaya as 'a plural society with no corporate soul . . . a glorified commercial undertaking rather than a State'.[6] In spite of its wealth, Malaya was obviously regarded as a peripheral problem by British policy-makers.

The Borneo territories did not even experience the attempt at major administrative adjustment, nor the political stirrings, which were evident in the peninsula. Although the British government considered the idea of purchasing the British North Borneo Company at the time of Clementi's proposals, nothing was done about it. Yet the Borneo peoples were not unheeded. Both in Sarawak and Sabah local administration rested largely on village headmen. Sarawak introduced a system of elective village councils among the Ibans in 1928. In Sabah, the Chiefs' Advisory Council, which steadily pressed the government to change certain policies, provided a political training ground, and a number of leaders of stature, such as Mohammed Saman, were recognised. A significant change occurred in 1934, when the chartered company decided to recruit former colonial servants from Africa rather than rely on Malay civil servants. Sir Douglas Jardine, with experience in Nigeria and Tanganyika, proposed adapting the doctrine of 'indirect rule' to Borneo. He began an experiment at Bingkor in 1936 by entrusting the Dusun chief, Sedoman, with the collection and expenditure of revenue in an area of twelve villages. But the experiment was a small one and the region never became fully autonomous.

Rajah Vyner Brooke made a more radical change in Sarawak, although in some ways a less practical one. He celebrated the centenary of the white raj in 1941 by proclaiming a constitution. But, although the goal of ultimate self-government was announced by granting power to a new supreme council of five and an enlarged Council Negri of twenty-five, he merely transferred his personal powers to bodies nominated by himself. There was no question of elections. The system existed for only a few months before the Japanese invasion.

The Japanese landed at Kota Bharu in the peninsula on December 8, 1941; they attacked the Sarawak oil fields on December 17, and the peaceful façade of British control collapsed. Since England's own independence had recently been threatened, resources were limited and in Asia they were concentrated on the defence of the Middle East and India. Few reinforcements were spared for the defence of Malaya; Sarawak, Brunei and Sabah received none. In addition to this, Japanese air superiority was overwhelming. Thus Kuching was occupied on Christmas Day 1941, Labuan fell on January 1, 1942, and Sandakan followed by January 19. The rearguard action on the Malay peninsula lasted fifty-four days, and the 'impregnable fortress' of Singapore surrendered on February 15, after a two weeks' siege.

It will be many years before a balanced account of the period of Japanese occupation can be written. Personal feelings must colour the attitudes of the generations who participated in the events of 1941–5. Yet it is clear that the war marks the watershed in the recent history of Asia. In Malaya it was also a vital stage in the political evolution of the various communities. The Japanese never completely subjugated the Malay peninsula, nor were they very clear as to their ultimate aims there. Throughout the war well-organised Chinese, and some Malay, guerrillas maintained units in the jungle. These formed links with a few British 'stay behind' parties, and eventually communications were opened with South-east Asia Command as it planned the reoccupation. Towards the end of the war the guerrillas co-operated with 'Force 136' parties who dropped into Malaya by parachute.

During the last days of the battle for Singapore, the governor belatedly called

145

upon the Chinese to mobilise, and briefly both Communist Party and Kuomintang supporters fought side by side. After the surrender the Kuomintang was disbanded. The communists 'went underground' and played a leading part in all the Malay states in the Malayan People's Anti-Japanese Army, which throughout the war combined military training and action with ideological preparation for a future independent Malayan people's republic.

The Japanese, however, were slow to adopt the idea of Malayan independence, in contrast to their policy in other parts of the 'Co-prosperity Sphere'. Well developed nationalist movements indicated a policy of granting some form of independence, which was given to pro-Japanese governments in Burma and the Philippines in 1943. A Provisional Government of Free India was created in Singapore. Indians in Malaya were encouraged through Indian Independence Leagues to regard themselves as a spearhead in the liberation of India, and the Japanese recruited an Indian National Army in Malaya. But after handing back the four northern states to Thailand in 1943, the Japanese regarded the rest of Malaya's future in the context of a Greater Indonesia. For example, the 150 imprisoned leaders of the pro-Indonesian Union of Malay Youths were released by the Japanese and their leader, Ibrahim bin Haji Ya'kob, was appointed commander of the Japanese-sponsored Malay Pembela Tanah Ayer ('Avengers of the Country') Army. Although it was intended at first that the rulers should be forced to give up their lands and peoples to the Japanese emperor, in 1943 the titles, property and religious authority of the sultans were confirmed. Thus the Japanese were evidently intent upon dividing the communities in Malaya. While various attempts were made to win over the Malays, and the Indians were directed to the invasion of their homeland, the Chinese, particularly communists, were harshly treated. The Europeans were interned. But when Japanese collapse was imminent in 1945 a decision was made to stimulate national consciousness in Malaya and Indonesia. To eliminate racial and communal differences, the Union of Peninsula Indonesians (Kesatuan Rakyat Indonesia Semenanjong), or KRIS movement, was encouraged. After a chance meeting with Sukarno on August 12, 1945, the party's leader, Ibrahim, gained the impression that when Indonesia was granted independence by the Japanese, all Malaysia would be included. But when the Republic of Indonesia was proclaimed, Malaya and British Borneo were excluded. Ibrahim shortly quit Malaya for Djakarta, but the KRIS movement went ahead with a conference at Kuala Lumpur on August 17, 1945, and decided to found the Malay Nationalist Party.

Although some of the leaders of these war-time parties were imprisoned briefly when the British returned to Malaya, the political activities of the war years contributed to the markedly changed atmosphere which gradually became

146

evident when the British Military Administration restored freedom of speech. Moreover, since the dropping of the atomic bombs on Japan had precipitated the cease-fire of August 15, 1945, and the surrender on September 2, there was a time-lag before the British landing on September 5. This meant that the British did not return as they had intended as a victorious liberating army. It has been argued that this unexpected situation destroyed the carefully worked out plan of the Colonial Office Malayan Planning Unit for the post-war development of Malaya[7].

Whereas the general trend of pre-war policy had been to preserve the Malay rulers and to avoid the complications of democratic institutions, during the war this view was reversed. The Association of British Malaya urged a unification of the governments, and Tan Cheng Lock, the veteran leader of the Overseas Chinese Association, in exile in India, proposed a United Malaya and Straits Settlements with the goal of full self-government in the Commonwealth, and with equal citizenship rights for the inhabitants. The Colonial Office decided that the pre-war system was too cumbrous and that 'although the special position of the indigenous Malays needed to be safeguarded, reforms were overdue in the system of representation in order to permit the claims of other races, Chinese and Indian . . . to receive reasonable satisfaction'.[8]

Thus from October to December 1945, Sir Harold MacMichael toured the Malay states and secured the signatures of the rulers to documents which super-seded the old treaties and provided, now for the first time, that 'full power and jurisdiction' would be vested in the British Crown. With these powers, the British government created a Malayan Union with a common Malayan citizen-ship. Singapore became a separate Crown colony. Mr Malcolm MacDonald was sent out as governor-general to co-ordinate policy in the Union and Singa-pore, and also in Labuan, Brunei, Sarawak and Sabah.

The Japanese hold over the Borneo territories was gradually removed during the summer of 1945. The Australians landed in Labuan and Brunei Bay on June 10; Kuching was occupied on September 11, Sandakan on October 19. But al-though the white rajah returned to Sarawak on a visit, and a senior chartered company servant headed the civil administration in Sabah, these two 'private enterprise empires', curious relics of the Victorian era, did not survive. During the war, Vyner Brooke decided to cede Sarawak to the Crown, and he issued a proclamation to this effect on February 6, 1946. On July 1, Sarawak, in spite of considerable opposition voiced by a good proportion of the representatives of its peoples in the Council Negri, was annexed as a Crown colony. Two weeks later, the territory of the British North Borneo Company, with Labuan now added to it, became another Crown colony. The chartered company had also realised that it could not afford the responsibility of post-war reconstruction, and, in return for compensation, it ceded its rights to the Crown.

In 1946 it appeared then, on a superficial view, that the fifty-year-old trend of unifying the governments of the Malaysian territories was about to be fulfilled. The goal of self-government in Malaya had been announced. A clear idea of official trusteeship was accepted in Sarawak and Sabah. Singapore was still regarded as a vital strategic base, but it was granted a more representative constitution. However, the policy-makers in Britain had underestimated the political resilience of the leaders of Malay society, the preservation of whose rights had been one of the main themes of the inter-war years. Thus, the Malayan Union provoked such opposition that it became the starting point for the new political system of the Federation of Malaya. The ensuing controversy accelerated the movement to independence, and this meant that unity in Malaysia could not be achieved under the British, but only under Malayan auspices.

10

Communism and the Emergency

ANTHONY SHORT

It is perhaps a moot point whether a chapter on 'Communism and the Emergency' should be included in the history or politics of Malaysia. Certainly the Emergency is an event so recent that it cannot be decently interred in the pages of history; on the other hand, except for the officers of the Police Special Branch and the Ministry of Internal Security, it was, until the problem of confrontation arose, generally regarded as an experience so remote as to belong to the pre-natal phase of independent Malaya.

As a popular political force, communism in Malaya is a dead letter; on the other hand it is the long shadow over the whole of Asia. On the principle that the whole is greater than the part, the Malayan experience of guerrilla communism has often been subject to generalisations about the pattern of subversion and insurrection in the rest of Asia. As one would expect, there are, in fact, similarities—before, during and after the Second World War—but if one points to a series of post-war revolutions in South-east Asia, it is at most a discrete series and the better approach is to regard the insurrection in Malaya as a unique event.

The history of the Malayan Communist Party (hereafter the MCP) can be considered in five phases of which the fourth and the fifth are the most important.

PHASE ONE, 1930 TO 1941

This period saw the building of the party on the foundations which had been laid by communist elements of the Kuomintang and, after the purge of 1927 in China, by representatives of the China Communist Party. In 1930, at a conference in Singapore (attended by the Annamite communist who was later known as Ho Chi Minh) the Nanyang (South Seas) Communist Party and the Nanyang General Labour Union were dissolved—or, rather, there was a change of prefixes by which 'Malayan' replaced 'Nanyang'—and the general effect was to remove control of the MCP from the Chinese Communist Party and put it in the hands of the Far Eastern Bureau of the Communist International.

In part, this reorganisation may have been due to the realisation—Ho Chi Minh certainly pointed to the truth of it—that it was an advantage for communist parties to be built up on a national basis rather than serve exclusively as the instrument for executing the policy of international communism. Apart from the ideological link, there was, however, a racial link between Malayan communism and the outside world: it was predominantly Chinese. In November 1925, writing from Moscow, the Indonesian communist and official Soviet propagandist for the Pacific area, Tan Malaka, admitted that so far not the slightest advantage was to be seen from the work of his propagandists either in Singapore or Penang. The only people interested in economics and politics, he said, were the Chinese and if any movement were to begin in Malaya it would come not from the Malays but from the Chinese and the Indians.

The overwhelming majority of the MCP are, were and always have been Chinese. From the outset, true, or ideological, north was in Russia. Magnetic, or affinitive, north was in China. Of the two influences it seems to have been the second that was more important, and although fairly quick to follow the United Front policy laid down by the Comintern in 1935 and to foment trouble in the 'imperialist' war after the Nazi-Soviet Pact in 1939, the party line of the MCP changed a year before it would have done had it been geared to Russian policy. In July 1940, as a result of fresh instructions from the China Communist Party which had reached agreement with the Chungking government, anti-British movements and strike agitation were called off. Instead, the MCP were urged to concentrate on an anti-Japanese National Salvation Front; an anti-imperialist policy was permitted only if it did not encourage anti-British activities.

These instructions were frequently ignored, particularly on the labour front, and the MCP, even after Russia's entry into the war, continued to regard the expulsion of the British from Malaya as their primary objective. Until December 1941, however, the problem of collaborating with an imperial power against fascist aggression was essentially academic; after the Japanese invasion it became a matter first of urgency and then of self-preservation. All-out co-operation with government was offered and accepted. Several hundred volunteers were trained in sabotage and guerrilla warfare and one semi-regular unit sustained heavy casualties in the defence of Singapore.

PHASE TWO, 1942 TO 1945

In a matter of three months the MCP had moved into its second phase: war communism and the resistance movement. This, as far as the Emergency was concerned, was to be its formative phase, and from 1942 to 1945 was a period of material and psychological preparation. As a guerrilla force supplied and equipped in the later stages of the war by long-range aircraft from Ceylon, the Malayan Peoples Anti-Japanese Army, which was largely the MCP in battledress, was neither required to nor did it achieve a high degree of operational efficiency and combat experience. But it was, in a sense, the alternative government for Malaya, two stages removed. First the Japanese had to be defeated. This would be done in conjunction with allied forces; and what would work against the Japanese would also work against a re-established colonial administration. The colonialist-capitalist structure would collapse because of internal contradictions; and there was always the more or less vague assumption that troops from mainland China would assist in the liberation. Indeed, in several villages at the end of the war—which seems to have taken South-East Asia Command and the MCP by surprise and to have confounded one as much as the other—triumphal arches were built to welcome Chinese forces and some of the guerrillas themselves believed that this would actually be the pattern of occupation.

It is difficult to exaggerate the importance of the war and the Japanese occupation in Malaya. In its simplest terms it represented the defeat of European colonialism and the triumph of Asian nationalism. The Japanese victories in 1942, although half-expunged in 1945, had created a sense of possibility. When the colonial powers returned to Asia after what, at least for Malaya, was a bloodless victory, independence was the basic premise of all political activity.

PHASE THREE, 1945 TO 1948

Many advantages were now held by the MCP in the third, or constitutional, phase of its activity which lasted from September 1945 to June 1948. It was a tightly organised party. It possessed, at least comparatively, a high level of political consciousness and determination. And its policy on one level offered the most advanced political program while, on another, it was based on the implicit assumption of an extension of Chinese power.

An extension of Chinese power was also the assumption that was implicit in London and would have been effected had the proposed Malayan Union come into existence. The consequence of this proposal, however, was to arouse if not to create a heightened sense of Malay nationalism, and its obvious affinities with the Indonesian struggle plus some ugly outbreaks of communal butchery would, by themselves, have been enough to occupy the attention of the Malayan security services. In fact, they seem to have been almost preoccupied with the prospect of militant Malay nationalism and although very conscious of the efforts, mostly successful, of the MCP to subvert trade unions, one can see, for example in the importance that was given to Singapore, evidence of a primary concern with imperial considerations.

151

In this constitutional phase of its existence the MCP achieved its greatest though temporary success. By a mixture of promises and intimidation it gained control of union after union and in the Pan-Malayan Federation of Trade Unions it had a weapon which was potentially capable of wrecking the economy. By 1947, a year in which there were three hundred strikes and almost three quarters of a million working days were lost, the MCP had a firm hold on the organised labour force in Malaya. At the same time, its internal organisation was in ruins.

In March 1947 the secretary-general of the MCP disappeared. For some months previously there had been increasing criticism of his 'right-wing' policy and an ugly rumour was circulating that he had been at least a Japanese agent and probably a British agent as well. His disappearance led to an immediate crisis within the party and a majority of its Central Committee was apparently in favour of instant insurrection. Even when the furor had died down the crisis of confidence continued, particularly in the south, and apart from increasing criticism of the leadership there were many defections from the party as well.

This is part of the background against which the decision of the MCP to begin the armed struggle must be judged. Militant trade union activity had been curbed by a recent government ordinance; economic recovery had begun; and there was declining confidence within the party. The more time that elapsed the less likely was it that the Old Comrades' Association of the Anti-Japanese Army would respond to a mobilisation order; and in the event it was shown that three years of peace had greatly reduced the number of potential revolutionaries. There is, however, a widespread belief that the order for an insurrection came from Moscow; that it was obeyed in Malaya; and that it formed part of an integral Soviet pattern for insurrection in South-east Asia.

A good deal of circumstantial evidence has accumulated to support this belief and among the more or less well known items are Zhdanov's article in the Cominform's journal; Chou En-lai's letter to Chin Peng, the secretary-general of the MCP who replaced Loi Tak; the Calcutta communist youth conference of February 1948; and the discussions which the Australian communist, Sharkey, had with the MCP in Singapore shortly afterwards. Against this can be offset this basic appreciation from a Malayan intelligence source.

It may be concluded, therefore, that internal friction and discontent within the Party, the declining influence of the MCP in politics, the improving economic and constitutional situation in Malaya generally, led the MCP leaders to the decision that a radical change of policy was essential if they were to maintain their prestige and influence within the Party. The necessity for a change in policy coincided in period of time with renewed activity on the part of the Soviet in S.E.-Asia, with the S.E.-Asia Youth Conference and the

India Communist Conferences in February and March, 1948. The actual form which the change of policy assumed corresponded to the active and armed revolt upon which the India and Burma Communist Parties had already embarked. The Armed Revolt in Malaya, which probably would have taken place eventually in any case, thus neatly dovetailed into the Soviet scheme, and became part of a policy of revolt intended to embrace all countries of the Far East and South-east Asia.

PHASE FOUR, 1948 TO 1960

Whatever the sufficient cause, the 'armed struggle' between the MCP and the government began in June 1948. In the fourth phase of its history the purpose of the MCP was to disrupt the economy; to engage and defeat the police and the army; to win local support; and thus accomplish its task of overthrowing the colonial government. Compared to the Warsaw Rising of the Polish Home Army in 1944 or to the Jewish campaign in Palestine the Malayan insurrection was badly organised and did not even achieve the first of its objectives: the disruption of the Malayan economy. It would not have been a difficult task to murder practically every European planter and tin miner in the country. Had it been done, had a number of government officials been assassinated and had there been more acts of deliberate sabotage, particularly demolition, the economic mechanism of Malaya would have come to a halt.

This presupposes, however, a high degree of mobilisation, control and efficiency on the part of the MCP forces and this was something that manifestly did not obtain. It was comparatively easy to send a small killer squad into a village, even in daylight, for the purposes of murdering a Kuomintang official or a Chinese detective; and it was not too difficult to muster a hundred and fifty men for an attack on, though seldom the capture of, an isolated rubber estate. Similarly, the natural advantage of surprise attack on small military units, particularly in unarmoured lorries, in country most of which might have been designed for ambush and concealed movement, could usually be pressed home and, in fact, continued throughout the Emergency. But the operational order to which the MCP were soon working called for something far more ambitious: the establishment of 'liberated areas'. A half-hearted attempt was made by certain guerrilla 'regiments'—as these were often no greater than company strength they are better thought of as regional designations—to move into three designated areas but natural infelicities as much as anything caused them to be abandoned.

With their abandonment came a new strategic formula. Stage one was straightforward guerrilla fighting at platoon and section strength. Its purpose was to damage the economy; to inflict heavy casualties on the security forces; and to capture large quantities of arms and ammunition. Stage two was to begin

153

when the guerrillas—now self-styled as the Malayan Races Liberation Army—were strong enough to overrun small Security Force outposts which, it was assumed, would be abandoned by the government. The guerrillas would then be able to operate in company strength from small bases, and the Min Yuen, their supply organisation, would be able to organise the collection of food both from villagers and from their own cultivation areas. Phase three would follow when the 'dominated areas' of phase two were joined up to form a 'liberated area' as a result of increasingly heavy attacks on the security forces; and the last phase, the MCP's Armageddon, would take the form of pitched battles at what was described as Army Corps strength and colonialism would be annihilated.

This was the strategic intention of the MCP. The reality was very different. For the first six months the guerrillas were on the offensive. Estates, mines and police stations were attacked, security forces ambushed, civilians murdered. By the end of the year the objects of attack had held firm, the impact was absorbed, and the MCP had lost its first and greatest opportunity of success. Its frustration, in large part, must be attributed to the decision of the commissioner general in South-east Asia, Malcolm MacDonald, that the available security forces—a police force of some 9,000 men and approximately eight full strength British, Gurkha and Malay infantry battalions—should be used to guard installations that were vital to the 'life, economy and employment of the country'. In this period the security forces for the most part were fighting blind and although they reduced the scale of their operations to platoon and section level—which was the scale of Malayan jungle warfare—much quicker than some reports suggest, they were operating on a skeletal and disarticulated intelligence framework and the contacts between them and the guerrillas were, in so far as the security forces were concerned, largely fortuitous.

Nevertheless, the MCP never got beyond stage one of its strategic plan and by the beginning of 1949, on account of its initial failure and disruption, its armed units withdrew into the jungle to reorganise, recruit and retrain. Confidence in the power of government to withstand the MCP assault was to some extent re-established in 1949 when the emergency measures which had been taken at the outset—the raising of a large force of Special Constables for the guarding of mines and estates, and the arrival of reinforcements in the shape of ex-Palestine police-men and the Brigade of Guards—were strengthened by the more effective imposition of the Emergency Regulations proper.

Perhaps the most drastic of these regulations was the power of mass detention and deportation which, in 1949, resulted in the deportation of six thousand Chinese. Powers of arrest and detention were considerably increased, new crimes, such as consorting with bandits, were written into the statute book, dawn to dusk curfews were introduced throughout the Federation and restrictions of all kinds were imposed to deny support to the armed guerrillas and masses organisation of the MCP.   Nevertheless there was still a binomial quality to government policy and such integration as there was between the military and the civil functions of government was essentially on an *ad hoc* basis.

In April 1950, General Sir Harold Briggs arrived in Kuala Lumpur to take up his post as the first director of operations.   His arrival coincided with the mounting of an increasingly powerful communist offensive which, for the next two years, was to keep the country at full stretch.   That it was withstood at this time and subsequently is in large part due to the analysis which Briggs made and the plan which he submitted to the British Defence Co-ordination Committee on May 24, 1950.

This was a counter-guerrilla classic.   Guerrillas, whether in Spain, Mexico, Yugoslavia, China, Cuba or Malaya, rely upon popular support.   Without it, they wither and die.   The popular support in Malaya was engineered by the Min Yuen, the 'masses organisation', and this, said Briggs, was able to exist and function in populated areas mainly because the population as a whole lacked confidence in the ability of the forces of law and order to protect them against communist extortion and terrorism.   Information—intelligence, in the military sense—which was essential if the Min Yuen and the guerrillas (here Briggs used the fashionable understatement 'bandits') were to be eliminated, was quite inadequate.   The problem, as Briggs saw it, was to extend effective administration and control of all populated areas.   The domination of these areas and the creation of a feeling of complete security within them, would yield a steady and increasing flow of information from all sources.   This would contribute to the breaking up of the Min Yuen; guerrillas would thereby be isolated from their food and intelligence organisation; and be finally destroyed as they were forced to attack the security forces on their own ground.

Effective administration, domination and control of all populated areas meant, in short, the establishment of more or less popular government over the whole country: the less consent, the more control that was necessary, until government in totality was sometimes indistinguishable from the totalitarian form.   One sector of the population that had been conspicuously immune to government was the 'squatters', some 500,000 Chinese who had been leading a peasant's existence since and largely on account of the Japanese occupation.   Their small-holdings of a few acres of vegetables and fruit, a few pigs and ducks had been cleared from secondary jungle and abandoned plantations on what was still state land.   But the cause of concern was not their technically illegal (though often socially profitable) occupation.   It was the fact that they provided the guerrillas with their principal support.

Squatter resettlement was therefore one of the priorities of the Briggs Plan—

155

optimistically, it was thought that the essential resettlement program would have been completed by the beginning of 1952—but an equally important part was the integration of military and civil functions from top to bottom of the administration. At the top, a Federal War Council was created while at the level of states and settlements and districts, War Executive Committees were made responsible for executive action.

Strategically, the plan was to clear the country from south to north and the army order of battle called for thirteen battalions in the states of Johore, Negri Sembilan and south-west Pahang. Tactically, the army's job was to dominate the jungle up to about five hours' journey from the guerrilla supply areas with the object of forcing them to fight, disintegrate, or leave the area.

Throughout 1950 and 1951 the security forces were fighting a war of attrition. Reinforcements continued to arrive from the Commonwealth. Police forces, special constabulary and home guard continued to expand within the country— too fast at one point as was shown by heavy casualties and loss of weapons—while weapons and military supplies also arrived in increasing quantities. But militarily this was a patrol war: ten or twelve men on either side, hundreds of hours walking, waiting, wading, slithering, climbing and the few seconds of combat with a fleeting enemy. It was sustained, on the one side, by the professional pride of the regular soldiers, by the knowledge, for the national serviceman, that his was a limited engagement of eighteen or twenty-four months, and above all, for the Malay policemen, by the determination to destroy the armed insurrection of an alien race.

For the guerrilla, hungry, sick, uncertain whether his next round would fire or his last grenade explode, constantly hunted and for whom a serious wound meant capture or a lingering death, determination or fanaticism may have been enough to keep him in the jungle but hope was essential if he was to continue fighting and, moreover, to have thoughts ever of emerging from it. For the Asian communist, 1950 and 1951 were the years of hope. In fact, from 1948 onwards the Emergency in Malaya has to be seen in relation to the rising tide of communism, its greatest quantitative victory in China and a massive and temporarily successful intervention in the Korean war. If this was the wave of the future, if Chinese communism was destined to reassert its influence over the Nanyang Chinese, then the effects were twofold. First, it was a material and tangible reinforcement for the inevitable, but distant triumph that was built into Marxist dialectical logic. Second, it reinforced the attractions of domestic neutralism for the Chinese community at large—unless and until an alternative focus for Asian, and principally Chinese, loyalty could be found.

From 1946 onwards, more or less vague intentions of independence had been evident on the part of the British government. In 1946 the Malayan Union proposals envisaged 'that political adjustment' which would offer the means and

156

prospect of developing Malaya's capacity in the direction of responsible self-government, and although this 'adjustment', which would have been favourable to the Chinese, was aborted by Malay opposition, the revised Agreement of 1948 again mentioned self-government and spoke of 'election of members of the several legislatures' as soon as circumstances and local conditions would permit. In the event, these elections did not take place for seven years but when they did, they were the prologue to independence rather than a manipulated routine to support some puppet régime; and in the meantime, although well over a million Chinese were excluded from citizenship, and thus debarred from voting, representative government had begun at the lowest levels—local councils—particularly in the 'New Villages'.

'New Villages' was the name given to the four hundred resettlement areas ranging in size from less than a hundred to well over ten thousand inhabitants which were, for the most part, what their name announced: entirely new villages. They were enclosed by barbed wire, guarded, and provided, eventually, with elementary social services and a form of self-government. The determination to turn what were often poor prototypes into viable and acceptable models and to transform the Briggs design into a going concern was perhaps the most enduring contribution that General Templer made to the political infrastructure of the new Malaya, although he is more often remembered for his violent impact on the country.

Templer arrived in Malaya in February 1952 at a time when the country's morale was probably at its lowest. Three months earlier, Sir Henry Gurney, the high commissioner, had been killed in a road ambush and, although a fortuitous guerrilla success, it coincided with a bad month—heavy casualties in another ambush, evidence of bad resettlement, premonitions of racial strife—and it was followed, in November, by the worst week of the Emergency. Accompanying these guerrilla successes was the hint of government failure. The director of intelligence had resigned: a result of personal differences. The commissioner of police left so hurriedly that there could be no doubt that he had been fired. And, instead of promoting Gurney's deputy—which local experience alone would have suggested—the government brought in Templer, an entirely new man, to combine the roles of high commissioner and director of operations.

There is no denying the drive, indeed the ruthlessness, which Templer brought to his job as supreme commander. Civil servants were shaken out of their routine, the European business community were indicted for complacency and racialism, the inefficient were dismissed. All over the country Templer ranged in search of the wicked, the timorous and the slothful. 'Put up your hands, those of you who are communists', he said at one New Village meeting. The response, not surprisingly, was negative; and this, in turn, brought a reduction

157

in the rice ration and a house curfew of twenty-two hours out of twenty-four. His critics declared that Templer's methods were going to lose the war. When he left, at the end of 1954, it was obvious that the war was being won and a year later, when the MCP triumvirate emerged from the jungle at the border town of Baling, it seemed that the end of the insurrection was in sight.

To understand the Baling meeting, however, it is necessary to go back to September 1951 and one of the rare meetings of the Central Committee of the MCP. What emerged from this meeting was a political and ideological paper— the 'October Directives'—which was recovered; and probably an operational order, which was not. The former were a confession of failure: as communists and guerrillas. As guerrillas they had cut themselves off from the masses: a mistake and a consequence which was inherent in their 'inadequate mastery of Marxism-Leninism'. In the past, said the Central Committee, the party had suffered from both 'rightist 'and 'leftist' deviation and only the year before, in its *Guide to the Anti-Resettlement Struggle,* the Central Politburo had, they confessed, 'caused the masses to suffer more losses and evoked their doubts regarding the correctness of Party leadership and even dissatisfaction against Party leadership'. Henceforward, the supreme criterion was whether party tasks and policies as well as activities were supported and accepted by broad sections of the masses; and where in the past they had alienated the masses by stealing their identity cards, burning buses and slashing rubber trees (throwing grenades into a crowded cinema show and similar incidents were tactfully left unmentioned), in the future they were to concentrate their military activities against the Security Forces.

A year later, these directives had seeped down to the smallest of the guerrilla formation, and from September 1952 there was a marked drop in civilian casualties. The party as a whole had gone over to a variant of the United Front policy—for example it was stated that no excessive demands should be made upon the petty-bourgeoisie in the 'workers' and peasants' struggle'—but as part of the 'development work' more effort was to be made to subvert existing (legal) trade unions while illegal ones should be created in rural areas. In general, the MCP was trying to reintegrate itself in the community; it recommended a study of Mao Tse-tung as a specific against the deviations of the past; and it pinned its hopes on a favourable international situation.

All this was no doubt necessary, both as an ideological purge and in order to make 'correct' decisions in the future, but it was hardly enough for the armed units. From the change of tactics which followed the October Directives one may reasonably infer, however, that there was a fresh operational order, three consequences of which were: the setting-up of deep jungle bases for reorganisation and retraining as well as for jungle cultivation which was to be the main source of food supply; making use of the sizeable aborigine population to help in jungle cultivation and to provide a human radar screen around the deep jungle bases; and the merging of the Min Yuen and the armed guerrilla units into what are still called Armed Work Forces—which meant the disbandment of most of the regular units.

For the next four years the MCP attempted, with modifications, to make this policy work. Jungle cultivation, however, was immune neither to poisonous chemicals sprayed from the air nor to security forces launched from helicopters or dropped by parachute—not to mention the ravages of wild animals. Aborigine supporters of the guerrillas could also be won over, and where resettlement of these nomads had failed, sometimes disastrously, they responded to the security provided by 'jungle forts' and even more to the social, and especially medical, services that went with them.

By 1955, the MCP's fortunes were waning at all three levels of its activity. The number of major public incidents had dropped from the 1951 average of two hundred a month to less than twenty. In the jungle, another 'fine and private place', their organisation was disrupted by unceasing attacks. While on the third level, that of subversion and penetration, although achieving some local successes, notably in Singapore, they had succeeded neither in disrupting the economy nor in subverting the major political parties that were emerging in Malaya.

In this lay their last chance—or would have done if communists ever admitted that there was such a thing. With the elections of 1955, Malaya was on the threshold of independence; and at the end of 1955 the MCP made its last major attempt to reintegrate themselves in the community and to attune themselves to the national aspirations. After a good deal of hesitation, havering and apprehension, the principal ministers of Malaya and Singapore, Tengku Abdul Rahman, Dato' Sir Tan-Cheng Lock and Mr David Marshall, met Chin Peng at Baling in December 1955. Chin Peng, it seems in retrospect, was under an illusion: that it would be possible for the MCP to lay down their arms (which did not apparently mean surrendering them) and to continue as a legitimate political party. To go back, in effect, to square one.

When this proved impossible, the MCP issued this statement: 'As soon as the elected government of the Federation attains control of internal security and local armed forces we will end the hostilities, lay down our arms and disband our forces': one which they must surely have regretted since. For eighteen months it would have been possible to maintain the fiction that Malaya would not, in fact, become truly independent. But with independence an accomplished fact on August 31, 1957, the last support was knocked away from the MCP's pretensions to be the party of national liberation. This was not, of course, something that was admitted immediately by the party and its armed supporters and in the

159

interim period between Baling and Merdeka they had singled out Chinese Home Guards as an object of attack in Johore and, in the same state, had surprisingly still been able to attract a number of recruits from Chinese schools.

A state of Emergency still existed; but with MCP confidence at its lowest ebb it was virtually over by 1958. Military operations were based on the principle of the concentration of forces and continuous patrol effort while on the civil side the population continued to be rewarded for its co-operation with government. In two senses: by the policy of 'white areas' where the Emergency Regulations were lifted and people could enjoy something like a normal existence; and by a realistic but unpleasant policy of paying heavily for all information that led to the 'elimination' of guerrillas. Other things being equal and making allowance for some hair-raising exploits by the Special Branch, it was the prospect of bringing in so many hundred thousand dollars 'on the hoof' that led to at least some of the spectacular mass surrenders of 1959 where ranking members of the MCP brought their comrades out with them.

PHASE FIVE

Today, the remnant of the organised MCP is to be found, as they occasionally are, in the five hundred neo-guerrillas on the Malayan border with Thailand. For the most part they have given up their guerrilla activities and have become political bandits: levying contributions on the local population, posing as their champions against haphazard government, murdering occasionally in cases of non-payment or betrayal, but for the most part keeping to themselves. They are a sort of Sherwood Forest branch of the MCP and in the conceivable future they might serve as a nucleus of a resurgent guerrilla communism in Malaya. What is far more likely, however, is that theirs is essentially a country membership, useful but expendable, and that the MCP is now in the fifth phase of its existence: the return to subversion. The Emergency is over. The political struggle continues.

TABLE 11. STRENGTH OF GUERRILLA FORCES 1950–1*

Malayan Races Liberation Army	3,250
Min Yuen Units (partly armed service corps)	3,800
'Masses executives' (intelligence and material support units outside jungle)	7,400

* The guerrillas were probably at their greatest strength at this time.

TABLE 12. CASUALTIES DURING THE EMERGENCY

	Killed	Wounded	Captured or Missing	Surrendered
Guerrillas	6,711	n.a.	1,289	2,704
Security Forces	1,865	2,560	—	—
Civilians	2,473	1,385	810	—

PART THREE

Society and Culture

11

The Peoples of North and West Borneo

TOM HARRISSON

In 1958, during excavations organised by the Sarawak Museum at Niah caves, 300 miles north-east of Kuching and 100 miles south-west of Brunei,* we found what is almost certainly the oldest known Asian skull of *Homo sapiens*, 'Modern Man', at a level well below 35,000 years ago.[1]   Hitherto, only the remains of earlier 'ape men' (like Java Man) had been discovered in South-east Asia—except for considerably more *recent* skulls and skeletons in the caves of Malaya and elsewhere, the oldest not yet dating back beyond 10,000 years.

This is not to claim any special position for the history and prehistory of man (and woman) in west Borneo.   Certainly, more thorough archaeological search on the mainland will reveal people with modern brain capacities of early date over a much wider area.   What is important about the Niah skull is that it establishes, for the first time, the fact that a 'modern' type of man was present in this part of the world much longer ago than previously supposed.   It had been thought that he (we) developed over a great period in the Middle East and elsewhere, only reaching the Far East much later.   That view is no longer acceptable.   The ancestors of our present-day population were present, even in a remote corner of Borneo, back at the very beginnings of civilisation as we now understand it.

This and other new results from cave excavations are beginning to document a continuous story of human occupation and development over three hundred centuries.   It is becoming clear that this was on a much larger scale and much more diversified than we had thought.   The picture of a few timid savages, upon

---

* Throughout this chapter, reference is made, where necessary, to the peoples of the state of Brunei for purposes of comparison with the peoples of Sabah and Sarawak.

163

whom descended waves of migrants with ever-increasing degrees of sophistication, is now too thin as a theory for the growth of Malaysian population.

In this chapter, I wish to approach the problems of human diversity particularly from the Borneo angle.[2] I choose this angle because—largely for geographical reasons to be discussed presently—a wide range of civilisation has grown up
throughout this great island, often almost independently of passing outside influences. In Malaya itself, the picture is not so clear. In particular, Islam has been
longer and much more fully established on the peninsula. The remaining non-
muslim peoples are few, scattered, and in important respects culturally impoverished. These groups, generally and rather unfortunately classed as 'aborigines'
in Malaya, include plenty of Negritos. There are, however, no living Negritos in
Borneo. But there are strong indications that they did exist in the late stone age,
and were subsequently swamped by and merged into bigger-bodied and more
virile folk, as part of the unceasing flow and change of Borneo's immense human
dynamic.

The nearest thing to the Malayan aborigine in Borneo is the nomadic Punan.
There are some 15,000 Punans, mostly in Kalimantan (Indonesian Borneo). They
move in small groups over very large jungle areas, and detest coming out into the
sunlight. They live—and often live well—principally on wild sago and the game
they shoot with well made hardwood blowpipes. Although timid and hard to
know, the Punans are immensely tough, intelligent and perceptive. And they
make exquisitely patterned black and white mats of the highest quality, perhaps
the finest craftsmanship of any Borneo people and among the finest mats made in
the world. These nomads are very far from being barbarians.

Malaya itself is, today, a country without any large native population other
than the Malays. It can accurately be described as a Malay country. Borneo is
not a Malay country in the Malayan sense, and for the successful achievement and
survival of Malaysia, it is very necessary to face this fact clearly and at all times.
The total population of the island is uncertain, but probably is now about four
million. Of this, under half a million *regard themselves* as Malays. This question of
self-regard is crucial as we shall see below. Other groups are muslim. But this
does not necessarily mean that they consider themselves to be *Malays*. In fact,
among some of these other muslim groups, there is a tendency to dissociate
from the Malays or regard them as *very* different. Thus the Bajaus in Sabah are
probably closer to the Dusuns than to the adjacent coastal Malays from Brunei.
And the 13,000 muslim Kedayans, within Brunei itself, were one major factor in
causing the revolt against the government in this muslim state, with whom this
minority was out of sympathy.[3]

Accurate figures on religious and other groupings are only available for the three 'British' territories from a complete census undertaken in 1960. Fuller reference will be made to the implications of this census later on. For the moment, here are the figures for the three main religious groupings:

TABLE 13. RELIGIONS IN 1960 AS PERCENTAGES OF ALL FAITHS GIVEN

State	Muslim	Christian	Animist, etc.	Muslim Increase/Decrease since last Census
Sarawak	23·4	15·8	60·8	−1·2 (since 1947)
Sabah	37·9	16·6	45·5	+3·9 (since 1951)
Brunei	60·2	8·1	31·7	−6·9 (since 1947)

On the other hand, the crude statistics obscure two important other facts. Firstly, that the muslim faith is much more uniform (*Sunni*) and deeper-seated than the rest. Second, that well over 95 per cent of all Borneo Malays are strictly island people and not of immigrant Malayan origin.

Although western Borneo was almost the last and furthest place from Mecca to receive the message of Islam (about AD 1440), the faith has since grown slowly but relatively undisturbed.[4] Owing to the tormented geography of the interior, however, it seldom spread further inland than the coastal plain. A large part of the inland population, under Brunei's nominal rule for centuries, remained animist pagan. It is only since the Japanese War (1941–5) and under British Colonial Office rule that the elaborate systems of interior animism have been suddenly influenced by christian missionaries. Conversions of whole 'tribes' have taken place, largely assisted by the use of small aircraft and other modern technological devices.

However, considerable confusion has been caused in that not one but *several* christian sects have been competitive over the same interiors. At one stage, in the early 1950s, intersectarian competition was so intense that it was possible for there to be three independent services in a large long-house on the same Sunday and a fourth the following Saturday (Seventh Day Adventists). This sudden series of impacts is now producing some curious reactions. Perhaps the most conspicuous is a reversion, especially among the Kayans, to a new agglomeration of both christian and animist attitudes: the *Bungan Malan* cult (from the Kenyahs' benevolent goddess of that name).[5]

The second qualification to the above table is equally significant, at another level. The present-day Malay and other muslim population almost entirely lives along the monsoonal west coastline and the broad belt of mangrove swamps, or on the sandy flatland behind the coast. This is not, as so many writers assume, a population which has migrated *en masse* into Borneo from *outside* as either Malays or muslims. On the contrary, in some cases whole groups and more often many individuals (cutting across groups) have been converted to Islam over the last five centuries from out of the indigenous, previously pagan, population. The present-day sultanate of Brunei has been muslim for twenty-eight successions: some of them extremely brief! But the first sultan was a converted pagan, perhaps of the Bisaya group, and the sultanate dates back at least another seven centuries and was centred on the wonderfully rich habitation site of the old capital, Kota Batu.[6]

There is also documentary evidence in the curious bamboo 'manuscripts' of the Philippines, the *Maragtas*, that probably before AD 1350 the Brunei Bay aristocracy split. A powerful minority led by Datu Puteh or Pateh sailed north in long boats and established an upper crust of higher culture in the southern islands of the group, involving millions of people now called Visaya (cf. Bisaya).[7]

Further south-west in Borneo, even along the coastal plain, Islam spread comparatively slowly, largely owing to the difficulties of navigation by sailing in these waters, and to opposition from scattered but powerful pagan groups. The aristocratic Malays of Kuching, capital of Sarawak, mainly trace descent from a marriage between the royal houses of Johore and 'Jawa'; but most ordinary Malays trace direct back to Dayaks, particularly Melanaus, who still occupy large areas of coastal plain as the world's primary sago producers (over 40,000 of whom are still pagan: 1960 census). Malay family trees also show early Chinese associations; for instance, the second muslim sultan of Brunei married the daughter of the Ming admiral, Ong Sum Ping, who led a junk fleet to Kota Batu about AD 1460.[8]

Against this background, it is natural enough that Borneo Malays share many common attitudes and ways of life with their neighbours, irrespective of religion, and sometimes on quite a local basis. This situation has been maintained by continuing difficulties in communications and slow day-to-day intercourse over a terrain which is much more complicated than any other in South-east Asia, at least until we reach as far east as New Guinea. This complex of historical and geographical factors in and around Borneo has produced special patterns of living and surprising variations, both along the fifteen hundred miles of coastline from Tawau to Tanjong Datu and equally far inland along the vast mountain meander of the Kalimantan border.[9]

One result is that most Sarawak Malays, for instance, have a more variable and in some respects more 'Dayak' outlook than their namesakes elsewhere on the mainland. This can be seen if the reader looks at Dr Raymond Firth's standard study of fishermen in Malaya, in conjunction with our figures for man-days at three of the largest coastal 'fishing villages' in south-west Borneo.[10] The data cover altogether just over 470,000 man-days for 1962.[11]

TABLE 14

| | Percentage of sample man-days gainfully spent at work mainly on: | |
Village	Water	Land
Santubong	65	35
Bako	67	33
Sematan (bauxite)	19	81

Bako is the nearest to a 'pure' fishing village in the area. Yet a third of the main effort in 1962 was spent on such jobs as:

TABLE 15

Land Job (Sample)	Man-days
Rubber Tapping (own)	9,582
Coconuts (own and Chinese)	8,954
Mixed Gardening (tapioca, bananas, etc.)	8,672
Jungle Produce and Hunting	5,459
Swamp Produce (mangrove and nipah)	5,403
Durians (local 1962 crop failed)	277

For the whole Sarawak river delta zone, parallel figures give an annual man-day work count averaging out about 41 per cent fishing and boats, 34 per cent agriculture (over a quarter of this is own rubber) and swamp produce collecting.

Time spent in resting, holidays and sickness has not been included in the present consideration: it can be a large factor (e.g. during Bulan Puasa).

At many places up the seemingly endless Bornean coastline, long stretches of seemingly good land and teemingly rich sea are still empty of human activity. This is in part a reflection of the very gradual growth and extension of coastal civilisation in Borneo. Also, it reflects the correspondingly slow build-up of other peoples inland, separated by long and often difficult stretches of a river which until very recent times have been the only forms of ordinary communication over most of the whole island. Thus it comes about that the lowlands are, with some notable exceptions, seldom fully populated: this despite the early growth of an impressive, if 'primitive', form of civilisation around Niah caves and at other sub-coastal points where there was a great flowering of human energy in the stone age.

Anyone who flies across Borneo will equally be struck by the enormous expanses of virgin jungle, unbroken green forest canopy, which pass below for twenty or even thirty minutes at a time. Over seventy per cent of the land is still under rain forest which has never been felled. Much of this wild land is only hunted by small bands of nomadic Punans with their *pi* dogs and poisoned darts. Nevertheless along the lines of the great navigable rivers, and again on the far interior uplands, table-lands and plateaux between 1,000 and 4,000 feet, large and successful groups have come to anchor and stayed to develop local cultures and languages unlike anything else seen beyond themselves. Although these inland peoples have much in common, to the outsider the differences between them usually appear more striking than the similarities. Thus, while nearly all of them (except southern Dusuns) live in long-houses, the enormous riverside Kenyah houses, which are basically arranged on a graded class structure (both socially and physically), are almost dramatically different from the smaller, but extremely well-planned and psychologically taut long-houses of the mountain Kelabits, with their elaboration of individual, family, kin, friendship and group living under a common roof.[12]

There are almost as many ways of considering the classification of Bornean human groups as there are anthropologists and others ready—sometimes eager— so to classify. 'Cultural' criteria have been popular in recent times. From my own knowledge, in all four of the Borneo territories, there are so many other factors complicating, overlaying, occasionally undercutting the cultural pattern, that in the end, whenever a really thorough study along this line is complete, one tends to find oneself back where one started: in a sort of cultural haze! Particularly in a country like this, it is hopelessly artificial to try and isolate the living cultures of today simply *in the present*. It is essential to understand how they have grown up. It is needful to recognise the intricacy of exchanges: exchanges of ideas and things just as much as of people and words. These have gone to make up all sorts of equations and intermixtures, sometimes in quite simple and sometimes manifestly very complex groupings.

Among the more complex groupings, prior place might perhaps be given to the Melanaus, a people with a very rich cultural background, extending back in time to the Painted Cave at Niah through the dynamic local climax of the T'ang dynasty and trade with China; and in place to the remote Njadgu people of southeast Borneo, whose religious and related activities have fortunately been the subject of one of the very few really thorough and adequately understood depth-studies yet undertaken in this part of the world.[13] But even the people clearly recognisable as Melanaus today—all speaking a common language—have been, as it were, culturally hung, drawn and quartered in the past two or three centuries. For one thing, a broad wedge of aggressive and expanding Iban Sea Dayaks from the south and Kayans from the north-east (c. 1800–80) drove into Melanau territory and bisected the main grouping into divided geographical areas, with no physical contact between them. One of these relic groups, remaining essentially Melanau, is the so-called Kajang in a dozen or so poor long-houses, physically intermixed with quite 'other' peoples around Belaga up in the headwaters of the Rejang river.

The large element of Melanaus who moved out on to the coastal plain partly to escape from these and some earlier pressures, have themselves been bisected—and one segment lost to the Melanau people as such—by the advance of Islam along the coast. There is the well known story of the two twin boys born to pagan Melanau parents in the sago country of the great Rejang delta. The elder boy, by a few minutes, grew up to marry a Melanau girl. His offspring are Melanau. The fractionally younger boy falling in love with a Malay girl in a nearby village, married her, '*masok melayu*', became a muslim. His children are Malays. He is no longer Melanau. Latterly this situation has been further confused by a considerable growth in Roman Catholicism through the lowland Melanau country; and a burst of activity by an Australian Baptist mission operating on the far inland segment at Belaga since 1950. To this, for accuracy, we must add a very important influence, especially on smaller outlayers of the Melanaus, from adjacent different language groupings. Thus the Belaga segment is scattered over a very wide stretch of two rivers, interspersed among Kenyahs and Kayans of separate growth, with a distinctive class and long-house system, other sets of omens, death and agricultural beliefs, rituals, etc.

Where, as in the case of the Belaga Melanaus, the group as a whole is not strong and numerous enough to live on its own cultural, social and marital resources, in varied degree it influences and is influenced by such neighbours. This is particularly so where there is a strong traditional upper class. The intermarriage of aristocratic Kenyans/Kayans into—and sometimes over the heads of—the Melanaus, has played quite an important part in reorientating the cultural development of the groups.

Thus, while it is possible to get a fairly coherent and simplified picture of a particular aspect of Melanau culture by sticking to a small group of houses—or one set of customs—the moment we start to extend and try to reach a comprehensive idea of 'Melanauism' in general, we find ourselves faced with a multiplicity of definitions, categories and qualifications. We are then confronted with the impossibility of interpreting these results except in terms of historical origin and development—and indeed, to be adequate, prehistorical as well. This involves not only the Melanaus, but the whole island context. Of course, this sort of difficulty is not in any manner of means confined to Borneans. But it is unusually difficult in Borneo. This is partly so because of already mentioned factors of geography, linked to the very long local traditions and origins in prehistory, back to the very root-stock of Niah *Homo sapiens*.

If, then, at this stage in our knowledge we have to admit a measure of defeat in trying simply to analyse or categorise Borneo's human groupings on cultural

169

terms, it would seem alternatively hopeful to use the criteria of physical anthropology. Unfortunately, here again, the more we learn, the less satisfactory the rather oversimplified initial picture becomes. The more we measure and observe, the more overlaps appear. This is particularly so when a detailed analysis is made, for instance, of human teeth, both over a wide arc of west Borneo and over a wide time-span of history and prehistory. Satisfying distinctions between even such big categories as 'mongoloid' and 'melanoid' dentitions are, due to recent research based largely on the rich Niah caves material, looking very shaky now (1963). In fact (and not to put too fine a point upon it), the long established science of physical anthropology has not to date spoken out a single valid message for a place like Borneo. I suspect, in fact, far too much has been made of too little strictly objective and measured evidence.

In using physical criteria, also, secondary and usually irrelevant considerations can often confuse the observer. Thus, the habit of chewing betel-nut, or the use of a head-band in carrying padi baskets, can produce important secondary transformations in facial physique which have no genetic origin. Take away the throat tattoo from an Iban Sea Dayak youth, cut his hair short and sew up the incisions in his ear-lobes, and it is magical how he ceases to look Dayak at all. Recently, I undertook some simple tests to try and clear the mind's eye a little in this respect. Though further work of the same kind is of course needed, my initial impression is simply this: if you mix up Kayan, Iban, Melanau, Dusun, Land Dayak, Malay and Sibu Chinese, take all young men of the same age, and line them up in an identity parade, it is doubtful if any anthropologist in the world could guess their 'races' even fifty per cent correctly. The chances of being accurate may well be about the same as statistical chance itself.[14]

Not that there is anything very mysterious about this. As I have been trying to indicate, the fundamental underlying characteristics are very different—so different that the people holding one set of such characteristics may in the final challenge be prepared to kill (or be killed) in support of maintaining these over against another group with a different set of nevertheless similar standards. The present distribution and differentiation of peoples in Borneo can only be understood if this is always appreciated as part of a process which has gone on for thousands of years past and which—to a much larger extent than is perhaps realised—remains under the surface today.

A third promising approach is the linguistic one. There are at least forty distinct Borneo languages. These are distinct in that a Kayan put down among Kelabits will not understand a word. Even among peoples often treated as speaking minor dialect-variants of a common tongue, the differences may be very large: for example as between the Selakau (Mount Poi) and Bidayuh (Kedup) branches of 'Land Dayak'. There is no common Borneo language or word base, except in so far as 'bazaar Malay' is widely understood—and Iban is fairly near some Malay. Once more, the subject is a big one; and it has not been systematically tackled to provide clear definitions up to the present. If anything, the recent attitude has been to neglect the smaller languages—naturally enough—and hope some common form (or sense) may appear out of the present Babel. Meanwhile, the problems posed, even at the simple levels of informing the people about new nationalisms and goals, are severe. As Drs Cense and Uhlenbeck have well said, in a recent authoritative survey:[15]

> Published data consist mainly of incidental remarks of explorers and travellers, who in their works occasionally also included word lists, terms for various institutions and sometimes a few set phrases or isolated words. The most important contribution to the knowledge of many Bornean languages is due to missionary effort. The Bible translations and other translations of Christian literature, valuable when no original texts are available, are for many languages often practically the only source of information. It is impossible to provide a reliable picture of the present linguistic situation on the island by means of these data.

Another approach to this vexed complex is through *origins*, group traditions, whence they came, how; and how they kept together (or fell apart). Here the people themselves sometimes help, by keeping detailed genealogies, integrated with fine and protracted sung folk-sagas, spelling out in detail a mixture of legendary and real deeds performed by their ancestors back into the mists of myth and monstrosity. This type of information has proved to relate factually to archaeology on a number of occasions during our Sarawak Museum studies, since 1947. Many a folk-lore reference to a place or incident has subsequently been supported by the stratified evidence of excavation *in situ*. I have come to respect a large amount in the spoken and sung epics of the hitherto illiterate (in written terms) islanders as directly based on, if not always reflective of, actual events in the past. Only, one must not take their actual *sequences* as reliable without outside confirmation.

Three main conclusions to be drawn from this sort of 'original' data deserve emphasis here. From these it will be clear that again the final outline is far from simple and that this approach to Borneo peoples remains incomplete as well as intricate. I should add that attempts to arrange and clarify peoples by folk-lore content, special ethnographical traits and so on, have so far all proved ineffective to deal with the richly intertwined inland cultures and their long, long story of physical mobility plus physiological interchange.

1. There is precious little evidence, at any period, for any *orderly* and successive or logically spaced *waves of migrants*, that is to say bodies of men, who are supposed—

by nearly every authority—to have moved along, through or past Borneo in prehistorical times. One writer has repeated the next with tiresome monotony, adopting gross assumptions about race, purpose and route. We shall have to discount most of this writing (and this whole way of thinking) to get at a true idea of how such a complex human society was built up, since the start of *Homo sapiens* at Niah.

2. In my view, the migratory wave approach in general has been much over-done. Instead, we need to look far more for movements of population develop-ing from internal numerical growth and other dynamics within Borneo itself and in the *immediately* surrounding places (notably the Celebes, southern Philippines, Sumatra and—across the sea—the gulf of Siam round to the Yellow River). Much of this influence has been sporadic, or of few actual persons, or of persons coming and going (e.g., in seasonal trade traffic). A single man could bring a new set of ideas—just as did the first Arab sheikhs to Brunei in the fifteenth cen-tury, and four Australian Bible-thumpers to central Borneo in the middle of the twentieth.

3. As we fill in the archaeological picture, we see that in protohistorical times a great disturbance and shift of peoples occurred through the island, affecting the first full 'Sarawak Malays' about 16 generations ago, the Sea Dayak push from the south-east over into west Borneo (19–20 generations), and even the Murut-Kelabits in the further hinterlands (*circa* 16–17 generations).

But if any group appears to be culturally and topographically stable—indeed isolated and 'cut off from outside impact'—it is the Kelabits. In reality, no group anywhere in this huge, tangled tropic island (a cultural *continent* it is) ever really stayed out of any main or side stream for long. The impacts were multiple, though maybe eccentric, erratic, or frankly incoherent.[16]

One of the best documented human moves of a more 'logical' character is the spread of the Iban Sea Dayaks north-west across from the Kalimantan Kapuas headwaters into what is now southern Sarawak. Look at one of the many Iban genealogies in the Sarawak Museum's ethno-archives; this one collected by generation number 29 herein. One can incidentally see how inappropriate the term 'Sea Dayak' really is for the story of a people moving for centuries across the mountains from the immense hinterland of south-east Borneo over to the west, ending up (in this case) at Sarawak's tidewater head of culture and commerce, the capital Kuching. Where descent is in the female line the name is italicised below:

1. Beji—who lived in the lower Kapuas (Kalimantan).
   |
2. Nisi—who moved up the Kapuas.
   |

172

3. Antu Berambayan—who lived in the middle river.

   |

4. Telichi—whose wife (*Dara Sia*) owned the first of the ancient *rusa*, Chinese
      stoneware jars.

   |

5. Gila Gundi Sepit.

   |

6. Retak Dai—who colonised the upper Kapuas headwaters.

   |

7. Serapoh—who introduced new death rites (cf. *Sarawak Museum Journal*, x, 1962.
      19).

8. *Remi.*

   |

9. Menggin—who married the daughter of the great cult hero, Singalang
      Burong (while she was still the spouse of Katupong, the Rufous
      Piculet of high omen).

   |

10. Surong Gunting—who led the first migration over the waterhead into the
       Batang Lupar, east of Engkilili (= Sarawak, ? c. AD 1500).

   |

11. Surong Kempat.

   |

12. *Ridoh* m. Bada.

   |

13. *Gupi* m. Gerasi.

   |

14. Geraman ('Ensoh').

   |

15. *Beragai* m. Chundau.

   |

16. Beti.

   |

17. Talak.

   |

18. *Badas* m. Girik.

   |

19. Belaki.

   |

20. Penyut.

   |

21. *Juring* m. Busu—who colonised the lower Paku (Saribas).

|

22. Uyut.

|

23. *Pala* m. Renggi.

|

24. Kalanang—who killed off the Brunei tax collectors.

|

25. Uyut—who continued anti-Brunei.

|

26. Linggir—Penghulu under the regime of the first Brooke rajah.

|

27. *Umang* m. Garran—who drove back other tribes round Kapit (Rejang).

|

28. Attat.

|

29. Benedict Sandin—Museum Research Assistant.

|

30. *Umang* m. (1962) Edmund Sumbang.

|

31. *Cherembang* b. 1964.

These genealogies, many of which are recorded in Iban *tusut* lore, regularly correspond back to the level of Menggin (generation 9), who also appears under different guises as a similarly migratory ancestral hero of some of the Land Dayaks (Serian and Bau districts). The earlier figures are shadowy, as is even more the case with interior Kayan and Kenyah family trees. But all the available proto-historical evidence adds up to a reasonable supposition that the Ibans, now the biggest single ethnic unit in west Borneo, first entered 'Sarawak' about 20 generations ago (450 years by Iban early-marriage calculation?) back from Benedict Sandin's elder daughter Umang. At least, that is the most they themselves claim for their indigenosity.

Enough has, I hope, been said to suggest how such origins and movements have helped to build up the human complex existing at the present time. It is not necessary to reiterate the lack of simplicity in such data, if it is considered free of prejudgement or the only-too-human craving to fit all the (suitable) facts into one acceptable social theory—even if the fitting requires intellectual brute force!

What, then, remains to be said on this sore but crucial (for the future) subject of group classification? In terms of modern administration, taxation and United

Nations ideology, it is no longer enough that men should be men and women mothers. They have all to have labels, self-identifying (in theory, at least). From the long experience of many government and other officers in the Borneo territories, it also remains inevitable that, on present knowledge, the only *workable* criteria for considering human groups with valid feelings of their or any entity is by the verbal classification *either* (a) that they give themselves; *or*—failing this—(b) that others (preferably their friendly neighbours) give them.

In Sarawak and Sabah over modern decades and a succession of census numerations, groupings of type (a) have become fairly well established and agreed. In the 1947 Sarawak census I wrote an appendix explaining the system then proved reasonably adequate; and this classification was used in an improved form in the 1960 census. In Sarawak, even where a group name has no original meaning—or sense—its gradual recognition by outsiders has become part of the self-expression for those inside! The movement from (b) to (a) is part of emerging modernism as well as of a very ancient historicism. The meaningless term Kelabit is a case in point.

The 'ideal' group is then one which all members call themselves and by which outsiders likewise call them. The non-ideal is one which not only does not think of itself as such, but resents being so called by outsiders. This can become a live—in fact, a dangerously explosive—issue in a country like Borneo, where smaller or remoter groups feel their entity and differences yet have the former over-ridden and the latter ignored by some other larger group nearer the centre of 'classificatory power'. Specially is this a social danger if religious or other spiritual issues are involved.

A good example of the non-ideal process was supplied by the 1960 Census of the state of Brunei. For political reasons, in Brunei the planning of census categories was left to a local, non-specialist officer as superintendent. The procedure naturally got coloured by the outlook of a small, separate and single-minded muslim state. The final report was written up by the 'census adviser', Mr L. W. Jones, who was both first-class superintendent and author at all stages for Sabah and Sarawak.[17]

Let me summarise three of the key sets of figures which I have extracted from the Brunei Census reports for particular focus here:

TABLE 16

| Brunei Census | Percentage of 'Indigenous' (only) Population classed as: | | | |
	'Tutong'	'Kedayan'	'Malay'	Total
1921	10·0	19·8	57·0	86·8
1931	10·2	21·9	55·5	87·6
1947	7·8	21·6	53·7	83·1
1960	0	7·3	76·2	83·5

According to these official returns, there was a truly sensational *increase* in the population of Malays in Brunei between 1947 and 1960, with a corresponding drop for both pagan Tutong and Kedayan: the only two cases of group *decline* in any of the three Borneo territories. Yet (as we have seen in table 13) the percentage of muslims in Brunei has decreased by 6·9 per cent since 1947.

The text of the 1960 Census makes fairly heavy weather of what any reader might well notice as curious. Reversing the detailed approach used in the two neighbouring territories, the Brunei commentary declares (p. 27, my italics):

> ... any attempt to differentiate too finely between one small community and another is not only a waste of time, but is likely to be *misleading*. The Kedayans are unlikely to be dying out despite the above figures; the explanation for the decline in their numbers which caused them to fall back from being 22 per cent to a mere seven per cent of the indigenous population is that some number of them have now chosen to *call themselves* Malays.

What seems to have really happened is that those organising the Census, surely honourable but short-sighted, classified as Malays a lot of Kedayans and all the Tutongs, although the former have a very distinct and 'non-Brunei' group feeling (ex-Indonesia) and the latter privately consider themselves much closer to the Bisaya-Melanau peoples of the adjacent territories.[18] This widely held Malay attitude—expressed in the long-time running of Brunei as a strictly 'muslim state'—materially assisted in producing those reactions which led to a largely Kedayan-led revolt in Brunei on December 9, 1962, and to the severance of Brunei from the Federation of Malaysia.

Here it might be well to remember that a previous revolt staged mainly by Kedayans, in the reign of the thirteenth muslim sultan, lasted twelve years. It is more than *misleading* to move men of blood from one category to another without the fullest understanding of both parties. To obscure the origins of even quite tiny communities can be worse than misleading in Borneo; it can be disastrous, as we have seen. A big responsibility lies on social scientists who may have to be concerned in this even from an apparent 'practical politics' approach of immediacy.

Having thus aired some of the main and in part perhaps insoluble problems of present-day Borneo Man (as I see him), I will conclude with a more succinct presentation. In the following table I have reanalysed, from the original tables, all the human categories for each country, based as nearly as I can on the Sarawak group approach, while freely recognising all the resultant defects and overlaps.

TABLE 17. TOTALS OF ALL 'RACES' BASED ON THE 1960 CENSUS FOR THREE BORNEO TERRITORIES, AS CORRELATED BY THE PRESENT WRITER—TO NEAREST HUNDRED[19]

	Sarawak	Sabah	Brunei	Comment
(a) *Peoples of the Coastal Plain*				
Malay	129,300	25,100	33,500	Incl. 'Brunei'.
Kedayan	7,200	7,900	13,000	See main text above.
Other Muslim Indigenous	0	90,000	400	Mostly Bajau, Sulu, Tidong.
'Indonesians'	3,200	24,800	300	Border-area concentrations.
(a–b) *Both Coast and Inland*				
Bisaya	2,800	10,100	7,000	Incl. Brunei 'Dusuns'.
Dusun (=Kadazan)	0	145,200	0	Sabah Bisayas excluded.
Melanau	44,700	0	400	Pagans; Bisayas are closely related.
(c) *Inland and Hinterland Only*				
Kelabit and Murut	7,300	22,100	0	Many more in Kalimantan.
Kenya and Kayan	16,000	100	0	„ „ „ „
Sea Dayak (Iban)	237,700	1,800	3,900	Spread to lowlands recently.
Land Dayak	57,600	0	0	—
Punans and Nomads	4,700	0	100	Many more in Kalimantan.
(d) *Anywhere Folk*				
Indians, Europeans, etc.	4,900	13,000	2,900	Incl. Eurasians.
Chinese	229,200	104,500	21,800	See native-born % (Table 18)
Total	744,259	454,421	83,877	Incl. small number not classifiable on present basis, except in Sarawak.

In conclusion it should be emphasised that some of the races, notably Indian and Chinese, though now regarded as 'non-native' or 'expatriate', have been associated with west Borneo over very long periods of time.

Earliest fully proven dates for racial contact include:

AD 723   *Chinese* at Kota Batu, Brunei, and soon with major trading posts along the west coast and at Niah Caves, etc; later they had pepper gardens and gold mines far inland.

AD 900   *'Indians'* on small scale only, but with significant influences on song, folklore, etc.

AD 1521   *Europeans* reach Brunei (and meet the fourth muslim sultan, the great Nakoda Ragam, who features also in Malayan sagas); by 1600 there are several Catholic missions in west Borneo; the first travel book on the area in English is published in 1718.

Few Europeans but most Indians in west Borneo were born here. For the Chinese the figures are:

TABLE 18

	Percentage of Chinese native-born, 1960
Sarawak	80
Sabah	77
Brunei	50

The synthesis of all these peoples—including very small but proud, ancient and remote ones—presents some headaches for the years ahead in Malaysia. The value the group *attaches to itself* regardless of 'outside logic', even at times of own self-interest, must never be underestimated as a living reality in Borneo, and one likely to continue for some time to come. This great island has in it some of the spirit of a smaller one which has given the expatriate English centuries of anxiety. As the Irish song goes:

> The sea, oh, the sea, the glorious sea,
> Long may you roll between England and me,
> God help the poor Scotchmen—they'll never be free,
> But we're entirely surrounded by water.

12

Religion and Culture of the Modern Malay

WAN A. HAMID

Anthropologists speak of Late and Early Malays, or of Proto- and Deutero-Malays. The Proto-Malays are the tribes to be found in the interior forests among the foothills of the Malay archipelago, while the Deutero-Malays live along the river banks and the coastal regions. The Deutero-Malays are also referred to as the civilised or modern Malays. They have come in contact with Hindu and, later, with European influences in historical times. But anthropology does not find the Proto-Malays pure and the Deutero-Malays are certainly composite. The difference between Proto- and Deutero-Malays 'belongs to the field of cultural (rather than physical) anthropology'.[1] The word 'modern' in the context of this chapter relates only to the Malays of the twentieth century, particularly of the last decade or two. Unless it is necessary to draw some distinction or for the sake of emphasis, the word 'modern' will not be repeated *ad nauseam*, and subsequent references to the Malays will be primarily about the Malays of this century.

It is obvious that in one chapter it is impossible to treat of all aspects of the culture, the social heritage or the way of life of the Malays, if by culture is meant all the manifestations of social habits of a community, the reactions of the individual as affected by the habits of the group in which he lives, and the artifacts of human activities fashioned by members of the group. A selection of the cultural elements to be discussed has to be made, and the basis of that selection may not satisfy the social scientist, because it is purely a personal selection, although it is by no means haphazard. The cultural elements that will be mentioned are those that are of topical interest in contemporary Malaya and Singapore, that form the subject of discussion and are occupying the thoughts of the Malays themselves.

When speaking of the culture of the modern Malay, one has to treat of his

179

religion, which is the foundation of his beliefs and the frame of reference of his evaluation of what is happening around him, and consequently influences his attitudes to his fellow-men and to institutions.

One has to mention his language, the vehicle for the communication of his ideas, since the Malay language has assumed in Malaya today a special significance which is crystallised in the slogan *Bahasa Jiwa Bangsa* (language is the soul of a nation), of which no one can fail to be aware even after a brief acquaintance with the political situation in Malaya. Indeed the language issue is a lively one and it can be summed up as the agitation to make Malay the national language of Malaya and of Malaysia. To the overwhelming majority of the Malays of Malaya at least, the success or failure of that agitation is equated with the survival or the obliteration of the Malays as an ethnic group.

Besides his religion and his language, mention must also be made of the customs of the modern Malay. Throughout the centuries, the Malays have worked out a framework of expediency in which those customs which are incompatible with his religion are observed and perpetuated as *adat* (custom). They take their *adat* so seriously that they have a proverb which says *Biar mati anak, jangan mati adat* (Let the child perish, but not the *adat*). A contemporary call to reverse this proverb so that it reads *Biar mati adat, jangan mati anak* (Let the *adat* perish, but not the child) has not led to a conscious onslaught on the citadel of *adat*; rather the structure is being undermined by the impact of economic forces.

Mention of some of the artifacts and items of dress that are regarded as typically Malay is made if only because some of them have acquired a certain emotional significance as symbols of the Malay race. It is perhaps an understatement to say that the Malays are as much concerned with symbols as with reality.

It is commonly stated that the Malays belong to a community that is culturally homogeneous, and this observation is based on a few facts. Firstly, all the modern Malays are followers of Islam. Secondly, they speak their own language: the Malay language. Thirdly, they have their own customs and beliefs which set them apart from the other peoples of Malaya. Fourthly, they have stood together as a community in politics *vis-à-vis* the British on the one hand, and the non-Malay population of Malaya on the other, during the struggle for independence, and especially when they were opposing the imposition of the Malayan Union by the British government during the period 1945-8.

It must have been these facts that influenced those who wrote the Constitution of the Federation of Malaya in the latter part of the 1940s to define a Malay as 'a person who professes the Muslim religion, habitually speaks the Malay language and conforms to Malay customs' (Article 160 (2) of the Constitution of the Federation of Malaya).

While that definition may well serve the needs of the Constitution, it never-theless is oversimplified. On closer examination, it will be found that the modern Malays are made up of peoples of diverse racial origins among whom cultural, social and economic distinctions are becoming more evident, to such an extent, indeed, as to invalidate the statement that they belong to a community that is culturally homogeneous. This is even more apparent if by the term Malay one has to include not only the Malays in Malaya, but also those of Malaysia and Indonesia. Furthermore, even in Malaya alone, there are already indications that the politics, customs and beliefs of the Malays are diversifying and changing, and this process of change has affected even their religion in which schisms already existed, although the difference is more of opinions on rituals rather than of fundamental doctrine.

For centuries the Malays have intermarried quite freely with peoples who are racially akin to them, like the Javanese and the Bugis, with peoples who share a common religion with them, like the Indians, Pakistanis and Arabs, and in recent decades with peoples who have come either to settle or to work in Malaya, among whom we can include the Chinese and the Europeans. While anthro-pologists may still attempt to delineate the characteristic features of the Malay, it is not always easy to identify all the modern Malays that one sees walking about the street in the towns and villages of the country. Indeed, the diversity in the skin colour and in the physical features of the modern Malay is such that one of the sultans, remarking that he could not identify his Malay subjects as easily as formerly, enjoined them to put on their caps so that they could be clearly dif-ferentiated from his non-Malay subjects. But alas, there are many non-Malay Muslims who habitually wear the caps that are regarded as the hall-mark of the Malays! Today the Malay cap has become an item of dress that is supposed to distinguish citizens of Malaya who represent their country at international con-ferences and are donned by people who would normally object to being mistaken for Malays.

Some historians go so far as to deny the existence of any indigenous civilisa-tion in South-east Asia before the coming of the Indians and the introduction of Hinduism. G. Coedes for instance writes that 'Outer India did not enter history except in as far as it had been civilised by India'.[2] Others are more cautious; Wertheim, for example, when writing about cultural dynamics in Indonesia, is of the opinion that 'Beyond question, Indonesian civilisation, like that of Further India, has throughout the centuries kept its peculiar character, because of the "local genius" of the population, despite the strong cultural impulses derived from Hindustan',[3] and that 'it would be erroneous ... to consider the Indonesian court civilisation as a Hindu import. Rather Indonesian society had to create conditions under which Hindu influences could operate.'[4]

It should be remembered that before the advent of the Indians, the Malays in the archipelago were engaged in agriculture of a highly developed type based on the cultivation of padi in *sawah* (irrigated fields) and where *sawah* cultivation prevailed 'a definite social order came into existence, for this form of agriculture requires the close co-operation of all the inhabitants of each separate village under common leadership'.[5] The *gotong-royong* system that has been much publicised throughout Malaya is essentially the outcome of this type of agriculture, and it includes the obligation of individuals to help each other in time of distress as well as in the seasonal chores that are concomitant with padi cultivation.

The Malays as a race were animists before they came under the influence of Hinduism and Islam. To them as animists everything, animate and inanimate, has a *semangat* (soul) or *penunggu* (guardian spirit). Thus *semangat besi* is the soul of iron that is responsible for the special qualities of iron, and homage has to be paid to it if the Malay weapon, the *keris*, made from it is to gain and retain its virtue. Padi has its own *semangat* and if padi used for the following year's sowing is to retain its vitality or life-force, the ears of padi have to be cut with a special reaping knife called a *tuai* which consists of a framework of wood in the shape of an arc in the outer centre of which is sandwiched a blade. The stalks of the ripening padi are drawn against the blade between the fingers. The underlying idea is not to let the padi grains see the knife and thereby lose their *semangat* through fright. The belief in the *semangat* is in fact quite contrary to the teachings of Islam but the modern Malay still retains this belief and where, centuries ago, his ancestor would utter the magic words at the rituals associated with reaping in the Malay language, the Muslim Malay of today would incorporate also verses from the Koran. The belief in magic is still so prevalent as to lead thousands of people to visit a recently discovered spring outside the town of Kuala Lumpur in search of miracle cures even though in one instance at least the magic spring turned out to be a burst water main!

To the Malays, spirits are of two kinds: the evil ones are *hantu* and the not so evil ones are *jin* or genie. To the Muslim Malay a *hantu* is still a *hantu* today, but a *jin* may be an evil *jin* in which case he is a *jin kafir* (an infidel *jin*), or a good *jin* who is a *jin Islam* (Islamic *jin*). When the pupils of an Arabic school were haunted by several *hantus* or *jins* (no one was quite sure which), the school was closed down temporarily. All over Malaya many Malay girls have one of their fingers painted red with henna which is supposed to ward off evil spirits.

Because the animist Malay had his collection of spirits and his belief in magic, it was not difficult for him to accept Hindu tantrism and Muslim mysticism when the time came. 'Between the primitive beliefs and practices of the Malay and those of the Hindu there was much in common.'[6]

Hindu incantations were introduced into Malay rituals and the Sanskrit term *puja* came to mean the utterance of a *pawang* or an expert in any art believed to need the use of magic. The modern Malays of the east coast state of Kelantan still hold an annual festival of *puja pantai* on the beach to mark the beginning or opening of the fishing season after the north-east monsoon. The ceremony is to invoke the help of the guardian spirits of the sea so that the fishermen may be protected from evil and that they may have big catches during the following season.

Historians have given us some indication of the period during which Islam was introduced into the Malay archipelago. J. C. van Leur quoting other sources mentions that 'there are allusions to Arab settlements or colonies on the west coast of Sumatra as early as AD 674, and that Arab tombstones dating from 1082 on Java . . .'[7] have been found. These provide evidence of the existence of Arab settlements but whether or not they indicate that some of the inhabitants of the area had embraced Islam is not so certain. The discovery of tombstones in Perlak, in northern Sumatra, and in Trengganu, in Malaya, are offered as evidence of the introduction of Islam because Arabic is the language and script of the Koran and the graves were believed to be those of some local inhabitants.

It is by now fairly well substantiated that by the fifteenth century Islam was a major religion in the Malay archipelago. The ruler of Malacca who visited China in 1419 bore the name of Muhammad Iskandar Shah and this 'shows that the ruling family of Malacca either had gone over to Islam, or had been replaced by a new Moslem dynasty. The tombstones of the Malaccan rajahs of the early fifteenth century corroborate Chinese reports.'[8]

On the question of how Islam spread in the Malay archipelago two theories have been put forward. According to the first, groups of Muslims came and colonised parts of the archipelago and from such colonies they spread their faith. According to the second, Islam was spread by traders who came primarily to trade in the ports of the area and by individual men of religion, some of whom came at the invitation of the local potentates. There seems to be more evidence of the second theory than of the first. For lack of the equivalent of a Church to centralise and direct missionary activities, Islam has spread and indeed is being spread today very much by individuals. J. C. van Leur maintains rightly that 'Islam does not have an exclusive, magical charisma of the priest such as that of Catholic Christianity, but has remained a missionary community in the early christian sense. Because of the expansive missionary nature of Islam, every Moslem is a propagandist of his faith.'[9] This is true of the spread of Islam in our time as it was centuries ago, although there are moves to institutionalise missionary activities by the creation of organisations through which it is hoped to channel proselytising work. But to date there has not been much evidence to suggest that such work is being carried out to any large extent. Those Muslim missionary societies that exist have mainly concentrated on welfare and evangelical work among the already converted, and new converts to Islam have, so to speak, been introduced to it by individuals or else through contracting marriages with Muslims. If, in the future, Muslim missionary societies decide to intensify their proselytising activities, they will have to look for converts primarily among the pagan hill tribes, but the Christian missions have had a good start among such peoples, especially among the tribal peoples of the Borneo territories. The Christian missions are prohibited by law in Malaya from converting Muslims to Christianity.

There is no doubt that Islam will acquire greater significance as a result of its political status in Malaya at any rate, where it is the state religion and the king is head of the Muslim religion in the state. In the constitutional arrangement for Malaysia, however, the king has not been given in Malaya the position of head of the muslim religion, as in the Borneo territories. In Malaya 'state law may control or restrict the propagation of any religious doctrine or belief among persons professing the muslim religion'[10] but in the Borneo territories the same provision could only be made by a two-thirds majority of the total membership of the state's Legislative Assembly.

It is difficult to generalise on the attitude of the modern Malay to his religion. Much depends upon his education. It is a common belief that those who are educated primarily in the English schools do not have the same reverence for their religion as those who spend much of their school days in the Malay or Arabic schools. But many Malays who are educated in English find much intellectual satisfaction from writing about Islam or talking about it on the radio, although they are not necessarily shining examples of devotion to the faith. Other Malays, with improvement in their political and consequently economic well-being, make the pilgrimage to Mecca, albeit by the easier and quicker way, namely, by air. But in spite of their apparent concern for their religion, many if not all of them do manage to keep their zest for life as uninhibited as before their pilgrimage.

In spite of the lapses of the few, the great majority of the Malays contend that Islam comprises everything to be wished for in the way of democracy and socialism, and that it is a complete guide to life on this earth. In the present century, with the breaking down of the subsistence economy and the self-contained village community with the introduction of the capitalist mode of production, the Muslims are increasingly called upon to direct their thinking to the incompatibilities of capitalism with some of the tenets of Islam. With the insistence on the economic development of Malaya and the active participation of the Malays in commerce and industry as the major and declared aims of the present government of the Federation, ways and means must be found to justify economic development based on capitalism, and the creation of a capitalist class among the Malays themselves.

As modern banking involves the granting of loans and the charging of interest in financing economic projects, a way has to be found to overcome the Koranic prohibition of *riba* (literally 'increase', technically 'usury and interest'). There are Malays who will not accept even the dividends they are entitled to when they keep their money in the Post Office Savings Bank. While controversy centering around *riba* will no doubt continue among the theologians, for the present at any rate the Malay language has come to the rescue by replacing the old Malay word for interest, *bunga*, which is frowned upon even socially, by the word *faedah* (literally 'benefit') which seems to be more acceptable to the Malay conscience.

Recently Muslim theologians met in Kuala Lumpur to deliberate on the question of whether financial grants from the Social Welfare Lotteries Board could be used for the construction of mosques and other houses of worship. Because a lottery is regarded as a form of gambling and therefore prohibited by religion, the proceeds from a lottery are unacceptable for financing the construction of a mosque. The theologians decided that the proceeds from the lotteries of the Board should first be paid into the general revenue of the state and an allocation then made to the Ministry of Rural Development which in turn could make grants for the construction of mosques and other houses of worship. A direct grant from the Social Welfare Lotteries Board was found unacceptable.

Islamic reformism[11] in Malaya from the beginning of the twentieth century saw its task as primarily religious and educational, and not political, but the formation of the Pan-Malayan Islamic Party has changed the situation because one of its declared aims is to set up a state based on the Koran and the Hadith (a collection of the actions and sayings of the Prophet Muhammad and his companions: the whole body of the sacred tradition of Islam). In Malaya, the Pan-Malayan Islamic Party is in power in Kelantan.

It is not the purpose here to trace the roots of Malay nationalism. But it can be said that nationalism as a motivating and unifying factor in politics embracing the whole Malay population of Malaya is of very recent origin. Certainly the growth of nationalisms in India, the Middle East and Indonesia during this century has attracted the attention of many Malayans, but only the Indonesian political struggle against the Dutch has strong emotional echoes in the breasts of Malays, particularly those of Indonesian extraction. Nevertheless, it was the opposition to the Malayan Union imposed by the British when they returned to Malaya after the Second World War that was the immediate cause which unified the Malays of Malaya under the leadership of the late Dato' Onn bin Ja'afar. British administrators who used to think of the Malays as a docile and contented people were surprised to see the latter making a united and concerted stand against the Malayan Union and demanding complete independence from Britain. It was this political awakening that stimulated the search for banners round which the Malays could rally, and one of these was the Malay language. It was the practical need to put across political ideas to the masses that gave an added impetus to the use of the Malay language, apart from the obvious demand of nationalism for a language in which to express itself.

There are about 170 languages spoken in the Malay archipelago; they 'belong with few exceptions to the Austronesian (Malay-Polynesian) language-group. Its Indonesian section may be sub-divided into two groups: to the first belongs the Achinese and several other languages of the interior of Sumatra, Borneo and Celebes; to the other, the Batak, the Malay-proper, the Javanese and Balinese. The latter are closely related to each other and also to the Malagassi of Madagascar and the Tagalog of Luzon. The geographic distribution of the two groups suggests that the languages belonging to the second one were introduced into the archipelago at a much later date than those of the first one. Their close affinity with Malagassi and Tagalog indicates that the people who spoke them were great seafarers in an early age and probably had risen far above the level of civilisation popularly connected with the epithet "neolithic", a conclusion which is also borne out by social ethnology.'[12]

Although Malay proper is the mother tongue of only a few of the one hundred million people of the Malay archipelago, it is today understood and spoken by the vast majority of the people of the region, especially now that its variant Bahasa Indonesia (the Indonesian language) has been made the national language of the Republic of Indonesia. Malay had for many centuries past been the lingua franca of the archipelago, and Vlekke, for instance, ventures the opinion that 'the use of Malay as the language of trade dates much further back than to AD 1400, perhaps even to the sixth century'.[13]

In Malaya today, the Malay language is referred to as Bahasa Kebangsaan (national language) and not so much as Bahasa Melayu (the Malay language). This change in nomenclature is purely to avoid undue emphasis on Malay as the language of the Malays since it is sought to stress its suitability as the national language of a nation comprising peoples of different racial origins. It is hoped to unify the peoples of Malaya through a common language.

The demand for a national language is not peculiar to Malaya; it is characteristic of the national-liberation movements throughout much of Asia. In Indonesia 'the oath to support one country and one language, the Bahasa Indonesia, went back to the 1928 conference of Pemuda Indonesia (Young Indonesia), the all-Indonesia youth organisation. The following year this oath had been taken over by the chief political parties and religious social organisations. After that all official nationalist publications were in the *Bahasa Indonesia*.'[14] In Malaya the culmination of the agitation to make Malay the national language was the incorporation in the Constitution of Malaya in August 1957 of Clause 152 (1) which stated that: 'The National language shall be the Malay language and shall be in such script as Parliament may by law provide.'

Although Malay was proclaimed the national language, the Constitution stipulated that, notwithstanding the provisions of Clause 152 (1), 'for a period of ten years after Merdeka Day, and thereafter until Parliament otherwise provides, the English language may be used in both Houses of Parliament, in the Legislative Assembly of every State, and for all other official purposes'. In effect this clause gives the Malay language a period of ten years during which to develop and supplant the English language as the official language of the country.

There has been opposition to making Malay the national and sole official language of the Federation of Malaya by 1967. This has been based on what the critics regard as the inadequacies of the Malay language to perform the functions of a national and an official language of a modern state, and also on political grounds. The critics argue that all the four main languages spoken in Malaya (namely Chinese, English, Malay and Tamil) should have official recognition in a multiracial and a multilingual society. In the state of Singapore, these four languages can be used in the State Assembly.

It is not generally known that Malay is a very versatile and flexible language and this is shown by the fact that it was able to survive repeated onslaughts by several vigorous European languages from the fifteenth century onwards, while it has always to contend with other languages in the Malay language-group itself such as Javanese. In spite of the competition, it has managed not only to survive but also to extend its influence in the archipelago to the point where it has been chosen as the national language of the biggest political unit in the area, Indonesia.

That the Malay language has to be developed after years of being relegated to second place in its own country is not denied. But the development of a language cannot be divorced from the culture of the people speaking it. Malay does not have the vocabulary of science and technology, but this is also true of most if not all oriental languages, and the consideration should be whether a language is capable of developing further and meeting the needs of the community. In this the Malay language has shown its capabilities and there is every reason for being optimistic about its future as the national and official language of Malaya.

In order to centralise and direct the work of coining new words in the Malay language, the Dewan Bahasa dan Pustaka (Language and Literature Agency) was incorporated in 1959 and given the following tasks:

1. to develop and enrich the national language;
2. to develop literary talent, particularly in the national language;
3. to print or publish or assist in the printing or publication of books, magazines, pamphlets and other forms of literature in the national language and in other languages;
4. to standardise spelling and pronunciation, and devise appropriate technical terms in the national language;
5. to prepare and publish a national language dictionary.[15]

Terminological committees comprising persons trained in the sciences and language experts meet regularly to coin new words and these words are gradually being introduced into the textbooks written in the national language for the schools of the country. The Dewan Bahasa dan Pustaka is itself a publisher.

The standardisation of the spelling in *Bahasa Melayu* (Malay language) and *Bahasa Indonesia* (Indonesian language) has been agreed upon and the agreement is awaiting ratification by the governments of Malaysia and Indonesia.

Every year a National Language Month is organised in order to direct public attention to the need for extending the use of Malay in administration, commerce and industry. As a result road names and shop signboards are being written in the national language, and more and more non-Malays are learning the language. Besides the slogan *Bahasa Jiwa Bangsa* mentioned earlier, the National Language Month movement is also responsible for the coining of another slogan, *Bahasa Kebangsaan Bahasa Perpaduan* (the National language is the language of Unity). Much hope is placed on the national language as a means of unifying the peoples of Malaya. The danger of putting too much faith in slogans is that they may breed complacency and a false sense of achievement. The truth is that, while being indispensable as a means of communication among human beings, a language does not *per se* create unity. The confrontation policy launched by Indonesia against Malaysia is a bitter reminder of the fact that although the Malayans and the Indonesians speak the same language, this language does not engender unity. Only common ideals and principles can bring unity, and language plays its part merely in communicating such ideals and principles to the peoples of Malaysia.

It should be evident from what has been said above that the modern Malay is at the centre of many cross-currents. Modern reformism in Islam is attempting to sweep him in one direction while orthodoxy is restraining him to one spot. His customs and beliefs rooted in his past are daily being challenged by his modern education. His family and clan ties are chiefly in the countryside but the towns with their factories and their neon lights are beckoning him to leave his farmstead. His subsistence economy is being undermined by the necessity to sell his produce in a money economy as his needs and wants multiply. His *gotong-royong* society is breaking up with the penetration of private enterprise into the country-side. He feels his position threatened by immigrants who are asking for equal rights and privileges. He knows that time is not on his side because he has to catch up in many fields with people who are not standing still.

Two courses of action are open to him: he may turn ultra-nationalist and develop an aggressive attitude towards all things foreign, or he may yet be per-suaded to see his advancement in co-operation with the non-Malays of the country. But whichever course of action he takes, he will have to create new ties and alignments because his feudal society is cracking up and his salvation lies in thinking in class terms rather than in racial terms. The modern Malay has time yet to take his bearings.

13

The Chinese in Malaysia

VICTOR PURCELL

The Overseas Chinese in South-east Asia were estimated to number in 1960 about 12 million in a total population of some 220 million.[1]   In no country, except the state of Singapore (which became a unit of the Federation of Malaysia in August 1963), are the Chinese in a majority.   In Malaya they account for some 38 per cent of the total, and in Thailand perhaps 10 per cent.   Elsewhere they are in a very great minority, and there can therefore be no question of a physical 'take-over' by the Chinese—without, of course, the military participation of Communist China, which in the foreseeable future is highly unlikely.   Moreover, by its treaties with Indonesia and in other ways the Chinese government has been at pains to insist that (unlike the Kuomintang government before it) the Chinese People's Republic has no territorial ambitions in South-east Asia or elsewhere. Some of the South-east Asian governments (e.g., of Burma and Indonesia) have shown a disposition to believe them; others (notably those of Thailand and the former Federation of Malaya) have declared themselves as more than sceptical on this score.   The fact is, however, that the Chinese minorities in all these countries have on the whole evinced a strong desire to come to terms with the indigenous peoples among whom they live.

In the new Federation of Malaysia there is now (1964) the largest Chinese minority in South-east Asia and one that numbers about 4·4 million in a total of 10·4 million.   In Malaya the Chinese represent 2·7 million in a total of 7·35 million; in Singapore, 1·35 million in a total of 1·77 million; in Sarawak, 0·24 million in a total of 0·76 million; and in Sabah, 0·11 million in a total of 0·48 million.

I have said that the Chinese in these territories are trying to come to terms with their environment and to identify themselves with the countries in which they live, but the cultural pulls of China are the greatest obstacle to the achievement of this aim. Communism is one thing and Chinese nationalism another, and the Chinese overseas have shown a disposition to educate their children in Chinese, which is bound to have the effect of inducing them to look in the direction of mainland China since it is there that the bulk of the literature is produced to which education in Chinese opens the door. Nevertheless, Chinese politicians who urge a closer association of this community with the indigenous communities claim that a knowledge of Chinese is no impediment to multilingualism. Lee Kuan Yew, for example, the prime minister of Singapore, welcomed the adoption of Malay as the 'official language' of Singapore, and Chinese politicians in the Federation of Malaya have shown similar agreement that Malay should be the official language of the Federation and should be taught in all schools. But it must be pointed out that most of the Chinese leaders who are well disposed towards the dominance of the Malay language in the curriculum are English-educated (as is Lee Kuan Yew) while the Chinese-educated Chinese are afraid that the extension of the number of hours devoted to teaching Malay will render it difficult for a Chinese pupil to obtain a high standard in his own language.

The educational problem is undoubtedly the key difficulty in Sino-Malaysian relations. The repeated demonstrations by Chinese teachers and students in the middle schools in Malaya and Singapore over the years have demonstrated an emotional commitment to Chinese. The political and economic difficulties are, it seems, less of an obstruction to the eventual assimilation of the Chinese into the local communities. How the problem is being tackled in Malayan schools is therefore worthy of more detailed attention.

The Malayan Education Ordinance of 1957 stated the government's aim 'to establish a national system of education acceptable to the people as a whole . . . with the intention of making the Malay language the National Language of the country while preserving and sustaining the growth of the language and cultures of peoples other than Malays living in the country'. Primary education was available in four languages: Malay, English, Chinese and Tamil. English was the medium of instruction in the University of Malaya, but the government, in collaboration with the university, was examining the feasibility of the gradual introduction of the Malay medium into some university courses. In Singapore (whose population was nearly eighty per cent Chinese) the principle adopted was 'to make all schools highways to citizenship, and all languages must be broad bridges to Malayan loyalty'. Emphasis was placed on education *for* Malays and *in* Malay for all communities. The first secondary schools in Malay were formed. Free education for Malays was provided at all levels of education in Singapore.

The above examples drawn from the Federation of Malaya in which the Malayan Chinese Association was associated with Malays and Indians in the

191

governing party in power, the Alliance Party, and from Singapore where the governing party, the People's Action Party, though organised on a non-communal basis, was mostly composed of Chinese, are sufficient to indicate the willingness of the Chinese to compromise in the key matter of education in the interests of the cultivation of a 'Malayan' outlook.

Having stressed the paramountcy of the educational problem, I must now turn to certain social aspects of the Chinese community in Malaya and the Borneo territories.

Chinese immigration into Malaya had mostly taken place during the British period when immigrants from south China had flocked in to take part in the opening up of the country. They were employed on the tin mines and (in much smaller numbers) on the rubber estates, but were mostly urban, being engaged in trade, as artisans, or in the hundred and one occupations of an urban society. The Malays, on the other hand, were mostly peasants working their smallholdings of rice, fruit, and cash crops. Immigration since the Second World War, however, had virtually stopped (being confined to certain very limited categories) so that the Chinese community relied almost exclusively on natural increase to maintain or extend its numbers relative to the other communities. Before the war the ratio of the sexes had been about three males to one female, but since the war the sexes had approached very near to numerical equality and the rate of natural increase was not greatly different from that of the indigenous peoples. (It is true that the Chinese rate of increase was higher than that of the native communities in Singapore and some of the Borneo territories, but not to such a degree as to support a belief that the Chinese were greatly out-multiplying the natives.) Before the war, it might have been much more plausibly argued that the Chinese were swamping the natives when the Chinese immigrants greatly outnumbered the emigrants.

The Overseas Chinese originated almost exclusively from the southern provinces of China, and the pre-war pattern of distribution of Hokkiens, Cantonese, Hakkas, Foochows, Hailams (Hainanese), etc, remained largely unaltered—the Hokkiens being most numerous in Singapore, Penang and Malacca (the old Straits Settlements), the Teochius the most numerous in Kedah, the Hainanese the most numerous in Trengganu, the Hakkas in Sabah, etc. But although the several tribes tended to keep together, there was a good deal of intermarriage and intermingling between them. Moreover, the Chinese community as a whole was the product not of a single wave of immigration but of many waves. It was therefore to be expected that it would differ in many respects from the several parent communities in China.

Freedman[2] concluded that, while Chinese society to be seen in Singapore takes its culture directly from south-eastern China, the economic and political conditions of the colony were totally alien to those of the home setting, and the social organisation of Chinese in Singapore cannot be understood simply as a branch of society in China. At the same time as agnatic kinship was reinterpreted in Singapore, the powerful bias of the homeland system in favour of the 'patriline' was modified overseas by the removal of local groups based on kinship.

There were many modifications, too, consequent on the more 'modern' outlook of the Overseas Chinese (influenced by the West), and in Singapore, for example, while preferring to seek their wives within their own dialect groups, they treated the new marriage as a matter concerning only the bridal couple and their fellow household members. There had also been a change in the relative status of primary and secondary wives (the 'principal wives' and 'concubines' of the older European literature on China) such that the latter often assumed a significance probably unknown in China. At the same time, the definition of secondary wife had become blurred, and there was a shading of polygamy into mistress-keeping. The forms of marriage had proliferated, and various combinations of traditional and modernist ceremonial made it difficult to make any general statement as to the essentials constituting a Chinese marriage.

It should be emphasised that, generally speaking, the Chinese intermarried within their own community, marriage between Chinese and Malays being practically unknown owing to the taboos of the muslim religion. This was in contrast to the situation in Thailand and Burma, where the religion was buddhist and marriage between Chinese and Thais or Burmese was common. The state of affairs in muslim countries meant, of course, that the community problem could not be solved by assimilation, and the only solution was a *modus vivendi* between races with different customs, religion and standards of living.

The mention of differing 'standards of living' draws attention to the economic factor in intercommunal relations in Malaya and the Borneo territories. The Malay aristocracy inherited many economic and political advantages from their past which had been preserved under British rule, but the great bulk of the Malays were peasants whose standard of living was that of Asian primary producers. That is to say, they were assured of enough to eat, but their cash income was very low. The Chinese, on the other hand, were mostly wage earners who, with the development of the trade unions, were able to demand wages which had some direct relation to the price of the main export products: rubber and tin in the case of Malaya. Moreover, a section of the Chinese controlled a considerable sector of the entrepreneurial activities of both Malaya and the Borneo territories. In 1951, the combined incomes assessed for tax of 5,195 Chinese in the Federation amounted to $M 62 million (£7·2 million) as compared with 773 Malays whose combined incomes assessed for tax amounted to $M 8·1 million (£0·92 million).

These figures give a very fair idea of the comparative distribution of money wealth.

The economic gulf between the Malays and Chinese was in the British period a source of dissatisfaction among the former, though the Malays enjoyed certain important privileges as the 'people of the country', including the reservation to them of the best rice land (1913) and eligibility of their aristocracy for admission to the Malayan Civil Service. But it appeared that their separate and often opposing interests would prevent them at any time from making common cause politically.

The study of another Chinese community in Malaya, namely the rural Teochius of Province Wellesley, also brings out the modifications which Chinese society has undergone, and is undergoing, in South-east Asia.[3]

The Teochiu Chinese (like the other Overseas Chinese) regard themselves as a part of the larger Chinese society and they therefore aim at conforming to the values which they believe hold the wider Chinese society together: the emphasis on the Chinese written language, Chinese family organisation, and the recognition of the homeland as the source of their beliefs and ideas. Yet, although they themselves were scarcely conscious of it, their villages had departed in many ways from the traditional pattern of those in China. There was, for example, among the Teochius of Province Wellesley, an absence of strong class organisation. Whereas the family system in China was represented as a 'virilocal, patrilineal one with the emphasis on males to the almost total exclusion of females from important positions of direct authority in the family', in the village of 'Treacherous River' (Sungei Derhaka) a high proportion of economic families consisted of elderly males living alone, deserted by their sons. Another difference was due to the fact that whereas a China-born Teochiu regarded himself as being an outpost of his village in China and remitted money to support his relatives living there in order to acquire prestige when he returned, the Malayan-born Chinese tended to spend his money in Malaya on other things, such as gambling, watches, wine and property (there has been a marked increase in gambling and horse-racing since the war, says W. H. Newell). Young Chinese were excluded from the main wedding feasts and ceremonials by their parents and when they became adults it was doubtful whether they would carry on the same customs. Already it was laid down that a bridegroom must see his bride before betrothal at a special local ceremony held for the purpose: a custom which did not obtain in the ancestral village in China.

But while cut off to a great extent from China, the Province Wellesley Teochius did not make up for the deficiency in models offered them by borrowing the neighbouring Malay communities. Practically nothing was taken from this source. In China, the agent for supplying the village with up-to-date ideas was the student educated in Kuo Yü (Mandarin), and no doubt also in communist principles, whereas in Malaya the cleverer and more advanced students of the upper middle school level were nearly all educated in English and rapidly lost touch with their local community. Thus the local communities were left without leaders who understood the wider society and such peasant leaders as there were represented only those special groups of vegetable-growing farmers who spoke Teochiu and who were members of local Chinese associations. This special group was not linked in any way, economic, social or linguistic, with the Malays, not even with the Malay farmers in the same village.

Religion, too, among the Province Wellesley Teochius showed signs of considerable divergence from the homeland pattern. The China system of a hierarchy of gods and officials, each receiving orders from the stage above, was too inflexible for a society which had to face a series of unpredictable accidents. As a result, the *Kuei* (spirits of the dead, as distinguished from the *Shen*, the gods or supernatural spirits) had gained an importance in the religious system greater than in the homeland. They had the characteristics of the men they once were, and stepped in to protect the community against the economic uncertainties of life.

The absence of traditional Chinese methods of organising a village society, shown by the lack of class and inter-village associations and their replacement by an elaborate framework of informal contacts, reflects an inability by the inhabitants to organise their society as they believe it was organised in China. While outwardly supporting traditional Chinese values, in fact they are building a new type of society.

Adaptation to local circumstances was also apparent in the cultivation of the arts among the Malayan Chinese. The cultural renaissance which had been in progress in China since 1949 was naturally reflected in Malaya, but owing to local conditions and political requirements it assumed a modified character.

This fact is apparent particularly in the activities of the China Society centred on Singapore. This body endeavoured not only to stimulate interest in the progress of the arts in China itself but to act as an intermediary between the Chinese, Malay, Indian, western and other cultures.

In mainland China there were two distinct styles in painting: the Traditional School and the so-called Socialist Realist School which came from Russia and which was the official communist line in art. There was also a third and more popular art represented by the wood-cuts and New Year paintings. It seems, however, that among Malayan Chinese artists the Traditional School was uppermost, and painting which had a propagandist motive was generally ignored. This was in keeping with the 'neutral' line of the Overseas Chinese, a majority of whom, in actual fact, were probably neutral in external politics. The traditional artists followed the two main schools: the *Kung pi*, or 'fine workmanship', and the *Hsieh*

195

yi, or 'expression of the spirit', and some very fine work was exhibited at the exhibitions. But, as in China, directly a fusion of the Western and Chinese methods (involving the adoption of Western 'perspective') was attempted the result was a failure. The Singapore Academy of Art, however, sponsored by the China Society, conducted separate classes in Chinese Painting and Western Art.

There was a considerable 'folk' element in those cultural activities. Moreover, other cultures were represented too. For example, at a rice-dumpling party held by one of the China Society's vice-presidents, Dr Chen Su Lan, to celebrate the Dragon Boat Festival, there was a recital of Peking operatic singing, while at another party, given by another vice-president, Mr V. Pakirisamy (an Indian, be it noted), there was a vegetarian dinner followed by a performance of Indian dancing. The president and Mrs Lee Siow Mong played hosts to members on the occasion of the Moon Cake Festival when a new program of verse chanting was introduced: poems by famous Chinese poets such as Li Po and Tu Fu were chanted in Mandarin and translations of the poems were chanted in English, Malay and Tamil.

The careful selectiveness of the Singapore Chinese was again apparent at a Peking Drama Night at the Theatre of the Adult Education Centre. The plays chosen were *The Fisherman's Revenge* and *Lady Precious Stream*: not, be it noted, modern plays with a communist propaganda element ('agitprop') such as (say) *A Single Spark Starts a Prairie Fire*, about a peasant's revolt in 1928, such as was popular in Peking.

Other cultural features, including folk dancing, flower arrangement and Chinese 'judo', were also encouraged by the China Society.

It will be seen that in spite of attempts on the higher social levels to effect a synthesis—or at least a mutual appreciation—between the rival cultures of Malaya, the communities for the most part remained isolated. Yet from 1953 onwards the Malay and Chinese leaders combined to seek independence. This was achieved for Malaya in 1957 by an alliance between the United Malay National Organisation (UMNO) and the Malayan Chinese Association (MCA), to which the Malayan Indian Congress (MIC) was later added. And this Alliance was still in power in 1964.

I have illustrated these problems of racial relationship mainly by examples from Malaya and Singapore, but they existed in varying degrees of urgency in the Bornean territories. In Sabah, as in Sarawak, there was a promising background of friendly race relations under the British to help the Federation of Malaysia, and one encouraging development (not, so far, repeated in Malaya) was the intermarriage that was taking place in the interior of Sabah between the Chinese and the Dusun (or Kadazan) peoples.

196

It should be clear from the above that the Chinese in Malaysia had to adjust themselves to a number of different settings. How far do the facts fit the picture of the Overseas Chinese as a 'spearhead' or 'fifth column' for the invasion by China of South-east Asia?

To be an effective instrument of Communist China's ambitions (if such indeed exist), it would be necessary for the majority of the Chinese in Malaysia to be communists or 'fellow travellers'. There can be no doubt that the communist element among them is strong, especially in a densely populated urban centre like Singapore. Nor did the Malayan Communist Party and its affiliates in Malaya and the Borneo territories neglect any opportunity for furthering their aims and exploiting the political situation in the region. But there was plenty of evidence also that a large proportion of the Chinese were anxious to come to an understanding with the native peoples among whom they lived. It must not be forgotten that an ever increasing proportion of them were born in Malaya or Borneo and, now that immigration has virtually stopped, in due course all of them would be Malaya- or Borneo-born. And while it is clear from examples such as the 'Babu' Chinese of Malacca and Penang or those of Semarang (in D. E. Willmott's study[4]) that however long a Chinese community is domiciled in South-east Asia, and even when it forgets its own language, it remains 'Chinese', it is also true that it becomes also 'Malayan', 'Indonesian', 'Bornean', etc, and sees its interests, not in terms of China, but of its adopted country.[5]

The one link with China that remains is education in the Chinese language. As was inevitable, this education (whatever precautions are taken to prevent the use of communist textbooks) is influenced by trends in education in the Chinese People's Republic, and much of the literature to which such education opens the way is bound to be largely that which has been published in China since 1949. But a sentiment in favour of a Chinese education does not necessarily betoken communist sympathies and the education itself does not necessarily induce a communist outlook.

The Chinese in Malaysia, as in South-east Asia generally, are anxious to keep free from political entanglements, especially abroad. This is particularly true of those engaged in business,[6] and the majority, directly or indirectly, are so engaged. They are working within a capitalist framework and have to keep on good terms with it. At the same time many Chinese still have relatives in China, and for their sakes it is expedient not to antagonise the authorities in the Chinese People's Republic. The latter, for its part, as is consistent with both its foreign policy and its marxist principles, is unwilling to extend protection to the Overseas Chinese when they are in conflict with any of the South-east Asian governments over legislation discriminating against entrepreneurial enterprise (as proved to be the case when Chinese retailers were prohibited as 'aliens' from carrying on retail trade in the rural areas of Indonesia). The only hope of the Chinese businessmen is that, as capitalists, the South-east Asian governments, in their own interests as well as in equity, will not discriminate against them. And when they happen to be citizens of the country (often with roots of more than a generation) there is no excuse at all for such discrimination.

If the Chinese of Malaysia are granted equal rights everywhere with the indigenous peoples, and are free from the interference from China (which was not the case under the Kuomintang which continually interfered in South-east Asian affairs for the alleged 'protection' of the Overseas Chinese between the wars) there is every chance that they will consider themselves, and come to be considered, first and foremost as 'Malaysians'. To achieve this end short of miscegenation (which, as we have seen, is still in process though handicapped by religious and other obstacles) the Overseas Chinese will have to submit to systems of education in which the 'official language' (usually Malay) is given priority. This will mean that they cannot expect to reach the same standard in Chinese as those whose sole education is in that language. They would nevertheless be able to keep Chinese as a cultural bond with their country of origin. There is meanwhile a strong case for the retention of English as a medium of intercommunication. The administrative systems of Malaya are founded largely on British models, the laws are mostly enacted in English, and English is still for the most part the language of administration. The association of English with 'colonialism' has led to a reaction against it on nationalist grounds, but with the political withdrawal of the British from the whole of Malaysia, this prejudice should diminish to nothing as the years pass by. Moreover, it is to be noted that in Malaya and Singapore the English-educated Chinese have proved the most effective in helping 'Malayanisation', since they cannot be accused of affiliation with Communist China in a country which is notably 'anti-communist'.[7]

It must be emphasised that the Overseas Chinese, with the exception of 'pockets' of militant communists, are on the defensive. They are either mercantile or dependent indirectly on commerce and are therefore unlikely to 'quarrel with their bread and butter'. And even if it is still argued that they are aggressive and a threat to the local governments, it must be pointed out that they are unarmed. The armed forces and the police both in Malaya and the Borneo territories are recruited from the indigenous peoples. A 'spearhead' needs a sharp point and cutting edges to qualify for the description. It is to be hoped that in the interests of Malaysia the alleged spearhead of the Malayan Chinese will continue to be blunt.

14

Education and Problems of Nationhood

R. H. K. WONG

Although the political merger of the four territories of Malaya, Singapore, Sabah and Sarawak to form Malaysia became an accomplished fact only on August 31, 1963, it is but the last link in a chain of associations, historical and cultural, which these countries have had with one another over a period of years. Moreover, in each of the four territories, British influence has left its mark on the administrative and educational pattern, whether it was through a chartered company, or the benevolent rule of a British family as exemplified by the Brookes of Sarawak, or through an established colonial government.

It is not surprising, therefore, that educational endeavour, with some degree of local variation because of local needs, has followed a strikingly similar pattern in its development and problems in all four territories. Before the Second World War, against the common multiracial and multilinguistic background, there arose three main and separate systems of education perpetuated through the efforts of the government, of the missions and of independent Chinese school boards.

The initiative in education was generally not taken by government but rather by religious missions and independent groups, or even by public spirited individuals. For example, Penang Free School was founded in 1816 by the colonial chaplain of Penang. To the missions goes the credit for having established some of the best English-medium schools in this area. The Chinese with their high regard for learning set up their own schools as a necessary concomitant of settlement in a new country. Their enterprise in education might well have been the expression of a culturally induced acceptance of Confucian social-prestige rating (scholar, farmer, labourer, merchant, in that order). The order of prestige may, in today's materialistic society, have undergone a change, but the premium on scholarship remains. Nanyang University in Singapore stands today as a monument to the ceaseless quest of the Chinese for education.

While the missions devoted their efforts largely to giving education in the English medium (and in this venture government also had a part), government more particularly sponsored Malay education. This, however, met with indifferent success. Except in Malaya, where the Malay College at Kuala Kangsar was set up at the turn of the century to prepare high-ranking Malays for entry into the administrative service of the government, and the Sultan Idris Training College and the Malayan Women's Training College opened for the training of Malay schoolteachers, Malay education in the other territories did not develop much beyond the primary school stage. There were different reasons for this.

In Singapore, the population has always been largely Chinese. Progress in education in the Malay medium naturally fell behind in pace by comparison with education in English or in Chinese. Actually, the first training college for Malay schoolteachers was established in the island in 1878, but did not survive like those in Malaya. So far as Sarawak and Sabah are concerned, Malay education, before the last war and even after, has not been much sought after. For, apart from a heavy concentration of Chinese in the coastal towns, there is a large indigenous non-Malay population consisting of Dayaks, Dusuns, Muruts, Bajaus and Melanaus by whom Malay has never really been regarded as the *lingua franca*.

For the first half of this century, certainly, the situation with respect to education, as it obtained in a large part of Malaysia, was not satisfactory. The three separate systems described above meant that the aims of education were subject to divisive influences. Lack of integration in the education service affected the quality and recruitment of teachers. For Malay schools the resources for the training of teachers were to be found only in the two Malay colleges on the Malayan mainland. More than half of the teachers in Chinese schools were recruited from China; a great number of teachers in both mission and Chinese schools remained untrained. There was marked disparity in terms of service with the different systems, with government service offering the best inducements.

Furthermore, textbooks with a local content were not to be found; there were no common syllabuses. English-medium schools looked to Britain for materials and texts for the classroom, while the Chinese-medium schools similarly looked to China as the natural source of supply. Thus it was that a local child in an English school would recite Wordsworth's lines on the daffodils, never having seen them, sail up the Thames in imagination, accompany Bonnie Prince Charlie through Scottish burns and braes, and pay for imaginary purchases in pounds, shillings and pence. His opposite number in the Chinese-medium school, on the other hand, referred to the 'Middle Kingdom' as 'My Country'. He was taught to repeat the will of Sun Yat Sen, founder of the Chinese Republic, and he learnt to sing the Chinese national hymn. His cultural heritage came from China; his aspirations and loyalties remained, not with the land of his birth, but with the land of his fathers.

To enhance invidious comparison, occupational opportunity with government departments opened its doors widest to those who had had an English education. In such a context it was not possible to consider the demands of a 'common loyalty' even within each separate territory.

The immediate post-war years were characterised by the feverish activity of reconstruction. The Japanese occupation had left chaos in many places in so far as school buildings were concerned. Besides, a bottleneck had developed with respect to children and youths whose educational careers had been arrested by the outbreak of the Second World War. But the problems discussed above were not allowed to pass unnoticed. Steps were taken to examine and remedy the situation and a great impetus was given to education, resulting in a gathering of momentum in progress, particularly noticeable in the last decade.

In 1956, two committees—the Razak Committee in Malaya and the All-Party Legislative Committee in Singapore—made significant recommendations. For the first time there was mention made of a 'national system of education' and an emphasis on the need to foster a common loyalty. More specifically, the Razak Report set out the importance of this in its views on common content syllabuses:

> We cannot overemphasise our conviction that the introduction of syllabuses common to all schools in the Federation is the crucial requirement of educational policy in Malaya. It is an essential element in the development of a united Malayan nation. It is the key which will unlock the gates hitherto standing locked and barred against the establishment of an educational system 'acceptable to the people of Malaya as a whole'.

Almost simultaneously, the All-Party Report in Singapore hit the same note: 'Schools should use syllabuses and textbooks with a common content designed to build up a Malayan loyalty.'

Syllabuses and textbooks committees were set up in each place to draw up common content syllabuses for use in the different kinds of schools. In Sarawak, the McLellan Report of 1959 on Secondary Education showed how lacking the Chinese school textbooks were in local content. 'The curriculum was still very much the same as that laid down by the Nanking Ministry: so too were the syllabuses. . . . In short the picture throughout was one seen through the eyes of a Chinese in China.' There, in 1961, the Sessional Paper on National Secondary Education, approved by Council Negri, set out the need for a common medium of instruction (English) and a curriculum with a common content for all types of secondary schools. In Sabah also, it was felt 'necessary to ensure that the content

201

of teaching was geared to the needs of the country, and this was particularly true in the approach to social studies'. By the end of 1960 the major part of the work on curriculum revision had been completed in Malaya, Singapore and Sabah. According to the Annual Report of Singapore's Ministry of Education in 1960, thirty-seven approved common syllabuses were ready for implementation. There is great activity in local publishing enterprises and every encouragement is being given to local writers to produce sound textbooks of good quality. In Sarawak, the Borneo Literature Bureau plays a valuable part in the production of textbooks with a local content.

THE SYSTEM OF EDUCATION AS IT IS TODAY

Malaysia, as it stands on the threshold of nationhood, shows promise of a vigorous coming-of-age. Not that adolescent troubles are entirely over: in the anticipation of impending changes, racial issues have been made more conspicuous than necessary by reason of their very absence formerly. But in education, timely changes have brought together children of all races in a system which aims at parity of treatment irrespective of race.

No longer do three separate systems of education exist in mutual exclusiveness. Through a system of grants all assisted schools come under the control of a central authority in each state, particularly with respect to standards of maintenance. An independent and professionally qualified inspectorate of schools is established in each place to ensure that instruction is on a level acceptable to the education authorities concerned. Salaries for teachers in aided schools are exactly the same as those for teachers with similar academic qualifications in government schools. Under improved conditions of planned enterprise, educational development is moving on apace. At present, the pattern of education is multilingual, subject to variations in policy in the different component territories of Malaysia.

Malaya

In Malaya, there are only two types of schools at primary level and both under the same system. There are Standard Schools where the medium of instruction is Malay, and Standard-type Schools where medium of instruction is one of English, Chinese or Tamil. The last mentioned language medium is necessary because of a sizeable South Indian population which has grown, partly through immigration and partly through the practice, in the past, of employing from time to time an indentured labour force from India. A parent in Malaya may now register his child at a primary school using the language medium of his choice.

Both in the Razak Report of 1956 and in the Talib Report of 1960, which reviewed the education policy recommended in the former, it was emphasised that while the national system was to be 'acceptable to the people as a whole', that is, cater for the multicultural aspects of the Malayan community, there was every intention of making Malay the national language and the main medium of instruction, 'except that other languages and literatures might be taught at least in their own media'.

In the light of this intention, Malay has been made a compulsory subject of study in all schools in Malaya. In a Standard School, and in an English-medium Standard-type School, English and Malay are studied together from the first year, whereas in other Standard-type Schools, Malay is studied from the first year and English is compulsory for the last four years of primary school. This implies that a Malay child will, in the first instance, learn two languages in his primary school years. If his parent so chooses, and if parents of fifteen of his peers also so decide and request, he may also be taught either Chinese or Tamil or both. The child in a Standard-type School, other than the English-medium school, besides studying the language used as the medium of instruction, must study both Malay and English. He may study the fourth language if his parents so wish it.

The dual form of education at primary level carries over into the secondary, with schools falling either into the category of National or National-type School. The former is the secondary equivalent of the Standard, as the latter is of the Standard-type, primary school. The ultimate intention of making Malay the main medium of instruction in all government schools with English as a compulsory second language is kept well in view. But the development towards this end is wisely gradual, since it is difficult, not only to train enough teachers to teach in Malay, but also to find enough teachers to teach it as a second language. The conversion of government schools into National Schools has entered upon its first phase with the introduction of Malay streams into such schools as soon as appropriately trained teachers are available. The compulsory study of Malay as a subject has increased the pool of school-leavers who have a reasonable command of the language. As the ripples of change go out in ever widening circles, more teachers can be trained at both training college and university level. The suggestion is already mooted of introducing the Malay medium into some university courses, and it is highly probable that, if the system of primary and secondary education is carried to its logical conclusion, higher institutions of learning, such as the Technical College and the University of Malaya, will also become bilingual.

Singapore

Generally speaking, the pattern of education in Singapore is the same as that in Malaya, but there is a major difference in educational policy. The Singapore government continues to establish schools at both primary and secondary levels in the four language media. There is no attempt to convert or confine government schools to a single type. Malay education was brought into line with other streams with the opening of the first Malay secondary school, the Sang Nila Utama Secondary School, in 1961. Secondary school classes in the Malay and Tamil media, however, had already been started in selected schools in 1960.

Sarawak and Sabah

Curiously enough, the 'national system of education' in Sarawak and Sabah is being defined in quite a different way. There, although the majority of government primary schools were originally established in the Malay media, the process of conversion is from Malay to English. The reason for this is best expressed in the words of Sarawak's governor in his speech in December 1960, before the Council Negri:

> Now it is apparent that multiracial schools can only function satisfactorily if there is a common medium of instruction. . . . In the circumstances of Sarawak today, English is undoubtedly the most acceptable language for educational purposes. It has been employed for many years as a medium in a number of Aided Secondary Schools where its use has enabled pupils of different races to study together. It has immediate advantages in obtaining employment for school-leavers and even greater advantages in the field of further education as it has made it possible for Sarawak students to enter universities and training colleges in increasing numbers. Many more such trained persons are required and it has clearly become a matter for concern to parents that the exclusive use of other media fails to provide opportunities outside the limited occupations open to the products of communal education.

To the indigenous peoples in the Bornean territories, particularly the Dayaks, the realisation has come that English is essential for the effective participation of their children in today's affairs. Perhaps lingering in the background is also an emotional issue, pride of race, which prefers to eschew anything that savours of an association of earlier days when the Dayaks were under the domination of the Brunei Malays. In the peak of the current demand, and because of their new-found enthusiasm for education, many local communities have established on their own initiative native voluntary schools (in Sabah) and self-help schools (in Sarawak). These suffer from poor facilities; their staff are generally inadequate and untrained. Their multiplication is carefully watched and controlled by the state government and as government plans develop and more help is given in financial aid and in the supply of qualified staff, the situation will be effectively remedied. Mission and other non-government schools are generously assisted by grants made from the Central Education Fund (Sabah) and benefited by the Grant Code of 1956 (Sarawak). In this way many primary schools have been opened.

Although a majority of primary schools in the Bornean states are still using Malay as a medium of instruction, the transition phase has already begun with the introduction of English into native schools as a subject of study from the first year. By the third year, English replaces the native dialect as the medium of instruction. In Malay schools, English replaces Malay by the fifth year, at the latest, as a medium of instruction. The policy with respect to Malay schools is to convert, by degrees, the teaching of all school subjects (if parents so desire it) from the Malay to the English medium while retaining Malay as a compulsory subject of study. The governments concerned have not seen fit to discard Malay from the curriculum since it is still the regional language of the area. English has been made a compulsory subject of study for Chinese schools.

Secondary schools in both Sarawak and Sabah are either English- or Chinese-medium schools. Recently established government schools are all in the English medium except two in Sabah where, in the period 1958 to 1960, one junior secondary school using Chinese, and one containing two parallel streams, using English and Chinese, were established. Chinese secondary schools in Sarawak have been invited to convert over a period of years to the use of English as a medium of instruction in all subjects 'except in the study of Chinese languages and literature which will be maintained'.

Educational expansion in the Bornean territories is slower and, comparatively speaking, more expensive than in either Malaya or Singapore. Because of the difficult terrain and lack of communication facilities despite rapid improvements in recent years, boarding schools continue to be in great demand, particularly where rural children have to travel long distances to avail themselves of the benefits of education. Thus, while six years of primary education are now given free at public expense to every child of the correct school-going age in both Singapore and Malaya, such education is not yet quite free or compulsory in the other territories. According to the 1960 Census for Sabah, 30,000 children of primary school age (a large number being indigenous children) were still not in any school as against 46,957 in schools. In Sarawak, there were places for only about fifty per cent of the school age population in 1961.

VOCATIONAL SCHOOLS

An important forward step has been the greater attention paid to the need for diversification in the education offered at secondary level. Until very recently, the curriculum has been heavily biased towards an academic content. In all regions some attempt has now been made to set up classes, at least, of a technical or vocational nature, if not to establish trade and technical schools. Commercial streams are also introduced into some academic-type schools. Trade schools are aimed at training artisans and semi-skilled craftsmen and workers. Intake of students for these occurs at the immediate post-primary level. Technical schools prepare technicians. It has been stipulated that students for such schools must have passed the Lower Certificate in Education with credits in mathematics and science. The snag about this sort of education (which is urgently necessary in the face of rapid progress towards industrialisation) is that it is very expensive and specialised. Equipment is difficult to procure and staff difficult to recruit. As an example, two secondary technical schools were built in 1956 in Singapore, but never really differed from the ordinary academic-type secondary school in much of the curriculum offered until 1960. They only received their full equipment in 1961.

Schools in the past have tended to be concentrated in urban areas. This kind of situation meant the almost total exclusion from any sort of education of the rural sector of the population. Singapore alone is the exception. As a commercial city it depends largely on commerce and industry to remain viable.

To promote a healthy rural economy, rural areas have to be developed, less wasteful methods of farming introduced, and, to make this effective, rural dwellers have to be educated. This points to the fact that education cannot remain the preserve of the urban dweller. For this reason, the Sekolah Lanjutan Kampong (Rural Secondary School) was set up in Malaya in 1958. There are eight such schools offering courses with a rural bias. Girls will also be enrolled in these schools to study domestic science. It is significant that adult education in Malaya is now the responsibility of the Ministry of Rural Development. Such integration in planning for youth and adult education as is possible would bring the best results in rural development. Unfortunately, the Bornean states, while needing this sort of education most, through force of circumstances (lack of trained personnel, lack of equipment, difficulties in communication) have hardly made a start in this direction.

SOME SPECIFIC PROBLEMS

Like many another young nation, Malaysia has had to face the problem attendant upon a sudden upsurge in the demand for education brought about both by the needs generated by the responsibilities of nationhood and by a heightened awareness of the importance of education on the part of the masses. Quantitatively speaking, the new Federation has already gone beyond the first halting steps to meet such demands through planned expansion. But ever present are the problems connected with the requisites for maintaining the line in qualitative standards of the educational output. Foremost among these are teacher supply, multilingualism, and selection.

1. *The problem of teacher supply*

At independence, the teaching profession was clearly a ready-to-hand source of educated and experienced administrators. Competitive recruitment within and without the Education Service drains resources already slender. Added to this, rapid expansion and the demands of a new multilingual educational pattern impose a strain on existing schools of pedagogy. Multiplication of these schools intensifies and adds a further dimension to the problem, *viz.* the question of how to recruit, from an internationally limited market, staff trained for the training of teachers. It is very clearly pointed out in the Report of the First Commonwealth Education Conference at Oxford, 1959, that the possibility of assistance in the form of trained personnel from any source external to the newly emergent country would be slight.

It is noteworthy that under the existing circumstances teacher training in Malaysia has not been hide-bound by precedent. Singapore's only Teachers' Training College has suspended its full-time courses and gives training in all four language media to part-time students who are teachers in primary schools. It also trains teachers for vocational and technical schools in conjunction with the Balestier Trade School and the Singapore Polytechnic which supply the trainees with the practical experience. But part-time training does not hold all the answers. It is almost entirely out of the question for the Bornean states where travel is difficult because of lack of communication facilities.

In the case of Malaya there has been wise planning to avoid duplication of aims or of activities and courses offered in the different training colleges. Yet the rate of expansion is such that with all colleges in all of Malaysia operating at full capacity, and despite 'crash programs' and innovations in training procedures, a great number of untrained teachers have still to be used. For example, consulting the statistics for Singapore as at June 1962, the ratio of trained to untrained teachers in primary schools at a rough calculation was 2 : 3; in secondary schools the ratio was 3 : 1. The ratio 2 : 3 shows a disturbing inadequacy of trained staff at a level where, because of the complex nature of multilingual education, it is most crucial.

Time lag in respect of training of teachers for vocational and technical schools is the greatest. The lack is due in fact to the absence of adequate facilities to supply the practical experience, knowledge and skills which are the prerequisites of training for teachers.

With education a federal responsibility, planning will be integrated. Perhaps then it would be pertinent to consider priorities in which training for the voca-

207

tional and technical aspects of education and language teaching will take precedence. Perhaps around a few well equipped and strategically placed vocational and technical centres, school classes could be set up so that students in their final years at these centres could serve both a practical and professional apprenticeship. This presumes that such training would be full-time; so should the training of language teachers who should study not only the language and the usual psychological principles associated with general practice, but also be given training in the diagnosis of linguistic difficulties.

Since each territory in Malaysia is already spending from fifteen to twenty per cent of the state budget on education, it is hardly likely in the context of national development that unlimited funds would be available. The concentration on the vocational, technical and linguistic aspects of education would necessarily divert funds from other kinds of training. Here novices training for the academic-type school could well serve a practical apprenticeship with selected teachers of proven merit to whom recognition could be given in some suitable form. The content of their professional course could be given by correspondence.

Even in the best of circumstances, teacher-training in its formalised state is inadequate. Knowledge multiplies so fast today that regular refresher courses are necessary. Thus, at a period of sudden demand, it might be better to concentrate on the practical aspects, assuming that there is a level of academic attainment below which content preparation would be considered unacceptable and when demand has stabilised, the career-long inservice training such as that mooted by L. J. Lewis in the Report of the African Summer Study could be considered.

2. The problem of multilingualism

While there is research evidence to show that in a stable language environment children acquire phonemes with much more facility than adults, there is also evidence that word-concept retardation is a much greater danger to the bilingual, and even more to the multilingual, than to the monolingual child. This implies that the teacher of language must not only be fluent in the language himself, but also be specially trained to appreciate the difficulties of the children whom he teaches. The use of Rumi (a romanised script for Malay) confuses the child who is being introduced to the written form of both Malay and English simultaneously. As an example, the Malay word 'dan' has the same meaning and component letters as the English word 'and'. Spelling difficulties increase as the child makes the acquaintance of Malay words borrowed from the English. The Malay word 'pos' comes from the English 'post'; similarly 'opis' corresponds to 'office'. If a child's language environment at home and with his peers does not happen to be stable there is every likelihood that he will incorporate the word 'opis' into his English instead.

208

The differences in idiomatic expression and syntactic usage pervade the study of language. The Chinese sentence is sometimes an inverted form of the corresponding English sentence. 'Where are you?' is literally in Chinese, 'You in where?'

Effective language learning is the necessary concomitant of intellectual growth. To minimise word-concept confusion it may be feasible to confine the first two years of a child's school life to speech bilingualism or trilingualism with study of the written form confined to one language. Research is urgently necessary to discover the specific difficulties of the local child in the study of a language which is not his mother-tongue so that remedial work may be more effective.

3. *The problem of selection*

The introduction of diversification at secondary school level necessarily raises the question as to who would best profit by what kind of education offered. Furthermore, the broad base of primary education is not maintained at secondary level. In the Report of the Commission of Inquiry into Vocational and Technical Education in Singapore (1960), the recommendation is made for channelling post-primary students into the various types of secondary schools in the following proportions: Academic type 20 per cent; Commercial 8 per cent; Technical 7 per cent; and Vocational 65 per cent. The Malayan Ministry of Education has also stated in its report for 1962 its intention to stabilise the intake into secondary schools (including rural secondary schools) at 30 per cent of the number sitting the Secondary Entrance Examination.

Selection at all levels (Primary VI level, Lower Certificate in Education level, School Certificate and Higher School Certificate level) has been chiefly by examination; sometimes, as in the selection for teacher-training, the oral interview is also used. There is great need for the testing of tests which can be validly used in the local context, for follow-up studies to consider the predictive value of the various selection procedures adopted, and for studies of the differential aptitudes of local children.

The problems outlined above are but a few of those which have to be considered. In what way can education promote desirable attitudes with respect to national goals is another question of urgent importance. The challenge to education is great; much new ground has to be broken in practice and research, but what economists call 'investment in education' will bring its best rewards if characterised by bold vision and wise planning, untrammelled by overconsideration of past practices or too hasty an assimilation of imported ideas without due adaptation to local circumstances.

15

Trends in Modern Malay Literature

MOHD. TAIB BIN OSMAN

Modern Malay literature is the product of a society which has undergone changes as the result of contact with the West. The changes which affected traditional Malay society started with British colonial expansion into the Malay peninsula during the nineteenth century and the first phase of the growth of modern literature coincided with the period of British rule up to the outbreak of the Pacific War. The Japanese occupation between 1942 and 1945 saw little literary activity, but like the political changes brought about by the war, the seeds of further changes in Malay literary tradition were sown. Since 1945, we have seen the birth of a new and dynamic spirit in Malay literary activity. Not only has there been a serious effort at literary creativity, but the modern literature of this period has also won for itself a place in the life of the society.

But before we can fully appreciate the importance of recent trends, we should look briefly at traditional literature and the beginnings of a modern outlook. Traditional Malay literature[1] was the product of Malay society before the impact of modern western civilisation during the late nineteenth century. Until this period, Malay cultural contacts were mainly with two great Asian civilisations, that of India from about the first century AD to the thirteenth or fourteenth centuries and then that of the Islamic world. These contacts left permanent marks on the life of the Malays, particularly on life in the royal courts which were the focal points of traditional society. It was at these courts that literature flourished and this is the reason why traditional Malay literature is often referred to as 'kraton-centric' (*kraton* means palace).

It needs to be stressed, however, that traditional literature as known today is the literature written in the Perso-Arabic script known as *Jawi*. Its use dates from the acceptance of Islam by the Malays beginning from the fourteenth or fifteenth century. Besides the written literature which was almost the monopoly of the royal courts, we have to bear in mind the existence of folk tales which, as a form of literature, were never written down but were perpetuated and kept alive orally from one generation to the next. There was also literature inspired by the Indian heritage of the pre-Islamic period. Epics like the story of Rama and stories from the *Mahabarata* still found favour in muslim Malay courts. Islam brought with it not only theological writings, but also stories of the prophets and romances of muslim heroes which came from Persia via India. Somehow, the elements of pre-Islamic and Islamic literature mingle harmoniously. Not only in the folk-tales but also in the written romances, we find princes and princesses bearing hindu and muslim names, hindu gods, muslim prophets and local heroes, in-digenous beliefs, hindu ethics and muslim teachings: all blended together in the *hikayat* or story. Another type of literary product which is more local in character is the *sejarah* or histories of the local sultanates. They relate stories and happen-ings in the courts usually glorifying the reigning monarchs. Such works are more literary than historical because their authors were not obliged to record history but to eulogise their patrons.

Perhaps it is in traditional poetry that the Malay language finds itself fully exploited as an artistic expression, with its rhythm, rhyme and imagery. Besides the Persian verse-forms which are to be found in some isolated works of Perso-Indian origin, there are the famous *pantun* and the narrative *sha'ir* which, to the Malays, are the literary heritage they cherish most. The *pantun* can be considered as folk-ditty; it is used on almost all occasions in Malay life: at festivals, weddings, betrothals, in courtship, or whenever an occasion arises where poetic expression can add lustre to the occasion. The *pantun* is a quatrain and is unique in structure. The first two lines are usually meaningless except to provide the rhyming scheme for the last two lines which actually convey the message. The message, often disguised in metaphors and similes, can be anything: an expression of love, a riddle, a reflection of one's mood or fate, or just a wise saying about the ups and downs of human life.

In contrast to the *pantun* which is everybody's property, the *sha'ir* is a long narrative poem made up of quatrains rhyming *a-a-a-a*. Unlike the *pantun*, each quatrain of the *sha'ir* conveys an idea from the first to the last line. The *sha'ir* not only tells stories of the usual romances of heroes, princes and princesses, but also the 'histories' of the local sultanates and conveys the teachings and ideas of religion. Though it was common for a *sha'ir* to be copied over and over again until we do not know how it came to be written, we cannot doubt that a *sha'ir*, unlike the *pantun*, is a creation of the poetic genius of an individual.

Such were the antecedents of modern Malay literature, antecedents usually ignored and misunderstood by most of the young writers today in their en-thusiasm for creating new traditions. As for the beginnings of modern writing, these can be dated from Abdullah bin Abdul Kadir Munshi (1797–1856). Abdul-lah's works are considered the forerunner of modern literature, not so much in the style and language which deviate from earlier conventions, but more in the content and subject-matter. It was his criticism of traditional Malay society which made him different from his predecessors. We might consider his writings as representing the first step forward, but his ideas did not receive acceptance in his own time and were not taken up again until the twentieth century.

However, Abdullah did not entirely break away from the older Malay literary traditions. Though, generally speaking, his style is less cramped than the style of his predecessors and his language is almost free from conventional clichés, he was still fond of the time-worn proverbial sayings of the Malays. As a social critic, Abdullah could not help being a moraliser, and it was in moralising about human goodness and frailties that he found the richness of Malay proverbs. He was also fond of the traditional Malay verse-forms—the *pantun* and the *sha'ir*. But in this, he seems to be less capable than those before him. Abdullah did not look with favour on the content of traditional literature, but, he said, it was to the language of the *Sejarah Melayu*[2] that the Malay language should look for inspiration. This does appear to be a retrogressive view, for today his own style is regarded as the changing point of literary style, from the traditional to the modern. Perhaps Abdullah did not realise that he was himself forging a change in the Malay language; but during his time, what was traditional and what was modern seemed to overlap.

THE BEGINNINGS OF THE MODERN TRADITION

In the period before the outbreak of the Pacific War, the significance of Abdul-lah in innovating Malay literature was not given full recognition in Malaya because the activity which gave rise to modern literary expression was not motivated by a consciousness for the need to create a literature befitting a chan-ging society. It was different, however, across the Straits of Malacca. As early as 1920, a young western-educated Sumatran nationalist, Muhamad Yamin, wrote essays evoking the name of Abdullah as the harbinger of a new life to Malay literature, while at the same time experimenting with new forms of poetic expres-sion in Malay. Muhamad Yamin chose the sonnet as the form to write his modern poetry in Malay.[3] It was with him and his colleagues in the organisation called the 'Jong Sumatranen Bond' (The Association of Young Sumatrans) that the first conscious attempt to give a new life to Malay literature on modern lines was made. Thus in Indonesia, Abdullah was a source of inspiration to the con-scious efforts in creating a modern literature in Malay,[4] whereas in Malaya, the

212

presence of an Abdullah on the literary scene would have made the birth of a modern Malay literature more meaningful.[5] The appearance of the so-called first novel in Malay in 1926 can hardly be said to be the result of a new conscious-ness in literary activity; its appearance was more a by-product of a socio-religious awakening in the society.

Literary activity which produced work bearing distinctive characteristics different from those of traditional literature started roughly from 1925. Prior to this, the factors which shaped the character and trends of the activity were formed. Within sixty years of Abdullah's death, British rule had practically covered the whole of Malaya, and this brought in its wake modern western civilisation. However, the changes brought by western civilisation were not met without resistance. First to the fore were the religious-educated elite. While realising that the tide of change could not be stopped, this group chose to meet the impact by kindling a new outlook and spirit based on the true teachings of Islam. This was interpreted as a way to challenge the progress of the western christian nations by introducing modernity with true Islamic teachings as the base. In Malaya, this movement was an offspring of the Islamic reform which was sweeping the muslim countries in the Middle East, especially Egypt, in an earlier period. It is significant that it was the same situation—contact with the West bringing with it a challenge towards progress—that gave rise to the spirit of religious reform and awakening in Egypt. The idea of Islamic reform can there-fore be interpreted as a defence against a total acceptance of western civilisation by the muslim nations. In this the printing press played an important role. The journal *Al-Imam* (which appeared in 1906) was the first of the series of publications used as a vehicle to propagate the aims and views of the movement. Right from its first issue, it had taken upon itself the task of exhorting the Malays to wake up and work for progress following the path of Islam. This campaign was pursued with vigour by *Al-Imam* and was followed up, even until the present day, by various other journals. The role played by this movement in the rise of a modern literature in Malay was to introduce to Malay society modern Egyptian literature. And it was modern Egyptian literature which exerted a great influence on early Malay literary activity.

Most Malay literary historians claim that when an Egyptian novel was adapted into Malay in 1926 by Syed Sheikh Al-Hady, one of the men connected with *Al-Imam*, it marked the first beginning of a truly modern literature since Abdullah. This was the first time that the novel as a literary genre was intro-duced into the world of Malay literature. Thus the criterion seems to be the introduction of literary genres such as the novel, the short story, and other forms of literature to be found in western literary traditions. Abdullah had introduced modern themes into Malay literature because he brought the reader from the domains of the *hikayat* to the world of everyday life. But Abdullah did not write novels, nor did he introduce the sonnet because, it is said, '. . . the contact (with the West) during Abdullah's time was not an "intellectual" contact between the dynamic western civilisation and the feudal Malay society; for if it were the case, there would certainly have been an "intellectual revolution", even in a small way, towards the modernisation of Malay literature. And this would mean that fiction, as a new western literary genre, would also have developed in Malay literature (at that time).'[6] However, this novel (*Faridah Hanum* as it is known in Malay) does not deviate very much from the characteristics of the *hikayat* for it is 'as entrancing as the *Hikayat Gul Bakawali* except that its setting is modern'.[7] Fiction purely as the product of imagination is to be found in the *hikayat* and the folk-romances, but fiction as a literary genre would come to mean here a story from imagination about ordinary man and his problems in contemporary everyday life. Thus, though *Faridah Hanum* is a story of ideal characters in the background of modern but far-away Egypt (and in this respect it is not unlike the stories of princes and princesses of far-away lands of Persia, India or China, or even the heavenly kingdom, of the *hikayat*), the social problems implied in this novel are not only in line with the ideas of Islamic reform but also relevant to contemporary Malay society at that time. The emancipation of women in modern society, the need to educate women, the pre-marital code of conduct between young men and women, and the ideas of patriotism and national pride, are some of the questions raised by this novel. And these reflect some of the questions confronting Malay society in the course of readjusting its cultural and religious values to the needs of modern times. As a novel, of course, these questions are entwined around the central theme—love—for *Faridah Hanum* is actually a love story.

Fiction, it is said, can either be to entertain (to give pleasure to the reader) or to instruct, or both. The pattern of Malay fiction following *Faridah Hanum* seems to fulfil these requirements, though in technique the novels were still in a raw and unpolished stage of development. It was not until 1929, when an original novel called *Kawan Benar* by Ahmad bin Abdul Rashid appeared, that we get the beginning of novels with local Malay characters set in a contemporary Malay social background. Until the outbreak of the Pacific War, Malay novel writing can generally be said to comprise on the one hand works translated from Egyptian sources and popular western literature, and on the other original novels with Malay characters in a local setting. Whether original or otherwise, the novels were either for entertainment or for introducing new ideas; not only the authors' views on the problems confronting Malay society, but also those touching vaguely on Malay nationalism. It is suggested that the late introduction of the novel as a modern literary genre in modern Egyptian literature is reflected also by its late introduction into Malay literature.[8] The influence of Egyptian literature is further reflected by the fact that the large number of newspapers which came out during the 1930s often carried translations of stories appearing in Egyptian newspapers; and this was not confined to Egyptian works like the historical romances or the novels featuring social problems, but also western works which were translated into Arabic, especially from French. This might well be a journalistic device to make the newspapers more palatable to the readers, but undeniably it reflects a close contact with the Egyptian literary scene. The newspapers seem to have had an important role in the literary activity of that time, for it was through the medium of the newspapers that most of the literary productions first found expression, whether they were original, translated or adapted. Most of the stories were at first serialised in the newspapers and then compiled to be sold as novels.

While we have to mention the great contribution made by the new Egyptian literature on the growth of modern Malay literature, we must also note that works in English also left some impressions on the writing of Malay novels during that time. But it was popular literature in the form of penny novels, thrillers and adventure stories rather than the serious works of English literature that left a mark. Detective stories, the adventures of Tarzan, and romantic love stories, were translated and adapted, while attempts at emulating the style of such works were made.[9] This tendency arose because there had been only incidental contacts with literature in English and no direct contact with real English literary values and traditions. Urbanisation in the country had brought some of the Malays to the towns; it was in the towns that the incidental contacts took place. Though English literature was a subject taught in the English stream of education in Malaya, contact with English literary traditions was so superficial that the finer points of English literary values were often missed by the students. Those Malay writers who had some familiarity with English literature did not show in their writings that they had actually benefited from their experience. It is significant to note that those writers in Malaya (Malays or non-Malays) who write in English, especially after the war, are mostly those who have studied English literature at the University of Malaya.

At about the same time, too, beginning from 1925 or thereabouts, short stories began to appear in the newspapers and magazines. These did not grow out of any conscious effort at creating a new literary genre, but rather out of a journalistic endeavour to provide entertaining reading in the newspapers. However, as in the case of the novels, topics such as social criticism, religious reform or suggestions for the progress of society came into focus more and more. Thus, though there was a fair share of literary output with the intention of providing reading for pleasure, a tendentious bias ever present in Malay literary efforts of the time led to short stories being used as an alternative medium to essays on social problems.[10]

It is interesting to note that the same trend was manifest in the early development of modern Indonesian literature. In the 'twenties, the novels discussed problems which reflected the situation in which the old *adat* (customs) came into conflict with the new order, while in the 'thirties, under the leadership of the *Poedjangga Baroe* movement, the cry was for the creation of a new Indonesian culture based on a unity transcending regional and racial barriers. In Malaya, the themes chosen by the religious-educated writers reflect their concern for the social and moral crises which they thought were confronting society. Thus their novels and short stories discuss themes like the adverse moral effects of a liberal mixing between young men and women, an over-westernised way of life, too much freedom for women and other problems which are supposed to touch on the sensitivity of the traditional moral code of the Malays. On the other hand, among the more politically conscious writers—especially the Malay-educated and English-educated writers—the tendency was to write on themes reflecting the political factors affecting Malay society at that time. Besides exhorting the Malays to seek advancement, they also suggested the ways and means to better society, or even, as in the case of Ishak Haji Muhammad, touched on the nature of British colonialism. Urbanisation had brought many young Malays into towns. The writers warned that life in town was full of temptation from places of entertainment and other distractions; they took it upon themselves to warn the young people of these dangers. On the other hand, the writers saw that modernism brought advancement, at least materially, and comparing the advancement achieved by the other races in Malaya, they had to exhort their people to strive for progress, but without discarding their own traditional cultural and religious values.

As an illustration, I shall mention some representative writers who belong to the period under discussion. The first is Abdul Rahim Kajai, who is today regarded as the 'father' of modern Malay short stories. His short stories which appeared in many of the newspapers of the 'thirties conveyed the same messages to be found in the writings of people like Syed Sheikh. Even in his style and language, he was a close follower of Syed Sheikh. In fact, Syed Sheikh's tradition was even carried into the period after the war, especially in the writings of Ahmad Lufti, whom I shall mention later. Rahim Kajai was essentially a journalist; between 1930 and 1942, he was the editor of some of the more important newspapers of that period. In his newspapers, Rahim not only wrote editorials on themes centering around social problems, but also short stories which reflected the same problems.

Besides Kajai, Ishak Haji Muhammad can be said to be another representative writer of the period. Ishak was English-educated and a member of the most radical Malay nationalist movement before the war. It is significant to note that

216

a person like Ishak who displays deep political insight in his novels, probably because of his educational background, wrote in a style not much different from the Malay novels of his time. It is often said that the English-educated Malays have made very little contribution to the growth of modern Malay literature. The educational system channelled the English-educated Malays into the civil service, from the clerical to the junior administrative posts. Though the early political movements attracted this group, most of them, except for a few who were more radical in their anti-colonialism, confined their political outlook to the preservation of Malay rights and privileges against the encroachment of the other races. In literary activity, though some took up writing in Malay either as journalists or as translators of western works, no attempt was made by this group to initiate modern writings on the lines of western literature. Ishak Haji Muhammad, for example, after completing his secondary English education, joined the Civil Service as anyone else in his position would have done. But he resigned after a few years and took up journalism. It was as a journalist that he started writing short stories and novels, which, in both style and content, did not reflect any impact of western literary traditions.

The Malay-educated group and those educated in religious schools did not have the opportunity to learn of western literary traditions because they lacked a knowledge of English. If they had such, it was through reading translated works or through popular literature. For the Malay-educated elite, this was a vacuum filled by works published in Indonesia. This is evident from the works written by writers belonging to this group. Harun Muhamad Amin, for example, mentions in his first novel, *Melor Kuala Lumpur*, which was written in 1930, an early Indonesian novel he had read. However, judging from his novel, Harun did not seem to grasp fully the message conveyed by the Indonesian novel in question. Whereas the latter reflects the conflict between the old and the new orders in Indonesian society, Harun placed more emphasis on the love element found in the novel. Abdullah Sidek, another writer belonging to this group, also showed traces of Indonesian influence in his novels. Contact with modern Indonesian literature left some impressions on the writings of Malay writers, but it was not enough to create the same dynamic spirit as existed in Indonesian literature. Though the same motivation was to be seen, writers in Malaya lacked clarity of purpose. The conflict between the old and the new orders was clearly reflected in the Indonesian novels; but novels in Malaya only touched the fringes of such questions. The *Poedjangga Baroe* movement was not unknown in Malaya,[11] but the strong nationalistic drive which gave the literary activity of the movement a purposeful character did not have much influence in Malaya. In 1934 there was born a Malay literary organisation which was first engendered in the columns of Syed Sheikh's newspaper, *Saudara*. But this organisation, called *Persaudaraan Sahabat Pena*, did not foster

217

the same degree of literary consciousness as did the *Poedjangga Baroe* movement, though it succeeded in forming branches all over the country.

In the field of poetry, *pantun* and *sha'ir* were still the poetic forms of the day. The newspapers regularly featured *pantun*—even *pantun* competitions—and *sha'ir*. Auspicious occasions called for specially composed *sha'ir* and this became a journalistic tradition of pre-war Malay newspapers. However, towards the end of the 'thirties, there appeared attempts at experimenting with new poetic forms, especially in journals like the *Majallah Guru* and *Saujana*,[12] the publications of the Malay schoolteachers' associations. To what extent this can be attributed to influence from Indonesia it is difficult to say, but modern Indonesian *sajak*—as this new free verse form is called—did actually appear in *Majallah Guru* as early as 1934. In this endeavour the leadership was not from the writers educated in religious schools but rather from the Malay-educated writers. The Malay-educated elite can be said to consist of the graduates of the Sultan Idris (Teachers') Training College, the highest seat of learning in Malay before the war (about the level of secondary school), and those other teachers who did not have the opportunity to go to the College. However, new poetic forms appeared only once in a while in those journals and, generally speaking, did not leave a permanent mark on the Malay literary scene. Even in Indonesia, though Muhamad Yamin had been writing sonnets as early as 1920, and was followed by new poets like Roestam Effendi and Sanusi Pane in the late 'twenties, it was not until the 'thirties that the new free verse form came not only to be appreciated, but also to be something to work for.[13] Thus though its beginnings can be traced before 1941, the new spirit of poetic expression rightly belongs to the period after the war.

In Indonesia, it is said that the birth of modern Indonesian literature was partly at the instigation of the Office of Popular Literature (*Balai Pustaka*) which was set up by the government to provide reading material for the people. A body having nearly similar aims was set up by the British government in Malaya in 1924. This was known as the Malay Translation Bureau attached to the Sultan Idris Training College. Besides producing textbooks for school use, the Bureau translated some works of authors like Shakespeare, Jonathan Swift, Robert Louis Stevenson and Sir Arthur Conan Doyle. But these translated works did not have a great impact on the Malay-educated writers except perhaps in arousing the desire to write.[14] They were regarded rather in the same way as the *hikayat*—as merely stories. As O. T. Dussek says of the Bureau of which he was the founder: 'We have spent the last one hundred years in producing reading materials for children',[15] for the books did not go much further than being supplementary readers for the children in Malay schools.

Modern Malay literature until the outbreak of the Pacific War did not achieve a high literary standard because there was no consciousness of literature as a form of creative art. Literature was regarded more as a medium—an alternative medium—for expressing the writer's ideas about things closely related to his life and his society. Whatever his affiliations—be he religiously oriented, or of the Malay-educated elite, or an English-educated nationalist—he did not treat the novel or short story as a literary form but as a medium to express his thoughts. If he was not motivated by this end, he lacked the intuition and insight to produce works of high literary merit. Concomitant with the new literary writings, the traditional literature still held its sway. But, in spite of this, it is undeniable that the new writings did begin to meet the literary needs of a society which was undergoing transformation.

THE POST-WAR PERIOD

Literary activity during the Japanese occupation can be passed over briefly. During this three and a half year period, the traditional *pantun* and *sha'ir* were still widely featured in the newspapers and magazines, though some young people, including Masuri S.N. who is today recognised as the pioneer of modern poetry writing, were beginning to transform the traditionally impersonal *pantun* into a poetic form conveying their own personal thoughts and feelings.[16] As for the novel, hardly one is known to have been written during this period. It was the short story which came to the fore as a favourite and popular form of fiction. The two main periodicals of this time, *Fajar Asia* and *Semangat Asia*, and the newspaper *Berita Malai*, carried short stories fairly regularly. These however, perhaps unavoidably, had a strong flavour of Japanese propaganda. Typical is a short story called *Ubi Kayu* (Tapioca) by Samad Ismail which ends: '. . . plant much more tapioca!'[17] Though literary activity during the Japanese occupation was rather limited in scope, nevertheless the post-war writers attribute the beginnings of the changes in the post-war period to the situation created by the Japanese occupation, especially in bringing modern Indonesian works closer to the Malay reading public.[18]

The forging of a new literary tradition in Malaya after the war did not make a sudden impact on society. In the early post-war years, the tradition of pre-war literature still had a hold on the Malay reading public, especially the novels which still bore pre-war characteristics. Most of these novelists were those who were quite familiar with the post-war literary scene. One of them, Ahmad Lufti, can be said to be the last of Syed Sheikh's followers. He has written more than ten short novels; though the first two novels deal with themes far removed from contemporary social problems, the others are directly in the tradition of the pre-war didactic novels. These novels can be said to be an exposé of social ills and moral degradation in Malay society seen mostly from the point of religion, but they contain almost no prescription for these problems. So preoccupied was

219

Lufti with such ideas that the theme of his novels tends to follow very closely the topic of the day discussed in the country. For example, when the question of Malay women playing hockey was discussed in the newspapers, out came Lufti's novel *Hockey*, giving a somewhat lopsided view of the subject.

Harun Muhamad Amin, whom we have mentioned earlier, is another writer of the pre-war tradition. His are romantic stories, but it is in him that we get traces of novel-writing not so much as an instructive occupation, but more for the sake of writing a story. His recently written historical novels, *Panglima Awang* (1956) and *Anak Panglima Awang* (1961), still show Harun's flair for writing a story for its own sake, though Harun could not really stay aloof from contemporary trends and in his later novels we get an undertone of nationalism, evoking the great bygone days of the fifteenth-century Malay empire of Malacca.

Ishak Haji Muhammad also continued to write in the tradition of his pre-war novels. His new novels also keep very close to social questions; but unlike Ahmad Lufti who sees the problems mainly from the point of religious sanctions, Ishak is more concerned with the fate of the common people in the prevailing political and social conditions. Modern Malay literature, according to Ishak, should inspire the people to work and improve their lot.[19]

Besides these three—Lufti, Amin and Ishak—there were other younger writers who could not help but follow the same trend of novel-writing. Apart from those expressing the same sentiments as Lufti and Ishak, especially on themes displaying nationalistic feelings, there were also writers of romantic stories and thrillers. However, like the pre-war novels, these novels are usually short, poor in technique, mediocre in content, and above all badly presented. With bright but sketchy illustrations on the cover, they take the appearance of penny novels, and, in some cases, they are just that.

While the pre-war traditions are being perpetuated in the novels, young writers have emerged, who, in the chosen medium of short stories and poetry, have given a new and vigorous life to Malay literature. The growth of post-war Malay literary activity has gone hand in hand with new social and political awareness among the young people. The changes occurring all over the world after the end of the Second World War affected Malaya and not only were happenings outside the country exerting their influence but also the situation prevailing in the country. The opposition of the Malays to the Malayan Union in 1946–7, the labour unrest in Singapore, the Emergency and the independence movement are all reflected in the new writings. But above all, the drive in literary activity was the result of an increasing nationalist consciousness. It was the desire to have a rich literature in their own language which spurred this consciousness. No longer was literature taken for granted. It was realised that literature can be a source of pride, not only to an individual but to the whole nation. This reminds us of what took place in Indonesia in the 'thirties when the *Poedjangga Baroe* movement consciously worked for a modern literary tradition with the intention of making it a cultural manifestation of a united Indonesian nation. But post-war Malay literary expression is still close to society; in fact, even more so than in the case of pre-war writings, because now it is written with definite ideas behind it and with a better display of insight into the problems the writers are portraying. In the short story and also in poetry, this trend was not discernible immediately. In the early post-war years, as in the case of the novels, romantic and sentimental love themes were still evident.[20] At the time of the struggle against the establishment of the Malayan Union, political inclinations were not expressed in a direct manner but shrouded in romantic themes. Typical of such themes is the expression of love for country and nation overcoming love for a woman.[21]

It was not until a group of young writers in Singapore banded together in 1950 and formed an organisation called *Angkatan Sasterawan '50* (Generation of Writers of the 'Fifties) or in short *Asas '50* that we get a definite consciousness of literary creativity and also the formulation of new trends which greatly influence contemporary writings. Unlike the *Poedjangga Baroe* which was a loosely formed association centering on its journal of the same name, this body of young writers was a closely knit group. As an organisation, *Asas '50* inspired a new spirit of group identification. The influence which this group has exerted on the growth and trends in Malay literature today cannot be underrated. Although the body as an organisation is moribund now, its leadership is still very much alive. Writers belonging to the group, especially Masuri S.N. and Tongkat Waran in the field of poetry and Keris Mas in short-story writing are still looked up to even though they are not as prolific as they were during the heyday of the organisation. The most productive period of *Asas '50* was between 1950 and 1954; after that, though some of the members still wrote, it was not as active.[22] In its wake came a younger set of writers; but the traces of *Asas '50* in their efforts are still very much in evidence. Although *Asas '50* was formed primarily as a literary group to pool the resources of young writers in order to instil a new life and spirit into Malay literature, its underlying motivation was nationalism. *Asas '50* not only produced literary works, but also dealt with political questions, social problems, language and cultural matters. This can clearly be seen in the various papers submitted by this body to the Language and Literary congresses held in the country.[23] All these questions are really inseparable. They are well defined in the slogan of *Asas '50*: 'Art for Society.' Though this led to a split in the group and some of the members who were afraid of literature being used as propaganda left the organisation,[24] the concept of literature as an instrument for the betterment of society is the most influential idea in post-war Malay literature.

Judging from what has been written, there is little indication that this slogan has been inspired by the social realism in western literature. It is clear that the group was motivated by feelings of nationalism and the desire to expose and if possible to correct the ills prevailing in the society. This is not new, and may be observed in writings ever since Abdullah; but with the *Asas '50*, it becomes clearly defined and emphasised. The influence of this movement is particularly to be seen in short stories and poetry. This is no accident because the three leading members of the organisation were editors of *Utusan Zaman* and *Mastika*, the most influential literary media at the time.[25] It was through these publications and to some extent through the radio that prominent members of *Asas '50* expounded their views and concepts. Thus, the desire to create a literature which would befit the age they lived in went together with the desire to instil a new spirit and outlook among the Malays, and new social and political ideas, especially those related to the struggle for independence and the fight for social justice. In their enthusiasm, they rejected traditional beliefs and attitudes and also the old literary traditions. Their view of traditional literature is reminiscent of Abdullah's; to them as to him, traditional forms and styles are not expressive of the contemporary and the real in everyday life. As Tongkat Waran says, '. . . the duty of the New Generation now is to destroy ideas which are outmoded and stale . . . and to promote ideas which are emphatic, precise, forceful and vigorous. That is the way to give enlightenment to the people towards a pure, progressive and independent tendency. . . .'[26] Perhaps it is not their fault that they cared little for their own literary traditions and took the old literature only on their own terms: that is, literature should be written to make people aware of the political and social conditions prevailing in their society at the time. Thus, conscious though they were of literary creativity, they tended to overlook the literary values to be found in traditional Malay literature.

The wealth of post-war literary output is to be seen in the short story and in poetry. But drama too has been gaining popularity especially in Singapore, where a play is staged almost every month. Though a dearth of novels is greatly felt, there have appeared recently novels which, at least in length and technique, can be said to be an improvement on the pre-war novels. The new novels like *Salina* by Samad Said and *Hari Mana Bulan Mana* by Salmi Manja have the same themes as those to be found in the short stories—themes centering on social and political problems. It has been a long established tradition of Malay Sunday newspapers to feature at least a short story and two or three *sajak* (free verse compositions). First begun by the *Utusan Zaman*, it was taken up by the *Berita Minggu*. Today these two newspapers are not only the main media for literary efforts, but have become the place where literary recognition is to be won. It used to be the aim of aspiring young writers to have their efforts published in the *Utusan Zaman* and its monthly magazine *Mastika*, but now the field has broadened slightly with the addition of *Berita Minggu* and also its daily *Berita Harian*, which carries a hundred-dollar prize for short stories published every Thursday. Malay literary activity is very much confined to the newspapers and magazines, and the media through which the young writers can express themselves are still limited.[27] Even so, the place given to Malay literature by the reading public is encouraging; much of it is due to the recognition that literary activity is important to the life of society. Besides literary works, criticism is also a feature which reflects the healthy state of literary consciousness. Unlike the period before the war, Malay literature is now a subject in the school curriculum and also at the university; this gives a new importance to literary creativity. Even before independence, there had already been plans to establish a body responsible for the development of Malay language and the encouragement of literary efforts in Malay. This body grew up to be the *Dewan Bahasa dan Pustaka* which, among other things, has organised short-story and novel-writing competitions. However, the improved conditions for aspiring writers have not solved many basic problems. Writers as yet cannot live off their writings and literature remains a part-time occupation. The lack of publication media also has a stifling effect on literary growth. Recently, some publishers stated that though they would help young writers, they were still guided by 'names' because only works by well-known writers would guarantee good returns.[28] The newspapers and the publishers still do not pay writers well; one of the motives for the formation of *Asas '50* had been to safeguard the writers' interests.[29]

At the beginning, the young writers were mostly Malay-educated, but in the last seven years or so, the English-educated, including university students and graduates, have also started writing. If Indonesian works had been the first inspiration, now the horizon has become wider; great literary works, both western and oriental, have become new sources of inspiration for the younger writers. It is not uncommon to find short stories reflecting sentiments of authors like Balzac, Tolstoy and Hemingway. Literary concepts and movements in the West have also received attention.[30] Besides short stories, poetry has undergone vast changes, almost amounting to the rejection of the *pantun* and the *sha'ir*. Though the appeal of *pantun* is still strong, the *sajak* has become the accepted new form. Unlike the *pantum* and the *sha'ir*, which are governed by rather rigid forms, the *sajak* is usually free verse. At first the influence of the *pantun* form could still be seen, but gradually the *sajak* has drawn away from any recognised traditional forms, not only in the prosody, but also in the imagery and diction. The content, following the short stories, has also become topical; political situations, not only in the country but also outside, find expression in modern Malay

223

sajak.[31] In recent years, especially after independence, poetry has become increasingly subjective, and at times the *sajak* are rather obscure.[32]

The question of a Malayan literature has been discussed on many occasions. Besides literature in Malay, there are in Malaya writings in English, Chinese, and Tamil. Though in recent years writings in Malay have been translated into English, Chinese and Tamil, not much from the other languages has been translated into Malay. Though the National Union of Writers is supposed to be a national body, the membership is almost exclusively Malay. There has been very little effort to bring the writers of the different language groups together, though seminars like the one organised by the Singapore *Dewan Bahasa dan Kebudayaan* in 1962 are sometimes held. Whether writings in Malay will be regarded as Malayan to the exclusion of others because the national language is Malay is something which will have to be thrashed out. But it is undeniable that the spirit of the young nation is fully and richly reflected in the literary activity of the young Malay writers.

PART FOUR

The Economy

16

The Plantation Industries—The Estates

D. W. FRYER

Plantation industries[1] form the bedrock of the Malaysian economy. In Malaya they account for nearly forty per cent of gross national product and for some sixty per cent of export income; they produce about one half of the export income of Sarawak if petroleum re-exports are excluded, and about forty per cent of that of Sabah, although these figures may show considerable fluctuations from year to year. The organisation of the plantation industries is of greater complexity than is often supposed and though it is customary to distinguish between an estate and a smallholder division, the definition of both an estate and a small-holding is far from easy and it is not really surprising that there has been no uniformity between the various Malaysian territories. In Malaya and Sabah estates and smallholders are of approximately equal importance in terms of planted area, although estate output is considerably the greater; in Sarawak, however, smallholders are of much greater significance.

Estate agriculture is not, therefore, as dominant in Malaysia as is commonly supposed in the world at large, but it is impressive enough; in Malaya it can sometimes produce more than forty per cent of export earnings, it provides employment for some 300,000 workers (about the same as the number of smallholders) and accounts for around sixty per cent of the foreign investment in the country. It is, nevertheless, far from a monopoly of overseas capital; forty per cent of the planted area of rubber estates is on properties owned by Asians, the great majority of whom are permanent residents in the country.

ESTATE AREA AND CROPS

It is probable that the Chinese were the first to begin estate operations in Malaysia, as was also the case in what is now Indonesia. Sugar estates were established in Province Wellesley in the first half of the nineteenth century but there was little European interest before 1840. Such a labour-intensive industry presented special difficulties in the pioneering environment of Malaya and led to the importation of Indian workers, the first of a growing stream of Indian immigrants without whose labour the estate industries could never have attained their subsequent importance. European planters, however, sought for crops that would be less demanding both on labour and on soil; tea, tobacco, gambier, pepper and cinchona were all tried, but it was coffee that created the first planting boom. The first European estate in Selangor, the Weld Hill estate (now a residential area of Kuala Lumpur), had 150 acres planted to Liberian coffee in 1881 and within a few years the influx of planters and capital from the disease-ridden coffee plantations of Ceylon had made coffee the dominant estate crop. By 1896 there were 72 European-owned estates with 10,835 acres under cultivation in Selangor while in Perak over 35,000 acres were being opened up for estate planting.[2] The estate coffee industry is now virtually defunct, being confined to one small property in Trengganu, the last Selangor estate having ceased operations in 1962. Rubber, though introduced into Malaya in 1877, long remained a novelty; the first commercial planting of Hevea braziliensis was made in 1895 by Tan Chay Yan on Bukit Lintang, behind Malacca town. This estate, however, was interplanted with Ficus elastica, another rubber-yielding plant. The first unmixed stand and the first rubber commercially planted in Selangor was made in 1895 by the Kindersley brothers on what is now part of the Inch Kenneth estate near Kajang. Thereafter development was rapid and within two decades rubber had come to dominate the Malayan economy.

The late nineteenth century saw the introduction of another plant to Malaya, the oil palm, which was for many years used only for decorative planting. The first commercial planting did not take place until 1917 and initial development was slow. Since the end of the Second World War, however, the pace of expansion has quickened considerably and, although the oil palm is never likely to challenge rubber, it is clear that it is destined to become a crop of considerably greater significance than at present. This period has also witnessed the first commercial planting of two other crops, cocoa and abacá (Manila hemp), though both crops have long been known in Malaysia.

There is no uniformity in the definition of estates, either between crops or between the various Malaysian territories themselves. The Statistics Department of the former Federation of Malaya defined rubber estates as 'land contiguous or non-contiguous, aggregating not less than 100 acres in area, planted with rubber or on which the planting of rubber is permitted and under a single legal ownership'.[3] Holdings of less than this magnitude are regarded as smallholdings, although by the device of registering different lots under different names, usually those of relatives, many local owners are able to enjoy the privileges of small-holders (such as a higher replanting grant than that allowed estates) even though they may possess more than 100 acres. The total number of estates so defined is certainly larger than is recorded in the Department's annual Handbook of Rubber Statistics.[4] For the 1960 Census of Agriculture the Federation Department of Agriculture defined an estate as 'an area of 100 acres or more of *cultivated land* which is managed as a single agricultural unit operating its own set of financial accounts'.[5] In the case of crops other than rubber, however, the Census admitted to some uncertainty, and for such crops information on plantings of less than 100 acres was also collected. In Sarawak the term estate is confined to properties exceeding 1,000 acres (holdings of from 100 to 1,000 acres being considered as 'medium holdings'), and in Sabah to those over 250 acres.

The total number of estates in the Malaysian territories appears to be around 2,500, of which all but a handful are located in Malaya. Seven types of cultivated estate land use were recognised by the Malayan Census of Agriculture; wherever a particular crop occupied three-quarters or more of the total estate cultivated area, the estate was assigned to that category of land use, but if less than three-quarters of the cultivated area was planted to any one crop, it was regarded as a 'mixed estate'. Table 19 shows the number and distribution of estates using these criteria and Table 20 summarises the information available on estates in the Borneo territories. The most striking points that emerge are that only about four per cent of the total estate cultivated area is located in the Borneo territories; that rubber is by far the most important crop, accounting for about ninety per cent of the total number of estates and for over eighty-eight per cent of the estate culti-vated area; and that Malaysian estates are essentially monocultural. About ninety per cent of all estates reporting some rubber land and about forty per cent of those reporting land under oil palms possessed no other cultivated land at all.

There is, nevertheless, a distinctive group of about a dozen large estates which practise multiple cropping on a considerable scale in Malaya, and about three in Sabah. Most of the former were established about the turn of the century, either as coconut estates or for the production of coffee and lowland tea, occasionally as offshoots of Ceylonese companies, and all are located along the lower Perak, Bernam, Selangor and Langat rivers. With the introduction of more profitable crops, land has been diverted from coconut or coffee production into rubber and oil palm. The largest of these multiple crop estates is the Jugra and Carey Island estate to the south of the Langat river, which has almost 10,000 acres under rubber, over 6,000 acres under coconuts and almost 1,000 acres respectively under oil palm and lowland tea. Temporary multiple cropping is visible along several portions of the Perak and Selangor coastlands, for the greater profitability of oil palm as compared with rubber is encouraging estates to make the changeover wherever physical conditions are suitable. This development also reflects the desire of estate companies to insure against increasing competition from synthetic rubber, and the fact that since 1956 replanting grants have also been allowed to estates desirous of diverting rubber land into alternative cropping.

TABLE 19. NUMBER AND AREA OF ESTATES, FEDERATION OF MALAYA, 1960

| Land Use | No. | Unmixed Estates* | | | All Estates Reporting Some Land in Each Category | |
		Total Area (acres)	Planted Area by Category (acres)	Total Cultivated Area (acres)	No.	Planted Area (acres)
Rubber	2,206	2,137,989	1,843,582	1,903,579	2,287	1,905,871
Coconuts	57	68,594	59,331	62,415	250	88,423
Oil Palm	32	133,186	98,864	109,760	68	131,105
Tea	8	9,004	5,508	5,678	16	8,305
Pineapples	6	19,758	14,122	14,487	7	15,082
Other Crops	6	5,201	2,056	2,184	132	7,275
Mixed	62	147,573	116,940	122,863		
Cleared Land	5	1,256				
Total	2,382	2,522,561	2,143,163	2,221,957	2,760	2,156,061

* Estates with three-quarters or more of cultivated area in any category including plantations of less than 100 acres for crops other than rubber.
Source: Agricultural Census 1960, Preliminary Report No. 16; Table 1321.

TABLE 20. ESTATES IN THE BORNEO TERRITORIES, 1960

	No.	Planted Area (acres)
Sarawak		
Rubber*	5	13,385
Sabah		
Rubber**	n.a.	76,000
Abacá	3	4,430
Cocoa	1	900
Oil Palm	2	1,000

* Estates of more than 1,000 acres only.   ** Estates of more than 250 acres only.
Source: Annual reports.

The principal objection to multiple cropping is that it denies estates the advantages of specialisation; in particular it obstructs the optimum deployment of the labour force. Limitations of space, however, permit no more than a brief reference to the labour situation. It is generally true that workers on Chinese

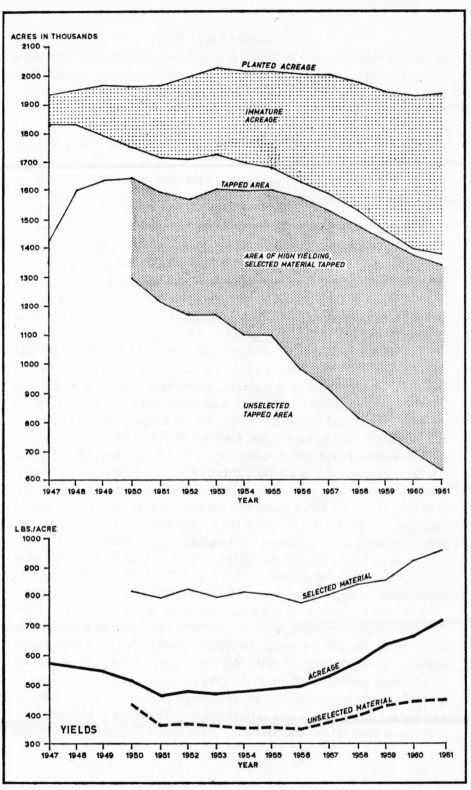

Figure 6: Acreage, Type of Material, and Yields of Rubber for Estates

estates are either Chinese or Malay and that on European estates resident workers are mainly Indian. But about one fifth of the total labour force employed in rubber estates consists of contract workers, of whom more than seventy per cent are Chinese.[6] Many European estates in fact employ considerable numbers of non-resident contract Chinese workers, and in this way make a considerable saving in overheads; in old established mining areas and in the vicinity of urban centres—the districts where such labour is likely to be available—Chinese contract workers may amount to one half or more of the total labour force on European estates, and occasionally may comprise the entire tapping force.

DISTRIBUTION AND SIZE

The earliest estates were established along the rivers of the accessible west coast in Province Wellesley, Perak and Selangor, where some of the best soils of Malaya are to be found. Later alienations took place along roads connecting tin mining districts and along the developing railway systems of Perak and Selangor. Many roads were constructed to open up land for estates, and form the nucleus of the road system of the western portion of the country.

The present geographical distribution of estates, and indeed the size and ownership pattern, are largely explicable in terms of the pace and nature of land alienation. In the cultivation of rubber Europeans had a decided initial advantage for they had the capital resources to meet the seven-year gestation period before the trees commenced to yield. Nevertheless, in Malacca, where the rubber industry may be said to have begun, there was already a large and prosperous Chinese community controlling substantial areas of land, formerly under tapioca. The Settlement was thus not initially attractive to the European planters, and it was in Perak and Selangor, with their large areas of unoccupied land and their early acceptance of British advisers, that the planters found the most congenial environment. From Selangor and Perak planters moved into Negri Sembilan; these three states of the old Federated Malay States still contain nearly forty-five per cent of the total estate cultivated area and are, as they always have been, areas in which European-owned estates predominate. The development of estates in Johore came later than in the three western states of the FMS, but once begun it was particularly rapid and was still proceeding during the inter-war period when the estate situation in other states was virtually static. Johore is particularly notable for the fact that the average size of estates, both in the European and Asian sectors, is considerably larger than the Malayan average. There is little doubt that the reason for both these facts lies in the more generous land policy in relation to non-indigenous economic activity, for a smaller proportion of state land has been set aside for Malay reservations than elsewhere. The creation of large Malay reservations after 1912 in the western states of the FMS tended to freeze the existing pattern of predominantly European interests, while in the eastern states the enormous areas allocated to Malay reservations and extremely poor communications acted to discourage European and Asian enterprise alike.

TABLE 21. CULTIVATED AREA OF ESTATES AND DISTRIBUTION BY SIZE OF ESTATE, FEDERATION OF MALAYA, 1960

	Total Cultivated Area (acres)	Percentage Distribution by Size of Estates			
		Under 1,000 acres	1,000–3,000 acres	3,000–5,000 acres	Over 5,000 acres
Johore	635,000	16·5	23·8	21·8	37·9
Kedah	208,087	25·0	30·9	22·7	21·4
Kelantan	44,514	27·4	46·6	14·2	11·8
Malacca	118,712	27·9	28·9	22·4	18·8
Negri Sembilan	278,604	32·2	28·6	16·1	33·1
Pahang	126,907	32·0	31·6	31·7	4·7
Penang and Province Wellesley	46,828	48·5	21·4	6·8	23·3
Perak	341,676	29·0	40·7	13·0	17·3
Perlis	2,251	100·0			
Selangor	369,138	13·7	43·2	22·2	20·9
Trengganu	23,180	41·2	6·4	52·4	
Federation of Malaya	2,221,957	23·7	31·6	20·2	24·5

Source: Agricultural Census 1960, Preliminary Report No. 16; Tables 1309–19.

In the Borneo territories the location of estates is still very similar to that of late nineteenth-century Malaya; estate developers have looked for areas of suitable soil at the mouths or along the lower courses of navigable rivers.

The size of Malaysian estates varies considerably between crops and also between the types of ownership. Estates producing crops which require elaborate processing tend to be of larger size than those whose crops need only simple treatment. The processing of rubber can be either simple or elaborate, however; small estates usually produce only ribbed smoked sheet, but larger ones may also produce crepe and a variety of latex products and there is a marked tendency for the latter to become of increasing importance. The most capital-intensive crop by far is the oil palm for which a heavy initial outlay on factory equipment necessitates large scale operations. Thus while the average size of oil palm estates is just over 3,000 acres, rubber estates tend to be of considerably smaller size, the national average for Malaya being a little less than 900 acres.

There is, nevertheless, a considerable difference between the situation in the European-owned and the Asian-owned sectors. Nearly 85 per cent of all Asian-owned rubber estates have a planted area of less than 500 acres, but less than ten

233

per cent of all European estates fall into this category (Table 21). There are, however, some giants among both sectors. Malaya's largest rubber estate is the Tanah Merah estate of United Sua Betong Ltd near Port Dickson, of almost

TABLE 22. TOTAL ACREAGE PLANTED WITH RUBBER, MALAYA AND SINGAPORE, 1961

	European		Asian		Number of Estates	Total Acreage Planted
	No. of Estates	Total Acreage Planted	No. of Estates	Total Acreage Planted		
Johore	84	277,864	406	272,771	490	550,635
Kedah and Perlis	51	129,367	233	83,241	284	212,608
Kelantan	10	28,100	53	15,669	63	43,769
Malacca	22	65,453	110	48,585	132	114,038
Negri Sembilan	60	180,400	204	92,984	264	273,384
Pahang	25	45,521	158	72,132	183	117,653
Penang and PW	6	11,975	52	15,007	58	26,982
Perak	100	166,610	291	93,501	391	260,111
Selangor	117	249,474	196	71,465	313	320,939
Trengganu	3	8,840	37	8,473	40	17,313
Singapore	4	2,892	22	4,532	26	7,424
Total	482	1,166,496	1,762	778,360	2,244	1,944,856

Source: Handbook of Rubber Statistics, 1961; Table 4.

TABLE 23. ESTATE ACREAGE UNDER RUBBER BY SIZE GROUP AND OWNERSHIP,
FEDERATION OF MALAYA, 1961

Size Group (acres planted with rubber)	European			Asian		
	No. of Estates	Mature Area (acres)	Immature Area (acres)	No. of Estates	Mature Area (acres)	Immature Area (acres)
0– 499	42	8,836	2,137	1,397	205,690	65,768
500– 999	61	33,896	12,416	212	106,486	47,835
1,000–1,999	172	180,551	73,240	102	93,733	43,858
2,000–2,999	76	134,446	56,951	25	39,880	20,351
3,000–4,999	80	223,363	88,556	14	34,214	18,093
Over 5,000	51	247,763	104,341	12	74,419	28,033
Total all estates	482	828,855	337,641	1,762	554,422	223,938

Source: Handbook of Rubber Statistics, 1961; Table 3.

18,000 acres, of which over 14,000 are under rubber. The Ladang Geddes property of Dunlop Malayan Estates Ltd near Bahau is almost as large and also has over 14,000 acres planted. These giants may be compared to the Chuup estate of Cambodia managed by Socfin, claimed to be the world's largest rubber estate with

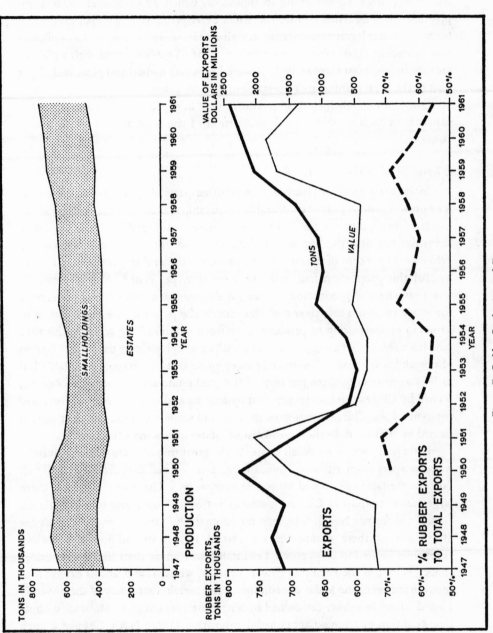

Figure 7: Rubber Production and Exports

over 25,000 acres planted, and the Wingfoot estate of Goodyear in East Sumatra, the largest single rubber estate in Indonesia, which also has over 14,000 acres planted. Among Asian estates, the Kulai Besar property of Ko Plantations Ltd, formerly under Japanese ownership and situated near Kulai, Johore, has a planted area exceeding 10,000 acres. Nevertheless of the 63 rubber estates with a planted area exceeding 5,000 acres in 1961, 51 were European-owned and possessed 77 per cent of the total planted area of estates in this size category.

Some of the Sabah estates are also of very large size, but in contrast to the situation in Malaya only a small proportion of the total area of estate land is cultivated.

OWNERSHIP AND CONTROL

Estate agriculture in Malaysia, as in all other parts of the inter-tropical world, is a non-indigenous importation and its ownership and control are entirely in the hands of immigrant peoples.[7] European interests strongly dominate the estate industries but over the past decade their share, in one sense, has declined. In 1953 seventy per cent of the rubber estate area was under European ownership but by 1961 this proportion had fallen to some sixty per cent.[8] Nevertheless, the European share of production has been maintained at about seventy per cent of the estate total and it is clear that this reflects the policy of the European companies in endeavouring to produce more from a diminishing acreage; this they have been able to do through replanting with very high yielding material. Figures of a breakdown of the Asian-owned rubber estate area are no longer available, but in 1953 some twenty-three per cent of the total estate acreage under rubber was owned by Chinese and seven per cent by Indians and others. Almost forty-five per cent of the Chinese-owned estate area and some fifty-nine per cent of that owned by Indians and others consisted of estates of less than 500 acres.

Little is known about Asian estates as the great majority are owned privately, whereas apart from a few insignificant privately owned properties, virtually all European estates are owned by public companies. There are, however, three large concentrations of Chinese ownership, two in Johore and one in Malacca. One of the former has already been mentioned; the other is Lee Rubber Estates Ltd. Both of these companies are owned by private milling and dealing companies located in Singapore. Lee Estates, with more than 18,000 acres under rubber, is part of the Lee Kong Chian complex, whose ramifications extend into many branches of the Malayan economy. It is certain that many of the privately owned estates in Johore are owned by Singapore residents. In Malacca, with its long tradition of Chinese agricultural enterprise, Unitac Ltd, a Chinese agency house, manages nearly 22,000 acres of rubber land.

The most distinctive feature of the European estate industries is the dominant position of the agency houses, which between them control a substantial share of the economy of Malaysia. The fourteen leading agencies together control more than a million acres of rubber land in Malaysia, almost 85 per cent of the total planted area on European estates. Their share of the oil palm area, which is almost entirely in European hands, is only a little less. The agency houses originated before the establishment of the rubber industry, but prospered greatly from the planting boom, when their specialised knowledge of Malayan conditions enabled them to get a firm grip of companies floated in London and elsewhere. Ownership, however, is widely diffused. Although British interests predominate, American, French, Belgian, Danish, Swiss and other European capital is represented, while a not inconsiderable equity is also held by Malayan residents; as local trading facilities improve, the equity proportion held by the latter may be expected to enlarge.

Through a complex of holding companies, cross-company investments and interlocking directorates, the agency houses have maintained a strong grasp on the estate industries. They have not lacked critics, and have not infrequently been attacked as a principal reason for the high overhead cost-structure of estates and for the general inflexibility of estate output in the face of price movements.[9] It must be conceded that competitive conditions do not apply in the European sector of the estate industries, but neither do they in a considerable range of manufacturing industries; competitive conditions, in fact, are often associated with technological stagnation. It might well be doubted if the natural rubber industry would have made the technical progress it undoubtedly has were it organised on competitive lines. There are several famous estates where research, and particularly the propagation of new clonal rubbers,[10] is the principal activity; some serve a group of agency houses, such as the well known Prang Besar estate. The major houses possess a wealth of centralised scientific and technical ability which can be made available to any estate company in their control. Moreover, the Malayan situation is paralleled in many parts of the world where plantation agriculture is encountered, and in several of these the Malayan houses also have considerable interests.

Table 24 shows the distribution of the interests of the agency houses and of the other sections of the European estate industries. It is clear that there are several differences between the pattern of interests of the two largest houses, Harrisons & Crosfield Ltd and Guthrie & Co. Ltd. The first is by far the larger but it does not differ essentially from all the others except in being considerably bigger. Guthrie, however, appears a much more specialised organisation; it controls relatively few companies and far fewer estates than many smaller rivals. The properties under its management, however, are of large and not infrequently of very large size, including both the largest rubber and oil palm estates in Malaya. The

237

TABLE 24. AGENCY HOUSE AND OTHER INTERESTS IN MALAYSIAN ESTATE INDUSTRIES

Agency/Interest	Number of Companies	Number of Estates	Planted Area (acres)					Total Area (acres)
			Rubber	Oil Palm	Coconuts	Others*	Total	
British Houses								
Harrisons & Crosfield	42	111	180,540	19,800	22,310	8,530	231,180	360,430
Guthrie	22	39	152,680	27,210	—	2,910	182,800	213,980
Boustead-Buttery	37	58	118,490	1,630	1,750	—	121,870	149,250
REA—Cumberbatch	37	55	93,200	2,530	1,830	—	97,560	120,310
T. Barlow	19	42	86,190	6,100	10,050	100	102,440	111,600
Sime Darby	23	30	73,470	250	110	70	73,900	81,400
Oriental Estates	14	19	55,140	—	—	—	55,140	69,210
Plantation Agencies	10	29	48,040	—	—	—	48,040	55,030
Whittall	22	28	34,480	2,340	9,390	—	46,210	47,410
Harper, Gilfillan	16	18	34,130	1,430	—	—	35,560	39,790
Ethelburga Agencies	1	9	27,860	—	—	—	27,860	30,660
J. Warren	16	21	24,370	1,290	—	410	26,070	30,230
Other Agencies**	5	7	21,040	—	—	—	21,040	23,450
Non-British Houses								
Socfin	6	10	34,400	28,110	—	—	62,510	75,060
East Asiatic	4	4	21,100	—	—	—	21,100	23,360
Unitac	7	12	20,260	—	—	—	20,260	21,720
Manufacturers								
Dunlop	1	12	68,190	—	—	—	68,190	74,780
US Rubber	1	9	27,900	—	—	—	27,900	30,070
Unilever	2	2	—	11,000	—	—	11,000	21,000
Other European Interests								
United Plantations	2	4	940	13,620	6,590	390	21,540	23,660
Independent	18	25	40,840	—	—	—	40,840	65,000
Total	305	544	1,163,260	115,310	51,980	12,410	1,343,010	1,685,850

* Tea, cocoa, abacá. ** Grummit, Reid, Paterson Simons, Osborne & Chappell.

Source: Zorn & Leigh-Hunt, Manual of Rubber Planting Companies, 1960. Straits Times Directory, 1962.

geographic distribution of its interests is very different from that of the largest house; nearly three-quarters of the planted area managed by Guthrie is located in Johore and in Negri Sembilan as against only thirty per cent in the case of Harrisons & Crosfield. All the other houses resemble the largest in having (1961) their main interests in Perak and Selangor, which with Negri Sembilan and Kedah are the only states in which European-owned estates exceed in area that of the Asian-owned sector. (See Figure 15, page 266.) By virtue of its large Labis estate, however, the Franco-Belgian house Socfin also has a larger than average proportion of its planted area located in Johore. Guthrie & Co. have taken a leading part in the swing towards oil palm cultivation and its companies are extremely closely knit together.[11] In many ways it can be regarded as the leader of the European estate industries.

The greater part of the estate industries outside the control of the agency houses consists of the 'captive estates' owned by manufacturing companies, whose interest in production arises from their desire to insulate themselves from fluctuations in the prices of their raw materials and to ensure a continuity of supply. The largest of these manufacturing interests is the Dunlop Malayan Estates Ltd, which has nearly 70,000 acres under rubber. The Dunlop properties resemble those of Guthrie in also being of considerably larger size than the average for European estates and it is also similar in having all but a small fraction of its planted area located in Johore and Negri Sembilan. The largest American tyre manufacturers, despite a substantial interest in natural rubber production in Indonesia and West Africa, have not elected to establish estates in Malaya, an omission they may have regretted. The smallest of the American 'Big Four', US Royal, however, possesses over 27,000 acres under rubber and is unique among large companies in having most of its planted area in Kedah. Outside the rubber industry, the only important captive estate is the Pamol estate of south Johore, a Unilever property with over 11,000 acres planted to oil palms. Unilever has also acquired about 10,000 acres at the mouth of the Labak river near Sandakan, Sabah, for oil palm cultivation. The Cadbury company, in association with Harrisons & Crosfield, has an interest in a cocoa estate in Trengganu, but this is largely an experimental undertaking. This attempt to establish a new estate crop has encountered considerable difficulties, especially 'die-back', a disease that still awaits a satisfactory remedy.

One large organisation independent of agency houses or manufacturers exists in Perak; this is United Plantations Ltd, a Scandinavian group with substantial interests in oil palm and coconut cultivation. Of the unattached companies of Table 24, however, it may be remarked that several have secretarial firms common to those managed by agency houses. Largest of the unattached companies is the Duff Development Co., successors to a large land grant made to a

Captain Duff by the sultan of Kelantan before the transfer of sovereignty from Thailand in 1909; in owning large properties in this state, which has allocated enormous areas to Malay reservations, the Duff Co. is also unique. Finally it may be noted that locally registered companies, many of which are also managed by the agency houses, account for only a minute proportion of the European estate acreage—and this, moreover, is declining. In 1948 locally registered public companies held nearly 64,000 acres of rubber land, but by 1963 this had fallen to only a little over 48,000 acres.[12]

The Indonesian government acquired a considerable estate area as part of the assets inherited from the Netherlands Indies government; since 1958 it has considerably added to these by expropriation of former privately owned Dutch estates. The lack of any direct government interest in estate production in Malaya has occasioned some comment, but even research interests have not been pressed as far as they should be. The Rubber Research Institute has a well equipped field testing station and estate of over 3,000 acres at Sungei Buloh near Kuala Lumpur, but there is now no official research centre for oil palm cultivation or processing, even the collection of material at the College of Agriculture at Serdang having been dispersed. It is common knowledge that the government's interest in agricultural research has been mainly limited to those crops that are of major significance to smallholders, a situation that reflects the political power of the rural voter. There is some indication, however, of a revision of outlook, and a renewal of interest in crops that seem best suited for large scale production is greatly to be desired. In Sabah, however, the British government, through the Colonial Development Corporation, has a considerable interest in estate production. The Corporation, in association with Harrisons & Crosfield, has pioneered with abacá production three estates in the Tawau district possessing a mature area totalling a little more than 4,000 acres in 1961.

PROGRESS IN REPLANTING

There are very substantial differences in the yield per acre between rubber estates of various size categories and between estates in different parts of the country, and to a considerable extent these reflect differences in the ownership pattern. European estates of every size category have a higher productivity than their Asian counterparts; in some categories the disparity is almost two to one. The reason is simple: as a result of vigorous replanting policies European estates of every size category have a higher proportion of their planted acreage under high yielding material than their Asian counterparts. In the words of the Mudie Mission, appointed in 1953 to investigate all sections of the rubber industry of the Federation: 'Malaya can do nothing about the price of synthetic rubber; it can only conform to it.' By replanting to high yielding clones, some of which have

240

shown themselves capable of yielding more than a ton of rubber per acre per annum, and by improved methods of tapping, involving high tapping with the aid of ladders, European companies have endeavoured to maintain, or even to increase, output with a diminishing acreage, thus increasing the productivity per worker and reducing labour and other direct costs. Estates that could not be replanted or which presented difficulties in replanting have been sold off, often to be cut up into nominal or real smallholdings in order to take advantage of the $M 200 margin between the replanting grants allowed to smallholders and estates.

Asian estates, which tend to be mainly of the smaller size categories, have lagged behind in replanting. The Mudie Mission estimated that in 1953 48 per cent of all trees on rubber estates were over 28 years old and that no less than 35 per cent were over 33 years old.[13] As the economic life of a rubber tree is generally considered to be about 30 years, after which there is likely to be a marked falling off in output, the consequences of this unfavourable age distribution appeared extremely serious. Moreover, only 36 per cent of the planted acreage consisted of high yielding trees. Working on an average replanting rate of 3 per cent of the planted area per annum (admittedly only a rough guide) and a seven-year gestation period, the Mission considered that some 21 per cent of the estate planted area should consist of immature material. Most European estates now expect to bring rubber into bearing within five years of planting, so that a figure of 21 per cent for immature material may be excessive. Between 1948 and 1953, however, the Mission found that only some 47,000 acres had been replanted out of a desired total of 60,000 acres. This had mainly taken place on the larger European estates; those under 500 acres had achieved very little replanting, nor was the situation much better in those of the 500 to 999 acre category.

As a result of the report of the Mudie Mission, the Malay Federation finally introduced its own replanting scheme for assisting estates to replant with high yielding material. Between 1958 and 1962 $M 168 million were allocated to aid estates to replant or to new plant up to 21 per cent of their total acreage. The estate replanting program has been administered by the Rubber Industry (Replanting) Fund Scheme Fund A, financed through a cess on exports, and provides assistance at a rate of $M 400 per acre, payable in instalments (see Chapter 17, page 257). The scheme has achieved a considerable measure of success. In the period 1948–53 the backlog of estate replanting as against the desired rate of 3 per cent per annum continually mounted, and in the last year of the period the cumulative deficit was 77,000 acres.[14] Between 1953 and 1961, however, this was reduced to 29,000 acres, while new planting had been carried out on nearly 116,000 acres, more than twice the total of that achieved in the earlier period.[15] As a result, the proportion of high yielding to unselected trees has been dramatically transformed; in 1953 64 per cent of the planted area on rubber estates consisted

241

of ordinary trees and only 36 per cent of high yielding, but by 1961 these proportions had been almost exactly reversed and the percentage of the immature to the total planted area had virtually doubled.[16] The replanting scheme was also successful in the most needed direction, i.e. on the Asian estates of less than 500 acres; these had 42 per cent of their planted area under high yielding trees in 1961 as against less than 16 per cent in 1953.

As a result of the replanting and new planting programs the yield per tapped acre on rubber estates rose from 470 lbs per annum to 719 lbs between 1953 and 1961 and the upward trend will be continued as the large immature area comes into bearing; the Malayan average of 965 lbs in 1961 for all high yielding material (over 1,000 lbs for such material on European estates) indicates the scope for further increases in productivity. Considerable regional differences in productivity remain, however; Negri Sembilan, Malacca, Selangor and Perak all substantially exceed the national average estate yield per tapped acre. The reason for this situation is clear: three of these states possess an estate industry that is predominantly European-owned, while in Malacca, where Asian-owned estates exceed the area of those under European control, there are many very large Chinese properties managed with a high degree of efficiency.

The Borneo territories have also endeavoured to bring about a more favourable ratio of high yielding to ordinary trees by assisted replanting and new planting schemes. In Sarawak some eighty per cent of all mature trees are estimated to consist of unselected material. The emphasis in the Borneo territories, however, has been mainly on new planting rather than on replanting as there is nothing comparable to the investment in roads, housing, services, etc, in western Malaya, and has mainly been directed at the smallholder. By 1961 Sarawak estates had accounted for only 1,134 acres of the total of nearly 52,000 acres planted under the Rubber Planting Scheme introduced in 1956.

ESTATE CROPS OTHER THAN RUBBER

Of the estate crops other than rubber only one is of any considerable importance. This is the oil palm, which occupies a little less than 135,000 acres, almost all of which is located in Malaya itself. It is quite possible, however, that the planted area in Malaya could reach 200,000 acres before 1970, while considerable new plantings are also planned for Sabah.

The palm oil industry at the time of writing is experiencing a mild boom; on favourable soils such as those of the Selangor Coastal Series it is more than twice as profitable as rubber or coconut, and it is hardly surprising that in such conditions some European estates are replacing their other crops with oil palm at a rate of 300 acres or more per annum. The troubles of Malaya's principal competitors, the Congo (Leopoldville) and Indonesia, the increasing world demand for fats and oils, and the progressively wider dissemination of synthetic rubber manufacture have all combined to create interest in the oil palm.[17] The crop has a number of attractive features: it starts to bear within three years of planting as compared with five for rubber and yields continuously until the height of the trees and the growing costs of harvesting make replanting desirable. Nevertheless, although it can be grown on a variety of soils, its mineral requirements are more substantial than those of rubber; the tree cannot be neglected or left unharvested, a fate that often befalls rubber in periods of low prices, and above all, the industry requires a heavy capital investment in factory equipment. The latter consideration has been mainly responsible for the fact that oil palm cultivation is almost entirely reserved to large European estates.

The first commercial planting of oil palm did not take place until 1917[18] and the growth of the industry was slow until the middle 'twenties; in 1925 there were 12 estates with a total planted area of nearly 8,600 acres, about three quarters of which was located in Selangor. From then on development was more rapid. In 1929, 29,000 acres of land in Johore was alienated for oil palm cultivation and in the following year Johore became the leading state for oil palm cultivation, a position it has held ever since.[19] In the same year Perak also exceeded the planted area of Selangor, where the industry began, but since 1953 Selangor has regained the second position as a result of large post-war planting.

The minimum size for the profitable operation of an oil palm factory was estimated at about 2,000 acres in the mid 'twenties, but the economies of scale that were expected to ensue from the production of a high quality oil with a low free fatty acid content of about 2–3 per cent and from bulk handling resulted in subsequent estates being of much larger size. The Ulu Remis estate of Oil Palms of Malaya Ltd near Layang Layang, Johore, and the Labis estate of Socfin, also in Johore, are respectively the estates with the largest planted area and the largest total area in Malaysia. There is reason for believing, however, that the economies of large-scale operations were overestimated, and estates of around 5,000–8,000 acres are probably closer to the optimum size at present. Until 1930 all estates used the centrifugal process of oil extraction, but in that year the first hydraulic press went into operation on the Elaeis estate of Oil Palms of Malaya Ltd, near Layang Layang, Johore. The 1960 Census of Agriculture reported 20 estates using centrifuges as against 13 using hydraulic presses, but the latter are preferred on large estates. Lack of a local market for the residue has so far retarded the extraction of palm kernel oil, most kernels being exported for crushing overseas.

Oil palms produce about 16 to 25 cwt of fruit per acre after about 9 years and modern methods of processing give an oil to bunch extraction rate of 17 per cent. Even unselected seedlings yield well and the industry has not recorded any major development to match that of the new high yielding rubbers. All estates, however, participate to some extent in research and in seed selection, and many received planting material from Serdang when official interest in oil palm research was terminated. The great majority of Malaya's oil palms are of the 'dura', or Deli type, moderately thick-shelled, but with a good oil-yielding pericarp. Harvesting is carried out every seven days, so that a continuous labour input is possible, as is the case with rubber. After harvesting the fruit must be processed as soon as possible and all large estates have light railways to transport the fruit to the factory; the largest possesses more than fifty miles of line. Oil palm estates follow a different replanting pattern from that on rubber estates in that mature and immature plantings are intermingled; this arises from the practice of replanting half the old stand every year as the trees grow too tall to be harvested economically.

The distribution of the agency house interests in oil palm cultivation differs greatly from that in rubber; two of the largest houses, Boustead-Buttery and REA-Cumberbatch, have less than 3 per cent of their planted area under oil palm at present. The leader among the British houses is clearly Guthrie & Co. which controls over 27,000 acres of oil palms in Johore, and is planting adviser to the large Pamol estate of Unilever in the same state. Some non-British houses are even more specialised, Socfin having forty-five per cent and United Plantations over sixty per cent of their respective planted areas under oil palm (Table 24). It is not easy to account for this different pattern of interest, but the three leaders of the oil palm industry have been noted for their enterprise and their willingness to back an intuitive sense of future market possibilities. United Plantations' large planted area in the Teluk Anson area of Perak is all converted rubber land, and its example is being followed by several agency houses. The pattern of interest in the oil palm industry is thus likely to reflect that of the estate industries as a whole within the next decade.

Little can be said of the remaining estate crops. Coconuts are predominantly a smallholder crop, but of the 90,000 acres of coconut land recorded in the 1960 Malayan Census of Agriculture about half appears to be under European control. Only 14 estates exceed 2,000 acres and these account for about fifty-five per cent of the total 'estate' area.[20] About a dozen large estates in the Bagan Datoh peninsula of Perak and along the lower Bernam in Selangor account for the greater part of the European interest in coconut cultivation. Tea covers a little over 8,000 acres in Malaya, over half of which is located on three large estates in the Cameron Highlands of Pahang; four estates in Selangor produce lowland tea, but these are essentially rubber estates. Pineapple production as an estate activity is entirely in Chinese hands and apart from one estate in Perak and Selangor respectively is restricted to the peatlands of west Johore.

. . .

THE PLANTATION INDUSTRIES—THE ESTATES: D. W. Fryer

Perhaps the most remarkable feature of Malaysia's estate industries has still to be mentioned; it is that the large foreign-owned estate is accepted and can still play an important part in the development of the national economy. Some political groups, it is true, clamour for nationalisation of the estate industries, but their appeal at present is small; the unhappy situations of Indonesia and Ceylon are a warning of the consequences of elevating dogma above economic efficiency. Nor need Malaysia take very seriously the threat of certain leaders of the estate industries to transfer their operations to Africa because they do not like certain aspects of Malaysian nationalism. The new Africa appears extremely unfruitful soil for the expansion of large scale foreign agricultural enterprise, whatever concessions it may be prepared to make to industrialists. The Malaysian estate industries cannot claim to achieve the world's highest levels of efficiency and incomes per worker; that distinction belongs to the estate industries of Hawaii, but mainly because they have unrestricted access to the large protected market of the United States. Apart from British preferences on minor crops, the Malaysian estate industries have to compete on the world market on the basis of their own unaided competitive efficiency. There is every indication that both government and the estate industries themselves are determined to maintain that level of efficiency as high as possible.

17

Smallholding Cultivation of Cash Crops

JAMES C. JACKSON

Cash crops[1] were being cultivated in several parts of the territories which make up the new Federation of Malaysia by the early nineteenth century. However, it was not until the beginnings of European estate expansion in the 1880s, at that time mainly for coffee cultivation in Malaya and tobacco in Sabah, that a distinction could be made between 'estates' and 'smallholdings' with regard to cash crops production. Throughout most of Malaysia, 100 acres is taken as the upper size limit for smallholdings, and this division will be followed in the following account.

1. RUBBER

Rubber is the most important cash crop produced in the Malaysian territories. In Malaya approximately 64 per cent of the total cultivated area is planted with rubber, in Sabah approximately 54 per cent, and in Sarawak almost 40 per cent.[2] In each territory the greater part of the area planted with rubber consists of smallholdings, in which it is the only cash crop of major importance. This situation reflects the following facts: of all the important tropical cash crops, rubber is the only one that is tolerant of a very wide range of soil conditions; it will grow in most topographical locations below about 1,000 feet; it is sufficiently hardy to withstand a considerable amount of neglect and is relatively free from pests and diseases; and it provides an assured and regular source of income for the smallholder.

An overwhelming proportion of the total acreage planted with rubber (more than ninety per cent) is located in Malaya. In 1961 approximately 51 per cent of the total acreage of rubber in Malaya was in the hands of smallholders who produced about 42 per cent of the total Malayan output, or roughly 14 per cent of the total world natural rubber production. Despite this fact, attention in much of the literature dealing with the rubber industry in Malaya has been focused on estate cultivation. This situation has arisen partly because there is a lack of suitable or reliable information, and partly because by its very nature as a 'peasant' industry, the mainstay of a large part of the multiracial Malayan rural economy, small-holding rubber cultivation is a difficult and demanding field of study. The nature of the information available, and the fact that 'the past ten years have witnessed one of the most ambitious replanting and new planting programmes ever undertaken in Tropical Agriculture',[3] mean that the present situation can only be fully understood in the light of the developments of the last decade.

Smallholding Rubber Cultivation in Malaya: The Situation in 1952[4]

In 1952, 44·7 per cent of the total rubber acreage in Malaya lay on small-holdings, which produced 41·5 per cent of the total output of rubber. Figure 8 shows that while in every state of Malaya, except Negri Sembilan and Selangor forty per cent or more of the planted rubber acreage lay on smallholdings, in only four states was there a larger acreage on smallholdings than on estates.

A rubber smallholding can vary from less than 1 acre to 99 acres in size, and each of the ethnic groups found in Malaya is represented amongst smallholders. Thus although the average size of a rubber smallholding in 1952 was 4·11 acres, the patterns of size and ownership were extremely complex. Tables 25 and 26 represent attempts to rationalise the facts available on these aspects of the small-holding sector of the Malayan rubber industry in 1952. Over eighty per cent of the total smallholding acreage consisted of holdings of less than 25 acres of rubber; of these most were less than 4 acres in size, the average size of holding in this group for the whole country in 1952 being 3·42 acres. This category of rubber smallholding has been appropriately termed 'peasant holding'.[5] In contrast are the much larger holdings of between 25 acres and 100 acres in size. These hold-ings have been rightly called 'medium holdings' in official publications; the average size of medium holdings for the whole country in 1952 was 43·32 acres.

The 'typical' peasant and medium holdings varied noticeably in size from state to state in 1952 (Table 26). Only three states recorded an average size of peasant holding as large as, or greater than, the national average: Johore, Pahang and Kedah. Five states had an average figure of less than 3 acres, the smallest occurring in Kelantan where the average size of peasant holding was 1·8 acres. On the other hand, six states recorded an average size of medium holding greater than the national average. The smallest medium holdings were recorded for Pahang (27·2 acres) and Kedah (28·8 acres).

Table 25 reveals that 55·5 per cent of the rubber acreage on peasant holdings was Malay-owned, and that these holdings had the smallest average size (3·13

247

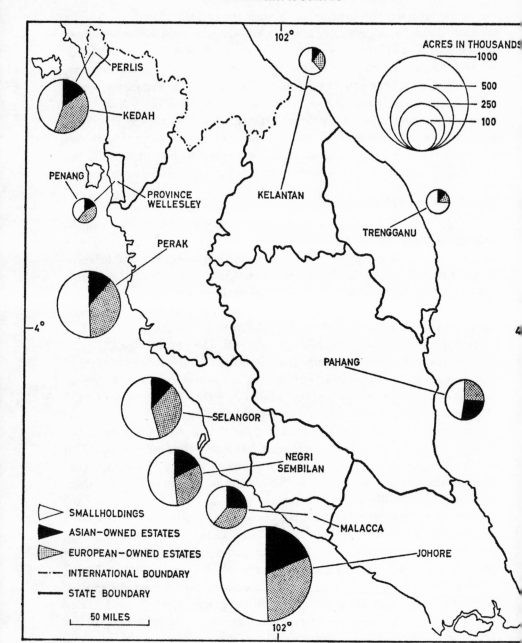

Figure 8: Rubber Cultivation in Malaya, 1952
Based on information contained in *Handbook of Rubber Statistics 1952*, Alor Star, 1953

248

TABLE 25. RUBBER SMALLHOLDINGS IN MALAYA, 1952: SIZE AND OWNERSHIP

	Peasant Holdings, less than 25 acres				Medium Holdings, 25 acres to less than 100 acres				Total Smallholdings			
	Number of Holdings	Planted Acreage (a)	Average Size of Holding	Per cent over (b)	Number of Holdings	Planted Acreage (a)	Average Size of Holding	Per cent over (b)	Number of Holdings	Planted Acreage (a)	Average Size of Holding	Per cent over (b)
Malay	161,426	504,899	3·13	55·53	345	9,771	28·32	5·23	161,771	514,670	3·18	46·9
Chinese	63,086	330,284	5·24	36·32	2,907	123,338	42·43	65·99	65,993	453,622	6·87	41·4
Indian	12,553	56,449	4·50	6·21	650	28,565	43·95	15·28	13,203	85,014	6·44	7·8
Others	2,323	17,551	7·55	1·94	423	25,225	59·63	13·50	2,746	42,776	15·58	3·9
Total	239,388	909,183 (b)	3·80	100·00	4,325	186,899 (b)	43·21	100·00	243,713	1,096,082 (b)	4·50	100·0
Not included in records	146,933	410,372	2·79		2,520	109,639	43·51		149,453	520,011	3·48	
Grand Total	386,321	1,319,555	3·42		6,845	296,538	43·32		393,166	1,616,093	4·11	

Adapted from information contained in *Rubber Statistics Handbook, 1952*, Alor Star, 1953; Table 28, ii; several Districts were 'unable to supply information as to nationality of ownership, and the table is therefore incomplete'.

TABLE 26. DISTRIBUTION OF RUBBER SMALLHOLDINGS IN MALAYA, 1952

State	Total Acreage Alienated for Smallholding Rubber Cultivation	Peasant Holdings, less than 25 acres			Medium Holdings, 25 acres to less than 100 acres			Total Smallholdings		
		Number of Holdings	Planted Acreage	Average Size of Holding (acres)	Number of Holdings	Planted Acreage	Average Size of Holding (acres)	Number of Holdings	Planted Acreage	Average Size of Holding (acres)
Johore	549,259	96,407	453,183	4·7	1,752	88,057	50·2	98,159	541,240	5·5
Kedah	157,310	26,895	109,021	4·05	1,125	32,480	28·8	28,020	141,501	5·05
Kelantan	103,955	33,277	60,188	1·8	99	4,920	49·7	33,376	65,108	1·9
Malacca	102,365	19,356	57,808	2·9	598	29,336	49·05	19,954	87,144	3·9
Negri Sembilan	136,520	38,735	93,718	2·4	858	34,493	40·2	39,593	128,211	3·2
Pahang	112,436	20,599	86,050	4·17	455	12,403	27·2	21,054	98,453	4·7
Perak	327,904	87,493	268,280	3·06	828	41,839	50·5	88,321	310,119	3·5
Perlis	6,941	1,830	4,583	2·5	3	194	64·7	1,833	4,777	2·6
Province Wellesley	21,297	4,731	13,857	2·9	138	5,978	43·3	4,869	19,835	4·07
Selangor	176,140	43,122	129,603	3·0	689	34,128	49·5	43,811	163,731	3·7
Trengganu	56,639	11,727	35,194	3·0	268	11,585	43·2	11,995	46,779	3·9
Penang	n.a.	n.a.	n.a.	—	n.a.	n.a.	—	2,181	9,195	4·2
Total	1,750,766	384,172	1,311,485	3·42	6,813	295,413	43·32	393,166	1,616,093	4·11

Adapted from Appendix 'A' Table 1, Smallholdings Planted Area—1952, The Rubber Industry (Replanting) Board Scheme No. 3 for the Administration of Fund 'B', *Report on Operations for the Year 1961 by the Replanting Officer*, Kuala Lumpur, 1962, p. 25.

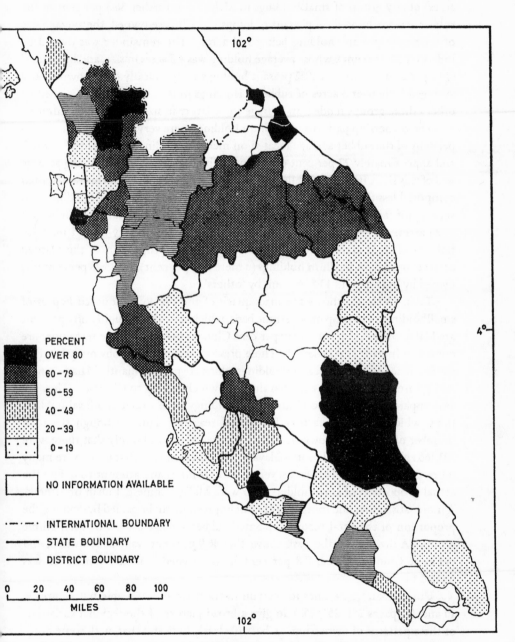

Figure 9: Malaya: Percentage of Total Smallholding Rubber Acreage Owned by Malays, by District, 1952
Handbook of Rubber Statistics 1952, Table 28, ii, 79–82.

251

acres) of any group of smallholdings in Malaya. A further 36·3 per cent of the rubber acreage located on peasant holdings was Chinese-owned, the average size of a Chinese peasant holding being 5·24 acres. The remainder was owned by Indians (6·21 per cent), whose average holding was 4·5 acres in size, and by 'others' (1·94 per cent). Thus, in 1952 peasant holdings were typically Malay-owned, and averaged little over 3 acres of rubber. Holdings in the same category owned by other ethnic groups tended on average to be larger in size and fewer in number.

The ownership patterns of medium holdings were very different. Almost 66 per cent of the rubber acreage located on medium holdings was Chinese-owned, and approximately 27 per cent of the total Chinese-owned smallholding acreage was of this size category. While the total planted acreage which this represented comprised less than ten per cent of the total acreage in rubber smallholdings, it is very significant. The average size of Chinese-owned medium holdings was 42·43 acres, which contrasts markedly with the 'typical' Malay-owned medium holding of 28·32 acres. Malays owned the smallest proportion of the planted acreage located on medium holdings (a mere 5·23 per cent), for 15·28 per cent was owned by Indians, and 13·5 per cent by 'others'.

Table 25 clearly shows the inadequacy of the previously quoted figures of smallholding ownership on an ethnic basis, which state that 'roughly fifty per cent are Malay-owned, thirty to forty per cent Chinese-owned, and the remainder are owned by Indians and others'.[6] These previous estimates are obviously based in the first place only upon peasant holdings which are predominantly Malay-owned, and ignore medium holdings, two thirds of which belong to Chinese. They are also, apparently, based upon 'number of holdings' as recorded in official publications, which are unsatisfactory for several reasons. Thus, although the total 'number of holdings' shown in Table 25 (page 249) would imply that there were 393,166 rubber smallholders in Malaya in 1952, it is unlikely that there were many more than 250,000.[7] This fact severely compromises any attempt to define the actual proportion of smallholders who were Malay, Chinese, Indian or 'others'. A more satisfactory and more meaningful impression can be gained by defining the proportion of the total recorded planted rubber acreage owned by each ethnic group. A division on this basis shows that 46·9 per cent was Malay-owned, 41·4 per cent Chinese-owned, 7·8 per cent Indian-owned, and the remainder was owned by 'others'.[8]

Unfortunately, statistics for certain districts are not available but Figures 9, 10 and 11 (pages 251, 253, 256) do give a broad picture of the regional variations of these patterns of ownership. Chart 10 clearly indicates that, with some noteworthy exceptions, the majority of the smallholding acreage in northern Malaya was owned by Malays. The records are less complete for the southern half of the country and only four districts can with certainty be said to have had more than

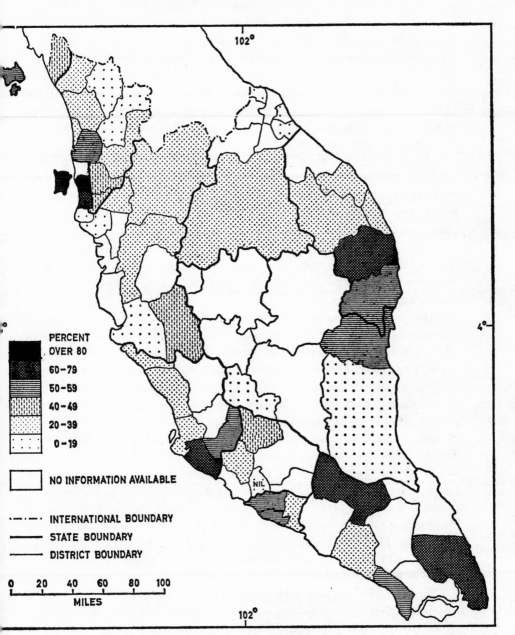

Figure 10: Malaya: Percentage of Total Smallholding Rubber Acreage Owned by Chinese, by District, 1952
From *Handbook of Rubber Statistics 1952*, Table 28, ii, 79–82

half of their smallholding acreage Malay-owned: Pekan and Bentong (Pahang), Rembau (Negri Sembilan), and Batu Pahat (Johore). It is, however, probable that if records were available for much of the remainder of Negri Sembilan and Pahang these would also fall into the same category. On the evidence available four notable areas of almost solely Malay ownership emerge: Rembau, Pekan, Sik (Kedah), and the recorded districts of the Kelantan delta—all areas of traditional Malay settlement. In each of these areas more than ninety per cent of the total smallholding acreage was Malay-owned; these must therefore have been areas with a marked concentration of peasant holdings.

Figure 10 suggests that all the areas in which the greater part of the smallholding rubber acreage is Chinese-owned possess two features in common. They are all close to large urban centres, and each is a region of long-standing Chinese settlement. It is, incidentally, probable that many Chinese smallholdings in Johore are, in fact, owned by residents of Singapore.

Indian ownership was a relatively unimportant feature of smallholding cultivation (Figure 11). In only two districts of those for which records exist did Indians own more than one fifth of the total smallholding acreage: Kubang Pasu and Kulim, both in Kedah.

The yields obtained by smallholders in 1952 were relatively low. On the total planted smallholding rubber area, the average yield was a little over 300 lbs per acre as against a yield of 480 lbs per tapped acre on estates in the same year. For only two states, Kelantan and Perak, did the average yield per acre on smallholdings exceed 400 lbs per acre, and it exceeded 300 lbs per acre in only three others: Pahang, Kedah and Penang and Province Wellesley. These figures may give a slightly more unfavourable picture than was actually merited for they are calculated on the basis of 'total planted acreage' and it is possible that not all smallholding rubber in existence in 1952 was being tapped. The 'planted acreage' would include immature rubber not yet in tapping and probably also many holdings on which the rubber trees were too old to make tapping economic except in periods of very high prices. However, since a mere 20,000 acres of smallholding rubber were replanted in the period 1947–52 (representing less than 1·5 per cent of the 'total planted acreage' in 1952), almost the whole of the acreage recorded in 1952 must have consisted of mature rubber, and therefore at least capable of being tapped.[9]

The reason for the low yields achieved by smallholders in 1952 was that a large part of the total smallholding acreage was planted with very old, unselected rubber trees. A great many smallholdings were planted between the boom of the early 1910s and the Stevenson scheme of the 1920s; many others were planted in the brief interval between the two inter-war restriction schemes. Thus, by 1952 rubber trees on many smallholdings were either past, or fast approaching, an

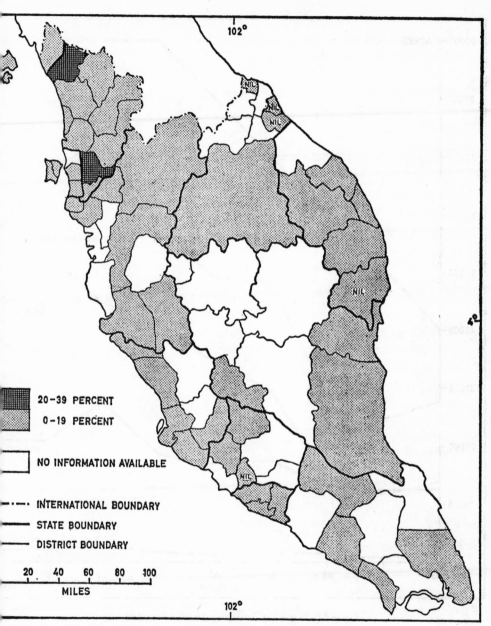

Figure 11: Percentage of Total Smallholding Rubber Acreage Owned by Indians, by District, 1952
Handbook of Rubber Statistics 1952, Table 28, ii, 79–82

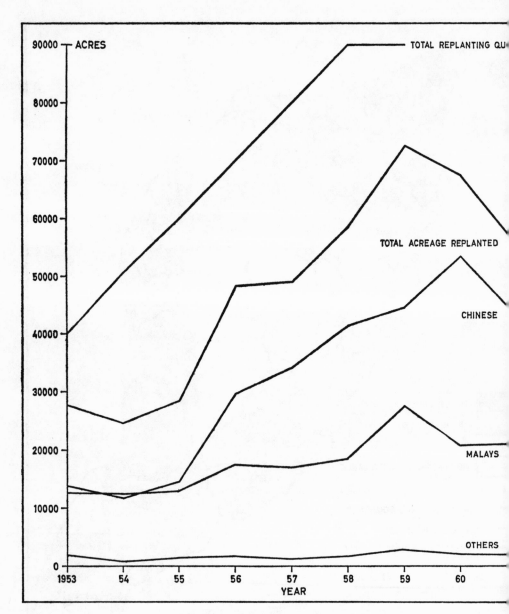

Figure 12: Progress of Replanting Smallholdings, 1953–61

age when output decreases noticeably, for it is generally accepted that the rubber tree has a productive life of from 30 to 35 years. Indeed, it is probable that by 1952 as much as two thirds of the total smallholding acreage was planted with trees which were over 30 years old.

The History of Replanting Schemes in Malaya, 1950–61

A Rubber Smallholdings Enquiry Committee appointed to review the situation submitted reports to the government in 1950 and 1951. These reports indicated that if smallholding yields were to be improved, it was necessary to replant a large proportion of the existing trees.[10] Replanting was also desirable in order to replace existing old low yielding rubber by the new high yielding varieties. These facts were emphasised by a government statement issued in 1955 which stated that 'the age of the tree and the type of tree are major determinants of yield, and although other factors such as soil fertility, tapping intensity, etc, are also of importance, it is by increasing the yield per acre by planting new high yielding material that the greatest reduction in the cost of producing rubber can be made'.[11]

As a result of the recommendations of a Smallholders Replanting Sub-Committee formed by the Rubber Producers' Council, an interim scheme, known as Scheme No. 1, came into operation on September 1, 1952.[12] On January 1, 1953, this interim scheme was replaced by Scheme No. 2 for the Administration of Fund 'B'. The whole replanting scheme was to be financed by the imposition of a cess on all rubber exported from the Federation of Malaya. The money so collected was to be allocated to two funds: Fund 'A' for the payment of grants to estates, and Fund 'B' for the payment of grants to smallholders. Initially under Scheme No. 2 'assistance was confined to cover the replanting of not less than one acre or more than one third of the total holding or holdings, provided that smallholders owning 15 acres of rubber or less could be assisted to replant up to 5 acres'.[13] Although at first the scheme provided for a grant of $M 400 per acre it soon became apparent that this was insufficient, and in October 1954 this grant was increased to $M 500 per acre, with retrospective effect from January 1, 1953.

In April 1956, a government Replanting Scheme for smallholders[14] came into operation, under the management of the administrators of Scheme No. 2. This new scheme provided for the payment of an additional grant of $M 100 per acre to those participating in Scheme No. 2. Henceforth smallholders replanting their rubber under these schemes would receive a total grant of $M 600 per acre. The new government scheme also allowed the smallholder who participated in Scheme No. 2 'to be assisted to replant or new plant an additional acreage equivalent to the acreage for which he was receiving grants under Scheme No. 2 under

257

Fund 'B', or up to a maximum of 5 acres, whichever is less, provided he owned not more than 30 acres of rubber land',[15] for which he would also receive a grant of $M 600 per acre.   On January 1, 1960, Scheme No. 2 was replaced by Scheme No. 3, which carries on the work of its predecessor.

The Progress of Replanting on Rubber Smallholdings in Malaya, 1953–61

The initial aim of these schemes was to effect the replanting of approximately one third (480,300 acres) of the 1952 acreage in the seven-year period 1953–9. Targets were established for total replanting each year, together with yearly quotas for each individual state.

Unfortunately, the target for total replanting was not achieved in any single year, and only 317,821 acres (i.e. two thirds of the target) of smallholding rubber were replanted in the period 1953–9 (Chart 12, page 256).[16]   For the country as a whole the peak year of replanting was 1959, the last year of Scheme No. 2.   In all states, except Malacca and Negri Sembilan, 1959 was the year of greatest activity. In Malacca the peak years were 1956, 1958 and 1960, and in Negri Sembilan, 1956.

Only Malacca succeeded in achieving the quota; Johore, Pahang, Kedah and Perlis achieved less than half.   Malacca was also the only state which consistently exceeded its quota;[17] the only other states to replant more than was stipulated in any one year were Negri Sembilan in 1956, Perak in 1953, and Trengganu in 1956 and 1958.

Several interconnected factors help to explain the failure of smallholders to achieve these replanting quotas.   In the first place, it may well be that the authorities established unduly optimistic targets at a time when large scale replanting on smallholdings had not been previously attempted.   Another important contributory factor is the general conservatism of peasant farmers, and the suspicion with which they view any government action; many were 'hesitant about applying for assistance until they were fully satisfied that it did not involve governmental control of their holdings'.[18]   The early failures of the scheme are certainly connected with the fact that for some time many smallholders were not aware of their eligibility for grants to aid them replant, and after they did discover their eligibility many were undoubtedly discouraged by delays in the payment of subsidies.   In some instances smallholders showed an interest in replanting but were frustrated by the length of time it seemed to take the authorities to deal with their cases.   Multiple ownership of smallholdings also hindered replanting, for all the owners might not agree to replant, or might not be immediately available to give their consent.   'Most field studies suggest, however, that the major factor arises from the hesitancy of many smallholders to replace existing rubber stands, that continue earning a certain income, however inefficiently, for future yield prospects over six years away in time.'[19]

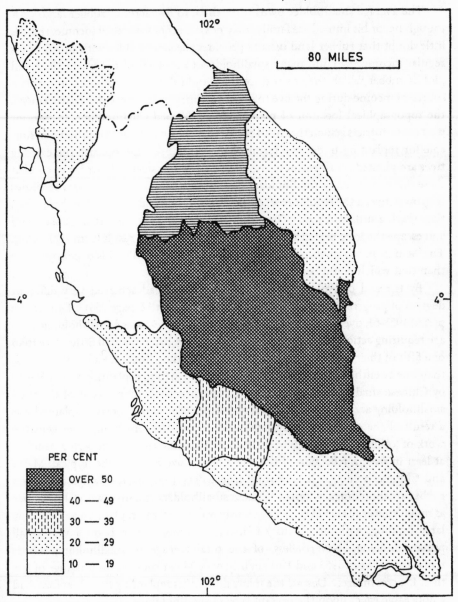

Figure 13: Malaya, Increases in Smallholding Rubber Acreage by States, 1952–61

The average smallholder owns from three to five acres of rubber land. Although he, or his immediate family, may possess other sources of income, there is little doubt that rubber land usually provides the smallholder with much of his regular income.[20] Thus, many smallholders cannot afford to replant the small plot of rubber which they own since this would deprive them of an immediate source of income during the five to seven year maturation period. Furthermore, the topographical location of many long-established smallholdings in interior west coast districts is such that in all probability they would not be considered suitable for replanting under the terms of the official scheme because the existing trees are planted on slopes now considered to be too steep. In order to combat these difficulties many smallholders have preferred to allow self-sown seedlings to grow between the regular rows of the original trees and begin to tap these when they reach a sufficient size. Thus, they maintain output from their rubber land and escape the long period without income which would result from replanting. The yield from the mixture of old trees and self-sown seedlings is of course lower than that which could be obtained by replanting.

By the end of 1961 the various ethnic groups had achieved very different degrees of progress in the matter of replanting (Chart 12, page 256). During the period 1953–61, over forty per cent of the total Chinese-owned smallholding acreage requiring action was replanted, whereas Malays had replanted little more than one fifth of their total acreage, and 'others', including Indians, had replanted less than one twelfth.[21] Thus, most progress with regard to replanting was achieved by Chinese smallholders who replanted approximately 62 per cent of the total smallholding acreage affected. Thirty-five per cent of the acreage replanted was a result of the efforts of Malay smallholders, and the remaining 3 per cent the work of 'others'. There can be little doubt that this variation in performance is, at least in part, a reflection of the difference in size between the 'typical' Malay and Chinese holding. It is broadly true to say that Malays own the smallest rubber smallholdings, whereas Chinese smallholders usually own at least twice as much rubber (Table 25). It is obviously much easier to replant on a reasonably large holding, without seriously reducing income, than it is on a very small peasant holding. Nevertheless, of the total acreage of smallholding rubber replanted between 1953 and 1961 slightly over 79 per cent lay on holdings of less than 15 acres in size. Despite the many difficulties replanting has, therefore, had a noticeable effect upon the peasant type of smallholdings.

The Expanding Smallholding Rubber Acreage in Malaya, 1952–61

Apart from the replanting with high yielding material of almost 22 per cent of the total acreage, the other significant change in the period 1952 to 1961 is the marked expansion which has taken place in the smallholding acreage which is summarised in Table 27. In terms of area alone, smallholdings had become more important than estates.

The greatest relative increase in the smallholding rubber acreage during this period occurred in Pahang, Kelantan and Negri Sembilan; the smallest occurred in Penang and Province Wellesley, and Perak (Figure 13, page 259, and Table 27). Apart from Pahang the greatest absolute increases occurred in west coast states, the largest figure being recorded by Johore.

These increases have resulted either from subdivision of estates, or by new planting undertaken by individuals or block planting schemes. These processes have had markedly different effects in different parts of the country. The increases in the case of all west coast states (including Johore) were chiefly the result of estate subdivision, although most of the new planted acreage is also located in these same states. Except in Johore and Malacca, the expansion resulting from subdivision was made solely at the expense of European-owned estates. In Malacca slightly less than one third of the increase caused by subdivision was produced by the break-up of Asian-owned estates, and in Johore subdivision only occurred on Asian-owned estates (compare Figures 8 and 15, pages 248 and 266). In the east coast states of Pahang, Trengganu and Kelantan virtually all the expansion in the smallholding acreage resulted from new planting of rubber.

For many smallholders new planting has proved much more attractive than replanting. As long ago as 1949 Benham wrote: 'There can be no doubt that new planting, provided that suitable land is available not too far away, is much better for smallholders than replanting; they can continue to tap their existing trees for their livelihood while the new ones come into bearing.'[22] In the period 1952–61 slightly over 200,000 acres of rubber were new planted on smallholdings, 119,750 acres under various block planting schemes since 1956, and 83,600 acres as a result of new planting by individual smallholders. Individual smallholders new-planting rubber have been assisted under the terms of the replanting scheme; those participating in various block planting and fringe alienation schemes have received grants of $M 400 and $M 200 per acre, and loans covering the complete cost of new planting are granted on Federal Land Development Authority schemes.

One of the factors already noted as militating against smallholding replanting is the small size of many existing holdings. In some areas an attempt is being made to overcome this problem by allotting smallholders a further, previously uncultivated, plot of land within a small block on which high yielding material is planted. The original plot provides an income until the new trees reach maturity when it too can be replanted. The blocks of land for such schemes— known as Fringe Alienation Schemes—are selected as close to the existing holdings

261

TABLE 27. MALAYA: CHANGES IN SMALLHOLDING RUBBER ACREAGE, 1952-61

State	1952 Acreage	Additions, 1952-61				1961 Acreage	Actual Increase 1952-61 (acres)	Percentage Increase 1952-61
		Fragmentation from Estates (acres)	Block New Plantings (acres)	Individual New Plantings (acres)				
Johore	541,240	61,887	40,226	12,883		656,236	114,996	21·2
Kedah/Perlis	146,278	23,381	6,721	13,128		189,508	43,230	29·5
Kelantan	65,108	4,836	13,187	11,113		94,244	29,136	44·7
Malacca	87,144	12,818	8,754	1,401		110,117	22,973	26·3
Negri Sembilan	128,211	30,300	12,125	6,046		176,682	48,471	37·8
Pahang	98,453	13,079	23,285	21,485		156,302	57,849	58·7
Penang/Province Wellesley	29,030	3,101	—	65		32,196	3,166	10·9
Perak	310,119	29,259	7,696	11,530		358,604	48,485	15·6
Selangor	163,731	36,287	2,889	412		203,319	39,588	24·2
Trengganu	46,779	1,952	4,867	5,538		59,136	12,357	26·4
Total	1,616,093	216,900	119,750	83,601		2,036,344	420,251	26·0

Adapted from Table 44, Estimated Distribution of Smallholders' Acreage, December, 1961, in *Annual Report, Rubber Research Institute of Malaya, 1961*, Kuala Lumpur, 1962, p. 117.

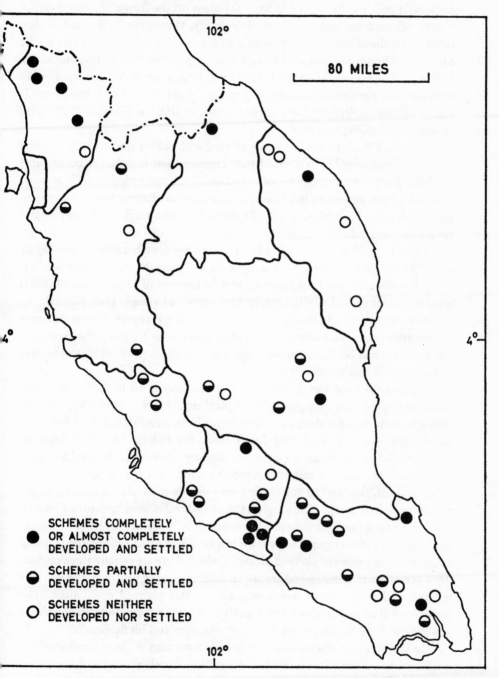

Figure 14: Malaya, Federal Land Development Authority Schemes, 1962

263

as possible and usually consist of irregular areas on the fringe of existing settlements. Contractors fell, clear and, if necessary, terrace the land which is allocated to smallholders in lots of from 2 to 6 acres, according to the size of the existing holding. The smallholders are then responsible for planting and maintenance. The remainder of the value of the total grant of $M 200 per acre on such schemes consists of planting material and fertiliser. During 1961 alone 37 Fringe Alienation Schemes were implemented, resulting in a total of 19,242 acres of new smallholding rubber.[23]

Some 63,000 acres have been new planted with rubber under block planting schemes administered by individual state Development Boards, the participants receiving grants of $M 400 per acre. Such schemes cover blocks of 250 acres or more which are developed in phases, the clearing and planting being undertaken by contractors. Each block is initially opened up as a single entity but is later subdivided into individual holdings usually consisting of 6 acres each. At Sungei Lui, Kuala Pilah District, Negri Sembilan, for instance, such a scheme was begun in 1960 by over 500 smallholders (mainly Malays). Here the state government has set aside 4,000 acres for new planting, and by the end of 1961 532 smallholders were participating and approximately 2,500 acres had already been planted. In this case, when the whole block has been planted it is expected to be run on a co-operative basis, with a central processing factory, so as 'to obtain the maximum profit which will be shared among the participants in proportion to the area owned by each smallholder'.[24]

The Federal Land Development Authority, established in 1956, is now the principal organisation engaged in block planting. These schemes begin by the state governments allocating a block of virgin land, usually of about 4,000 acres, for the purpose and requesting funds from the Federal Land Development Authority to finance the development and settling of the area. When the scheme is approved, the selected area is surveyed to certify that it is suitable for smallholding agriculture and to ensure that no valuable minerals exist which might require exploiting later. The jungle is then felled and cleared by contractors who usually also have the right to extract any commercially useful timber. Frequently contractors are also engaged to prepare the land and plant rubber, the planting taking place in a series of planned phases of which there are usually three or four. After access roads, housing and service facilities have been provided, the specially selected settlers are moved into a centrally situated planned new village. The families are then expected to work together under the supervision and guidance of a Federal Land Development Authority manager and his field staff.

On almost every scheme between 60 and 80 per cent of the agricultural land is devoted to rubber, the remainder being planted with a variety of foodcrops, amongst which fruit trees are prominent. Each settler is allotted a total holding

264

of 10¼ acres. In the early schemes this consisted of 6 acres of rubber, 2 acres of *dusun*,[25] 2 acres of rice, and a ¼-acre house lot, but in more recent schemes the allocation has been 8 acres of rubber, 2 acres of *dusun*, and a ¼-acre house-lot.[26] The initial provision of housing materials, food, planting materials, and cash comes from the Federal Land Development Authority grant. The cost of these advances is debited to the account of each settler who will repay in monthly instalments when the crops begin to yield. Although most of these schemes are based upon rubber as the cash crop, on the schemes at Kulai (Johore) oil palm is being planted as the major crop. At the end of 1962 49 Federal Land Development Authority schemes had been approved, although 13 of these were neither developed nor settled; of the remainder 20 were either almost completely or partially developed and settled (see Figure 14, page 263). When completely developed it is expected that these schemes will add between 80,000 and 100,000 acres to the total smallholding rubber area in Malaya.

Smallholding Rubber Cultivation in Sarawak

Possibly as much as ninety per cent of the estimated 300,000 acres planted with rubber in Sarawak in 1961 was located on smallholdings.[27] Rubber cultivation in Sarawak is therefore essentially a smallholding industry, still mainly Chinese-dominated, in which the typical holding is of the peasant category, most being less than 5 acres in size.

In the early 1950s almost the whole of the smallholding acreage was planted with old unselected seedling rubber trees nearing the end of their economic life. It was therefore desirable that the proportion of the total smallholding rubber acreage which was both immature and planted with high yielding material should be increased. As a result the Sarawak Rubber Planting Scheme came into existence on January 1, 1956, and for a number of reasons was back-dated to 1955. Initially the scheme established a target of not less than 10,000 acres to be either replanted or new planted with high yielding material in the subsequent five years, and provided for the payment of a grant of $M 450 per acre to both estates and smallholders who replanted, and $M 200 per acre to those new planting. The primary object of this scheme was 'to expand and diversify a smallholding agricultural economy based on rubber as the cash crop and not to replace traditional systems of agriculture with one wholly dependent on rubber'.[28] At first, to provide the necessary capital, a sum of one million Malayan dollars was set aside in the 1955–9 Development Plan. With the ready response given to the scheme it was revised later in 1956, and the capital sum increased to four million dollars.

From the start the scheme proved to be extremely successful, and the original target of 10,000 acres to be planted in five years 'was well encompassed in less than half that time'.[29] In 1957 the planting target was increased to 40,000

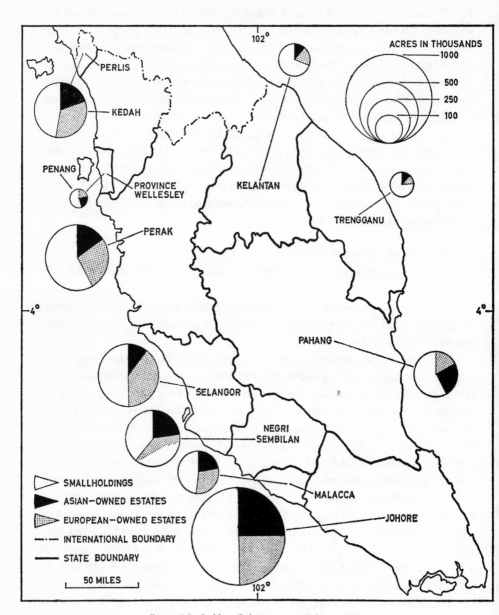

Figure 15: Rubber Cultivation in Malaya, 1961

acres, and in 1958 to 60,000 acres. The target was once again increased in 1959 to stand at 90,000 acres of high yielding rubber to be planted before 1964. Since January 1, 1959, a cess has been levied on all rubber exported from Sarawak to help finance the scheme; this has allowed the grant for new planting to be raised from $M 200 to $M 250 per acre. Almost seventy per cent of the total estimate set aside for agricultural development in the current Sarawak Development Plan (1959–63) will be devoted to the improvement of the rubber industry.

In the early stages of the Rubber Planting Scheme most enthusiasm for both replanting and new planting was evinced by Chinese smallholders, who by the end of 1956 had planted a little over nine tenths of the total acreage affected at that date. However, in more recent years Dayaks, and particularly Land Dayaks in the First Division, have participated increasingly in the scheme, almost entirely for the purpose of new planting. Thus, of the total of 30,700 acres new planted by smallholders between 1956 and 1959 45 per cent was undertaken by Chinese and 41·5 per cent by Dayaks (Table 28).

Apart from planting by individuals, the scheme now gives top priority to 'communal, mixed racial and block plantings'.[30] Several noteworthy block planting projects are at present in progress. At a Foochow Chinese settlement near Bintulu (Fourth Division), almost 4,000 acres had been planted by 168 families by 1959; 97 acres have been planted at a Malay settlement at Engkilili (Second Division), which will later be divided into five-acre lots; a considerable number of Dayak block plantings have been undertaken, particularly in the First and Third Divisions.[31]

Replanting of existing rubber has proved far less popular amongst small-holders in Sarawak than new planting. Of the total area planted with high yielding rubber by the end of 1959 less than one tenth represented replanting. Most of the replanting so far achieved has been concentrated in the First Division, and 88 per cent of the total replanted acreage is the result of Chinese efforts (Table 28 and Figure 17, page 269).

Under the terms of the scheme slightly over 50,000 acres had been planted with high yielding rubber by smallholders by the end of 1961; thus, with three years to go, 55 per cent of the target had already been achieved. By the end of 1961 probably between fifteen and twenty per cent of the total smallholding acreage was planted with immature high yielding material.

Smallholding Rubber Cultivation in Sabah

About 173,460 acres were planted with rubber in Sabah at the end of 1960, with 75–80 per cent of the total acreage concentrated in the west coast and interior residencies (particularly in the districts of Papar and Beaufort respectively).[32] Between one half and three fifths of the total rubber acreage is located on

TABLE 28. SARAWAK: NEW PLANTING AND REPLANTING OF RUBBER BY SMALLHOLDERS, 1956-9

Division	Chinese Acres Planted		Malay Acres Planted		Dayak Acres Planted		Others Acres Planted		Total Acres Planted	
	New Planting	Re-planting	New Planting	Re-planting	New Planting	Re-planting	New Planting	Re-planting	New Planting	Re-planting
First	1,640	2,379	166	25	4,350	93	25	12	6,181	2,509
Second	774	12	199	36	3,667	119	21	1	4,661	168
Third	3,809	380	98	6	3,606	2	—	—	7,513	388
Fourth	6,402	20	881	3	877	—	1,552	—	9,712	23
Fifth	1,206	126	521	54	245	—	662	39	2,634	219
Total	13,831	2,917	1,865	124	12,745	214	2,260	52	30,701	3,307
% of Total Area Planted	45·0	88·2	6·1	3·7	41·5	6·5	7·4	1·6	—	—

Adapted from Appendices 'F1' and 'F2', Government of Sarawak, *Annual Report of the Department of Agriculture for the Year 1957*, Kuching, 1959, pp. 67-8.

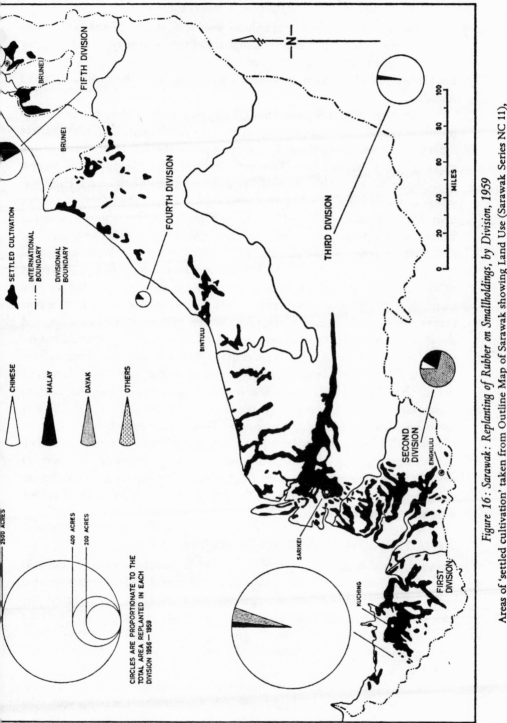

Figure 16: *Sarawak: Replanting of Rubber on Smallholdings, by Division, 1959*

Areas of 'settled cultivation' taken from Outline Map of Sarawak showing Land Use (Sarawak Series NC 11), by permission of Director of Lands and Surveys, Sarawak

smallholdings, and in 1960 smallholders produced almost 57 per cent of the total rubber output. Most smallholdings are of the peasant type, and probably more than two thirds of the total smallholder rubber acreage is Chinese-owned; the average size of a peasant holding on which rubber is the main crop is 7·3 acres.[33]

As early as 1950, a Rubber Fund Board was established in North Borneo mainly to supply improved planting material and fertiliser free to rubber growers —particularly smallholders—and thereby improve the future prospects of the industry. As in Sarawak most of the high yielding rubber is being planted on new land (Figure 17, page 271). In 1954 the Rubber Industry Replanting Fund was established, and a cess levied on all rubber exported from the colony to finance planting. This enables grants of $M 160 per acre (consisting wholly of planting material and fertiliser) to be made to smallholders undertaking new planting, and those replanting receive the same plus a cash grant of $M 240 per acre spread over a four-year period. By 1960 it had become the policy of the Board to plant 10,000 acres with high yielding material annually. In response to this encouragement, the total area planted with rubber in Sabah increased by thirty-five per cent between 1956 and 1960, mainly as a result of new planting by smallholders, and the proportion of the total acreage planted with high yielding material has increased from approximately fifteen per cent in 1956 to almost forty per cent in 1960.

Most of the new planted acreage is located in the West Coast Residency (where new planting has been most active in the districts of Papar and Tuaran-Tenghilan), and in the interior (particularly in Tenom district). In the east coast residencies new planting has been confined almost entirely to the districts of Sandakan (Sandakan Residency) and Semporna-Tawau (Tawau Residency). Besides new planting by individual smallholders, government development schemes have done much to effect this increase in acreage (e.g. the Keningau Plain Development Scheme, Interior Residency, on which 8,065 acres of rubber were planted during 1960 alone).[34]

2. SMALLHOLDING CASH CROPS OTHER THAN RUBBER

Of the total cultivated smallholding acreage in Malaya recorded in the 1960 Agricultural Census, 44 per cent is planted with rubber and 45 per cent is devoted to padi and other non-cash crops. Amongst the crops grown on the remaining area which may be termed cash crops are coconuts and pineapples; all others are of minor significance.

Coconut

Whilst coconuts are the second most important cash crop produced by smallholders in Malaya, they are of relatively little significance. Coconuts grown by

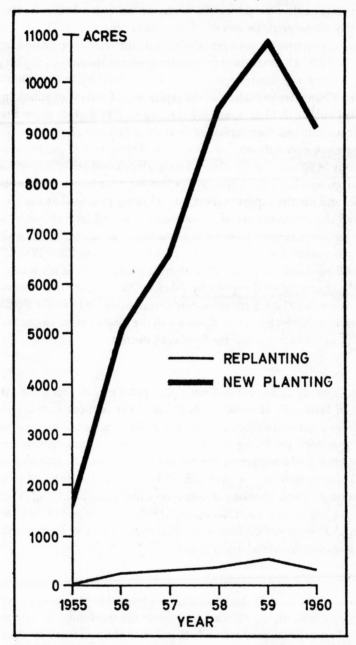

Figure 17: Sabah: Progress of Replanting and Planting in Smallholding, 1955–60

271

Malayan smallholders are principally for home use or local sale, although some enter international trade by way of oil processing centres.

Coconuts occupy 8·5 per cent of the total cultivated area located on small-holdings in Malaya and are most frequently grown as the major crop on peasant holdings. They are most important as a smallholding crop in Johore and Selangor. Grants are provided for the replanting of several smallholding crops other than rubber in Malaya, and by the end of 1961 slightly more than 7,000 acres of coconuts had been replanted (mainly in Selangor, Johore and Perak).

In Sarawak coconuts occupy an estimated total area of 50,000 acres (there being about 34,500 acres in the First Division alone), and are exclusively a small-holder crop, which, as in Malaya, are grown both for home consumption and local sale, and for the export market, the oil being processed at Kuching. It is considered that coconuts are of considerable potential importance in Sarawak and a subsidised Coconut Planting Scheme began in January 1959, which now aims to plant 20,000 acres during the current Development Plan (1959–63).

In 1960 copra, coconut oil and fresh nuts produced in Sabah accounted for about 3·5 per cent of total exports by value.[35] At that date coconuts occupied approximately 50,000 acres, the main concentrations being in Kudat district (West Coast Residency), which contained about half the total acreage, Tawau and Lahad Datu (Tawau Residency), and the Sandakan district.

Pineapple

Some 9,000 acres are planted with pineapples in compact areas on small-holdings in Malaya.[36] However, only about 17 per cent (or 1,544 acres) of this total acreage is devoted to the cultivation of pineapples for canning purposes, the remaining acreage producing pineapples for home consumption or local sale. Smallholdings producing pineapples for canning purposes in 1960 were concentrated predominantly on the peat soils of Johore (1,327 acres), and to a much lesser degree on those of Selangor (190 acres), the pineapples being processed at canneries in Johore Bahru and Klang respectively. By the end of 1961 3,600 acres of pineapples (both for canning and other purposes, and located entirely in Johore) had been replanted under grant.

Pepper

In Sarawak six to seven thousand acres are devoted to pepper which is entirely a smallholder crop, grown on what is probably the most intensive system in the world.[37] Pepper prices have generally been low in the post-war period, causing a decrease in average yield,[38] and producing a tendency for smallholders to replant part of their holdings with rubber. In the period 1956–60 there was a continuous decline in the amount of pepper produced, and whereas Sarawak produced 38 per cent of all pepper entering world trade in 1956, by 1960 this had fallen to about 5 per cent.[39] In 1959 a cleaning and grading plant was installed at Sarikei (Third Division), which has done much to improve the quality of pepper exported.

To sum up: smallholder cash crop cultivation is almost monocultural in nature; and in comparison with rubber every other crop is insignificant in terms of area occupied, number of people employed and value of exports. In each territory Chinese smallholders occupy a position with regard to the production of export crops which is disproportionate to their total numbers in the population. Finally, the last five to ten years have witnessed in each territory a remarkable expansion and improvement of smallholding cash crop production (particularly of rubber) in response to very similar government schemes. The cultivation of cash crops by smallholders appears likely to be of increasing importance in the Malaysian territories.

18

Problems of Agriculture

K. T. JOSEPH

Agriculture in Malaysia is largely the agriculture of economic perennial crops (i.e. crops with a life span greater than ten years) producing for export the following major raw materials: rubber, copra, coconut oil and palm oil. It is clear that there is a heavy dependence upon agriculture since the vast majority (57 per cent) of the active labour force is engaged in agriculture and agriculture is estimated to be responsible for at least 50 per cent of the national income in this region.

Tables 29, 30 and 31 show the distribution of crops grown in the territories comprising Malaysia and illustrate the position of agricultural commodities in the export and import trade of these countries, respectively.

The main crops on an acreage basis (Table 29) are clearly rubber, padi, coconut, sago and oil palm. The crops of importance in terms of export trade are rubber ($M 2,001 million), oil palm ($M 61 million), coconuts ($M 32 million), pineapples ($M 26 million), pepper ($M 17 million), abacá ($M 5 million), and sago ($M 3 million). It should be noted that timber accounted for $M 190 million in the 1960 export trade.

The salient features of the cropping patterns in Malaysia are the pivotal position of rubber and the fact that the territories in the Federation do not produce more than 50 per cent of their domestic food requirements. This is clearly shown for example by the fact that 21 per cent of the total cultivated area only provides approximately two thirds of the total rice requirements for this region. Table 31 indicates that imports of food commodities and animal feedstuffs amount to a quarter of the total imports of this region and most of these foods and feedstuffs could be produced locally. Palm oil (from 2 per cent of the total cultivated area) had double the export trade value of copra (from 10 per cent of total cultivated area). Pineapples in Malaya are mostly grown on peat, a medium that has not yet been utilised as profitably with any other crop. Padi in Malaya is almost entirely wet padi, whereas in both Sarawak and Sabah it is mostly dry padi. In Sarawak two thirds of the total padi area of 268,000 acres and in Borneo one third of total padi area of 93,000 acres is dry hill padi. The cultivation of dry hill padi not only leads to soil erosion but also gives yields which are extremely low (one half the average yield of wet padi of 480 gantangs per acre). The animal population from a meat production point of view is insignificant apart from pig husbandry

TABLE 29. DISTRIBUTION OF CROPS, 1960

Crop	Area in Thousands of Acres				Percentage of Total Cultivation Area
	Malaya	Sarawak	Sabah	Total	
Rubber	3,400	300	173	3,873	62·8
Coconut	520	38	51	609	9·9
Oil Palm	135	—	2	137	2·2
Padi	932	268	93	1,293	21·0
Sago	7	150	4	161	2·6
Pineapple	43	—	—	43	0·7
Pepper	1	8	—	9	0·1
Tobacco	6	—	2	8	0·1
Coffee	15	—	3	18	0·3
Tea	9	—	—	9	0·1
Abacá	—	—	4	4	0·05
Sugar Cane	3	—	—	3	0·05

Source: Annual Reports of the Federation of Malaya, Sarawak and North Borneo, 1960 (1961).

TABLE 30. EXPORT TRADE, 1960

Commodity	Export in Million Dollars (Malay)		
	Malaya	Sarawak	Sabah
Total Exports	2,927	203	188
Rubber	1,829	122	50
Timber	55	44	91
Palm Oil	61	—	—
Copra	24	—	8
Pineapples	26	—	—
Pepper	—	17	—
Abacá	—	—	5
Sago	—	3	—
Agricultural Products as a percentage of Total	68	92	82

Source: Annual Reports of the Federation of Malaya, Sarawak and North Borneo, 1960 (1961).

which is increasing. The supplies of meat in Malaya are hardly sufficient to meet local demand as is also the case with poultry requirements in terms of eggs and meat. Fish, both marine and fresh-water, as well as meat and eggs, are still inadequate to provide minimum levels of animal protein so essential in the diet of the peoples of this region.

Agricultural expansion in these territories can be brought about in two ways: firstly by extending the areas under various existing and new crops, and secondly by increasing the crop and animal productivity in existing cultivated areas.

TABLE 31. IMPORT TRADE, 1960

Commodity	Import in Million Dollars (Malay)		
	Malaya	Sarawak	Sabah
Total Imports	2,150·6	204·9	195·9
Rice	134·8	14·1	8·4
Milk, Condensed and Dried	64·5		
Meat and Fish	60·4		
Sugar and Sugar Preparations	67·5	45·8	25·8
Fats and Oils	—		
Fruits and Vegetables	62·9		
Feeding Stuffs for Animals	28·0	—	—
Others	140·0	—	—
Total Food Imports	558·1	59·9	34·2
Food and Feeding Stuffs as a percentage of Total	26	29	17

Sources: Statistics of External Trade, 1960. Federation of Malaya, Annual Reports of Sarawak and North Borneo, 1960 (1961).

INCREASING CROP ACREAGE AND DIVERSIFICATION

Land Use Survey and National Land Policy

First we have to decide whether or not the present 'spectrum' of crops is ideal both in terms of width and distribution. Should there be expansion in all crops or should this be confined to a few specific crops? This is largely a question of economics. However, quite apart from economic considerations, some diversification of crops is possible if not essential from purely ecological considerations alone. The ideal type of crop husbandry is, to a certain extent, predetermined by the ecological variables. For example, the possible alternative crops suited to inland swamps are limited to wet padi or sago palm; rubber would be incompatible. Steep land areas are best utilised for timber production from forests. (Export trade in timber amounted to $M190 million in 1960.) Destroying the native forests to supplant them with any crop is disastrous. The resulting increase in soil erosion and run-off from catchment areas (with consequent flooding elsewhere) bring about an enormous wastage of the land resources in these territories, and land (unlike labour, capital and management) is irreplaceable.

The maximum area available for the choice of alternative crops must be delineated, that is, the various technological possibilities need to be presented for the prevailing ecological variables. To do this efficiently, a land use survey for Malaysia must first be carried out and a planning commission set up to promulgate a national land policy. This body, to be effective, should consist of a group of individuals with diverse interests, but all capable of assessing land usage in these areas.

Some preliminary advances in this connection have been made. A soils map of Malaya has been produced by the Soil Science Division of the former Federal Department of Agriculture[1] and soil surveys are being carried out in Sarawak and Sabah. A land use survey of Malaysia can be undertaken and completed in a relatively short time provided good topographical maps are available. It does not involve much elaborate work since a broad scale reconnaissance survey would suffice. In Malaya soils have been categorised into various fertility classes. For a land use survey this is unnecessary. Chemically the fertility of soils can be changed—it is a matter of 'additives'. From a soil chemical point of view, most of the soils in Malaysia are poor by world standards and the use of fertilisers is basic to the culture of any crop in these areas. A land use survey on the broader aspects of the physical properties of the soil, e.g. drainage conditions, the presence or absence of any physical barrier which might significantly impede root development, would provide not only a more rational basis for the designing of patterns of crops for the areas under consideration but also speed up the survey for land use.

The possibilities in terms of land use are limited since the range of ecological differences is small. From a soil point of view, the Malaysian territories can be divided into four or five zones or categories for possible alternative crops in the manner suggested by Joseph.[2] The choice from any number of alternatives compatible with the various zones should be made only after critically examining both economic as well as sociological factors.

Unless and until a land use survey of Malaysia is undertaken to formulate a national land policy, it would be difficult to make any objective statements as to the directions in which expansion could take place except to make certain generalisations based on present information.

The steep land areas (all land above the 250 ft contour is a suitable criterion) should remain forested and legislation to this effect has to be made to stop the devastation of existing land resources. In Malaya steep land amounts to nearly 50 per cent of the total land area. The potential areas for expansion in Malaya

277

are largely in south Johore and Pahang. In Sarawak the potential land areas are largely restricted to the alluvial and swampy coastal plain. There is also the area of rolling country intersected by mountain ranges and here a system of tree crop husbandry—for example rubber or oil palm—appropriate to the soils of the area would be possible. The mountainous region in the interior should remain undisturbed. In Sabah, only 6 per cent of the total area is under cultivation. Unfortunately much of Borneo is mountainous although on the west coast there is an extensive coastal plain. Expansion in both Sabah and Sarawak in the areas not too steep for agriculture is again seriously limited by poor communications. A land use survey would indicate the zones suitable for development and a system of roads would then be needed to open up such zones for agriculture.

The Ministry of Rural Development has made some headway in providing the stimulus for expansion in Malaya in the building of roads and by organising settlement schemes under the Federal Land Development Authority. The lessons gained from these experiences in Malaya would be invaluable in Sarawak and Sabah. If the same mistakes are to be avoided, a land use survey and a national land policy must first be adopted. The size of the new farms in accordance with the agricultural potential of the land and economic returns in order to provide a decent living standard for prospective settlers in new settlement schemes must also be determined.

The drainage and irrigation schemes on the west coast of Malaya have provided spectacular results in respect to both padi cultivation and rubber, coconut and oil palm. Table 32 illustrates the acreages in Malaya under irrigation and drainage and demonstrates the increased areas under padi production as a result of these schemes. The capital outlay as well as maintenance costs for these irrigation and drainage schemes amounts to a small fraction of the additional earnings which result from these schemes. Likewise the swamp areas along the coast in Sarawak and Sabah provide for expansion in wet padi cultivation and thus the expansion and development of the Drainage and Irrigation Department in Sabah and Sarawak are matters of top priority for extending wet padi cultivation.

TABLE 32. PADI DRAINAGE AND IRRIGATION SCHEMES—MALAYA, 1959–60

	Padi Acreage				Yield of Rice in tons
	Under Irrigation	Controlled Drainage	Substandard and Under Construction	Total	
Prior to Scheme	130,000	21,000	188,000	339,000	
Resulting from Scheme	134,000	11,000	44,000	189,000	
Total after Scheme	264,000	32,000	232,000	528,000	337,000

The expansion of wet padi cultivation is particularly important in Sarawak and Sabah, since there is a need to work towards the total abolition of dry land padi cultivation in view of the erosional hazards which this system invariably incurs. Self-sufficiency in rice in these territories can be attained by wet padi cultivation alone provided that irrigation and drainage facilities are adequate and appropriate to the environment.[3]

Need for Diversification

The rubber industry is still the life blood of Malaya and Sarawak; about two thirds and a half respectively of the total export earnings are derived from rubber (in Sabah a quarter). In Malaya in the first five-year development plan some expansion in rubber acreages took place in the way of new land development schemes for smallholders under the aegis of the Ministry of Rural Development. This course of action was justified by the prevailing rubber prices at the beginning of the first plan, but since the end of the plan, the price of rubber has dropped by over 25 per cent and the future is uncertain in view of the ever increasing competition from synthetic rubber. It is possible by raising productivity that falling rubber prices may be borne. No one can predict with certainty to what level the rubber price will eventually fall and Malaysia, eager for growing prosperity, cannot have a non-viable economy. The old saying, 'too many eggs in one basket', has a resounding ring in this context and the task is therefore to broaden the base of the economy. The diversification of agriculture in Malaysia is vital to the future prosperity of this young nation.

There is general agreement on the need and wisdom of diversifying agriculture, but the direction in which this is to take place is complicated and less well defined. There are few beacons to light the path towards greater diversification. What other crops can we grow that will yield as good economic returns as rubber does at present? If there are, do we possess the know-how and experience to ensure the success of such diversification?

On the basis of the present prices of rubber and palm oil, there is not much doubt that the oil palm is a real economic alternative to rubber. The price of palm oil on the world market, unlike that of rubber, has not been subject to turbulent fluctuations and if the downward trend of rubber price continues, then the financial return from oil palm will be substantially greater. Further, it is a crop Malaya has much practical experience of, albeit only as an estate crop.

However, it must be borne in mind that the oil palm does not have quite the wide adaptability to the soil conditions in the region as the rubber plant although it is not as delicate as some believe.

There are considerable potential areas for the expansion of oil palm in Malaysia. The oil palm flourishes in the marine clays on the west coast of Malaya.

279

In these areas therefore, old rubber plantings could give way to oil palm. There are other areas as yet undeveloped where oil palm should grow well, e.g. the soils of volcanic origin in Sabah and Pahang in Malaya. This is by no means the limit for the crop as considerable areas suitable for oil palm also exist in Trengganu and elsewhere. As a matter of fact, provided that the soil is free-draining, has a reasonable clay content (greater than 30 per cent) and no laterite, the oil palm, contrary to popular belief, is being satisfactorily grown.

A substantial acreage in Malaya (Table 29) is devoted to the cultivation of coconut which is mainly concentrated in the coastal areas of west Johore and Bagan Datoh in Perak. Coconut is predominantly a smallholder crop but in Bagan Datoh and elsewhere there are some estates. The industry has not quite recovered from the recession in 1959 and production from smallholdings in west Johore particularly is low. From an economic point of view, there is much evidence to indicate that even with fairly good yields, the income from coconut per acre per annum is very much lower than that from oil palm, as shown in Table 33. In view of the fact that most of the soils in Bagan Datoh and west Johore are marine clays, it would be more rational to switch over to oil palm. Naturally, a number of problems will be encountered in any move to change the smallholders' crop.

TABLE 33. RETURNS FROM OIL PALM AND COCONUT

Crop	Expected Yield per acre per annum	Price	Gross Income per acre per annum
Coconut	8 pikuls copra	$M 25 per pikul	$M 200
Oil Palm	5 tons fresh fruit bunches	4 cents per lb.	$M 448

The first problem is social rather than technical. Most of the area under coconut is cultivated by smallholders and they will be reluctant to alter their rhythm of life by changing to the more exacting culture of oil palm. However, given financial backing and the force of economic considerations the smallholders may be won over to this new crop. The second problem is technical since the smallholders will have to be shown how to grow and manage the crop. Perhaps the experience of the oil palm estates can be drawn upon for designing a program of technical aid to potential oil palm smallholders.

There is still the problem of providing oil palm factories for the extraction of palm oil. The capital outlay is heavy and in a predominantly smallholding area of oil palm, some form of a government-aided co-operative factory will be needed. In areas where large estates already exist and in new oil palm schemes, an arrangement whereby fruit from smallholders may be processed at the estate factory can be worked out. Such an arrangement will operate in the near future in Kulai, Johore, and its success will determine the launching or otherwise of similar projects elsewhere. Notwithstanding all these difficulties, there is no doubt that oil palm expansion must take place in Malaysia as an integral part of diversification.

In the padi areas, provided irrigation water is available during the off-season, possibilities of diversification also exist. In the long run, continuous double cropping with padi may bring adverse effects such as the greater incidence of pests and diseases and deterioration of soil conditions. Cash crops like maize, sugar cane, vegetables and soya bean may become off-season or rotation crops.

The potentialities for expansion in pineapple cultivation are almost unlimited. The large peat areas in Malaya (estimated at one million acres), Sabah and Sarawak (extensive, but as yet unsurveyed) provide opportunities for expansion. The limited work on peat in Malaya with a number of crops has so far demonstrated that the pineapple is the only crop that can be successfully grown on peat. Viewed purely as an export there are problems of competition in world markets, chiefly from Australia, Hawaii and Formosa. Only a powerful organisation to discover better techniques of production and processing of pineapple as exists in Hawaii and Australia will be able to stand up to this challenge.

Tea, both lowland and highland, is grown largely on an estate basis in Malaya and total production and exports have been steadily rising over the last ten years. (Production figures are 4·19 and 5·36 million lbs for 1953 and 1959 respectively.) Some expansion in estate acreage is taking place in Cameron Highlands and possibilities for estate expansion may exist in the highlands of Sabah and Sarawak.

The implications of agricultural diversification stretch far beyond the promotion of one or two crops already grown to some extent in Malaysia. It will involve the introduction of crops hitherto little known in the region. The little experience that we have had with new introductions, in particular cocoa, has bred caution before their extensive release for cultivation.

As a preamble to crop diversification, plantings of Trinitario cocoa in Malaya were carried out experimentally in 1948 by the Department of Agriculture on its stations. In the years 1950 and 1951 Trinitario cocoa was substituted with a variety Amelonado from West Africa. The early results appeared favourable and the first commercial planting was made by an estate in Trengganu in 1953. Up to the year 1957, the prospects for cocoa in Malaya remained fairly bright (Heath, 1958), but in early 1958 a disease called 'die-back' set in affecting most areas, and yields were a third of what was really expected. Efforts to discover the cause of 'die-back' have been unsuccessful and as a result cocoa has not been recommended as a crop for diversification. Owing to the shortage of staff, research on cocoa is now minimal although there is some evidence that an introduced Brazilian variety may be less prone to the malady.

The failure to establish cocoa as a major crop in Malaya cannot be laid at the feet of the Department of Agriculture as failure is as much a part of experimentation as success. After all, it is possible that we do not have the environment for cocoa but this can only be settled by future research. Be that as it may, one major criticism can be made and this is directed at the inadequate planning and research that went into the effort. More detailed studies should have been conducted on the suitability of climate, soil and culture of the crop. In particular, factors such as shading, varietal differences and yield performances should have been tested over a sufficiently long period. If all the efforts made to introduce cocoa are not to be written off as a complete loss, then it is incumbent on us to salvage what information we can.

Sugar cane cultivation has been suggested (see note 2) for parts of Kedah that have a distinct dry period of a few months each year. The crop requires this dry period for maturation or otherwise the cane will have a low sugar content. Where such climatic conditions exist elsewhere in Malaysia, it appears that sugar cane merits consideration as a crop for diversification. The plant is a prolific producer of leafy material which will thus form a mulch and enrich the organic matter content of the soil, and this is particularly desirable in soils of low organic matter content, a dominant feature in Malaysia.

In Malaya, the sandy soils of the east coast (approximately 200,000 acres) can be exploited for coconut. It would appear that a system of legume/grass and grazing animals on these sandy soils in conjunction with coconut husbandry would offer a practical solution to the development of these soils. In this connection, the legume, *Stylosanthes gracilis*, has shown considerable promise.

The expansion in systems of mixed farming in Malaysia needs to be encouraged; for example, in Sabah, pig husbandry is carried out in Chinese coconut, sago and padi holdings where coconut meal, sago waste and rice bran respectively constitute the main source of feed for the animal.[4] There is a need to design systems of farming whereby plant residues and by-products can be exploited for animal feed. In this context, Joseph has suggested that sugar cane cultivation on some soils of Kedah could be integrated with some form of animal husbandry (see note 2).

A field that offers unlimited scope for development is fresh-water fish culture. Fish protein provides a practical solution to the problem of protein deficiency in the diet of the rural people. Experiments at the Tropical Fish Research Institute in Malacca indicate that yields of fresh-water fish can be raised by breeding, stocking ponds with suitable fish at optimum rates, excluding predators and competitors and stimulating the supply of fish food by the use of fertilisers.[5] At the Institute, the natural unimproved crop of fish of 20 to 50 lbs per acre per annum has been increased to approximately 1,500 lbs per acre per annum by the use of fertilisers alone. Thus land too poor or too costly to be drained can be profitably used for fish culture. The Department of Fisheries is actively engaged in finding practical ways and means of introducing fish culture into the agricultural scene.

The crux of all these problems of diversification is that adequate and appropriate research of a fairly long term nature must be carried out before deciding whether a new crop can be grown successfully on a wide scale in Malaysia. For example, manila hemp is also a possible crop for diversification but before firm recommendations can be made, the following parameters have to be determined: suitability of climate, the soils best suited (hence the land use survey), the agronomic and management requirements of the crop, the best varieties, susceptibility to pests and diseases, yield performances over a sufficient period (say five years) and finally the economic returns per acre per annum.

To do this efficiently, the best plan is to establish special experimental stations on a number of representative soils in Malaysia where new crops proposed for diversification, e.g. manila hemp, sugar cane, citrus, cocoa, etc, are tested for the information mentioned above. In point of fact, such an experimental station in miniature already exists on peat in the Malayan Department of Agriculture but the scheme needs modification and extension to other soils. Unless crop and animal testing are placed on a rational basis, we may be landed with a number of defunct 'groundnut schemes'. Had all this research been performed ten or more years ago, valuable information would have now become available. In the absence of such research, the formulation of a sound diversification policy for agriculture is fraught with difficulties.

Any policy of agricultural diversification in Malaysia should also take due cognisance of the human element, for hundreds of thousands of people will be affected by proposed changes to new crops. There is bound to be considerable reluctance to change to a new form of farming since most people have little wish to have their tempo and pattern of living upset, however rational a scheme may be. Human beings are not expendable, therefore it behoves policy makers to prepare by education the mass of our smallholder farmers for the new challenges ahead. Their co-operation and goodwill are as vital as a sound blueprint for a flourishing agriculture in the future.

INCREASING PRODUCTION PER ACRE

By and large, this is a question of raising crop or animal production per unit area by both estates and smallholders. New and better husbandry techniques, such as the planting of high yielding material, proper manuring, drainage and crop protection developed through research, contribute to agricultural progress in the form of increased production, but the magnitude of this increase depends mainly on the extent to which these new methods are put into practice.

Where estates and smallholdings are found producing the same crop, it is common to find that estates are ahead of the smallholders in production per acre. In the field of crop production, a study of yield figures for major crops like rubber and coconut reveals that there is considerable room for levelling all yields up to those of better estates and knowledge does exist to make this possible. For example a recent survey[6] in Malaya has shown that the average yield of rubber from one group of smallholders is estimated at 470 lbs per acre per annum whereas that of estate-owned rubber is of the order of 800 lbs per acre per annum. Since a large proportion of the total acreage of rubber in Malaysia is under smallholders (about 50 per cent), we can expect substantial increases in yields through the adoption by smallholders of present techniques alone, e.g. replanting with high yielding clones of rubber. The future of the Malayan rubber industry as a whole is the more secure because of the heavy replanting program that has been earnestly undertaken particularly by the large estates. Today, more than half the acreage of rubber in Malaya has been replanted but the fly in the ointment of this bright endeavour is the much slower rate of replanting in the smallholdings. The urgency of overcoming this problem is reflected in the extension of the replanting scheme recently announced by the Malayan government. There is little time to lose to bring the smallholders up to schedule and much of the responsibility falls on the extension service to accelerate replanting as well as to persuade them to implement latest methods.

From the yield point of view, the figure of 800 lbs per acre per annum is by no means the ceiling of potential rubber yields for some estates in Malaya have recorded yields exceeding 1,000 lbs per acre per annum. Substantial advances in this direction will depend on research, and present work carried out by the Rubber Research Institute on yield stimulants indicates that yields up to 2,000 lbs per acre per annum may be achieved in the foreseeable future. In the battle between natural rubber and synthetic, there can be no let up in research efforts.

Padi yields in Malaya vary markedly from as low as 1,400 lbs per acre to as high as over 5,000 lbs per acre; the national average is about 2,000 lbs per acre. In Kedah—the rice bowl of Malaya—the average yields vary between 2,500 and 2,800 lbs per acre whereas in the Tanjong Karang area of north-west Selangor, yields often exceed 5,000 lbs per acre. This prompts one to ask if such high yields are already found within Malaysia, why are not all areas made to yield as well? This vast difference in yield is due to many factors such as soil fertility, husbandry methods, water control, etc. Only long term research will help to unravel the specific factors controlling yield and thereby raise yields throughout Malaysia to those now obtained in Tanjong Karang.

This does not imply that significant short term improvement in padi yields cannot be achieved. Current breeding and agronomic research carried out by

284

the Department of Agriculture in north-west Malaya has indicated that by the use of high yielding varieties developed, proper planting techniques and correct timing and quantity of fertiliser application, increases in yield may soon be obtained. This information will be made progressively available to farmers and success will depend on the implementation of such information, for which the role of the extension service is vital.

Malaya still imports more than a third of its total consumption of rice (valued at $M 135 million in 1960, Table 31) and this is true for Sabah and Sarawak as well. The practice of double-cropping padi seems to offer a short cut to the attaining of self-sufficiency in rice. Traditionally, only one padi crop is taken off the land in Malaya because the fields are dependent on the rain for water and the rainfall distribution only allows for one crop a year. This is particularly true of Kedah and Kelantan but in some relatively smaller areas, such as mainland Penang where irrigation water is available throughout the year, double-cropping is already practised. However, the total area double-cropped only amounts to less than five per cent of the total acreage of padi land in Malaya.

The supply of irrigation water is the *sine qua non* of double-cropping in the major areas of Kedah and Kelantan. To irrigate an area of nearly half a million acres calls for gigantic irrigation projects and the one proposed for Kedah (the Muda scheme) will cost more than $M 150 million. The initial expenditure is certainly enormous and there will be difficulties in finding funds to finance such projects, but with the envisaged doubling of productivity resulting from the scheme, there is good reason to believe that the money will be recovered within a fairly short time, certainly within a decade.

Apart from these purely agricultural considerations, there are grave social and economic problems in the padi areas of Malaya such as the endemic poverty of the peasant farmers, smallness of holdings, systems of land tenure, etc.[7] For real advancement, these problems must be tackled simultaneously with those of agriculture. Even if padi yields can be doubled, or trebled for that matter, within the next decade, will this provide a decent living standard for the average padi farmer with a holding of only two acres? Social and economic reforms are as important as technical innovations in striving to improve living standards, a fact many countries with agrarian societies have come increasingly to appreciate.

After rubber, the next major crop grown for export is oil palm. It is encouraging that the industry in Malaysia is a vigorous one. In Malaya, it is almost entirely an estate crop being located on the fertile coastal alluvial clays along the west coast and free draining inland soils. Yields are good and in fact Malayan yields in terms of palm oil per acre are amongst the highest in the world and are definitely above those obtained in West Africa. On the coastal alluvial clays, spectacular increases in yields in the near future are unlikely but, in the long term,

285

evolving high yielding palms through breeding will probably be the most promising line of research to pursue. On the other hand, where the oil palm is grown on inland soils—a feature which may increase in prominence in future—agronomic research should continue to effect large increases in yield.

Unlike oil palm, the coconut industry has declined. Malayan exports of coconut oil in terms of value have been falling over the past years. This is particularly serious in the smallholder area of west Johore in Malaya. A survey by Wilson[8] showed that the average yield of copra was only 4 piculs per acre compared with the expected yield of 8 piculs. Bad drainage, poor management and pests, in particular the rhinoceros beetle, have contributed to the decline. There is now a program of replanting and drainage but the real issue is whether to replant with coconut or some other crop such as rubber or oil palm. This problem has been discussed in an earlier section of this paper.

With regard to animal production, data are unfortunately even scarcer than for crop production. However, it is known that local supplies of eggs, meat and milk products are inadequate to meet demands (see Table 31). These products are sources of protein so essential in the human diet. Nutritional surveys conducted by the Institute of Medical Research in Malaya[9] have highlighted the shortage of protein in the diet of the rural community and indicated that the dietary levels of protein intake must be materially raised. Table 34 shows the estimated intake of calories (carbohydrates) and protein as a percentage of recommended allowances by Malayans in the low income group.[10]

TABLE 34. ESTIMATED MONTHLY INTAKE OF NUTRITIONAL CONSTITUENTS
as a Percentage of Recommended Allowances for Malayan Households
(Based on Household Budget Survey)
Income Group $M 1–$M 150

	Malay		Chinese		Indian	
	Rural	Urban	Rural	Urban	Rural	Urban
Calories	81	76	83	63	88	87
Protein	63	58	55	52	64	65

To increase meat production in Malaysia is rather more difficult than to increase crop production because research on animal husbandry in Malaysia, particularly into the nutrition and management aspects, is rudimentary, and because, unlike the rubber industry, there is not the example of efficient large scale animal farms for smallholders to follow. There is an urgent need to promote and accelerate investigations into the feeding and management of pigs and poultry to increase their production. The optimum levels of nutriment for maximum growth rates have to be determined as well as the nutritive values of various feedstuffs. A great deal of animal feed is now imported into the country (see Table 31, page 276). It will be sounder practice to utilise all available local waste products for feeds. For example, copra, tapioca and oil palm kernel residues should be exploited together with feeds such as maize and sweet potatoes which can be grown successfully here. For milk or meat production, cattle and goats require fodder of a high nutritive quality. This means that fodder crops, i.e. legumes and grasses, need to be introduced much more widely into Malaysian farming.

In Malaya, certain legumes such as *Centrosema pubescens*, *Pueraria javanica* and *Stylosanthes gracilis* have been successfully grown. The first two legumes are utilised mainly as cover crops in rubber estates but have not yet been exploited as animal feed. In the poorer soils, *Stylosanthes* has shown considerable promise[11] and can be cut for fodder. A number of grass species have been tested in agricultural stations by the Malayan Department of Agriculture and of these Guinea grass (*Panicum maximum*) appears worthy of attention. On the whole, there is a dearth of information on the establishment and utilisation of tropical grasses and legumes as animal fodder in Malaysia. Again, the urgency for research along such lines needs little emphasis.

EDUCATION AS A SOLUTION TO THE BASIC PROBLEM

The problems of agriculture in Malaysia are many and varied. Economic problems are complex. It is not just a question of increasing the customary categories of inputs into the productive process—land, labour and capital; there are marketing, money-lending and rent problems.[12] As has just been mentioned, sociological factors are important and cannot be excluded. There is no intention here to delve into the economic and sociological problems of agriculture but rather to consider how the technological problems of agriculture may ultimately be resolved.

Technologically, increased agricultural productivity may be brought about by improving husbandry methods in respect to crops as well as animals. As we have seen this can be done by (i) implementation of existing knowledge of crop and animal husbandry by the farmer; (ii) translation of both existing and new knowledge (as it develops through research) to the farmer via the extension service, and (iii) building up new knowledge through research in order to discover improved methods of crop and animal husbandry. These three endeavours are closely interlinked and make for efficient agriculture.

Therefore, the basic task in Malaysia is to develop and bring closer together all these three groups of people: farmers, extension workers, researchers who are engaged in agriculture, and particularly the farmers, through agricultural education.

287

The smallholder in Malaysia has had little or no education. He is born poor and remains so in everything material. Smallholders are predominant in Malaysia as shown in Table 35. In Sarawak and Sabah practically the whole of agriculture is practised by smallholders.

TABLE 35. FARMERS IN MALAYA

Size of Farm acres	No. of Farmers		Total Cultivated Area thousand acres	
$\frac{1}{4}$ to $14\frac{3}{4}$	434,600	95·6%	1,960	42·4%
15 to $99\frac{3}{4}$	17,800	3·9%	427	9·2%
Over 100	2,500	0·5%	2,240	48·4%
Total	454,900		4,627	

Source: Malayan Census of Agriculture 1960: Preliminary Reports.

Surveys carried out in Malaya have shown that yields of padi, coconut and rubber[13] from existing smallholdings are low. Increased yields can be expected in all these situations from superior husbandry methods such as improved methods of cultivation, use of superior planting material, proper use of fertilisers, weed control, the elimination of useless animals, better animal feeding practices and the development of better breeds of animals. Existing knowledge alone (in Malaysia this is certainly less advanced than in the temperate countries) if applied can make marked advances possible. In this connection references to rubber, padi and coconut have already been made.

It is necessary therefore to establish in Malaysia a more 'sophisticated' farming community. An imaginative education policy appropriate to the situation needs to be formulated and adopted. This in itself is a big problem. Should the educational attack be made on the present or future generation or both? Practically all inhibiting prejudices originate in past generations and are held by the present. Even if succeeding generations come under an effective system of education, it must be borne in mind that they will still be influenced to a certain extent by the present generation. Rural education for future generations would appear to be the most effective system. The need for agricultural education in rural areas is real. This problem although grave enough in Malaya is even more acute in Sarawak and Sabah where large areas have been devastated and made useless by erosion arising from the practice of growing dry land padi on steep slopes in a system of bush fallow. That these practices are so ingrained in some of the peoples of Sarawak and Sabah is exemplified by the following quotations from Cook writing in the annual report of the Sarawak Department of Agriculture.[14] 'The production of dry land padi on the steep slopes of the interior . . . is traditional and is integral in the way of life of the interior peoples', and 'the fact must be faced that this sytem will be practised for many years before there are any major changes'. He goes on to say: 'There is, on the other hand, little tradition in regard to wet padi cultivation . . . standards of cultivation are poor, the use of animal drawn implements and the principles of drainage and irrigation almost unknown and yields correspondingly low.'

The relationship of education appropriate to agricultural development is critical if we are to make the transition from tradition to modernity. This could effectively be carried out by creating farm schools in rural areas to teach practical agriculture. In Malaya the scene is set for such a development to begin. In 1961 out of a total of 20,021 candidates who sat for the Lower Certificate of Education Examination in Malaya (average age 14–15 years) only 11,062 were promoted. This means that nearly fifty per cent of these students had to leave school, thereby terminating their formal education.

Although the distribution of students in Table 36 has not been divided into rural and urban or in terms of race, it is indicative nevertheless of the tremendous wastage of young human potential that is taking place and will continue to do so increasingly with time. In spite of the limitations of the table presented below, it demonstrates the existence of student material that could be channelled for exposure to an elementary agricultural education.

TABLE 36. LCE EXAMINATION, 1961

Promoted	Passed	Failed	Withdrew	Total
11,062	3,939	4,754	266	20,021

Source: Controller of Examinations, Ministry of Education, Federation of Malaya.
Note: Candidates who passed normally have to leave school in addition to those who failed. A pass in LCE merely entitles a candidate to a certificate.

The time has come for some rethinking on the type of education required in these territories. The large number of students who have to leave school at the LCE level presents the nation with a social and economic problem. The provision of technical and agricultural training facilities for these young people would enable a great number of them to play a fuller role in society. In the rural areas farm schools provide not only a means of absorbing these students for further education but also, in the long term view, provide the raw material from which our more 'sophisticated' farmers might evolve. A system of rural farm education has to be created whereby practical agriculture, particularly in regard to the major crops of this area, forms the basis of the training. Details of the location for these schools, their course, and staff can be worked out once the need is recognised and these ideas accepted.

The translation to the farmer via the extension service of existing knowledge and the new knowledge as it develops is important in agriculture. In Sabah and

Sarawak the problem of translating knowledge to the farmer is even graver than in Malaya. Since in these territories, in the words of Cook, 'The absence of an efficiently run estate industry from which example might be taken by the small-holder is manifest and thus, while comparatively efficient holdings (in rubber) do exist, the majority is badly planted, maintenance is poor, tapping and processing primitive, and the end product of low quality' (see note 14).

The basic ingredient for technical efficiency in agriculture is the translation of information on improved farming techniques to the farmer. This must be carried out by trained personnel who are in close contact with farmers to advise them on agricultural matters. For effectiveness in this process of 'translation' to the farmer, there must be an adequate number of such trained personnel for this task. Whatever index is used, be it 'number of farms' or 'farmers per extension worker', the ratio is hopelessly inadequate throughout Malaysia. The training and supply of this important category of personnel needs development both in terms of quantity as well as quality. The training required for this group of extension workers must be entirely practical in scope. What we need here are agricultural technicians, trained in and for the Malaysian environment. Where are these trained personnel to come from? Throughout Malaysia there is but one agricultural college, that at Serdang in Malaya where the number of students enrolled is only of the order of 25 a year for the whole region. The numbers required for agricultural development in Malaysia would necessitate a marked expansion in intake of students to about 100 or 150 per year (five times the number entering the University of Malaya to read Agricultural Science). This will, of course, involve increased capital costs for buildings, and increases in the teaching staff and so on. Investment of money for the expansion of the Agricultural College at Serdang is essential in view of the important role that this institution must play in the agricultural development of Malaysia. This it is unlikely to accomplish in its present form. The College at Serdang needs a complete over-haul and reorientation in outlook. The course at Serdang should be geared to produce agricultural technicians with sound, practical knowledge of crop and animal husbandry, relevant to these territories. The College should be geared to the practical needs rather than aspiring to the academic. Therefore, as one of the priorities for development in Malaysia, this College must be reorganised and expanded so as to be able to produce men and women with practical skills. It is hoped Serdang College will ultimately produce the bulk of our extension 'corps'. It must also provide the teaching staff for the rural farm schools discussed previously, and the farm managers for the various land development schemes. For agricultural expansion in Malaysia and especially in Sarawak and Sabah, government-sponsored land development schemes will assume more and more significance and suitably trained managers would be essential for their success.

The college at Serdang must now be changed to prepare it for its greater role ahead.

The need for research in order to discover improved methods of crop and animal husbandry is as great as the need for training the technical service for extension and the creation of a more enlightened farming community. The technical problems of agriculture raised here can only be resolved by intensive research. Financial support for agricultural research in Malaysia should be increased and should be looked upon as a sound investment as in technically advanced nations. At present, the major organisations responsible for agricultural research in Malaysia are the Departments of Agriculture in Malaya, Sarawak and Sabah and the Rubber Research Institute. The last mentioned however is solely confined to the rubber crop. Apart from the recently established Pineapple Industry Board which is now responsible for pineapple research in Malaya, and a few fairly small commercial experimental stations on rubber and oil palm, the Departments of Agriculture bear the heavy burden for research on all the remaining crops and animals.

There is ample opportunity for expansion in research efforts in Malaysia, and in this connection, it is hoped the newly instituted Faculty of Agriculture of the University of Malaya will ultimately play a dominant role. As well as training people for senior extension and estate managerial posts in Malaysia, the Faculty of Agriculture must at the same time conduct independent research and produce personnel for the various research organisations.

Research in agriculture in Malaysia is in its infancy. Agricultural research workers trained in temperate countries have a problem of adapting themselves to the local scene. Far too often the extension of western educational techniques into the underdeveloped tropical countries in the various branches of agriculture has not taken full account of the needs there. For a variety of reasons, writes M. F. Millikan,[15] 'Our export educational product has both during the colonial and post colonial eras placed even more emphasis than our domestic product on rote learning, preparation for fixed subject matter examinations and memorisation of a body of knowledge of limited relevance to local needs.' It is hoped that the Faculty of Agriculture of the University of Malaya will have as its central goal a system of training appropriate to our environment and always geared towards an educational attitude for problem solving. It must not be merely a process of transmitting a body of information from one student generation to another but rather a process of creating a set of attitudes and talents conducive to finding new and more effective ways of doing things.

Properly designed education at all three levels—the farm school, the technical level (Serdang and similar colleges) and the university—will require the government of the Malaysian territories to devote a considerable proportion of its financial resources. Given the stimulus of increased financial aid and a properly designed education for these three distinct levels, agricultural development in Malaysia should make substantial progress. Advances in agriculture can only take place in Malaysia provided a proper land use policy is adopted, and the standard of farming is raised through the creation of better farmers, an efficient extension service and active research.

19

The Mining Industry*

YIP YAT HOONG

Any appraisal of the mining industry of Malaysia must be confined largely to Malaya which at present accounts for almost all the mineral production of the area (Table 37). Mineral production is of no importance in Singapore and Sabah and of negligible importance in Sarawak. In Malaya, mineral production contributed to about 7 per cent of the gross national product in 1959. In Sarawak, where the first and only gross national product estimate was made in 1955, mineral production was only one per cent (Table 38). In terms of direct employment, only 2 per cent of the economically active population of Malaysia is engaged in mineral production (Table 39), a proportion insignificant when compared with agriculture and less important than services, commerce, manufacturing, transport and communications or building and construction. However, in terms of indirect employment this proportion, particularly in Malaya, is likely to be very much higher. And further, where contribution to total exports and to government revenue is concerned, mineral production is of significant importance. In 1960 exports of mineral products from Malaysia accounted for 20 per cent of the total exports, a third as important as rubber and nearly as important as all the other exports put together (Table 40). In Malaya export duty on mineral products alone made up about 7 per cent of the total government revenue in 1960.

Of the various minerals produced in Malaysia, tin and iron in Malaya dominate the whole mining industry (Table 41). These two together made up 95 per cent of the total value of mineral production in 1960, tin accounting for two thirds and iron more than one quarter of the total. The production of other

---

* Because of the importance of oil produced in Brunei to the Malaysian economy, figures for Brunei, wherever possible, are included in this chapter for purposes of comparison.

TABLE 37. VALUE OF MINERAL PRODUCTION, BY COUNTRIES, 1938, 1949, 1956–60

(in $M million)

Countries	1938	1949	1956	1957	1958	1959	1960
Malaya[1]	70·6	274·5	477·5	455·6	319·2	364·8	502·0
Singapore	—	—	—	—	—	—	—
Sarawak[2]	n.a.	n.a.	5·4	5·3	6·7	8·6	10·1
Sabah	—	—	—	—	—	—	—
MALAYSIA	—	—	482·9	460·9	325·9	373·4	512·1
Brunei[3]	5·5	60·1	309·3	313·7	300·4	292·6	240·1

n.a. = not available.

Sources: 1. Federation of Malaya, Annual Reports, Kuala Lumpur; Department of Mines, Federation of Malaya, Bulletin of Statistics relating to the Mining Industry, 1956–60, Kuala Lumpur, Table 2, p. 2. 2. Sarawak, Annual Reports, Kuching. 3. State of Brunei, Annual Reports, Kuala Belait.

Note: Actual value of production is used as far as possible; where this is not available, value of exports has been used instead. For Malaya, the value of mineral products is based mainly on actual production; for Sarawak, mainly on the value of exports (excluding re-exports) but also on the estimated value of production; and for Brunei, entirely on exports.

TABLE 38. CONTRIBUTION OF MINERAL PRODUCTION TO GROSS NATIONAL PRODUCT, BY COUNTRIES

(in $M million)

Countries	Year	Gross National Product[1]	Mineral Production Value[2] ($M million)	% of GNP
Malaya	1959	5,411[a]	365	6·7
Singapore	1955	1,625[b]	—	—
Sarawak	1955	375[c]	5	1·3
Sabah	1960	n.a.	—	—
Brunei	1960	n.a.	240	—

n.a. = not available.

Sources: 1. United Nations, Economic Survey for Asia and the Far East, 1961, Bangkok, Asian Economic Statistics, Table 7, p. 172; the Colombo Plan, Fifth Annual Report of the Consultative Committee, Wellington, December, 1956, p. 73. 2. Department of Mines, Federation of Malaya, Bulletin of Statistics, 1956–60, op. cit., Table 2, p. 2; Sarawak, Annual Report, 1955, pp. 59–60; State of Brunei, Annual Report, 1960, p. 23.

Notes: a. Gross domestic product at market prices. b. Gross national product of Singapore was obtained by taking 25 per cent of the gross national product of Malaya and Singapore for 1955 on the assumption that one fourth of the total was attributed to Singapore, as stated in the Colombo Plan, Fifth Annual Report, op. cit., p. 73. c. First and only gross national product estimate to date.

TABLE 39. DISTRIBUTION OF ECONOMICALLY ACTIVE POPULATION, BY INDUSTRIES, 1960[a]

(in thousands)

Industries	Malaya[1]	Singapore[2]	Sarawak[3]	Sabah[4]	Total No. of Persons	Total % of Total
Agriculture, Forestry and Fishing	1,244·8	40·2	239·6	142·1	1,666·7	54·3
Services	319·7	161·3	16·3	10·1	507·4	16·5
Commerce	195·2	121·5	13·8	7·7	338·2	11·0
Manufacturing	135·7	66·8	11·5	6·7	220·7	7·2
Transport and Communications	74·8	50·3	5·6	4·7	135·4	4·4
Building and Construction	67·8	24·6	4·6	4·5	101·5	3·3
Mining and Quarrying	58·5	1·6[b]	—	—	60·1	2·0
Electricity and Water Supply	11·6	5·6	—	—	17·2	0·6
Other Industries	18·1	—	2·9	0·8	21·8	0·7
Total	2,126·2	471·9	294·3	176·6	3,069·0	100·0

Sources: 1. Department of Statistics, Federation of Malaya, *1957 Population Census*, Kuala Lumpur, Report No. 14, p. 31. 2. Singapore, *1957 Census of Population*, Singapore, Preliminary Release No. 12, paper presented to the Legislative Assembly, Cmd. (New Series) 24 of 1959. 3. Jones, L. W., *Report on the Census of Population of Sarawak*, 1960, Kuching, January, 1962, p. 110. 4. Jones, L. W., *Report on the Census of Population of North Borneo*, 1960, Kuching, March 1962, p. 113.

Notes: a. Malaya and Singapore figures are based on their 1957 reports of census of population.
b. Mainly in quarrying.

TABLE 40. VALUE OF MAIN EXPORTS, 1960

(in $M million)

Main Exports	Malaya[1]	Singapore[a]	Sarawak[2]	Sabah[3]	Total $M million	Total % of Total	Brunei[4]
Mineral Products	647	—	8[b]	—	655	19·7	240
Rubber	1,829	—	122	50	2,001	60·2	5
Other Agriculture	165	—	64	141	370	11·1	—
Other Exports	287	—	9	3	299	9·0	10
Total	2,928	—	203	194	3,325	100·0	255

Sources: 1. Federation of Malaya, *Official Year Book*, 1961, Kuala Lumpur, Appendix III, Table 30, p. 470. 2. Sarawak, *Annual Report*, 1960, p. 26. 3. North Borneo, *Annual Report*, 1960, Jesselton. 4. State of Brunei, *Annual Report*, 1960, p. 23.

Notes: a. Singapore has no export industry of importance. Its exports consist mainly of re-exports, about one third from the Federation of Malaya, but also a significant proportion from Indonesia and Sarawak. b. Excludes re-exports of oil from Brunei.

minerals is insignificant by comparison. Bauxite, which is the main mineral product of Sarawak, made up less than 3 per cent of the total value in 1960 while the rest added up to only 2 per cent of the total.   In Malaya tin and iron (roughly three quarters and one quarter respectively) made up 97 per cent of the total value of its mineral production in 1960.   Thus any appraisal of the mining industry of Malaysia must be confined largely to tin and iron mining.

TABLE 41. VALUE OF MINERAL PRODUCTION, BY MINERALS, 1960

(in $M million)

Minerals	Malaya[1]	Singapore	Sarawak[2]	Sabah	Total $M million	% of Total	Brunei[3]
Tin	343·8	—	—	—	343·8	67·1	—
Oil	—	—	2·7	—	2·7	0·5	240·1
Iron	143·8	—	—	—	143·8	28·1	—
Bauxite	8·1	—	5·0	—	13·1	2·6	—
Gold	2·1	—	0·4[a]	—	2·5	0·5	—
Ilmenite	3·0[b]	—	—	—	3·0	0·6	—
Coal	0·2	—	—	—	0·2	0·0	—
Other Minerals	1·0	—	2·0[a]	—	3·0	0·6	—
Total	502·0	—	10·1	—	512·1	100·0	240·1

Sources: 1. Department of Mines, Federation of Malaya, *Bulletin of Statistics*, 1956–60, *op. cit.*, Table 2, p. 2. 2. Sarawak, *Annual Report*, 1960, p. 87. 3. State of Brunei, *Annual Report*, 1960, p. 23.

Notes: a. Estimated value. b. Declared value of exports.

TIN MINING

Malaya produces consistently about one third of the world production of tin, nearly twice as much as Indonesia, the next largest producer, but consumes a negligible amount of it. Consequently virtually the whole of this output is exported. At the same time Malaya is the lowest-cost producer, firstly, because the tin deposits in Malaya, unlike those in Bolivia for instance, are alluvial which are relatively easy and cheap to exploit, and secondly, because the concentrates mined in Malaya contain a percentage of metallic tin higher than those found in most other producing countries. On a free world market, Malaya is capable of competing very favourably with any other tin producing country.

Tin mining dominates the whole mining industry of Malaya (Table 42). It accounts for 70–85 per cent of the total mineral production, employs about 85 per cent of the industry's labour force and contributes 80–90 per cent to the total duty collected on mineral exports.

TABLE 42. PRODUCTION OF TIN-IN-CONCENTRATES, EMPLOYMENT AND EXPORT DUTY PAID, MALAYA, 1956–60

Year	Production (in $M million)		Employment (in thousands)		Export Duty Paid (in $M million)	
	All Minerals	Tin	All Minerals	Tin	All Minerals	Tin
1956	478	405	44	39	65	59
1957	456	372	42	37	61	54
1958	319	239	28	23	36	30
1959	365	250	29	24	46	36
1960	502	344	37	29	69	55

Source: Department of Mines, Federation of Malaya, Bulletin of Statistics, 1956–60, op. cit., Table 2, p. 2; Table 8, p. 12; Table 29, p. 31 and Table 64, p. 72.

Early Developments

The early development of Malaya was owed almost entirely to the developments of its tin mining industry. It was Malaya's wealth in tin which first attracted the Chinese and then the Europeans before the turn of this century and which in later years produced the funds for the country's rapid economic progress. Although its relative importance to the Malayan economy has declined considerably in the last fifty years as a result of the country's general development, in absolute amount its contribution to government revenue and to the gross national product remain substantial.[1] Until the turn of the century, tin mining in Malaya was entirely in the hands of the Chinese.

The inter-war years were a period of significant changes in the Malayan tin mining industry. The first half of this period saw the rapid introduction of western techniques of mining, principally the dredge, and the development of large-scale operations in tin mining which led to the rise of the European and the decline of the Chinese sector of the industry. The early 1930s saw a slump in the world tin industry, caused partly by a temporary fall in world demand as a result of the Great Depression but mainly by the vastly increased world production during the late 1920s. In Malaya the increased production had come chiefly from European-owned mines. As a result the average tin price in 1931 fell to one third of its level in the boom year of 1926. From 1931 further decline in the tin price was prevented by drastic export control among the principal producers in the world in the form of the International Tin Agreement. An artificial tin price was thus maintained until the outbreak of the Second World War. In effect, the operation of the International Tin Agreement prevented the elimination of high cost producers like Bolivia and worked generally to the disadvantage of Malaya, a low cost producer.[2]

297

Post-War Developments

Malaya came under the Japanese occupation between 1942 and 1945. Despite severe disruptions to the tin mining industry under the Japanese occupation the recovery of tin production in Malaya in the immediate post-war years was remarkable. By 1948 production had almost reached the 1939 level and by 1956, in spite of serious disturbances under the emergency which came into force in mid-1948, the industry returned to its pre-control productive capacity of the late 1920s.

To some extent, the rapid progress of the industry in the post-war years was the result of the financial assistance offered by the Malayan government for the rehabilitation of the mines immediately after the war. But more important was the encouragement given to the industry in the form of a continuous high tin price which culminated in the Korean War boom of 1951–2. In 1949 the average tin price was twice that of 1946 and nearly three times that of 1939. During 1951–2 this was three times that of 1946 and five times that of 1939. No doubt production costs during the years after the war had risen considerably in all the producing countries. But in Malaya the post-war tin price, especially during 1951–2, still left a wide enough margin of profit to encourage the rapid introduction of new productive capacity in the industry.

An important influence on the post-war world tin market has been the United States strategic stockpiling policy. The United States, which has no tin resources of its own, began stockpiling tin for strategic purposes in 1939 but continued with the policy even after the war. As early as the end of 1947 the post-war recovery of tin production in Malaya (and also in Indonesia) had been so rapid that world production had caught up with world commercial consumption. During the following years 1948–55, there was a continuous substantial excess of production over commercial consumption and it was chiefly the heavy buying of the United States for its strategic stockpile during this period which removed this substantial excess from the world market and maintained a high price of tin throughout this period.

After 1956, the United States reduced substantially its strategic stockpile purchase of tin. But even before that it had become clear that the high post-war tin price was only temporary. As soon as the United States had achieved its stockpile target a world tin surplus similar to that of the 1930s would emerge. Consequently in 1956, the International Tin Agreement was revived in an attempt to maintain the high tin price artificially, if necessary by export control. The scheme was successful in keeping the average tin price above £730 per ton throughout 1956–60, but in the process export control was introduced between late 1957 and 1960. As a result between 1956 and 1958–9 world production fell by nearly 25 per cent. In Malaya the effects of export control were more serious. Between 1956 and 1958–9 production fell by about 40 per cent, employment by more than one third, the export duty on tin by nearly one half and about 40 per cent of the mines were put out of operation. In recent months a further element of uncertainty in the world tin market has been caused by the desire of the United States to release part of its strategic stockpile acquired during 1948–56 on to the world market.

Methods of Mining

About 95 per cent of Malaya's tin output is won from alluvial deposits. The principal alluvial mining methods are dredging and gravel pumping which together in 1960 accounted for over 90 per cent of the total output. Other alluvial mining methods are hydraulicing and open-casting but these are relatively unimportant. Underground mining produced less than 5 per cent of the total output in 1960.

Dredging is the largest single producer in the industry. In 1960 it was responsible for 54 per cent of the total output. Dredging entails a very high initial fixed capital outlay (to equip a site with a dredge and requisite buildings, etc, would probably require an investment of $M 7 to 8 million at the present cost of labour and material) so that it is confined only to large scale, heavily capitalised mines, mainly European-owned. Although dredging produced more than half of the total output in 1960, only 69 mines or about 12 per cent of the mines in the industry were dredges. But the annual output per dredge was more than ten times that of a gravel pump mine. Dredging has the advantage of a lower average operating (or variable) cost which is lower than all other methods of mining and is as little as about half that of gravel pumping.

Gravel pumping is the commonest mining method in Malaya (80 per cent of the mines in 1960 were gravel pump mines) but produces only about one third of the total output. Ownership is mixed—both Chinese and European, although the former is predominant. But although Chinese gravel pump mines are the more important (90 per cent of the total gravel pump output in 1960 came from Chinese mines), they are usually small compared with European gravel pump mines whose average production is about four times that of the Chinese. Taken as a whole, gravel pumping has the lowest average output among the recognised mining methods in Malaya. Because of its relatively small expenditure on equipment and development (the capital cost of starting a gravel pump mine is estimated as between $M 100,000 and $M 150,000), gravel pump mining is particularly popular with the small producers who can give close personal supervision to its actual operation. As a method of mining gravel pumping is ideally suited to the type of entrepreneurial skill common among the Chinese in Malaya.[3]

299

The Problem of Export Instability

As an export commodity, tin is subject to extreme price instability which presents a serious problem for the Malayan economy. For various reasons the world tin price is very unstable. The supply and demand for tin are relatively inelastic which means that under competitive conditions relatively small changes in its supply or demand can cause substantial fluctuations in its price. The demand for tin is a derived demand because ordinarily tin is not used alone, so that its value is only indirectly reflected in the value of the manufactured products of which it forms a part, usually only a negligible part. For instance, in the canning industry which absorbs about two fifths of the primary tin consumed in the world, the cost of tin in a can of meat does not come to more than 5 per cent of the total cost of production. On the other hand, unlike the resources in industrial or agricultural production, those engaged in tin mining are generally less readily re-employed for other purposes. In Malaya, for instance, both dredges and gravel pump mines are known to continue producing more or less the same quantity of tin ore even when the price has undergone some changes over a period.

This export instability is all the more significant because in Malaya tin exports form a considerable proportion of the total exports of the country (15 to 20 per cent) as well as represent a fairly important share of its gross national product (5 to 7 per cent). This heavy dependence on tin (as well as on rubber) exports has rendered Malaya's balance of payments highly vulnerable to the fluctuations of income and employment of the industrial countries. This had tended to tie the Malayan economy to the industrial activity of western countries, to their prosperity and depression as well as to their peace and war.

All this presents special difficulties to Malaya in terms of financing its economic development. With its present low *per capita* income and high marginal and average propensity to import (and consume), any reduction in its export receipts during a recession must therefore be borne at the expense of its economic development program. Furthermore, the effects of export instability do not end with the balance of payments but are also reflected on the overall internal economy. Yet in Malaya today, internal income stabilisation measures are generally ineffective because (although institutions like the Central Bank have recently been set up) there is still a lack of experience in the field of fiscal and monetary policy. Not unnaturally, this has led to inflationary and deflationary difficulties in the country in the past.

In the tin industry, the post-war revival of the International Tin Agreement has not proved to be a solution. During the last five years, it has succeeded in maintaining a high tin price and somewhat reduced its fluctuations to within a

300

narrower range. But this has failed to stabilise export proceeds whose average annual fluctuation between 1956 and 1960 was 32 per cent. This was higher than that over the pre-control period 1948–56.[4]

Under these circumstances economic development in Malaya must necessarily proceed by fits and starts according to the market supply and demand conditions of tin (and, more important, rubber). Yet continuous and steady development is vital if we are to achieve the development targets set out in the Second Five Year Plan.

IRON MINING

Iron ore is the second largest mineral product of Malaysia (Table 41, page 296). In 1960 iron mining accounted for nearly 29 per cent of the total value of mineral production in Malaya and employed almost 18 per cent of the mining industry's labour force (Table 43). But its importance to the Malayan mining industry and the prospects of its future development must not be over-emphasised. Its development became significant only during the last five years or so. No doubt iron ore production (and employment in iron mining) had more than doubled between 1956 and 1960, but its relative importance in the Malayan mining industry was to a large extent raised by the temporary decline in tin ore production, particularly during 1958–60, the years of export control.

TABLE 43. PRODUCTION OF IRON ORE AND EMPLOYMENT IN MALAYA, 1935, 1940, 1949–50, 1956–60

Year	Production			Employment	
	Tons (million)	Value ($M million)	% of Total Value of Mineral Production	No. (thousands)	% of Total Employment in Mining Industry
1935	1·41	n.a.	—	n.a.	—
1940	1·96	n.a.	—	n.a.	—
1949	0·01	0·13	0·1	n.a.	—
1950	0·50	8·92	2·4	2·24	4·2
1956	2·44	52·44	11·0	3·10	7·0
1957	2·97	66·73	14·6	3·73	8·9
1958	2·80	67·45	21·1	3·38	12·2
1959	3·76	99·51	27·0	4·37	14·9
1960	5·64	143·83	28·7	6·59	17·9

Sources: Department of Mines, Federation of Malaya, Annual Reports, 1939–49; and Bulletin of Statistics, 1950–5, 1956–60.

Historically, iron mining has neither the importance of tin mining nor even the importance of coal or gold mining in Malaya. Although iron mining on a large scale began in the early 1920s (in Johore in 1921 and in Trengganu in 1925) and was carried on throughout the 1930s, iron ore production was insignificant

301

by comparison with tin ore production and was second to coal and gold mining. Between 1935 and 1940, the annual iron ore production in Malaya was consistently between 1½ and 2 million tons. In 1940, the year of peak pre-war production, just less than 2 million tons of iron ore were produced. Post-war recovery began slowly and production was not restarted until 1949. Only since 1950 has iron ore production in Malaya been more important than coal and gold production.

The method of iron mining in Malaya is mainly open-cast. Trengganu has been responsible for about two thirds of the total production but in recent years Perak has become increasingly important as a producer. In 1960 Trengganu still accounted for about half of the total output and Perak one third.

The prospects of development of iron mining in Malaya are not bright. On the one hand, development is hindered by a narrow domestic market. Apart from a few hundred tons a year used in tin mining, little, if any, iron ore is used at all in Malaya. The consumption of pig iron too is relatively small, The lack of a substantial domestic market and the absence of coking coal in the country remove any possibility of a steel industry being established in Malaya. Today, as it was before the war, the iron mining industry is dependent upon external markets, particularly Japan.

On the other hand, although iron ore deposits occur widely in Malaya there are only a few areas where they are large enough to be profitably exploited. The report of the International Bank for Reconstruction and Development of Malaya estimated the total proved reserves of iron ore in Malaya in 1955 at only 25 million tons, with a further 20 million tons in the 'probable' and 'possible' categories.[5] Between 1955 and 1960 no less than 20 million tons of iron ore had been mined in Malaya. Thus at the average production rate of 3 to 4 million tons per annum, iron mining in Malaya will, according to the International Bank report, cease to be important by 1970 unless fresh deposits are discovered before then. Yet the possibility of there still being large iron ore deposits in Malaya is remote. It would seem unlikely, therefore, that the future development of the mining industry of Malaysia could depend very much upon iron ore production in Malaya.

OIL PRODUCTION

Oil production in Sarawak was worth only half of one per cent of the value of all mineral production in Malaysia in 1960 (Table 41, page 296). It is discussed here only because it cannot really be separated from oil production in Brunei. Also, it is necessary for the understanding of Malaysia's mining industry to have a clear idea of Brunei's oil industry as compared with the meagre supplies from Sarawak (Table 44).

TABLE 44. CRUDE OIL PRODUCTION IN NORTHERN BORNEO, 1911–60
(in thousand US barrels)

Year	Sarawak	Brunei		Total for Brunei
	Miri	Seria	Jerudong	
1911	1	—	—	—
1920	1,061	—	—	—
1930	5,114	25	—.	25
1940	1,094	6,267	—	6,267
1946	19	2,032	—	2,032
1950	414	30,543	—	30,543
1955	472	38,879	4	38,883
1956	509	41,994	82	42,076
1957	475	41,372	191	41,563
1958	410	38,489	22	38,511
1959	395	39,565	111	39,676
1960	433	33,457	114	33,571
Cumulative Production up till 1960	75,943	518,644	524	519,168

Source: Geological Survey Department, British Territories in Borneo, *Annual Reports*, 1949–60.

Growth of the Industry

Oil in small quantities was produced from seepages by individuals in Brunei as early as the nineteenth century, but it was only during the years preceding the First World War that oil exploration in northern Borneo began in earnest when various companies belonging to the Royal Dutch-Shell Group, the Standard Group and others began to explore the area and drill for oil. The first important discovery was made by the Royal Dutch-Shell Group at Miri in Sarawak in 1910. The other companies were less successful and after 1918 most of them abandoned their search for oil in this area. But the Royal Dutch-Shell Group, encouraged by their Miri discovery, stayed on, acquired many of the leases relinquished by the other companies and was eventually rewarded in 1929 by the discovery of a much richer oilfield at Seria in Brunei. After the Seria discovery, no other important oilfields were found in northern Borneo in spite of increased efforts at exploration. In 1955 oil was discovered at Jerudong in Brunei but this has proved to be of little importance. Since 1959 exploration of the off-shore areas has been intensified with the use of a mobile drilling barge.

Oil production in northern Borneo during 1911–60 is shown in Table 44. Development in the Miri oilfield was slow. Production reached its peak during 1924–30 with an annual average output of around 5 million US barrels. Production declined rapidly during the 1930s partly because of reduced demand in the early years of the decade as a result of the Great Depression but mainly because of

303

the rapid exhaustion of the oilfield. By 1940 production at Miri had returned to its level two decades ago. In the post-war period its annual output has remained under half a million US barrels.

By comparison, the development of the oilfield at Seria in Brunei was rapid. Within half a decade after its discovery its output had surpassed that at Miri which was then already declining. Peak pre-war production of over 6 million US barrels was reached in 1940. But the real expansion of production at Seria came during the post-war years. The highest output of nearly 42 million US barrels was recorded in 1956. Throughout 1955-9 its annual production was around 40 million US barrels. By 1960 almost 600 million US barrels of crude oil had been extracted, some 87 per cent of this from the Seria oilfield alone (Table 44).

Control of the Industry

The oil industry of Sarawak (and Brunei), unlike the tin industry of Malaya, is a 'vertically' integrated one; that is, an industry controlled at all levels, production, refining, transportation, etc., by one company or a group of companies and subsidiaries. Three oil companies operate in northern Borneo and they are all associates of the Royal Dutch-Shell Group. These are Sarawak Shell Oilfields Limited which operates the Miri oilfield in Sarawak, Brunei Shell Petroleum Company Limited which operates the Seria and the Jerudong oilfields in Brunei, and Shell Company of North Borneo Limited which at the moment is involved only in exploration drilling in Sabah. The crude oil produced in all the three oilfields in northern Borneo is refined at and exported through Lutong in Sarawak. Refining and shipping facilities at Lutong are controlled and provided by Sarawak Shell Oilfields Limited.

This high degree of vertical integration from production to export has created a partial monopoly in the oil industry which has tended to discourage the entry of new firms both from within and without the area. So far none of the big oil company groups in the world has attempted to enter into oil production in northern Borneo. On the other hand, competition from local firms is unlikely because of the high fixed capital expenditure involved, particularly in exploration. Between 1947 and 1957, for instance, the Royal Dutch-Shell group of companies in northern Borneo spent on exploration over $M 168 million or 20 per cent of the total fixed capital outlay. During 1953-7 the annual expenditure on exploration alone averaged over $M 25 million.[6]

Thus, unlike the tin mining industry of Malaya where numerous small producers working on a small scale, each with a little fixed capital investment, contribute a substantial proportion to the total tin output, the oil industry of Sarawak (and Brunei), from production to export, is exclusively in the hands of a few companies working on a large scale.

DEVELOPMENT PROSPECTS

In the mining industry of Malaysia, any assessment of its development prospects must remain with tin mining. While the expansion of production of the other minerals cannot be altogether ruled out, it is improbable that this expansion in future years can be of a magnitude sufficient to offset the consequences of any appreciable decline in tin production.

What, then, is the future of tin production in Malaysia? In the past, the expansion of tin production had contributed significantly to Malaya's economic development. But it seems unlikely that tin production can continue to expand at a rate substantial enough to remain an important element in Malaya's (indeed, in Malaysia's) future economic development. On the contrary, the immediate problem facing the tin mining industry is one of actual decline of production, due to the difficulty in Malaya of finding new tin-bearing lands while the existing ones are being rapidly exhausted. For over 60 years tin production in Malaya has been practically stationary over the long run although it has fluctuated widely from year to year. Since the end of the last century no major tinfields like the Larut or the Kinta have been discovered and much of the tin produced throughout this period has in fact come from reworking some of the 'worked-out' areas by superior techniques, chiefly the dredge. The question that needs to be asked here is, how much longer will existing tin ore reserves in Malaya last at the present rate of exhaustion?

In the past, various estimates of Malaya's tin ore reserves have been made. In 1939 Fermor estimated the total known reserves at about one million tons of tin metal.[7] From then until 1960 over 750,000 tons of tin ore or over 550,000 tons of tin metal had been recovered in Malaya. Thus according to Fermor's estimate, tin production in Malaya at the present rate of production will cease to be important by about 1975. However, in a more recent estimate given in the Paley Report in 1953, Malaya's total known tin ore reserves were placed at one and a half million tons of tin metal or about one third of the total tin ore reserves in the 'free world'.[8] This will give Malaya another thirty years or so of tin production at the present rate of exhaustion.

Thus the long-term prospects of the industry will depend largely upon finding new tin-bearing lands within Malaya. This is an urgent problem. At present the area leased for alluvial mining is less than one per cent of the total area of Malaya. For over thirty years there have been severe restrictions to tin prospecting in Malaya. First, there were the export controls associated with the international restriction schemes which began in 1931 and continued actively until the outbreak of the Second World War; then there was the Japanese occupation of Malaya and the rehabilitation of the industry that followed; and finally, there was the Emergency which began in 1948 and lasted for eleven years which increased the difficulty of prospecting in many parts of Malaya. The result of all this has been a marked reduction in the average grade of ground worked. The International Bank in its report gave the recovery of tin concentrates by dredges in Malaya in 1955 as ranging from 0·28 lb per cubic yard to 0·97 lb per cubic yard, with an overall average of 0·46 lb per cubic yard.[9] In 1915 the average recovery of tin concentrates by dredges in Malaya was 0·82 lb per cubic yard, ranging from 0·65 lb per cubic yard to 1·28 lbs per cubic yard.[10] No ground yielding less than half a pound of tin ore per cubic yard was then considered profitable to work. No similar figures are available for comparison in gravel pumping although it is generally known that, before the First World War, no Chinese miner would work a ground yielding less than one *kati* (i.e. one and one third pounds) per cubic yard. A yield of several *katis* per cubic yard was then not uncommon and at one mine—the Tambun mine—the average recovery of tin concentrates during 1902–3 was 26 *katis* per cubic yard![11]

There are at present in Malaya still large areas of Malay reservations, forest reserves, river reserves, agricultural lands and other holdings, many of which may be rich tin-bearing lands. On these the future production of tin in Malaya will depend. When the whole country has been thoroughly prospected it is not impossible that the total tin ore reserves in Malaya might well be double the estimate of the Paley Report of one and a half million tons of tin metal.

To sum up, tin production in Malaya is on the decline and unless new and additional reserves are discovered soon, this decline will reduce the relative importance of mineral production in Malaysia and will thus reduce the funds now available for supporting its various development programs.

20

Economic Development and the Goals of Government in Malaya

GAYL D. NESS

Economic development has emerged as a universally accepted and highly important value especially in the new nations of the modern world. The desire for development is an important element in all modern nationalist movements, and the (alleged) lack of fulfilment of this desire has been a strong element in modern anti-colonial ideologies.

Accompanying the emergence of this value is a new theory of development that dictates a new role for government in the development process. The economic development or industrialisation[1] of the western world was accompanied by a theory of growth that prescribed for government a passive rather than an active role. It was assumed that the maintenance of order and the exercise of minimal restraints by government would produce the most rapid economic growth. In the new nations of the twentieth century, the emphasis on economic development is accompanied by a theory that prescribes an active role for government in stimulating development. It is now assumed that government must do more than maintain order; it must do even more than to produce the social and economic overhead capital required for development. It is assumed that government must play an active role in stimulating and controlling investment and consumption in the broadest sense in order to provide for development.

Since the role government actually plays in development will be a function of the goals it sets for itself, any analysis of modern development in the new states must at some time be concerned with the goals of government. In a new state such as Malaysia, only now in the process of emerging, an analysis of the goals of government can assist in our understanding of that emergence, and can also present some indication of what the future may hold, given specified conditions.

The argument of this chapter is that in Malaya itself the coming of political independence was accompanied by a shift in the goals of government from *order* to *economic* or *development* goals.[2] This shift brought an increase of government efforts to stimulate national economic development, with particular emphasis upon the rural sector. For the past few years the Borneo territories have been experiencing some of the same changes and pressures for change that marked Malaya's immediate pre-independence period. Thus the Borneo territories can be seen as representing different stages in an historical process, the broad patterns of which have already been traced in Malaya's modern development. In this respect the coming of Malaysia will probably mean for the Borneo territories a shift in the goals of government similar to that experienced in Malaya.

MALAYA

In the decade 1950–60, the goals of government in Malaya changed from *order* to *developmental* goals. This was a broad change in the orientation of government that brought a different and increased emphasis upon economic development. It was made up of many smaller and more specific changes, the most important of which were the following:

1. A change in fiscal policy from an emphasis upon a balanced budget to an emphasis upon an expanding economy.
2. A change from an emphasis upon urban development to an emphasis upon rural development, largely to provide for the uplift of the Malays.
3. A change in the position of social services, from a place of low priority to a place of high priority; this included a redefinition of education as investment rather than consumption.
4. A change in the organisation of planning and co-ordination from an unspecialised to a specialised departmental basis.

It will be useful to examine these changes in some detail to gain a greater understanding of the broad forces of change that were manifest in this goal change. Since Malaya obtained a legislature with an elected majority in 1955, achieving independence in 1957, it is possible to see two distinct legislative policies, corresponding with the first and second halves of the decade. We shall refer to these as the 'colonial' legislature or policy and the 'independent' legislature or policy.[3]

1. *Changes in Fiscal Policy*

The budget speeches of the financial secretaries in the first half of the decade clearly reflect the importance government placed upon balancing the budget.

In the first three years the speeches were extremely short. A statement of the budget had been issued to the press before the budget debate and government saw no particular need to elaborate its policies in the legislature, apart from making explicit its commitment to balancing the budget. With the large deficit budget of 1954 ($M 222 million), a new finance secretary began elaborating government policy at greater length in the budget speech. This official recognised that the large deficit would not be accepted easily, but argued that it was necessary for the prosecution of the Emergency. He further reaffirmed government's policy '. . . to get rid of this deficit and bring the budget back into balance'.[4]

The budget speeches of the independent government immediately reflected a radical change in fiscal policy. The Federation's first finance minister, Colonel H. S. Lee, clearly articulated the fiscal policy of the independent government in his first budget speech.[5]

> . . . we set ourselves two pillars of economic and financial policy, namely a
> basically sound economy and a balanced budget. We have based our plans
> on an expanding economy. In order to achieve it, we accept for the time being
> deferment of our second aim. We are budgeting for a deficit in 1957. . . . I
> opened my speech by saying that the government has budgeted for a deficit.
> This unbalance arises not as a result of deliberate policy. . . . Nevertheless it
> has a basis in policy, the policy of an expanding economy. Malaya is still only
> a partially developed country. It is capable of much further development
> which we seek to foster and encourage by our public investment programme.
> To this development we look for the future increase in the national wealth
> and the national income which, when it is reflected in the public revenue as
> it should be, will give us surpluses in the good years to offset the deficits
> which may still arise when the state of our trade is unfavourable to us. This
> is the balance at which we aim.

The basic outlines of this policy have been reiterated in each budget speech since 1956. Government plans for an expanding economy. Public investment is required for this expansion and government is willing to engage in deficit financing for this end. Finally, the balance desired in the budget is a balance over the trade cycle rather than a year-to-year balance.

In the yearly budget debates there was clear support, though not without opposition, for the policies of both the colonial and independent governments. In the colonial legislature some of the most outspoken members were the appointed European members. In all cases they gave unqualified support to the value of the balanced budget, equating it with good business practice. To a large extent the arguments of the Europeans were echoed by the indigenous members, though in the latter traces of a nationalistic opposition to government can be seen.[6] This was most dramatic in the large deficit budget of 1954, when a European member cast the only dissenting vote on acceptance of the budget in the entire decade. In all 27 members (of a total of 47) took part in the debate on that budget. All three European debaters opposed the deficit, and 14 of the 24 indigenous members who took part in the debate opposed the deficit.

In the budget debates of the independent government there has been almost no opposition to the budget deficits, not even from the Europeans who remained as appointed members until the first fully independent elections of 1959. In the first few years of independence there was nothing but praise for the industry of the new government in carrying out its promises of development, even at the expense of considerable deficit financing.

The independent government's acceptance in theory of the necessity of deficit financing for public investment was matched by its actions in regard to the public debt. In 1946 the total public debt of the federal government was $M 146·7 million; by 1962 it had reached $M 1,582·5 million. In broad lines this demonstrates the willingness, either begrudged or easy, of both governments to engage in deficit financing in pursuit of their goals. For the colonial government the deficit was accepted largely for the prosecution of the Emergency; in pursuit of *order* goals. For the independent government the deficit was accepted to obtain capital for public investment: in pursuit of *development* goals.

Along with the increase in the public debt went an important change in fiscal procedures to control and utilise borrowed money. Until 1958 loans had been authorised in the legislature by individual bills that included a schedule of projects and their costs for which the money was to be used. In 1958 the finance minister introduced the Malayan Development Fund Bill, establishing a fund into which all money for development would be placed, regardless of whether they came from loans or from current revenues. Money for any development project approved by the legislature would be taken from this general fund. The minister explained that this was a break from policies characteristic of dependent territories; it would give greater power and flexibility to the legislature to control development. He further pointed out that this would not make more or less money available for development, but by showing that the country was doing its utmost to stimulate its own development, it would '. . . assist in maintaining conditions favourable to investment of such finance in the Federation . . .', which was the cardinal principle of government policy.[7]

In the budget speeches, the budget debates, and in the movement of the public debt, there is a clear distinction between the policies of the colonial and the independent government. Behind each policy lies an implicit theory of economic development which dictates the proper function of government. For the colonial government Malaya was an underdeveloped country, which by definition meant that there was insufficient local capital available for development. Development required the influx of foreign capital. To encourage this influx it was the duty of government to maintain order, to demonstrate its fiscal responsibility through balancing the budget yearly, and to keep taxation to the minimum. For the independent government the overriding necessity was to build up the social and economic overhead capital that was considered a prerequisite of sustained indigenous development. This would demonstrate government's commitment to development. Perhaps because they were themselves businessmen and investors rather than bureaucrats, the new men in control of finances did not make a sharp distinction between foreign and local investors. For them investment required not so much confidence in the present responsibility and stability of government as confidence in the future of the economy. They felt that government could best provide this climate of confidence in the future by demonstrating its own commitment to national economic development.

2. From Urban to Rural Development

After the war the major task of government development lay in reconstruction. Normal services and both mines and estates had suffered considerable decay under the Japanese and it was necessary to reconstruct these to make the economy viable. Roads and bridges had to be repaired, the railways needed reconstruction and extension, and services such as security, communications and utilities had to be restored and extended. This reconstruction involved primarily the modern sector: mines, estates and urban areas. It was a development that left the traditional sector, that of the Malay peasant and fisherman, largely untouched.[8]

There was general support given to the value of rural-Malay development in almost every official statement of the government after the war. However, this value was clearly subordinate to the value of fiscal stability. Rural development under the colonial government continually suffered from lack of funds and a lack of a sense of urgency. The Emergency only exacerbated this condition, for during the first half of the 1950s government followed each statement of its commitment to rural development with the observation that the Emergency was draining away immense sums that could otherwise be used for rural development.

Throughout the decade pressure mounted for more attention to rural-Malay development. This pressure arose from two basic conditions. In the first place there was the simple political pressure that accompanies increased popular representation. The Malays were the first to demonstrate their ability to organise modern legitimate political structures. They had the power of the electorate, in which for a number of reasons they have been considerably over-represented.

311

This gave them the legitimating support of the theory of representative government: government must do what the majority of the people desire. The second, and more explosive, source was a communal one. The resettlement program that broke the supply line of the communist insurgents relocated Chinese squatters in New Villages. Partly out of sheer necessity, and partly to win the minds of the Chinese, government provided them with amenities they had never known as squatters. Schools, roads, utilities and land were made available to the New Villagers. This caused considerable resentment among the Malays who argued that while they were carrying the brunt of the fighting against the communists, who were largely Chinese, it was the Chinese who were getting all government's attention. The Malays observed that red tape could be cut for the New Villagers while the Malays in the *kampong* were being neglected. One legislator ended a forceful speech on this issue in the Council with the poignant question, 'What price loyalty?'[9]

This increased pressure for rural-Malay development was not without effect on government activities. The first formal move in the direction of rural development came with the formation of the Rural and Industrial Development Authority in 1950–1. RIDA operated on a relatively small budget of $M 5 million a year, engaging in a large array of activities among the rural Malays. Though it has been one of the most troublesome and least successful of government efforts in rural development, it has enjoyed the public image of a rural-Malay oriented organisation, and it drew off some of the pressure against government in the first half of the decade. With the independent government the attention to rural development increased considerably. The first manifestation of this (apart from developments in education, which are discussed below) was the creation of the Federal Land Development Authority. The FLDA was organised in 1956 and was designed primarily to provide new land for landless Malays, though Chinese and Indians have not been completely excluded. The latest and most important move came in 1959 with the formation of the Ministry of Rural Development. Acting essentially as a super district office, the Ministry is concerned with increasing the activities of all government agencies in rural development. Under the direction of the deputy prime minister, Tun Abdul Razak, the Ministry has achieved considerable success in directing government investment to the development of overhead capital in the rural areas. In official statements and in actual practice, rural development is one of the dominant values in Malaya today.

3. *The Priority of Social Services*

The colonial government displayed an ambivalent attitude towards social services, especially towards education. Expenditures on health clearly had the advantage of supporting the plantation economy, and education was necessary to provide clerks for the bureaucracy. In a more general and more altruistic sense these expenditures wᵉre also for things considered 'good', for services that made man's life better and more elevated, so that they were easily subsumed under the proper functions of governments.

At the same time these services were defined as *social* services and distinguished from *economic* services by the fact that they gave no immediate and direct returns. Though these services were accepted as good and necessary things, it was also argued that the country could only have as much as it could afford. Higher priority was given to economic services, for it was argued that from this kind of investment economic growth would ensue. The consequent increased income could then be used to buy more social services. To the extent that national income accounting was understood, it provided theoretical support for the lower priority of the social services. Economic development requires increased investment and decreased, or at least stable, consumption. Social services are classed as items of consumption rather than investment in the national income account (except for buildings and plant). Thus an increase of expenditures on social services could be defined as an obstacle to economic development. These arguments were all explicit in the budget speeches and debates during the first half of the last decade.

The independent government greatly increased the commitment of resources to social services, and to education in particular. In the budget session controlled by the first elected government, the outgoing British finance secretary closed his last budget address with the observation that '... the Alliance government would dearly have liked its first budget to be a balanced one, but the present needs are such that this goal is not attainable'.[10] This was followed by the budget address of the new chief minister, Tengku Abdul Rahman, who gave some indication of what these present needs were. The Tengku remarked that this was a standstill budget because the government had not yet had time to translate its policies into fiscal directives, but some things had been accomplished none the less. The first thing he mentioned was that there would be 8,000 new places in school the next year. Actual expenditure on education had climbed steadily to $M 86·3 million in the last year of the colonial government (1955); the independent government increased this to $M 186·3 million in its first year in office (1956). Education expenditures have continued to increase since 1956, and for most years education has been the largest single item on the budget. The change in health expenditures has been in the same direction, but of a lesser magnitude.

As with the shift to rural development, the increased emphasis on education was largely the result of the changing political pressures associated with independence. The popular demand for rural development included a demand for more schools, especially for the Malays.

The Alliance Party demonstrated its sensitivity to this popular demand in the 1955 elections when it promised to give education top priority. When it was elected to power, the party placed its most able and powerful administrator, Tun Abdul Razak, at the head of education to direct the increase of resources to this field. There was, of course, more than mere political expediency in this change of priorities. If the new men of power did not have a very clear vision of the new society they wanted to build, they did have a strong aversion to certain characteristics of the old colonial society that they desired to change. In large part this included making greater opportunities for all, especially for the Malays, who had been left behind in the modernisation of the country. This new desire was supported by the new theory of economic development, elements of which have already been discussed. Again it was the finance minister, Colonel Lee, who gave the most articulate expression to this new theory. In justifying the great increases in education expenditure, he argued that the country needed skilled technicians, administrators and workers for its development. It was in part the purpose of education to provide this skilled manpower. The new independent government thus came to view education as an item of investment, and to act on this view by increasing its investment in pursuit of its new development goals.

4. *Planning and Co-ordination for Development*

Malaya's first development plan, the Draft Development Plan, was prepared by the Economic Department of the Office of the Finance Secretary in 1949–50. It was drawn together somewhat hastily to plan for the spending of a grant of about £5 million expected under the United Kingdom Colonial Development and Welfare Act of 1945. The Plan was little more than a list of departmental projects designed to make use of available money. In 1951 the Office of the Economic Adviser to the High Commissioner was formed. This office was to be concerned with trade and commerce, and with economic development. Under the Economic Adviser, the Draft Plan was revised and a progress report issued in 1952. With the Emergency taking the major part of government resources and energies, however, little more was done in planning until the independent government came to power in 1955.

During this first half of the decade, the legislature witnessed vague rumblings of dissatisfaction with planning and development. There were repeated requests for organised efforts at long-term planning and at co-ordinating planning and development efforts. There was also criticism of government's narrow fiscal approach to development. These were all vague and unsophisticated demands and criticisms. Though they displayed no real competence in analysing planning and development needs, they did display a growing discontent with colonial development policies, especially with the lack of a sense of urgency, the lack of co-ordination and the lack of long-term planning.

The independent government moved in the direction of satisfying these demands, though it was a few years before the present structures for co-ordination and planning emerged. The Economic Adviser to the High Commissioner became the head of a new office, the Secretariat of the Economic Committee of the Executive Council (a pre-independence cabinet). The Secretariat produced Malaya's First Five-Year Plan (1956–60), which like the Draft Plan was prepared quickly and as the result of an external stimulus in the form of pending talks with the British government on financing Malaya's development. Though the plan was not much better than the Draft Plan of the colonial government, it was important that it was produced in an organisation removed from direct control of the minister of finance. The importance and extent of this separation were seen in the recession of 1957–8 when the Secretariat came into conflict with the Treasury over the control of development expenditures. Alarmed by the recession's potential effect on revenues, the Treasury wanted to curtail development expenditures. The Secretariat argued that the recession was not severe and that it was important to continue the pace of public investment for development. Each organisation claimed legitimate control over development spending. With formal control over planning removed from the centres of fiscal power, the way was cleared for the more rational performance of the planning function. At present the Secretariat has developed into the Economic Planning Unit in the Prime Minister's Department. It is rapidly gaining greater professional and organisational competence to do the job of planning that seems to be desired by the independent government.

The demands for better co-ordination of development efforts have largely been satisfied by the creation of the Ministry of Rural Development under the deputy prime minister, Tun Abdul Razak. As the most powerful among equals, the Ministry has demonstrated a great capacity to co-ordinate the activities of all government departments and to mobilise and direct the resources of government in pursuit of its declared goals.

5. *The Actual Allocation of Resources*

The actual allocation of government resources over the past decade reflects the changing goals described above. Table 45 shows the per cent allocation of actual expenditures by Malayan departmental categories.

The most dramatic changes in the allocation of resources occur in the increase of total expenditures, the increased proportions to education and health, and the decreased proportions to military and police. Less dramatic, but not less important, is the steady increase to agriculture and irrigation, rural development,

TABLE 45. PER CENT ALLOCATION OF TOTAL STATE AND FEDERAL GOVERNMENT EXPENDITURES IN MALAYA, 1950–60

	1950	1951	1952	1953	1954	1955	1956	1957	1958	1959	1960
Total											
(million $M)	399	614	756	873	810	817*	853	928*	1,106*	1,077	1,133
Federal[1]	340	549	672	790	714	712	740	813	988	980	997
State[2]	59	65	84	83	96	104	113	114	117	97	136
Agriculture[3]	1·7	1·8	2·1	1·8	1·9	2·0	2·3 }	4·0	3·5	3·4	4·4
Irrigation	1·3	1·2	1·2	1·2	1·4	1·4	1·6 }				
Public Works	13·6	15·3	14·0	15·6	13·2	12·8	13·4	10·0	11·4	10·8	20·6
Rural Development[4]	—	—	0·5	0·6	0·9	0·5	0·9	0·6	—	—	1·0
Commerce and Industry	—	—	—	—	—	—	—	0·8	5·5	6·4	4·4
Education[5]	7·1	7·9	8·9	8·9	11·3	10·6	21·3	22·2	13·6	14·8	15·8
Health[5]	6·7	6·8	6·5	5·8	4·5	6·8	12·1	10·4	6·5	7·1	7·5
Sub-total	30·4	33·0	33·2	33·9	33·2	34·1	51·6	58·0	40·5	42·5	53·7
Military Police[6]	22·2	28·7	26·8	31·7	28·5	25·9	23·1	22·6	20·2	18·3	15·7
Total	52·6	61·7	60·0	65·6	61·7	60·0	74·7	80·6	60·7	60·8	69·4

Notes: 1. Including Development Expenditures for 1957–60, years for which the Development expenditures are separated from the ordinary budget. 2. Excluding federal grants to the states to eliminate double counting. 3. Including Forestry, Fisheries, and Veterinary. 4. Before 1960 this is primarily for the Rural and Industrial Development Authority; for 1951 and 1958–9 this is included in other categories and could not be separated easily. 5. Including Social Welfare. 6. Including the designated cost of the Emergency for 1954–5, when it was shown separately in the Financial Statement.

* Components do not equal the total due to rounding.

Source: Federation of Malaya yearly Financial Statements.

and commerce and industry, the majority of expenses for which are incurred for rubber replanting. The allocations not listed here can in a gross form be taken as the cost of administration. The secular trend is for this cost to decrease in proportion to total expenditures.

Development expenditures in the three plans show some of the same general changes. The level of public investment increased considerably. It was $M 856 million under the Draft Plan, $M 1,149 million under the First Five-Year Plan, and $M 2,150 under the Second Five-Year Plan. The entire social sector received greatly increased proportions of total investment under the three plans: 11 per cent, 18 per cent and 23 per cent. Education and health have grown at about the same rate, each doubling its proportionate allocation.

It could be argued that the Emergency alone is sufficient to account for the heavy commitment to *order* in the first half of the decade, and the cessation of the Emergency sufficient to account for the reduction in *order* expenditures and subsequent increase in *developmental* expenditures in the second half of the decade. That is, the change of goals may be a spurious explanation for what is really only a change in the external conditions demanding the resources of government. The importance of the Emergency cannot be denied. However, the case presented here rests not alone on the actual allocation of expenditures. Far more importance is placed upon the theoretical or ideological changes in the new men of power. The new commitment to development is explicit, as is the importance placed upon investment even if it requires deficit financing.

The actual increase in total ordinary and development expenditures indicates a large change in the ability of government to mobilise resources in pursuit of its goals. With the cessation of the Emergency, it would have been financially possible to reduce taxes, reduce expenditures, and return to a balanced budget. That the government chose to do otherwise gives support to the interpretation of changed goals. The point is that the theoretical changes and the changes in the stated goals of government were accompanied by charges in the actual allocation of resources. It is all of these things taken together that produce the picture of a change in the goals of government.

SARAWAK AND SABAH

Since the end of the Second World War the governments of Sarawak and Sabah have shown tendencies of goal-change similar to, but less pronounced than, those experienced in Malaya. Total government expenditures have increased considerably. The most rapid growth has been in education, and agricultural and infrastructure[11] development. There has been some movement in the direction of planning with mild emphasis on rural development and in Sarawak a separate office for economic development has been formed.

317

Total government expenditures in Sarawak have increased from about $M 20 per head of population in 1947 to about $M 125 in 1960. In Sabah, expenditures have increased from $M 83 per head in 1954 to $M 141 in 1960. In the pre-war decade the Sarawak government allocated an average of 0·4 per cent of its total expenditures to education. There were no expenditures on education until 1939, the allocating being about 1 per cent in the last three years before the war. Just after the war 2·5 per cent of expenditures were allocated to education; in 1960 the figure was almost 14 per cent. In Sabah, expenditures on education increased from about 3 per cent of the total in the early part of the 1950s to about 9 per cent in 1960. The increased emphasis on education can also be seen in the proportion of the total population in school and in government expenditures per school attendant.

In Sarawak's pre-war decade, an average of about 25 per cent of total government expenditures was spent on agricultural and infrastructure development; by 1960 this had increased to 45 per cent. In Sabah the proportion increased from 35 per cent early in the 1950s to 45 per cent in 1960.

Along with these changes, the proportionate allocation on the maintenance of order has decreased steadily.[12] In Sarawak the decrease was from an average of 9 per cent in the pre-war decades to an average of about 5 per cent in 1959–60. In Sabah the percentage has decreased from 7 per cent in 1954 to 5 per cent in 1960. It also appears that there has been a decrease in the proportion spent in general administration, though it must be admitted that this is a residual category and it may not be an accurate representation of the administrative function.[13] In Sarawak administration averaged 50 per cent in the pre-war decade, and fell to about 29 per cent in 1960. The figures for Sabah were 42 per cent in 1954 and 33 per cent in 1960.

TABLE 46. CHANGING EMPHASIS ON EDUCATION IN SABAH AND SARAWAK

	Sarawak		Sabah	
	1949	1960	1954	1960
Percentage of total population at school[a]	6	13	7	11
Government expenditure per schoolchild[b] ($M)	8	130	34	112

Sources: Annual Reports, North Borneo and Sarawak. Sabah's 1954 population is estimated by straight line projection from the censuses of 1951 and 1960.

Notes: a. This slightly understates the increase because the total population is getting younger; most of the increase in population is in ages below school-attending age. b. Education expenditures include both ordinary and capital expenditures.

Along with this increased emphasis on 'building up the territory' has come an increased emphasis on planning, though this varies considerably in the two territories. Both territories have development plans that bear close resemblance to Malaya's first Draft Development Plan of 1949–50. The plans are simply collections of departmental projects. Both are oriented outward for sources of capital, and both have a strong 'fiscal' orientation, beginning with a consideration of what finances will be available for the plan period. Finally, in both territories the plans are prepared by the financial secretaries.

Of the two territories, however, Sarawak appears to be the more advanced with respect to planning. There is a specialised office for planning under the finance secretary and an explicit commitment to rural economic development has been made. In this respect Sarawak has taken a leaf from Malaya's recent planning. Sarawak's plan for the period 1964–8 places emphasis on rural development, and has ordered the formation of the local development committees that have been a significant part of Malaya's Red Book operations.

Sabah's orientation is clearly external and fiscal. 'Local Development planning is related closely to the period of the United Kingdom Colonial Development and Welfare (Amendment) Act. . . . Planning has been based on: (a) finance which can reasonably be expected to be available during the period; (b) proposals of Residents and Heads of Departments.'[14] The external capital orientation has not changed despite the greatly increased power of the colony's own financial resources. The current plan originally envisaged an expenditure of $M 61 million, of which $M 26 million (43 per cent) was to come from the Colonial Development and Welfare Grant. In two subsequent Council papers in 1960 and 1961, it was announced that additional allocations could be made from current revenues so that of the revised total expenditures of $M 109 million, $M 83 million (76 per cent) would come from government revenues. Finally it can be stated that, in interviews with the author, Sabah financial officials have expressed open hostility to planning. They prefer 'to get on with the work that everyone can see needs to be done'. And they dislike planning because 'plans are no sooner made than they have to be revised'.

It appears that only a relatively small part of this gradual shift in the direction of developmental goals is the result of increased popular pressure for development. The pressure does exist in an objective sense. There is a growing sense of dissatisfaction among indigenous leaders in both territories over the lack of a sense of urgency in government's development efforts.[15] In education indigenous peoples are creating considerable problems for government by going ahead with building their own schools and even with assuming responsibility for paying part of teachers' salaries. Few government officials seem aware of the growing resentment over this lack of urgency, however. Education officials are more than aware of the increased demands for education, but they are hampered both by a lack of teachers and funds and by an insistence upon maintaining high standards. Thus

319

it can be said that, while the popular demand for development is increasing, government is not acutely sensitive to this demand. It can be expected that with the emergence of an *elected* government under Malaysia this sensitivity to popular demand will increase tremendously, just as it did in Malaya.

With current developments in the Borneo territories paralleling recent developments in Malaya other specific changes will undoubtedly come from increased government sensitivity to popular demands, following upon the acquisition of power by elected representatives. One can expect great increases in the emphasis on education and on rural development. In planning and implementation, it can also be expected that control will move out from under pure fiscal offices and will be lodged more directly under the control of elected executives and legislators. This will probably be accompanied by the creation of specialised agencies for both planning and the actual implementation of development schemes. Following Malaya's example, it can be expected that increased responsibility for planning and for control of development will be lodged in local committees. Finally, though finance will always be a problem, at least in the minds of finance officials, it can be expected that the territories will be at least as successful as the colonial governments, if not more so, in mobilising more internal resources to finance their own development. It seems likely that the availability of capital for public investment will be far less a problem than the technical and administrative capacity to spend, and to spend wisely, the capital that will be available.

SINGAPORE

Singapore has been excluded from this analysis largely by limitations of space. Singapore has already passed through a marked change in the goals of government, and is now firmly committed to development. However, as an almost purely urban and Chinese territory, its course of development is somewhat removed from that of the other territories. Although the differences are only those of specific details of development and could be easily analysed with the same framework used above, this would require more space than is here available.

PART FIVE

Politics and Government

21

Politics and Government

R. S. MILNE

Informed comment on the working, as opposed to the structure, of politics and government in the Malaysia territories is slight. Apart from the writings of Swettenham, Purcell, Silcock, Emerson, Mills, Pye and a few others, there is little of substantial value.[1] Up to now a few intelligent roving academics have been let loose on the Malaysian scene to capture, record and analyse its politics and only one of the universities in Malaysia carries out systematic teaching and research in political science.

MALAYA

This chapter is devoted mainly to Malaya for three reasons: it is the only unit of the new Federation which has enjoyed full independence; it is the largest unit; its constitution and machinery of government will serve as a 'frame' for Malaysia. There are three main sections: an outline of how some features of the 1957 Malayan Constitution seem to be developing; an account of some of the social and political features which underlie, and bedevil, the political process in Malaya; a very brief estimate of the effects of the inclusion of Singapore and the Borneo territories in the new Federation of Malaysia.

Main Constitutional Features

In its external appearance the political system of Malaya roughly resembles that of Britain. It is even closer to that of India, on which it was explicitly modelled.[2] In it are found such familiar features of the 'parliamentary' system of government as a non-political head of state, a legislature composed of two houses, one directly elected, a cabinet responsible to that house, a neutral civil

323

service and an independent judiciary. Some differences are also obvious. Practices which in Britain have resulted from the development of constitutional conventions have been inserted and spelled out in the Constitution of Malaya: which powers of the head of state are discretionary; that the prime minister must sit in the popularly elected house of the legislature; the preconditions for dissolution and resignation. But, although the 'blueprint' of the constitutional model is drawn in greater detail than the British, its actual design is not so complex. For example, the lower house has its Public Accounts Committee, but it lacks committees to scrutinise the estimates or to report on the government's use of delegated legislation. Some deliberate departures have been made from the British model. For instance, in an effort to minimise possibilities of political patronage in the public services, independent commissions have been set up to regulate appointments and conditions of service, after the fashion of India and some other Commonwealth countries.

But beneath the smooth constitutional surface of parliamentary democracy are the contours of traditional Malay rule, and also of British colonial administration, as exemplified in the district officer. In rural areas the influence of the *penghulu* (headman) is still considerable. In one major instance the old fabric of government has not been concealed by the new. On the contrary the new edifice is 'crowned' by the sultans. In nine of the eleven states in Malaya the head of state is the ruler: the head of state of the whole country (the Yang di-Pertuan Agong) is one of the nine chosen by his peers for a term of office of five years. Together with the governors of Penang and Malacca the nine, in their capacity as 'Conference of Rulers', have certain limited powers, as a 'third house' of the legislature, over such subjects as the alteration of state boundaries, religious observances, the special position of the Malays, and their own 'privileges, position, honours or dignities'. The political and social role of the rulers cries out for analysis, although detailed research might encounter certain obstacles. To what extent are the rulers a symbol of government or a focus of loyalty in the eyes of older Malays, younger Malays, members of other races in Malaya? In so far as the rulers *are* regarded as symbols, is the effect a strengthening of national unity or of state particularism? Are the rulers a convenient means of tempering the impact of desirable social changes or, as relics of indirect rule, do they constitute a drag on change?

Federalism in Malaya can be attributed only to the belief that the rulers and the states attract powerful loyalties, partly in their role as 'protectors of Islam', at least from Malays. Clearly none of the classic arguments for federalism applies for instance, size or great variations in climate, crops or way of life.[3] Even the racial 'Quebec-type' argument for federalism is irrelevant; except in the north-east the races in Malaya are not sufficiently distinct geographically to justify federalism for this reason. Apparently in practice the emphasis has been laid on the 'establishment of a strong central government' rather than on giving the states a 'measure of autonomy'.[4] Thirty years ago an observer of the inter-war wrangles on centralisation and decentralisation, pleaded either for an 'honest' centralised bureaucracy or for creating the 'realities as well as the forms of state government'.[5] Today it would seem that the forms of state government are more impressive than the realities. This view is supported by such considerations as the importance of the powers allocated to the federal government, and the comparative unimportance of the county-council-like powers given to the states, in the federal Constitution; by the limited degree to which checks exist on the amending power of the federal legislature;[6] by the constitutional provisions that the agricultural and forestry officers of the states must accept professional advice from federal officers.[7]

Liaison between federal and state governments is also secured through the National Finance Council, the National Land Council and the National Council for Local Government, on which all the governments are represented. The National Land Council plays an important role in ensuring some federal control of land policy in spite of the fact that, by the constitution, land is a state subject. Where the same political party is in control of the federal government and a state government, constitutional and legal channels are supplemented by political party ties. When the state government is in the hands of a different party (Trengganu from 1959 to 1961 and Kelantan since 1959) interesting frictions may be observed. The Kelantan government request for a $M 5 million loan for a bridge to cross the Kelantan river was turned down by the federal government on the ground that the plans had not been properly drawn up and that the federal Public Works Department had not been consulted. Kelantan has refused to give up land for the federal Land Development Authority to open up, and has gone ahead with its own land development program without federal aid. In Trengganu in 1960 an Alliance-dominated local government council (Kemaman) was apparently able to circumvent the PMIP state government and obtain financial help direct from the federal (Alliance) government. The state government had cut down two major road schemes put forward by the Kemaman council. The council appealed to the federal government through informal channels, obtained $M 67,000 and finished work on its two roads before many of the schemes in PMIP-controlled councils in Trengganu were anywhere near completion.[8] The limits of federal constitutional power over the states should be noted. Late in 1961 the prime minister lamented the fact that there was no constitutional provision for ensuring that the Trengganu state government could be forced to carry out its functions properly, for instance by the federal government's having been given the power to suspend it.[9]

As far as can be ascertained, the structure and working of the cabinet broadly follow British lines. However, the number of ministers is smaller than the number of departments, and several ministers hold more than one portfolio. For instance, the deputy prime minister is minister of Defence and also minister of Rural Development. All ministers are members of the cabinet; outside it are assistant ministers. An unhealthy development is that two out of a cabinet of fourteen are ministers without portfolio, who are members of the House of Representatives and at the same time represent Malaya abroad. This arrangement seems to have been designed to serve particularist, rather than universalist, interests.

Although, if a minister cannot agree with his colleagues on a point of substance, 'resignation is the only honourable course open to him',[10] one minister's views of collective responsibility were eccentric. When the prime minister decided to transfer Inche Abdul Aziz bin Ishak from being minister of Agriculture and Co-operatives to being minister of Health in July 1962, Inche Aziz refused to move and had to be dismissed from the cabinet in October. The delay was probably attributable partly to the prime minister's patience and also to his preoccupation with Malaysia. The prime minister said that in the past his authority had never been questioned and that he did not think it likely that it would be questioned in this case.[11] Yet this is just what Inche Aziz was doing. It is pleasant to be able to record that when eventually Inche Aziz was dismissed he had arrived at the opinion that he was happy to leave.[12]

At present the chief defect of the House of Representatives is the weakness of the opposition. True, the situation is less one-sided than before the 1959 election, when there was only one elected opposition member. But even now the Alliance has nearly three quarters of the seats. The opposition groups rarely combine, although in March 1963 they formed a common front to oppose the government's plan for Malaysia. It has been alleged that the government is averse from accepting suggestions made by members of other parties, as is shown by its reluctance to make use of select committees in the House. The government has also been criticised for not encouraging the growth of healthy opposition 'instead of merely condemning other parties as subversive, communal, racialist, chauvinist or communist'.[13] The predominance of the government is also symbolised by the fact that, although opposition members are active and capable in the proceedings of the Public Accounts Committee, the chairman of the committee is a government member and not from the opposition, as in Britain. Such criticisms are to the point. Even so, any government, while aware of the desirability of encouraging an effective opposition, also has the over-riding obligation of working for national unity—or at any rate for those things which will divide the country least. Governmental behaviour in the House is a reflection of its general policy in the country: to set a limit to expressions of communalism and, mindful of the disruption caused by the Emergency, to repress any activities which it regards as subversive.

The Senate is composed partly of members chosen by state legislatures, partly of nominated members. Expectations that the 'state' members would contribute to the federal pattern by acting as spokesmen for the interests of their states have not been realised. The Senate's impact on the political life of the country has been negligible.

The Civil Service is dealt with in another chapter. In grossly oversimplified terms, the problem has been to preserve previous standards of efficiency and incorruptibility during 'Malayanisation', while also 'Malayanising' in the sense of changing the image of the civil service as the aloof representative of an alien power.[14] It would require several thousand words to give an account of local government in Malaya which was reasonably complete and even semi-intelligible. To sacrifice completeness at least, the day-to-day working of local authorities is within the competence of the state governments, although the National Council for Local Government enables the federal government to ensure some uniformity by formulating a national policy for the promotion, development and control of local government. Before 1913 some elections on a limited franchise were held in the Straits Settlements. But after that date it was not until 1950 that an Ordinance authorised local elections. Eventually it is intended that all local authorities will be financially autonomous and will contain only directly elected members. But various authorities have made different degrees of progress towards these goals and either goal may be attained before the other.

The development of local government has not been uniformly smooth. Quarrels have occurred between local authorities and state governments when the same party does not control both, for example Seremban and Negri Sembilan. And it has been alleged that discussion of the 'local' functions of some councils has been swamped by acrimonious disputes on intractable *national* issues, such as education policy.

Social Features

In contrast to the institutional approach the political system may be examined by considering some underlying social features. The society is not only transitional, on the way from traditional to modern: it is also multiracial, or plural.[15] There is little loyalty to a general political system, but rather loyalties to particular groups. There is little consensus, but well-defined cleavages.[16] Some of these exist, to a minor degree, *within* broad racial groups. Some 'Malays' are in fact Malaysians from the neighbouring areas of Indonesia, although such immigrants are rapidly assimilated. The 'Indians' are mostly from the south of India,

327

but include Sikhs and Ceylonese; some of them are muslims. More obviously the Chinese belong to some half-dozen major dialect groups, to say nothing of the distinctive Straits Chinese. The major racial cleavages into Malay, Chinese and Indian coincide largely with cleavages in religion, language and way of life, thus making consensus especially difficult. The cleavages in Malaya are probably as deep as those in almost any other country, a complicating factor being that the two main groups, Malays and Chinese, are comparable in size.[17] The cleavages were also apparent, perhaps especially apparent, among the rebels during the Emergency,[18] in spite of the claim that the rebellion had a national character.[19] To make things worse the cleavages are intensified by external pressures and attractions, particularly on some Chinese from mainland China and Taiwan and on some Malaysians from Indonesia. It could still be true that in Malaya there is far more Chinese nationalism, Indonesian nationalism and Indian nationalism than there is Malayan nationalism, although it need not take the form of working for the absorption of Malaya into these countries.[20]

The British have been generally blamed for this situation, but sometimes for not quite the right reasons. Tan Cheng Lock accused them of following what he called the Machiavellian maxim of divide and rule.[21] But this is to attribute too positive a role to the British. More correctly, their creed was 'laissez-faire and let rule'. It resulted from a '. . . basic attitude of separate obligation to almost any group which felt itself to be different, providing its interests did not conflict too strongly with the basic purposes for which power was secured in the first instance'.[22] Arithmetically, the sin of the British was not deliberate division, but rather insouciant addition, of immigrants. Tan Cheng Lock was nearer the mark when he complained that one of the basic defects of British administration was its lack of adequate planning and thought.[23] The inter-war years of 'no politics' in Malaya were a wasted period of relative prosperity when the British made no serious effort to absorb immigrants into the social system or to build up a constructive political tradition.[24]

Communal feeling, largely latent before the last war, was aroused both during the war and afterwards during the Emergency. The cleavages in the society are now so deep and so pervasive in their effects that practically every issue acquires communal implications. This is obviously true of policies on citizenship, language and education. It is also true of political parties, because it appears that the only way of building an effective 'non-communal' party is through a federation of parties which are communal. Exploitation cannot be attacked without consequences which follow from the fact that most middlemen are Chinese.[25] Equality cannot be advocated in vacuo without the audience being aware that Malays possess special privileges, safeguarded by the constitution.

Recently protests have been made about certain types of land development which have been alleged to produce too little benefit for Malay settlers and too much advantage to Chinese contractors. Electorally the provisions for drawing up of boundaries and the 'independence' of the Electoral Commission have been influenced by 'political' arithmetic, in turn dependent on communal considerations. At the highest level the existence of communal cleavage is shown by the (on some premises quite understandable) lack of support from Chinese in Malaya for the prime minister's 'Save Democracy Fund' to help India after the Sino-Indian border fighting in 1962. On a more trivial plane it is illustrated by the perpetual itch of students to annotate any reference in library books which could conceivably be construed as 'communal'.

In the face of these difficulties, the 1957 constitution and subsequent government policy may be viewed as a compromise designed to achieve a rough balance between Malay political power and the economic power of the Chinese. In effect a 'bargain' has been struck between the Malay and Chinese partners in the ruling Alliance Party. An increasing number of Chinese have been made citizens, thus raising the proportion of Chinese in the electorate. On the other hand, after a transitional period, Malay is to be the only official language, and this advantage is to be reflected in the pattern of development of the educational system. Malay privileges as regards land are safeguarded, and their 'special position' is recognised, *inter alia*, for entry into the Civil Service and for certain types of trade and business licences.

A disputed feature of the 'bargain' has been the period for which Malay privileges should be retained. They have been written into the Constitution without any provision for review.[26] However, it is equally difficult to give any estimate of the length of time necessary for Malays to achieve anything like parity with Chinese in the economic sphere. Taken as a whole the bargain is generally fair. But it is all too easy for a member of one community to point to any one feature of the arrangement and to claim plausibly that it is unfair, without also drawing attention to the rough equilibrium of the whole. The bargain is therefore wide open to plausible communal attacks on the ground that it is communally biased.

Nevertheless, the communal 'balance' which has been achieved is only an arithmetical and mechanical product. It has not yet blossomed into national unity. Even among the Malays nationalist feelings were aroused later than in most areas of South-east Asia. Intercommunal cleavages made it inevitable that the Legislative Council's discussions in 1957 concerned not the constitution of a united Malayan nation but merely proposals *designed to promote the growth* of a united nation.[27] This situation was inescapable. It is not true that in plural societies self-government has to be 'the expression of a unity which must be felt and not the instrument for creating it'.[28] Nowadays the strength of anticolonialism and

329

the desire to follow the example of neighbouring independent countries dictate that often self-government must come first.

One indirect approach to the problem of creating national unity is suggested by the hypothesis of Lipset that national unity is hardest to achieve when lines of cleavage tend to coincide; for instance, in Malaya, race, language and religion. It might be argued, from this analysis, that it would be desirable to promote other lines of cleavage, for instance, economic ones, to minimise the influence of the existing coincident cleavages. Consequently new economic groupings and divisions should be welcomed and promoted. Whatever their desirability for other reasons, trade unions, Malay capitalists and political parties based on economic not communal foundations should be encouraged. It is hoped that communal considerations would eventually disappear.

As an academic exercise the analysis is persuasive. But it does not allow for the circumstance that in Malaya ideological lines of cleavage are not entirely separate from communal ones. Communism may have a special appeal to some Chinese in Malaya just because it is felt to be a movement of, by and for the Chinese.[29] It is also likely that there would be a very long period of transition before communal considerations were replaced by economic ones. At present both appear to be at work in the party system, although the former seem to be the more important. Socialist Front speakers have had difficulty in getting across the point that when they say they support special rights for Malays they mean only for *poor* Malays, because they are poor.[30] Consequently the line-up of parties in Malaya today is a little reminiscent of those in the French Third Republic, with communal divisions corresponding to the French divisions on clericalism and education. There are an economic axis and a communal axis, as indicated in Table 47, in which allied parties are joined by dotted lines.

Positively, national unity may be encouraged in the long run through the national language and through a Malayan focus in the content of education. 'Revivalist nationalism',[31] dependent on myths from the past, is out of the question, because Malays and Chinese do not share 'a heritage of common suffering and common rejoicing in the past . . .'[32] However, some common elements and symbols may be given emphasis. In government business and proceedings citizenship should be stressed rather than race.[33] The Yang di-Pertuan Agong could become an effective symbol of national unity, especially if the term of office were made longer than five years.[34] The prime minister, Tengku Abdul Rahman, himself partly Thai by birth, has set a fine example of promoting racial unity by adopting two Chinese children. Other symbols of nationhood, such as the flag and the role played by Malayan troops in the Congo, should be given extensive publicity. The Rural Development Program with its well-publicised 'Operations Room' has considerable potential as a symbol. The government's 1962 decision to extend rural development to the new villages (largely occupied by Chinese) could make this into a truly national symbol, not just a Malay one. Malaya is too small, too non-aggressive and too subject to centrifugal forces to use an aggressive foreign policy in order to build up national feeling. Perhaps, in a mild way, the Malaysia project is an approach to such a policy. A major problem is to discover potent Malayan symbols conducive to national unity which are not exclusively *Malay*. Some countries have the task of assimilating small minorities with an obviously less elaborate heritage of civilisation than the majority. But, decidedly, these conditions do not apply to the Chinese, or to the Indians, in Malaya.

TABLE 47. [35]

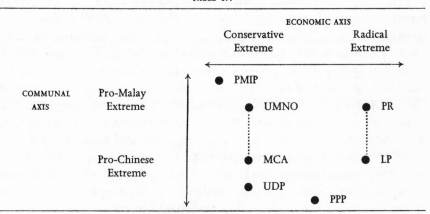

PMIP:	Pan-Malayan Islamic Party
UMNO:	United Malays National Organisation
MCA:	Malayan Chinese Association
UDP:	United Democratic Party
PPP:	Peoples Progressive Party
PR:	Parti Rakyat
LP:	Labour Party

There is one reason for not being too defeatist about the struggle for national unity. Lipset has observed that some countries which have lacked 'legitimacy' (which seems to be largely dependent on a feeling of national unity or a common 'secular political culture') have survived for varying periods largely because of the 'effectiveness' of their governments.[36] France between the wars and until recently a number of well-governed colonies would come into this category. Malaya, with its relatively high standard of life and high level of bureaucratic performance, is now in the same situation. Whether it remains there or not will depend on the future of rubber and tin (and the measures taken to develop new products and industries) and on the maintenance of peaceful relations with its neighbours. Prolonged effectiveness over generations, according to Lipset, may even confer legitimacy on a political system; that is, if Malaya is consistently more prosperous and better-managed than its neighbours this may in the long run tend to produce feelings of national unity.

SINGAPORE, SABAH AND SARAWAK

There is no space to describe pre-Malaysia politics and government in Singapore and the Borneo territories in detail. All that can be done is to mention a few of the circumstances relevant to their inclusion in Malaysia and hazard a guess at some consequences.

Singapore

There are no *institutional* obstacles to Singapore's union with Malaya; the general structure of government is similar. The main political problem is that three quarters of Singapore's population are Chinese, most of whom are Chinese-speaking and have little Malayan consciousness. Instead, they have different degrees of attachment to things Chinese and to China itself—or at least to memories or images of it. 'Any man in Singapore who wants to carry the Chinese-speaking people with him cannot afford to be anticommunist. The Chinese are very proud of China.'[37] Hence the government of Singapore has been captured by successively more left wing parties and it has been widely accepted that there are no enemies on the left. Until now Singapore governments have always wanted merger with Malaya. The People's Action Party in particular has worked hard to foster a Malayan national consciousness so that the Chinese in Singapore would be 'ready, willing and able to be absorbed as one Malayan people . . .'[38] But it was only in 1961 that the Malayan prime minister came to favour it, largely impelled by the imminent danger of a *very* left wing or pro-communist government coming into power in Singapore. In the terms for merger Singapore, unlike the existing states in the Federation of Malaya, is to be allowed to keep control of education and labour policies, a substantial concession in view of the Federation's education policy. But the impact of the Chinese in Singapore on Malaysia will be cushioned in two ways. Malaya tightened up its citizenship regulations, possibly to prevent citizens of Singapore from gaining Malayan citizenship and exercising political rights there too easily. And Singapore's retention of powers over education and labour was given as a reason for its slender allocation of fifteen seats in the new federal Parliament. Sabah and Sarawak with a much lower population than Singapore have been given a total of forty seats.

Sabah and Sarawak

Politically Sabah and Sarawak are so little developed that a 'crash program' will be needed to fit them easily into Malaysia. Sabah has been one of the least advanced of all British dependent territories.[39] The first elections were those held, on a local level, in 1962. Sarawak has gradually evolved a system of local authorities, all members of which are elected. At two removes the local councils elect some of the members of the Council Negri (Legislative Council). But until 1963 these indirectly elected 'unofficials' constituted only a slight majority in the Council Negri. The Council Negri in turn elects some of the members of the Sarawak Executive Council. It is less than two years since the 'member system', by which some members of the Executive Council are associated with policy decisions, was introduced in Sarawak. The intention is that Sabah shall develop along a similar pattern. Consequently, when the first general elections take place for the federal Legislature of Malaysia in 1964, the members from Sabah and Sarawak will not be directly elected but will be chosen by the state legislatures.

There has also been a tropical growth of political activity, expressed in the formation of a large number of political parties. Four years ago there was only one properly constituted party in either of the two territories, the (largely Chinese-led) Sarawak United People's Party, and the governor had publicly expressed doubts whether the formation of parties would assist the progress of Sarawak.[40] Since then the number of parties has grown rapidly, largely in response to the proposals for Malaysia. In each territory there is now an 'Alliance' of pro-Malaysia parties.

Brunei's 'independence' and wealth dictated that negotiations on joining Malaysia would begin later than the talks with Sabah and Sarawak. In December 1962 a revolt broke out in Brunei led by A. M. Azahari whose Parti Rakyat controlled all the elective seats in the Legislative Council, although they were outnumbered by the non-elective members. This resulted in further delay, although it was agreed that Brunei would join by August 1963. Two months before that date, however, Brunei decided not to join.

Racially the picture resembles a more fragmented version of the Balkans. Strictly, only a sixth of the population of Sarawak, and a minute proportion of the population of Sabah, are Malays. But the term, 'Malay' is often used, not ethnically, but to refer to those who profess Islam.[41] (38 per cent in Sabah, 23 per cent in Sarawak.) Many Malays are conscious of their former dominant position under the sultanate of Brunei and the Brooke rajahs in Sarawak.[42] The Brunei rebellion of 1962 would have commanded much more support from Malays than it did if the sultan had been convincingly represented as having supported it. Paradoxically, the attachment of some Malays to Brunei has had the consequence that much of the most vocal opposition to union with Malaya has come from Malays. Correspondingly, some other communities, such as the Dusuns, look back with revulsion on previous rule by the sultans of Brunei. In the Borneo territories the Chinese constitute only about a quarter of the population, although

333

their percentage increase is spectacularly higher than that of any other community.[43] It is the general impression that, compared with Malaya, the Chinese are rather less isolated from the life of the other communities.

As in Malaya in a slightly earlier period, the British did little to encourage racial integration in the Borneo territories, except latterly in Sarawak at local council level.[44] Nor did they push through proposals to unify the territories and Brunei in a single unit.[45] They were content to set up piecemeal or *ad hoc* links through the Commissioner General for South-east Asia, a single Supreme Court, conferences of governors and so on. The British might even have scanned the political horizon with a wider view. In 1945 it did not need the vision of a Cecil Rhodes but merely the calculation of 'any tidy-minded non-British administrator' to see the advantages of a federation of the three Borneo territories with Malaya and Singapore.[46]

In the absence of vision or calculation, the British established a tempo of political advance for Sabah, Sarawak and Brunei which would have been entirely appropriate to the circumstances of the 1930s. It took external pressures in the shape of the communist threat and the rising tide of opinion against colonialism to accelerate the coming of independence.[47] 'Independence' is, in practice, to take the form of inclusion in Malaysia. The Cobbold Commission Report tried to estimate the degree of support for Malaysia in Sabah and Sarawak,[48] but the margin of error must have been very wide. As in Malaya itself, few feelings of Malaysian national unity already exist in the Borneo territories; they remain to be created. Present constitutional, administrative and economic links and similar traditions of government may help. So may the fact that Malay is a lingua franca throughout most of the territories. Members of the Cobbold Commission have pointed to the interest and admiration which Malaya's rural development programs have aroused in Sabah and Sarawak.[49] If the program is extended to these territories it could become a symbol making for consensus. Other persuasive symbols are hard to find. Perhaps Malaysia, like Malaya, will have to rely mainly on 'effectiveness'.

The non-Malay and non-muslim local communities have been insistent that they should be provided with certain safeguards, particularly on religion, language and education, immigration and employment in the civil service. These were necessary conditions for obtaining their agreement, but (like the 'special position' of the Malays in Malaya) they rule out some of the more direct approaches towards building national unity.

To conclude, the creation of Malaysia will make the delicate and complex politics of Malaya even less predictable. The Federation of Malaysia is dedicated to the proposition that the political process can remain substantially democratic in a system in which communism and the cruder expressions of communalism are outlawed. But the strains on the system will be increased by the inclusion of leftist Chinese from Singapore and electors of many races, whose voting power is high in relation to their degree of political sophistication, from the Borneo territories. At the same time external reactions to Malaysia seem certain to have unfavourable internal effects. Some will be directly damaging to national unity. Others, such as increases in defence costs with a consequential reduction in the rate of economic development, will impose financial burdens and lessen effectiveness. Superb statesmanship, and considerable luck, will be required to prevent the effectiveness of the system from being destroyed and the long-term prospects for national unity from being imperilled.

Editor's Note: This paper was completed before Malaysia Day, September 16, 1963. For more recent data on the politics of Malaysia, see the editor's preface.

22

Political Parties and Pressure Groups

K. J. RATNAM

Some important factors need to be borne in mind when discussing political parties and pressure groups in Malaya.[1] There is first the division of the Malayan society into Malay and non-Malay compartments, each having its own ideas of what constitutes an 'equitable compromise' in the political bargaining process. Briefly, the Malays want to safeguard their 'special position' and establish for themselves a position of priority in the country's political and social life;[2] the non-Malays on the other hand want to extend the limits of their 'legitimate interests', thereby bringing about a gradual termination of the advantages at present enjoyed by the Malays. There are, in addition, significant internal divisions within these two main groups, especially that between the extreme communalists and those willing to compromise.

Next, there is the resurgence of Malay nationalism.[3] Sections of the Malay community have continued to express dissatisfaction with the benefits which independence has brought them, both in terms of absolute material improvements and in terms of their status *vis-à-vis* the non-Malays. There has also been considerable activity on the part of non-Malay communal groups, expressed in the form of dissatisfaction with those sections of the constitution which give Malays certain preferences and privileges and revealed also by the continued insistence on multilingualism and a different education policy.

Finally, certain basic national policies still remain to be commonly accepted. While the different communities may agree on general principles, details of implementation continue to provide the basis for bitter controversy.

Prior to the introduction of elections in 1952[4] political parties in many ways acted as pressure groups attempting to influence official policy without thinking of direct participation in government. The need which arose after 1952 to compete with each other with a view to winning elections naturally had a profound effect on the goals and methods adopted by the different parties.[5]

Yet another phase might have been anticipated in the development of party politics from 1957, the year of independence. While ideas about the most suitable constitutional arrangements for the country were a very natural feature of party activity before that date, preoccupation with the constitutional demands of the different communities might have been expected gradually to cease after it, giving way to a rivalry based on different policy preferences within the framework of the constitution. However, most parties have continued to be preoccupied with changing the constitution to the advantage of their own communities.

In the general area of politics, the rival attractions of communalism and intercommunal politics have a most decisive effect on public opinion. Consequently, party rivalries have very considerably been shaped by the conflict between, on the one level, communalism and intercommunalism, and, on the other, Malay and non-Malay communalism. Arising from this, a convenient classification of the major parties would depict the Alliance as an intercommunal party, the Pan-Malayan Islamic Party (PMIP) as a Malay communal party, the People's Progressive Party (PPP) as a non-Malay communal party and the Socialist Front (SF) as a party which, although based more on ideological than communal inspiration, is compelled also to emphasise its intercommunal outlook. However, needless to say, each of these parties also reflects certain other features, although the dominant characteristic is fairly pronounced in every case.

Discussion will have to be limited to the four parties just mentioned. They are the most important, and among them they represent the main political trends in the country.[6]

THE ALLIANCE

Although the Alliance contests elections as a single body, its constituent organisations continue to function on communal lines, being responsible to their own members. Further, it is only these organisations which have individual members and collect subscriptions. The Alliance as such exists only at the various co-ordinating levels, receiving specified contributions from the member groups. The party is therefore an intercommunal organisation, and not non-communal as is often claimed. Also, while the national leadership continually emphasises intercommunal goals, candidates and officials at the lower levels, as members of the United Malays National Organisation (UMNO), the Malayan Chinese Association (MCA) and Malayan Indian Congress (MIC), espouse, in varying degrees, communal views—presumably because they may otherwise lose their following to others who openly rely on a communal appeal, However, the intercommunal approach is clearly the party's main image and, in order to

337

preserve it, compromises, however painful and prolonged, are always attempted when deciding on important issues.

In its efforts to reconcile communal with broader interests, the Alliance has encountered two main difficulties. The first of these is a direct result of the continued (even if considerably modified) communal functioning of the member organisations. The leaders of each group are often too preoccupied with the interests of their own organisations. Consequently, selfishness often stands in the way of maximising the party's support, a fact most evident in the type of bargaining which accompanies the selection of candidates at election time. Secondly, attempts at intercommunal partnership, by necessitating compromises, have also led to accusations that the partners of the Alliance are sacrificing the interest of those whom they claim to represent. Thus, while sections of the Malay community accuse the UMNO of 'selling out' the interests of the Malays, many Chinese find the MCA more concerned with placating UMNO demands than with fighting for Chinese rights. The defence, as already indicated, has revolved around efforts to emphasise the need for and desirability of intercommunal co-operation, and at the same time to satisfy each community that its own interests are being well looked after.

Despite these difficulties, the Alliance continues to be by far the most powerful political party in the country. It benefits from its better organisation and considerably better funds, its record of opposition to the colonial government culminating in the attainment of independence under its leadership, and the popular intercommunal appeal of its leader, Tengku Abdul Rahman.

THE PAN-MALAYAN ISLAMIC PARTY (PMIP)

The PMIP is the most extreme Malay communal party in the country, deriving its support mainly by encouraging Malay fears of non-Malay domination, by advocating a policy of 'Malaya for the Malays' and by channelling dissatisfaction with Alliance policies into a program aimed at communal solidarity. Arguing that the attainment of independence has been nothing more than an empty victory for the Malays, its leaders have emphasised that Malay nationalism still has an important role to play in the country; they have, consequently, attempted to stir the Malay community into an exaggerated view of its own rights. The party also advocates a theocratic state where 'Islamic principles of administration' would be adhered to, although nothing definite has yet been said about what this really means. However, with the help of rural religious leaders and teachers, the party appears to have had some success in explaining its political objectives in terms of Islamic doctrine (e.g. the belief that, for muslims, there should be no separation between religion and politics). Its most dramatic victories were scored at the 1959 federal elections, when it made an almost complete sweep in Kelantan

338

and Trengganu having only a few months earlier gained majorities in the legislative assemblies of these states.[7]

Although appearing to be the most important explanation, religious slogans
are not the only reason for the PMIP's appeal: its attempts to attribute the
economic grievances of the Malay community to the generous treatment accorded to the non-Malays (thereby pointing a condemning finger at the UMNO's
partnership with the MCA and MIC in the Alliance) are also of some consequence.

To speculate on the party's prospects in the future, two possible developments
will have to be considered. First, should certain national policies (e.g. those over
education, special Malay rights, and so on) continue to breed controversy, communal tensions may well harden; then parties like the PMIP will gain strength as
champions of communal rights. On the other hand a successful program in
economic development and education by the present federal government may
well weaken the influence of some of the factors which appear to have contributed
to the PMIP's success. Kelantan and Trengganu are characterised by isolation,
predominantly Malay populations, economic backwardness (accompanied by a
great resentment of Chinese middlemen and moneylenders) and a general simplicity of life. They also represent the most traditional areas in the country
where religious leaders exert a great deal of influence in social and political life.
With economic development not only may geographic isolation be gradually
overcome, but the composition of the society may itself change as a result of the
growth of towns and the influx of more non-Malays. Concerning education
policy, religious teachers have in the past been able to play an active political role
because much of the teaching (especially religious instruction) in the *kampongs* was
conducted without government assistance and control. With the spread of
government-sponsored education, however, more and more teaching will be
done by government teachers who, by the terms of their employment, cannot
actively participate in politics.

THE PEOPLE'S PROGRESSIVE PARTY (PPP)

If the PMIP lies on one end of the Malay versus non-Malay continuum, the
PPP lies on the other. Most of its support, which is largely confined to the Ipoh
area in Perak, arises from its successful exploitation of Chinese sentiment, particularly dissatisfaction with the status given to Chinese education. Judging from
the party's 1959 Election Manifesto, the four most important items in its platform
appear to be:

    (a) the recognition of Chinese and Tamil as official languages, while accept-
        ing Malay as the national language;

    (b) the retrospective application of the principle of *jus soli* in citizenship;[8]

(c) the abolition of the 'special position' of the Malays; and

(d) the amendment of education laws so as to give equal treatment to all communities.

All these are in direct contradiction to the claims of the PMIP (which condemns the government for not taking more effective steps to establish Malay as the *only* official language as soon as possible, deplores the liberal citizenship terms, and advocates greater emphasis on Malay education and an extension of the privileges now given to the Malays), and show how deep the conflicts between Malay and non-Malay communal attitudes are.

It may be argued that since the PPP is only advocating equality, its stand cannot be considered communal. While this should ideally be true, there is also a very good case to be made (on historical and economic grounds, as indicated elsewhere) for the granting of certain priorities to the Malays. For the present, non-communal politics would imply the advocacy of equal rights and privileges for everyone, with 'equality' defined in such a way as to assume a few (defined) privileges for the Malays.

THE SOCIALIST FRONT (SF)

The SF comprises the Parti Rakyat and the Labour Party of Malaya, the former essentially Malay and the latter largely non-Malay. This makes the Front in some respects an intercommunal alliance and it is not surprising that, arising from this, it has a number of problems in common with the Alliance Party. The most difficult of these, a problem which will have to be faced by any party which wants to base its appeal on socialism, is that of uniting the predominantly Malay peasantry and the largely non-Malay industrial working class. At present the fact that the former is suspicious and jealous of the latter is, as already indicated, an important reason for the PMIP's popularity. The Front's support, by and large, appears to be confined to the urban areas.

Further, it will not be sufficient for the SF to have a program based on economic policies alone, however attractive they may be. Some stand will have to be taken on the essentially 'communal' issues leading, as in the case of the Alliance, to attacks from sections of both the Malay and the non-Malay communities. The need to take a clear stand on these issues has on occasions led to friction between the two member organisations of the SF and their respective leaderships.

Although some of the difficulties at present faced by the SF are caused by internal defects (such as misunderstandings between the local branches of the two member organisations), many of them are of general significance for the future of party politics in the Federation of Malaya: no socialist party can hope to achieve widespread popularity as long as communal affiliations override economic interest.

FEDERAL ELECTIONS 1955, 1959

The present discussion of political parties will probably benefit from a brief outline of performances at the 1955 and 1959 federal elections.

The communal composition of the electorate in 1955 was a gross distortion of that of the population as a whole: of a total of just over 1,280,000 who ultimately registered as electors,[9] about 84·2 per cent were Malays, 11·2 per cent Chinese, and the remaining 4·6 per cent mainly Indians. On a constituency basis, the distribution was even more uneven: out of a total of 52 constituencies the Malays constituted a majority in 50, the Chinese in 2 and the Indians in none. Three factors account for these figures: the decision (taken as a matter of principle, with reference to the problem of nation-building) not to consider communal factors in drawing up constituencies; the very obvious fact that the Malays formed a good majority of federal citizens at this time; and the fact that about three quarters of Chinese and Indian citizens were under 21 years of age and hence ineligible to register as voters.[10]

Given a purely communal approach to politics, these figures could well have resulted in a legislature in which 50 of the 52 elected members were Malays and the remaining 2 Chinese. Fortunately the party at the helm of the nationalist movement, the Alliance, improved the situation by nominating 15 Chinese and 2 Indian candidates, in addition to 35 Malays. All but one (a Malay who lost to a PMIP candidate) were successful. Table 48 gives a communal classification of the candidates, and the percentage of total votes polled by each party.

TABLE 48: FEDERAL ELECTION, 1955

Party	Total No. of Candidates	Malays	Chinese	Indians	Percentage of Total Votes (Spoilt Votes Excluded)
Alliance	52	35	15	2	79·6
Party Negara	30	29	1	—	7·6
PMIP	11	11	—	—	3·9
Labour Party[11]	4	—	2	2	2·0
National Association of Perak	9	8	1	—	0·5
Perak Malay League	3	3	—	—	0·4
Perak Progressive Party[12]	2	1	—	1	0·1
Independents	18	16	1	1	3·0
Total	129	103	20	6	

In contrast, the communal composition of the electorate in 1959 was reasonably representative of that of the general population; out of a total of about 2,144,000, about 56·8 per cent were Malays, 35·6 per cent Chinese, and 7·4 per cent Indians. This swelling of the non-Malay vote was very largely the outcome of a further relaxation of the citizenship laws in 1957 and the coming of age of a large number of non-Malays who had been between the ages of 18 and 21 in 1955. Except in the case of the Indians (who still did not have a majority in any constituency), the overall predominance of communities by constituencies was also more even: the Malays formed the majority or the most numerous group in 63·5 per cent of the constituencies (now raised to 104) and the Chinese in the remaining 36·5 per cent. For the Alliance this meant not only that it was no longer necessary deliberately to make up for any deficiencies caused by the electoral system, but also that the UMNO now became more concerned with preserving its own power within the party than with making generous gestures. Generally, there was a great increase in the proportion of non-Malay candidates who stood for elections. Another important feature of the elections was the increased proportion of votes which went to opposition parties, although the Alliance's strength in Parliament was still most impressive.

TABLE 49: FEDERAL ELECTION, 1959

Party	Total No. of Candidates	Malays	Chinese	Indians	No. of Seats Won	% of Valid Votes	
						Overall	In Constituencies Contest
Alliance	104	69	31	4	74	51·5	51·5
PMIP	58	58	—	—	13	21·2	36·2
Socialist Front	38	11	20	7	8	13·0	34·8
PPP	19	1	9	9	4	6·4	32·2
Party Negara	10	10	—	—	1	2·2	22·2
Malayan Party	2	—	1	1	1	0·9	41·5
Semangat Permuda Melayu	1	1	—	—	—	Negligible	
Province Wellesley Labour	1	—	1	—	—		
Independents	26	7	17	2	3	4·8	20·4
Total	259	157	79	23	104		

An interesting feature is the extent to which the election results showed the regional basis of party popularity.[13] The Alliance won all the seats in Kedah, Perlis, Pahang and Johore, and lost 14 of the 16 seats in Kelantan and Trengganu;

the PMIP won all its 13 seats in Kelantan and Trengganu; the PPP won all its 4 seats in Perak; and the SF won its 8 seats in Selangor and Penang. While this is no doubt very striking, crude results in the form of seats won can give an exaggerated picture of popularity especially when a multiparty system is accompanied by single-member constituencies.

The fact that no single community forms a majority of the population could lead to interesting developments in the evolution of party politics. Since it is likely that communal considerations will continue to be politically relevant for some time, there may be a continuing tendency for intercommunal parties to be formed—assuming, of course, the continued functioning of parliamentary democracy. Only a well organised and well financed intercommunal organisation can hope, on its own, effectively to challenge the supremacy of the Alliance. The 'intercommunal' aspects of such an organisation must be stressed, for a totally non-communal party is not likely to enlist much sympathy for the time being.

PRESSURE GROUPS

In briefly discussing pressure groups, it may be convenient to begin by making a few comments on the trade union movement.

A certain amount has been written on trade unions in Malaya,[14] giving a fairly adequate account of their organisational functioning. While there was undoubtedly a high political content in the activities of unions during the immediate post-war years, the extent to which these activities were circumscribed after the declaration of the Emergency in 1948 has had a lasting effect, to a point where one gets the impression today of a trade union movement which is anxious to avoid open political commitments. Provided that this show of 'responsibility' is not in any way inspired by fear of reprisals, it is possible to argue that such a state of affairs will in the long run be beneficial not only to the interests of the country as a whole but to those of organised labour as well.[15] On the other hand, the view has also been expressed in Malaya that only a well organised and effective trade union movement which has not disavowed political goals can lure the working classes away from their preoccupation with communal politics.[16] While there may be some truth in the latter assumption, it is also possible that attempts by the trade union movement to advocate particular points of view on communal issues may have little effect. On the other hand, such attempts, especially if persisted in, could also lead to more damaging consequences like the loss of confidence in the movement or the emergence of communal 'wings' within it, each preferring attachment to a different political party. Economic interests are still only of dubious value as an aid to political unification.

There are, within each community, various interest associations which often act as pressure groups on the political system. The best examples of this in the case of the Chinese community would be the various guilds, chambers of commerce and educational groups (like the All-Malaya Chinese School Management Committees Association and the United Chinese School Teachers Association). Both in 1947 when the Federation of Malaya Agreement was being drawn up and in 1957 when the present constitution was being decided upon, the guilds and chambers of commerce made serious attempts to improve the constitutional status of the Chinese. Although the MCA claimed to have incorporated their demands when making its own proposals to the Alliance in 1957,[17] there were obvious signs that these bodies were not satisfied with the outcome. As a final attempt they sponsored a delegation to London to present their four main claims: citizenship by birth; relaxation of the residential qualifications for those wishing to become citizens by registration; equal rights for all citizens; and the establishment of a multilingual legislature. The delegation was unsuccessful.

As for the educational groups, a good example of their activities as a pressure group was their public protest in 1959 against the government's education policy. Although this particular protest was touched off by the question of whether or not those educated in Chinese schools should write their government examinations in Malay, several other grievances were brought to light so as to support the claim that Chinese education was not being given a 'fair deal'.[18] Coming only a few months before the federal elections (and aided by dissatisfaction with the Alliance's selection of candidates) this incident, by provoking public disagreement between the government and influential Chinese groups, contributed to the defection of some important MCA leaders. The inability of the MCA, as a partner in the Alliance, satisfactorily to aggregate the interests of the Chinese community seems to have led to considerable dissatisfaction. A Chinese newspaper observed when the 1957 Constitution was being drawn up:

> We feel that we can no longer rely on the MCA to accomplish this task [of fighting for Chinese rights] because it is a political party and not an organisation to represent public opinion. Moreover, because of its association with the Alliance, it has many difficulties in this matter. . . . This is to say that MCA will support the common views of the Alliance and can do nothing else. Unfortunately, the views of the Alliance and the demands of the Chinese are still greatly divided.[19]

Accusations of this kind are also made against the other partners in the Alliance by parallel organisations in the other communities.

Among the Malays, teachers and religious leaders appear to be the groups with most political influence. Together they represent the areas of Malay culture which are politically the most consequential today; this makes their grievances, often presented as symbolic of those of the Malay population at large, valuable as aids to the propagation of Malay nationalist ambitions. It is in these terms that their value to the PMIP can best be appreciated. At the same time, it may be misleading to view the relationship between religious-cultural interests and the PMIP as that between pressure group and political party. Their relations are in many ways symbiotic, the latter mainly being the formal organisation through which the former can undertake political activity. It should however also be pointed out that the teachers have their own organisations which often make representations to the government. For its part the Alliance has tried its best to show a keen interest in their welfare, no doubt knowing well the extent to which the Malay community as a whole is sensitive to this issue and therefore realising that a sympathetic treatment of the claims of these organisations is necessary to combat the PMIP's appeal among a very influential group.

It therefore seems apparent that the type of activity one generally associates with functionally specific groups in most western democracies is generally lacking in Malaya. While interest articulation as such is not absent from the political process, such articulation (especially that part of it which is most significant politically) is essentially a component of the more general attempts by each community to further its own interests. However, although most political parties are also classifiable by the positions they occupy in the Malay versus non-Malay continuum, there is no clear picture of direct and obvious affiliations between pressure groups and specific political parties, with the exception of the link between religious interests and the PMIP.

Editor's Note: This paper was completed before Malaysia Day, September 16, 1963. For more recent data on the politics of Malaysia, see the editor's preface.

23

Policy Formulation, Policy Execution and the Political Elite Structure of Contemporary Malaya

ROBERT O. TILMAN

The present chapter represents an exploratory attempt to identify categories of Malayan political elites, to analyse the recruitment of these elites, and finally to hypothesise on the inter-relation of the various elite groups and on their roles in the political process. For various historical, political, and economic reasons, the precise power relationships among these elite groups are not clear. Moreover, recruitment studies must be based almost as much on personal observation and intuition as on empirical data at the present time. In several cases biographical material is almost impossible to obtain without the assistance of government, and it does not seem probable that academic researchers will gain access to this information in the near future. Thus, the present essay must be regarded primarily as a set of tentative propositions that should invite refutation as much as corroboration.

My point of departure is the concept of a political elite, but the meaning of neither 'political' nor 'elite' is universally accepted in the literature of the social sciences. 'Politics' for the Greeks had to do with the ideal or 'good' life; for later students it implied a study of the 'state'; and for many modern writers—heavily indebted to Machiavelli—the term suggests a contest for 'power', either among individuals or among groups. The simple fact is that political scientists have not yet agreed on what is meant by 'political'.

As a working definition, 'politics' is taken here to mean the interplay of relationships among individuals and groups within and around the structures of government, which are motivated primarily by the objective of influencing the formulation of goals and the selection of means for the political system. Yet, as Mosca oversimplified the problem four decades ago: 'In all societies—from societies that are meagrely developed and have barely attained the dawnings of civilisation, down to the most advanced and powerful societies—two classes appear, a class that rules and a class that is ruled.'[1]

There is general recognition by all but the most devout marxists that society must inevitably be stratified, and the social sciences—particularly the discipline of sociology—have amassed an abundance of literature on social stratification. Since not all individuals or all groups play equal roles in the political process, we can arrive at a working definition of a political elite: individuals or groups clustered within or around the structures of government who are able to exert influence disproportionate to their numbers in the formulation and implementation of government policies.[2] In this sense, then, 'political elite' is viewed as a generic classification under which might be subsumed the more specific categories of elites discussed in the following section.

THE CATEGORIES OF MALAYAN POLITICAL ELITES

In the preparation of this chapter, no *pro forma* method has been found entirely satisfactory for determining who appropriately might be considered a political elite. Many studies on the recruitment of elites begin from the assumption (sometimes explicit, sometimes implicit) that all persons filling certain posts in government or society are by definition members of the elite.[3] It is sometimes preferred to assume that the elite are those whose pronouncements appear most often in the press, while some writers merely hold that 'the political elite is the top power class',[4] thus leaving the selection of the elite to the researcher's ingenuity in ferreting out the power centres of the political system. To be sure, if an elite group did not wield disproportionate power it would not be an elite, but the question of who holds power and who is responsible for decision-making is not an easy one. There seems to be no completely acceptable formula for identifying the political elite, and the present study will therefore employ in part all three approaches. It is proposed to consider as elites those persons filling offices that are, according to the author's observations, so situated in the governmental structure as to be able to influence the formulation and execution of official policies.[5] On this basis, it seems possible to identify four major categories of political elites in Malaya.

1. *Elected and Party Elites.* In this category I have undertaken to analyse the Alliance cabinet and the office holders of the three constituent parties of the Alliance: the United Malay National Organisation, the Malayan Chinese Association,

347

and the Malayan Indian Congress. No attempt has been made to include opposition political leaders, whose pronouncements and opinions may often appear in the press, because the nature of parliamentary decisions strongly suggests that the loyal opposition has had little influence on policy formulation in the Dewan Rakyat.[6] Moreover, the selection of individuals has been restricted to exclude all but the Alliance front-benchers. The high degree of unanimity usually observed in the parliamentary alliance suggests that the real give and take of politics might be centred in extra-parliamentary caucuses rather than in the Dewan Rakyat, and thus the party role (and, more important, the interlocking cabinet-party role) is likely to be a better estimate of political influence than the more apparent fact of popular election.

2. *Bureaucratic Elites.* I have limited my analysis here to members of the Malayan Civil Service. Perhaps there are some few individuals not of the MCS who should be incorporated into this category, but it seems probable that they are statistically insignificant. While other senior bureaucratic services are confined largely to one (or at most to several) ministries, officers of the MCS are to be found staffing key posts in almost every ministry. Only in the Ministry of External Affairs do MCS officers not hold the permanent secretaryships, and throughout the government it is rare for the senior MCS officer of a ministry to be subordinate in rank to a colleague of the professional services.[7] While I have concentrated here on the most senior MCS personnel—some fifty officers—I have also found it necessary to comment briefly on the general characteristics of the subordinate segment of the service (numbering some 200 Malayan officers). The MCS is in a state of transition, and the orientation of the younger officers might be expected to differ from that of their superiors. Since by bureaucratic practice in Malaya it seems probable that most of the junior officers will rise on the promotion ladder by seniority, it is desirable not to ignore this group of potential elite.

3. *Military Elites.* It is a formidable task to collect biographical data on the military officer corps of Malaya. Throughout the world the military is often one of the most security-conscious groups of government. Moreover, independent Malaya has been fortunate in enjoying a military that has refrained from creating sensational news, and thus information is not readily available either to the general public or to the academic researcher. Yet, in view of experiences elsewhere in the new states of Asia, it is perilous to exclude the military from all consideration, however impressionistic the treatment of them must be.

4. *Symbolic Elites.* In the making of day-to-day policy decisions and in the execution of these policies, it is probable that the Malay royalty of the peninsula exert little influence. In this sense they could not be called a political elite, but they do serve the function of legitimatising political decisions made elsewhere in

the system and must be considered within the total structure of Malayan political elites. It would present a distorted picture of Malayan government if the Malay rulers were excluded for formal reasons.

THE PROCESS OF POLITICAL SOCIALISATION AND RECRUITMENT

Political socialisation is the process by which individuals become inducted into the environment surrounding the political system. In a sense, it involves both learning the rules of the political game and accepting the limitations of the game itself.[8] Certain generalisations may be made about the process of political socialisation and the avenues of elite recruitment, which are empirically verifiable in the case of all but the military elite, and which personal observation suggests may also be valid for the latter.

1. *The language of socialisation has been English.* Rarely has an individual succeeded in gaining a place of political prominence after coming through a vernacular or traditional stream of education in Malaya. Direct recruitment into the MCS requires an academic degree from an acceptable English-language university (in practice, usually a Commonwealth university) or satisfactory completion of the Bar Final Examination, which is conducted in English and is based on imported English law and practice. Recruitment by promotion from the junior services is also possible, but, as it will be shown later, here too the senior bureaucracy draws only from the English stream of education in Malaya. In the case of the elected and party elites, note the following distribution according to stream of education.

TABLE 50. ELECTED AND PARTY ELITES: MAJOR LANGUAGE OF EDUCATION*

	Cabinet-Party n = 13	Cabinet n = 18	Party n = 33	Total Elite n = 38
English	100**	100	67	71
Vernacular/traditional	Nil	Nil	6	5
Vernacular/traditional and English	Nil	Nil	21	18
Unknown	Nil	Nil	6	5

* Source: These tabulations have been compiled from various newspaper and biographical sources contained in the National Archives, Singapore, and the library of the University of Singapore. ** Throughout this essay all tabulations are given in percentage figures for comparative purposes. Attention should be drawn, however, to the small number of the sample in some cases.

While the symbolic elite is generally associated with the more traditional way of life in Malaya, it should not be supposed that the Malay rulers have shunned opportunities for western education. On the contrary, apparently unlike the pre-independence muslim religious and political leaders of India and Northern Nigeria, Malay royalty have enthusiastically pursued English-language education,

349

and the sultans were among the first to send their sons to the British-established English-language secondary schools.

TABLE 51. SYMBOLIC ELITE: EDUCATION AND LANGUAGE*

	n = 11	Percentage
English Secondary School		82
(Malay College	55)	
(Other	27)	
University Education in English		18
Unknown		18**

* Source: See Table 50. ** All formal education has been considered here; thus, the total is equal to more than 100 per cent.

2. *The bureaucracy has served as a major avenue of recruitment of elites.* Lateral recruitment into segments of the senior bureaucracy is almost without precedent in Malaya; thus to persons thoroughly immersed in Malayan government it may seem almost tautological to suggest that bureaucratic elites have been drawn almost exclusively from the bureaucracy. However, in view of the practices of other states, this is an important point to note.[9]

TABLE 52. BUREAUCRATIC ELITE: ADMINISTRATIVE SERVICE BACKGROUND*

n = 53	
Years of Prior Service	Percentage
0–5	9
6–15	9
16–25	45
26–35	40
36–40	4
Unknown	2

* Source: Compiled from Federation of Malaya, *Staff List, 1st January 1962* (Kuala Lumpur, 1962), pp. 2–7.

Given Malayan practices, it is not surprising that the bureaucracy itself has been the avenue of recruitment of bureaucratic elites, but the role played by the bureaucracy in the recruitment process of other elite groups is perhaps somewhat more unexpected.[10]

TABLE 53. ELECTED AND PARTY ELITE: AVENUES OF RECRUITMENT*

	Cabinet-Party n = 13	Cabinet n = 18	Party n = 33	Total Elite n = 38
Bureaucracy	46	50	39	42
Professional	23	22	15	16
Business	23	22	24	24
Other	0	0	12	11
Unknown	8	6	9	8

* Source: See Table 50. Some individuals have of course combined several of these categories in the course of their careers. I have attempted here to select the category that seemed most appropriate, generally because of longest association.

POLICY FORMULATION: R. O. Tilman

The influence of the bureaucracy in imparting the values basic to the present Malayan political system cannot be underestimated. The usual stepping stones to success (which was generally defined as eventual promotion to the MCS) were through an English-language secondary school, thence into the Malay Administrative Service, and finally into the MCS for a small percentage of the officers. Created in 1910 with the expressed intention of utilising Malay officers to staff subordinate administrative posts, the MAS originally drew cadets only from Malay College at Kuala Kangsar—an English-language secondary school organised along the lines of a British public school.[11] During their stay at the College and throughout their careers in the MAS, the conduct of Malay officers both on and off their jobs would have been carefully scrutinised, and promotion to the MCS was almost as dependent upon 'social fitness' as on administrative competency.[12] Such emphasis on the acquisition of British tastes and habits could not fail to leave its mark on the personalities of the present elites.

3. *Universities have played a significant role in elite recruitment and their influence is likely to increase considerably.* To the present time, the influence of the universities has been most pronounced in the case of the elected and party elite, and, in fact, among those holding the key cabinet-party posts, more than three quarters have had some university experience.

TABLE 54. ELECTED AND PARTY ELITE: EDUCATIONAL BACKGROUND*

	Cabinet-Party n = 13	Cabinet n = 18	Party n = 33	Total Elite n = 38
University degree (including Inns of Court)	53	50	27	29
University or college: no degree	23	22	18	18
Maximum of secondary education	23	28	36	37
Unknown	0	0	18	17

* Source: See Table 50.

As suggested earlier, and as Table 55 demonstrates, the Malay Administrative Service has been the major avenue of recruitment of the bureaucratic elite, and to this junior administrative service the usual stream of recruitment has run not through the universities, but through the English-medium secondary schools. However, while the MAS continues to be an important reservoir for future administrative bureaucrats, the pattern of recruitment has been changing rapidly as young university graduates are becoming available. The first indigenous officers recruited directly into the MCS did not enter until 1953, but at the present time the universities have become the major supplier of young MCS officers—the potential bureaucratic elite of Malaya of several years hence. Note the following

351

comparison of the path of recruitment for the present elite and the future elite.

TABLE 55. AVENUE OF RECRUITMENT OF MCS OFFICERS*

	Present Elite n = 53	Potential Elite n = 204
Promotion through MAS	79	44
Direct from universities	2	43
Promotion through State Civil Services	11	14
Promotion through other services	8	0

* Source: See Table 56. Some material has also been drawn from University of Singapore records and from personal interviews.

While the young officers entering the administrative services directly from the universities have demonstrated less inclination to emulate expatriate practices and mannerisms, there is as yet no evidence to suggest that the socialisation process is producing individuals with markedly different political values. On the whole, given the policies and practices discussed in the following section, this group is likely to be among the most conservative of the university students. Institutional safeguards in the bureaucracy largely prevent the recruitment of individuals not firmly committed to the present order, and political realities at the present time would make it difficult for a non-conformist to achieve high status among the elected and party elites.

4. *Chinese and Indians are entering the government in ever increasing numbers, but the elites are still primarily Malay in composition.* Of the 38 individuals representing the elected and party elite, 24 are Malay, including eight of whom are members of the inner group with interlocking membership in UMNO and the cabinet. The symbolic elite at the present time is entirely Malay.[13] However, since an element of discretion was inevitable in the selection of the elected and party elites, and since the Malay character of the symbolic elites is almost part of the definition, it is perhaps more revealing to analyse the composition of the present and potential bureaucratic elites, where selection has been based largely on institutional criteria.

Since the MCS was not opened to direct local recruitment until 1953, it was possible for Malayans—with only minor exceptions—to enter the Service only through the MAS, and the MAS was and still is a purely Malay service. Thus, until 1953, when non-Malays were first recruited, the MCS was entirely Malay and expatriate in composition. At the present time, therefore, the 53 Malayan bureaucratic elite analysed in this study represent all Malays with the exception of only three officers: the two Chinese and one Eurasian who were taken into the MCS from subordinate services on January 1, 1953.

Non-Malays are now entering the total bureaucracy of modern Malaya in impressive numbers, but a constitutionally sanctioned recruitment quota of four Malays to each non-Malay ensures that the MCS will retain its predominantly Malay character indefinitely. The following table shows the communal composition of the total MCS for the period since Merdeka.

TABLE 56. MALAYAN CIVIL SERVICE, BY COMMUNITY, 1957–62*

	1957	1958	1959	1960	1962
Expatriate	220	154	104	55	26
Malay	128	123	166	195	219
Chinese	9	11	13	16	17
Indian	3	4	9	12	15

* Source: This table has been prepared by the author by tabulating the annual *Staff Lists* of the Federation Establishment Office for the years indicated. A relatively insignificant category, 'others', has been omitted.

Any analysis of the process of socialisation of the military elite must be largely intuitive, but certain evidences are abundant enough to suggest similarities to the processes observed in other elite groups. To a far greater extent than the bureaucracy, the military is still subject to the direct influence of expatriate officers. The most senior officers of the Malayan military have often had experience in the British armed forces; many younger officers are graduates of Sandhurst, and the Federation Military College at Port Dickson is itself largely patterned after the Sandhurst model. Malayan officers often seem even more anglicised than their expatriate colleagues, enthusiastically adhering to accepted practices, habits, and mannerisms that have long been traditions of the British military. This, of course, cannot serve as empirical proof, but it does seem strongly to suggest that the military have accepted the same social rules—and, by extension, perhaps the same political rules—that guide the other elite. It seems probable that the generalisations extrapolated in analysing the other groups can, in essentials, also be applied to the military.

THE ELITE AND THE POLITICAL PROCESS

While many of the elites share a common background in Malay tradition, on the whole the present groups owe their emergence to the Malayan colonial experience. Colonialism provided the environment; colonial officers introduced the seeds of political change; government-sponsored education and government service provided the means of political socialisation; English was the language of political communication; and the present elites of Malaya are those who passed through this socialisation process. Even those of the present elite who retain the traditional trappings—the symbolic elite—have largely shared a common colonial experience that includes an English-language education, often travel abroad, and —less tangible but probably as important—shared English taste and habits that

353

have caused the royalty to identify themselves almost as much with the English social environment as with Malay society.

When Macaulay in 1835 said that it should be the goal of British educational policy to create Indian-Englishmen,[14] the groundwork was laid for the creation of the present elites of the former British colonies and protectorates, including Malaya. None would probably agree with the reasoning behind Macaulay's arguments today, and few would be willing to accept the exaggerated process to the extent of calling the citizens of the former colonies hyphenated Englishmen. Malayans are no more Malayan-Englishmen than Senegalese are Senegalese-Frenchmen, and no one—particularly among the Malayans and Senegalese—would want it any differently. Nevertheless, the present elites of Malaya are those who were politically socialised into the British colonial environment, and, as Macaulay suggested, it is they who have served as the liaison group, or in the colourful phrase of Josef Stalin, as the 'transmission belt'.

The political, bureaucratic and military elites have been able to work hand-in-hand, all the while enjoying legitimacy within the constitutional framework, which in turn is sanctioned by the symbols of the state as represented by the symbolic elite group. All of the four groups of political elite are playing approximately the same political game, and they are abiding by generally the same rules of the game. The institutions of government are those patterned after the British model, and the elites have all been socialised into an environment similar to the one in which such institutions evolved. The elites have therefore been able to utilise these institutions to effect the political, social and economic programs of the Federation, while others outside the game have been at a political disadvantage.

It is easy to recognise that the English-educated elite groups are dominating the political process today, but it is another thing entirely to decide which of the political elite groups are politically superior to the others. Classic democratic theory holds that the political leaders, responsible to an electorate, make policies that are then executed by a perfectly neutral Weberian bureaucracy. In contrast, there is the modern tendency to suggest that the new states—schooled in colonial practices—are 'administered governments'. To be sure, the bureaucracy of Malaya has played a vital role in the successful transition from colonialism to independence, but it would be difficult to argue that this constitutes an 'administered government'. Yet pure democratic theory also seems inadequate. While the bureaucracy (and probably the military as well) is neutral under the present political regime, it is difficult to make the assumption that this represents absolute neutrality in the Weberian sense. So long as all the elite groups share common goals and agree on the selection of similar means, it is virtually impossible to estimate power relationships. However, should the character of one of the elite groups change in the future, then these relationships should become more apparent. While change may not be foreseen at the present time, it seems reasonable to conjecture that in a democratic government it is the elected and party elite that is most vulnerable, for it is the only elite group that does not enjoy an entrenched position in the political system.

24

Constitutional Problems

H. E. GROVES

Whatever form the Constitution of Malaysia takes, and in much of its structure it is expected to be the same as the Constitution of Malaya,[1] one paramount constitutional problem will be present. It is a problem crucial in nearly all governments of new or emerging nations endeavouring to follow the Westminster model of democracy; it is a problem which, unsolved in many new nations in Asia and Africa, has left them with only the shadow or pretence, or less, of democracy. It is a problem for which a satisfactory solution must be found and continue to persist in Malaysia, as in any other country, for parliamentary democracy as it has developed in England to be able to survive. The problem is, of course, that of devising and working the constitutional machinery which enables an effective opposition to exist, i.e., the problem of the dissentient political voice. Embodied in this overriding problem are, among others, the issues of free expression, of emergency powers of government, of detention without trial, of the right of free travel throughout all of the country, of citizenship, of electoral constituencies, and the like.

Western democracy and the dominance at any given period of time of a monolithic party are not necessarily inconsistent concepts. It may well be that the nature of the polity is such that at some time or times one party can largely embrace the existing spectrum of political views. This is very often the case when a nation has just emerged from colonial dominance, when most political energies have been directed towards the one great goal of freedom, the achievement of which customarily demands unity and a suppression of the divisive views which form the normal range of political, economic, social, religious and other beliefs, prejudices and aspirations of men.

The issue for constitutional democracy is not whether at any particular time one party has been able to command the loyalty and express the views of the majority, even the vast majority, of the population. The democratic issue is that of the means by which this result is achieved, with the corollary of the means by which those with other views are enabled to reach and to seek to win over the electorate to their differing positions. Ancillary issues include those of the coincidence of the electorate with the adult population, which raises such questions as citizenship and the relative weight of votes. Attention must also be given to the matter of whether the constitutional machinery operates to ensure a smooth transition upon a change of party control of government.

When one speaks of the rights of the dissentient view, it is not necessarily to argue that every voice must be given the public ear, whatever its cry, although there is exceedingly respectable opinion that this absolute is an essential concomitant of democracy, to be limited only when expression becomes action likely to bring about the overthrow of the government by other than constitutional means, i.e., by force and violence.[2] If one takes England as the political model, an obvious choice for those who have taken its parliamentary form of government,[3] it will be seen that in peace-time the widest range of political expression is tolerated, limited only by little-used laws of sedition and treason. Or if one looks to the United States, the first, and considered by many a successful, if imperfect, descendant of English parliamentary democracy, it will be seen that, except for the extreme communist view (an exception which lies uneasily on the nation, as exemplified by the division of views in the Supreme Court, where these issues come for resolution),[4] the Constitution also permits the political dissenter great latitude to create and increase a following.

In Malaya, too, political expression has been essentially free.[5] A wide range of political parties has developed; and if one takes the major party, the Alliance,[6] as the 'centre', it is apparent that views both 'left' and 'right' have succeeded in persuading a sufficient percentage of the electorate to have been able to win both local[7] and state[8] elections. But while Malaya has fairly stood as a model of emerging democratic nations, it must be kept in mind that its history has been short. Of course, nations which have arisen since Malaya have witnessed the collapse of democratic institutions. But variations in the level of economy, education, administrative skills, social and political sophistication and many other features from country to country render comparisons of doubtful utility.

For Malaysia its first period of major stress and strain, apart from the Emergency period which accompanied the birth of the Federation of Malaya, has developed out of the very activity of forming itself into the broader geographical entity. One may hope that the new Constitution, both in the formalism of its terms and the spirit of its implementation, will accommodate itself to the reality the English type of democracy, which is structured on the rights of the loyal opposition, 'loyalty' being interpreted to mean only the eschewing of force and violence to achieve its ends and bearing no necessary relationship to the degree, or lack of it, of agreement with the policies, in whatever realm, of the government of the day.

Turning to the existing Constitution of Malaya, three articles seem to offer a measure of protection to the political dissenter, while ten articles appear in some form antithetical to this basic right. These will be discussed under their several heads.

EXPRESSION, ASSEMBLY AND ASSOCIATION

Fundamental to the right of political dissent are the rights of free expression, assembly and formation of associations. Obviously, for a dissenting view to have political reality it must be possible to communicate it to others. Just as obviously, such communication may need to take several forms, particularly writing and speech; and if groups are to be persuaded, groups often need to be spoken to, hence the importance of assembly. Likewise for the dissenting policy to impress itself upon the body politic associations are customarily essential for the transforming of ideas into political change. All of these freedoms appear in Article 10 (1) which provides: 'Subject to Clause (2)—(a) every citizen has the right to freedom of speech and expression; (b) all citizens have the right to assemble peaceably and without arms; (c) all citizens have the right to form associations.' It is, however, totally unrealistic to believe that these rights have ever been entrenched in the Constitution of Malaya; for the overriding Clause (2) states:

> Parliament may by law impose—(a) on the rights conferred by paragraph (a) of Clause (1), such restrictions as it deems necessary or expedient in the interest of the security of the Federation, friendly relations with other countries, public order or morality and restrictions designed to protect the privileges of Parliament or of any Legislative Assembly or to provide against contempt of court, defamation, or incitement to any offence; (b) on the right conferred by paragraph (b) of Clause (1), such restrictions as it deems necessary or expedient in the interest of the security of the Federation or public order; (c) on the right conferred by paragraph (c) of Clause (1), such restrictions as it deems necessary or expedient in the interest of the security of the Federation, public order or morality.

To make unmistakably clear that the 'rights' referred to in Article 10 (1) exist only so long as and to the extent that Parliament chooses, Article 4 (2) (b) provides: 'The validity of any law shall not be questioned on the ground that it imposes such restrictions as are mentioned in Article 10 (2) but those restrictions were not deemed necessary or expedient by Parliament for the purposes mentioned in that

Article.' Thus, these basic rights have been without effective constitutional protection. Their security has lain in the will of a presumably transitory parliamentary majority.

Expression of one kind, that which occurs in proceedings in Parliament, is partially protected by Article 63 (2), which provides: 'No person shall be liable to any proceedings in any court in respect of anything said or any vote given by him when taking part in any proceedings of either House of Parliament or any committee thereof.' This section does not provide protection against non-judicial action by government, such as revocation of the citizenship of one who is a citizen by registration or naturalisation; nor does it protect one against administrative detention without trial, both subjects of which are dealt with below.

MOVEMENT

Several characteristics may distinguish a federation of states from a confederacy, the latter term being normally employed to describe two or more states associated for some common purpose, usually external, but with the sovereign powers and internal structure of the states remaining otherwise unaltered. An expected feature of a confederacy would be the retention of their parochial characteristics by political parties. An essential feature of a true federation is that political parties have unfettered opportunity to operate at both state and national level. And such operation might be expected to require the free movement of political leaders, party organisers and even voters.[9] One can conceive of some political parties in a parliamentary democracy espousing the overthrow of lawful government by force and violence, thereby placing themselves and their members outside the protected area of essential constitutional freedoms. But it would be utterly inconsistent with the principle of federalism for such prohibitory laws to be otherwise than national in character; and it would be the height of federal anomaly for a party lawful in one state to be other than lawful in all.

As in the case of the 'rights' mentioned in the preceding section, the Constitution of Malaya has spoken of, but not guaranteed, the rights of free movement and residence throughout the Federation. Article 9 (2) provides, 'Subject to any restriction imposed by any law relating to the security of the Federation, public order, public health, or the punishment of offenders, every citizen has the right to move freely throughout the Federation and to reside in any part thereof.' But, again, to make unmistakable that this is a parliament-controlled 'right' and not a constitutional one, Article 4 (2) (a) provides, 'The validity of any law shall not be questioned on the ground that it imposes restrictions on the right mentioned in Article 9 (2) but does not relate to the matters mentioned therein.'

Nor are the portents hopeful that the freedoms of travel and residence will be as extensive in either law or fact in the new Federation of Malaysia as they were in Malaya. One assurance repeatedly given the Borneo territories has been that those states will be permitted to control immigration into their areas, even from other states of the nation of which they are a part.[10] And one potential Malaysian state, on the basis of a revolutionary uprising in a second, has established the precedent of barring the entry of citizens and residents of a third for reasons of membership in a political party never declared unlawful; moreover this action of political interdiction has been applauded by ministers and members of Parliament of the fourth and most powerful state—all of which are potential partners in the new Federation.[11] That political parties and such politically sophisticated organisations as trade unions are not unmindful of the necessity of national freedom of action is apparent from public statements already reported.[12] Free movement and residence would seem to be a *sine qua non* of federalism and, therefore, completely inconsistent with the principle of state control of immigration from within the nation.

EQUALITY

Article 8 (2) provides, 'except as expressly authorised by this Constitution, there shall be no discrimination against citizens on the ground only of religion, race, descent or place of birth in any law or in the appointment to any office or employment under a public authority or in the administration of any law relating to the acquisition, holding or disposition of property or the establishing or carrying on of any trade, business, profession, vocation or employment'. Some might wish, so long as the Constitution was to speak in this broad way to the matter of equality, that political activity would have been included among the protected subjects. For while, after one has assumed certain public employment, political activity of some types might be fairly forbidden, employment in the first instance might well be independent of past lawful political activity, and certainly one would hope that acquiring, holding or disposing of property or the establishing or carrying on of any trade, business, profession, vocation or employment would in no sense be prejudiced by one's lawful political activity, past, present or future.

Amendments to the Constitution in 1962 authorised discrimination between citizens in a field not covered by Article 8 (2).

Prior to 1962 the Constitution had respected the one man one vote principle, a result which it achieved through requiring electoral constituencies of approximately equal size.[13] The impartiality of delimitation of constituencies was sought to be assured by placing all such matters in a constitutionally created Election Commission with the independence of a judicial body. In 1962 an amendment to the Constitution made it possible for 'rural' constituencies to have as little as one half the number of electors as 'urban' constituencies, thus enabling a 'rural' vote to equal twice that of an 'urban' dweller. The amendment neglected to define the vital words 'rural' and 'urban', which are not elsewhere defined in the Constitution either. Moreover, delimiting the constituencies is no longer within the control of the Election Commission; but that body now makes recommendations to the prime minister. And the final determination as to the boundaries of the constituency lies with the House of Representatives. Will this important power to gerrymander districts be used by a party in control of government for the benefit of the opposition?

CITIZENSHIP

The Constitution of Malaya treats 'citizenship' as a unitary concept for both federal and state elections. Article 119 provides, '(1) Every citizen who—(a) has attained the age of twenty-one years on the qualifying date; and (b) is a resident in a constituency on such qualifying date or, if not so resident, is an absent voter, is entitled to vote in that constituency in any election to the House of Representatives or the Legislative Assembly . . .' The Interpretation Article 160 says ' "Citizen" means a citizen of the Federation.' Oddly the important term 'resident' is not defined or described in the federal constitution. In spite of the apparent oneness of 'citizenship', two kinds of citizenship have been recognised, in fact, by the Constitution of Malaya, i.e., federal and state citizenship. All of Part III is concerned with the acquisition and loss of federal citizenship and incidents of that citizenship. But Article 8 (3) takes cognisance of the fact that there is a status known as a subject of the ruler of a state. And more particularly, Article 8 (5) (d) provides: 'This Article [establishing the principle of equality] does not invalidate or prohibit—any provision prescribing residence in a State or part of a State as a qualification for election or appointment to any authority having jurisdiction only in that State or part, or for voting in such an election.' This is essentially all that is contained in the phrase 'dual citizenship' as used in the United States to distinguish certain rights and obligations applicable to a resident or 'citizen' of one state, independent of his rights and obligations of national citizenship.

The state constitutions vary considerably in the precision with which they deal with the question of state 'citizenship'; but the concept is implicit, if not explicit, in all of them. The Constitution of Kelantan defines a 'subject of His Highness' as 'any person who under the written law for the time being in force in the State is a subject of His Highness the Ruler of the State of Kelantan'. It is thus apparent that definition of this important status is a matter of state statutory law only. 'Residence' is not defined in the Kelantan Constitution, nor in the others; yet typical is the Kelantan Article XXX providing: 'Every citizen of or over the age of twenty-one years who is a resident in the State is qualified to be a member of the Legislative Assembly . . .'

361

Further constitutional clarification of the terms 'citizen', state and federal, 'subject', 'resident' and 'national' of the Federation[14] of Malaysia may be hoped for.

Perhaps the greatest threat to political opposition in the citizenship provisions of the Constitution of Malaya lies in Article 25 (1) (a), which states, 'The Federal Government may by order deprive of his citizenship any person who is a citizen by registration under Article 17 or a citizen by naturalisation if satisfied that he has shown himself by act or speech to be disloyal or disaffected towards the Federation.' Procedure for administrative appeal is provided the affected citizen. Article 27 states:

(1) Before making an order under Article ... 25 ... the Federal Government shall give to the person against whom the order is proposed to be made notice in writing informing him of the ground on which the order is proposed to be made and of his right to have the case referred to a committee of inquiry under this Article. (2) If any person to whom such notice is given applies to have the case referred as aforesaid the Federal Government shall, and in any other case the Federal Government may, refer the case to a committee of inquiry consisting of a chairman (being a person possessing judicial experience) and two other members appointed by that Government for the purpose. (3) In the case of any such reference, the committee shall hold an inquiry in such manner as the Federal Government may direct, and submit its report to that Government; and the Federal Government shall have regard to the report in determining whether to make the order.

It is apparent that a citizen is subject to lose this most basic of all political rights, his citizenship, without even the benefits of the judicial safeguards that customarily surround a trial for petty crime. He is entitled to have his case heard by a committee. But the committee can have no claim to judicial impartiality. It is a committee of government appointees and can be *ad hoc*. Moreover, the government directs the manner in which the committee shall hold the inquiry. Which is to say that such fundamental safeguards as confrontation of witnesses, representation by counsel, and indeed all other procedural safeguards, which have been embedded into the English common law and the constitutional law of some countries, are a mere matter of governmental grace here. And, finally, whatever the committee may report, the government is only directed to 'regard' it and may, of course, reject the report completely.

The relevance of this striking power in government to opposition thought in a country like Malaya, where such a large proportion of the population has secured its citizenship by registration or naturalisation, is apparent. It cannot but inhibit legitimate political activity among such citizens. To begin with, the criteria are both broad and vague. What is disaffection towards the Federation? Governments are not infrequently sensitive to criticism. And political parties long in power may easily drift into the habit of thought that an attack upon their long-held and long-pursued policies is an attack upon the nation. If the party in power, as here, is to determine for itself, and exclusively, what is disaffection towards the nation, how safely can any citizen who is so by registration or naturalisation express his dissenting political views?

SPECIAL POWERS AGAINST SUBVERSION, AND EMERGENCY POWERS

By far the greatest threat to the voice of the opposition lies in Part XI of the Constitution, wherein are contained the special powers against subversion and emergency powers, with the reality of the threat of the former exceeding the latter. The emergency powers are more sweeping than those dealing with subversion. While a Proclamation of Emergency is in force, the executive authority is greatly increased and the Fundamental Rights provisions are suspended. But the very sweep of these powers is some protection against their use. And the wide publicity which their employment necessarily attracts, both domestically and abroad, argues against their retention beyond the period of need. Governments which profess democracy are usually not comfortable in the admission of failure implicit in the invocation of emergency powers, especially if the occasion has not been forced by external events, such as war.

The danger to political dissent in the special powers against subversion is greater than in the emergency powers provisions for a variety of reasons. Extending to fewer people, they may seem less harmful to a larger proportion of the population. They may be employed less dramatically and publicly than in the procedure of a declaration of emergency. Operative through statutes, they may take on a kind of respectability through apparent commonplaceness in the large section of the populace which tends to political apathy. Article 149 (1) of the Federation of Malaya Constitution enshrines these large and arbitrary powers. It provides:

> If an Act of Parliament recites that action has been taken or threatened by any substantial body of persons, whether inside or outside the Federation—(a) to cause, or to cause a substantial number of citizens to fear, organised violence against persons or property; or (b) to excite disaffection against the Yang di-Pertuan Agong or any Government in the Federation; or (c) to promote feelings of ill-will and hostility between different races or other classes of the population likely to cause violence; or (d) to procure the alteration, otherwise than by lawful means, of anything by law established; or (e) which is prejudicial to the security of the Federation or any part thereof, any provision of

363

that law designed to stop or prevent that action is valid notwithstanding that it is inconsistent with any of the provisions of Article 5, 9 or 10,[15] or would apart from this Article be outside the legislative power of Parliament; and Article 79[16] shall not apply to a Bill for such an Act or any amendment to such a Bill.

This is, of course, the constitutional sanction for legislation permitting administrative detention without trial.[17]   As in other provisions which jeopardise individual freedoms,[18] most that is fearful in Article 149 lies in the combination of breadth and vagueness of the descriptive language and the removal of the consideration of the fairness of its application by an independent judiciary.   Parliament need only follow the simple permissive formula of the Article, and any repressive legislation whatsoever, whatever the basis for it in fact, may be enacted, and this will be legislation beyond the reach of any court.   A party in control of a government which uses such power against opposition parties, whatever its understanding of the justification of the use, must have cause to speculate on the security of its own party leaders and members should control slip away from them and this weapon of repression fall into the hands of others.

No one could examine the Constitution of Malaya, the expected model for the Constitution of Malaysia, without observing its very great concentration of power in the government of the day.   That the Federation government has never yet made the fullest use of its arbitrary strength is a credit to those in whose hands these controls have been lodged.   To expect that all politicians into whose hands these great weapons could constitutionally come will always employ them with even some benignity is to take a most hopeful view of the future.

No person should seek to deny a government's concern with the line between freedom and anarchy.   But no government should wonder at the individual's concern with the line between reasonable control and a totalitarian state.   Democracies which fail to find the middle way unfortunately, but by definition, cease to be democracies.

25

Malaysia, South-east Asia and World Politics

ZAINAL ABIDIN BIN ABDUL WAHID

Of late, Malaysia has attracted world attention primarily because of recent Indonesian opposition against its formation and, to a lesser extent, because of the Philippine claim over Sabah.[1] Both Indonesia and the Philippines have expressed their opposition on the grounds of security and neocolonialism. They claim that Malaysia would not contribute towards the stability of South-east Asia and that it would only perpetuate colonialism in a new guise.

The accusations levelled against the creation of Malaysia seem to contradict what the promoters of this plan have said they hope to achieve. Malaya considers the Malaysia plan as a means to eradicate colonialism from the British Borneo territories. It is meant to create a more viable economic unit by federating the fifteen states and thus establishing a much bigger and stabler state which could prove to be a bulwark against communist expansion in South-east Asia. The British government, the other party in this promotion, has little choice in this matter. While wishing to retain British control over the three Borneo territories as long as possible, it realises that it has to bow to the trend of politics since the Second World War and grant independence to its dependent territories. Realising that it has to move out of Borneo in the not too distant future, the Malaysia proposal must have been a most welcome move to the British government. For Malaysia, under the prevailing political conditions in Malaya, Singapore and the Borneo territories, would provide the best protection for British interests in the three Borneo territories. In fact it has been argued that Malaysia could possibly have been the result of subtle British suggestions.[2]

In discussing the reasons for the establishment of Malaysia, one important factor has not been accorded its due place. This is the inherent desire of the people in the Malaysian territories to get united and become independent. This feeling is particularly true amongst the indigenous peoples. Actually, Tengku Abdul Rahman's Malaysia proposal only provides the channel for the expression of this latent feeling. Malaysia serves as the rallying call for unity and independence. If this were not the case, how else could one explain the tremendous support given by the Borneo peoples to the Malaysia plan? The pro-Malaysia Sabah Alliance won 98 per cent of the votes in the election held late in 1962.[3] In Sarawak, political parties favouring Malaysia enjoy a majority support among the people. The Sarawak United People's Party which opposes Malaysia[4] claims a membership of 61,000.[5] The pro-Malaysia Party Negara of Sarawak claims that it has 72,000 members.[6] While one may question the correctness of these figures, it is safe, however, to assume that they are of about equal strength. But, besides the Party Negara, there are other pro-Malaysia political parties, for example, the Sarawak National Party, the Barisan Anak Jati Sarawak, the Sarawak Chinese Association and the Parti Pesaka Anak Sarawak.[7] It is only in Brunei that there has been strong opposition to Malaysia.[8] Even then, the pro-Malaysia political parties in Brunei are gradually gaining strength.[9] For Malaysia to gain such a backing in less than two years, it must be something which harmonises with the wishes of the people. After all the British government has, in the last eight years, attempted to federate the three Borneo territories without success.[10]

Much can be said for Malaya's contention that Malaysia could prove to be a weapon against communism. It is in this aspect of the problem that lies one of the major reasons for the creation of Malaysia. The whole communist issue centres on Singapore.

After the defeat of the People's Action Party (PAP) at the Hong Lim by-election in early 1961, there was a feeling of uneasiness among the government circles in Kuala Lumpur. The activities of Lim Chin Siong and his colleagues indicated that all was not well with the PAP government in Singapore.[11] This was finally confirmed by the defeat of the PAP candidate at the Anson by-election in July 1961. The formation of the Barisan Sosialis put matters in their correct perspective, both in terms of the strength of the extreme left wing elements and the future of Singapore politics.[12]

It was believed that the communists and the pro-communist elements could take over the government of Singapore constitutionally, if the political trend then were to continue in the same direction. June 1963 was the target date for a revision of the present constitution of Singapore.[13] In all likelihood, the scheduled constitution revision would be followed by a general election which, it was calculated, could result in a victory for the Barisan Sosialis. It was to avoid this possibility that the Malaysia plan was put forward, for a Barisan Sosialis victory would ultimately mean a communist-controlled Singapore. This would give the communists a most valuable foothold in South-east Asia, controlling a strategic island, an important communication centre and a flourishing entrepôt port. Singapore would provide the communists a very congenial base for their operations in South-east Asia. Once Singapore came under the control of the communists, it would not be long before the people became orientated into their line of thinking. Such a possibility could *not* be allowed to happen. Malaya does not wish to see a 'Cuba' three quarters of a mile away from it.[14]

Under the circumstances, Malaysia is considered to be the best solution to this problem. It is hoped that Malaysia would be able to contain Singapore politics. The granting of autonomous status to Singapore, both in Education and Labour, has not been purely because Singapore and Malaya have had divergent developments in these two fields. It is also a measure which gives Singapore a special position; but this position would limit the eligibility of its citizens to stand for elections outside Singapore.[15] Singapore's partial autonomy also restricts its representation in the Malaysian Federal Parliament,[16] thus avoiding any possible left-wing domination from Singapore in the foreseeable future. In short, the semi-autonomous status of Singapore is a means to contain Singapore politics.

But to take Singapore alone into the fold of Malaya would not be politic for the Malayan government. The Malays in Malaya would certainly object to such a move, a move which would upset the balance of population against them. Thus it was thought that the British Borneo territories could provide one of the ways out. The inclusion of the Borneo territories, with the indigenous peoples forming two thirds of its population, is regarded as a means to correct the demographic imbalance that would be created if it were only a merger between Malaya and Singapore. At the same time, the slogans of 'independence for the colonised' could also be used to advantage.

However, the inclusion of the Borneo territories has produced new problems. In the early stages, Indonesia was not opposed to the formation of Malaysia, at least not publicly. Subandrio wrote a letter to the *New York Times* to the effect that Indonesia did not oppose the concept of Malaysia.[17] He reiterated this statement in the General Assembly of the United Nations.[18] The Philippines too did not at first consider the Malaysia proposal as a neocolonialist move. In fact President Macapagal went as far as to say that he regarded the Malaysia project as 'a powerful bulwark against communism'.[19] But their views changed. Both Indonesia and the Philippines later alleged that Malaysia was a threat to the peace and stability of their countries and that it was a neocolonialist venture.[20] Malaya was then accused of being a neocolonial power.

It is, to say the least, strange that Indonesia and the Philippines have found common ground on the problem of security. Indonesia's argument on the security question is untenable. Indonesia claims that Malaysia would endanger the security of Indonesia because it has a defence treaty with Britain. Actually the former position was worse. As British colonies, both Sarawak and Sabah could be used by Britain for SEATO purposes as of right which, in fact, Britain had already done, whereas, under Malaysia, Britain could not even keep one soldier either in Sarawak or Sabah unless the Malaysian government agreed to it. After all, what can ten million Malaysians do against a hundred million Indonesians? Malaysia does not have even a single fighter plane, whereas Indonesia is equipped with jet fighters and bombers.

It is difficult to understand why the Philippines considers Malaysia a threat to its security. President Macapagal said, 'I am convinced that Malaya would not be able to resist the communist onslaught.'[21] Surely Macapagal knows Malaya's attitude towards communism and its success in defeating the communists' insurrection during the Malayan Emergency!

As far as the allegation that Malaya is neocolonialist goes, there appears to be a failure to understand the purposes behind the establishment of Malaysia. Under Malaysia, Malaya will lose its identity. There will no longer be a state known as the Federation of Malaya. How then could it be possible for Malaya to colonise the Borneo territories?

If the Indonesians and the Filipinos are thinking of neocolonialism through the British then it must be remembered that Malaysia is pledged to uphold parliamentary democracy. As such, the voters of Malaysia have the opportunity to express their approval or disapproval of a government through the ballot-box.

The overwhelming victory of the Sabah Alliance, whose major platform is the formation of Malaysia, should have belied any accusation that Malaysia is a neocolonialist venture, at least with regard to Sabah.[22] In Sarawak, it has been shown earlier that it is safe to assume that the majority of the people prefer Malaysia. The Cobbold Commission has, to a certain degree, indicated a majority support for Malaysia, both in Sarawak and Sabah.[23] Sarawak and Sabah have not been forced, or even coerced, to join Malaysia.[24] Donald Stephens, leader of the United National Kadazan Organisation in Sabah, and Datu Bandar Abang Haji Mustapha, president of the Party Negara in Sarawak, did, at first, oppose Malaysia on the ground that it was a Malayan attempt to colonise the Borneo territories.[25] But once they came to know the actual reasons behind this plan, they gave their wholehearted support to it.[26] These two and many others in Sabah and Sarawak, like Datu Mustapha bin Datu Harun, the president of the United Sabah National Organisation, are leaders who have the interests of their countries at heart. It is difficult to imagine them supporting Malaysia if Malaysia is really an attempt to colonise them.

In Brunei, the situation was different. Here the issue was not confined to Malaysia alone. The Brunei Parti Rakyat (People's Party) had been unhappy with the constitutional progress in that country. It wanted a faster pace towards a more representative form of government.[27] To judge from what is known, one would have thought that the Brunei Parti Rakyat would have supported the Malaysia proposal, since it is clear that this would bring independence to the territory. Besides, the party leaders would have seen the trend of events in Malaya with regard to the position of the sultans. One of the major items on the Parti Rakyat program was to make the sultan of Brunei a constitutional ruler.

Yet, when the Malaysia plan was announced, the Parti Rakyat of Brunei came out with a vehement condemnation of it.[28] The motive behind this violent opposition is worth looking into. A. M. Azahari, the president of the Parti Rakyat, condemned Malaysia as a means whereby Malaya would colonise Brunei. It would have been a natural reaction from the Parti Rakyat had it quietened down after the initial outbursts.[29] But Azahari refused to accept the explanation given to him.

It could have been that he sincerely believed that Malaysia was neocolonialist, but this is doubtful. There are, however, other conjectures, the likelihood of which seems to have been borne out by events. Though Azahari might have realised that Malaysia would quicken the pace to democratise Brunei yet, at the same time, he knows that Malaysia would open Brunei to the influence of political forces from outside, particularly from Malaya. For example, the conglomeration of right-wing political parties in Brunei would then be able to obtain greater assistance from the Alliance in Malaya. This could undermine the political sway that had been exercised by the Parti Rakyat. There would also be competition in terms of personalities. A new, dynamic figure could enter the political arena of Brunei. Until the December 1962 revolt, Azahari dominated the Brunei political scene. Had a full election been held then, his Parti Rakyat would have become the ruling party.[30] In short, personal ambition played a significant part in Azahari's arithmetic of Malaysia.

In trying to get a more representative form of government established in the state, a government in which he would occupy a dominant position, Azahari had not found it unwise to ally himself to forces that might ultimately prove to be opposed to his dreams. He established contacts with some people in Indonesia and Malaya who, it appears, had promised him massive assistance. The premiership of Kalimantan Utara must have been too tempting a bait for Azahari to bother about the motives of his allies. However, there were some missing pieces in the puzzle and when Azahari started his rebellion in December 1962, it failed miserably.[31]

Had Azahari merely wanted to democratise the system of government in Brunei, he could have done so constitutionally. He had already won all the contested seats, except one, in the 1962 elections.[32] Even the sole independent member had pledged his support for Azahari. In a council of thirty-three,

Azahari had the backing of sixteen members.[33] He was in a strong position to bargain. He could have also obtained outside sympathy for his professed cause, had he tried to achieve it constitutionally. Yet Azahari resorted to the use of force.

It is not inconceivable that Azahari's often-expressed opposition against the inclusion of Brunei into Malaysia fits into another scheme of things. He could have prevented the entry of Brunei into Malaysia through constitutional means; for it would be difficult for the Brunei government to ignore the voice of the elected opposition when the former had only a slender majority of one. Azahari's intention, therefore, seemed to be not only to keep Brunei out of Malaysia but to frustrate the formation of Malaysia itself.

Three groups of people would not like to see the emergence of Malaysia. They are Indonesia, the Philippines and the communists. The Philippines tolerated, if not actually condoned, the extended stay of Azahari in Manila, while Indonesia now provides a haven and other amenities for him. The arguments against the neocolonialist and the security aspects of the allegations have already been stated. What is it then that makes Indonesia and the Philippines keep harping on the same tune? It is believed that both these countries are seriously concerned over the role which could be played by that segment of the Malaysian population who are of Chinese origin. Looking into the domestic policies of the Philippines and Indonesia, the Chinese problem appears to be the only common denominator that is significant enough to make the two countries the 'strange bedfellows' that they have become.

Indonesia's fear is, I believe, more psychological than strategic. It has been argued in some circles in Indonesia that Malaysia would only mean the enrichment of the non-indigenous people in the three Borneo territories.[34] They further contend that Malaysia should only be formed when the indigenous people are in the position to compete equally with the non-indigenous. While this contention is laudable in itself, it must, however, be related to the actual, existing conditions. As it stands, the indigenous people in Sarawak and Sabah are much more economically and educationally backward than the non-indigenous. The trend of events to date is not in favour of the indigenous; in fact, their conditions are getting worse, whereas under Malaysia, they would occupy a 'special position' which could gradually improve their economic and educational status.[35]

Perhaps what really worries Indonesia most is the increased general welfare that would be brought by Malaysia to the Borneo territories. The impressive economic and rural development projects, educational and health facilities and the ability to live under the rule of law in Malaysia will make too unfavourable a comparison with the deplorable economic and generally chaotic conditions prevailing in Indonesia. The Indonesians would become more discontented with their plight when they saw their counterparts in the bordering Malaysian areas buying all their rice, bread, butter, jam, clothing and other necessities of life just from the local store. And all this happened so soon after independence, without having to go through 'guided democracy', Manipol, Usdek, Nasakom, etc.[36] While in the pre-Malaysian days it could be argued that the economic well-being of the peoples in Sarawak and Sabah was one enjoyed under colonial bondage, the same could not be said after Malaysia. The possibility of the two territories becoming the showcase of democracy to Indonesian Kalimantan must have considerably disturbed the Indonesian leaders. The example of a successfully working democracy right at their doorstep and practised by people akin to themselves would seem to be too much for these leaders to take. An additional cause for discontent to an already dissatisfied population could not be allowed to go unchallenged.

There is yet another argument against the Indonesian contention. This also applies to the Philippines. To delay Malaysia, for whatever reasons, would mean to prolong British colonialism in Sabah and Sarawak. While this prolongation would, in certain aspects, help to prepare the peoples of this area more fully for self-government, it provides at the same time a better opportunity for the communists to influence the masses by appealing to anti-colonial slogans and identifying themselves with the genuine nationalists. In fact, one of the major arguments put forward by Malaysia is that the Indonesian government's opposition to Malaysia results from the pressure applied on it by the communist countries, through the Partai Kominis Indonesia.[37] There is no doubt that Indonesia is heavily indebted to Russia[38] and that Sukarno has to accommodate the PKI to a certain extent in order to counterbalance the influence of the Indonesian Army, thus somewhat stabilising his own position. Opposition to Malaysia therefore does not only serve Sukarno's interests but also those of his creditors whom he does not wish to displease, at least for the present.

In actuality, it is very difficult for Indonesia not to oppose Malaysia. Malaysia is the living example of what the Indonesian leaders have repeatedly proclaimed as unattainable or unsuitable in a South-east Asian context. The liberal parliamentary democracy of Malaysia is working successfully while Indonesia has to resort to guided democracy. Federalism has been considered as unsuitable by Indonesia and yet Malaysia has adopted a federal type of government. Malaysia's liberal economic policy has brought prosperity and progress to this country; whilst Indonesia's guided economy has only brought poverty and hunger to that country. Then, Indonesia believed that it would be a sin to co-operate with its ex-colonial power. On the other hand, Malaysia has not severed relations with its ex-colonial power; instead, has continued co-operation to the mutual advantage of both. Thus one finds that on all counts the Indonesian leaders would find it most difficult to justify their position *vis-à-vis* the Indonesian people unless they resort to illogical and extreme measures.

With regard to the Philippines, its concern for the adverse role that could possibly be played by the Chinese in Malaysia seems to lack perspective. It is worth noting that under the proposed Malaysian constitution, Sabah and Sarawak would have special powers to regulate immigration into their territories. At present, there are less than half a million people of Chinese origin in the two areas. This appears to me to be a lesser source of danger than the flourishing Indonesian Communist Party which has a following of more than five million.[39] The present anti-communist policy of the Malayan government should provide an assurance to the Philippines.

But whatever is the argument for or against Malaysia, the fact remains that it has been a source of friction between Malaya, Indonesia and the Philippines, resulting in the building up of tension in the South-east Asian area. Indonesia's confrontation policy, President Sukarno's sabre-rattling and President Macapagal's assertion that Malaysia is a neocolonialist move and a threat to the Philippines' security have jeopardised amicable relations in this area. However, the meeting between the officials of the Foreign Offices of the Philippines, Indonesia and Malaya in Manila in June 1963 and the somewhat unexpected 'summit' between Sukarno and Tengku Abdul Rahman in Tokyo in May–June had reduced the tension between Indonesia and Malaya. The Tokyo 'summit' seemed to reveal that Indonesia was not opposed to the concept of Malaysia as such but to the way it was introduced.[40]

Though Indonesia has not dropped its opposition to Malaysia, yet the understanding arrived at in Tokyo certainly helped to create a more amicable atmosphere for the meeting of the foreign ministers of the three countries in Manila. At the Manila meeting, held from June 7 to 11, 1963, accord seemed to have been obtained. Indonesia and the Philippines expressed their readiness to 'welcome the formation of Malaysia provided the support of the people of the Borneo territories is ascertained by an independent and impartial authority, the Secretary-General of the United Nations, or his representative'.[41] Malaya then undertook to consult the British and the Borneo governments with a view to meeting the wishes of Indonesia and the Philippines. The foreign ministers' conference was to prepare the way for a summit meeting between the heads of states of the three countries.

Meanwhile, the different governments involved in the formation of Malaysia proceeded with their consultation and negotiation, in preparation for the final meeting in London where an agreement was to be signed. Difficulties arose between Malaya and Singapore, and between Malaya and Brunei. The Malaya-Singapore problems were sufficiently solved as to enable them to proceed to

London for further talks; but, with regard to Brunei, negotiation broke down. Apparently it was due to the question of revenues from oil and local taxation. Despite this breakdown, however, a Brunei delegation also went to London.

More meetings were held in London. Through many gruelling sessions, the representatives of the governments concerned managed to find a compromise solution to the Singapore problems. In the case of Brunei, it appears that the keen desire of the different delegations to reach a settlement was not equally shared by that of Brunei. Malaya conceded on almost every point at issue except on the question of precedence for the sultan of Brunei *vis-à-vis* his eligibility to become the Yang di-Pertuan Agong (Paramount Ruler).[42] In this particular issue the Malayan delegation was not in the position to give its consent since decision on such matters could only be made by the Conference of Rulers.[43]

It may be noted that the prime minister of the Federation of Malaya had, during the Malaya-Brunei negotiations in Kuala Lumpur, suggested to the sultan of Brunei that the question of his precedence be referred to the Conference of Rulers. The sultan did not agree to it.[44] It was therefore a great disappointment to many when Brunei decided not to join Malaysia on the scheduled date, i.e. August 31, 1963. The other fourteen states, however, signed the Malaysia Agreement.

The refusal of Brunei to be a member state of Malaysia would not only be to Brunei's own disadvantage but could also provide the communists with the opportunity to establish a beachhead in this region. Brunei would now have to depend on Britain to a much greater extent. The 'colonial' nature of Brunei would become more pronounced. As it stands, Brunei has to move at a much faster pace in order not to be left too far behind the political progress of its neighbours, particularly that of Sarawak and Sabah. Thus Brunei could provide the communists with the opportunity of camouflaging their real intentions by identifying themselves with genuine anti-colonial and nationalist forces struggling for the independence of Brunei.

It is difficult to imagine that the Brunei leaders have not foreseen these rather grim possibilities. After all, the Azahari rebellion could certainly serve as a pointer. One would have thought that the incessant anti-colonial, anti-imperialist, and anti-neocolonialist pronouncements of the Indonesian leaders would have been taken as a warning against any attempt to maintain the *status quo* or even to adopt a 'less haste more speed' attitude. Also, apart from the issue on precedence, one could perhaps note that the hardening of attitude of Brunei appears to have coincided somewhat with the reports of the new discovery of oil deposits off Seria.[45]

The signing of the Malaysia Agreement in London by the representatives of Malaya, Sabah, Sarawak and Singapore on July 9, 1963, evoked strong criticism from Indonesia and to a lesser degree from the Philippines. The two countries considered it premature for Malaya to agree to sign the Malaysia Agreement as it would anticipate the summit meeting between the three countries. It did appear that the meeting between the heads of governments of Malaya, the Philippines and Indonesia would not be able to revive the cordial atmosphere permeating the foreign ministers' meeting, though a kind of working arrangement on the basis of agreeing to disagree could probably be worked out.

Malaysia has not become, and is unlikely to be, a major international issue, though it did threaten to break Malayan-Indonesian relations and, to a lesser degree, the existence of ASA—Association of South-east Asia, comprising Thailand, the Philippines and Malaya. However, the alignment of forces for and against Malaysia is already defined. Excluding the Philippines and Indonesia, the anti-communists and many of the non-aligned countries support Malaysia,[46] while the communists are opposed to it. The arguments put forward by the supporters of Malaysia have already been discussed. Some of them view it from the economic aspect, i.e. the creation of a more viable economic unit, some from the security angle—a bulwark against communist expansion in South-east Asia—, while others consider Malaysia as a move for colonial freedom. These factors do, of course, overlap.

The United Nations is also favourably disposed towards Malaysia.

The communists consider Malaysia as a form of neocolonialism in which Britain is using Malaya 'to suppress the democratic and patriotic movements of the peoples in these five countries which aim at the attainment of genuine national independence and freedom from imperialism' and that Malaysia 'will strengthen the position of the imperialists in South-east Asia in implementing their SEATO activities which are also aimed against Indonesia'.[47] The Indonesian Communist Party's criteria for independence certainly differ from the generally accepted standards, for it still considers Malaya as not independent. It would be repetitive to argue the case against the neocolonialist allegation. Even in relation to SEATO, it has been shown that the pre-Malaysian position would be worse for Indonesia. Malaysia has no treaty relations with SEATO and the movements of British and Commonwealth forces in Malaysia is under the control of the Malaysian and British governments. To invoke any item in the Malaya-Britain defence treaty requires the agreement of the two governments. But it is not too remote to think that the interests of Malaysia may, on occasions, coincide with the aims and objectives of SEATO. National interest is the fundamental basis of foreign policy.*

---

* Written in July 1963.

26

Malaysia and the Commonwealth: An Inquiry into the Nature of Commonwealth Ties

ROBIN W. WINKS

When Malaya became independent on August 31, 1957, it became a member of the Commonwealth of Nations[1] by virtue of having provided for such membership in its Constitution, and through the assent of the other members of the Commonwealth. The preamble to this document, the Federation of Malaya Agreement, 1957, declared that 'Her [Britannic] Majesty and their Highnesses [the Rulers of Malaya] and the . . . Ruling Chiefs have agreed that the said Federation should become an independent country within the Commonwealth with the Constitution hereinafter provided for.'[2] Leaving the Commonwealth thus requires a constitutional amendment.

While there was some talk in Malaya before 1957 of shaking off Commonwealth ties after independence, and while certain political leaders, perhaps most notably Onn bin Ja'afar and Dato' Sir Tan Cheng-Lock, publicly reserved judgement on the question of membership during the pre-independence period, there was no real public opposition of an organised kind.[3] The parting with the British was a friendly one for most, a parting of form rather than substance, and there seemed to be no sufficiently good reason for renouncing the Commonwealth mantle which could be so easily, because automatically, assumed. Commonwealth membership cost nothing and demanded little; it was based on co-operation and consultation; and if it did not provide Malaya with a circle of thoroughly committed friendly nations, it at least provided a forum in which the new nation could demand and would receive attention. Caught in the midst of the Emergency, and situated in a rapidly changing, unstable area of the world, Malaya had good reason to let nature, evolution and British constitutional practice take their course.

This automatic and natural tie with the Commonwealth has been strengthened since independence, so that today the political elites—if not the people—of Malaya (and to a lesser extent, of the Borneo territories and, lesser still, of Singapore) feel a strong bond with 'the Commonwealth idea'. This bond, and a particular (and proper) conception of this idea, were evident when the Malayan prime minister, Tengku Abdul Rahman, actively worked to oust the then Union of South Africa from the Commonwealth at the Prime Ministers' Conferences in 1960 and 1961 because of South Africa's *apartheid* policy, which all Asian and most African members found insulting to themselves and to their idea of the Commonwealth. And it was the prime minister and his deputy who led all attempts in Malaya to establish more firmly the idea of the Commonwealth at the local level. The prime minister made frequent public references to 'the intimate friendship and accord which come about so naturally between the member countries of the Commonwealth', and he promised that 'Malaya and its people will do all they can to make the Commonwealth a living force. . . .'[4] The Tengku initiated the opening of a branch of the Royal Commonwealth Society in Kuala Lumpur and arranged for the secretary-general of the society to visit Malaya, and he has seen to it that the new Federation makes full use of the machinery for advice and consultation within the Commonwealth.[5]

The Tengku has good reason to promote the Commonwealth tie, for on the whole the people of Malaysia seem to have comparatively little knowledge of, or interest in, the Commonwealth beyond a rather uninformed awareness of the fact of membership itself. Although the same might well be said for most member nations, there are particularly urgent reasons why Malaysia must take steps to inform its populace of the nature of the Commonwealth. Not the least of these reasons is the fact that nearly sixty per cent of the population of Malaysia is under twenty-one years of age. This youthful group will remember comparatively little of the British period of Malaysian history, and while they can afford to be less anti-British than the previous generation, which participated in the post-war wave of nationalism in Malaya, they also will have less reason to remember the Emergency, which helped align Malaya with the anti-communist Commonwealth nations, and less regard for many of the ties that link their elders to the Commonwealth. Then, too, the incorporation of Singapore into Malaysia has raised the Chinese proportion of the population to nearly half: Malays, having no other homeland, may reasonably be expected to be interested in the Commonwealth, and Indians doubly so, since either of their loyalties represents a Commonwealth tie. But the Chinese, if they look to China or even to a general Nanyang sentiment, look away from the Commonwealth. To foster a stronger sense of Malayan nationhood, the Malay-dominated government of the Federation promotes the use of Malay as the national language, and to the degree that this program succeeds, English will be endangered as the lingua franca of the region. The decline of English may not occur, but if it does one of the most vital of ties to the Commonwealth will have been weakened.

The Malayan Prime Minister, although committed to the promotion of Malay as the *Bahasa Kebangsaan*, seems well aware of the dangers. The present writer asked the Tengku, in a lengthy interview in February 1963, which of the ties usually cited—common law, parliamentary government, the English language, a common historical experience as ex-dependencies of Britain, the Queen, or links of trade and finance—most closely bound Malaya to the Commonwealth? The reply, unhesitatingly but thoughtfully given, was 'the English language'. However, when officials in the High Commissioners' offices of Canada, Australia, New Zealand, India, and the United Kingdom, as well as officers of the British Council, were interviewed, all equally unhesitatingly (and perhaps less thoughtfully) replied 'trade'. The suggestion was made by two of these officers that many Malayan politicians were not genuinely interested in the Commonwealth but declared themselves so because it was politic to follow the Prime Minister's lead, and one high official was of the opinion that interest in the Commonwealth was limited to the chief minister and his deputy, and to higher ranking military officers who worked with the Commonwealth Strategic Reserve forces in Malaya.

In any case, whatever the ties that bind might be, there is little evidence that the people of Malaysia are, as a nation, aware of them, and there is virtually no evidence that anything is being done to inform the new generation of the nature of these ties. An examination of back files of sixteen secondary school annuals, of all known literary and historical journals, and of a year's run of English-language newspapers in Kuala Lumpur, Singapore, Penang, Ipoh and Jesselton, as well as of student publications from Malaysia's three universities, revealed not a single student article on the Commonwealth, and very few newspaper articles except for those dealing with the Common Market. Since students usually write what they have been encouraged to write, one must conclude that little is done in the schools to promote Commonwealth awareness. Instruction is offered in English, and in Imperial and Commonwealth history, but seldom in terms of the recent Commonwealth. An examination of the texts most commonly used in Malaysian schools shows that all but two are, in effect, of pre-independence vintage, and all place heavy emphasis on the growth of the Empire and give little attention to recent developments relating to the Commonwealth.[6] A year's file of the Singapore *Radio Weekly* shows no information program devoted to the Commonwealth, except for those broadcast by the BBC's General Overseas Service.

Informational and propaganda measures about the Commonwealth were being taken by the government of the United Kingdom, and British non-governmental organisations were working towards the same ends. But it is significant that in 1963, and excepting the Tengku's personal efforts, no Malaysian-based non-commercial bodies seemed interested in explaining the nature of the Commonwealth to Malaysians. In 1962, in the so-called Cobbold Report on attitudes towards the Malaysian federation in Sabah and Sarawak, the Commission of Inquiry wrote of the latter: 'We were made aware of the high respect and affection in which Her Majesty the Queen is held, more especially among native populations in the interior. There was genuine gratification that the Commonwealth links would be maintained with Malaysia.'[7] But gratification does not necessarily denote understanding.

At present most information on the nature of the Commonwealth relationship comes from London, from the several ministerial departments concerned, from the Central Office of Information, and from many non-governmental or extra-governmental bodies. The British government is the only one that promotes in any effective way the collective whole of the Commonwealth as a viable institution. Malaysia is bound to the United Kingdom and the Commonwealth by many strands, some major and most minor. The latter range from the personal visits of British statesmen to Malaysia, to the Queen's annual message to the Commonwealth, traditionally broadcast each Christmas.[8] Annual conferences draw interest groups together: Malaya has been represented regularly at conferences of Commonwealth Auditors, of Commonwealth and British Chambers of Commerce, of the Commonwealth Press Union, of Commonwealth Parliamentarians, and many others. Malaysia sends teams to the Commonwealth Games and displays to the Commonwealth Institute in London, receives members from the Voluntary Service Overseas group (the British original of the US 'Peace Corps') and provides scholarly speakers for the Royal Society. Malayan students study in Britain and until 1963 the Federation government maintained two teachers' training colleges in England. A Malayan Art Society of Britain contrasts at the unofficial level with the Commonwealth Advisory Committee on Defence Science at the official. The Royal Overseas League, Malaysia's membership of the Commonwealth Telecommunications Board, and the prospect of a finished cable system connecting Malaysia to Britain by 1965, all literally or figuratively serve to bind Malaysia into the Commonwealth.[9]

'CIRCUMSTANTIAL' TIES

But what, if any, are the non-institutional, underlying ties of which this host of conferences, organisations, and clubs may be taken as symptoms or symbols? What are the ties of education, of trade, of defence, of political form, not only as a whole but in terms of specific ties with specific members, that constitute the Commonwealth of Nations? And what are the forces, within Malaysia and without, that serve to loosen these ties?

The least evident, but possibly most important, ties between Malaysia and the Commonwealth are those which we may label 'circumstantial'. These arise from conditions largely unique to Malaysia and therefore not applicable to a discussion of the Commonwealth as a whole. Five such factors of circumstance are of particular note.

1. The Commonwealth has many racial tensions within it: Sinhalese-Tamil in Ceylon, Fijian-Indian in Fiji, Arab-African in Zanzibar, Greek-Turk in Cyprus French- and Anglo-Canadian in Canada, Hausa-Ibo-Yoruba in Nigeria, and Malay-Chinese-Indian in Malaysia. The plural nature of Malaysian society makes acceptance of the Commonwealth, itself a plural society, easier and also more practical, since the Commonwealth provides one means for the exchange of information on the easing of interethnic tensions. Although the point is controversial, it can be argued that the main steps towards inter-racial harmony in Malaysia were taken during the British period and that the present delicate balance between the groups depends upon a continued use of procedures established by the British. (Others would argue that the British increased racial tensions by a 'divide-and-rule' policy and by importing Indian labourers for the rubber plantations.)

2. Malaysians may also find other Commonwealth nations easier to understand than do either the affluent, western members or the poorer Eastern members, for Malaysia has the highest *per capita* income in Asia, after Japan, is experiencing a considerable boom based on western conceptions of production, and is more 'westernised' than any other Asian member. But Malaysia is an Asian nation, capable of understanding its fellow Asian members more readily than its fellow western and Pacific members. The Malaysian prime minister, when interviewed by the present writer, declared that he felt closer to and understood better the United Kingdom or Australia, and certainly Pakistan, than the African states, which seemed less culturally and economically advanced.

3. Malaysia, as the only elective monarchy in the Commonwealth, stands midway between the monarchical members and the republican members; not itself a Crown Dominion (as New Zealand is, for example), it is nevertheless able to understand the mystique of monarchy.

379

4. Malaysians (unlike other Commonwealth members except those African states adjacent to units of the French Community) have seen a local attempt at an imposed type of commonwealth relationship fail. In 1949 the Dutch forced the then United States of Indonesia to accept membership in a Dutch-Indonesian union which was nothing more than an attempt to salvage an empire by creating a commonwealth through 'administrative fiat, rather than by evolutionary development'.[10] Malaysians were in a position to see that, however unjustified British imperialism may or may not have been, it was a less harmful variety than French, Portuguese or Dutch imperialism, and that the Commonwealth had the virtue of being open-ended, voluntary in membership, variable under the impact of Asian leadership (the decision to include republics having been made at India's request), and the product of organic developments. The Commonwealth permits new countries to learn new techniques gradually, and it decreases diplomatic costs for new nations since few diplomatic appointments need be made or few legations opened initially, the Commonwealth High Commissioners and British embassies and legations handling such matters.

5. The circumstance of a very youthful population, with little memory of 'the days of the British raj', and the circumstance of a western-educated leadership group, although hardly unique, enter into any calculation of the nature of the Commonwealth tie. A western-educated leadership generally wishes to initiate large-scale economic and social changes, changes that produce cultural variations and move a nation in the direction of a more highly developed technology. Where emphasis is placed on technological skills, faces will continue to be turned towards the West (although in the future communist China may well be in a position to play the role of technological leader).[11]

Any organisation or grouping which is favoured by these circumstances may expect a friendly hearing from Malaysia. For this reason, Malaysia is a member of several international groups and has itself been among the founders of others. While some might remark that the Tengku, who has taken the lead in obtaining Malayan membership in the United Nations, in ECAFE (the European Commission for Asia and the Far East), in the Colombo Plan, in ASAS (the Association of South-east Asian States), and in creating Malaysia, is a kind of international Rotarian, a joiner, a believer in greater safety through greater memberships, one can also point out that where the circumstances do not favour such membership —as in the case of SEATO (the South-east Asia Treaty Organisation)—Malaysia has not joined. The Tengku's purpose, under the thrust of circumstances, is to create what a political scientist, Karl W. Deutsch, would call a 'security community', and membership in SEATO might well jeopardise such a community, while membership in the Commonwealth, by creating a web of mutually responsive security measures, is well calculated at present to serve Malaysia's ends.

DEFENCE TIES

Malaya's refusal to join SEATO is evidence that it regarded the Commonwealth ties, and the specific defence agreements and measures that are wholly within the Commonwealth, as sufficient for the moment. Although involving fellow Commonwealth members, SEATO receives its chief motive power from outside the Commonwealth, and it represents the entry into the South-east Asian power balance of a nation not previously present: the United States. For this reason the Malayan prime minister could, in 1960, find SEATO 'ineffective, negative, outmoded and under the stigma of Western domination'[12] without being either anti-American or anti- any other SEATO member.

Still, rhetoric and the record sometimes do not coincide. The Anglo-Malayan defence treaty of 1957, and the presence of a Commonwealth Strategic Reserve force in Malaya, made up of troops from three SEATO members, Britain, Australia, and New Zealand (together with British naval units at Singapore), were to provide for the defence of the Malaysian area.[13] At the time of the Brunei rebellion, additional troops were rushed from the United Kingdom. During the Emergency Commonwealth troops stationed in Malaya were used to combat communist terrorists. But these Commonwealth forces in Malaya cannot be used to fulfil members' SEATO commitments, although they may be redeployed to SEATO bases. The Borneo territories were included in 1949 in the ANZAM area of co-ordinated defence planning between Australia, New Zealand and the United Kingdom.[14]

This writer finds it difficult to avoid evidence of *de facto* Malayan participation in SEATO. One feels that a child psychologist, with his concept of 'parallel play', would recognise the situation. Two children may sit side by side, playing the same game, perfectly aware that it is the same game, quite content and without playing directly together. SEATO goals were served by the war on the terrorists, and redeployment of Commonwealth troops to SEATO bases may be achieved so quickly as virtually to make Malaysia a staging area for SEATO operations. Of course, with the incorporation of the more strongly neutralist, left-wing Singapore, and the independence within Malaysia of the Borneo territories, the nature of these defensive ties to Commonwealth members, as well as Malaysian attitudes towards SEATO, have been altered, especially as a result of Indonesia's policy of 'confrontation'. Any tendency to lessen the defensive ties for ideological reasons, however, was offset in 1963, at least, by continued worry over relations with Indonesia, over Brunei, and over a Philippine claim to Sabah.[15] The Commonwealth troops in Malaysia will remain a very real tie to the Commonwealth of Nations, as will the Anglo-Malayan Defence Agreement, however ambiguously these arrangements may interlock with Commonwealth members' obligations.

CONSTITUTIONAL TIES

Even if and when changing power situations throughout the world modify the defensive ties out of recognition, Malaysia will have ties of a constitutional nature to the Commonwealth. Although an elective monarchy, Malaysia is governed by the parliamentary democratic system inherited from Britain, is administered by cabinet government, and draws its laws (outside questions of religion) from the great reservoir of English common law: the basis of the judiciary system in every Commonwealth nation except Ceylon. In addition, Articles 24, 155, and 160 of the Malayan constitution stated that a citizen of Malaya (and of Singapore) is a Commonwealth citizen under the law of the United Kingdom, in common with citizens of other Commonwealth countries. The constitution was amended in 1962 to clarify the meaning of Commonwealth, so that 'part of the Commonwealth' means 'any Commonwealth country, any colony, protectorate or protected state, or any other territory administered by the Government of any Commonwealth country'. However, this does not impair the Federation's control over entry of Commonwealth citizens.[16]

One must not assume that parliamentary forms, cabinet government or the common law are indissoluble ties to the Commonwealth, especially since the Malayan constitution, like that of Pakistan and India (although by the operation of different principles), is an autochthonous one: a constitution which may be considered to have 'sprung from the land itself'.[17] Parliamentary forms, for example, have evolved from a common English root, but the evolution has taken different courses in different countries. Privileges, precedents and practices which are well established in the British House of Commons do not necessarily apply in other Commonwealth legislatures, unless established by the constitution or assumed by later legislation. Certainly parliamentary government may be practised in different ways in different countries, just as federalism has evolved in a different manner or as the conception of collective ministerial responsibility may be applied differently. That such is the case in Malaysia is indicated by the proceedings of the Legislative Assembly of the State of Singapore, in 1960, to hold one of its members in contempt of Parliament; by the fact that migration between units of the Federation of Malaysia is restricted; or by the circumstances under which Aziz bin Ishak, the minister of Agriculture and Co-operatives, left the Malayan cabinet towards the end of 1962.[18] Ties of law, form and precedent are real, but they must not be sentimentalised or overemphasised.[19]

CULTURAL TIES

Cultural links with the western members of the Commonwealth are obvious but difficult to assess. English dress and, unfortunately, food, and English amusements (especially soccer and cricket) are much in evidence, and an English system of education and the use of the English language as the medium of social mobility and international commercial exchange are of lasting significance. The 1957 Constitution provided for the retention of English for ten years as the official language, and its replacement by Malay after that date, but there has been a growing demand for English instruction even as the *Bahasa Kebangsaan* also grows in use. The British Council actively promotes the English language, and membership in its libraries in Kuala Lumpur, Singapore and Penang is growing. Use, especially of technical manuals, is increasing even faster than membership: the Kuala Lumpur library, with 28,000 volumes, circulated 100,000 books in 1960, 130,000 in 1961, and 160,000 in 1962, while membership grew from ten to twelve thousand. The Commonwealth Education Bureau, the English-Speaking Union, the Books for the Commonwealth Scheme started by the Countess of Ranfurly in 1959 to make English books available in book-poor countries, membership on the part of Nanyang University, the University of Malaya and the University of Singapore in the Association of Universities of the British Commonwealth, and the fact that the universities of Singapore and Malaya draw most of their staff from Commonwealth countries, and that most higher degrees held by staff members are from universities in the United Kingdom—all add to the educational ties between Britain and Malaysia. Not only have thousands of Malaysian students studied in Britain, but also thousands more who have not been to Britain have used British texts in their classrooms.[20]

Whether the operation of such educational forces is entirely calculated to strengthen Commonwealth ties is, however, open to question. Malaysian students who have studied abroad often find readjustment to Malaysian society difficult. Trained in skills which they cannot always use in Malaysia, and schooled in concepts which may be of little use in rural areas, for example, these students may find that their overseas experience is not valid for Malaysian conditions.[21]

These ties of security, law, governmental practice, language and education are real but tenuous, since many of them can make little impression at the local village level. The cultural similarities that link Malaysia with the western members of the Commonwealth are largely urban similarities, and they are more than offset by the continuing vitality of the local and indigenous cultures. So that these ties to the Commonwealth may be strengthened, major efforts of an educational, informational and propaganda nature must be undertaken by all of the parties, governmental and private, concerned with fostering them.

PROMOTING COMMONWEALTH RELATIONS

There is, therefore, a considerable body of literature calculated to inform

Malaysians of the nature of the Commonwealth, and of the benefits they receive from membership. Much of this literature is informational only, intended to give the reader a feeling of pride in belonging to a particular group. A psychologist might well expect to find evidences of national 'role-taking' in such literature, and in the past the United Kingdom often used organic metaphors borrowed from biology, especially in references to 'the Mother Country'. Such metaphors are not popular in Asia, however, since Britain was not a Mother, organically or culturally, to the new national governments of Malaya, India, Pakistan and Ceylon. More often one finds the literature emanating from the United Kingdom today referring to Britain as the 'senior partner' of the Commonwealth. This metaphor, borrowed as it is from the world of business, is less objectionable and has, one might conclude, the virtue of an unintended near accuracy, since many of the major ties binding Asian members to the Commonwealth are economic.

Whatever metaphor is chosen, one feels that the Commonwealth is bound together, to the extent that it is bound, only with the aid of the many printing presses that produce the journals, general and specialist, which make it their business to promote a Commonwealth image. That most of this literature comes from the United Kingdom is natural. The British Information Service issues a fortnightly digest, *Commonwealth Facts and Figures*, which contains a regular section on 'Malayan Affairs in Britain', locally printed in Kuala Lumpur. The Service also issues *Commonwealth Survey*, a fortnightly, and most important, *Commonwealth Today*, an undated monthly illustrated magazine which, in Malaysia, appears in Chinese and Malay (*Commonwealth Hari Ini*) as well as in English. All are available for free distribution and are to be found in most schools and rest-houses in the Federation.[22]

There also are numerous semi-official and private journals that foster the Commonwealth tie, and some that do not.[23] Of particular interest is the monthly journal of the British Association of Malaya. Ably edited, *Malaya* is a link between those 'Europeans' or 'expatriates', as they are called in Malaysia, who have returned to Britain and those who remain in the Federation. Much of the magazine reads like an 'old boys' annual, with news of marriages, promotions and sales, directed to Britons 'at home'. It is not blimpish and does its job well, but its job is not apparently to promote Commonwealth awareness, least of all in non-British Malayans.

Perhaps it is natural that the burden of promoting the Commonwealth idea among educated Malaysians falls most heavily on the United Kingdom, just as the burden of the entire Civil List falls on Britain. Other Commonwealth members promote information media and have their own instruments of propaganda, but the content of such propaganda is almost always bi- rather than multilateral. Australian (and Canadian or New Zealand) publications in Malaysia, both governmental and commercial, do virtually nothing to further the idea of Australian-Malaysian relations as an aspect of a broader Commonwealth tie, but concentrate on the one-to-one relationship between the two nations as sovereign peoples. The result is that the United Kingdom alone must propagate the idea of the whole, while the other individual members are free to promote, not the Commonwealth, but their own specific relationship with Malaysia. In this sense Australian, New Zealand and Canadian propaganda, and even aid, in Malaysia cannot truly be reckoned among the means by which a general Commonwealth consciousness may be created. New Zealand's attempts at self-promotion in Malaysia, for example, have been notably successful, but the reward appears to be increased Malayan-New Zealand friendship and not increased Malaysian-Commonwealth awareness. These Commonwealth members that take from Britain but do not give, in terms of the nature of their support in Malaysia for the Commonwealth idea, no doubt would reply that their efforts to strengthen their bonds with Malaysia automatically strengthen the Commonwealth. But the present writer, on the basis of discussion with many Malaysian students, politicians, business and professional men, must conclude that there is no evidence to support this defence. When a Malaysian thinks of Australia, he thinks of the Commonwealth of Australia, not of the Commonwealth of Nations.

MALAYSIA'S INTER-COMMONWEALTH RELATIONS

1. New Zealand

In terms of specific national promotion projects in Malaysia, stemming from Commonwealth membership, New Zealand must be judged by far the most successful. Similar in size to Malaya and Singapore, well known for a policy of racial acceptance of its indigenous Maori, and clearly not in a position either strategically or economically to be a 'neocolonial power', New Zealand begins its relationship with none of the disadvantages of Canada, so distant and so large, or of Australia, with its immigration policy which, though no more restrictive than New Zealand's, is so ineptly named. In addition, New Zealand has implemented its program of aid within the Colombo Plan and its general informational campaign with great good sense. Its diplomatists in Malaya have been well chosen, and the fact that New Zealand sent a Maori, Colonel C. M. Bennett, to Malaya as High Commissioner showed good judgement. Quite apart from his own abilities, the fact that New Zealand could entrust such a post to a non-European was taken as evidence in Malaya of racial harmony in New Zealand. New Zealand's troops in Malaya also have won a particularly good reputation.

New Zealand has achieved more visual (and propaganda) impact with its money than other Commonwealth (or Colombo Plan) nations. New Zealand's capital grants have centred around three projects: building a civil service training centre in Kuala Lumpur, financing buildings and equipment for the School of Agriculture at the University of Malaya, and part-financing of 'kampong New Zealand'. Each project was finished on time, with no strings attached, to local satisfaction. Whether by design or accident, each project is visually prominent and is completely identified with New Zealand. In addition, the Dominion has accepted many students under the Colombo Plan, publishes a special fortnightly *New Zealand Newsletter* in Kuala Lumpur which is by far the best prepared of such publications issued by Commonwealth offices in Malaysia; and the High Commissioner's office distributes numerous brochures and maps, including Malay and Chinese translations. It is not surprising, therefore, that the number of inquiries received at the High Commissioner's office for information on New Zealand showed a fifty per cent increase in 1962 over 1961.[24] These ties are, of course, confirmed and strengthened by a trade pact signed in 1960 and by increasing New Zealand consumption of Malaysian rubber, tin, and pineapple.[25]

In contrast to New Zealand, Canada and Australia have fared less well in their information and propaganda activities, although the Canadian program, at least, must be considered a moderate success.

2. *Canada*

Canada receives frequent and favourable mention in the Malaysian English-language press, and there is an increasing amount of trade between the two countries, as well as some Canadian investment in Malaysia. The substantial trade in rubber, tin and pineapple helps tie the two countries together. Canada has provided considerable aid to Malaysian development, including equipment for the Engineering School at the University of Malaya, expert advice for surveying an east-west road across Malaya near the Thai border, and teaching assistance. Malaysian interest in Canada also has quickened, if statistics relating to the number of pieces of informative literature distributed from the High Commissioner's office in Kuala Lumpur are reliable: in 1959, 1,004 pieces; in 1960, 2,759; in 1961, 3,756; and in 1962, 2,920 in the first three quarters.[26] This material is well prepared, and special sets are available for headmasters. However, none of the material is in Malay or Chinese.

Canada's attempts to become better known in Malaysia are further limited by the requirement imposed by the Canadian government on Colombo Plan administrators that aid be primarily in terms of technical skills and equipment purchased in Canada.[27] But this restrictive requirement is somewhat offset by the fact that Canada's trade connections reach well back into the century, a Trade

Commissioner for Canada having been appointed to Singapore as early as 1921, and by cultural ties. Interestingly enough, the Federation's national anthem, 'Malaysia Forever', was written by a visiting Canadian.

3. *Australia*

Australia is in a special position. This position is not special in the same sense that the more emotional propagandists for the Commonwealth would have us believe, nor is it special in quite the way most Australians apparently think or wish. Derek Ingram, in a leading popular book on the Commonwealth, sees an organic tie developing between the two nations.[28] 'The birth of Malaya highlights another happy development in the Commonwealth—the way in which the older countries are beginning to act as uncle to young nephews.' This kind of familial metaphor obscures rather than illumines, for most educated Malaysians have not been slow to ask, What kind of uncle is it that permanently bars his nephew from entry into his home?[29] The special relationship between Malaysia and Australia is based on trade and on mutual responsiveness: both nations need each other if they are to feel strategically secure in a rapidly changing world in which they share Indonesia as a neighbour. This situation would exist whether or not either nation were a member of the Commonwealth.

To the Australian government Malaya and Singapore are key points in a farflung security system. Before the Second World War the Australian tie with Malaya was a flimsy one: the basic pre-Pacific War study of Australian policies in the Far East does not mention Malaya.[30] But the so-called fortress of Singapore was viewed as the pillar of Australian defence. The war demonstrated that Singapore could not be viewed, strategically or militarily, except in a broader Malaysian context. The approach of Malayan independence and the victory of the communist regime in China made apparent the need for thinking in terms of a single defence system for South-east Asia and Australia. In 1949 Australia, New Zealand and the United Kingdom agreed to plan defences jointly in the ANZAM region (which included Malaya and British Borneo), and in 1955 Australian troops were stationed in Malaya.[31]

From the Australian public's point of view, this was the first peace-time basing of troops overseas, but from the Malayan (and the troops') point of view it was not a time of peace, since Malaya was in the midst of the long undeclared war with the Malayan communists which officially lasted from 1948 to 1961. The United Kingdom, Australia and New Zealand supplied troops, and those of Australia were of particular importance, not only in their contribution to the Commonwealth Strategic Reserve but in terms of creating news copy in the traditionally parochial Australian press. Australia became aware of the peninsula behind Singapore through the Emergency and the numerous Australian-written pamphlets, articles and novels inspired by that Emergency.[32] Because Singapore both then and since was a centre of left-wing movements, and because the Alliance government of Malaya seemed conservative and secure, Australia had intensified reasons for giving moral and diplomatic support to this new member of the Commonwealth when it became independent in 1957.[33]

This support continued as ties of trade and mutual defensive need added to the common fear of communism. Indonesia was the catalyst. As Indonesia pressed its case against the Dutch for West New Guinea, or Irian Barat, Australia began to realise that it had a potentially powerful, clearly ambitious and heavily populated nation to the immediate north. Malaya, where the Malays spoke a language very similar to Bahasa Indonesia, and where they adhered to the same muslim religion, and yet where English also was commonly spoken and where British governmental procedures were understood, might well be a bridge to understanding Indonesia.

As Malayan relations with Indonesia deteriorated, especially after the idea of the broadened Federation of Malaysia received British support, Australia went through a period of equivocation. Would it support Malaysia and thus offend Indonesia? Would it simply remain silent on the issue, in the hope that it could remain neutral? For many months Australia seemed to have chosen the latter course, although towards the end of 1962 the government expressed its general sympathy with the Malaysian idea if it were not to prove unduly disruptive in South-east Asia. But as it became increasingly clear that the United Kingdom was adamant on Malaysia, and that Malaya expected Australia's moral support, and as talk of 'appeasement' of Indonesia was bruited in Canberra, the Menzies government apparently decided to clear the air. Australia had withheld formal support because, in case Malaysian federation did not eventuate, it wished to avoid needless offence to Indonesia. In March 1963 the British Commissioner for South-east Asia, Lord Selkirk, conferred with the Australian prime minister, Robert Menzies, to make it clear that Britain would not back away from the plan despite Indonesian and Philippine objections. British pressure, a changing Australian conception of its own national self-interest, growing fears of communist influence in Indonesia, concern for Australian New Guinea, and perhaps the ties of the Commonwealth relationship combined to varying degrees to lead to an announcement on March 6 of limited Australian support for Malaysia. At the same time the flagship and half the strength of the Royal Australian Navy set out for Malayan waters to reinforce the Commonwealth Strategic Reserve.

Australian support remained without clear definition, however, as was shown less than a week later when the Malayan prime minister declared at a public meeting in Malacca that Australia would defend Malaya in case of war with Indonesia. The Australian government refused to comment on this announcement, but it obviously was embarrassed. A. A. Calwell, leader of the opposition Labour Party, promptly stated that he and his party opposed any commitment of this nature. The Malayan prime minister in turn publicly apologised for his remark, changing his phrase to the ambiguous statement that Australia, as a member of the Commonwealth, 'would rally to our help'. But an observer in either Malaysia or Australia would have continued to find it difficult to understand exactly what commitments Australia felt it had towards Malaysia. A flurry of generally well-informed articles in Australian periodicals discussed Malaysia (although most Australian newspapers seemed ill-informed in contrast), and once again mutual awareness between the two nations was increased by a matter of strategic and military importance.[34] Again, however, any Commonwealth component to this awareness seemed slight; even if neither country were a member of the Commonwealth, relations probably would have developed in a similar pattern.

In any case, the relationship between Australia and Malaysia did not differ from that between Malaysia and Canada or New Zealand, in that Australia's information outlets were intended to promote the interests of Australia rather than of the broader entity to which it belonged.[35] That Australia does value a favourable image in Malaysia is apparent from the quality and number of publications distributed throughout Malaysia by both its High Commissioner and its Trade Commissioner. The latter issues a well-prepared monthly journal, *Austral News*, which is distributed freely, while the former supplies booklets and posters in Malay and Chinese as well as English. An Assistant Trade Commissioner in Singapore has a separate staff, including a Trade Publicity Officer. From Canberra have come no less than seven different newsletters, including one for children. Numerous film strips are available; Radio Australia broadcasts in English and Mandarin to the whole of Malaysia; and official exhibitions of contemporary Australian art have been well received in Malaya and Singapore.[36]

In the private sphere ties are becoming closer, although both peoples remain ill-informed about each other. The *Bulletin* of Sydney, once a staunch advocate of white supremacy, is now selling in Malaysia and shows a generally liberal face to South-east Asian readers on the subjects about which they care most. Christian missionary activity, particularly in Borneo, continues.[37] Most productive of all is the steady flow of Malaysian students into Australian secondary schools and universities. At March 31, 1962, there were 5,700 Malaysian students in Australia; well over half of these were university students. Australia thus provides university education for as many students as are at present enrolled in the University of Malaya itself. Thirteen per cent of the total number of Colombo Plan students in Australia are from Malaysia, and at certain institutions the percentage is far higher: at Adelaide University, eighty per cent of the Asian students in 1962 were from Malaysia. Malaysians continue to covet an Australian education, especially if they wish to study in the sciences.[38]

A reverse flow was slower to develop in Australian university circles, but such a movement was very much in evidence by 1964. Australian and New Zealand Commonwealth scholars were pursuing higher degrees in Malaysia; Malay was being taught in five of the ten Australian universities; and four of the universities provided instruction in Malaysian (as distinct from Indonesian) history. Significantly, both chairs of history in Malaysia, at Kuala Lumpur and Singapore, were held until 1963 by Australian-born and trained scholars with primary interests in South-east Asia.[39]

The ties of trade, of mutual defensive needs, of scholarly interest, of increasing tourism, of consciously nurtured 'public images', and of education, together with the flow of Australian Colombo Plan aid—of law books, technicians and diesel railway engines—have given some reality to the 'special relationship' between these two Commonwealth members. The two prime ministers have exchanged goodwill visits; more and more Australian businessmen are to be seen and heard on the streets of Kuala Lumpur and Singapore; Australians have invested heavily in Malayan tin; and the flow of precise English from Malayan students continues to be heard in the classrooms of Sydney or Melbourne. But the future of this developing relationship is clouded by the so-called 'White Australia policy'.

Among Asian university students in both Malaysia and Australia, there is general resentment of Australia's immigration policy, and general condemnation of its popular, if somewhat erroneous, title of 'White Australia'. These students will soon be in positions of prominence in Malaysia, for in countries where technical skills and professional training are in scarce supply and high demand, socio-economic pressures lead to rapid promotion. Whether their educational experiences in Australia or New Zealand will lead to their tightening the bonds with the Commonwealth, or whether their memories of the 'White Australia policy' and of the potential it held for direct discrimination against them (even if not applied) will lead to a growing sense of estrangement, cannot be guessed, but many Malaysians will be faced with divided loyalties, with a choice between a people they found to be individually friendly and an experience personally rewarding, and a nation which collectively let them know that the colour of their skin barred them from permanent residence. And what of the vast majority of Malaysians who have not experienced the former and who know only of the latter, especially through sometimes garbled news reports?

The *Times of Indonesia*, in January 1958, observed: 'The Asian is not good enough to become an Australian, but once that principle is grasped and acknowledged, the Australian cannot do enough to show how much Australians like Asians in absentia. The Colombo Plan and other schemes are a kind of blood-money paid by the Australian to silence his guilty conscience towards Asians and Africans.'[40] Malaysians do not publicly echo this statement, but many share its feelings none the less.[41] In Asia the 'White Australia policy' is resented because it is considered to be a racial rather than a cultural restriction; all Asian countries limit immigration, and Malaysia is particularly stringent in this regard, but none do so on the basis of skin colour alone. Australia's reply that Asians are restricted for cultural, not racial, reasons is not accepted, for many Malaysians are more 'westernised' in the sense of having identified themselves with traits of western culture than are some Australians, but they still find entry into Australia barred. The deputy prime minister of Singapore and the *Straits Times* of Kuala Lumpur and Singapore have spoken out against the policy, and even the prime minister of Malaya, who has bigger fish to fry in that Australia's friendship, even if equivocal, is more important at this juncture, has indicated that Australia could be expected to amend its immigration policy 'in good time'. Although the Tengku also observed that 'Australia had no racial prejudices', he did not defend the 'White Australia policy'.[42] And near the end of 1961, when Australia attempted to deport two Malay pearl divers who were working at Darwin under contract, Malaysian newspapers looked on with bitter interest.[43] But Malaysia, itself alert to ethnic issues because of its plural society, and perhaps because of the restraint Commonwealth ties do place on criticisms, has been less vocal than other Asian countries, including Australia's SEATO allies, about 'White Australia'.

4. *Asian Commonwealth Countries*

In addition to such direct ties with the Pacific members of the Commonwealth, Malaysia has also many ties with the Asian members: Pakistan, India and Ceylon. All three maintain High Commissioners' offices in Kuala Lumpur. Ties of religion link Malaysia and Pakistan; ethnic ties link India and Ceylon with Malaysia's substantial Indian and Ceylonese minorities. Ties of interest have come to link India and Malaysia, both having reason to fear Communist China. Ties of mutual concern over the position of tea in the Common Market link Malaysia and Ceylon. Ties based on opposition to anti-Asian racial policies, whether practised in the mild form of Australia or the virulent form of the Republic of South Africa, link all four. An increasing exchange between the universities of the four nations, goodwill visits, a steady rise in tourism, and trade all serve to strengthen this Commonwealth relationship in Asia.[44]

5. *The Colombo Plan*

Among the ties that bind Malaysia to the Commonwealth as a whole may be included the Colombo Plan. The Plan was the creation of Commonwealth members, and while it now includes, both as donors and as recipients of aid, nearly as many non-Commonwealth nations as Commonwealth, and while a major contribution to the Plan is made by the United States, most Malaysians continue to regard the Plan as one of Commonwealth origin and character. This view is, on the whole, a legitimate one, for the original participants in the Plan in 1950 were Australia, Canada, New Zealand, India, Pakistan, Ceylon and the United Kingdom, with Malaya (not then independent), Singapore, North Borneo, Brunei and Sarawak in an associated status. In addition, the Plan was born at a meeting of representatives from Commonwealth governments in a Commonwealth country. However, it was not intended that the Colombo Plan should be exclusive to the Commonwealth, as was indicated by the entry of the United States the following year.

As envisaged in 1950, the heaviest expenditure on programs of national development was to flow into India and Pakistan with the Malaysian area following next in terms of total aid.[45] The Plan originally was limited to six years, but at the 1955 annual meeting of the group's Consultative Committee, held in Singapore, an extension by four years was accepted, and a further extension for five years was agreed to at the Djakarta meeting in 1959. At the same meeting Singapore was made a full member of the Plan; Malaya had become a full member at Saigon in October 1957. When the thirteenth meeting of the Committee was held in Kuala Lumpur, in celebration of the tenth year of the Plan, the full impact of this valuable Commonwealth tie was made abundantly clear to Malaysians by a specially arranged and well attended exhibition.[46]

Colombo Plan aid involves capital projects to improve basic facilities, commodity assistance and counterpart funds, technical assistance, and the exchange of students. One major benefit of the Plan is that it has enabled Asian Commonwealth countries to co-ordinate their development needs and to analyse them more fully than before. In addition, one may suppose that the aid provided by the Plan also has primed the pump in the sense that it has enabled Malaysia to launch projects which, in turn, attract more money. Malaysia has received loans from the United Kingdom government, the American Development Loan Fund, the government of Brunei, and the Commonwealth Development Finance Company, as well as direct Colombo Plan aid from Japan and the United States, outside the Commonwealth.[47]

Such ties, subject to the normal incidence of loosening because of a proud nation's regret over needing aid at all, or because of personal factors, such as the occasions of discrimination, real or imagined, felt by Malaysian students overseas, obviously are important ones. They are practical demonstrations, often at the village level, of the value of Commonwealth membership. While Malaysia would continue to receive such aid even if not a member of the Commonwealth, there is a general assumption that the aid comes more easily and in larger quantities because of membership.

MALAYSIA'S TRADE RELATIONS WITH THE COMMONWEALTH

The Malayan prime minister has pointed to cultural factors, such as the spirit of the Colombo Plan, or the English language, as the most important links to the Commonwealth; representatives of other member nations have singled out trade. As is the case with educational and cultural interchange, there is an entire network of house organs and trade journals calculated to tie Commonwealth countries together. Few mention the Commonwealth as such, preferring to emphasise the direct relationship between Malaysia and the country, agency or company sponsoring the media. As one reads file upon file of such publications, one is more and more convinced that trade (and a commonly shared special relationship with Britain) is of particular—although not prime—importance to the Commonwealth as a whole.

However, in Malaysia's case one must be careful not to overemphasise the Commonwealth as the most important factor in these trading links. Malaysia maintains a considerable trade with Commonwealth members in Asia, for example, and in particular with India. But such trade is to be considered largely in terms of traditional trading patterns dating back to the pre-European centuries, and in terms of the mutuality of Asian interests.[48] The ties of trade are proportionately less important to Malaysia than to many other Commonwealth nations. Sarawak's pre-1963 trade statistics, it is true, show exports mainly to Commonwealth members (although Sabah's chief buyer is Japan), but these members were Singapore and Malaya. Rubber and tin together accounted for sixty-five per cent of Malaya's total exports in 1960, and the proportion of Malaya's total income derived from trade is unusually high, but this rubber and tin by no means flow chiefly to Commonwealth nations. (No statistics are yet available for Malaysia.) Singapore does have good reason to look to the Commonwealth and its various economic systems, especially as relations with Indonesia deteriorate, but as an entrepôt Singapore also looks to its regional affiliations.

In 1961 Singapore took 45·7 per cent of its imports from, and sent fifty per cent of its exports to, members of the sterling bloc; most of this trade was with Commonwealth members. In terms of individual countries, Malaya, the United Kingdom and Sarawak ranked first, third and sixth respectively in terms of total trade. However, with the absorption of Singapore, Malaya and Sarawak into the enlarged Federation of Malaysia this trade has become internal.

Malaya's trade followed a somewhat different pattern, with independent Commonwealth members figuring more prominently in the statistics. In the last month (October 1962) for which detailed commodity and destination figures were available at the time of writing, Malaya sent 21·3 per cent of its exports to Singapore (which, in turn, re-exported them, predominantly to the United

393

States, the United Kingdom, the Soviet Union, West Germany, Japan and Canada, in that order[49]), and the rest to the United States, Japan, the United Kingdom, West Germany, Canada, Italy, Australia and India.[50] As an importer, Malaya bought from the United Kingdom, Singapore, Thailand, Indonesia, Japan, the United States and Australia in descending order. Obviously while Commonwealth trade is important to Malaysia, it is not, with the exception of the exchange with the United Kingdom, really crucial.[51]

Malaysia and Commonwealth Preference

The Commonwealth has been described as 'the world's largest preferential trading organisation'. Commonwealth exports reached £9,000 million annually in 1960 and imports exceeded £10,000 million, or thirty per cent of the world's trade.[52] But the preferential tariff system is widely misunderstood outside the Commonwealth, for popular belief holds that preferential tariffs are mutually given. This is not always the case. West and East African members do not give preferences to Britain, and Britain grants preferences on only half of its imports. The preferential system operates in a manner that is, according to a recent authoritative investigation, 'partial and haphazard'.[53] The most recent comparative statistics for the entire Commonwealth are for 1956; in this pre-independence year Malaya was reversing the normal Commonwealth trend by becoming more rather than less dependent on Britain, largely because of concentration on rubber and tin. None the less, in 1956 Malaya and Singapore were lower in percentage of exports to the United Kingdom than were any independent Commonwealth members, and they were in a median position in terms of trade with other members. In the same year only Canada was lower in terms of total imports from the United Kingdom. Malaya's trade clearly was out of the ordinary, for the normal pattern is for Europe, the United States and Japan to take seventy per cent of Commonwealth exports and to provide sixty-five per cent of the imports. Malayan trade is shifting increasingly to the Commonwealth norm, but the trade pattern remains unique. Geography and commodity composition, rather than Commonwealth ties, account for both the pattern and the shifts within it.

Also not generally understood is the fact that most preferences quoted by Commonwealth countries to the United Kingdom are based on *ad valorem* duties, and that most of the preferences which Britain gives are specific. Thus, a 15 per cent preference to Commonwealth exporters in the 1930s might be a 5 per cent preference in the 1950s. This 'erosion of preference margins', together with changes in tariff schedules and cuts made during international negotiations through GATT, has led to a considerable decline in the preference idea as a Commonwealth tie. In Malaya's case, 17 per cent of its exports were granted preferences: the lowest percentage of any Commonwealth member. In turn,

Malaya gave generous preferences but only on a very few items: electrical machinery, cotton and wool textiles, rayons, clothing and automobiles; and Singapore gave none except on automobiles. None the less, in 1960 the *Economist* Intelligence Unit could find that preference retained considerable importance because it was 'one of the few concrete instances of special treatment for Commonwealth products and its abolition would . . . signify a grave weakening of Commonwealth ties'.[54] This argument is a highly circular one, however. In effect it argues that the Commonwealth exists because of such ties as the preferential system; that the preferential system continues because of Commonwealth ties; and that in any case, when practically applied, these ties are few and slight, at least in the case of Malaysia.

The private capital Malaysia has attracted has not been predominantly British, excluding from consideration grants from the United Kingdom during the Emergency. As Malaya launched a major program of governmental borrowing, placing emphasis on the government as an instrument for developing basic services and industries, it has looked to Britain for less. Private investment has tended to follow the line of public borrowing. Malayan tin is smelted at home and then goes to Japan or the United States; Malayan iron ore goes to Japan and rubber to Europe and North America. Sarawak's trade is with Malaya and Singapore. As one follows the course of a particular commodity from source to market, one is reminded of a billiard table in which the ball cannons about, falling into the side pocket marked 'Commonwealth' far less often than it falls into the end pockets.

Still, Commonwealth preference continues to have both real (if limited) and ideological (if misunderstood) meaning, and trade as a Commonwealth tie is reinforced by other strands of an economic nature. Once a trading pattern is established it tends to remain, depending upon how elastic the market is and how responsive to consumer demand the retailer is. Consumer demand in Malaysia is less sophisticated and less changeable than in western countries. The old ties with the United Kingdom persist. There is a high degree of British ownership in the plantation economies of Malaysia. The great agency houses—Harrisons and Crosfield, Ltd, Guthrie and Company, and Edward Boustead and Company—continue to link Malaysia to Britain. Before the Second World War a third of tin production was controlled by the Anglo-Oriental Corporation, a subsidiary of the London Tin Corporation, while three of the four leading banks—the Hongkong and Shanghai, the Chartered Bank, and the Mercantile Bank—were British. Ties of this nature, although diminished, continue.[55]

Counter to these ties runs the fact of Britain's relative economic decline. Weakened in ability to foster and maintain overall Commonwealth bonds, the

British government must think in terms of priorities; clearly, India will be put ahead of Malaysia. And the British businessman, despite the machinery which gives him ready access into Malaysia, is losing ground to his Australian, Japanese, Hong Kong, West German and American counterparts. By 1961 British sales had declined so seriously in Singapore and throughout South-east Asia in general, that the Federation of British Industries sent a five-man trade delegation to the region. The reasons for decline had little to do with the Commonwealth, nor could the Commonwealth offset them: 'a broadening of the sources of supply following political autonomy; ... the non-competitive tendency of certain British consumer goods; and . . . inability to tender successfully and deliver in time in the case of capital equipment.' Many British manufacturers had sent no executive on a visit to South-east Asia in eighty years and had lost touch with what the people wanted, even though tastes remained conservative and 'a strong preference for British goods . . .' was noted.[56]

Perhaps the most important financial feature of Malaysia's membership in the Commonwealth will be its continued affiliation with the sterling area. Such membership in the early years of independence made it possible for Malaya to maintain 'long-standing financial orientations' and to give confidence to the Malayan dollar.[57] Revenue surpluses and government funds were invested in Commonwealth government securities. Malaysia can make a favourable balance of American dollars available to sterling bloc countries. Malayan delegates regularly attended the Commonwealth Sterling Area Balance of Payments Conferences, and the Malayan dollar (which is also the currency of Singapore and the Borneo territories) is, of course, freely convertible into sterling. The sterling bloc is not coincidental with the Commonwealth, for it does not contain all Commonwealth members and, in turn, includes several nations that are not members of the Commonwealth. Nonetheless, it is dominated by its Commonwealth members, and it may quite properly be thought of as a tie to the larger community.[58]

Malaysia and the Common Market

Because of its favourable trading position, and as a result of its dependence on the two basic commodities of rubber and tin, Malaysia has been able to stand apart from the controversy concerning Britain's proposed entry into the European Common Market, a controversy that has placed heavy strains on the Commonwealth ties. While it is not true that 'Malaya has nothing to fear from the Common Market',[59] as one assessment concluded, it is quite true that Malaya has little to fear, since the destruction of imperial preferences will not touch rubber and tin, commodities that generally have had no preferences in any case. Rather, success of the Common Market, and any contribution Britain could make to that success, would be welcomed by most Malaysian businessmen in the hope that the

Economic Community might need more natural rubber.[60] On the other hand producers and distributors of palm oil, coffee, tea, pepper, coconut oil, canned pineapples and sawn timber might well suffer.[61] Malaya felt strongly enough about the position of the last three commodities to hint that it might send its own representatives to the so-called Brussels talks, held in the latter part of 1962, concerning British entry into the Common Market.[62]

Nonetheless, Malaya did not appoint such representatives, and when the Commonwealth prime ministers met in London at their annual conference in September 1963, the Malayan delegation, led by the deputy prime minister, Tun Abdul Razak bin Hussein, did not join in the massive assault launched by the chief ministers of Canada, Pakistan, India and Australia against the carefully argued pro-Common Market views put forth by the British prime minister, Harold Macmillan. Tun Abdul Razak made it clear that he was not willing to contribute to any move that might weaken the Commonwealth. Since one view held that attempts by Commonwealth members to prevent British entry would weaken the Commonwealth, while a second view held that British insistence on entry would alienate the members, Tun Abdul Razak had, in effect, announced that Malaya would, for the time being, take no position on the issue. The press in Malaya, however, tended to favour British entry, both during the conference and later, when French intransigence finally brought the Brussels talks to a collapse.[63]

Tun Abdul Razak did not find the fence on which he sat crowded. The premier of Singapore, Lee Kuan Yew, publicly supported the move by the leader of Britain's Labour Party, Hugh Gaitskell, to oppose Britain's entry into Europe.[64] Since all other independent Asian members of the Commonwealth, as well as the Pacific members which were regarded as having a 'special relationship' with Malaya, opposed Britain's attempts to enter the Common Market on the terms then being discussed, Malaya stood alone within the Asian-Pacific region.

While recognising and even supporting Britain's need to enter the European community, Malaya did express concern even before the Prime Ministers' Conference over the position of its lesser commodities. In 1961 Britain had taken 28 per cent of Malaya's exported palm oil, 27·1 per cent of the Federation's coconut oil, and 29 per cent of the total export of timber. Malaya sent crude glycerine to the United Kingdom and obtained a ten per cent preference; Malaya and Singapore between them supplied most of Britain's sago flour (for use in industrial starches) and received a five per cent preference. Sabah sent tobacco. Even more important were tea (60·9 per cent of Malaya's 1961 export going to Britain), and canned pineapple (44 per cent of which went to the British market). At the time of the Prime Ministers' Conference it was not clear how some of these commodities would be affected, although it was assumed the effect would be adverse in varying degrees; timber, for example, was to be subject to a duty of ten per cent. On the other hand, although the Treaty of Rome had provided for a three per cent duty on natural rubber, it was widely understood that the duty would not be enforced. Such might be the case with other commodities, and Malaya's delegation to the conference had good reason to be watchful, cautious and silent—at least publicly.

Malaya therefore chose to make a public issue of but one commodity: canned pineapple. While tea was important, Ceylon could be expected to take the lead in this regard. Pepper was primarily of moment to Singapore, which re-exported to the United Kingdom increasing amounts of Sarawak and a decreasing amount of Indonesian pepper, and to the Borneo territories, which exported to Singapore and also directly to Britain, France and West Germany. Canned pineapple remained without a specific defender, and on this one commodity Malaya could press for special treatment without appearing to oppose Britain's policy in general. Malaya had taken up the question earlier in 1962, as was revealed in June when the annual report of the Metal Box Company of Malaya, Ltd was released. In November Britain did what it could, proposing at Brussels that the Common Market should open negotiations for a trade agreement with the future Federation of Malaysia, and that canned pineapple exports should be granted a duty-free quota. The only relatively important Malayan product that appeared to be threatened, therefore, was coconut oil. In any case, in January 1963, the Brussels talks had collapsed and the question of the Common Market was in abeyance.[65]

There are, then, ties both apparent and real, ties of the spirit and of the mart, that link Malaysia to the Commonwealth, ties often sentimentalised outside Malaysia and often misunderstood by Commonwealth members as well as non-members, but bonds that are of both historical and contemporary importance. Ties of circumstance and of precedence, ties of language, law, education, defence and trade are strengthened by a massive, if sometimes inefficient, machinery of informational support. If most Malaysians seem ill-informed about the Commonwealth, and if the Malaysian prime minister remains its most vocal champion; if most of the 'ties that bind' seem to run bilaterally between Malaysia and specific Commonwealth members rather than multilaterally to all members at once; if the ties do not, in fact, bind but more properly act as points of contact, the intellectual or ideological significance of the Commonwealth for Malaysia, and of Malaysia within the Commonwealth, is not diminished. One has but to look to Indonesia to see how isolated a nation is that turns its back, rightly or wrongly, by force of circumstance or by decision of will, on its past. In India Nehru has remarked that membership in the Commonwealth 'since it involves no commitments, can do no harm'. This is but a half-truth. Membership surely can do no harm and by the processes of consultation and co-operation much good; but membership does involve commitments, commitments of mind, of spirit, and of the assumption of a commonly shared, if ambiguous and unclearly defined, goal. In the international context Malaysia's membership in the Commonwealth is of great significance whether or not image and reality coincide. In 1956 Tengku Abdul Rahman remarked, 'We will either float or sink with our Commonwealth friends.' He is probably correct.

List of Contributors

D. K. Bassett received his BA from the University of Wales and his PhD from the University of London. He is now Senior Lecturer in History at the University of Malaya.

D. W. Fryer took his MSc (Econs) from the London School of Economics, his MCom from Melbourne University and his PhD from the University of London. Before returning to the University of Malaya, where he is now Reader in Geography, he also taught at the University of Nottingham and the University of Melbourne.

H. E. Groves, BA (Colorado), JD (Chicago), LlM (Harvard), is now Visiting Professor of Constitutional Law and Head of the Department of Law, University of Singapore.

Hamzah-Sendut, BA (Malaya), MCD (Liverpool), is a Lecturer in Urban Geography at the University of Malaya who is now on secondment as Specialist in Urbanisation, United Nations Headquarters, New York.

Tom Harrisson, DSO, OBE, is the author of several studies of the peoples and cultures of ancient and modern Sarawak. He is now Government Ethnologist and Curator of the Sarawak Museum.

Robert Ho, MA (London), DipArts, received his education at Raffles College, Singapore, and at King's College, London. He is now Professor of Geography at the University of Malaya.

J. C. Jackson, BA (Sheffield), MA (Leicester), received his specialist training in historical geography. He is now Lecturer in Geography in the University of Malaya.

K. T. Joseph took his BAgrSc (Hons) from the University of Western Australia and his MAgrSc from the University of Adelaide. Before he joined the University of Malaya as Lecturer in Soil Science, he had been Soils Chemist in the Malayan Government.

ALASTAIR LAMB, MA, PhD (Cantab), has written on Sino-Indian relations and the Tibetan question as well as on the archaeology and early history of Malaya. He was Reader in History at the University of Malaya before recently joining the Australian National University as Senior Fellow.

T. G. McGEE was educated in New Zealand and received his BA from the University of New Zealand and his MA from Victoria University of Wellington. He was Lecturer in Geography at the University of Malaya, before joining the Victoria University of Wellington.

DAVID McINTYRE received his BA from Cambridge University, his MA from Washington University, Seattle, and his PhD from the University of London. He is now Lecturer in Commonwealth and American History in the University of Nottingham.

LORD MEDWAY, MA (Cantab), PhD (Birmingham), has worked in Indonesia and Sarawak before coming to the University of Malaya. He is now Lecturer in the Department of Zoology.

R. S. MILNE, BA, MA, was educated in Glasgow and Oxford. He is now Professor of Political Science at the University of Singapore. Before he came to Singapore, he had taught at the University of Bristol and was Professor at the Victoria University of Wellington.

MOHD. TAIB BIN OSMAN, MA (Malaya), was one of the first graduates of the Department of Malay Studies, University of Malaya. He is now Lecturer in Malay Studies and specialises in Malay literature.

GAYL D. NESS is a sociologist who received his PhD from the University of California in Berkeley. He is currently doing research in South-east Asia as a Fellow of the Institute of Current World Affairs, New York, and is now at the Department of Sociology in the University of Michigan.

M. E. D. POORE, MA, PhD (Cantab), has served as Senior Scientific Officer with the Nature Conservancy, Edinburgh, and as Consultant Ecologist in the Middle East. He is now Professor of Botany in the University of Malaya.

VICTOR PURCELL was educated in Cambridge before joining the Malayan Civil Service. He later received both his PhD and DLitt from Cambridge. He has recently retired from his lectureship in Far Eastern History at the University of Cambridge. He is the author of two pioneer studies of the Chinese in South-east Asia.

K. J. Ratnam, BA (Malaya), MA (British Columbia), PhD (London), is now Lecturer in Political Science in the University of Singapore. He has lately completed a work on political problems in post-war Malaya.

Anthony Short, BSc [Econ] (London), MA (Virginia), BLitt (Oxon), is Lecturer in History at the University of Malaya. He is now writing a history of the Emergency in Malaya.

Robert O. Tilman, PhD (Duke), is a professor of political science at Tulane University, New Orleans. He has travelled widely in Malaysia and is the author of a study on the public services of Malaya.

C. M. Turnbull received her education at the University of London where she took her BA before joining the Malayan Civil Service; later she received her PhD while she was a Lecturer in History at the University of Malaya. She now lives in Singapore.

Wan Abdul Hamid was educated at the University of Malaya from which he graduated with a BA (Hons) in Geography. He was a graduate assistant at the University and then a senior member of the Johore Civil Service. He is now the Secretary of the Dewan Bahasa dan Pustaka (Language and Literature Agency), Kuala Lumpur.

Wang Gungwu, MA (Malaya), PhD (London), is Professor of History at the University of Malaya. In 1961–2, he was Rockefeller Research Associate at the School of Oriental and African Studies, University of London.

Robin W. Winks, MA (Colorado), PhD (Johns Hopkins), is Associate Professor of History at Yale University and specialised in Commonwealth History and Literature. He was Smith-Mundt Visiting Professor to the University of Malaya in 1962–3.

Ruth H. K. Wong, BA (Belfast), EdD (Harvard), first received her education at Raffles College, Singapore. She has been Senior Lecturer in Education in the University of Singapore and is now Professor and Head of the School of Education at the University of Malaya.

Yip Yat Hoong, MA (Malaya), is a Lecturer in Economics in the University of Malaya. He is about to complete his PhD thesis on the tin industry in Malaya for the London School of Economics and Political Science.

Zainal Abidin b. Abdul Wahid, MA (Queensland), is now Lecturer in History at the University of Malaya. Before joining the University, he served in the Ministry of External Affairs, Federation of Malaya. He is now preparing a study on the formation of Malaysia.

Bibliographical Notes

NOTES TO CHAPTER 1   *25–43*

1. Fisher, C. A., 'Some aspects of the political Geography of Greater Malaysia', *The Journal of Tropical Geography*, XVII (1963).
2. East, W. G. and Spate, O. H. K. (eds), *The Changing World, Studies in Political Geography* (London, 1956).
3. Hodder, B. W., *Man in Malaya* (London, 1959). For this section see Watts, I. E. M., *Equatorial Weather* (London, 1955).
4. Ho, R., *Man, Land and Environment in Malaya* (Kuala Lumpur, 1963).
5. Dale, W. L., 'Surface temperatures in Malaya', *The Journal of Tropical Geography*, XVII (1963).
6. Robequain, C., *Malaya, Indonesia, Borneo and the Philippines*, trans. E. Laborde (London and New York, 1958).
7. Dale, W. L., 'The Rainfall of Malaya (Parts I and II)', *The Journal of Tropical Geography*, XIII (1959) and XIV (1960).
8. Mohr, E. C. J., *The Soils of Equatorial Regions* (Ann Arbor, 1944).
9. Department of Civil Aviation and Meteorological Services, British Territories in Borneo, *Rainfall Statistics of the British Borneo Territories, 1896–1957* (Jesselton, 1961).
10. Gan Tong Liang, 'A study of some heavy rainspells on the east coast of Malaya during the northeast monsoon season', *Memoir of the Malayan Meteorological Service No. 6* (Singapore, 1962).
11. Hydrographic Department, British Admiralty, *China Sea Pilot II*, 2nd edn. (London, 1950).
12. Dale, W. L., 'Wind and drift currents in the South China Sea', *The Journal of Tropical Geography*, VIII (1956).
13. Ommanney, F. D., *Malayan offshore trawling grounds* (London, 1962).
14. Watts, I. E. M., 'Rainfall of Singapore Island', *The Journal of Tropical Geography*, VII (1955).

15. Watts, I. E. M., 'The line squalls of Malaya', *The Journal of Tropical Geography*, III (1954).
16. van Bemmelen, R. W., *The Geology of Indonesia* (The Hague, 1948).
17. van Bemmelen, R. W., *Mountain Building* (The Hague, 1954).
18. Alexander, J. B., 'Geology and palaeontology in Malaya', *Nature*, CLXXXIII (1959), pp. 230–2.
19. Ho, R., 'The evolution of the Indo-Malaysian region', *Proceedings of the Centenary and Bi-Centenary biological Conference* (Singapore, 1958).
20. Liechti, P., et al., *The Geology of Sarawak, Brunei and the western part of North Borneo*, Geological Survey Department, British Territories in Borneo, Bulletin No. 3 (Kuching, 1960).
21. Umbgrove, J. H. F., *Structural History of the East Indies* (Cambridge and New York, 1949).
22. Fitch, F. H., *Annual Report of the Geological Survey Department, British Territories in Borneo 1960* (Kuching, 1961).
23. Fitch, F. H., 'Evidence for Recent emergence of the land in east Pahang', *Journal of the Malayan Branch, Royal Asiatic Society*, XXII (1949), pp. 115–22; Richardson, J. A., 'Outline of the geomorphological evolution of British Malaya', *Geological Magazine*, XXIX (1958).
24. Hodder, *Man in Malaya* (London, 1959).
25. Collenette, P., 'A physiographic classification for North Borneo', *The Journal of Tropical Geography*, XVII (1963).
26. Scrivenor, J. B., *The geology of Malaya* (London, 1931).
27. Walker, D., 'Studies in the Quaternary of the Malay Peninsula I', *Federation Museums Journal*, I and II (1957).
28. Geological Survey Department, British Territories in Borneo:
    Haile, N. S., *The geology and mineral resources of the Strap and Sadong Valleys, West Sarawak*, Memoir 1, 1954; Wilford, G. E., *The geology and mineral resources of the Kuching-Lundu area, West Sarawak*, Memoir 3, 1954; Haile, N. S., *The geology and mineral resources of the Lupar and Saribas Valleys, West Sarawak*, Memoir 7, 1957; Kirk, H. J. C., *The geology and mineral resources of the upper Rajang and adjacent areas*, Memoir 8, 1958; Wolfenden, E. B., *The geology and mineral resources of the Lower Rajang Region, Sarawak*, Memoir 11, 1960.
29. Panton, W. P., 'The 1962 Soil Map of Malaya', *The Journal of Tropical Geography*, XVIII (1964); Andriesse, J. B., *Field Classification of the soils of Sarawak, 1st approximation*, Soils Division, Department of Agriculture, Sarawak, Technical Paper No. 1 (1962).
30. Anderson, J. A. R., 'The structure and development of the peat swamps of Sarawak and Brunei,' *The Journal of Tropical Geography*, XVIII (1963); and two articles by Coulter, J. K., in the *Malayan Agricultural Journal*, 'Development of the

peat soils of Malaya', xl (1957), and 'The Kuala Langat (North) Forest Reserve', xxxix (1956); also see Coulter, J. K., McWalter, A. R. and Arnott, G. W., 'The Trans-Perak Swamp', *Malayan Agricultural Journal*, xxxix (1956).

31. Wall, J. R. D., 'Topography-Soil relationships in Lowland Sarawak', *The Journal of Tropical Geography*, xviii (1964); McWalter, A. R., *Classification of Rice soils*, International Rice Commission of the FAO, 7th meeting, Ceylon, 1959; and Dennett, J. H., 'The western coastal alluvial soils', *Malayan Agricultural Journal*, xx (1932).

32. Panton, W. P., *Reconnaissance soil survey of Trengganu*, Department of Agriculture Bulletin No. 105 (Kuala Lumpur, 1958); Panton, W. P., 'Reconnaissance soil survey of Kelantan', *Malayan Agricultural Journal*, xliii (1960); Andriesse, J. P., *Podzols and podzolic soils in the lowlands of Sarawak and their fertility*, Soils Division, Department of Agriculture (Kuching, Sarawak, no date).

33. Burton, C. K., 'The Older Alluvium of Johore and Singapore', *The Journal of Tropical Geography*, xviii (1964).

34. Paton, T. R., *A soil survey of the Apas-Balung region of the Semporna Peninsula*, North Borneo Department of Agriculture (Jesselton, no date).

35. Joseph, K. T., 'The soils of Kedah', *The Journal of Tropical Geography*, xviii (1964).

36. Panton, W. P., 'Types of Malayan laterite and factors affecting their distribution', *Proceedings, 6th International Congress of Soil Science*, v (Paris, 1956).

NOTES TO CHAPTER 2 44-54

1. van Steenis, C. G. C. J., 'The delimitation of Malaysia and its main plant-geographical divisions', in *Flora Malesiana*, i (Noordhof-Kolff, Jakarta, 1950).

2. van Steenis, C. G. C. J., 'On the application of the terms Malaysia and Malaya in plant geography', *Gardens Bulletin, Straits Settlements*, ix (2), pp. 187–9 (1937).

3. van Steenis, C. G. C. J. Ed., in *Flora Malesiana*, i (Noordhof-Kolff, Jakarta, 1950). iv (1954). v (1958).

4. Wyatt-Smith, J., 'A note on the fresh-water swamp, lowland and hill forest types of Malaya', *Malayan Forester*, xxiv (2), pp. 110–21 (1961).

5. Corner, E. J. H., 'A tropical botanist's introduction to Borneo', *Sarawak Museum Journal*, x (17–18), pp. 1–16 (1961).

6. van Bemmelen, R. W., *The Geology of Indonesia*, Vol. i a. 'The general geology of Indonesia and adjacent archipelagos' (Government Printing Office, The Hague, 1949); Walker, D. W., 'Studies in the Quaternary of the Malay Peninsula. i. Alluvial deposits of Perak and changes in the relative level of land and sea', *Federation Museums Journal*, i and ii, pp. 19–34.

7. Federation of Malaya, *Report on Forest Administration for the year 1960* (Kuala Lumpur, 1962); Government of Sarawak, *Annual report of the Forest Department for the year 1961*

(Kuching, 1962); Colony of North Borneo, *Forest Department Annual Report, 1960*, (Govt Printing Office, Jesselton, 1961); State of Brunei, *Annual Report* (Kuching, 1955).

8. Wyatt-Smith, J., 'An ecological study of the structure of natural lowland evergreen rain forest in Malaya' (Typescript, 1947).

9. Govt of Sarawak, *Annual Report of the Forest Dept. for 1961* (Kuching, 1962).

10. Corner, E. J. H., *Wayside Trees of Malaya* (Singapore, 1940).

11. Holttum, R. E., *Plant Life in Malaya* (London, 1954).

12. van Bemmelen, R. W., as note 6.

13. Govt of Sarawak, as note 9.

14. Nye, P. H., 'Organic matter and nutrient cycles under moist tropical forest', *Plant and Soil*, XIII (4), pp. 333–45 (1961).

15. Govt of Sarawak, as note 9.

16. Wyatt-Smith, J., 'Shifting cultivation in Malaya', *Malayan Forester*, XXI, pp. 139–51 (1958).

17. Wyatt-Smith, J., as note 4.

18. Forman, L. L., 'A new genus in the Fagaceae', *Taxon*, XI (4), pp. 139–40 (1962).

19. van Steenis, C. G. C. J., 'On the origin of the Malaysian mountain flora. I. Facts and statement of the problem', *Bull. Jard. Bot. Buitenzorg*, III (13), pp. 135–262 and III (13), pp. 289–417 (1934 and 1935).

NOTES TO CHAPTER 3   55–66

1. Kloss, C. B., *Journal of the Federated Malay States Museums*, VII (1918), p. 245 footnote.

2. For example: Chasen, F. N., 'A handlist of Malaysian birds', *Bulletin of the Raffles Museum, Singapore*, XI (1935); Chasen, F. N., 'A Handlist of Malaysian mammals', *Bulletin of the Raffles Museum, Singapore*, XV (1940);   Delacour, J., *The Birds of Malaysia* (New York, 1947).

3. In, for example, Inger, R. F., and Chin, P. K., 'The fresh-water fishes of North Borneo', *Fieldiana: Zoology*, XLV (March 1962), pp. 237–49.

4. Hails, N. S., 'The snakes of Borneo', *Sarawak Museum Journal*, VIII (1958), p. 743.

5. Chasen, 'Malaysian Birds'.

6. Lord Medway, 'Checklist of the mammals of Borneo', *Sarawak Museum Journal* (in press).

7. Davis, D. D., 'Mammals of the lowland rain-forest of North Borneo', *Bulletin of the National Museum, Singapore*, XXXI (September 1962), pp. 19–20.

8. Corbett, A. S., and Pendlebury, H. M., *The Butterflies of the Malay Peninsula*, 2nd edn. (Edinburgh, 1956).

9. Tweedie, M. W. F., *The Snakes of Malaya* (Singapore, 1953).

10. Medway, 'Mammals of Borneo'.

11. Smythies, B. E., 'Checklist of the birds of Borneo', *Sarawak Museum Journal*, VII (June 1957), i–iv, pp. 523–818, 1 map.

12. Inger, R. F., *in litt.*

13. Hooijer, D. A., 'Prehistoric teeth of Man and of the Orang-utan', *Zool. Med. Museum, Leiden*, XXIX (1948), pp. 175–301, plates I–IX.

14. Lord Medway, 'The Malay Tapir in late Quaternary Borneo', *Sarawak Museum Journal*, IX (July–December 1960), pp. 356–60, plate XI.

15. Harrisson, T., Hooijer, D. A., and Lord Medway, 'An extinct Pangolin and associated mammals from Niah cave, Sarawak', *Nature*, CLXXXIX, No. 4759 (1961), p. 166.

16. Lord Medway, 'Niah Cave bone V: Recent additions', *Sarawak Museum Journal* (in press).

17. Corbett and Pendlebury, *Butterflies of the Malay Peninsula*, XXXV.

18. Harrison, J. L. 'A survey of common squirrels', *Malayan Nature Journal*, V (1950) pp. 79–83.

19. Banks, E., 'The Forms of Prevost's squirrel found in Sarawak', *Proceedings of the Zoological Society of London* (1931), pp. 1335–48.

20. The summary given below is derived largely from Inger and Chin, 'Freshwater fishes of North Borneo', pp. 237–49. Additional data may be found in Weber, M. and de Beaufort, L. F., *The Fishes of the Indo-Australian Archipelago*, I–VIII (Leyden, 1911–53).

21. Umbgrove, J. H. F., 'Geologic history of the East Indies', *Bulletin of the American Association of Petrology and Geology*, XXII (1938), pp. 1–70.

22. Harrison, J. L., 'Mammals of Innisfail', *Australian Journal of Zoology*, X (1962), p. 76, Table 6.

23. *Annual Report of the Institute of Medical Research, Federation of Malaya, 1960* (Kuala Lumpur, 1961), p. 78. Hereafter cited as *Annual Report, IMR, 1960.*

24. Harrison, J. L., 'The distribution of feeding habits among animals in a tropical rain-forest', *Journal of Animal Ecology*, XXXI (February 1962), p. 54.

25. Davis, D. D., 'Mammals of North Borneo', IX (see note 8).

26. Davis, *loc. cit.*

27. *Annual Report, IMR, 1960*, pp. 75–8.

28. See Table 8 in Lord Medway, 'The fauna of Pulau Tioman: Mammals', *Bulletin of the National Museum* (in press).

29. Chandler, N. and Heffer, A., 'Distribution of the Yellow-necked Mouse', *Transactions of the Suffolk Naturalists' Society*, IX, 1954–6 (1956), pp. 313–15.

30. Wade, Phyllis, 'Breeding season among mammals in the lowland rain-forest of North Borneo', *Journal of Mammalogy*, XXXIX (1958), pp. 429–33.

31. Lord Medway, '300,000 bats', *Sarawak Museum Journal*, VIII (1958), pp. 667–79. Also much unpublished data.

32. Lord Medway, 'The swiftlets (*Collocalia*) of Niah cave, Sarawak', *Ibis*, CIV (1962), pp. 45–66 and 228–45.
33. Burgess, P. F., 'Breeding of the White-bellied Swiftlet (*Collocalia esculenta*) in North Borneo', *Sarawak Museum Journal*, x (July-December 1961), pp. 264–8.
34. Harrison, J. L., 'Breeding rhythms of Selangor rodents', *Bulletin of the Raffles Museum, Singapore*, xxiv (1952), pp. 109–31. Also 'Data on the reproduction of some Malayan mammals', *Proceedings of the Zoological Society of London*, cxxv (1955), pp. 445–60.
35. Inger, R. F. and Greenberg, B., 'The annual reproductive pattern of the frog *Rana erythraea* in Sarawak', *Physiological Zoology*, xxxvi (January 1963), pp. 21–33.
36. Hendrickson, J. R. and Berry, P. Y., in Malaya; Inger, R. F. and collaborators in Borneo.
37. Harrisson, T., 'Notes on the Green Turtle (*Chelonia mydas*) Nos. 1–9', *Sarawak Museum Journal*, v, pp. 592–6; vi, pp. 126–8; vii, pp. 233–9 and pp. 504–15; viii, pp. 481–6 and pp. 772–4; ix, pp. 277–8; x, pp. 293–9. Also *Nature*, CLXIX (1952), p. 198; CLXXVIII (1956), p. 1479. Hendrickson, J. R., 'The Green Turtle *Chelonia mydas* (Linn). in Malaya and Sarawak', *Proceedings of the Zoological Society of London*, cxxx (1958), pp. 455–535.
38. (Anonymous), 'The Leathery Turtle or Luth', *Oryx*, vi (1961), pp. 116–25.
39. Reid, J. A., 'Secondary vectors, an obstacle to malaria eradication', *The Medical Journal of Malaya*, xiv (June 1960).
40. Wharton, R. H., 'Studies on Filariasis in Malaya: Field and laboratory investigations of the vectors of a rural strain of *Wuchereria bancrofti*', *Annals of Tropical Medicine and Parasitology*, LIV (April 1960), p. 89.
41. Macdonald, W. W. and Traub, R., 'Malaysian Parasites xxxvii: An introduction to the ecology of the mosquitoes of the lowland dipterocarp forest of Selangor, Malaya', *Studies from the Institute of Medical Research, Federation of Malaya*, No. 29 (1960), pp. 80–109.
42. Reid, J. A., 'Mosquitoes, insecticides and evolution', *Proceedings of the Centennial and Bicentennial Congress, Singapore, 1958* (1960).
43. *Annual Report, IMR, 1960*, pp. 84–8.
44. *Annual Report, IMR, 1960*, pp. 89–93.
45. *Annual Report, IMR, 1960*, p 116.
46. *Annual Report, IMR, 1960*, p. 70.
47. Wang Gungwu, 'The Nan-hai trade', *Journal of the Malayan Branch, Royal Asiatic Society*, xxxi, pt 2 (June 1958).
48. Harrisson, T., Chapter ii, in Smythies, 'Birds of Borneo'.
49. Harrisson, Barbara, *Orang-utan* (London and New York, 1962).
50. Medway, 'The Swiftlets of Niah cave', pp. 239–40.

NOTES TO CHAPTER 4

1. Unless otherwise indicated, the statistical data upon which this chapter is based have been taken from the following census publications:
   Fell, H., *1957 Population Census of Malaya, Report No. 14* (Kuala Lumpur, 1959); *1957 Census of Population, Singapore: Preliminary Releases Nos. 1–10* (Singapore, 1959–61).
   Jones, L. W., *North Borneo, A Report on the Census of Population 1960* (Kuching, 1962).
   Jones, L. W., *Sarawak, A Report on the Census of Population 1960* (Kuching, 1962).
   Some earlier censuses, not cited here, have been used in the construction of Table 1.

2. '1963 Yearbook', *Far Eastern Economic Review* (Hong Kong, December 1962), p. 47.

3. A factual background is given in Milne, R. S., 'Malaysia: A New Federation in the Making', *Asian Survey*, iii, No. 2 (February 1963), pp. 70–82.

4. Hanna, W. A., 'Malaysia, A Federation in Prospect. Part viii Billets for Ballots', *American Universities Field Staff Reports Service*, South-east Asia Series, x, No. 12: Brunei, Malaya, North Borneo, Sarawak, Singapore (New York, September 1962), pp. 1–9. See also Lim Tay Boh, *The Development of Singapore's Economy*, Background to Malaya Series, No. 14 (Singapore, 1960).

5. For studies on population in Malaysia see: Smith, T. E., *Population Growth in Malaya*, Royal Institute of International Affairs (London, 1952); Saw Swee Hock, *The Population of Singapore and its Social and Economic Limitations* (unpublished MA thesis, University of Singapore, 1960); Lee, Y. L., 'The Population of British Borneo', *Population Studies*, xv, No. 3 (March 1962), pp. 226–43.

6. This division into five main periods of population growth is based largely on that suggested in Smith, T. E., *op. cit.*, pp. 1–2.

7. Keesing, Felix M., 'Some Notes on Early Migrations in the Southwest Pacific Area', *Southwestern Journal of Anthropology*, vi, No. 2 (Summer, 1950), pp. 110–19.

8. Kernial Singh Sandhu, 'Chinese Colonisation of Malacca', *The Journal of Tropical Geography*, xv (June 1961), p. 6.

9. Winstedt, R. O., *Malaya and Its History* (London and New York, 1948).

10. For studies on migration see: Blythe, W. L., 'Historical Sketch of Chinese Labour in Malaya', *Journal of the Malayan Branch of the Royal Asiatic Society*, xx, pt 1 (June 1947), pp. 64–114; Kernial Singh Sandhu, 'Some Preliminary Observations of the Origins and Characteristics of Indian Migration to Malaya, 1786–1957', *Papers on Malayan History* (Singapore, 1962), pp. 40–72.

11. Lee, Y. L., 'The Population of British Borneo', p. 228 (see note 5).

12. Saw Swee Hock, *The Population of Singapore and its Social and Economic Limitations*, p. 35 (see note 5).

13. 'Singapore Population Census 1957', *Population Release No. 8, Table 1* (Singapore, 1960).

14. Although registration of births and deaths is probably fairly accurate in the urban areas of Malaya and Singapore, it is still doubtful how accurate registration figures are in the rural areas of Malaya and the Borneo territories. It is likely that there is considerable under-registration.

15. On urbanisation, see Chapter 5 of this volume.

16. Kernial Singh Sandhu, 'The Population of Malaya, some changes in the pattern of distribution between 1947 and 1957', *Journal of Tropical Geography*, xv (June 1961), p. 89.

17. Jones, L. W., *Sarawak: Report on the Census of Population taken on 15th June 1960* (Kuching, January 1962), p. 29.

18. See: McGee, T. G., 'The Malayan Elections of 1959, a study of Electoral Geography', *The Journal of Tropical Geography*, xvi (October 1962), pp. 70–100.

19. Defining the indigenous groups accurately is a difficult problem, and depends largely upon whether the worker in the field chooses to take the census definition or attempts some classification on the criteria of 'race' or some cultural aspect such as language. In general, for ease of computation, I have followed the census classification of the various territories. But this has presented certain difficulties. For instance, Malays in Sabah, who will unquestionably receive automatic citizenship in the coming Federation, are classified in the 'other races' group in the Census for Sabah. An even greater difficulty are the Indonesians, who in Sabah form a large percentage of the 'other races' group. In the past, in Malaya, they appear to have automatically received Malayan citizenship, but whether such generosity will be extended to them within the Federation, especially in view of the Indonesian government's belligerent attitude towards the Malaysian Federation, is an interesting question. For discussion of the problems of classifying the various tribes of the Borneo territories see Noakes, J. L., *Sarawak and Brunei: A Report on the 1947 Population Census* (Kuching, 1950). See also Chapter 11 of this volume.

20. *Report of the Commission of Enquiry, North Borneo and Sarawak* (Kuala Lumpur, 1962), p. 16.

21. Lee, Y. L., 'The Population of British Borneo', p. 230.

22. See: Polunin, Ivan, 'The Muruts of North Borneo', *Seed*, ii, No. 4, pp. 1–3.

23. On the aborigines of Malaya, see: Williams Hunt, P. D. R., *An Introduction to the Malayan Aborigines* (Kuala Lumpur, 1952); Cary, Iskandar, 'Aborigines and the Five Year Plan', *Seed*, i, No. 5 (1961), pp. 1–2.

24. See: Newell, William H., *Treacherous River: A Study of Rural Chinese in North Malaya* (Kuala Lumpur and New York, 1962); Purcell, Victor, *The Chinese in Modern Malaya*, Background to Malaya Series, No. 9 (Singapore, 1956); Tien Ju Kang,

The Chinese of Sarawak, London School of Economics and Political Science Monographs on Social Anthropology, No. 12 (London, 1953).

25. Del Tufo, M. V., *Malaya. A Report on the 1947 Census of Population* (Kuala Lumpur, 1949), p. 76.

26. Lee, Y. L., 'The Population of British Borneo', p. 241.

27. See: Hodder, B. W., 'Racial Groupings in Singapore', *The Journal of Tropical Geography*, 1 (October 1953), pp. 25-36, for a description of the various dialect groupings in Singapore in 1947. Also see my own account of the population in Kuala Lumpur for the manner in which such dialect groupings affect the demographic structure of the community: McGee, T. G., 'The Cultural Role of Cities: A Case Study of Kuala Lumpur', *The Journal of Tropical Geography*, XVII, pp. 178-96.

28. Jones, L. W., *Sarawak, Census 1960*.

29. Smith, T. E., *Population Growth in Malaya*, pp. 75-6 (see note 5).

30. These figures are taken from Saw Swee Hock, *Population of Singapore, and its Social and Economic Limitations* (see note 5).

31. It is, of course, possible that Singapore may have to impose some kind of restriction of movement into its territory as one measure to prevent population growth.

32. Cf. 'White Paper on Merger'.

33. *Report of the Commission of Enquiry, North Borneo and Sarawak* (Kuala Lumpur, 1962), p. 55.

34. See: Anglin, Douglas G., The Political Development of the West Indies, p. 56, in Lowenthal, David, *The West Indies Federation* (New York, 1960).

35. See: McGee, T. G., 'The Cultural Role of Cities', *op. cit.*

36. See: Kiser, Clyde W., Cultural Pluralism, pp. 307-20, in Spengler, J. J. and Duncan, O. D., *Demographic Analysis* (Glencoe, Illinois, 1956).

NOTES TO CHAPTER 5   *82-96*

1. All statistical data used in this chapter have been extracted from the censuses of the component territories of Malaysia:

   (a) Fell, H., *1957 Population Census of the Federation of Malaya, Report No. 14* (Kuala Lumpur, 1960).

   (b) Noakes, J. L., *1947 Population Census Report of Sarawak and Brunei* (Kuching, 1949).

   (c) Jones, L. W., *1960 Population Census Report of Sarawak* (Kuching, 1962).

   (d) Jones, L. W., *Report on the Census of Population of North Borneo, 1960* (Sandakan, 1962).

(e) Jones, L. W., *Additional Tables on the Census of Population of North Borneo, 1960* (Sandakan, 1962).

(f) *Preliminary Release No. 1, 1957 Census of Population of Singapore*, Department of Statistics (Singapore, 1959).

2. UNESCO, *Urbanization in Asia and the Far East*, proceedings of the Joint UN UNESCO Seminar, Tensions and Technology Series (Calcutta, 1957), Table 3, p. 101.

3. See Chapter 10.

4. Hamzah-Sendut, 'Resettlement Villages in Malaya', *Geography*, xlvii (January 1962), pp. 41–6.

5. See United Nations, *Economic Bulletin for Asia and the Far East*, 'Aspects of Urbanisation in ECAFE Countries', iv, No. 1 (May 1953), p. 8, where among other things it was said that in many South-east Asian countries tradition does not sanction the employment of women outside the home.

6. See Fell, H., *op. cit.*, p. 7.

7. For a study of this phenomenon in Malaya, see Hamzah-Sendut, 'Problems of rural-urban migration', *Community Development Bulletin*, xii, No. 3 (June 1961), pp. 86–90.

8. Hamzah-Sendut, 'Patterns of Urbanisation in Malaya', *Journal of Tropical Geography*, xvi (October 1962), pp. 114–30.

9. For some aspects of social disorganisation in a large Malaysian city, see McGee, T. G., 'The Cultural Role of Cities, a case study of Kuala Lumpur', *Journal of Tropical Geography*, xvii (May 1963), pp. 178–96.

10. For a comprehensive analysis of the types of problems which a big city in Malaysia faces, see *Klang Valley Plan*—summaries of the major recommendations of the United Nations Planning Adviser (Federal Department of Town Planning, Kuala Lumpur, 1962).

NOTES TO CHAPTER 6   *99–112*

1. The earliest dated inscription from Malaya is the Trengganu Stone. The text, which is Islamic, contains a fourteenth-century date, though exactly when in the fourteenth century is still a subject of controversy.

2. The best summary of early Chinese references to the Malaysia region is: Wang Gungwu, 'The Nanhai Trade', *Journal of the Malayan Branch of the Royal Asiatic Society* (1958). For a detailed study of the historical geography of the Malay peninsula before AD 1500, with full bibliography, see: Wheatley, P., *The Golden Khersonese* (Kuala Lumpur, 1961).

3. For the early history of Indochina, and for a bibliography relating to the

Dongson question, see: Coedès, G., *Les Peuples de la Péninsuie Indochinoise* (Paris, 1962).

4. See: Malleret, L., *L'Archéologie du Delta du Mékong*, III (Paris, 1962).

5. See: Quaritch Wales, H. G., *Towards Angkor* (London, 1937), for an exposition of the 'colonisation' theory.

6. Some of these early inscriptions are discussed in: Chhabra, B. Ch., 'Expansion of Indo-Aryan Culture during Pallava Rule', *Journal and Proceedings of the Royal Asiatic Society of Bengal*, 3rd series, I (1935).

7. van Leur, J. C., *Indonesian Trade and Society* (The Hague and New York, 1955).

8. Perhaps the most important piece of research on this subject is to be found in: Wolters, O. W., 'Early Indonesian Commerce and the Origin of Srivijaya' (unpublished PhD thesis in the University of London, 1962).

9. For some account of the commodities involved in Chinese trade with Southeast Asia, see: Hirth, F. and Rockhill, W. W., *Chau Ju-kua, his work on the Chinese and Arab trade in the twelfth and thirteenth centuries, entitled 'Chu-fan-chi'* (St Petersburg, 1911); Wheatley, P., 'Geographical Notes on some Commodities involved in Sung Maritime Trade', *Journal of the Malayan Branch of the Royal Asiatic Society* (1959). For Chinese trade with Borneo, see: Harrisson, T., 'Export Wares found in West Borneo', *Oriental Art* (1959).

10. For an account of both Takuapa and Pengkalan Bujang, see: Lamb, A., 'Miscellaneous Papers on Early Hindu and Buddhist Settlement in Northern Malaya and Southern Thailand', *Federation Museums Journal* (1961).

11. For the history of Srivijaya, see: Coedès, G., *Les États Hindouisés d'Indochine et d'Indonésie* (Paris, 1949); Nilakanta Sastri, *Sri Vijaya* (London, 1949); de Casparis, J. G., *Prasasti Indonesia I* (Bandung, 1950).

12. Wilson, A., *The Persian Gulf* (Oxford, 1924).

NOTES TO CHAPTER 7 113–127

1. This does not include two Malays sent to Brunei by the Batavia government in July 1650; van Dijk, L. C. D., *Neêrland's Vroegste Betrekkingen met Borneo, den Solo-Archipel, Cambodja, Siam en Cochin-China* (Amsterdam, 1862), p. 308.

2. 'Country' traders were private merchants or shipowners engaged in trade between Asian ports. The trade between Asia and Europe was monopolised by the East India Companies.

3. Cortesão, A. (ed.), *The Suma Oriental of Tome Pires* (London, 1944), I, p. 223, note 1., pp. 224–5, note 1. Meilink-Roelofsz reverses the relative positions of Laue and Tanjongpura, but Cortesão's evidence is more convincing. See Meilink-Roelofsz, M. A. P., *Asian Trade and European Influence in the Indonesian Archipelago*

between 1500 and about 1630 (The Hague, 1962), pp. 341, note 86, 349, note 205.

4. Cortesão, *Pires, op. cit.,* pp. 223–5; Meilink-Roelofsz, *Asian Trade*, pp. 85, 101.

5. Stanley, H. E. J., *The First Voyage round the World, by Magellan* (London, 1874), pp. 112–13, 114.

6. Stanley, *Magellan*, p. 114; Sinclair, W. F. and Ferguson, D., *The Travels of Pedro Teixeira* (London, 1902), pp. 4–5; Ijzerman, J. W. (ed.), *De Reis om de Wereld door Olivier van Noort, 1598–1601* (The Hague, 1926), pt I, p. 126; Forrest, Thomas, *A Voyage to New Guinea and the Moluccas from Balambangan . . . in the Tartar Galley . . . during the Years 1774, 1775 and 1776* (London, 1780), p. 380.

7. Stanley, *Magellan*, p. 114; Forrest, *New Guinea*, p. 381. Forrest compared the practice to a fleet of London wherries floating with provisions from London Bridge to Westminster and back again.

8. With the exception of Abdullah of Kampar, who joined the Portuguese.

9. For Mahmud's movements in 1511–26, see Macgregor, I. A., 'Johore Lama in the Sixteenth Century', *Journal of the Malayan Branch of the Royal Asiatic Society*, XXVIII (May 1955), pp. 67–74.

10. By the Treaty of Saragossa, April 1529, the line of demarcation between the Spanish and Portuguese spheres in Asia was placed 17° east of the Moluccas. The Spaniards claimed that this line did not extend north to the Philippines when they settled on Cebu (1565) and Luzon (1570).

11. Pires advocated the Borneo route as early as 1515 because Portuguese ships did not engage in port-to-port barter in Java as the Asians did. It is not clear, however, whether Pires was recommending the Brunei or south Borneo route. Cortesão, *Pires*, I, pp. 219–20.

12. Teixeira, Fr Manuel, 'Early Portuguese and Spanish Contacts with Borneo', *Proceedings of the Second International Conference of Historians of Asia* (Taipeh, 1962), pp. 27–30.

13. Teixeira, *op. cit.*, p. 27.

14. Blair, E. H. and Robertson, J. H., *The Philippine Islands, 1493–1803*, 55 vols (Cleveland, Ohio, 1903–9), III, p. 182; XXXIV, p. 297.

15. Blair and Robertson, *op. cit.*, IV, pp. 167–8, 173–4, 221–4.

16. 'So there is no export here, but what the Portuguese get in barter for some cloths that they carry thither.' Sinclair and Ferguson, *Pedro Teixeira*, p. 4.

17. Teixeira, 'Contacts', pp. 31–3; Blair and Robertson, *Philippine Islands*, VII, pp. 83–4. Teixeira may have mistaken the date because Santiago de Vera did not report the tragedy to Philip II until July 1589.

18. Three junks came to Malacca from Brunei in 1513 and two in 1518. Their owners were related to the *temenggong* of Portuguese Malacca, who was variously described as coming from Brunei or Luzon. Teixeira, 'Contacts', pp. 5–6; Cortesão, *Pires*, I, pp. 132–4; Meilink-Roelofsz, *Asian Trade*, p. 164.

19. 'It is a place of great trade, for many junks come here from all parts.' Brunei was mentioned by Urdaneta as importing camphor to Malacca. Markham, Sir Clements, *Early Spanish Voyages to the Strait of Magellan* (London, 1911), p. 81.

20. For the development of the Portuguese Far East trade see Boxer, C. R., *Hidalgos in the Far East, 1550–1770* (The Hague, 1948), and *The Christian Century in Japan, 1549–1650* (Berkeley, Los Angeles and London, 1951).

21. Moreland, W. H. (ed.), *Peter Floris, his Voyage to the East Indies in the 'Globe', 1611–1615* (London, 1934), p. 73.

22. Stanley, *Magellan*, pp. 110, 111–3, 117.

23. Meilink-Roelofsz, *Asian Trade*, p. 164. Goncalo Pereira was instructed to purchase cash during his visit of 1530.

24. Blair and Robertson, *Philippine Islands*, IV, pp. 131, 195.

25. Ijzerman, J. W., *Olivier van Noort*, pt I, pp. 105, 121–4.

26. Terpstra, H., *De Factorij der Oostindische Compagnie te Patani* (The Hague, 1938), p. 4.

27. Terpstra, *Patani*, pp. 21–2, 180; van Dijk, L. C. D., *Neêrland's Vroegste Betrekkingen met Borneo, den Solo-Archipel, Cambodja, Siam en Cochin-China* (Amsterdam, 1862), pp. 211, 215.

28. van Dijk, *op. cit.*, p. 284.

29. *Ibid.*, p. 212.

30. Hendrik Janssen to Directors, Oct. 20, 1614. Terpstra, *Patani*, p. 180; van Dijk, *Betrekkingen*, pp. 215–16.

31. van Dijk, *op. cit.*, pp. 277–9; Coolhaas, W. Ph. (ed.), *Generale Missiven van Governeurs-Generaal en Raden aan Heren XVII der Verenigde Oostindische Compagnie*, I (The Hague, 1960), pp. 458, 511, 534, 553, 560.

32. Brouwer and council to Directors, Jan. 4, 1636; van Diemen and council to Directors, Dec. 9, 1637; Coolhaas, *Generale Missiven*, I, pp. 541, 630. As corroboration of Dutch indifference to Brunei, consider the absence of any treaty with Brunei in the 950 Dutch treaties with Asian states catalogued in Heeres, J. E. and Stapel, F. W., 'Corpus Diplomaticum Neerlando-Indicum', *Bijdragen tot de Taal-, Land-, en Volkenkunde van Nederlandsch-Indie*, pts 57, 87, 91, 93, 96 (The Hague, 1907–38). For a history of the Banjarmasin factory see Noorlander, J. C., *Bandjarmasin en de Compagnie in de tweede helft der 18de Eeuw* (Leyden, 1935).

33. 'De H. I. Regering . . . "weinig dunk had van de voortbrengselen" van 't rijk van Broenei': van Dijk, *Betrekkingen*, p. 313.

34. Blair and Robertson, *Philippine Islands*, XXXIX, pp. 190–1; XLI, pp. 322–3; de la Costa, H., *The Jesuits in the Philippines, 1581–1768* (Cambridge, Mass., 1961), p. 540.

35. De la Costa, *Jesuits*, p. 545; Forrest, *New Guinea*, pp. 374–5.

36. The Brunei navy consisted of 50 galleys, of which De Sande captured 27. They were usually armed with a few swivel guns and culverins, but the galley of 'Soltan Lijar', the son of the old sultan, carried 20 pieces of artillery. De

Sande removed 170 artillery pieces, as well as the kathi's chair and a carved marble relief from the mosque. He estimated the muslim population at 4,000–5,000. Blair and Robertson, *Philippine Islands*, IV, pp. 126, 160–1, 167, 184; XXXIV, pp. 388–9.

37. Blair and Robertson, *op. cit.*, XLI, p. 298; XLIV, pp. 78–9.

38. *Op. cit.*, XVI, pp. 134–5, 185.

39. *Op. cit.*, XVI, pp. 177–85, 194–9. Cf. Chaunu's 'Mouvement unitaire annuel des entrées dans le Port de Manille (1577–1787)' and 'Hiérarchie en valeur des provenances à l'entrée du Port de Manille' (1586–1787) in Chaunu, P., *Les Philippines et le Pacifique des Ibériques (XVIe, XVIIe, XVIIIe siècles). Introduction Méthodologique et Indices d'activité* (Paris, 1960), pp. 147–219. These tables show that only 7 pinnaces or ships came to Manila from Borneo during that period (3 in 1690–2; 2 in 1707–9; 2 in 1757) and that their cargoes were an infinitesimal percentage of the imports of Manila.

40. Temple, Sir R. C. (ed.), *A Geographical Account of the Countries round the Bay of Bengal, 1669 to 1679, by Thomas Bowrey* (Cambridge, 1905), pp. 246, 268.

41. Foster, Sir W. (ed.), *A New Account of the East Indies by Alexander Hamilton* (London, 1930), II, p. 38.

42. Jourdain to Sulivan and de Souza, enclosure to Madras Select Committee, Feb. 10, 1772. *Sumatra Factory Records (SFR)*, XV, India Office Library (IOL), Commonwealth Relations Office, London.

43. Temple, *Geographical Account*, pp. 237, 262, 264; Foster, *New Account*, II, pp. 39–41, 50, 83. For a favourable view of the Malays see Wilkinson, C. (ed.), *Voyages and Discoveries by William Dampier* (London, 1931), p. 113, in which Dampier distinguished between the robberies of 'the pilfering poorer Sort' and the respectability of 'the trading *Malayans*, who love Trade and Property'.

44. Temple, *Geographical Account*, pp. 237–8; Foster, *A New Account*, II, pp. 84–5. Bowrey confessed that the 'Salettes' were 'Subject to noe manner of Goverment [*sic*]'.

45. 'Relation du Voyage du *Marquis de Prié* et du *Saint-Joseph*', MS. No. 674, Cod. gallic, f. 32, Bayerische Staatsbibliothek, Munich. His description is almost identical with Dampier's. See Wilkinson, *Voyages and Discoveries*, p. 11.

46. Foster, *A New Account*, pp. 81, 83; Temple, *Geographical Account*, p. 279. Junk Ceylon, however, had no surplus foodstuffs for export (Temple, pp. 246–7).

47. Temple, *op. cit.*, pp. 255–8.

48. Monckton to Madras Select Committee, April 22 and May 2, 1772. *SFR*, XV (IOL).

49. Wilkinson, *Voyages and Discoveries*, pp. 108–9; Hughes, T. D., 'A Portuguese Account of Johore', *Journal of the Malayan Branch of the Royal Asiatic Society*, XIII (October 1935), p. 125.

50. Foster, *A New Account*, pp. 51, 81–3.

51. Foster, *op. cit.*, p. 79.

52. Irwin, G. W., *Nineteenth-Century Borneo: a study in Diplomatic Rivalry* (The Hague, 1955), p. 22.

53. Monckton to Madras Council, October 12, 1772. *SFR*, xv (IOL).

54. Forrest, *New Guinea*, pp. 378, 381–3.

55. Foster, *A New Account*, pp. 82, 84.

56. They were in Siantan when Monckton visited Riau in August 1772. Monckton to Madras Council, October 12, 1772. *SFR*. xv (IOL). After van Braam conquered Riau, Raja Ali retired successively to Mampawa, Sukadana, Matan and Siantan. Netscher, E., *De Nederlanders in Djohor en Siak, 1602 tot 1865* (Batavia, 1870), pp. 209, 211.

57. Netscher, *op. cit.*, pp. 168–9.

58. Forrest, *New Guinea*, p. 365; also his *Voyage from Calcutta to the Mergui Archipelago* (London, 1792), pp. 83–5. When Forrest was at Passir the resident Bugis merchant community expelled the local Malay sultan without undue fuss.

59. de Hullu, J., 'A. E. van Braam Houckgeest's Memorie over Malakka en den Tinhandel Aldaar (1790)', *Bijdragen tot de Taal-, Land-, en Volkenkunde van Nederlandsch-Indie*, pt 76 (1920), pp. 285–8; also Harrison, B., 'Malacca in the eighteenth century: two Dutch Governors' Reports', *Journal of the Malayan Branch of the Royal Asiatic Society*, xxvii (May 1954), p. 31.

60. de Hullu, J., 'Van Braam Houckgeest's Memorie'; also his 'De Engelschen op Poeloe Pinang en de Tinhandel der Nederlandsche Oost-Indische Compagnie in 1788', *Bijdragen tot de Taal-, Land-, en Volkenkunde van Nederlandsch-Indie*, pt 77 (1921), pp. 605–14.

61. Harlow, V. T., *The Founding of the Second British Empire, 1763–1793*, i (London, 1952), pp. 63–72, 97–8, 100–1, 135–45.

62. Bassett, D. K., 'British Commercial and Strategic Interest in the Malay Peninsula during the late eighteenth century', *Festschrift for Sir Richard Winstedt* (Oxford U.P., 1963).

63. Harlow, *The Founding of the Second British Empire*, pp. 70–5.

64. Harlow, *op. cit.*, pp. 75–80.

65. Harlow, *op. cit.*, pp. 81–97.

66. Wright, H. R. C., *East-Indian Economic Problems of the Age of Cornwallis & Raffles* (London, 1961), pp. 268–72, 275–6.

67. For the reports of Monckton and Desvoeux see *SFR*, xv (IOL).

68. British Museum, *Add. MS.* 29,210, ff. 217–22 v., 225–30 v., 231–2 v.

69. Bassett, D. K., 'Thomas Forrest, an eighteenth century mariner', *Journal of the Malayan Branch of the Royal Asiatic Society*, xxxiv (2), (1961), pp. 115–19; also 'British Commercial and Strategic Interest', *Festschrift* (1963).

70. Cowan, C. D., 'Governor Bannerman and the Penang Tin Scheme, 1818–1819', *Journal of the Malayan Branch of the Royal Asiatic Society*, XXIII (February 1950), pp. 52–4; also Cowan, 'Early Penang and the rise of Singapore', *ibid.*, XXIII (March 1950), pp. 4–5, 6–7.

71. Wright, *East-Indian Economic Problems*, p. 284.

72. Wright, *op. cit.*, pp. 280–1, 285–6.

73. Irwin, *Nineteenth-century Borneo*, pp. 12–13, 15; Bastin, J., *Essays on Indonesian and Malayan History* (Singapore, 1961), pp. 126–7.

74. Wright, *East-Indian Economic Problems*, pp. 280, 285–6; Irwin, *Borneo*, pp. 13–16, 24–28; Bastin, *Essays*, pp. 120–3.

75. Irwin, *Borneo*, p. 29; Bastin, *Essays*, p. 123.

76. Irwin, *op. cit.*, pp. 30–1; Bastin, *op. cit.*, p. 130.

77. For his efforts in Sumatra see Bastin, *Essays*, pp. 164–71; J. S. Tay, 'The attempts of Raffles to establish a British base in South-east Asia, 1818–1819', *Journal of South-east Asian History*, I (2) (September 1960), pp. 33–41.

78. Irwin, *Borneo*, pp. 48–51.

NOTES TO CHAPTER 8 128–137

1. A detailed account of the diplomatic background to the negotiation of the treaty is given in Marks, Harry J., *The First Contest for Singapore, 1819–24* (The Hague, 1959).

2. The best study of European diplomatic rivalry in Borneo in the nineteenth century is Irwin, Graham, *Nineteenth Century Borneo* (The Hague and Singapore, 1955).

3. Tarling, Nicholas, 'British Policy in the Malay Peninsula and Archipelago, 1824–71', *Journal of the Malayan Branch, Royal Asiatic* (1957), *Society* XXX, pt. 3, gives a comprehensive account of the East India Company's relations with the Malay states.

4. The development of Sarawak under the Brooke family provides the theme for two recent books: Runciman, Sir Steven, *The White Rajahs* (Cambridge and New York, 1960), and Payne, Robert, *The White Rajahs of Sarawak* (London, 1960).

5. This project was reported and discussed with interest in the Singapore newspapers, notably in *Singapore Free Press*, June 3, 1858, and *Straits Times*, June 12, 1858.

6. Wong Lin Ken in 'A Study of Singapore's Trade, 1819–69', *Journal of the Malayan Branch, Royal Asiatic Society* (1960), XXXIII, pt. 4, provides an excellent analysis of the growth of Singapore's trade during the first half century of the port's history.

7. The structure of the early tin trade is examined by Wong Lin Ken in a PhD

dissertation on the Malayan tin trade prior to 1914, with special reference to Perak and Selangor (to be published).

8. Governor to Calcutta, October 31, 1863, *Straits Settlements Records* (National Library, Singapore), XLI, p. 183.

9. A detailed account of this struggle is given by Linehan, W., 'A History of Pahang', *Journal of the Malayan Branch, Royal Asiatic Society* (1936), XIV, pt. 2.

10. The background and a brief outline of this movement are given in Mills, L. A., in 'British Malaya, 1824–67', *Journal of the Malayan Branch, Royal Asiatic Society* (1925), III, pt. 2 (reprinted *ibid.*, 1960, XXXIII, pt. 3).

11. Two recent books provide complementary studies of the background to British intervention in the Malay states during the first ten years of colonial rule in the Straits Settlements: Parkinson, C. N., *British Intervention in Malaya, 1867–77* (Singapore and New York, 1960), and Cowan, C. D., *Nineteenth Century Malaya: the Origins of British Political Control* (London and New York, 1961).

12. Sadka, Emily (ed.), 'The Journal of Sir Hugh Low, Perak, 1877', *Journal of the Malayan Branch, Royal Asiatic Society* (1954), XXVII, pt. 4.

13. Thio, Eunice, 'The extension of British control to Pahang', *Journal of the Malayan Branch, Royal Asiatic Society* (1957), XXX, pt. 1.

14. The best and most concise account of the development of administration in the Malay states after British intervention is Emerson, Rupert, *Malaysia: a study in Direct and Indirect Rule* (New York, 1937). Emerson's term 'Malaysia' referred not to the present-day political entity of Malaysia, but to British Malaya and the Dutch East Indies.

15. Tregonning, Kennedy G., *Under Chartered Company Rule* (Singapore, 1958), covers the origins and development of the British North Borneo Company's rule.

NOTES TO CHAPTER 9 *138–148*

1. For text of agreements see Maxwell, W. G., and Gibson, W. S., *Treaties and Engagements affecting the Malay States and Borneo* (London, 1924).

2. The Dindings, a small area on the Perak coast, was also British territory. Labuan was a separate Crown colony, 1846–89; it was administered by British North Borneo Company from 1890 to 1906, when it was incorporated in the colony of the Straits Settlements, as part of Singapore. From 1912 it was a separate settlement of the colony, until it was added to North Borneo in 1946.

3. Runciman, Sir Steven, *The White Rajahs* (Cambridge and New York, 1960), p. 227.

4. Emerson, R., *Malaysia* (Harvard, 1937), p. 146.

5. *Ibid.*, pp. 174–5.

6. Purcell, Victor, *Malaya—Communist or Free* (London, 1954), pp. 12 and 39.

7. Silcock, T. H. and Ungku Abdul Aziz, *Nationalism in Malaya* (New York, 1950).

8. MacMichael, Sir Harold, *Report on Mission to Malaya* (Colonial Office 194, 1946).

NOTES TO CHAPTER 10   *149–160*

In a volume on Malaysia this is probably one of the very few chapters in which it is proper to confine attention to Malaya. There was an 'Emergency' of a sort in Sarawak—it lasted six months, from August 1952 to January 1953—but there has, in fact, been no communist insurrection in the other Malaysian territories. The more recent events in Sabah, Sarawak and Brunei come within a different category.

STUDIES

For the general background to communism see
> Brimmel, J. H., *Communism in South-east Asia* (London and New York, 1959).

On the Emergency itself, three books deal with the critical years 1948–54:
> Perry Robinson, J. B., *Transformation in Malaya* (London, 1956).
> Miller, Harry, *Menace in Malaya* (London, 1954).
> Purcell, Victor, *Malaya: Communist or Free?* (London, 1954).

A sociological interpretation is attempted by:-
> Pye, Lucian, *Guerrilla Communism in Malaya* (Princeton, 1956).

There is a small number of rather stereotyped military accounts which convey the impression of transmogrified fox-hunting. Two which do not are:
> Crawford, Oliver, *The Door Marked Malaya* (London, 1958).
> Slimming, John, *In Fear of Silence* (London, 1959).

For an account of the organisation of the war-time guerrillas, see:
> Chapman, F. Spencer, *The Jungle is Neutral* (London, 1949).

Lastly, for a rare insight into the Chinese community and its reaction to the Emergency:
> Han Suyin, *And the Rain My Drink* (London and Boston, Mass., 1956).

NOTES TO CHAPTER 11   *163–178*

1. For a fully illustrated description and discussion of the Niah Skull, see Brothwell, D. R., *Sarawak Museum Journal*, ix (1960) 15: pp. 323–50.

2. This chapter is based primarily on my researches in all four territories of Borneo, during the years 1932–3 and 1945–63. Some of this has been pub-

lished in the 4,400 pages of the *Sarawak Museum Journal*, post-war issues 1949–62, Nos. 1–20. There is a great deal of other literature about Borneo; but it has to be confessed that it is of distinctly uneven quality and poor coverage. Where no reference is indicated in the present text, the observation is from my own work; much of this is now in process of preparation either for publication or duplicate filing in Kuching and elsewhere.

3. See my booklet *Background to a Revolt* (Brunei, 1963) for the context of this event. In northern Sarawak the rebels were also mainly Kedayan, in the south-west corner of Sabah they were Bajaus (also muslim). I refer again to the Kedayans and their treatment as a group in the 1960 Brunei Census near the end of the present essay. I wish to record here my personal regard for the Kedayans at peace.

4. *Background to a Revolt*.

5. A series of notes and papers on this cult has been or is about to be published in the *Sarawak Museum Journal*, which also deals extensively with other of the race-group matters discussed here. The Bungan Malan cult was initiated by a middle-class Kenyah, Jok Apoi of the Batang Kayan, Kalimantan. The ruling 'pope' in west Borneo is Baleng Abun of Belaga, a Kayan chief; he is currently preparing his 'bible' in both Kayan and Malay for Sarawak Museum achives.

6. Harrisson, T. and B., 'Kota Batu', *Sarawak Museum Journal*, VIII (1956), 6: pp. 283–319.

7. Carroll, John, 'The Term Bisaya in Borneo and the Philippines', *Sarawak Museum Journal*, x (1960), 15: pp. 489–541.

8. *Background to a Revolt*, see note 3.

9. Harrisson, T., 'Explorations in Central Borneo', *Geographical Journal*, v (1949), 114: pp. 132–47.

10. Firth, R., *Malay Fishermen* (Cambridge, 1949). Over the last five years, Malay observers in Sarawak coastal villages have reported the daily work for a sample of average villages on every day of the year. Two preliminary accounts of this work have appeared in Sarawak and a full-length report is now in press.

11. The original material is filed in the Sarawak Museum; for a methodological introduction, see *Sarawak Museum Journal*, IX (1960), 16: pp. 655–70.

12. Lee, Y. L., 'The Long House and Dayak Settlement in British Borneo', *Oriental Geographer*, VI (1962), 1: pp. 39–60; Geddes, W. R., *Nine Dayak Nights* (Oxford, 1961).

13. Scharer, H., *Die Gottesidee der Ngadju Dajak* (Leyden, 1940); this key study is discussed by Harrisson, T., 'Death in Borneo', *Bijdragen* (Leyden), 118, (1962); pp. 1–41.

14. It is hoped to establish this method by photograph files presently.

15. Cense, A. A. and Uhlenbeck, E. M., *Critical Survey of Studies on the Languages of Borneo* (The Hague, 1958), p. 3.

16. Harrisson, T., 'Culture Contact and Change in South-east Asia', *Sarawak Museum Journal,* XI (1962), 19: pp. 460–85.

17. Each territory's census is the subject of a separate large volume published by the Government Printer of Sarawak (at Kuching) during various months in 1962. Mr L. W. Jones kindly allowed access to some additional material, by authority, prior to the destruction of the original returns as required by law.

18. For a general account of Brunei pagan groupings see *Sarawak Museum Journal,* VIII (1958), 11: pp. 293–321. Several of the very small sub-groups in the 1960 Sarawak census are not finally classified and one or two (e.g. Ukit) are not correctly placed. This involves *circa* 0·1 per cent of the total, but should not for that reason give any grounds for satisfaction. *Exact* groupings really *matter* in the present and future state of Bornean multiracialism.

19. In Sabah there is no administrative category for Malay; and all Brunei Malays are classed as 'Bruneis'. The same system was adopted for the 1960 Census, necessarily.

NOTES TO CHAPTER 12   *179–189*

1. Wertheim, W. F., *Indonesian Society in Transition: A Study of Social Change* (The Hague, 1956), p. 2. Chapters I, V, VI, and X of this book contain many references and discussions on Indonesian culture and society. Chapter X especially is devoted to 'Cultural Dynamics in Indonesia' and it discusses the whole complex of *sawah* culture. Chapter VIII deals with 'Religious Reform' in Indonesia and much that is said there is also true of Malaya, and for those who are interested in the subject, this Chapter could profitably be read with Mr W. Roff's essay (see note 11 below).

2. *Ibid.,* p. 280.

3. *Ibid.,* pp. 281–2.

4. *Ibid.,* p. 283.

5. Vlekke, Bernhard H. M., *Nusantara: A History of Indonesia* (Cambridge, Mass., 1943), p. 12.

6. Winstedt, R. O., *The Malay Magician* (London, 1951), p. 27.

7. van Leur, J. C., *Indonesian Trade and Society, Essays in Asian Social and Economic History* (The Hague and New York, 1955), p. 111.

8. Vlekke, *op. cit.,* p. 82.

9. van Leur, *op. cit.,* p. 114.

10. Article 11 (4) of the Constitution of the Federation of Malaya.

11. Roff, W., 'Kaum Muda-Kaum Tua: Innovation and Reaction among the Malays, 1900–41': *Papers on Malayan History*, edited by Tregonning, K. G. (First International Conference of South-east Asian Historians, Singapore, 1961). This paper 'tried to describe the conflict in Malaya between the Islamic reformers and, on the one hand, the religious hierarchy and the traditional elite, on the other the rural ulama and the predominantly conservative elements in Malay peasant society, and to suggest the way in which these conflicts carried wider implications of social and political change', p. 186.

12. Vlekke, *op. cit.*, pp. 10–11.

13. Vlekke, *op. cit.*, p. 401, note 6.

14. Kahin, George McTurnan, *Nationalism and Revolution in Indonesia* (Ithaca, N.Y., 1952), p. 97, note 101.

15. The Dewan Bahasa dan Pustaka Ordinance, 1959, Article 5.

NOTES TO CHAPTER 13   *190–198*

1. My provisional estimate for the new edition (1964) of *The Chinese in South-east Asia*.

2. Freedman, Maurice, *Chinese Family and Marriage in Singapore* (London, 1957).

3. Newell, William H., *Treacherous River: A Study of Rural Chinese in North Malaya* (Kuala Lumpur and New York, 1962).

4. Willmott, Donald E., *The Chinese of Semarang* (Ithaca, N.Y., 1960).

5. 'Malaya proves to be the only country which poses a difficult problem for the Chinese in the Nanyang [South-east Asia]. Elsewhere, even in Siam, the choice before a Chinese is simple. He has to seek assimilation or live as an alien and one day return to China'; Wang Gungwu, *A Short History of the Nanyang Chinese* (Singapore, 1959), p. 42.

6. See Fitzgerald, C. P., 'Overseas Chinese in South-east Asia', *Australian Journal of Politics and History*, May 1962.

7. In Sabah, there is a strong movement for the retention of English as the 'official language'.

NOTES TO CHAPTER 14   *199–209*

RELEVANT DOCUMENTS

Colony of North Borneo, *Education Department Triennial Survey*; (a) 1955–7; (b) 1958–60; Government Printing Office, Jesselton. *North Borneo Annual Reports*; (a) 1960; (b) 1961; Government Printing Department, Jesselton.

Colony of Singapore, *Progress in Education during 1956*; Government Printing Office, (Singapore, 1957).

State of Singapore, *Department of Education Annual Report 1958*; Government Printing Office, (1959).

State of Singapore, *Ministry of Education Annual Reports*; (a) 1959; (b) 1960; Government Printing Office, Singapore, 1961, 1962. *Report of the Commission of Inquiry into Vocational and Technical Education in Singapore*; Government Printing Office, 1961.

Sarawak, *Education Department Annual Summary*; (a) 1960; (b) 1961; Government Printing Office (Kuching, 1961, 1962). *Education Department Triennial Survey 1958-60*; Government Printing Office, (Kuching, 1961).

Federation of Malaya, *Educational Policy*; White Paper No. 67 of 1954; Government Press, Kuala Lumpur. *Report of the Education Committee 1956*; Government Press, (Kuala Lumpur, 1956). *Report of the Education Review Committee 1960*; Government Press (Kuala Lumpur, 1960). *Federation of Malaya Yearbook*; (a) 1961; (b) 1962; Government Press (Kuala Lumpur).

McLellan, D., *Report on Secondary Education*; Government Printing Office (Kuching, 1960).

Yong, N. L., 'Spring source of our nation: The Tasks Ahead, Part II'; *Petir* (Singapore, 1959), 35 pp.

Commonwealth Education Conference (First), Review of teacher training and teacher supply: *CEC Report*; Oxford, England, HMSO, 1959.

Educational Services Incorporated, Teacher training: *General Report of the African Summer Study*; Watertown, Massachusetts (mimeograph), 1961.

NOTES TO CHAPTER 15

1. For traditional Malay literature, see Winstedt, R. O., 'A History of Malay Literature', *Journal of the Malayan Branch of the Royal Asiatic Society*, XXXI, pt 3 (June 1958).
2. A *sejarah* purporting to have been written during the sultanate of Malacca, but known to have been edited in 1612 at Johore Lama.
3. Teeuw, A., *Pokok dan Tokoh* (Djakarta, 1953), p. 27.
4. See Amir Hamzah, 'Abdoellah', *Poedjangga Baroe*, August 1933, pp. 44-7.
5. Reviewing the literary scene in Malaya before the last war, an Indonesian journalist, writing in a Sumatran newspaper, *Pewarta Deli*, wrote: 'Someone like Abdullah must emerge in Malaya; one who will vitalise the Malay literature (in Malaya) is long awaited by the people of Indonesia' (quoted by *Majallah Guru*, November 1934).

6. Omar Mohd. Hashim, 'Perkembangan Cherpen Melayu Sa-belum Perang', *Dewan Bahasa*, August 1961, p. 344.
7. Zainal Abidin bin Ahmad, 'Modern Developments', *Journal of the Malayan Branch of the Royal Asiatic Society*, XVII, pt 3 (1939), p. 153.
8. Omar Mohd. Hashim, *Dewan Bahasa*, August 1961, p. 346.
9. See Zainal Abidin bin Ahmad, 'Recent Malay literature', *Journal of the Malayan Branch of the Royal Asiatic Society*, XIX, pt 1 (1941).
10. Omar Mohd. Hashim, *Dewan Bahasa*, August 1961, p. 355.
11. See *Poedjangga Baroe*, July 1934, p. 4.
12. Some of the poems are contained in Ali Haji Ahmad's *Puisi Melayu Baru* (Kuala Lumpur, 1959).
13. 'We do not want to retain the old form, we do not want to sing the *seloka* and *gurindam*, like our forefathers; we want to create new forms which are worthy of the spirit of our society . . .'—Armijn Pane, *Poedjangga Baroe*, August 1933, p. 43.
14. Abdullah Sanusi Ahmad, 'Pejabat Karang Mengarang', an unpublished academic exercise submitted to the Department of Malay Studies, Kuala Lumpur, 1960, p. 65.
15. *Ibid.*, p. 62.
16. See Masuri's earlier poems in the collection *Awan Puteh* (Singapore, 1958).
17. *Semangat Asia*, II, No. 3.
18. See Usman Awang (Tongkat Waran), 'Bahasa Melayu Dalam Lapangan Kesusasteraan', *Memoranda* (Kuala Lumpur, 1962), pp. 152–4.
19. Mohd. Taib Osman, *An Introduction to the Development of Malay Language and Literature* (Singapore, 1961), p. 51.
20. Omar Mohd. Hashim, 'Cherpen Melayu Moden Sa-lepas Perang', *Dewan Bahasa*, March 1962, p. 105.
21. *Loc. cit.*
22. Ismail Hussein, 'Pengarang2 Melayu Di-Singapura Sa-lepas Perang Dunia II', an unpublished academic exercise submitted to the Department of Malay Studies, Singapore, 1959, p. 16.
23. See *Memoranda* (Kuala Lumpur, 1962).
24. Syed Husin Ali, 'Pertubuhan2 Bahasa Dan Sastera Melayu (Di-Singapura) Selepas Perang Dunia II', *Bahasa*, March 1960, pp. 41–3.
25. *Ibid.*, pp. 48–9.
26. Quoted by Omar Mohd. Hashim, *Dewan Bahasa*, March 1962, p. 102.
27. According to Samad Said, who is the editor of *Berita Minggu*, there are many more short stories and *sajak* received in a week than the weekly can ever publish.
28. *Utusan Melayu*, March 19, 1963, p. 5.

29. See Syed Husin Ali, *op. cit.*, p. 22.

30. In *Dewan Bahasa*, for example, there is a series of articles on the various literary movements and concepts in the history of western literature.

31. For example, themes on the death of Lumumba, the nuclear war threats and the ideological conflict between the eastern and the western blocs.

32. See also the Introduction by Kirkup, James, to *Modern Malay Verse 1946–61* (Kuala Lumpur and New York, 1963).

NOTES TO CHAPTER 16   *227–245*

1. Originally a plantation was any planting of export-oriented cash crops but the word gradually came to be restricted to the large units for which the term 'estate' was unsuitable, since the European estate of the seventeenth and eighteenth centuries was typically a collection of tenancies, and therefore under multiple, as opposed to single management. The Commonwealth Economic Committee defines plantation crops as those cash crops formerly grown under plantation (i.e. estate) conditions, but which may now be grown either by estates or by smallholders or by indigenous farmers.

2. Jackson, R. N., *Immigrant Labour and the Development of Malaya* (Government Press, Kuala Lumpur, 1961), pp. 93–4.

3. Federation of Malaya, *Agricultural Census 1960, Preliminary Report No. 16, Estates* (Kuala Lumpur, 1963), p. v.

4. The total number of rubber estates at December 31, 1961, was given as 2,218 with a further 26 in Singapore. Federation of Malaya Department of Statistics, *Rubber Statistics Handbook 1961*, p. 9.

5. *Agricultural Census, op. cit.*, p. v.

6. *Rubber Statistics Handbook 1961*, p. 59.

7. There are some Malay owners of coconut estates, as such estates are not rigorously defined, and there are a number of Malays in government service and in private industry owning shares in European estate companies.

8. *Rubber Statistics Handbook 1961*, p. 10.

9. The most sustained criticism is contained in Bauer, P. T., *The Rubber Industry; A Study in Monopoly and Competition* (London, 1948).

10. A clone is a race of plants with a common genetic inheritance, and therefore with identical characteristics. One half of the total area of budwood nurseries is situated on estates with a planted area exceeding 3,000 acres. *Agricultural Census, op. cit.*, p. 67.

11. The larger Guthrie units (Labu Cheviot, Linggi, Malacca Plantations, Oil Palms of Malaya, Port Dickson-Lukut and United Sua Betong) have very large inter-

company holdings in each other. Some 48 per cent of the ordinary stock of Guthrie & Co. is owned by Malayan Rubber Loan and Agency Corporation Ltd, an investment company. Zorn and Leigh Hunt, *Manual of Rubber Planting Companies* (London, 1960), p. 158.

12. Personal communication from Miss R. Mamajiwala, Department of Economics, University of Malaya.

13. *Report of the Mission of Enquiry into the Rubber Industry of Malaya*: the Mudie Report (Kuala Lumpur, 1954), Appendix C.

14. *Taxation and Replanting in the Rubber Industry.* Statement of the Federal Government on the Report of the Mudie Mission (Kuala Lumpur, 1955), p. 15.

15. *Rubber Statistics Handbook 1961*, p. 20.

16. *Op. cit.*, p. 14.

17. Since 1945 Nigeria has become a large producer of palm oil as well as being the world's largest producer of palm kernels. Production is a smallholder activity and much fruit is gathered from wild palms; the free fatty acid content of Nigerian palm is high. The Nigerian success in upgrading smallholders' oil by premiums for quality oil and by the use of 'Pioneer' mills has encouraged the Federation government to investigate the possibilities of smallholder oil palm cultivation; the two schemes to be undertaken by the Federal Land Development Authority, however, will involve central processing and accounting at estate factories.

18. The early history of the oil palm in Malaya is obscure but seed for the first commercial development came from the Deli area of east Sumatra and was planted on an estate near Batang Berjuntai, Selangor. These trees provided the material for the first commercial estate planting on the Tennamaram estate nearby. See Jagoe, R. B., 'Deli Oil Palms and Early Introductions of Elaeis Guineensis to Malaya', *Malayan Agricultural Journal*, xxxv, January 1952, pp. 3–9.

19. Grist, D. H., 'Malayan Oil Palm Industry in 1929', *Malayan Agricultural Journal*, xviii, July 1930, p. 347.

20. *Agricultural Census 1960, op. cit.*, p. 73.

NOTES TO CHAPTER 17   *246–273*

1. The term 'cash crop' is taken to include *only* those crops grown by smallholders which enter into the external commerce of the territories. The term therefore *includes* rubber, coconuts, etc, but *excludes* padi, fruit trees, market garden crops, etc.

2. *Cash crops* cultivated by smallholders occupy extremely small areas in Singapore and these areas are therefore excluded from the present discussion.
3. *Federation of Malaya Official Year Book, 1962* (Kuala Lumpur, 1962), p. 299.
4. Production of rubber by smallholders increased noticeably during the boom in prices at the beginning of the Korean War (1950–3), the peak year falling in 1950. The increased production achieved by smallholders at this time resulted from the tapping of trees hitherto uneconomic, and by 'slaughter tapping'. Smallholding production declined in 1951 and subsequent years, but in the late 1950s began to increase steadily. This decline was caused by falling prices and 'because of earlier intensive tapping and the growing age of the trees' ('Malaya and British Borneo', p. 172, in Silcock, T. H. (ed.), *Readings in Malayan Economics* (Singapore, 1961). In some respects therefore 1952 may not appear to be a suitable starting point for this discussion; it is however of considerable significance for it was the year in which official schemes designed to rehabilitate the Malayan rubber industry began.
5. Ooi Jin-bee, 'Rural Development in Tropical Areas, with special reference to Malaya', *Journal of Tropical Geography*, XII (March 1959), p. 144.
6. Ooi Jin-bee, 'The Rubber Industry of the Federation of Malaya', *Journal of Tropical Geography*, XV (June 1961), p. 58.
7. This discrepancy arises because the so-called 'holdings' recorded in the official statistics were actually individual 'lots' planted with rubber, and a single smallholding can consist of one or more 'lots' of rubber, provided that the total acreage does not exceed 100 acres.
8. One of the reasons why it is advisable to begin this discussion of the smallholding sector of the Malayan rubber industry in the early 1950s is the fact that statistics which can be used to indicate ethnic ownership are no longer published. Fortunately, it is reasonably safe to assume that there will have been no major changes since 1952 in the patterns indicated here.
9. Figures of average yields have been calculated from information contained in *Rubber Statistics Handbook, 1952* (Alor Star, 1953).
10. The Rubber Industry (Replanting) Board Scheme No. 3 for the Administration of Fund 'B', *Report on Operations for the Year 1961 by the Chief Replanting Officer* (Kuala Lumpur, 1962), p. 1.
11. *Taxation and Replanting in the Rubber Industry*, Statement of the Federal Government on the Report of the Mudie Mission and on Certain Proposals made by the Rubber Producers' Council (Kuala Lumpur, 1955), p. 13.
12. Scheme No. 1 was started 'with the intention of getting things moving, and inviting applications for grants so that those accepted would have ample time to prepare their lands ready for planting up in the main planting season' (Rubber Industry (Replanting) Board, *Report on Operations for the Year 1961*, p. 3).

13. Rubber Industry (Replanting) Board, *Report on Operations for the Year 1961*, p. 4.
14. The Rubber Industry (Replanting) (Smallholders) Scheme.
15. Rubber Industry (Replanting) Board, *Report on Operations for the Year 1961*, pp. 4–5.
16. That so much should have been achieved is surprising when it is remembered that from 1948 to 1961 Malaya was in the throes of the anti-communist war, known as the Emergency.
17. Almost twice the actual target area was replanted in Malacca between 1953 and 1959.
18. Ooi Jin-bee, 'The Rubber Industry of the Federation of Malaya', p. 63.
19. Regional Conference of South-east Asian Geographers, *Guide to Tours* (Kuala Lumpur, April 1962), p. 28.
20. In March 1963 a survey of Chinese smallholders in part of Selangor was undertaken by the Department of Geography, University of Malaya, under the direction of Dr D. W. Fryer and Mr J. C. Jackson, to investigate, amongst other things, the sources of income which these smallholders possess in addition to their rubber land. The results of this survey, which are not yet available, will be published in due course.
21. These figures are based upon estimates of the *total* smallholding rubber acreage owned by each ethnic group in 1952. Since it has already been noted that less than 1·5 per cent of the total smallholding acreage existing in 1952 had been replanted, it can be assumed that a very large proportion was in dire need of action, and the figures therefore give a general impression of the amount of progress so far achieved by each of the ethnic groups in this particular direction.
22. Benham, F. C., 'The Rubber Industry', in Silcock, *Readings in Malayan Economics*, p. 288. This article first appeared in *Economica*, November 1949.
23. Rubber Research Institute, *Annual Report, 1961*, p. 119.
24. Rubber Industry (Replanting) Board, *Report on Operations for the Year 1961*, p. 13.
25. *Dusun* = orchard, or block of land planted with fruit trees.
26. Although it might be suggested that the Federal Land Development Authority schemes are doing little more than simply perpetuating and extending a situation in which the majority of Malays are small-scale agriculturists with a relatively low level of productivity, it must be admitted that the schemes are resulting in the planting of large areas of high yielding smallholding rubber which will eventually yield far higher profits for the smallholder than the pre-existing type of Malay-owned rubber smallholding.
27. *Sarawak Annual Report, 1961* (Kuching, 1962), p. 49. Unfortunately accurate agricultural statistics are not available for Sarawak. In recent years indiscriminate planting of unselected rubber has been prevalent in areas which are not readily accessible and it is therefore possible that the total acreage of rubber in Sarawak is in excess of the published estimates.

28. Government of Sarawak, *Annual Report of the Department of Agriculture for the Year 1957* (Kuching, 1958), p. 27.

29. Government of Sarawak, *Annual Report of the Department of Agriculture for the Year 1958* (Kuching, 1959), p. 8.

30. Government of Sarawak, *Annual Report of the Department of Agriculture for the Year 1959* (Kuching, 1959), p. 78.

31. It was noted in 1957 that since the scheme came into effect, Ibans in up-country districts had been following a system of block planting, 'obviously a reflection of their social structure'; *Annual Report, Department of Agriculture, 1957,* p. 29.

32. As with Sarawak, accurate agricultural statistics are not available for Sabah and in giving estimates of acreages for 1960 the Government Annual Report notes: 'These figures . . . are not based on a full and detailed survey, and entire accuracy is not claimed for them.' *Colony of North Borneo Annual Report, 1960* (Jesselton, 1961), p. 54.

33. However, rubber is the main crop on only about one quarter of all peasant holdings in Sabah with almost twice as many devoted to padi. These facts are derived from information obtained during the Population Census, 1960, quoted in *Annual Report of the Department of Agriculture for the Year 1960* (Jesselton, 1961), p. 37.

34. Colony of North Borneo, *Annual Report, 1960,* p. 55.

35. Published figures for exports of copra from Sabah include very large amounts re-exported under the barter trade from Indonesia and the Philippines; these have been excluded from the figures used to produce this estimate.

36. Federation of Malaya, *Census of Agriculture, 1960,* Preliminary Report No. 10, Permanent Crops: Compact Areas and Scattered Trees (Kuala Lumpur, May 1962), Table 664.

37. Sarawak, *Annual Report, Department of Agriculture, 1959,* p. 9.

38. The yield of dry black pepper from fully mature vines has decreased from an average of 8–12 lbs before the Second World War to less than 6 lbs in 1959.

39. It should be noted, however, that 10,950 tons of Sarawak pepper entered world trade in 1961; this compares very favourably with the 4,100 tons in 1960, and may indicate a resurgence of the industry. *Sarawak Annual Report, 1961,* p. 54.

NOTES TO CHAPTER 18 274–292

1. Panton, W. P., 'Provisional Soils Map of Malaya', paper read at the South-east Asian Conference of Geographers, 1962.

2. Joseph, K. T., 'The soils of Kedah in relation to their proposed utilisation for

various crops', paper read at the South-east Asian Conference of Geographers, 1962.

3. Akers, R. L., *Report of the Drainage and Irrigation Department for the years 1958, 1959 and 1960, Federation of Malaya* (Government Printer, 1961).

4. Berwick, E. J. H., *Annual Report of the Department of Agriculture for the year 1961* (North Borneo Government Printing Office, 1962).

5. Hickling, C. F., 'The Fish Culture Research Station, Malacca', *Nature*, CLXXXIII, p. 287.

6. Bevan, J. W. L., *A study of yields, labour inputs and incomes on rubber smallholdings in the coastal area of Selangor. (A preliminary summary of data)* (printed for private circulation, 1962).

7. Aziz, U. A., 'The causes of poverty in Malayan Agriculture', *Problems of Malayan Economy*, ed. Lim Tay Boh (Singapore, 1956); Wilson, T. B., 'The economics of padi production in North Malaya. Part I: Land tenure, rents, land use and fragmentation', *Department of Agriculture, Federation of Malaya Bulletin*, 103, 1958.

8. Wilson, T. B., 'The West Johore Coconut Production Survey', *Ministry of Agriculture, Federation of Malaya Bulletin*, 104, 1958.

9. Burgess, R. C. and Laidin Bin Alang Musa, 'A report on the state of health, the diet and the economic conditions of groups of people in the lower income levels in Malaya', Institute for Medical Research, *Report No. 13*, 1950; Simpson, I. A. (ed.), *Applied Nutrition in Malaya*, Institute of Medical Research, Kuala Lumpur, 1957; Thomson, Florence A., 'Child Nutrition. A survey in the Parit District of Perak, Federation of Malaya', Institute for Medical Research, Kuala Lumpur. *Bulletin* No. 10, 1960.

10. Wharton, C. R., Jr., 'Food Consumption Levels in Malaya: Some Income, Locational and Racial Aspects', *Rural Social Science Monograph No. 2 B. Malayan Series* (1962).

11. Vivian, L. A., 'The leguminous fodder "Stylo" or "Tropical Lucerne" in Kelantan (*Stylosanthes gracilis*)', *Malayan Agricultural Journal*, XLII, pp. 183–98.

12. Aziz, U. A., 'The causes of poverty in Malayan Agriculture', *Problems of Malayan Economy*, ed. Lim Tay Boh (Singapore, 1956); Wharton, C. R. Jr. (1962), 'Marketing, merchandising and moneylending: A note on middleman monopsony in Malaya', *Malayan Economic Review*, VII-2, pp. 24–44; Wilson, T. B., 'The economics of padi production in North Malaya. Part I: Land tenure, rents, land use and fragmentation', *Department of Agriculture, Federation of Malaya Bulletin*, 103, 1958.

13. Wilson, T. B., 'Malayan Census of Agriculture 1960. Preliminary Reports 6A, 7 & 9', Commissioner for Agriculture Census, Ministry of Agriculture and Co-operatives, Federation of Malaya.

14. Cook, J., *Annual Report of the Department of Agriculture for the year 1961*, Kuching, 1962.
15. Millikan, M. F., *Restless Nations: A Study of World tensions and development*, New York, 1962.

NOTES TO CHAPTER 19 *293–306*

1. Between 1880 and 1905, the export duty on tin alone made up one third to one half of the total revenue of the then Federated Malay States: cf. Swetten-ham, F. A., *British Malaya* (London, 1906), table on p. 300.
2. Yip Yat Hoong, 'Malaya under the pre-war International Tin Agreement', *Malayan Economic Review*, VIII, No. 1 (April 1963).
3. As Silcock, T. H., has pointed out in the *Economy of Malaya* (Singapore, 1954), p. 441, 'Unlike many underdeveloped countries Malaya is very far from lacking commercial enterprise. There are always tens of thousands of Chinese willing to use what savings they have and what credit they can acquire in establishing businesses as very small contractors, shopkeepers or hawkers, and the talent for finding suitable new business opportunities is highly developed. Malaya indeed probably suffers from an excess of enter-prise, since this is a factor which tends to disintegrate existing business.' This cannot be more clearly illustrated than in Chinese tin mining. The 'excess of enterprise' which 'tends to disintegrate existing business' serves to explain the large number of small Chinese gravel pump mines in the tin mining industry.
4. Calculations based on Department of Mines, Federation of Malaya, *Bulletin of Statistics relating to the Mining Industry, 1956–60* (Kuala Lumpur), Table 8, p. 12.
5. International Bank for Reconstruction and Development, *The Economic Develop-ment of Malaya* (Singapore and Baltimore, 1955), p. 254.
6. Geological Survey Department, British Territories in Borneo, *Annual Report*, 1958 (Kuching), Table 5, p. 21.
7. Fermor, L. L., *Report upon the Mining Industry of Malaya* (Kuala Lumpur, 1939).
8. President's Materials Policy Commission, *Resources for Freedom*, a Report to the President (US Government Printing Office, 1952), II, p. 51.
9. International Bank for Reconstruction and Development, *op. cit.*, p. 249.
10. Griffiths, H. D., *Bucket Dredging for Tin in the Federated Malay States* (London, 1917), Table I, p. 3. This data was based on the 11 dredges operating in the Federated Malay States in 1915.
11. Stokes, R., *Malay Tin-Fields* (Singapore, 1906), p. 10.

NOTES TO CHAPTER 20 *307–320*

1. Economic development means essentially a long term, sustained increase in human productivity. Since the nineteenth century economic development has everywhere been accompanied by industrialisation, the growing importance of factory production in the national economy. Thus for our purposes it is possible to treat these two movements as synonymous, though for other problems it may be necessary to separate them.
2. Following Etzioni, a three-part classification of goals is used: *order, economic* and *cultural.* See Etzioni, Amitai, *A Comparative Analysis of Complex Organisations* (Glencoe, 1961), ch. iv.
3. Despite the invidious connotations of these terms, they are preferred here for their descriptive qualities. It is the assumption here that the fiscal policies noted in Malaya prior to 1955 were basically similar to what can broadly be called British colonial economic or fiscal policy.
4. Federation of Malaya, *Legislative Council Proceedings*, November 25, 1953, p. 823. Hereinafter referred to as Legco.
5. *Ibid.*, November 7, 1956, p. 1687.
6. European members recommended only general cuts in government spending. Indigenous members called for a reduction of highly paid ex-patriate officers.
7. Legco, April 30, 1958.
8. An exception to this was the interest in rice production shown by government during most of this century. However, this was primarily the result of government's support of the plantation economy, requiring low food costs so that labour costs could be kept low. The interest in the peasant Malay economy was only incidental to the interest in food production.
9. Dato Haji Mohamed Eusoff, Legco, November 20, 1952.
10. Legco, November 30, 1955.
11. Agricultural and infrastructure development here include capital and recurrent expenditures in the departments of Agriculture, Forestry, Fisheries, Public Works, Survey, and Utilities.
12. *Order* expenditures include expenditures on Police, Defence, and Prisons.
13. This includes all expenditures not included in Agriculture and Infrastructure, Education and Health, and *order.*
14. Colony of North Borneo, *Development Plan 1959–64*, Legislative Council Paper No. 31 of 1959.
15. From interviews held in February 1962.

1. But see the notes to this and related chapters. Some good work, for instance the PhD thesis by K. J. Ratnam, 'Communalism and the Political Process in the Federation of Malaya', is still unpublished.
2. *Malayan Constitutional Documents* (Kuala Lumpur, 1962), Section x has a comparative table on the two constitutions.
3. E.g. Wheare, K. C., *Federal Government* (London, 1947).
4. *Report of the Federation of Malaya Constitutional Commission* (Kuala Lumpur, 1957), para. 3 (terms of reference).
5. Emerson, R., *Malaysia: A Study in Direct and Indirect Rule* (New York, 1937), p. 338, quoting *Straits Times*, July 15, 1933.
6. Article 159 of the Constitution notwithstanding. Hickling, R. H., 'The First Five Years of the Federation of Malaya Constitution', *Malaya Law Review*, IV (December 1962), pp. 201 ff.
7. Article 94 (i).
8. *Straits Times*, December 5 and 6, 1960; *Malay Mail*, December 23, 1961.
9. *Straits Times*, September 20, 1961. But see Article 71 (3) of the Constitution and (on emergency powers) Articles 149 and 150.
10. *Federation of Malaya, Official Year Book 1962* (Kuala Lumpur, 1962), p. 77.
11. *Straits Times*, August 10, 1962.
12. *Ibid.*, October 11, 1962.
13. Dr. Lim Chong Eu (United Democratic Party), *Straits Times*, May 1, 1962.
14. Lim Tay Boh, *The Development of Singapore's Economy* (Singapore, 1960), p. 59. For Civil Service, see Chapter 23 of this volume.
15. Furnivall, J. S., *Colonial Policy and Practice* (Cambridge and New York, 1948); Almond, G. A. and Coleman, J. S., *The Politics of the Developing Areas* (Princeton, 1960); Riggs, F. W., 'Agraria and Industria—Toward a Typology of Comparative Administration' in Siffin, W. J. (ed.), *Toward the Comparative Study of Public Administration* (Indiana, 1957); Riggs, F. W., *The Ecology of Public Administration* (London and New York, 1961); Ratnam, K. J., 'Government and the "Plural Society" ', *Journal of South-east Asian History*, II (October 1961), pp. 1–10; Milne, R. S., 'Comparisons and Models in Public Administration', *Political Studies*, X (February 1962), pp. 1–14; Jiang, J. P. L., 'Political Change and Pariah Entrepreneurship', *Philippine Journal of Public Administration*, VI (October 1962), pp. 289–98.
16. Lipset, S. M., *Political Man* (London and New York, 1960), especially ch. i.
17. For comparison see Pye, L. W., *Politics, Personality, and Nation Building: Burma's Search for Identity* (New Haven, 1962); Wriggins, W. H., *Ceylon, Dilemmas of a New*

Nation (Princeton, 1960). But Malaya differs from these two countries in two important respects: its two main races are roughly equal in numbers and *both* are decidedly susceptible to influence by external forces.

18. Pye, L. W., *Guerrilla Communism in Malaya* (Princeton, 1956), p. 207.
19. Hanrahan, G. Z., *The Communist Struggle in Malaya* (New York, 1954), p. 101.
20. Silcock, T. H., *Towards a Malayan Nation* (Singapore, 1961), p. 59.
21. Tan Cheng Lock, *Malayan Problems from a Chinese Point of View* (Singapore, 1947), pp. 77–8.
22. Silcock, T. H., *The Commonwealth Economy in South-east Asia* (Durham, NC, 1959), p. 77.
23. Tan Cheng Lock, *Malayan Problems*, p. 127.
24. Silcock, T. H., 'Forces for Unity in Malaya', *International Affairs*, xxv (October 1949), p. 460; Purcell, V., *Malaya: Communist or Free?* (London, 1954), pp. 43–4.
25. Puthucheary, J. J., *Ownership and Control in the Malayan Economy* (Singapore, 1960), p. 174.
26. *Report of Constitutional Commission*, para. 168; *Federation of Malaya Constitutional Proposals* (Kuala Lumpur, 1957), para. 55.
27. Mr Chelvasingham McIntyre, *Straits Times*, July 12, 1957.
28. Mr Oliver Lyttelton (Lord Chandos), 503 H.C. Deb. 5s., 2383.
29. Pye, *Guerrilla Communism*, p. 207.
30. E.g. Mr Lim Kean Siew, *Straits Times*, May 14, 1962.
31. Carnell, F. G., 'Communalism and Communism in Malaya', *Pacific Affairs*, xxvi (June 1953), p. 105; Silcock, *Towards a Malayan Nation*, p. 78.
32. Tan Cheng Lock, *Malayan Problems*, p. 119.
33. Silcock, *Towards a Malayan Nation*, p. 12 and *passim*.
34. Hickling, 'The First Five Years', p. 186.
35. There is room for argument on the exact position of some parties. The PMIP is socially conservative, but some of its views on equality could be classified as 'radical'.
36. Lipset, *Political Man*, pp. 80–2.
37. Mr Lee Kuan Yew, *Straits Budget*, May 21, 1955, quoted in Mills, L. A., *Malaya: A Political and Economic Appraisal* (Minneapolis, 1958), p. 123.
38. 'The Fixed Political Objectives of Our Party: a policy statement by the Central Executive Committee of the People's Action Party,' *PAP 6th Anniversary Celebration Souvenir* (Singapore, 1960), p. 2.
39. Baker, M. H., *North Borneo, the First Ten Years* (Singapore, 1962), pp. 67–8.
40. *Sarawak by the Week* (Kuching), No. 21/59 (May 24–30, 1959), p. 3.
41. *Human Relations Area Files, North Borneo and Sarawak* (New Haven, 1956), p. 38.
42. *Ibid.*, pp. 119–20.

43. *Report of the Commission of Enquiry, North Borneo and Sarawak* (Kuala Lumpur, 1962), p. 103; see Chapter 4 in this volume.

44. *Area Files*, pp. 67, 77, 93.

45. Baker, *North Borneo*, pp. 137–41.

46. Silcock, *Commonwealth Economy*, pp. 73 ff.

47. *Report of Commission of Enquiry*, p. 108. This reference is from a paper prepared by the North Borneo government. But it is in Sarawak that communist propaganda has been most active, especially in some schools.

48. *Ibid.*, pp. 49–50.

49. *Ibid.*, pp. 71, 88.

NOTES TO CHAPTER 22   *336–345*

1. While these may already be clear from reading the other contributions, their importance as background factors necessitates a brief restatement here. Much of what is said in this chapter is derived from my own PhD thesis: 'Communalism and the Political Process in the Federation of Malaya'.

2. This is reflected by their concern with matters like the strength of their representation in Parliament and in other prestigeful and consequential positions, and their desire to see the Malayan society reflect, as far as possible, a cultural uniformity based on Malay characteristics.

3. The term 'Malay nationalism' is here used in a somewhat wide sense. Although 'Malay communalism' or ' Malay regionalism' may in certain cases be more appropriate, the choice of 'nationalism' may be justified in terms of the tendency, common to communalists and regionalists alike, to believe that they are fighting a nationalist cause, convinced that Malaya should as far as possible be a Malay country.

4. Only municipal and town council elections were held between 1952 and 1955, the first general elections being held in July 1955.

5. For example, the joint decision of the United Malays National Organisation (UMNO) and the Malayan Chinese Association (MCA) to form an alliance (which soon led to the foundation of the Alliance Party, into which the Malayan Indian Congress was eventually incorporated) was primarily the result of an attempt to strengthen electoral prospects.

6. In fact the only parties not discussed are the Malayan Party, Party Negara and the United Democratic Party (UDP). Of these the first two are indeed insignificant, having one seat and none respectively in the federal Legislature and being without any influence at the state and local levels. The UDP on the other hand may merit some discussion since it probably will take away some

non-Malay support, particularly Chinese, from the Alliance. Its leadership is largely made up of prominent ex-MCA members who resigned as a result of certain disagreements within the Alliance in 1959. The UDP's leader, Dr Lim Chong Eu, was in fact the president of the MCA until his resignation. However, since it was formed only in 1962, the UDP has not had enough time to organise itself and to state its policies clearly, or to give any real indication of its following.

7. There have, however, been some significant reversals since then. In 1961, the party lost its control of the Trengganu State Assembly to the Alliance, while managing to hold Kelantan. In town council elections held during the same year, it lost heavily to the Alliance in both states.

8. The 1957 Constitution had conferred automatic citizenship only on those born in the Federation of Malaya *on or after* Merdeka Day.

9. Registration is voluntary.

10. Smith, T. E., *Report of the First Election of Members to the Legislature of the Federation of Malaya*, p. 11.

11. The Socialist Front had not been formed by this time.

12. The forerunner of the present People's Progressive Party.

13. In fact with the exception of the Alliance the different parties tended to concentrate their efforts in different areas, no doubt influenced by their own assessments of their popularity.

14. See for example Gamba, Charles, *The Origins of Trade Unionism in Malaya* (Singapore, 1962); Josey, Alex, *Trade Unionism in Malaya* (Singapore, 2nd edn., 1958); and Awbery, S. S. and Dalley, F. W., *Labour and Trade Union Organisation in the Federation of Malaya and Singapore* (Kuala Lumpur, 1948).

15. See the various sections on 'interest articulation' in Almond, G. A. and Coleman, J. S., *The Politics of the Developing Areas* (Princeton, 1960), for the relevant arguments.

16. See for example Josey, Alex, *Trade Unionism in Malaya* (1st edn., 1954), pp. 51–2.

17. Each of the member organisations submitted its own proposals, and these were jointly 'processed' into a single memorandum which was submitted in the name of the Alliance. All the main points in this memorandum were incorporated into the final Constitution.

18. In addition to the general question of the status of Chinese education and Chinese language, the policy statement which emerged from the meeting sponsored by these groups also emphasised that Chinese schools were not being given sufficient financial assistance.

19. *Daily Press Summary of Vernacular Papers*, April 10, 1957, pp. 1–2 (from the editorial of the *China Press* of the same date).

1. Mosca, Gaetano, *The Ruling Class* (New York, 1939), p. 50 [Turin, 1923].
2. In a sense elites can only select possible alternatives of action acceptable to the society. The range of choice is determined by the nature of the political system. In the model political democracy, alternative choices would be severely restricted, for the government must remain thoroughly responsible to the electorate; in the authoritarian model the range of alternatives would be broad, perhaps even limitless. However, the real world does not reach such extremes. In political systems accepted today as 'democratic' it would be difficult to support the contention that every individual is guaranteed an equal voice in government. At the other extreme, as the Chinese Mandate of Heaven and the doctrine of tyrannicide have demonstrated, the ultimate check on an authoritarian ruler is assassination.
3. This approach minimises the intrusion of the subjective discrimination of the researcher. Examples are numerous, but two, drawn from both sides of the Atlantic, must suffice:

    '. . . the political elite with which I shall be concerned are the occupants of political offices . . . , those who owe their power to election or appointment by elected authority . . .'; Guttsman, W. L., 'Social Stratification and the Political Elite', *The British Journal of Sociology*, xi (June 1960), p. 148, n. 1.

    'The bureaucratic elite of Canada is defined for the present study as senior federal public servants [of specified ranks] who held office during 1953 . . .'; Porter, John, 'Higher Public Servants and the Bureaucratic Elite in Canada', *Canadian Journal of Economics and Political Science*, xxiv (November 1958), p. 497.
4. See Lasswell, Harold D., Lerner, Daniel and Rothwell, C. Easton, *The Comparative Study of Elites* (Stanford, 1952), p. 13.
5. There are at least three deficiencies in the present study that the author must readily admit. First, it would be desirable to broaden the base of the groups analysed, particularly in the case of category one below, with a view to determining the representativeness of the sample. Second, the selection of these samples involved some arbitrariness and intuition on the researcher's part, which ideally should be eliminated. However, in Malaya biographical information is difficult to gather, and thus the resulting selectivity inevitably involves personal discretion. Third, it has proved impossible to find a rational basis for selecting political elites from among the commercial classes, and thus this group has not been considered in the present essay. Personal observation suggests, however, that this group should not be excluded in more exhaustive

studies in the future. Unless otherwise noted, all biographical information in this Chapter was collected in late 1962.

6. The parliamentary Alliance—generally well disciplined in the past—holds more than a two thirds majority in the Dewan Rakyat (House of Representatives). Thus, the passage of all Alliance supported bills is virtually assured.

7. The present chapter is limited to a discussion of national elites, but it might also be pointed out that MCS officers are posted to every state in the Federation, some filling important state posts such as the state secretaryships, while many are posted as District Officers. The latter posts may permit the exercise of considerable administrative discretion when the personality of the DO is dominant over that of the locally elected leader.

8. On political socialisation, see Hyman, Herbert, *Political Socialisation* (Glencoe, Ill., 1959). The analysis presented above is largely based on Almond, Gabriel A. and Coleman, James S., *The Politics of the Developing Areas* (Princeton, NJ, 1960), pp. 26–33. Almond and Coleman reply to the rhetorical question, 'what do we mean by the function of political socialisation?', in this manner: 'we mean that all political systems tend to perpetuate their cultures and structures through time, and they do this mainly by means of the socialising influences of the primary and secondary structures through which the young of the society pass in the process of maturation. . . . Political socialisation is the process of induction into the political culture. Its end product is a set of attitudes—cognitions, value standards, and feelings—toward the political system . . .' (pp. 26–7). While political socialisation describes the general process of induction into the political culture, recruitment implies the more specific process of induction into specialised roles in the political system (p. 31).

9. Lateral recruitment in the United States—and, to a somewhat less extent, in Canada—is the rule, not the exception. The tendency towards the creation of bureaucracies owing allegiance to a particular political leader—best demonstrated by the case of Vietnam—also represents a form of lateral recruitment. On Vietnam, see Jumper, Roy, 'Mandarin Bureaucracy and Politics in South Vietnam', *Pacific Affairs*, xxx (March 1957), pp. 47–58.

10. It should also be noted that five of the eleven members of the symbolic elite have had some bureaucratic experience.

11. Shortly after its creation, the report of the adviser on education in the Federated Malay States commented that 'from this school Government have great hopes that the sons of Malays of the Raja and higher classes will be educated and trained on the lines of an English public school and be fitted to take a share in the Government of their country': Straits Settlements, *Report for 1910*

on the Federated Malay States, p. 23 (in Great Britain, *Accounts and Papers, 1911,* LIII, Cd. 5902).

12. Older Malay officers of the MCS have sometimes remarked only half jestingly that the adroit manipulation of silverware was the crucial hurdle that all successful officers had to clear.   There were various techniques employed for judging social fitness.   For a number of years Malay officers were brought into Kuala Lumpur annually to attend a round of social events and confer- ences under the direction of the federal (or chief) secretary.   In addition, expatriate superiors were expected to entertain and be entertained by their Malay subordinates.   A report on social graces might then become an integral part of promotion recommendations.

13. The Malay rulers of the nine Malay States of the Federation are, of course, Malay by history, tradition, and definition.   The Constitution provides no communal requisite for the governors of Penang and Malacca, though at the present time both of these are also Malay.

14. The Macaulay Educational Minute was the most articulate (but dogmatic) statement of the supporters of English education in their lengthy parliamen- tary debate with the Orientalists.   Macaulay's reasoning ('a single shelf of a good European library [is] worth the whole native literature of India and Arabia') was based on his almost total ignorance of Asian literature, but the policies the Minute espoused won out and influenced the course of twentieth- century politics in the former colonies.   The policies advocated were basically twofold: (1) 'We have to educate a people who cannot at present be educated by means of their mother-tongue.   We must teach them . . . our own lan- guage. . . .'   (2) '. . . It is impossible for us . . . to attempt to educate the body of the people.   We must at present do our best to form a class who may be interpreters between us and the millions whom we govern; a class of persons, Indian in blood and colour, but English in taste, in opinions, in morals, and in intellect. . . .'   The Macaulay Minute has been conveniently reprinted in part in deBary, William T. (ed.), *Sources of Indian Tradition* (New York, 1958), pp. 596–601.

NOTES TO CHAPTER 24   *356–364*

1. *Report of the Commission of Enquiry, North Borneo and Sarawak,* 1962, p. 76.
2. See the dissenting opinion of Mr Justice Black in *Communist Party of the United States of America* v. *Subversive Activities Control Board,* 367 US 1 (1961).
3. Not infrequently, in many parts of the world, some comment is made of the necessity of adapting the English constitutional provisions to the local scene. Adaptation of the borrowed may, indeed, be necessary.   But too often the

unhappy truth appears that what is meant is the abandonment, by way of 'adaptation', of those restraints on government which are the very genius of constitutional democracy.

4. See note 2 above.

5. Restrictions on free expression do exist. See ch. III of the Internal Security Act, 1960.

6. While this party is composed of three largely communal parties, it has, as a party in control of government, exhibited the characteristics of a unitary, and not a coalition, party.

7. The Socialist Front in the George Town City Council.

8. The Pan-Malayan Islamic Party in the 1959 elections in Kelantan.

9. The principle of the necessity of free movement in a federation was established in the United States by the decision in *Crandall* v. *Nevada*, 73 US 35 (1868), which denied to any state the right to limit the movement of a federal citizen into or through its boundaries. The principle was reaffirmed in *Edwards* v. *California*, 341 US 160 (1941).

10. See e.g., the *Report of the Commission of Enquiry, North Borneo and Sarawak*, 1962. See, also, the reported assurance given by Tengku Abdul Rahman in the *Straits Times* of August 16, 1962.

11. See report of proceedings in the Federation of Malaya House of Representatives in the *Straits Times*, December 12, 1962, when the House applauded reference to the barring by the government of Sarawak of entry of members of the Barisan Sosialis Party of Singapore, following the revolution in Brunei.

12. See the *Straits Times* of November 19, 1962, reporting statements made by Tengku Abdul Rahman in Jesselton, promising efforts by the Federation of Malaya Alliance Party to 'woo' the voters of Sabah. See, also, the *Straits Times* of February 3, 1962, in which Mr C. V. Devan Nair is reported to have commented on the opportunity Malaysia would give to build up a powerful trade union movement.

13. A negligible variation, up to fifteen per cent, was permitted to take care of such factors as natural boundary lines.

14. The 'Memorandum Setting Out Heads of Agreement Between the Federation of Malaya and Singapore', Cmd. 33 of 1961 (Singapore), introduced the term 'nationals of the larger Federation', which appears a not entirely felicitous euphemism for the more accurate term 'federal citizen'.

15. Article 5 provides, *inter alia*, 'No person shall be deprived of his life or personal liberty save in accordance with law.' Article 9 protects citizens from banishment or exclusion from the Federation. Article 10 has been discussed elsewhere.

16. Article 79 requires a procedural delay of four weeks of bills proposing changes

in matters enumerated in either the Concurrent List or the State List of subjects of legislative competence.

17. The Internal Security Act, 1960.
18. E.g., Article 25 (1) (a), previously discussed.

NOTES TO CHAPTER 25

1. The merits and demerits of the claim of the Philippines over Sabah are not to be discussed here as such, but only when they fit into the general pattern of the article.
2. Singhal, D. P., 'The United States of Malaysia', *Asian Survey*, i, No. 8 (October 1961), p. 19.
3. Reuter, January 4, 1963, datelined Jesselton. One of the major items on the platform of the Sabah Alliance is its support for Malaysia.
4. Even the Sarawak United People's Party is not opposed to the concept of Malaysia but only to the present proposals. Reuter, May 16, 1963, datelined United Nations.
5. *Straits Times*, April 26, 1963.
6. *Sarawak by the Week*, April 21, 1963.
7. These last four political parties form the Sarawak Alliance, *Malayan Times*, March 22, 1963.
8. The sultan considers that Malaysia is in the interests of his people; Reuter, May 16, 1963, datelined United Nations.
9. van der Kroef, Justus M., 'Indonesia, Malaya, and the North Borneo Crisis', *Asian Survey*, iii, No. 4 (April 1963), p. 181.
10. *Straits Times*, June 27, 1961; *Sarawak Annual Report*, 1961 (HMSO, London, 1962), pp. 1–2.
11. *Sunday Times* (London), July 9, 1961.
12. *Sunday Times*, July 16, 1961. Eight PAP members who were members of the Singapore Assembly declared their support for Lim Chin Siong. This marked the break of the extreme left-wing elements from the PAP, resulting in the formation of the Barisan Sosialis by the former group.
13. Lee Kuan Yew, *The Battle for Merger* (Government Printing Office, Singapore, 1961), p. 37.
14. *Siaran Akhbar*, Jabatan Penerangan, Persekutuan Tanah Melayu (Malaya's Information Services), PEN 4/63/264 (DPM), p. 3.
15. *Memorandum Setting Out Heads of Agreement for a Merger between the Federation Malaya and Singapore*, Cmd. 33 of 1961 (Singapore), p. 4.
16. *Ibid.*

17. *Malay Mail*, November 18, 1961.
18. United Nations General Assembly, 16th Session Official Records, 1,058th Plenary Meeting, November 20, 1961.
19. *New York Times*, July 28, 1962.
20. Reuter, February 1, 1963, datelined Manila.
21. *Ibid.*
22. Reuter, January 4, 1963, datelined Jesselton.
23. The Cobbold Commission was a Commission of Enquiry into North Borneo and Sarawak to ascertain the views of the people of the two territories regarding Malaysia, and to make recommendations thereon. The Commission was set up by the Malayan and the British governments. *Report of the Commission of Enquiry, North Borneo and Sarawak* (Government Printer, Kuala Lumpur, 1962), p. 50.
24. The under-secretary of the United Nations, Mr Narasinham, stated that there was a big support for Malaysia in the Borneo territories; *Straits Times*, April 22, 1963; *Malayan Times*, April 27, 1963.
25. *Straits Times*, July 8, 1961, and July 18, 1961.
26. *Straits Times*, October 23, 1961.
27. *Straits Times*, July 7, 1961.
28. *Straits Times*, July 7, 1961, and July 10, 1961.
29. Donald Stephens and Datu Bandar dropped their opposition to Malaysia when the Malaysia proposals had been explained to them; see notes 25 and 26.
30. *Malyan Times*, August 31, 1962; *Straits Times*, September 1, 1962.
31. Judging from Azahari's statements when the rebellion started, he was expecting mass support from the peoples of Brunei, Sarawak and Sabah and some assistance from Indonesia. But the only real support he obtained was from some of the people of Brunei; *Sunday Times*, December 9, 1962; *Malayan Times*, December 9, 1962; *Straits Times*, December 10, December 11, December 12, 1962; van der Kroef, Justus M., *op. cit.*, p. 177.
32. *Malayan Times*, August 31, 1962; *Straits Times*, September 1, 1962.
33. The Brunei State Council has 33 members—17 nominated by the sultan and 16 elected.
34. Conversations with Indonesian visitors in April 1963.
35. 'Special position' as accorded the Malays in the Malayan Constitution; *Malaysia Report of the Inter-Governmental Committee 1962* (Government Press, Kuala Lumpur, 1963), p. 26.
36. Some of the principles on which the Indonesian government is based, e.g. Nasakom is a combination of the nationalists, religionists and the communists; they are supposed to work together, hence the demand for a Nasakom Cabinet by the Indonesian Communist Party.

37. *Siran Akhbar*, Jabatan Penerangan, Persekutuan Tanah Melayu, February 1, 1963; March 30–1, 1963.

38. *Annual of the Far Eastern Economic Review*, 1962. Hong Kong. Excluding Japan's War Reparations payment and credits, the foreign credits to Indonesia from the western bloc are $M 798.8 million, from the eastern bloc $M 641.2 million.

39. Ebon, Martin, 'Indonesian Communism: from Failure to Success', *The Review of Politics*, xxv, No. 1 (January 1963).

40. *Straits Times*, June 6, 1963.

41. *Papers on the Manila Talks*, issued by the Ministry of External Affairs, Federation of Malaya.

42. *Straits Times*, July 10, 1963.

43. *Malayan Constitutional Documents*, 2nd Edn, Vol. i, Chapter 2, Article 38 (Government Printer, Kuala Lumpur, 1962).

44. *Straits Times*, July 10, 1963.

45. *Straits Times*, June 6, 1963. *Sunday Mail*, June 30, 1963.

46. *Tokyo Shimbun*, August 2, 1962; *The Japan Times*, August 2, 1962; *The Yomiuri*, August 5, 1962; *Dawn* (Pakistan), August 4, 1962; *Sern Seri* (Thailand), August 4, 1962; *Krongdheb* (Thailand), August 7, 1962; *Swadesamitran* (India), August 3, 1962; *Thina Mani* (India), August 3, 1962; *Nara India* (India), August 3, 1962. These were some of the favourable reactions to the accord on Malaysia between Malaya and Britain.

47. *Documents of the Third Plenum of the Central Committee of the Communist Party of Indonesia* (Djakarta, end of December 1961).

NOTES TO CHAPTER 26 376–399

1. 'The Commonwealth of Nations' has different meanings for different purposes. In lay parlance it probably is meant to exclude the 'dependent territories', since a colony is not yet a nation. Such distinctions have become quite blurred, however, and the government of the United Kingdom uses the phrase generally to mean the whole of those territories associated with Britain, dependent as well as independent, in order not to exclude and perhaps discourage areas which are advancing towards independence. In section 36 of the 1950 Finance Act of the United Kingdom, 'Commonwealth' includes dependent territories; so too does section 10 (4) of the Medical Practitioners and Pharmacists Act, 1947. Some but not all non-independent territories are represented at the Commonwealth Prime Ministers' Conferences. When the present author writes of 'the Commonwealth', he is referring to both independent and dependent nations and territories, to colonies, protectorates, and

states (Singapore was a 'State'). The independent members of the Commonwealth as this book goes to press (January 1964) are Canada, Australia, New Zealand, India, Pakistan, Ceylon, Malaysia, Ghana, Nigeria, Sierra Leone, Tanganyika, Uganda, Zanzibar, Kenya, Cyprus, Trinidad and Tobago, Jamaica, Western Samoa, and the United Kingdom. Most members refer only to 'the Commonwealth of Nations', although Canada, Australia and New Zealand still commonly attach the adjective 'British' to the collective title. On these points, as well as others relating to the role of the Queen as Head of the Commonwealth but not Queen *within* all member nations, although Queen of some, see de Smith, S. A., *The Vocabulary of Commonwealth Relations*, University of London Institute of Commonwealth Studies, *Commonwealth Papers* No. 1 (London, 1954).

2. *Malayan Constitutional Documents*, i (2nd edn, Kuala Lumpur, 1962), p. 10.

3. Ball, W. Macmahon, *Nationalism and Communism in East Asia* (Melbourne, 1952), p. 146; The Economist Intelligence Unit, *The Commonwealth and Europe* (London, 1960), p. 399.

4. *Commonwealth Today*, no. 95 (n.d.), p. 2: also available in Malay and Chinese versions with the same numbering and pagination; Butwell, Richard, *Southeast Asia Today—and Tomorrow: A Political Analysis* (New York, 1961; London, 1962), p. 157.

5. Kuala Lumpur *Malay Mail*, Nov. 2, Dec. 6, 1962; Ginsberg, Norton and Roberts, Chester F., Jr., *Malaya* (Seattle, 1958), p. 498.

6. The most popular text in Malaya is Brett, S. Reed, *A History of the British Empire and Commonwealth* (new edn, London, 1959), followed by Williamson, James A., *The British Empire and Commonwealth: A History for Senior Forms* (4th edn, London and New York, 1962, but very little revised from the first edition of 1935). The best text this writer examined was Hilton, P. B. and Tate, D. J., *South-east Asia in World History*, Book Three: *The Modern World* (Kuala Lumpur, 1961), and yet (and despite its title) it contains no word on the Commonwealth. A course in Commonwealth history at the University of Malaya lapsed at the end of 1962.

7. *Report of the Commission of Enquiry, North Borneo and Sarawak* (Kuala Lumpur, 1962), p. 10, Sec. D, para. 26.

8. Central Office of Information, *Commonwealth Tours* (London, n.d.); *Malay Mail*, Dec. 4, 1962; 'The Sultan of Pahang in New Zealand', *Commonwealth Today*, no. 83, p. 19.

9. *Malay Mail*, Nov. 10, 25, 1962; Kuala Lumpur *Malayan Times*, June 22, Nov. 6, 1962; Colombo *Ceylon Daily Mirror*, May 28, 1962; Singapore and Kuala Lumpur *Sunday Times*, Nov. 18, 1962; *The Bulletin* (Sydney), lxxxv (Dec. 8, 1962), p. 33; Federation of Malaya Diplomatic and Consular Privileges Ordinance, 1957;

'The Parliamentary Heritage', *Commonwealth Today*, no. 88, pp. 3–9; 'The Commonwealth Partnership: Sharing Knowledge and Facilities on Defence', *ibid.*, no. 87, pp. 4–5; 'John Lee Joo For of Penang', *ibid.*, pp. 19–21; *Malaysian Statesman*, I (Oct. 17, 1962), p. 16; United States Information Service [Newsletter] (Canberra), March 28, 1963; *HRH the Duke of Edinburgh's Second Commonwealth Study Conference on the Human Consequences of the Changing Industrial Environment in the Commonwealth and Empire* (n.p., [1962]), pp. 40, 51–2, 55; Harvey, Heather J., *Consultation and Cooperation in the Commonwealth* (London, 1952), *passim*; and 'The Commonwealth Under Strain', *Current Affairs Bulletin* (Sydney), XXVII (Dec. 12, 1960), pp. 35–47.

10. Bone, Robert C., Jr., *Contemporary South-east Asia* (New York, 1962), p. 69. The Dutch seemed to have had difficulty in understanding that the Commonwealth and Britain were not one and the same. For succinct testimony to this, see van Mook, H. J. (the Lieutenant-Governor of Indonesia in 1949), *The Stakes of Democracy in South-east Asia* (London, 1950), in which the index curtly dismisses half a century of evolution with the entry, 'BritishCommonwealth, *see* Britain'.

11. [National Union of Conservative and Unionist Associations], *Wind of Change: The Challenge of the Commonwealth* (London, 1960), pp. 24, 29; Silcock, T. H., *The Commonwealth Economy in South-east Asia* (Durham, NC, 1959), pp. 77, 98, 141; Sarkisyanz, Emanuel, *Sudostasien seit 1945* (Munich, 1961), p. 50; and State of Singapore, *Annual Report, 1960* (Singapore, 1962), p. 27.

12. Modelski, George (ed.), *SEATO: Six Studies* (Melbourne, 1962; Vancouver, B.C., 1963), p. 43, n. 9; Australian News and Information Bureau, *Weekly News Letter*, XXI (Nov. 3, 1963), p. 3.

13. By the agreement of 1957 Malaya committed itself to the defence of Singapore, the Borneo territories and Hong Kong. With the creation of the Malaysian federation, this commitment extends only to self-defence and to Hong Kong. But such an undertaking has led one writer to observe that in extending defensive commitments outside Malaysia, the Federation 'has underwritten British colonialism' to a slight extent (Miller, J. D. B., *The Commonwealth in the World* (London, 1958), p. 285).

14. See *Straits Times*, June 27, 1962; *Manchester Guardian Weekly*, Jan. 31, 1963; Parmer, J. Norman, 'Malaya and Singapore', in Kahin, George McT. (ed.), *Governments and Politics of South-east Asia* (Ithaca, 1959), pp. 262, 303, 305–7; Rose, Saul, *Britain and South-east Asia* (London and Baltimore, 1962), pp. 184–6; 'Malaysia—Federal Experiment', *Current Affairs Bulletin*, XXX (Oct. 22, 1962), p. 181.

15. On this last episode of diplomatic history, see the pro-Philippine analysis by Meadows, Martin, 'The Philippine Claim to North Borneo', *Political Science Quarterly*, LXXVII (Sept. 1962), pp. 321–35; and a pro-British account by

Tregonning, K. G., 'The Claim for North Borneo by the Philippines', *Australian Outlook*, XVI (Dec. 1962), pp. 283–91.

16. Hickling, R. H., *An Introduction to the Federal Constitution* (Kuala Lumpur, 1962), pp. 76–9; S. Jayakumar, 'Citizenship in the Federation of Malaya', *Me Judice*, V (Oct. 1962), pp. 8–9; *Malayan Constitutional Documents*, pp. 120, 123. Consult Federation of Malaya Passports Act, 1960; Constitution (Amendment) Act, 1960; and Constitution (Amendment) Act, 1962.

17. On the nature of autochthony as a principle of constitutional thought, see the unfortunately garbled (because grotesquely misprinted) but perceptive remarks by Wheare, K. C., in *The Constitutional Structure of the Commonwealth* (Oxford and New York, 1960), pp. 89–113, and especially pp. 106–8.

18. For general discussions see Wiseman, H. V., *The Cabinet in the Commonwealth: Post-War Developments in Africa, the West Indies and South-east Asia* (London, 1958); Walker, Patrick Gordon, 'Federalism in the Commonwealth', *Journal of the Parliaments of the Commonwealth*, XLII (Oct. 1961), pp. 351 ff.; Wade, E. C. S., 'Contempt of Parliament in a Commonwealth State', *University of Malaya Law Review*, III (July 1961), pp. 1–7; and Campbell, Enid, 'Suspension of Members of Commonwealth Parliaments', *ibid.* (Dec. 1961), pp. 267–86.

19. Nor should one assume that these ties are very well understood. Consider the speech given by one distinguished Malayan delegate to the Seventh Commonwealth Parliamentary Conference held in London in 1961, on the theme of 'The Place and Function of the Commonwealth in the World', a speech replete with errors, including the misstatement of such simple and readily verifiable facts as the date of the Canadian Confederation (*Report of Proceedings of the Seventh Commonwealth Parliamentary Conference* . . . [London, n.d.], pp. 27–9).

20. Rose, *Britain and South-east Asia*, pp. 72–3, 137, 153, 171–2; *Malaya* (Dec. 1961), p. 41; *Commonwealth Universities Yearbook 1961* (38th edn., London, 1961); 'Malaya Today and the Commonwealth of Nations', *The Malayan Student*, V (Feb. 1961), pp. 13–14, 43; 'Visual Aids to Education: Commonwealth Teachers on Courses in London', *Teaching and Learning* (Singapore), I (Sept. 1962), pp. 15–17; 'Aids to the Study of the Commonwealth', *ibid.*, pp. 18–20; Romney, Hall, 'The Malayan Student in Britain', *Straits Times Annual for 1955* (Singapore, 1954), pp. 58–61; Silcock, T. H., 'Language Problems in South-east Asian Universities', *Vestes*, V (Dec. 1962), pp. 3–12; Malayan Students' Union, London, *Pemandu Pelajar ka-British Isles* (London, 1961).

21. For criticisms of overseas study, see Ungku Abdul Aziz, 'Prospects for Economic Growth in Asia', in Wilkes, John (ed.), *Asia and Australia* (Sydney, 1961), pp. 55–66; and Jennings, Sir Ivor, *Problems of the New Commonwealth* (Durham, NC, 1958), pp. 62, 74.

22. *Commonwealth Today* gives considerable attention to Malaysia, as an examination of a file for 1959–62 (numbers 66–96) shows. In thirty-one issues printed in these years, Malaysia was represented by twelve major stories, mentioned in fourteen other articles, and was featured in one way or another in seventy-four of the photographs used, not counting the illustrations for the Malaysian articles.

23. *Hemisphere: An Asian-Australian Magazine* (North Sydney), while not limited to the Commonwealth, often features Malaysia; *New Commonwealth* (London), an independent monthly which emphasises trade, contains a regular Overseas Survey with articles on Malaysia; *Commonwealth Development*, an industrial news memorandum, is published six times a year by Empire House, London. The Commonwealth Union of Trade's quarterly, *Commonwealth Calling*, and the Economic Research Council's monthly, *Commonwealth Digest and World Economic Review*, contain occasional articles on Malaysia, usually about rubber. The *Journal of Commonwealth Political Studies*, published twice a year in Leicester, and the *Journal of the Parliaments of the Commonwealth*, a quarterly sponsored by the General Council of the Commonwealth Parliamentary Association, are influential among scholars. Many other magazines, especially those devoted to travel or economics, regularly publish material on Malaysia; two examples are the *Far Eastern Economist* (New Delhi) and the English illustrated weekly, *Sphere*.

24. Statistics on inquiries were furnished by the respective High Commissioners' offices.

25. Feslier, Arthur, and Gupta, B. K., 'The Asians Among Us', *New Zealand Listener*, XLVIII (Feb. 15, 1963), p. 5; Auckland *New Zealand Herald*, May 22, 1962; *New Zealand News* (London), no. 919 (May 15, 1962), p. 6; *New Zealand Newsletter* (Kuala Lumpur), no. 20.62 (Sept. 26, 1962), pp. 3, 7–9; *ibid.*, no. 23.62 (Nov. 7, 1962), p. 8; *ibid.*, no. 26.62 (Dec. 19, 1962), p. 3; *Sunday Times*, Sept. 22, 1962; *Malay Times*, June 30, 1962; *Straits Times*, Jan. 28, 1963; 'Malaya-New Zealand', *Commonwealth Calling* (May 1960), pp. 44–5; Auckland *The Weekly News* (March 27, 1963), p. 43.

26. Such statistics are, of course, suspect, for they do not reveal the sources of the queries. The Canadian office maintains figures in terms of number of pieces sent out rather than number of inquiries (thus, a larger packet of materials, to a smaller number of people, would appear as an increase in interest).

27. *Canada and the Colombo Plan 1951–61* (Ottawa, 1961); Nicholson, N. L., 'Geographers Meet in Malaya', *Canadian Geographical Journal*, LXV (Sept. 1962), pp. 74–5; *Malay Mail*, Sept. 22, Oct. 9, 11, 12, 1962; *Malay Times*, Oct. 11, 1962 and Stuchen, Philip, 'Industrialisation Prospects for Malaysia', *Queen's Quarterly* LXX (Oct. 1963) pp. 324–50.

28. Ingram, Derek, *Partners in Adventure: A New Look at the Commonwealth Today* (London, 1960), p. 122.
29. Ingram goes on to damage his case further by drawing the same parallel between Canada and the West Indies; yet, even highly trained black West Indians find entry into Canada on a permanent basis difficult. This kind of reasoning may have its uses, but overemphasis on metaphors of this type merely serves to confuse further already difficult problems in Commonwealth history.
30. Shepherd, Jack, *Australia's Interest and Policies in the Far East* (New York, 1940), p. 109.
31. Ball, W. Macmahon, 'Australia's Political Relations with Asia since 1945', in Wilkes, John (ed.), *Asia and Australia* (Sydney, 1961), p. 70.
32. The most successful of the Australian novels of Malaya have been *The Durian Tree*, by Michael McKeon, and *The Dark Backward*, by Eric Lambert.
33. *Malayan Times*, June 30, 1962; *Malay Mail*, Aug. 18, 1962; Sydney *Morning Herald*, July 16, 1963; Webb, Leicester C., 'Australia and SEATO', in Modelski, George (ed.), *SEATO: Six Studies* (Melbourne and Vancouver, B.C., 1962), pp. 78–80; Budewig, Eckhard, *Wird Asien rot? Rubel und Dollar im Wettlauf mit Peking* (Stuttgart, 1961), p. 114. Budewig sees Singapore as a *'chinesische Demokratie'* that stands midway between the 'people's democracy' of China and the dictatorship of Chiang Kai-shek. See also the interesting but sometimes equally ill-informed Caldwell, John C., *South of Tokyo* (Chicago, 1957). Also of interest are 'New Horizons', *Commonwealth Development*, IX (Aug. 1962), p. 11; and Levi, Werner, *Australia's Outlook on Asia* (Sydney and East Lancing, Michigan, 1958), pp. 192–4.
34. On Australia's early expression of sympathy, see *Australia in Facts and Figures*, no. 75 [1962], p. 141. On the decision to give support to Malaysia, and the contretemps over whether 'support' included military aid in case of war, see Sydney *Morning Herald*, March 5–7, 12, 1963; Sydney *Sun*, March 5, 1963; *Straits Times*, March 11–13, 1963. For a sectarian view see 'Freedom of Religion Threat in Malaysia', *The Catholic Weekly* (Sydney), XXII (March 21, 1963), pp. 1, 6; and editorial, *Harvest* (April 1963), Marist Fathers' magazine. Among intelligent Australian periodical assessments of the situation see, in particular, 'The Lesser Evil', *Nation* (Sydney), no. 114 (March 9, 1963), pp. 7–9; Gale, W. M., 'Brunei's Oil Money', *ibid.*, no. 113 (Feb. 23, 1963), p. 7, and editorial, *ibid.*, p. 3; Mackie, J. A. C., 'Azahari's Young Men', *ibid.*, no. 110 (Jan. 12, 1963); editorial, 'Stopping the Slanging Match', *The Bulletin*, LXXXV (March 2, 1963), p. 5, and 'Lee Kuan Yew and India's War', *ibid.* (Dec. 8, 1962), pp. 26–7; 'Singapore—City State', *Current Affairs Bulletin*, XXVI (Sept. 19, 1960), pp. 145–60; and Josey, Alex, 'The Tunku', *The Bulletin*, LXXXV (Sept. 28, 1963), pp. 11, 13, 15. On investment see 'Industry's Role in Malaysia', *ibid.* (July 20, 1963), pp. 45–6.

35. In Australia one does not always find activity on behalf of broad Commonwealth ties coming from the institutions established for such purposes. An example is the New South Wales Branch of the Royal Commonwealth Society. See its journal, *Commonwealth Outlook*.

36. *Current Notes on International Affairs* (Canberra), xxxiii (Sept. 1962), p. 65; *ibid.* (June 1962), pp. 59–60; *Austral News*, vi (Jan. 1963), p. 12. *The Bukit Bulletin*, a twice monthly publication issued at the Terendak Camp for Australian and New Zealand troops stationed in Malaya, also is of considerable interest.

37. *The Bulletin*, lxxxv (Oct. 6, 1962), p. 5; *CMS* [Church Missionary Society] *News*, New South Wales edn. (March 1963), pp. 1–2.

38. *Straits Times*, June 27, 1962; Sydney *Morning Herald*, March 15, 1963; Harper, Norman, 'Asian students in Australia', *Vestes* (June 1963), pp. 87–97; *Progress: A Review of Malaya's First Year of Independence, 1958* (Kuala Lumpur, 1958), pp. 88–9; Borland, Frank T., 'Asian Students in Adelaide University', Adelaide University Graduates' Union *Gazette*, iii (Dec. 1962), pp. 1–3; Oen Ing Yat, 'Asian Students in Australia', *Asiana*, i (Autumn, 1957), pp. 43–8; 'A White Man's Burden: Professor S. H. Roberts and the Sydney University Quotas', *Nation*, no. 98 (July 14, 1962), pp. 10–11; Zanetti, Terry, 'The Malayan Student in Australia', *The Straits Times Annual for 1956* (Singapore, 1955), pp. 29–32; Sheppard, Haji Mubin, 'Malaya', in Bradley, Kenneth (ed.), *The Living Commonwealth* (London, 1961), pp. 280–1.

39. *Current Notes on International Affairs*, xxxiii (Jan. 1962), pp. 25–6; Sydney *Morning Herald*, Jan. 8, 1963; Bastin, John, 'Indonesian and Malayan Studies in Australia', *Bulletin of South-east Asian History*, i (Jan. 1958), pp. 32–4; Alexander, Fred, 'Survey of Recent Research: Australia', *International Studies: Quarterly Journal of the Indian School of International Studies*, ii (April 1961), p. 444.

40. Quoted in the Immigration Reform Group, *Immigration: Control or Colour Bar? The Background to 'White Australia' and a Proposal for Change* (Melbourne, 1962), p. 99.

41. These generalisations are based on many conversations with Malaysians about issues of race during the academic year 1962–3 when the author taught at the University of Malaya in Kuala Lumpur. During the year he travelled throughout Malaysia, including the Borneo territories. In turn, generalisations about Australia are supported by an extended visit to the Commonwealth, where the writer taught for two terms in 1963 at the University of Sydney and travelled to all of the Australian capitals. Subjective remarks concerning Indonesia and New Zealand are supported by travel in both countries.

42. The Tengku's speech seems to have been exploited in Australia for propaganda purposes by both opponents and defenders of the present immigration policy. Sydney newspapers, and a former Australian Minister for Immigration, A. R.

Downer, have cited this speech to indicate Malaysian acceptance of the policy. There is considerable difference between acceptance for present purposes and acceptance in principle and for the future, and by his qualifying phrases the Prime Minister clearly was not speaking of the latter. Also unfair are those who say that Downer spoke of the Tengku's 'defence' of the policy. Downer himself recognised that 'acceptance' was not a defence. However, when referring to sources of criticism of the policy in Australia, Downer included 'detached thinkers'. What this means is not clear; one would think that both detachment and thought are precisely what the situation needs in both countries.

43. Reform Group, *Immigration*, pp. 38, 47, 101, 155–62; Victorian Association for Immigration Reform, *Why Does White Australia Matter?* (Brighton, Victoria, n.d.), pp. 2–4; Samuel, Peter, 'The White Australia Policy', *Melbourne University Magazine* (Autumn, 1962), pp. 27–8, 30. On the background of Malay pearl-shelling in northern Australia, see Bach, J. P. S., 'The Pearlshelling Industry and the "White Australia" Policy', *Historical Studies: Australia and New Zealand*, x (May 1962), pp. 203–13.

44. *The Far Eastern Economist*, xxxix (Nov. 2, 1962), pp. 807–8; *ibid.*, xxxviii (March 23, 1962), p. 753; *Malay Mail*, Oct. 9, 1962; Mills, Lennox A. and associates, *The New World of South-east Asia* (Minneapolis, 1949), p. 208; Purcell, Victor, *The Revolution in South-east Asia* (London, 1962), p. 106.

45. 'The Colombo Plan', *Current Affairs Bulletin*, xiii (Feb. 15, 1954), p. 135.

46. *Commonwealth Today*, no. 87, pp. 12–13, and *ibid.*, no. 90, pp. 20–1; *The Colombo Plan Story: 10 Years of Progress, 1950–60* ([Washington?], n.d.), pp. 1, 4–14, 36, 39, 41; and the *Annual Reports* of the Consultative Committee of the Colombo Plan for Co-operative Economic Development in South and South-east Asia (London), especially *The Colombo Plan for Co-operative Economic Development in South and South-east Asia: Eighth Annual Report of the Consultative Committee* (Jogjakarta, 1959), pp. iii–iv, 102–4, 188–95, 199, 204; and *The Tenth Annual Report . . .* (Kuala Lumpur, 1962), pp. 109–23. *Commonwealth Digest and World Economic Review*, i (March 1960), pp. 50–1.

47. A few examples of the aid provided by Colombo Plan members who are also Commonwealth members will indicate the practical nature of this tie. The UK gave £809,000 for the University of Malaya in Singapore; £1,200,000 for the construction on the Paya Lebar airport in Singapore; £1,346,000 for roads and £459,000 for hospitals in Sarawak and Sabah; £191,700 for developing Kuching; £886,000 for constructing an east-west road in Malaya; and £506,000 for a technical college at Kuala Lumpur. Canada has made major contributions, although India and Pakistan have been Canada's particular interest. In 1960, for example, the Canadian government agreed to help Malaya develop

its fisheries industry on the east coast. In a typical year (1958) Australia supported a number of efforts, including £13,000 in equipment to help a village achieve a dependable water supply.

48. On Malaysian-Indian trade, which is outside the scope of this essay, see Sovani, N. V., *Economic Relations of India with South-east Asia and the Far East* (Bombay, 1949); and *Indian Chamber of Commerce Report, 1960, Singapore* (Singapore, [1961?]), which contains excellent appendices on Malaysian imports and exports of cotton and cotton piece goods, silk, rayon yard, and copra. See also Markandan, Paul (ed.), *Report on Finance, Commerce and Industry: Federation of Malaya 1960* (Singapore, 1960).

49. These particular figures are for August 1962.

50. The order does not change, although the relative distance between countries does, if one uses the value instead of the percentage of exports as a basis for comparison.

51. The above comparisons are faulty in that a single month is not an accurate basis for judging trade statistics because of seasonal variations. However, such statistics do indicate the relative importance of Commonwealth nations to that trade pattern. For the above statistics see *Singapore Trade* (Oct. 1962), pp. 52–3, and Bottomley, Anthony, 'Malaysian Tariffs and Singapore', *ibid.*, pp. 15–16; *Federation of Malaya Monthly Statistics of External Trade* (Oct. 1962), pp. 11–12, 14; *Monthly Statistical Bulletin of the Federation of Malaya* (Dec. 1962), pp. 89–92; and Silcock, T. H., 'The Economy of Malaya: Relevance of the Competitive Laissez-Faire Model', in Hoover, Calvin (ed.), *Economic Systems of the Commonwealth* (Durham, NC, 1961), pp. 329–73. This essay has been reprinted as 'Economic Systems of the Commonwealth: the Economy of Malaya', University of London Institute of Commonwealth Studies *Reprint Series*, no. 15 (London, n.d.). Also consult 'Advertising in South-east Asia', supplement issue of *Overseas Trading*, Melbourne, xiv (June 29, 1962).

52. Economist Intelligence Unit, *Commonwealth and Europe*, p. 1.

53. *Ibid.*, p. 10.

54. *Ibid.*, p. 20. For the above statistics, see pp. 4–5, 7, 14, 16, 17.

55. *Ibid.*, pp. 31–2, 34–5, 41, 135, 168–9, 190–2; Rose, *Britain and South-east Asia*, p. 63; Stahl, Kathleen M., *The Metropolitan Organisation of British Colonial Trade: Four Regional Studies* (London, 1951), pp. 70–80; Spengler, Joseph J., 'The Commonwealth: Demographic Dimensions, Implications', in Deener, David R. and Cole, R. Taylor (eds.), *Commonwealth Perspectives* (Durham, NC, 1958), p. 113.

56. Boland, Geoffrey, 'How to Regain a Market', *Singapore Trade*, i (May 1961), pp. 31, 33; Federation of British Industries, *A Trade in Transition: Reports of the South-east Asia Trade Delegation, 1960* (London, 1961), pp. 69, 70, 95.

57. Parmer, 'Malaya and Singapore', in Kahin (ed.), *Governments and Politics of South-east Asia*, p. 272; Silcock, *Commonwealth Economy in South-east Asia*, p. 136.

58. Ball, *Nationalism and Communism*, p. 135; *Sari Berita* (Kuala Lumpur), II (July 5, (1962), p. 4; Karnail Singh Nijhar, 'A Short Essay on the Malayan-British Borneo Currency Agreement, 1950', *Ekonomi*, I (1960), pp. 40–5.

59. de la Mahotière, Stuart R., *The Common Market: A Comprehensive Guide* (London, 1961), p. 98.

60. For general assessments of the Common Market, see Kitzinger, U. W., *The Challenge of the Common Market* (2nd edn, Oxford, 1961), and Kennedy, William, *Straits Times*, July 3, 1961. For specific applications of similar views to Malaysia, see Kannan Kutty, K. P., 'Some Aspects of the Foreign Trade of Malaya', *Ekonomi*, II (Nov. 1961), pp. 16–21; Foo Voon-Kai, 'Economic Co-operation and Common Market', *Journal of the Commerce Society* [of Nanyang University], I (Nov. 1961), pp. 13–14; and 'The Asian Commonwealth View', *Common Market*, II (Sept. 1962), p. 165.

61. Wolstenholme, Alan, 'Malaya and the ECM', *New Commonwealth*, XL (Aug. 1962), pp. 535–6. Malayan and Bornean undressed timber already was in some difficulty within the Commonwealth, for in 1961–2 exports to Australia fell seriously. See 'Changes in the Pattern of Australia's Overseas Trade', *Overseas Trading* (Melbourne), XV (Feb. 8, 1963), p. 37.

62. *Malayan Times*, Sept. 15, 1962; *Malay Mail*, Oct. 1, 1962.

63. *The Sunday Mail*, Sept. 23, 1962; *Sunday Times*, Sept. 16, 1962; *Straits Times*, Sept. 11, 1962; *Malay Mail*, Sept. 10, 22, 1962; *Commonwealth Today*, no. 96, p. 7.

64. *Straits Times*, Sept. 11, 1962.

65. See *The Sunday Mail*, Sept. 9, 1962, Feb. 10, 1963; *Malay Mail*, June 27, Oct. 1, Nov. 23, 1962; Feb. 2, 1963; *Malayan Times*, June 25, 1962; *Straits Times*, July 7, Oct. 11, 1962, Jan. 3, 1963; 'Facing the Commonwealth', *The Economist*, CCIV (Sept. 8, 1962), pp. 865–6, 868; and Economist Intelligence Unit, *Commonwealth and Europe*, pp. 155, 161, 260, 398, 458–9, 473–4; Dell, Sidney, *Trade Blocs and Common Markets* (New York, 1963), pp. 299–303.

INDEX

457